LISTENING TO
MUSIC

FIFTH EDITION

CRAIG WRIGHT

YALE UNIVERSITY

THOMSON

SCHIRMER

Australia • Brazil • Canada • Mexico • Singapore • Spain
United Kingdom • United States

THOMSON

™

SCHIRMER

Listening to Music, Fifth Edition
Craig Wright

Publisher: Clark Baxter
Senior Development Editor: Sue Gleason
Assistant Editor: Emily A. Ryan
Editorial Assistant: Nell Pepper
Technology Project Manager: Rachel Bairstow
Executive Marketing Manager: Diane Wenckebach
Marketing Assistant: Marla Nasser
Project Manager, Editorial Production: Trudy Brown
Creative Director: Rob Hugel
Art Director: Maria Epes
Print Buyer: Judy Inouye

Permissions Editor: Roberta Broyer
Production Service: Melanie Field
Text and Cover Designer: Diane Beasley
Photo Researcher: Stephen Forsling
Copy Editor: Tom Briggs
Cover Image: Josef Danhauser (1805–1845). *Franz Liszt at the Piano.* 1840. Oil on canvas, 119 × 167 cm. Photo: Juergen Liepe. Nationalgalerie, Staatliche Museen zu Berlin, Berlin, Germany. Bildarchiv Preussischer Kulturbesitz / Art Resource, NY.
Compositor: Thompson Type
Text and Cover Printer: Courier Corporation/Kendallville

Printed in the United States of America
1 2 3 4 5 6 7 11 10 09 08 07

Library of Congress Control Number: 2006906782

ISBN-13: 978-0-495-18973-2
ISBN-10: 0-495-18973-1

Thomson Higher Education
10 Davis Drive
Belmont, CA 94002-3098
USA

For more information about our products, contact us at:
Thomson Learning Academic Resource Center
1-800-423-0563
For permission to use material from this text or product,
submit a request online at
http://www.thomsonrights.com.
Any additional questions about permissions can be
submitted by e-mail to
thomsonrights@thomson.com.

Brief Contents

PART V

Romanticism 250

PART VI

Modern and Postmodern Art Music, 1880–Present 338

PART VII

American Popular Music 416

Detailed Contents

PART I The Elements of Music 1

PART II   *The Middle Ages and Renaissance, 476–1600* 74

PART III The Baroque Period, 1600–1750 108

PART IV   *The Classical Period,* 1750–1820   170

PART VI Modern and Postmodern Art Music, 1880–Present   338

PART VII   *American Popular Music*   416

Listening Exercises

Boxes

About the Author

Craig Wright (Bachelor of Music, Eastman School of
Music, 1966; Ph.D., Harvard, 1972) is the Henry L. and
Lucy G. Moses Professor of Music at Yale, where he has
taught for the past thirty-three years. He is the author of
numerous scholarly books and articles on composers
ranging from Leoninus to Bach. Wright has also been
the recipient of many awards, including a Guggenheim
Fellowship, the Einstein and Kinkeldey Awards of the
American Musicological Society, and the Dent Medal of
the International Musicological Society. In 2004, he was
awarded the honorary degree Doctor of Humane Letters
from the University of Chicago. He has coauthored
(with Bryan Simms) *Music in Western Civilization* (Thomson
Schirmer, 2006).

About the Cover

The painting that serves as the cover for this book is a fascinating artifact. Indeed, one could write a book about it alone. Executed in 1840 by a minor Austrian painter, Josef Danhauser, it is a fanciful depiction of a gathering of some of the greatest artistic luminaries of the nineteenth century. Engaged at the piano is the imposing figure of Franz Liszt ①, perhaps the most formidable pianist who ever lived. Standing immediately behind him are Gioachino Rossini ②, the famous opera composer, and Niccolò Paganini ③, a violin virtuoso whose playing was so extraordinary that he was widely thought to be in league with the devil. To their right is the French nineteenth-century lion of letters Victor Hugo ④. Below sits Alexandre Dumas ⑤, author of *The Three Musketeers* and *The Count of Monte Cristo.* To his left, cigar in hand, is Aurore Dudevant ⑥, the prototype of the nineteenth-century feminist and novelist of more than two dozen volumes under her pen name George Sand. Reclining under the sway of the music is Marie d'Agoult ⑦, herself a feminist author, playwright, and prize-winning historian. If one looks carefully at the painting on the wall, the profile of the recently deceased poet Lord Byron ⑧, romantic figure *par excellence,* comes into view. Finally, radiating the very spirit of music from Olympian heights, a bust of the great Beethoven ⑨ sits atop the piano—Beethoven the law-giver surrounded by his apostles. These eminent poets, playwrights, and novelists could easily have heard Liszt play while they continued to talk or read nearby. But they have paused and put down their books not merely to *hear* the music but to *listen* to it. We can see from their faces that listening intently has allowed music to touch their emotions. These guests are profoundly affected, indeed transfixed, by the power of music.

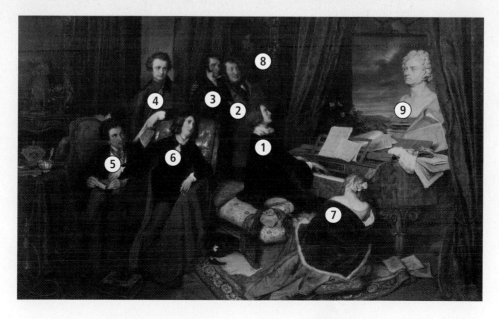

Preface

"Listening to music" is not just the title of this book and the theme of its cover. The aim of this textbook is to teach students to listen to music so that they, too, might become transfixed by its expressive power. As Josef Danhauser's scene on the cover suggests (see page xvii), music can be the most compelling of the arts.

Most music appreciation textbooks treat music, not as an opportunity for personal engagement through listening, but as a history of music. Students are required to learn something of the technical workings of music (what a tonic chord is, for example) and specific facts (how many symphonies Beethoven wrote) but are not asked to become personally engaged in the act of listening to music. What listening there is, is passive, not active. *Listening to Music*, however, is different. Here students are encouraged, indeed required, to become active participants in a musical dialogue, through a variety of means both within the covers of this book and beyond them.

NEW TO THIS EDITION

Although the goals of active listening have not changed, this edition of *Listening to Music* will appear physically different to those of you who have used it in the past. In response to your suggestions, the contents have been reconfigured into forty-one briefer chapters that students now can more easily read, study, and digest. In the process, jazz now occupies two chapters, and rock and Tin Pan Alley, one chapter each. In addition, new part openers preview each historical era and put the era's musical and historic events at students' fingertips in a richly illustrated timeline. At the end of each part, you will find a "Checklist of Musical Style" that reviews the key elements of music within each era's styles and lists representative composers and principal genres. All checklists in the book are previewed at the end of Chapter 7, where the concept of style is introduced.

An alternative volume—*Listening to Western Music*—is also available for those who prefer a text that is briefer and less expensive, and covers only Western (or "classical") music.

PEDAGOGICAL AIDS

Listening Exercises

Listening to Music is the only music appreciation text on the market to include Listening Exercises within the book. For the Fifth Edition, these exercises have been moved from chapter ends to their rightful place, immediately following the appropriate musical selections. By means of these, students will embrace hundreds of specific passages of music and make critical decisions about them. The exercises begin by developing basic listening skills—recognizing rhythmic patterns, distinguishing major keys from minor, and differentiating various kinds of textures. The exercises then move on to entire pieces in which students are required to become participants in an artistic exchange, the composer communicating with the listener, and the listener reacting over a long span of time. Ultimately, equipped with these newly developed listening skills, students will move comfortably to the concert hall, listening to classical and popular music with greater confidence and enjoyment. To be sure, this book is for the present course, but its aim is to prepare students for a lifetime of musical listening and enjoyment.

The instructor's enjoyment of the Fifth Edition has been enhanced as well, for now it is possible for students to take the Listening Exercises online, in ThomsonNOW (see below), to have them graded electronically, and to return the results to the instructor's electronic grade book. Instructors will find additional drills and self-tests in ThomsonNOW.

Listening Guides

In addition to the Listening Exercises, more than 100 Listening Guides appear regularly throughout the text to help the novice enjoy extended musical compositions. Within each guide are an introduction to the piece's genre, form, meter, and texture, as well as a "time log" that allows the listener to follow along as the piece unfolds. The discussion in the text, the Listening Exercises, and the Listening Guides have been carefully coordinated, minute by minute, second by second, with the CDs.

Because many pieces now contain internal tracks to cue important points in the composition, the timings in both Listening Guides and Listening Exercises have been carefully keyed to help students find and keep their place. The sample Listening Guide on page xx illustrates how the new keys work. First, gold and blue disc symbols representing the 6-CD and 2-CD sets, respectively, appear at the upper right of the Listening Guide and Listening Exercise. The first number below each disc symbol and before the slash indicates the appropriate CD number, and the number or numbers after the slash indicate track or tracks. Students can thus choose the correct CD and locate the tracks that they need, regardless of which CD set they own. Within all the Listening Guides and the multitrack Listening Exercises, track number reminders appear in small squares, color-coded in gold for the 6-CD set and in blue for the 2-CD set.

For pieces with multiple tracks, there are two timing columns. Those on the left are total elapsed times from the beginning to the end of the piece. Those to the right of the track number reminders and next to the comments are the timings that appear on a CD player's or computer media player's display.

The numbers in the discs indicate the 6-CD set and the 2-CD set. The numbers beneath them tell, first, the specific CD number within that set and, second, the appropriate tracks on that CD. Here, one needs CD 2, tracks 15–16, from the 6-CD set, or CD 1, tracks 17–18, from the 2-CD set.

Listening Guide

Joseph Haydn
String Quartet, Opus 76, No. 3, the "Emperor" Quartet (1797)
Second movement, *Poco adagio cantabile* (rather slow, song-like)

6 **2**
2/15–16 1/17–18

Form: theme and variations

THEME

(repeat)

(repeat)

0:00 [15/17]   Theme played slowly in first violin; lower three parts provide chordal accompaniment

VARIATION 1
1:19   Theme in second violin while first violin ornaments above

VARIATION 2
2:27   Theme in cello while other three instruments provide counterpoint against it

In this track number reminder, the top number indicates that the piece is now playing track 16 from the 6-CD set, and the bottom number indicates track 18 from the 2-CD set. The timing column on the right shows time elapsed within the track, as it would appear on a CD player. The first timing column, on the left, shows total elapsed times from the beginning of the piece.

VARIATION 3
3:45 [16/18] 0:00   Theme in viola; other three instruments enter gradually

VARIATION 4
4:58   1:13   Theme returns to first violin, but now accompaniment is more contrapuntal than chordal

 Use a downloadable, cross-platform animated Active Listening Guide, available at **www.thomsonedu.com/music/wright**.

Each Listening Guide reminds students that a downloadable Active Listening Guide is also available for their use, and each Listening Exercise carries a reminder that the exercise may be completed within ThomsonNOW, to receive feedback and to email answers to the instructor.

Over 150 additional Listening Guides, including those from previous editions, may be downloaded from the Book Companion Website and the instructor's Multimedia Manager.

Cultural Contexts

A series of boxed essays titled "Cultural Context" appears throughout the comprehensive volume of the book. They discuss aspects of the music of Ghana (West Africa), Islam, China, India, Indonesia, and Mexico, as well as Jewish klezmer music. Their aim is to set off in clear relief, and thereby call attention to, the special and often peculiar qualities of Western classical and popular music. Certainly, it is important to know something of non-Western music. But equally important, by studying the musics of other cultures, we can often learn much about our own.

Musical Terminology and the Glossary

As with medicine, law, and architecture, for example, music has its own vocabulary to express concepts unique to this discipline. To engage in a lively dialogue about music, we must all understand and be conversant with this musical vocabulary. All musical terms used in this book are defined in the Glossary (beginning on page 448). They are set in boldface blue type, usually at their first appearance in the text, and are included in the appropriate list of Key Words at the end of the chapter. When they recur in the text, an asterisk reminds readers that a definition can be found in the glossary. Finally, Thomson NOW includes flashcards with audio examples of many musical terms.

Repertoire

Every book about music aims to present the very best musical repertoire. But some musical works make better teaching pieces than others. Whenever possible it is important to emphasize that what students learn in this book is relevant to the music they hear in the real world. To this end, there are twenty-five works new to the Fifth Edition, spanning the centuries, from Dufay to Miles Davis, and for many pieces explanatory boxes elaborate upon the music's relevance today.

Students also need to know that not all music worth hearing was composed by "dead white men." Thus the coverage of women both as composers and as patrons of music remains substantial. Among the women treated in the Fifth Edition are Hildegard of Bingen, Beatriz of Dia, Barbara Strozzi, Clara Schumann, and Ellen Taaffe Zwilich.

Illustrations

Ironically, most beginning students feel more comfortable with the visual arts than with music. The reason for this is not difficult to fathom: Painting, sculpture, and architecture have an immediate appeal to our visual senses. But music cannot be seen or held. It is intangible, ephemeral, and mysterious. Because of this, our ways of thinking and talking about music are different from those used to address the visual arts. A new and separate set of concepts and vocabulary is needed. The notion of scales, chords, meters, and rhythms, for example, involves a technical understanding that can be intimidating initially. To help clarify things, this book uses the language of the visual arts whenever possible to explain musical concepts. In this Fifth Edition, nearly 300 color illustrations help transfer ideas already understood in the visual arts to the process of hearing music.

ANCILLARIES FOR STUDENTS

Introductory CD

Automatically packaged with each new copy of the book, and not sold separately, this CD contains all of the music discussed in Chapters 1–7 on the elements of music, as well as an interactive guide to "Instruments of the Orchestra," which presents the instruments and then tests students' ability to recognize the instruments by themselves and in various combinations. Following a demonstration of the various instruments and instrumental techniques, students may undertake a series of graduated Listening Exercises that test their ability to recognize the instruments.

2-CD Set

This includes a core repertoire of music discussed in the book. Each selection works with an interactive, cross-platform Active Listening Guide (available via website download) that demonstrates visually what students hear.

6-CD Set

This includes all musical selections discussed in the book. Each selection works with an Active Listening Guide (available via website download) that demonstrates visually what students hear.

Active Listening Guides

The Active Listening Guides feature full-color interactive listening guides for every selection on the CD sets.

Directions to Access the Active Listening Guides

1. Go to: http://thomsonedu.com/music/wright.
2. Click on "Active Listening Guides" under the BOOK RESOURCES tab on the left side of the screen.
3. The downloadable files for the CDs are listed for both PC and Mac users.
4. Click on the appropriate format and CD file to download and save it to your desktop/documents folder.
5. To play the Active Listening Guides with a CD, locate the file on your computer and open it, **making sure the corresponding CD is in your CD drive.**
6. See below for more detailed instruction for both PC and Mac users.

Once you've downloaded the CD's Active Listening Guides, you will never need to download them again. Just reopen the file on your computer and be sure to have the corresponding CD in the CD drive.

PC Users

1. Download and save the zip file for any CD.
2. Double click the zip file to open it.
3. Extract the contents of the zip file to your desktop.
4. You should now have a new folder on your computer.
5. Open this folder and launch the .exe program.
6. The application should now be running.

Mac Users

1. Download and save the StuffIt file for any CD.
2. Unstuff the file (this may have happened automatically when you downloaded it).
3. Locate the new folder on your desktop.
4. Open that folder and double click on the Mac icon.

You make also get assistance at 1-800-423-0563 and at *www.thomsonedu.com/support.*

ThomsonNOW

The new ThomsonNOW™ program, prepared in large part by Timothy Roden, of Ohio Wesleyan University, offers several challenging and interesting features. First, it allows for chapter-by-chapter self-study in which students take a Pretest to explore their knowledge of the topics presented in the chapter. The Pretest is followed by a personalized study plan made up of appropriate flashcards, topic summaries, text pages, and demonstrations—all determined by students' answers in the preview quiz. A Posttest follows.

In addition, ThomsonNOW contains interactive versions of the text's Listening Exercises; a video of a performance of Britten's *Young Person's Guide to the Orchestra*, in whole and by instrument families; a link to the downloadable Active Listening Guides; and classroom management for instructors.

vMentor

Live, one-on-one tutoring for students is available through vMentor. When instructors adopt this text packaged with vMentor, they give their students access to virtual office hours—one-on-one, online tutoring help from a subject-area expert, at no additional cost. In vMentor's virtual classroom, students interact with the tutor and other students using two-way audio, an interactive whiteboard, and instant messaging. (For proprietary, college, and university adopters only; for additional information please consult your local Thomson Schirmer representative.)

FOR INSTRUCTORS

Multimedia Manager with Instructor's Resources: A Microsoft® PowerPoint® Tool

This includes the Instructor's Manual and Test Bank, Resource Integration Guide, Exam View® computerized testing, and Microsoft PowerPoint slides with lecture outlines and images that can be used as offered, or customized by importing personal lecture slides or other material. ExamView allows you to create, deliver, and customize tests and study guides (both print and online) in minutes with its easy-to-use assessment and tutorial system. It offers both a Quick Test Wizard and an Online Test Wizard that guide you step by step through the process of creating tests, while its "what you see is what you get" capability allows you to see the test you are creating on the screen exactly as it will print or display online. You can build tests of up to 250 questions using up to twelve question types. Using ExamView's complete word-processing capabilities, you can enter an unlimited number of new questions or edit existing questions.

FOR STUDENTS AND INSTRUCTORS

Website

The *Listening to Music* Companion Website offers additional tools to aid student comprehension. Special features of this site include the free multimedia downloads that accompany the Introductory, 2-CD, and 6-CD sets. The multimedia downloads work with the audio CDs to provide an interactive learning environment for students and feature the following components: listening guides, elements of music tutorial, music style comparisons, and more. Visit *http://music.wadsworth.com* to find an aural dictionary that includes both audio and visual examples of musical terms, an Internet library of web links, and additional text-specific pedagogical devices.

WebTutor, for Blackboard and WebCT

This web-based teaching and learning tool is rich with study and mastery tools, communication tools, and course content. Use WebTutor to provide virtual office hours, post syllabi, set up threaded discussions, track student progress with the quizzing material, and more. For students, WebTutor offers real-time access to a full array of study tools, including flashcards (with audio), practice quizzes, online tutorials, and web links. Instructors can customize the content by uploading images and other resources, adding web links, or creating their own practice materials. WebTutor also provides rich communication tools, including a course calendar, asynchronous discussion, "real-time" chat, and an integrated email system. It is available to qualified adopters. Please contact your local sales representative for details.

ACKNOWLEDGMENTS

Part of the fun of teaching music appreciation comes from discussing with colleagues ways in which to introduce classical music to students who know little about music. What can students be reasonably expected to hear? What is the best terminology to use? Profs. Keith Polk (University of New Hampshire) and Tilden Russell (Southern Connecticut State University) have gently taken me to task for using the term "ternary form" where "rounded binary" is more correct; they are right, yet for fear of overloading the beginning student with too many new formal concepts, here I simplify and call both rounded binary and ternary forms just ternary. I am, nevertheless, grateful for their continuing support and attention to matters of detail. So too I am indebted to Profs. Anne Robertson and Robert Kendrick of the University of Chicago for their input on matters large and small. Five former students— Profs. David Metzer (University of British Columbia), Jess Tyre (SUNY at Potsdam), Marica Tacconi (Pennsylvania State University), Lorenzo Candelaria (University of Texas, Austin), and Laura Nash (Fairfield University)— continue to provide me with valuable criticisms and suggestions. Several colleagues made suggestions for specific improvements in content, for which I am grateful, namely Profs. James Ladewig (University of Rhode Island), Carlo Caballero (University of Colorado, Boulder), Bryan Simms (University of Southern California), James Sinclair (Orchestra New England), Mary Ann Smart (University of California, Berkeley), and Michael Tenzer (University of British Columbia). Finally, Prof. Timothy Roden (Ohio Wesleyan University), the author of the ThomsonNOW materials, Instructor's Manual, and Test Bank, has corrected errors and saved me from myself on numerous occasions.

The following reviewers also evaluated material or provided helpful information during the writing of this book:

Adeline Bethany
Cabrini College

D. E. Bussineau-King
University of the Incarnate Word

Andrew Byrne
Australian Music Center

Ann B. Caldwell
Georgia College and State University

Cheong L. Chuah
Cerro Cosso Community College

Kyle Cheong Chuah
Los Medanos College

Ginger Covert
Colla Modesto Junior College

Joseph Darby
Keene State College

Willis Delony
Louisiana State University

Hollie Duvall
Westmoreland County Community College

Harry Faulk
Fairmont State College

Fenton G. Fly
Alabama State University

Holly J. Gaines
Ursinus College

Nancy M. Gamso
Ohio Wesleyan University

Cliff Ganus
Harding University

Benjamin K. Gish
Walla Walla College

Stephanie B. Graber
University of Wisconsin, Stout

Larry N. Graham
Valencia Community College

David Grayson
University of Minnesota

Mary-Jo Grenfell
Salem State College

Patricia L. Hales
Purdue University, Calumet

Patricia Harden
Rockingham Community College

Marymal L. Holmes
Bowie State University

David Lee Jackson
Baylor University

Tido Janssen
Hardin-Simmons University

David Johansen
Southeastern Louisiana University

Benjamin M. Korstvedt
University of St. Thomas

Walter Kreiszig
University of Saskatchewan

Charles S. Larkowski
Wright State University

Mark Latham
Butte College

Bernard C. Lemoine
Mary Washington College

Gary Lewis
Midwestern State University

Ed Macan
College of the Redwoods

Michael Moss
Southern Connecticut State University

Sharon H. Nelson
Wright State University

Mustak Zafer Ozgen
Baruch College

Diane M. Paige
University of California, Santa Barbara

Linda Pohly
Ball State University

Thomas C. Polett
Culver-Stockton College

Julia M. Quick
South Carolina State University

Ronald Rabin
University of Michigan

Daniel Ratelle
San Diego Mesa College

Laurie A. Reese
Lebanon Community College

Rebecca Ringer
Collin County Community College

Steven Roberson
Butler University

Timothy J. Roden
Ohio Wesleyan University

Karl Schmidt
Towson University

Christine Larson Seitz
Indiana University South Bend

Richard Shillea
Fairfield University

John Sinclair
Rollins College

Jayme Stayer
Owens Community College

Lawrence Stomberg
University of Delaware

Larry Stuckenholtz
St. Louis Community College

Janet L. Sturman
University of Arizona

Gary R. Sudano
Purdue University

Timothy P. Urban
Rutgers University

Melva Villard
Louisiana State University at Alexandria

Susan Weiss
Johns Hopkins University

Carolyn Wilson
Chipola College

Graham Wood
Coker College

Barbara Young
University of Wisconsin, Eau Claire

Annette H. Zalanowski
Pennsylvania State University, Altoona

Ray H. Ziegler
Salisbury State University

I owe a special debt of gratitude to two individuals who contributed greatly to this Fifth Edition. Prof. Nathan Link (Centre College) critiqued the manuscript, provided many helpful ideas about contemporary musical culture, and generated text on specialized subjects. Sue Gleason (Thomson Schirmer) directed her exceptionally insightful attention to all aspects of this complex project: text, audio, website, and ancillary materials. Not to be overlooked is the important contribution of Prof. Andrew Tomasello (Baruch College, CUNY) who wrote the bulk of Chapter 41. I have also benefited from the help and good will of the staff of the Yale Music Library: Kendall Crilly, librarian; and Suzanne Lovejoy, Richard Boursy, and Evan Heater. Karl Schrom, record librarian at Yale, has been a source of good advice regarding the availability and quality of recordings for twenty years, and audio engineer Mateusz Zechowski (Studioteo) skillfully crafted a set of CDs of the highest quality. As always, it has been a privilege to work with publisher Clark Baxter and his experienced team at Thomson Schirmer—Emily Ryan, Nell Pepper, Diane Wenckebach, Rachel Bairstow, Trudy Brown, Tom Briggs, and Melanie Field—as well as Felicia Gearhart and Kirk Tsuye at Universal Records, and Tom and Lisa Smialek, developers of the Active Listening tools. My heartiest thanks to all of you! Finally, I thank my loving wife and attorney, Sherry Dominick, who might have sued me for "loss of consortium" during this project, but didn't.

PART I

The Elements of Music

Listening to Music

"It is perhaps in music that the dignity of art is most eminently apparent, for it elevates and ennobles everything that it expresses."
Johann Wolfgang von Goethe (1749–1832)

"It don't mean a thing if it ain't got that swing."
Edward Kennedy "Duke" Ellington (1899–1974)

We listen to music because it gives us pleasure. But why does it give us pleasure? Because it affects our minds and bodies, albeit in ways that we do not yet fully understand. Music has the power to intensify and deepen our feelings, to calm our jangled nerves, to make us sad or cheerful, to inspire us to dance, and even, perhaps, to incite us to march proudly off to war. Since time immemorial, people around the world have made music an indispensable part of their lives. Music adds to the solemnity of ceremonies, arts, and entertainments, heightening the emotional experience of onlookers and participants. If you doubt this, try watching a movie without listening to the musical score, or imagine how empty a parade, a wedding, or a funeral would be without music.

FIGURE 1–1

A medieval representation of how music was transmitted. Pope Gregory the Great (590–604) receives what is now called "Gregorian chant" from the Holy Spirit (a dove on his shoulder) and communicates it orally to a scribe who writes down the music on either parchment or a wax tablet.

Stiftsbibliothek, St. Gallen

HOW MUSICAL SOUND AND SOUND MACHINES WORK

When we listen to music, we are reacting physically to an organized disturbance in our environment. A voice or an instrument creates a vibration that travels through the air as sound waves, reaching our ears to be processed by our brain as electrochemical impulses (see boxed essay). Low-pitched sounds vibrate slowly and move through the air in long sound waves; higher pitches vibrate more rapidly and move as shorter waves.

While these principles of acoustics are invariable, our means for capturing and preserving sound have evolved over the centuries, with an ever-accelerating rate of change. Most early musical traditions were passed down by oral means alone. Not until around 900 C.E., when Benedictine monks began to set notes down on parchment to preserve their chants (Fig. 1–1), was a significant amount of music preserved in written notation. Thus, at first, only religious music was written down. Popular music—dances and troubadour songs, for example—first appeared in notation around 1250. As the centuries progressed, composers began to insert such directions as "dynamics" (indicating louds and softs) and "tempo" markings (showing how fast the piece should go), eventually producing the complex musical score familiar to classical musicians today.

Machines for capturing and replaying sound began to appear in the nineteenth century, with Thomas Edison's phono-

Music and the Brain

Mozart had an extraordinary musical ear—or, more correctly, musical brain. In April 1771, at the age of fourteen, he heard Gregorio Allegri's *Miserere*, a two-minute religious work, performed in Rome, and later that day wrote it down in all parts by memory, note for note, after just this one hearing. Obviously, he could process and retain far more musical information than can the rest of us. Mozart had a very keen sense of absolute pitch (the ability to instantly recognize specific pitches), a gift given to only one in about 10,000 individuals. But how, in simple terms, do we hear and remember music?

When a musician, such as virtuoso Sarah Chang, sings or plays an instrument, she creates mechanical energy that moves through the air as sound waves. These first reach the inner ear where the cochleae (one for each ear)

Sarah Chang playing the violin.

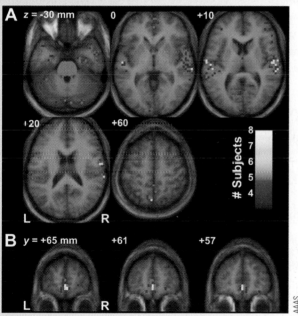

The brain at work while listening to music.

convert sound energy into electrical signals. These are then passed by means of neurons to the primary auditory cortex, located in the center of the brain, where the neurons are "mapped" in a way that identifies the pitch, color, and intensity of sound. How we feel about the music we hear—happy or sad, energetic or melancholy—is determined by different areas in this and other parts of the brain. Neurobiologists have observed increased levels of the chemical dopamine in our gray matter when pleasing music is heard, just as when we enjoy such experiences as eating chocolate. Thus, sound patterns enter our brain and incite specific neurological reactions that can make us feel relaxed or agitated, happy or sad. Oddly then, music alters the way we feel in much the same manner as a chemical substance, such as a candy bar, a medicine, or a drug. We can acquire the mechanism for a "mood-enhancing" experience, it seems, either over the counter or over the airwaves.

graph, patented in 1877, representing the most significant development. The twentieth century saw the advent of the magnetic tape recorder (first used to record music in 1936). In the 1990s, these earlier devices were superseded by the digital technologies of the compact disc (CD) and the MP3 file. In these formats, the pitch, intensity, and duration of any sound are converted into numerical data that can be stored on disc, hard drive, or any number of other digital media. When a digital recording is played, these numerical data are reconverted into electrical impulses that are amplified and pushed through audio speakers or headphones as sound waves (Fig. 1–2).

technology of recorded music

FIGURE 1–2
A student listening to an MP3 file on an iPod.

LISTENING TO WHOSE MUSIC?

Music is heard everywhere in the world. Numerous forms of art music, rooted in centuries of tradition, thrive in China, India, Indonesia, and elsewhere. Musical practices associated with religious ceremonies, coming-of-age rituals, and other social occasions flourish across Africa and Latin America. Dance music serves a central function for youth culture in nightclubs and discotheques across the globe. In the West, classical music still holds sway in concert halls and opera houses, while numerous idioms of Western popular music—rock, hip-hop, and country, for example—dominate the commercial landscape. Jazz, a particularly American form of vernacular music, shares traits with both Western classical and popular music.

What is more, the increasing frequency of "fusions" among musical styles illustrates the trend of musical "globalization" in recent years. Afro-Cuban genres draw upon musical traditions ranging from Caribbean styles, to jazz, to the music of old Spain. Classical cellist Yo-Yo Ma performs with traditional Chinese musicians on the *Silk Road Project,* while British pop singer Sting has collaborated with musicians ranging from jazz virtuoso Branford Marsalis to Algerian singer Cheb Mami. To be sure, there are plenty of styles, and fusions of styles, from which to choose. We might on occasion choose a certain kind of music—classical, traditional, or popular—according to its association with our own heritage, while at other times we might base our decision on our mood or activity at a particular moment.

CLASSICAL MUSIC–POPULAR MUSIC

Most of the music that will be discussed in this book is what we generally refer to as "classical" music. We might also call it "high art" music or "learned" music, because a particular set of skills is needed to perform and appreciate it. **Classical music** is often regarded as "old" music, written by "dead white men." But this is not entirely accurate: no small amount of it has been written by women, and many "high art" composers, of both sexes, are very much alive and well today. In truth, however, much of what we hear by way of classical music—the music of Bach, Beethoven, and Brahms, for example—*is* old. That is why, in part, it is called "classical." We refer to clothes, furniture, and automobiles as "classics" because they have timeless qualities of expression, proportion, and balance. So, too, we give the name "classical" to music with these same qualities, music that has endured the test of time.

What is a "classic"?

Popular music, as its name suggests, appeals to a much larger segment of the population. Pop and rock CDs outsell classical music recordings by more than ten to one. Popular music can be just as artful and just as serious as classical music, and often the musicians who perform it are just as skilled as classical musicians. Some musicians are equally at home in both idioms (Fig. 1–3). But how do classical and popular music differ?

- Classical music relies on **acoustic instruments** (the sounds of which are not electronically altered), such as the trumpet, violin, and piano; popular music often uses technological innovations such as electrically amplified guitars and basses, electronic synthesizers, and computers.
- Classical music relies greatly on preset musical notation, and therefore the work (a symphony, for example) is to some extent a "fixed entity;" popular

music relies mostly on oral and aural transmission, and the work can change greatly from one performance to the next. Rarely do we see performers reading from written music at a pop concert.

- Classical music is primarily, but by no means exclusively, instrumental, with meaning communicated through a language of musical sounds and gestures; most popular music makes use of a text or "lyric" to convey its meaning.
- Classical compositions can be lengthy and involve a variety of moods, and the listener must concentrate over a long period of time; most popular pieces are relatively short, averaging from three to four minutes in length, and possess a single mood from beginning to end.
- In classical music the rhythmic "beat" often rests beneath the surface of the music; popular music relies greatly on an immediately audible, recurrent beat.
- Classical music suggests to the listener a chance to escape from the everyday world into a realm of abstract sound patterning; popular music has a more immediate impact, and its lyrics often embrace issues of contemporary life.

Why Listen to Classical Music?

Given the immediate appeal of popular music, why would anyone *choose* to listen to classical music? To find out, National Public Radio in 2004 commissioned a survey of regular listeners of classical music. Summarized briefly below, in order of importance, are the most common reasons expressed by classical listeners:

1. Classical music relieves stress and helps the listener to relax.
2. Classical music helps "center the mind," allowing the listener to concentrate.
3. Classical music provides a vision of a better world, a refuge of beauty and majesty in which we pass beyond the limits of our material existence.
4. Classical music offers the opportunity to learn: about music, about history, and about people.

Classical listeners were given the chance to elaborate on why they prefer this kind of music. Here is just one typical response for each category:

1. "My work is pretty stressful, and when it gets really stressful, I turn to classical. It calms me down. It soothes the savage beast."
2. "It's very good for the brain."
3. "Enjoying a symphony takes me back to great childhood memories."
4. "I'm not educated in music. I'm like really stupid about it, but this is one way [listening on the radio] that I can educate myself, in my own stumbling, bumbling musical way."

From mental and emotional well-being, to increased concentration and enriched imagination, to deeper understanding of human culture and history, it would seem that classical music has something to offer virtually everyone.

Classical Music All Around You

You may not listen to classical music on the radio (found on the dial in most regions between 90.0 and 93.0 FM). You may not attend concerts of classical music. Nevertheless, you listen to a great deal of classical music. Vivaldi con-

© Lynn Goldsmith/Corbis

FIGURE 1–3

Trumpeter Wynton Marsalis can record a Baroque trumpet concerto one week and an album of New Orleans–style jazz the next. He has won nine Grammy awards, seven for various jazz categories and two for classical discs.

classical music good for the brain

certos and Mozart symphonies are played regularly in Starbucks. Snippets of Beethoven's Ninth Symphony introduce segments of the news on MSNBC. Traditional operatic melodies provide runway music as models strut in tele-thons for Victoria's Secret clothing, and a famous Puccini aria sounds promi-nently in the best-selling video game *Grand Theft Auto*, perhaps for ironic ef-fect. What famous composer has not had one or more of his best-known works incorporated into a film score, to heighten our emotional response to what we see? Classical music—composed by Bach, Beethoven, Copland, Verdi, and especially Mozart, among others—has also been appropriated to provide sonic backdrops for radio and television advertisements. Here it usually acts as a "high end" marketing tool designed to encourage rich living: to sell a Lexis au-tomobile or a De Beers diamond, advertisers realize, they must allow Mozart, not Kurt Cobain or Eminem, to set the mood.

everyday use of classical music

Attending a Classical Concert

There is no better way to experience the splendor of classical music than to attend a concert. Compared to pop or rock concerts, performances of classi-cal music may seem strange indeed. First of all, people dress "up," not "down": at classical events, attendees wear "costumes" or "uniforms" (coat and tie, suit, or evening wear) of a very different sort than they do at, say, rock concerts (punk, grunge, or metal attire). Throughout the performance, the classical audi-ence sits rigidly, saying nothing to friends or performers. No one sways, dances, or sings along to the music. Only at the end of each composition does the audi-ence express itself, clapping respectfully.

aspects of a classical concert

But classical concerts weren't always so formal. In the eighteenth century, the audience talked during performances and yelled words of encouragement to the players. People clapped at the end of each movement of a symphony and often in the middle of the movement as well. After an exceptionally pleas-ing performance, listeners would demand that the piece be repeated immedi-ately (an **encore**). If, on the other hand, the audience didn't like what it heard, it would express its displeasure by throwing fruit and other debris toward the stage. Our modern, more dignified clas-sical concert was a creation of the nine-teenth century (see page 254), when the musical composition came to be consid-ered a work of high art worthy of reveren-tial silence.

FIGURE 1–4

Symphony Hall in Boston. The best seats for hearing the music are not up front, but at the back in the middle of the balcony.

© Corbis

Attending a classical concert requires preparation and forethought. Most im-portant, you must become familiar in ad-vance with the musical repertoire. Go to a music library and listen to a recording of the piece that will be performed, or per-haps download it from iTunes. Hearing a recording by professional performers will prepare you to judge the merits of a live (perhaps student) performance.

Choosing the right seat is also impor-tant. What is best for seeing may not be best for hearing. In some concert halls, the sound sails immediately over the front seats and settles at the back (Fig. 1–4). Often the optimal seat in terms of acoustics is at the back of the hall, in the first balcony. Sitting closer, of course, allows you to watch the performers on stage. If you attend a concert of a symphony orchestra, follow the gestures that the conductor makes to the various soloists and sections of the orchestra; like a circus ringmaster, he or she turns directly to the soloist of a given moment. The conductor conveys to the players the essential lines and themes of the music, and they in turn communicate these to the audience.

where to sit

LEARNING TO BE A GOOD LISTENER

Most people would scoff at the idea that they need to *learn* how to listen to music. We think that because we can *hear* well, we are good *listeners*. But the ability to listen to music—classical music in particular—is an acquired skill that demands good instruction and much practice. Music can be difficult stuff. First of all, we must learn how it works. For example, how do melodies unfold? What constitutes a rhythm and what makes a beat? And how and why do harmonies change? Similarly, we must work to improve our musical memory. Music is an art that unfolds while passing through time; to make sense of what we hear *now*, we have to remember what we heard *before*. Finally, we will need to gain an understanding of the secret signs or codes by which composers have traditionally expressed meaning in music: the tensions, anxieties, and hostilities expressed in musical language, as well as its triumphs and moments of inner peace. To accomplish this, we must devote our complete attention to the music—using it as a mere backdrop to other activities simply won't do. We must concentrate fully in order to hear the mechanics of music at the surface level (the workings of rhythm, melody, and harmony, for example), as well as to understand the deeper, emotional meaning. The following discussions and their accompanying Listening Exercises will begin to transform you into disciplined and discerning listeners. At the same time, you will come to see that classical music—indeed all music—sometimes works its magic in mysterious and inexplicable ways.

learn how music works

focus solely on the music

GETTING STARTED: THREE MUSICAL BEGINNINGS

In a work of art that unfolds over time—a poem, a novel, a symphony, or a film, for example—the beginning is critical to the success of the work. The artist must capture the attention of the reader, listener, or viewer by means of some kind of new approach as well as convey the essence of the experience that is to follow. We can learn much about how classical music works by engaging just the beginnings of three strikingly original compositions.

Ludwig van Beethoven, Symphony No. 5 (1808)—Opening

The beginning of Beethoven's Symphony No. 5 is perhaps the best-known moment in all of classical music. Its "short-short-short-long" gesture is as much an icon of Western culture as is the "To be, or not to be" soliloquy in Shakespeare's *Hamlet*. Beethoven wrote this symphony in 1808 when he was thirty-

FIGURE 1–5

A portrait of Ludwig van Beethoven painted in 1818–1819 by Ferdinand Schimon (1797–1852).

Snark, Art Resource, NY

seven and almost totally deaf (Fig. 1–5; see Chapter 21 for a biography of Beethoven). How could a deaf person write a symphony? Simply said, he could do so because musicians hear with "an inner ear," meaning that their brains can create and rework melodies without recourse to externally audible sound. In this way, the nearly-deaf Beethoven fashioned an entire thirty-minute symphony.

A **symphony** is a genre, or type, of music for orchestra, divided into several pieces called **movements,** each possessing its own tempo and mood. A typical classical symphony will have four movements with the respective tempos of fast, slow, moderate, and fast. A symphony is played by an **orchestra,** a large ensemble of acoustic instruments such as violins, trumpets, and flutes. Although an orchestra might play a concerto, an overture, or a dance suite, historically it has played more symphonies than anything else, and for that reason is called a **symphony orchestra.** The orchestra for which Beethoven composed his fifth symphony was made up of about sixty players, including string, wind, and percussion instruments.

Beethoven begins his symphony with the musical equivalent of a punch in the nose. The four-pitch rhythm "short-short-short-long" is quick and abrupt. It is all the more unsettling because the music has no clear-cut beat or grounding harmony to support it. Our reaction is one of surprise, perhaps bewilderment, perhaps even fear. The brevity of the opening rhythm is typical of what we call a musical **motive,** a short, distinctive musical figure that can stand by itself. In the course of this symphony, Beethoven will repeat and reshape this opening motive, making it serve as the unifying thread of the entire symphony.

Having shaken, even staggered, the listener with this opening blow, Beethoven then begins to bring clarity and direction to his music. The motive sounds in rapid succession, rising stepwise in pitch, and the volume progressively increases. When the volume of sound increases in music—gets louder—we have a **crescendo,** and conversely, when it decreases, a **diminuendo.** Beethoven uses the crescendo here to suggest a continuous progression—he is taking us from point A to point B. Suddenly the music stops: we have arrived. A French horn (a brass instrument; see page 51) then blasts forth, as if to say, "And now for something new." Indeed, new material follows: a beautiful flowing melody played first by the strings and then by the winds. Its lyrical motion serves as a welcome contrast to the almost rude opening motive. Soon the motive reasserts itself, but is gradually transformed into a melodic pattern that sounds more heroic than threatening, and with this, Beethoven ends his opening section.

In sum, in the opening of Symphony No. 5, Beethoven shows us that his musical world includes many different feelings and states of mind, among them the fearful, the lyrical, and the heroic. When asked what the opening motive of the symphony meant, Beethoven is reported to have said, "There fate knocks at the door." In the course of the four movements of this symphony (all of which are included in the six-CD set), Beethoven takes us on a fateful journey that includes moments of fear, despair, and, ultimately, triumph.

a fateful musical journey

Turn now to this opening section (🔘/1) and to the Listening Guide. Here you will see musical notation representing the principal musical events. This notation may seem alien to you, but don't panic—the essentials of musical notation will be explained fully in Chapters 2–3. For the moment, simply play the music and follow along according to the minute and second counter on your player.

Listening Guide

Ludwig van Beethoven
Symphony No. 5 in C minor (1808)
First movement, *Allegro con brio* (fast with gusto)

(Intro 1)

0:00	▮ 1	Opening "short-short-short long" motive
0:22		Music gathers momentum and moves forward in purposeful fashion
0:42		Pause; French horn solo
0:45		New lyrical melody sounds forth in strings and is then answered by winds
1:04		Rhythm of opening motive returns
1:14		Opening motive reshaped into more heroic-sounding melody

Use a downloadable, cross-platform animated Active Listening Guide, available at **www.thomsonedu.com/music/wright.**

Peter Tchaikovsky, Piano Concerto No. 1 (1875)—Opening

All of us have heard the charming and often exciting music of Peter Tchaikovsky (1840–1893), especially his ballet *The Nutcracker,* a perennial holiday favorite. Tchaikovsky was a Russian composer who earned his living first as a teacher of music at the Moscow Conservatory and then, later in life, as an independent composer who traveled widely around Europe and even to the United States (see Chapter 30 for his biography). All types of classical music flowed from his pen, including ballets, operas, overtures, symphonies, and concertos.

A **concerto** is a genre of music in which an instrumental soloist plays with, and sometimes against, a full orchestra. Thus the concerto suggests both cooperation and competition, one between soloist and orchestra in the spirit of "anything you can do, I can do better." Most concertos consist of three movements, usually with tempos of fast, slow, and fast. Tchaikovsky's Piano Concerto No. 1 was composed in 1875 and premiered that year, not in Russia but in Boston, where it was performed by the Boston Symphony. Since that time, Tchaikovsky's first concerto has gone on to become what *The New York Times* called his "all-time most popular score."

The popularity of this work stems in large measure from the opening section of the first movement. Tchaikovsky, like Beethoven above, begins with a four-note motive, but here the pitches move downward in equal durations and are played by brass instruments, not strings. The opening motive quickly yields to a succession of block-like sounds called chords. A **chord** in music is simply the simultaneous sounding of two or more pitches. Here the chords are played first by the orchestra and then by the piano. Suddenly the violins enter with a sweeping melody that builds progressively in length and grandeur, a melody surely found near the top of every music lover's list of "fifty great

a Russian concerto premiered in Boston

classical melodies." Tchaikovsky's beginning makes clear the difference between a motive and a **melody:** the former is a short unit, like a musical cell or building block, while the latter is longer and more tuneful and song-like. As the violins introduce the melody, the piano plays chords against it. Soon, however, the roles are reversed: the piano plays the melody, embellishing it along the way, while the strings of the orchestra provide the accompanying chords. To make the music lighter, Tchaikovsky instructs the strings to play the chords **pizzicato,** a technique in which the performers pluck the strings of their instruments with their fingers rather than bowing them. Then, after some technical razzle-dazzle provided by the pianist, the melody sweeps back one last time. In this glorious, lush final statement of the melody by the strings, we experience the essence of musical romanticism.

the essence of musical romanticism

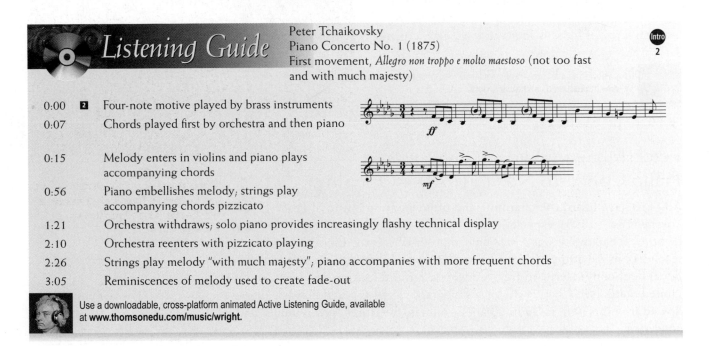

Listening Guide

Peter Tchaikovsky
Piano Concerto No. 1 (1875)
First movement, *Allegro non troppo e molto maestoso* (not too fast and with much majesty)

Intro 2

0:00	2	Four-note motive played by brass instruments
0:07		Chords played first by orchestra and then piano
0:15		Melody enters in violins and piano plays accompanying chords
0:56		Piano embellishes melody; strings play accompanying chords pizzicato
1:21		Orchestra withdraws; solo piano provides increasingly flashy technical display
2:10		Orchestra reenters with pizzicato playing
2:26		Strings play melody "with much majesty"; piano accompanies with more frequent chords
3:05		Reminiscences of melody used to create fade-out

Use a downloadable, cross-platform animated Active Listening Guide, available at **www.thomsonedu.com/music/wright.**

Richard Strauss, *Also Sprach Zarathustra* (*Thus Spoke Zarathustra;* 1896)—Opening

There were two important composers named Strauss in the history of music. One, Johann Strauss, Jr. (1825–1899), was Austrian and is known as "the Waltz King" because he wrote mainly popular waltzes. The other, Richard Strauss (1864–1949), was German and composed primarily operas and large-scale compositions for orchestra called tone poems. A **tone poem** (also called a **symphonic poem**) is a one-movement work for orchestra that tries to capture in music the emotions and events associated with a story, play, or personal experience. In his tone poem *Thus Spoke Zarathustra,* Richard Strauss tries to depict in music the events described in a novel of that title by the German philosopher Friedrich Nietzsche (1844–1900). The hero of Nietzsche's story is the ancient Persian prophet Zarathustra (Zoroaster), who foretells the coming of a more advanced human, a Superman. (This strain in German Romantic philosophy was later perverted by Adolf Hitler into the cult of a "master race.")

music inspired by a novel

Strauss's tone poem begins at the moment at which Zarathustra addresses the rising sun. The listener may sense in the music the dawn of a new age, the advent of an all-powerful superman, or simply the rising of the sun (Fig. 1–6).

While the imposing title *Thus Spoke Zarathustra* may seem foreign, and the mention of German philosophy intimidating, Strauss's music is well known to you. It gained fame in the late 1960s when used as film music in Stanley Kubrick's 2001: *A Space Odyssey*. Since then it has sounded forth in countless radio and TV commercials to convey a sense of high drama. The music begins with a low rumble as if coming from the depths of the earth. From this darkness emerges a ray of light as four trumpets play a rising motive that Strauss called the "Nature Theme." The light suddenly falls dark and then rises again, ultimately to culminate in a stunning climax. How do you describe a sunrise through music? Strauss tells us. The music should ascend in pitch, get louder, grow in warmth (more instruments), and reach an impressive climax. Simple as they may be, these are the technical means Strauss employs to convey musical meaning. Nowhere in the musical repertoire is there a more vivid depiction of the power of nature or the potential of humankind.

Cindy Davis

FIGURE 1–6

A fanciful depiction of the opening of Friedrich Nietzsche's *Thus Spoke Zarathustra* with the rise of the all-powerful sun.

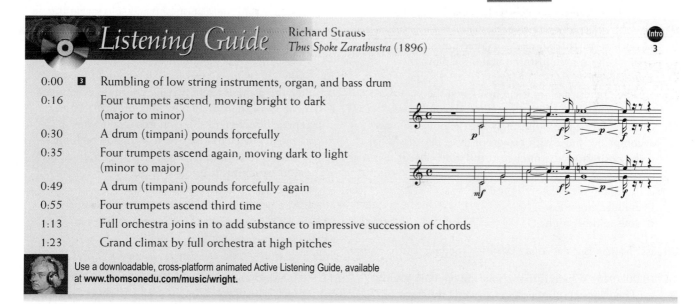

Listening Guide

Richard Strauss
Thus Spoke Zarathustra (1896)

Intro
3

0:00	**3**	Rumbling of low string instruments, organ, and bass drum
0:16		Four trumpets ascend, moving bright to dark (major to minor)
0:30		A drum (timpani) pounds forcefully
0:35		Four trumpets ascend again, moving dark to light (minor to major)
0:49		A drum (timpani) pounds forcefully again
0:55		Four trumpets ascend third time
1:13		Full orchestra joins in to add substance to impressive succession of chords
1:23		Grand climax by full orchestra at high pitches

 Use a downloadable, cross-platform animated Active Listening Guide, available at **www.thomsonedu.com/music/wright**.

Listening Exercise 1

Musical Beginnings

Intro
1–3

ThomsonNOW

To take this Listening Exercise online and receive feedback or email answers to your instructor, go to *ThomsonNOW* for this chapter.

This first Listening Exercise asks you to review three of the most famous "beginnings" in the entire repertoire of classical music. The following questions encourage

(continued)

you to listen actively, sometimes to just small details in the music. This first exercise is designed to be user-friendly—the questions are not too difficult.

Beethoven, Symphony No. 5 (1808)—Opening

1. (0:00–0:05) Beethoven opens his Symphony No. 5
1 with the famous "short-short-short-long" motive and then immediately repeats. Does the repetition present the motive at a higher or at a lower level of pitch?
   a. higher pitches
   b. lower pitches

2. (0:22–0:44) In this passage, Beethoven constructs a musical transition that moves us from the opening motive to a more lyrical second theme. Which is true about this transition?
   a. The music seems to get slower and makes use of a diminuendo.
   b. The music seems to get faster and makes use of a crescendo.

3. (0:38–0:44) How does Beethoven add intensity to the conclusion of the transition?
   a. A pounding drum (timpani) is added to the orchestra and then a French horn plays a solo.
   b. A French horn plays a solo and then a pounding drum (timpani) is added to the orchestra.

4. (0:42–0:44) Which combination of short (S) and long (L) sounds accurately represents what the solo French horn plays at the end of this transition?
   a. SSSSL   b. SSSSSL   c. SSSLLL

5. (0:45–1:02) Now a more lyrical new theme enters in the violins and is echoed by the winds. But has the opening motive (SSSL) really disappeared?
   a. Yes, it is no longer present.
   b. No, it can be heard above the new melody.
   c. No, it lurks below the new melody.

6. (1:13–1:21) Which is true about the end of this opening section?
   a. Beethoven brings back the opening motive.
   b. Beethoven brings back the material from the transition.
   c. Beethoven brings back the second, lyrical theme.

7. *Student choice* (no "correct" answer): How do you feel about the end of the opening section, compared to the beginning?
   a. less anxious and more self-confident
   b. less self-confident and even more anxious

Tchaikovsky, Piano Concerto No. 1 (1875)—Opening

8. (0:00–0:06) How many times does the French horn
2 play the descending motive?
   a. once   b. three times   c. five times

9. (0:07–0:14) Which instrumental force plays the chords first?
   a. The orchestra plays them first (then the piano).
   b. The piano plays them first (then the orchestra).

10. (0:15–0:43) As the violins play the melody, the piano accompanies them with groups of three chords. What is the position of the pitches of the three chords in each group?
   a. high, middle, low
   b. middle, high, low
   c. low, middle, high

11. (1:30–2:22) In the section of piano solo razzle-dazzle, which sounds more prominently?
   a. the four-note descending motive
   b. the long, sweeping melody

12. (2:26–2:54) During this final statement of the melody, the piano is again playing chords as accompaniment. Now there are many more of them, but the general direction of these chords is still what?
   a. moving high to low   b. moving low to high

13. (3:05–3:21) Tchaikovsky revisits which musical material to create this fade-out?
   a. the four-note descending motive
   b. the beginning of the sweeping melody

Strauss, *Thus Spoke Zarathustra* (1896)—Opening

14. (0:00–0:15) Which is true about the opening sounds?
3 a. The instruments are playing several different sounds in succession.
   b. The instruments are holding one and the same tone.

15. (0:16–0:20) When the trumpets enter and ascend, does the low, rumbling sound disappear?
   a. yes   b. no

16. (0:16–0:22 and again at 0:35–0:43) When the trumpets rise, how many notes (different pitches) do they play?
   a. one   b. two   c. three

17. (0:30–0:35 and again at 0:49–0:54) When the timpani enters, how many different pitches does it play?
   a. one   b. two   c. three

18. (1:15–1:21) In this passage, the trombones enter and play a loud counterpoint to the rising trumpets. In which direction is the music of the trombone going?
   a. up   b. down

19. (1:27) At the very last chord, a new sound is added for emphasis—to signal that this is indeed the last chord of the climax. What is that sound?

a. a crashing cymbal
b. a piano
c. an electric bass guitar
20. *Student choice:* You have now heard three very different musical openings, by Beethoven, Tchaikovsky, and

Strauss. Which do you prefer? Which grabbed your attention the most? Think about why.
a. Beethoven   b. Tchaikovsky   c. Strauss

Key Words

classical music (**4**)	orchestra (**8**)	chord (**9**)
popular music (**4**)	symphony	melody (**10**)
acoustic	orchestra (**8**)	pizzicato (**10**)
instrument (**4**)	motive (**8**)	tone poem
encore (**6**)	crescendo (**8**)	(symphonic
symphony (**8**)	diminuendo (**8**)	poem) (**10**)
movement (**8**)	concerto (**9**)	

Rhythm

Chapter
2

Music can be defined as sound that moves through time in an organized fashion. It involves, therefore, the interaction of time (expressed as rhythm, the subject of this chapter) and pitch (expressed as melody and harmony, the subjects of Chapters 3 and 4). Rhythm, melody, and harmony are the building blocks of music, and how they are arranged affects the color, texture, and form (the subjects of Chapters 5 and 6), and, ultimately, the meaning of every musical composition.

In discussing rhythm, melody, and harmony, we rely on terminology that has developed alongside the practice of notating music. Musical notation is a system that allows us to represent sound on paper by means of special signs and symbols. In Western musical notation, the passing of time (rhythm) is represented by notes placed on a horizontal axis (moving left to right), with black (filled) notes moving more quickly than white (empty) notes. Pitch (melody and harmony) is shown by a vertical axis (top to bottom) with the higher-placed notes representing higher pitches. Example 2–1A shows low, slow sounds that become progressively higher and faster, while Example 2–1B shows the reverse:

the terminology of musical notation

EXAMPLE 2–1A

EXAMPLE 2–1B

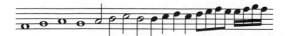

When we use musical notation, we in effect "freeze" a piece of music so that it can be reproduced exactly by performers at some later date. What is more, musical notation allows us to stop at any point. We can look at a composition as it "stands still," talk about its various parts, and learn something about how the music is put together. You can derive great pleasure from listening to music, of course, without being able to read musical notation. Indeed, musical notation is wholly absent from most musical cultures around the world. But the enjoyment of Western classical music in particular can be enhanced if you understand how this music works, and to see how it works, it helps to understand musical notation.

the advantages of musical notation

RHYTHM AND RHYTHMIC NOTATION

Rhythm is arguably the most fundamental element of music. When asked to sing a tune, most of us will recall the rhythm better than the melody. (To prove the point, try singing the theme song from *The Simpsons*.) We have a direct, even physical, response to rhythm. We can move to it, even dance to its pulse.

Rhythm, in the broadest definition, is the organization of time in music (Fig. 2–1). Rhythm divides time into long and short spans, and thereby gives shape to the pitches of the melody. Musical rhythms are supported and clarified by a beat. The **beat** is an even pulse that divides the passing of time into equal units. It may be strongly felt, as in a waltz or a straight-ahead rock 'n' roll tune, or it may be only vaguely sensed (because no instrument plays it strongly), as often happens in classical music. But whether immediately or distantly heard, almost all music has a beat. When we clap along with or tap our feet to music, we are reacting to such a beat.

The beat in music is most often represented by a unit of measurement called the quarter note (♩), a basic duration in music. Normally, the quarter note moves along at roughly the rate of the average person's heartbeat, sometimes faster, sometimes slower. As you might suspect from its name, the quarter note is shorter in length than the half and the whole note, but longer than the eighth and the sixteenth note. These other note values account for durations that are longer or shorter than a single beat. Here are the symbols for the most-used musical notes and an indication of how they relate to one another in length.

EXAMPLE 2–2

(whole note) 𝅝 = ♩ ♩   (2 half notes = 4 beats)

(half note) ♩ = ♩ ♩   (2 quarter notes = 2 beats)

(quarter note) ♩ = ♪ ♪   (2 eighth notes = 1 beat)

(eighth note) ♪ = ♬ ♬   (2 sixteenth notes = ½ beat)

To help the performer keep the beat when playing or singing, the smaller note values—specifically, those with flags on the vertical stem—are beamed, or joined together, in groups of two or four.

EXAMPLE 2–3

♩ ♪ ♪ ♬ ♬   becomes   ♩ ♫ ♩ ♬

FIGURE 2–1

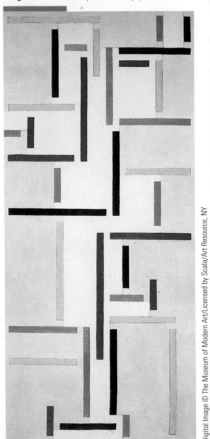

Rhythms of a Russian Dance (1918) by Theo van Doesburg. Rhythm in music is the rational organization of time into longer and shorter durations. The same process can be at work in the visual arts. Here the painter places units of color of different length to form complementary patterns.

Digital Image © The Museum of Modern Art/Licensed by Scala/Art Resource, NY

In vocal music, however, the beaming is broken when a syllable of text is placed below a note.

EXAMPLE 2–4

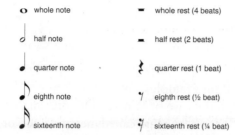

Jin - gle bells, jin - gle bells,   jin - gle all the way

In addition to notes that signify the duration of sound, there are other signs, called rests, that indicate silence. For each note there is a corresponding rest of the same value:

EXAMPLE 2–5

𝅝	whole note	▬	whole rest (4 beats)
𝅗𝅥	half note	▬	half rest (2 beats)
♩	quarter note	𝄽	quarter rest (1 beat)
♪	eighth note	𝄾	eighth rest (½ beat)
𝅘𝅥𝅯	sixteenth note	𝄿	sixteenth rest (¼ beat)

signs for the absence of sound

You will have noticed that, in their basic form, adjacent note values (and rests) in music all have a 2:1 ratio to one another: One half note equals two quarter notes, and so on. But triple relationships can and do exist, and these are created by the addition of a dot after a note, which increases the duration of the note to one and one-half its original value.

EXAMPLE 2–6

triple relationships

To see how the various note values indicate the rhythm of an actual piece of music, consider the well-known tune, "Yankee Doodle." First, the text is given to refresh your memory. Next, the rhythm of the tune is indicated by horizontal lines of different length, to show how long each pitch lasts. Then, the rhythm is presented in musical notation. Finally, the position of each beat in "Yankee Doodle" is indicated by quarter notes.

EXAMPLE 2–7

Here's the patriotic song "America" (first known in England and Canada as "God Save the King"—or "Queen") arranged the same way.

EXAMPLE 2–8

beat and rhythm

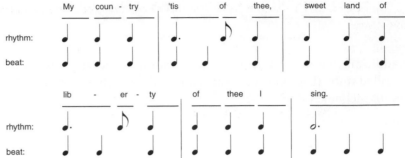

Meter

measure (bar)

Notice in the preceding examples how vertical lines divide the music into groups of two beats in the case of "Yankee Doodle" and into groups of three beats in "America." These strokes are called measure lines, or bar lines. A **measure, or bar,** is a group of beats. Usually there are two, three, or four beats per measure, although in some cases there can be more. The gathering of beats into regular groups produces **meter.** A musical composition does not usually present a steady stream of undifferentiated beats. Instead, certain beats are given emphasis over others in a regular and repeating fashion. The stressed beats are called strong beats, and the unstressed beats, weak beats. If we stress every other beat—ONE two, ONE two, ONE two—we have two beats per measure and thus duple meter. Similarly, if we emphasize every third beat—ONE two three, ONE two three—we have triple meter. Quadruple meter (four beats per measure) is common as well. Here is a familiar folk song notated in quadruple meter:

EXAMPLE 2–9

And here is an equally well-known tune in sextuple meter.

EXAMPLE 2–10

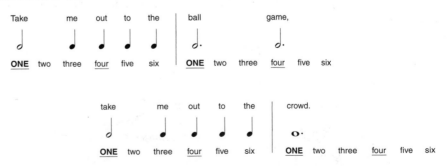

time signatures

Most music, however, is written in duple ($\frac{2}{4}$), triple ($\frac{3}{4}$), or quadruple ($\frac{4}{4}$) meter.
Meter in music is indicated by a **meter signature** (also called a **time signature**)—two numbers, one on top of the other, placed at the beginning of the

music to tell the performer how the beats of the music are to be grouped. The top number of the signature indicates how many beats there are per measure; the bottom number tells what note value receives the beat. Since, as we have said, the quarter note most often carries the beat, most time signatures have a "4" on the bottom. The three most frequently encountered time signatures are given here.

EXAMPLE 2–11

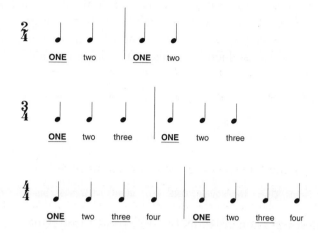

Having a time signature at the beginning of the music may be of great value to the performer, but it doesn't help the listener, unless he or she happens to be following along with the musical notation—following the **score,** as musicians call it. Without a score, the listener must of necessity hear and feel the meter. Most music, as we have said, is written in $\frac{2}{4}$, $\frac{3}{4}$, or $\frac{4}{4}$. Since $\frac{4}{4}$ is in most (but not all) ways merely a multiple or extension of $\frac{2}{4}$, there are really only two meters that the beginning listener should be aware of: duple meter ($\frac{2}{4}$) and triple meter ($\frac{3}{4}$). But how do we hear these and differentiate between them?

duple and triple meters

Hearing Meters

One way you can improve your ability to hear a given meter is to establish some sort of physical response to the music. As obvious as it might seem, it can be very helpful simply to tap your foot to the beat, while moving along with the music in a way that groups the beats into measures of two or three beats. Perhaps the most precise way to move with the music is to adopt the same patterns of motion that conductors use to lead symphony orchestras and other musical ensembles. These patterns are cut in the air with the right hand (a baton is optional!). Here are the patterns that conductors use to show $\frac{2}{4}$ and $\frac{3}{4}$ meter.

EXAMPLE 2–12

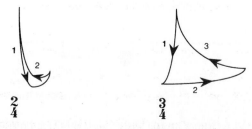

conducting patterns

Notice that in both of these patterns, and indeed in all conducting patterns, the first beat is indicated by a downward movement of the hand.

Accordingly, this first beat is called the **downbeat.** It represents by far the strongest beat in any given measure. In $\frac{2}{4}$ the downbeat is stronger, or more accented, than the **upbeat** (the beat signaled by an upward motion); in $\frac{3}{4}$ it is more accented than either the middle beat (2) or the upbeat (3). When listening to a piece of music, then, tap the beat with your foot, listen for the downbeat, and try to get your conducting pattern synchronized with the music (move your hand down with the downbeat). If you hear only one weak beat between each strong beat, the music is in duple meter, and you should conduct in $\frac{2}{4}$ time. If you hear two weak beats between each downbeat, on the other hand, you are listening to a piece in triple meter and should use the $\frac{3}{4}$ pattern. Try conducting "Yankee Doodle" and "America" in $\frac{2}{4}$ and $\frac{3}{4}$, respectively.

feel the downbeat

EXAMPLE 2–13

Yan - kee	doo - dle	went	to	town	rid - ing	on	a	po -	ny.
ONE	two	**ONE**	two		**ONE**	two		**ONE**	two

My	coun - try	'tis	of thee,	sweet	land of	lib -	er - ty	of	thee	I	sing.
ONE	two three	**ONE**	two three	**ONE**	two three	**ONE**	two three	**ONE**	two	three	**ONE** two three

One final observation about meters and conducting patterns: Almost all music that we hear, and especially dance music, has a clearly identifiable meter and a strong downbeat. But not all music *starts* with the downbeat. Often a piece will begin with an upbeat. An upbeat at the very beginning of a piece is called a pickup. The **pickup** is usually only a note or two, but it gives a little momentum or extra push into the first downbeat, as can be seen in the following two patriotic songs.

pickup to the downbeat

EXAMPLE 2–14

Oh	beau-	ti-	ful	for	spa-	cious	skies
two	**ONE**	two	**ONE**	two	**ONE**	two	**ONE** two

Oh	say	can you	see	by	the	dawn's	ear - ly	light
three	**ONE**	two three	**ONE**	two	three	**ONE**	two three	**ONE** two

To sum up: To identify whether the meter of a piece is duple $\left(\frac{2}{4}\right)$ or triple $\left(\frac{3}{4}\right)$, try using this simple three-step approach. First, tap your foot or hand to the beat. Second, identify where the downbeat is falling—where do you hear strong beats instead of weak beats? Third, conduct with the music and decide if you hear one or two weak beats between each strong beat. If there is only one weak beat between the strong beats, then the piece is in duple meter; if there are two, then it is in triple meter. Turn now to the Listening Exercise, which gives you a chance to practice conducting in $\frac{2}{4}$ and $\frac{3}{4}$ time and asks you to identify the meter of several musical works.

three steps to hearing meters

Listening Exercise 2

Hearing Meters

On your Intro CD, track 4, you have ten short musical excerpts, each played once. (You can replay them as many times as you wish.) Identify the meter of each excerpt. To do this, you should listen for the beat, count 1–2 or

1–2–3, and get your conductor's beat pattern in synchrony with the music (downbeat of the hand with downbeat of the music). If you do this correctly, the completion of each full conductor's pattern will equal one measure. All pieces are in duple ($\frac{2}{4}$) or triple ($\frac{3}{4}$) meter. Write "duple" or "triple" in the following blanks. There are five examples in duple meter and five in triple.

1. (0:00) Meter: _____ Chopin, Waltz in E♭ major

2. (0:18) Meter: _____ Mouret, *Rondeau* from *Suite de symphonies*

3. (0:45) Meter: _____ Claudin de Sermisy, *Tant que vivray* arranged for lute

4. (1:11) Meter: _____ Beethoven, Variations on *God Save the King*

5. (1:24) Meter: _____ Mozart, *A Little Night Music*, 1st movement

6. (1:50) Meter: _____ Verdi, "Un dì felice" from *La traviata*

7. (2:19) Meter: _____ Handel, Minuet from *Water Music*

8. (2:47) Meter: _____ Bach, Brandenburg Concerto No. 5, 1st movement

9. (3:21) Meter: _____ Tchaikovsky, Piano Concerto No. 1, 1st movement

10. (3:54) Meter: _____ Handel, "Hallelujah" chorus from *Messiah*

Syncopation

One of the ways to add variety and excitement to music is by the use of syncopation. In most music, the **accent,** or musical stress, falls on the beat, with the downbeat getting the greatest accent of all. **Syncopation** places the accent either on a weak beat or between the beats. The note that is syncopated sounds accented because it is played louder or held longer than the surrounding notes. A good example of syncopation can be found in the popular theme song to *The Simpsons*. The arrows show the moments of syncopation.

EXAMPLE 2–15

ONE two   **ONE** two   **ONE** two   **ONE** two   **ONE** two

Syncopation gives an unexpected bounce or lift to the music and is a prominent feature in Latin music and jazz.

TEMPO

The beat sets the basic pulse of the music. As beats are grouped into equal units, meter is created. Rhythm is the durational pattern of longs and shorts superimposed over the meter. **Tempo,** finally, is the speed at which the beats progress. While the tempo of the beat can be fast or slow, it usually falls somewhere in the neighborhood of 60–100 beats per minute. Tempo is indicated to the performer by means of a "tempo marking" placed at the beginning of the piece. Because tempo markings were first used in Italy, they are most often written in Italian. The following are the most common tempo indications, arranged from slow to fast:

tempo: the speed of the beat

grave (grave)	very slow
largo (broad)	
lento (slow)	slow
adagio (slow)	

Rhythm and Rap

Rhythm is without question an indispensable component of most classical music. Yet as we will see, melodic and harmonic features usually outweigh rhythmic elements as primary sources of interest in classical pieces. In many popular idioms and indigenous musical cultures, however, rhythm is primary. Certain traditional African musics, for example, which often feature relatively simple melodic and harmonic textures, offer rhythmic complexity that far surpasses that of most classical music.

Rap music is perhaps the most prominent popular musical genre to privilege rhythm over melody and harmony. In rap, while the bass and accompanying parts usually present some degree of melodic interest, the vocal line is delivered in a manner more resembling speech than song, rarely if ever offering discrete pitches that can be notated precisely on a musical staff.

The following four-bar excerpt, from the end of the second verse of Eminem's "The Real Slim Shady" (released 2000), illustrates the potential in rap music for highly sophisticated rhythmic textures and interactions. In the accompanying diagram, the arrows pointing up correspond to the regular musical beats* upon which we would expect the singer's musical emphases to fall most often. However, Eminem's vocal accents (indicated by bold text and downward arrows) align only rarely with these beats. Instead, they usually come off the beat, thereby creating syncopation*—a strong accent coming *between* rather than *on* the beat. Moreover, the stressed syllables in the vocal line most often appear in groups of three syllables, and these conflict with the duple meter that prevails in the accompanying drums, bass, and syn-

Eminem. Is he about to conduct a downbeat?

FIGURE 2–2

Marin Alsop (b1956), conducting the Baltimore Symphony Orchestra.

andante (moving)	moderate
andantino (slightly faster than *andante*)	
moderato (moderate)	
allegretto (moderately fast)	fast
allegro (fast)	
vivace (fast and lively)	very fast
presto (very fast)	
prestissimo (as fast as possible)	

Naturally, general terms such as these allow for a good deal of interpretive freedom. Conductors such as Marin Alsop (Fig. 2–2) and Leonard Bernstein (Fig. 2–3), for example, have had very different notions of just how fast a movement by Beethoven marked *allegro* (fast) should go. A movement conducted by Bernstein can last two minutes longer than one directed by Alsop. In addition, composers often called for changes in tempo within a movement by placing in the score commands such as *accelerando* (getting faster) and *ritardando* (getting slower). From this last Italian term we derive the En-

thesizer. Thus the nervous energy of this rap piece derives not only from the constant syncopations but also from the conflict caused when rhythmic units of three collide with units of two.

EXAMPLE 2–16

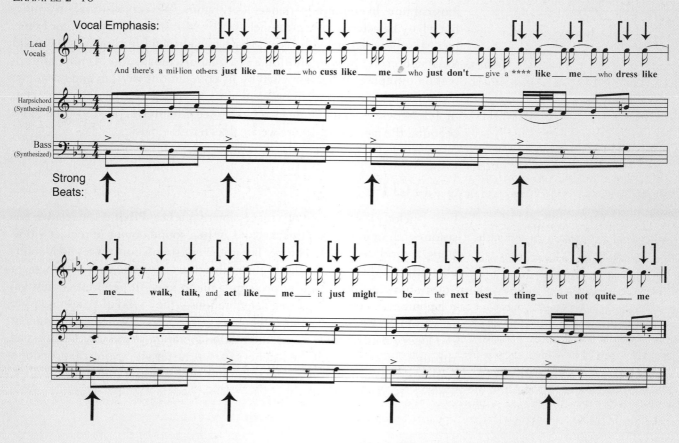

glish word for a slowing down of the music: **ritard.** Frequent changes in tempo can make it difficult for the listener to follow the beat, but they add much expression and feeling to the music.

FIGURE 2–3

Leonard Bernstein (1918–1990), one of the most forceful, and flamboyant, conductors of the twentieth century.

Key Words

music (**13**)
rhythm (**14**)
beat (**14**)
measure (bar) (**16**)
meter (**16**)
meter signature (time signature) (**16**)
score (**17**)

downbeat (**18**)
upbeat (**18**)
pickup (**18**)
accent (**19**)
syncopation (**19**)
tempo (**19**)
ritard (**21**)

ThomsonNOW

ThomsonNOW for *Listening to Music, 5th Edition,* and *Listening to Western Music* will assist you in understanding the content of this chapter with lesson plans generated for your specific needs. In addition, you may complete this chapter's Listening Exercise in ThomsonNOW's interactive environment, as well as download Active Listening Guides and other materials that will help you succeed in this course.

Melody

A **melody** is simply series of pitches arranged to form a cohesive, pleasing musical line. In common parlance, it's the tune. We can all think up a tune, but what characterizes the great melodies by Mozart or Beethoven, for example? Most beautiful melodies seem to have four elements in common: (1) a solid tonal center, (2) forward motion, (3) a goal or climax, and (4) ultimately, a feeling of repose. When enriched by its companions rhythm and harmony, melody can enchant us, even sweep us away, as it seems to do at the beginning of Tchaikovsky's Piano Concerto No. 1 (see Chapter 1, page 9). The more beautiful the melody, the more we are drawn to the music.

PITCH

faster vibrations produce a higher pitch

Every melody is composed of a succession of pitches. **Pitch** is the relative position, high or low, of a musical sound. When sound comes in regular vibrations, it produces a musical tone. But not every sound constitutes an identifiable pitch. When sound with regular vibrations is produced—by bowing a violin, blowing a trumpet, or pressing a piano key—it generates a musical tone. But if sound comes in irregular vibrations—the sound of a crashing plate or a barking dog, for example—then it is merely noise. When an instrument produces a musical tone, it sets into motion vibrating sound waves that travel through the air to reach the listener's ears. A faster vibration will produce a higher pitch, and vice versa. By grouping and ordering individual pitches, composers produce a melody.

THE OCTAVE

Have you ever noticed, when singing a succession of tones up or down, that the melody reaches a tone that sounds like a duplication of an earlier pitch, but at a higher or lower level? That duplicating pitch is called an **octave,** for reasons that will become clear shortly. Pitches an octave apart sound similar because the frequency of vibration of the higher pitch is precisely twice that of the lower. The string that produces middle C on the piano undergoes 256 vibrations or "cycles" per second, while the one generating the C an octave above vibrates 512 times per second. When men and women sing a melody together, they almost invariably sing "at the octave" (an octave apart from each other). While it may sound as if the men and women are singing the same pitches, the women are in fact singing an octave higher, with their vocal cords vibrating exactly twice as fast as those of their male counterparts.

octave duplications used in all musical cultures

All musical cultures, Western and non-Western, make use of the principle of octave duplication. But not all cultures divide the pitches within the octave the same way. In many traditional Chinese melodies, the octave is divided into five pitches. Some Arabic melodies, by contrast, make use of fourteen. Since ancient Greece, Western musicians have preferred melodies with seven pitches within the octave. The eighth pitch duplicates, or doubles, the sound of the first, and is thus called the octave.

During the early development of Western music, the seven notes within the octave corresponded to the white keys of the modern keyboard. Eventually, five additional notes were inserted, and these correspond to the black keys.

EXAMPLE 3–1

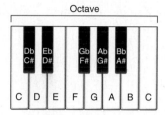

To get the sound of the octave in your ear, try singing "Over the Rainbow" and "Take Me Out to the Ball Game" (Ex. 3–2). Both begin with a leap up by an octave, regardless of starting pitch.

EXAMPLE 3–2

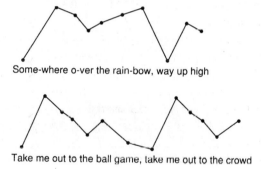

Some-where o-ver the rain-bow, way up high

Take me out to the ball game, take me out to the crowd

the octave is a large leap

NOTATING MELODIES

The type of notation used for the two tunes in Example 3–2 is useful if the singer merely needs to be reminded of how a melody goes, but it is not precise enough to allow him or her to produce the tune if he or she doesn't know it already. When the melody goes up, how *far* up does it go? More precision for musical notation began to appear in the West as early as the eleventh century, when notes came to be situated on lines and spaces so that the exact distance between pitches could be judged immediately. This gridwork of lines and spaces came to be called a **staff.** The higher on the staff the note is placed, the higher the pitch.

EXAMPLE 3–3

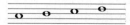

The staff is always provided with a **clef** sign to indicate the range of pitch in which the melody is to be played or sung (Fig. 3–1). One clef, called the **treble clef,** designates the upper range and is appropriate for high instruments like the trumpet and the violin, or a woman's voice. A second clef,

treble and bass clefs

called the **bass clef,** covers the lower range and is used for lower instruments like the tuba and the cello, or a man's voice.

EXAMPLE 3–4

FIGURE 3–1

G Clef (1935) by Josef Albers (1888–1976). The G clef (or treble clef) is so called because it centers around the line "G" and from this line all other pitches are reckoned.

names of the notes

sharps and flats

For a single vocal part or a single instrument, a melody could easily be placed on either one of these two clefs. But for two-hand keyboard music with greater range, both clefs are used, one on top of the other. The performer looks at this combination of clefs, called the **great staff,** and relates the notes to the keys beneath the fingers. The space between the two clefs is filled in by a short, temporary line called a ledger line. On the keyboard, it indicates middle C (the middle-most C key on the piano).

EXAMPLE 3–5

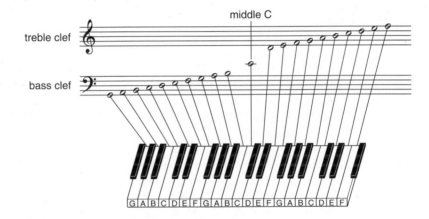

Each musical pitch can be designated by a letter name (like "C") as well as by a particular line or space on the great staff. We use only seven letter names (in ascending order A, B, C, D, E, F, and G) because, as we have seen, melodies were made up of only seven pitches within each octave. (These seven pitches, once again, correspond to the seven white notes of the modern piano keyboard.) As a melody extends beyond the range of a single octave, the series of letter names repeats (see Ex. 3–5). The note above G, then, is an A, which lies exactly one octave above the previous A.

As music grew increasingly complex, the spaces between the white keys were divided and additional (black) keys inserted. This increased the number of pitches within the octave from seven to twelve. Since they were not originally part of the staff, the five additional pitches were not represented by a line or space, nor were they given a separate letter name. Instead, they came to be indicated by a symbol, either a sharp or a flat, applied to one of the existing notes. A **sharp** (♯) raises the note to the key immediately above, usually a black one, whereas a **flat** (♭) lowers it to the next key below, again usually a black one. A **natural** (♮), on the other hand, cancels either of the two previous signs. Here, as an example of musical notation on the great staff, is a well-known melody as it might be notated for a chorus of male and female voices, the women an octave higher than the men. To keep things simple, the melody is notated in equal whole notes (without rhythm).

EXAMPLE 3–6

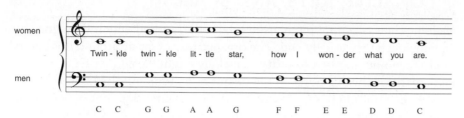

Twin - kle twin - kle lit - tle star,   how I   won - der what you are.

C   C   G G A A G   F F   E E   D D   C

Hearing melodies may be the single most important part of listening to music. Melodies contain the main musical ideas the composer wishes to communicate. Listening Exercise 3 asks you to respond to ten famous melodies drawn from the repertory of classical music and thereby to focus on melodic pitch.

Listening Exercise 3

Hearing Melodies

This exercise is designed to help you concentrate on the direction of, and approximate distance between, the pitches in ten famous melodies. On your Introduction to Listening CD, track 5, you will find ten melodies, first performed as the composer originally intended, and then played again in a more deliberate fashion to allow you to focus on the individual pitches. For each excerpt, select the pattern of x's that most accurately represents the pitches of the melody—the higher the x, the higher the pitch. (No indication of rhythm is given.)

1. (0:00) Beethoven, Symphony No. 5, 1st movement

2. (0:24) Mozart, Symphony No. 41, 4th movement

3. (0:46) Haydn, Symphony No. 94, 2nd movement

4. (1:10) Schubert, Symphony No. 9, 1st movement

5. (1:38) Beethoven, *Ode to Joy*

6. (2:03) Vivaldi, Violin Concerto in E major, the "Spring," 1st movement

7. (2:20) Beethoven, *Für Elise*

8. (2:35) Mozart, *A Little Night Music*, 1st movement

9. (2:55) Musorgsky, *Great Gate of Kiev* from *Pictures at an Exhibition*

10. (3:25) Handel, "Hallelujah" chorus from *Messiah*

TONALITY, KEYS, AND SCALES

tonality and key

Melodies have a central pitch, called the **tonic,** around which they gravitate and on which they usually end. The organization of music around this central pitch, the tonic, is called **tonality.** A melody might have C, or D, or F♯, or in fact any of the twelve notes in the octave as its tonic. In the case of *Twinkle, Twinkle,* the tonic pitch is C. As can be seen in Example 3–6, not only does the tune end on its tonic (as is generally the case), but it begins there as well. We can also say that it is written in the key of C major, meaning that its tonic is C and it makes use of the C major scale. A **key,** then, indicates not only the tonal center around which a piece is built but also the scale that it employs.

But what is a scale? A **scale** is an arrangement of pitches within the octave that ascends and descends according to a fixed pattern. Almost all Western melodies follow one of two types of scales—one major, the other minor. The image of the piano keyboard provided in Example 3–5 can help illustrate the difference between the major and minor scales. Notice that there are no black keys between B and C and between E and F. All the adjacent white notes of the keyboard are not the same distance apart. The difference, or distance, in sound between B and C is only half of that between C and D. B to C is the interval of a "half step," while C to D is the interval of a "whole step."

The major and minor scales are built on two distinctly different patterns of whole and half steps, each starting on the tonic note. The **major scale** has a succession of whole and half steps that proceeds 1–1–½–1–1–1–½. The **minor scale** goes 1–½–1–1–½–1–1. Both the major and minor scales use only seven of the available twelve pitches within each octave; once the octave is reached, the pattern can start over again. A major or minor scale may begin on any of the twelve notes within the octave, and thus there are twelve major and twelve minor scales and keys. Here are the notes of the major and minor scales as they start on C and then on A.

EXAMPLE 3–7

major and minor scales

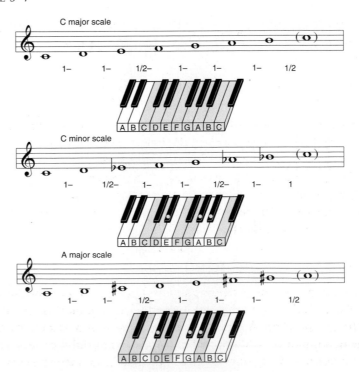

A major scale built on C uses only the white notes of the keyboard, as does a minor scale constructed on A. When begun on a note other than C (for the major scale) or A (for the minor scale), however, sharps and flats are needed so that the pattern of whole and half steps does not vary. The A major scale, for example, must raise or "sharp" the notes C, F, and G in order to keep the major scale pattern intact (see Ex. 3–7). Similarly, starting the minor scale pattern on C will require that E be lowered to E♭, A to A♭, and B to B♭ (see Ex. 3–7).

Composing a piece in A major would require writing out many sharps, just as one in C minor would require writing many flats. To avoid this labor, musicians have developed the custom of "preplacing" the sharps or flats at the beginning of the staff. These sharps or flats are then active throughout the entire piece. Preplaced sharps or flats are called a **key signature.**

EXAMPLE 3–8

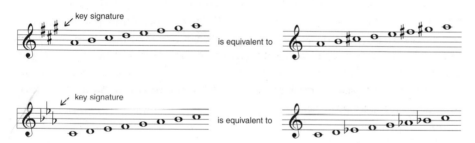

using sharps and flats

Key signatures indicate to the performer the key in which a piece is written; that is, they indicate the scale to be employed as well as the tonic pitch.

Modulation

Modulation is the change from one key to another. Most short popular songs don't modulate; they stay in one key. But longer pieces of classical music need to modulate so as not to bore the listener. Modulation gives a dynamic sense of movement to music. As the composer Arnold Schoenberg (1874–1951) said, "Modulation is like a change of scenery." Modulations are difficult to hear. The beginning listener may not recognize precisely when they occur, only that a general process of key change is at work.

Hearing Major and Minor

Scales are like colors on an artist's palette. A composer will choose what he or she believes is the right scale to achieve the desired musical mood or feeling for the composition. A melody in a major key sounds decidedly different from one in a minor one. Major-key melodies seem bright, cheery, and optimistic, whereas minor-key ones come across as dark, somber, and even sinister.

FIGURE 3–2

Contrasting Sounds (1924) by Wassily Kandinsky (1866–1944).

Try singing the following familiar major and minor songs to establish firmly in your "mind's ear" the difference between major and minor.

EXAMPLE 3–9

major and minor have a different sound

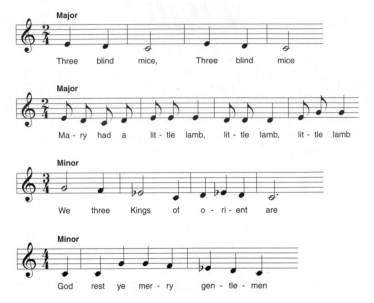

Composers over the centuries usually have chosen major keys to express positive emotions (joy, confidence, triumph, tranquility, love, and so on), but minor ones to convey negative feelings (fear, anxiety, sorrow, despair, and so on). Moreover, they have manipulated the way we feel about their music by switching from major to minor (C major to C minor, for example) or minor to major (F minor to F major, for example). Changing from major to minor, or from minor to major, is called a change of **mode**—from the major mode to the minor, or vice versa. Changing the mode certainly affects the mood of the music. To prove the point, listen to the following familiar tunes (your instructor can play them for you). In each the mode has been changed from major to minor by inserting a flat into the scale near the tonic note (C). Notice how all the happiness, joy, and sunshine have disappeared from these formerly major tunes.

EXAMPLE 3–10

changing the mood by changing the mode

Now turn to Listening Exercise 4 which tests your ability to distinguish between melodies composed in major or minor.

Listening Exercise 4
Hearing Major and Minor

ThomsonNOW™
To take this Listening Exercise online and receive feedback or email answers to your instructor, go to *ThomsonNOW* for this chapter.

Almost all Western melodies, popular as well as classical, are written using either a major or a minor scale. On your Introduction to Listening CD, track 6, you will find ten musical excerpts that will help you begin to differentiate major from minor. Pieces in major sound bright, cheerful, and sometimes bland, whereas those in minor seem darker, more somber, and even exotic. In the blanks below, indicate whether each melody is in major or minor. Five are in major and five in minor.

1. (0:00) Key: _____ Tchaikovsky, *Dance of the Reed Pipes* from *The Nutcracker*
2. (0:21) Key: _____ Tchaikovsky, *Dance of the Reed Pipes* from *The Nutcracker*
3. (0:39) Key: _____ Musorgsky, *Polish Ox-Cart* from *Pictures at an Exhibition*
4. (1:04) Key: _____ Musorgsky, *Goldenburg and Schmuyle* from *Pictures at an Exhibition*
5. (1:28) Key: _____ Musorgsky, *Great Gate of Kiev* from *Pictures at an Exhibition*
6. (1:55) Key: _____ Mouret, *Rondeau* from *Suite de symphonies*
7. (2:22) Key: _____ Handel, Minuet from *Water Music*
8. (2:51) Key: _____ Mozart, Overture to *Don Giovanni*
9. (3:12) Key: _____ Vivaldi, Violin Concerto, the "Spring," 1st movement
10. (3:21) Key: _____ Vivaldi, Violin Concerto, the "Spring," 1st movement

Chromatic Scale

In addition to the major and minor scales, there is a third important scale called the chromatic scale. Whereas each major or minor scale uses only seven notes within each octave, the **chromatic scale** employs all twelve. Chromatic (from the Greek *chroma*, "color") is a good word for this scale because the additional five pitches do indeed add color and richness to a melody. In the chromatic scale, all twelve pitches are just a half step apart.

EXAMPLE 3–11

every note within octave

In truth, rarely are pieces written entirely in the chromatic scale. Rather, a composer will momentarily substitute a chromatic scale for a major or minor one, to add extra "bite" or intensity to the melody. Irving Berlin began his popular holiday song "White Christmas" with a chromatic scale, before moving on to a major one.

EXAMPLE 3–12

MELODIC STRUCTURE

A great melody does not have to be a complex one. Ludwig van Beethoven demonstrated this when he fashioned his *Ode to Joy*, a melody he composed for the last movement of his Symphony No. 9 (1824). So beloved has this tune become that it has been used as a Christmas carol, a hymn for the United Nations, a film score (*Die Hard*), and background music in countless TV commercials. Below, the melody is notated in the bass clef in D major, the key in which Beethoven composed it, with the original German text translated into English.

EXAMPLE 3–13

Beethoven's Ode to Joy

(a)

Praise to Joy the God de-scend-ed, Daugh-ter of E - ly - si-um.

(b) 5

Ray of mirth and rap-ture blend-ed, God-dess, to thy shrine wel-come.

(c) 10

By thy ma-gic is u - nit-ed what tra - di-tion kept a-part. All __

(b) 15

__ hu-mans are peo-ple plight - ed where thy gen-tle spi - rit darts.

We can make a few general observations about Beethoven's melody. First, notice that it moves mainly by **step,** from one letter name of the scale to the next (D to E, for example), but rarely moves by **leap,** a jump of more than one letter name (D to F, or D to G, for example). The only leaps of any importance in *Ode to Joy* are the two at the end of phrase **c** (measure 12). Clearly, Beethoven wanted to keep this melody simple so that all the world could sing it.

a simple melody for all

Next, notice that there are in fact four melodic phrases here. A **phrase** in music functions much like a dependent phrase or clause within a sentence: it constitutes a dependent idea within a melody. Here four four-measure phrases form a complete sixteen-bar melody. The initial phrase (**a**) opens the melody and ends on a note *other* than the tonic (here the note E); the second phrase (**b**) answers this idea and returns the melody to the tonic (D). Two phrases that work in tandem this way are called **antecedent** and **consequent phrases.** Both phrases end with a cadence (see the horizontal brackets in Ex. 3–13). A **cadence** is the concluding part of a musical phrase—the last few notes that bring a phrase to an end.

Ode to Joy then pushes off in a new direction (phrase **c**). The music gains momentum by means of a repeating rhythmic figure in measures 10–11 and reaches a musical climax in measure 12 with the two leaps. The fourth and final phrase is an almost exact repeat of the second phrase (**b**), with the exception of one important detail (see * in Ex. 3–13). Beethoven brings the return of this phrase in one beat early—a bit of rhythmic syncopation*—thereby giving an unexpected lift to the melody.

balanced phrase structure

The melodic structure of Beethoven's *Ode to Joy*—balanced groups of four-bar phrases arranged antecedent–consequent–extension–consequent—is found frequently in the works of Haydn, Mozart, and Beethoven from the eighteenth and nineteenth centuries. Antecedent–consequent pairs also appear regularly in popular songs of nineteenth- and twentieth-century America. You may have been singing antecedent–consequent phrases all your life and not been aware of it. To prove the point, sing the following two well-known tunes:

"The Saints Go Marching In" (traditional)
Oh when the saints, go marching in, oh when the saints go marching in; (antecedent phrase)
Oh how I want to be in that number, when the saints go marching in. (consequent phrase)

"Oh Suzanna" (Stephen Foster)
Oh I come from Alabama with my banjo on my knee (antecedent phrase)
I'm bound for Louisiana my true love for to see. (consequent phrase)

Listening Exercise 5

Hearing Melodic Structure
Ludwig van Beethoven, *Ode to Joy* from Symphony No. 9 (1824)

ThomsonNOW

To take this Listening Exercise online and receive feedback or email answers to your instructor, go to *ThomsonNOW* for this chapter.

On your Introduction to Listening CD, track 7, you have an excerpt from the last movement of Beethoven's Symphony No. 9, in which his famous *Ode to Joy* can be heard. You are probably familiar with the tune already, but look at it again as it is given on page 30. Try to get the antecedent (**a**), consequent (**b**), and extension (**c**) phrases firmly in your ear. Now listen to the music on your CD. The melody is actually heard four times, first played softly by the low string instruments, then more loudly by the higher strings, then louder still by yet higher strings, and finally loudest of all by the trumpets and full orchestra.

Your task is to fill in the missing times in the listening chart below. Indicate the minute and second when each phrase is heard—by writing 1:23, for example. Notice that Beethoven actually repeats the extension (**c**) and consequent (**b**) phrases at the end of each of the four presentations of the melody. Many of the times of entry have been filled in to get you off to a solid start and keep you on track.

After you have filled in the blanks, go back and treat yourself to one final hearing in which you listen, unencumbered, to the growing power of Beethoven's melody.

Playing Number:	1		2		3		4	
	Low strings (double basses)		Higher strings (2nd violins)		Higher strings (1st violins)		Trumpets with full orchestra	
Antecedent	a	0:00	a	0:49	a	1:40	a	2:30
Consequent	b	0:09	b	0:58	3. b	_____	7. b	_____
Extension	c	0:17	c	1:07	4. c	_____	8. c	_____
Consequent	b	0:25	1. b	1:15	5. b	_____	9. b	_____
		(repeat)		(repeat)		(repeat)		(repeat)
Extension	c	0:33	c	1:23	c	2:13	c	3:03
Consequent	b	0:42	2. b	1:31	6. b	_____	10. b	_____

HEARING MELODIES AND PHRASES

As we have seen, melodies are made up of musical phrases. When listening to a piece of music, whether a classical symphony or a popular song, we follow the phrases. For the most part, we do this intuitively—we instinctively hear where a phrase begins and where it ends. Beethoven's *Ode to Joy* is composed of four symmetrical phrases, each four bars in length, and this is typical of the music of the Classical period (1750–1820) in music history. Symmetrical phrase structure is also typical of the repertory of popular songs written in early twentieth-century America, by composers such as Irving Berlin ("God, Bless America," "White Christmas," and "Alexander's Ragtime Band"). Such popular songs came to be known to jazz musicians as "standards"

FIGURE 3–3
Louis Armstrong at the age of 32.

© Michael Ochs Archives/Corbis

because they were frequently used as the basis for jazz improvisations. Jazz musicians from Louis Armstrong (1901–1971) to Wynton Marsalis (b1961) have found that the solid phrase structure of the standards offers a secure base for improvisatory flights of fancy. Having followed the phrase structure in Beethoven's *Ode to Joy,* go on now to do so in Louis Armstrong's version of the popular song "Willie the Weeper" (also known as "Co-caine Lil and Morphine Sue"). Perhaps because of its close attachment to standard tunes and because of its long-lasting popularity, this style of jazz is known as "classical" New Orleans jazz.

Listening Exercise 6
Hearing Phrases and Counting Measures

Intro 8

ThomsonNOW
To take this Listening Exercise online and receive feedback or email answers to your instructor, go to *ThomsonNOW* for this chapter.

Louis Armstrong was born in poverty in New Orleans in 1901 but went on to become the most famous jazz musician of the twentieth century (Fig. 3–3; for a biography of Armstrong, see page 424). Armstrong's powerful, "in-your-face" style of trumpet playing can be heard prominently in his setting of the song "Willie the Weeper," as can impressive solos by other members of Armstrong's band, the Hot Seven. Indeed, the solos by the various instruments help us recognize where one phrase ends and the next begins. Armstrong's "Willie the Weeper" is in a straightforward duple meter ($\frac{2}{4}$ time). Your task here is to count the number of measures, or bars, in each musical phrase. Sometimes there are eight bars in the phrase and sometimes sixteen. In the blanks, simply indicate the length of the phrase by writing the appropriate number (eight or sixteen). The answer for the first phrase is provided.

(0:00–0:03) Four-bar introduction
(0:04–0:24) Full band. Number of measures: <u>sixteen</u>

(0:25–0:45) Full band varies the tune. Number of measures: _____
(0:46–0:56) Trombone and tuba solo. Number of measures: _____
(0:57–1:06) Trombone and tuba repeat. Number of measures: _____
(1:07–1:27) Trombone solo. Number of measures: _____
(1:28–1:48) Extraordinary clarinet solo. Number of measures: _____
(1:49–1:58) Armstrong plays trumpet solo. Number of measures: _____
(1:59–2:08) Piano solo. Number of measures: _____
(2:09–2:28) Guitar solo. Number of measures: _____
(2:29–2:48) Armstrong plays trumpet solo. Number of measures: _____
(2:49–end) Trumpet, trombone, and clarinet improvise around tune. Number of measures: _____

Key Words

melody (**22**)	natural (♮) (**24**)	chromatic scale (**29**)
pitch (**22**)	tonic (**26**)	step (**30**)
octave (**22**)	tonality (**26**)	leap (**30**)
staff (**23**)	key (**26**)	phrase (**30**)
clef (**23**)	scale (**26**)	antecedent
treble clef (**23**)	major scale (**26**)	phrase (**30**)
bass clef (**24**)	minor scale (**26**)	consequent
great staff (**24**)	key signature (**27**)	phrase (**30**)
sharp (♯) (**24**)	modulation (**27**)	cadence (**30**)
flat (♭) (**24**)	mode (**28**)	

Melodies of the World

An Indian Melody for the Sitar

In the preceding chapter, we saw how Western classical and popular music makes use of major and minor scales, each with its own distinctive pattern of seven notes. We have also discussed how we in the West have, since the sixteenth century, generally associated the major mode with bright, happy feelings and the minor mode with darker, gloomier, more apprehensive sentiments. But these are particularly Western constructs—the rest of the musical world often has its own, and very different, ways of making music.

The classical music of India is marked by a remarkably complex, yet subtle type of melody. Perhaps more than any other musical culture, Indian music relies exclusively on melody for musical expression. There are no contrapuntal lines and no harmony other than a constant drone on the tonic and dominant notes of the melody. For an Indian musician, chords are thought to create too much sound at once and thus detract from what is truly important: the expressive nuances of the melody and the intricate rhythmic patterns of the accompanying drummer.

India, of course, is a vast, populous land of many ethnic and religious groups, with Muslims strong in the north and Hindus dominating the south. Indian music, too, is divided somewhat along regional lines. What is called **Hindustani-style music** is heard in the north, while **Karnatak-style music** prevails in the south. Among the many differences between the two is the fact that Karnatak music is almost always sung, whereas Hindustani music frequently makes use of an instrument called the sitar. The highly flexible quality of Indian melody can best be heard on this string instrument.

The **sitar** is a large, lute-like instrument with as many as twenty strings, some of which are used to play a melody, some simply to vibrate sympathetically with the melody strings, and some to provide a constant drone*. The strings are plucked by a plectrum, or pick, made of twisted wire, worn on the right index finger of the performer. As you can see in the illustration on page 34, the sitar is equipped with metal frets placed at right angles to the strings. The performer sets a pitch initially by pushing the string against the fret, and can slightly alter that pitch by pulling the string sideways along the fret—something sometimes done on our Western guitar. At each end of the instrument is a large, semicircular gourd that serves as a resonator to amplify the sound of the strings. A performance on the sitar is typically accompanied by a **tabla,** a pair of tuned drums. The left-hand drum can produce almost any low pitch, depending on the amount of pressure the drummer applies. The right-hand drum is set to a fixed pitch, usually tonic or dominant, that is important in the sitar melody.

Every melody in Indian classical music makes use of a raga. Like our Western scale, a **raga** is a basic pattern of pitches. But it is more. A raga expresses feeling—the mood of the piece. It has been called "the mystical expressive force" at the heart of every Indian composition. To the trained ear, *Raga Jogeshwari,* which we will hear, has the mood of love and pathos. Here the octave is divided into six pitches (C♯, E, E♯, F♯, A♯, and B [C♯]), not seven as in the Western major and minor scales (see Ex. 3–14).

Raga Jogeshwari sounds different to our ears because it employs a six-note scale. It also sounds "non-Western" because the performer "bends" the pitches by subtly pulling the strings of the sitar as the pitch is sounding. In Western classical music, we move along a scale from one specific pitch to the next. We have the notes, yet nothing in between. In much of the music of the world, however, great beauty is found between pitches. Small microtones (less than the smallest interval on our keyboard) give expressive power

EXAMPLE 3–14

Listening Guide

Raga Jogeshwari
Gat II (Theme II)
(performed by Ravi Shankar, sitar, and Alla Rakha, tabla)

6
6/15

0:00	15	Scale of raga (basic melody) played as quick *arpeggio*
0:08		Sitar presents the raga three times against beat in tabla
0:45		Alternation of the raga with free improvisations
1:17		Ascending and descending improvisations on scale of raga
2:11		Strong cadence for tabla
2:40		More elaborate patterns repeated on successive degrees of scale
4:18		Tempo increases
4:45		Strumming on drone strings of sitar
5:00		Sitar explores half steps that occur naturally in ascending version of raga
5:50		Tabla mimics rhythmic patterns of sitar

Use a downloadable, cross-platform animated Active Listening Guide, available
at **www.thomsonedu.com/music/wright**.

Ravi Shankar performing on the sitar. Shankar is the father of
Grammy award–winning pop singer Norah Jones.

© Bettmann/Corbis

sitar player. Shankar has been called "the god-father of world music." His work with The Beatles during the 1960s did much to introduce the sound of the sitar, and classical Indian melody generally, to Western ears. Shankar personifies an ideal of traditional Indian music: composer and performer are one and the same. Indeed, *Raga Jogeshwari* is his own creation. Yet each new performance of this raga results in a new composition because so much of the performance is improvised. For an Indian classical musician, then, composition, improvisation, and performance occur simultaneously.

to the music. In the course of *Raga Jogeshwari*, the melody becomes increasingly saturated with melodic ornaments and gradations of pitch, all growing out of the basic six-note scale.

The performance of *Raga Jogeshwari* that you will hear is by **Ravi Shankar** (b1920), India's legendary

A Chinese Melody for the Erhu

China is rapidly becoming one of the great economic powers of the world. Soon, even Chinese automobiles will be sold in the United States. But China is also arguably the world's oldest and richest continuing civilization. Many of the inventions that altered the course of Western history—gunpowder, printing, paper, silk, the nautical compass, and the dictionary, for example—first appeared in China. China has a musical history that extends back thousands of years. A mathematical theory for the generation of all musical pitches was known in the third century B.C.E.; orchestras with twenty and more performers played at court during the Tang dynasty (618–907); and full-fledged opera developed during the Yuan period (1271–1368), centuries before it did in the West.

As is the case in Indian music, traditional Chinese music places far more emphasis on melody than on harmony. In China, too, the melodies are subtle and involve microtones not possible on our modern keyboard. In general, the Chinese instruments that play these melodies are more "natural" than those in the West, meaning that the materials from which they are made are readily found in nature. The Chinese flute, for example, is usually a section of bamboo with air holes (as opposed to the Western flute made of metal and supplied with an elaborate key mechanism). Most distinctive among Chinese melodic instruments is the **erhu** (pronounced "R-who"). The player of the erhu passes the bow between the two fixed strings while twisting the instrument. A sound box, covered with snakeskin, helps the erhu to resonate with a vibrato-rich sound, a strange, veiled tone of great beauty.

The special quality of Chinese melody can be heard in *Erquan yingyue* (*The Moon Reflected on the Second Springs*) by Hua Yanjun (c1893–1950), known today simply as Abing. **Abing** was a blind street musician from the city of Wuxi, about seventy miles west of Shanghai, who played both the erhu and the **pipa** (a four-string lute). Like almost all Chinese folk musicians, he worked without benefit of written music, playing and improvising by ear. Abing's music survives in large measure because he recorded six of his creations shortly before his death in 1950. One of these, *The Moon Reflected on the Second Springs*, was originally conceived for erhu alone. Its subsequent history, however, is like that of a folk melody. It is known in many different versions and arranged for many different combinations of instruments including orchestra, string quartet, and even the Western piano. The title refers to an ancient pool, called Erquan Pool, in a park near Abing's home city of Wuxi.

As we listen to Abing's composition, several characteristics of Chinese music immediately become apparent. First, Chinese bowed string instruments are

The erhu is played by passing a bow between the two strings and continually twisting the instrument so that the bow can move from one string to the other. Playing is Min Hui-Fen of Shanghai, China.

Courtesy of Prof. Yu Zigang, Conservatory of Music, Beijing

infinitely flexible with regard to pitch. The solo erhu and the supporting orchestral strings seem to play as much between pitches as on them. (Compare this to the Western practice of moving from one discrete pitch to the next.) Second, there is almost no harmony in Chinese music. What may sometimes sound like harmony is usually two or more instruments playing the melody simultaneously in different ranges—an octave* higher or lower. Often the melody is doubled at the octave by an instrument playing with **tremolo,** a shaking or vibrating technique that produces a shimmering effect. Perhaps most important, Abing's

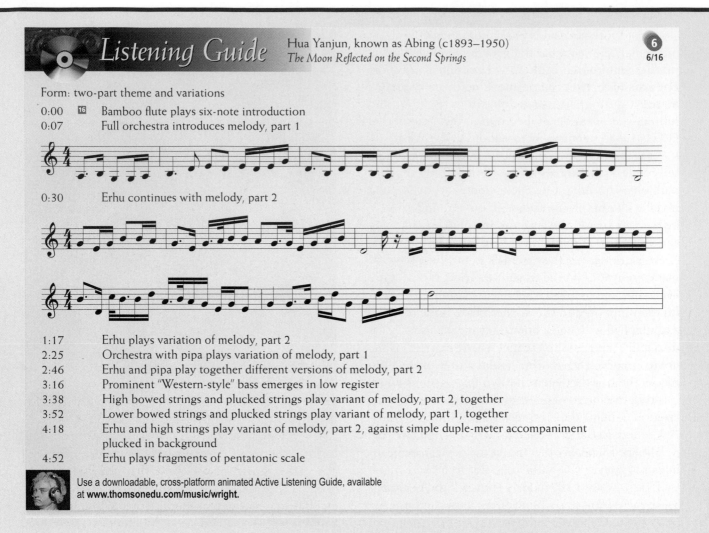

Listening Guide

Hua Yanjun, known as Abing (c1893–1950)
The Moon Reflected on the Second Springs

6
6/16

Form: two-part theme and variations

0:00   🔟   Bamboo flute plays six-note introduction
0:07   Full orchestra introduces melody, part 1

0:30   Erhu continues with melody, part 2

1:17   Erhu plays variation of melody, part 2
2:25   Orchestra with pipa plays variation of melody, part 1
2:46   Erhu and pipa play together different versions of melody, part 2
3:16   Prominent "Western-style" bass emerges in low register
3:38   High bowed strings and plucked strings play variant of melody, part 2, together
3:52   Lower bowed strings and plucked strings play variant of melody, part 1, together
4:18   Erhu and high strings play variant of melody, part 2, against simple duple-meter accompaniment
            plucked in background
4:52   Erhu plays fragments of pentatonic scale

Use a downloadable, cross-platform animated Active Listening Guide, available
at **www.thomsonedu.com/music/wright**.

melody is constructed around a **pentatonic scale,** one with five pitches within each octave. Here the five pitches are G, A, B, D, and E [G]. These five notes, however, are only the point of departure. By using them in different registers (different octaves) and applying to them a multitude of rhythmic values, Abing extends his basic melody in a variety of ways. His melody has two parts. Usually the orchestra plays or varies part 1, and the erhu plays or varies part 2. What we have here is not so much a "composition"— a fixed piece—as understood in our Western classical tradition, but rather a record of continual improvisation and variation around a given melody, a musical practice found among street and folk musicians across the globe.

Jewish Klezmer Music

Every musical culture around the world makes use of the octave. Its two similar sounding pitches, one higher, the other lower, serve as poles at opposite ends of the scale. Yet, as we have seen, Indian classical music sometimes has scales with only six pitches within the octave, while Chinese music often makes use of a pentatonic* (five-note) scale. Western classical and popular music divides the octave into seven pitches (the eighth duplicates the first, so the interval is called an "octave"). Moreover, we in the West have two specific and unvarying patterns for those seven-note scales within the octave: the major and the minor mode (see page 26). Other cultures make use of seven-note scales, but the patterns of these differ from the Western major and minor.

One such musical culture is that of klezmer music. **Klezmer music** is the traditional folk music of the Jews of Eastern Europe. It dates back to at least the seventeenth century and originated in countries such as Poland, Romania, Russia, Lithuania, and the Ukraine. Usually klezmer music is played by a small band, drawing on a variety of instruments including clarinet, trumpet, violin, accordion, and double bass, along with a singer. Some klezmer music is associated with Jewish religious rites, but most of it is heard at social events, particularly weddings. Although klezmer music, like the Jews themselves, was once threatened with extermination in Eastern Europe, it enjoyed a huge revival in the late twentieth century, particularly in Western Europe, Israel, and the United States. Klezmer music has managed to survive, and indeed flourish, by adopting elements of Western popular music—specifically, rock, funk, and jazz.

The Klezmatics, a popular klezmer band, has been successful by blending traditional klezmer tunes with contemporary rock idioms.

The lively sounds of klezmer music can be clearly heard in *Fun Taschlich*, a tune associated with the High Holy Days. On the Jewish New Year (*Rosh Hashana*), Jews walk to the nearest sea, lake, or stream and symbolically wash away their sins by casting bread on the water. This ceremony is called *Taschlich*. *Fun Taschlich* means "returning from the casting away of sin," for now it is time to dance and rejoice. This joyful tune is made up of three separate melodies (labeled **A**, **B**, and **C** on next page). Each is in duple meter and each is repeated to extend the dance. Most important, each phrase has its own particular scale pattern, or mode*. None of the three modes, however, exactly corresponds to our Western major or minor mode: melody **A** is similar, but not identical, to our D minor scale; melody **B** has much in common with our F major scale; while melody **C** approximates a mixture of our F and D minor scales. As you listen to melodies **A** and **C**, you will hear a decidedly exotic sound. It is the augmented second (three ½ steps or 1½ whole steps),

an interval that occurs in much Eastern European and North African music, but not in our two Western scales. The most striking moments of *Fun Taschlich* come at the shift between the minor-like **A** melody and the major-like **B** tune. Finally, note that this Eastern European piece is a happy dance, yet it is written mainly in what sounds like our minor mode. While music in a minor key may sound sad to Western ears, to more Eastern ones it can have happy connotations. Humans' emotional response to music is not conditioned by the physical properties of sound, but rather by each group's cultural traditions and musical habits.

Melody **A**
  Scale: D, E, F, G, A♭, B, C, D
  Pattern: 1, ½, 1, ½, 1½, ½, 1 steps

Melody **B**
  Scale: F, G, A, B♭, C, D, E♭, F
  Pattern: 1, 1, ½, 1, 1, ½, 1 steps

Melody **C**
  Scale: F, G, A♭, B, C, D, E♭, F
  Pattern: 1, ½, 1½, ½, 1, ½, 1 steps

EXAMPLE 3–15

Melody A

Melody B

Melody C

★ = augmented second

Listening Guide

Fun Taschlich
Traditional klezmer tune performed by the Klezmatics

6
6/17

0:00	17	Introduction: bass clarinet solo above North African–like drum pattern
0:42		Melody **A** played by bass clarinet
1:06		Melody **A** played by electric violin alternating with muted trumpet and bass clarinet
1:21		Sudden mode shift of mode for melody **B** played by bass clarinet, supported by electric violin and muted trumpet
1:38		Melody **C** played by electric violin and muted trumpet
1:54		Melody **A** played by all melodic instruments
2:10		Melody **B** played by bass clarinet, supported by electric violin and muted trumpet
2:26		Melody **C** played by electric violin and muted trumpet
2:44		Free improvisation around notes of modes 1 and 3 (melodies **A** and **C**)
4:21		Melody **A** played by all melodic instruments
4:35		Melody **B** played by bass clarinet, supported by electric violin and muted trumpet
4:51		Melody **C** played by electric violin and muted trumpet
5:07		Fade-out with opening motive

Use a downloadable, cross-platform animated Active Listening Guide, available at **www.thomsonedu.com/music/wright.**

Key Words

Hindustani- style music (**33**)	tabla (**33**)	pipa (**35**)
	raga (**33**)	tremolo (**35**)
Karnatak-style music (**33**)	Ravi Shankar (**34**)	pentatonic scale (**36**)
sitar (**33**)	erhu (**35**)	klezmer
	Abing (**35**)	music (**37**)

Harmony

Melody provides a lyrical voice for music, rhythm gives vitality to that voice, and harmony adds depth and richness to it, just as the dimension of depth in painting adds a rich backdrop to that art. Although melody can stand by itself, most often it is supported by a harmony, an accompaniment that enriches it. Melody and harmony work gracefully together, the one carrying the central idea above, the other supporting it below. Sometimes, however, discord arises—as when a singer strumming a guitar fails to change the chord to make it agree with the melody. The melody and harmony now clash; they are out of harmony.

As the double sense of this last statement suggests, the term *harmony* has several meanings. In the broadest sense, harmony is the peaceful arrangement of diverse elements (Fig. 4–1). When applied specifically to music, **harmony** is said to be the sounds that provide a support and enrichment—an accompaniment—for melody. Finally, we often speak of harmony as if it is a specific event in the accompaniment; for example, we say the harmony changes, meaning that one chord in the accompaniment gives way to the next. Thus, we might say that the song "Oh, What a Beautiful Morning" from the musical *Oklahoma* is a "harmonious" (pleasant-sounding) piece, "harmonized" (accompanied) in the key of C major, and that the "harmony" (chords used to accompany the melody) changes eight times.

FIGURE 4–1

Claude Monet, *Waterlily Pond: Pink Harmony* (1900). Monet's painting of his famous bridge at Giverny, France, reveals not only the harmonious qualities of nature, but also the painter's ability to harmonize various colors into a blend of pastels.

Musée d'Orsay, Peris/Lauros/Giraudon/The Bridgeman Art Library

EXAMPLE 4–1

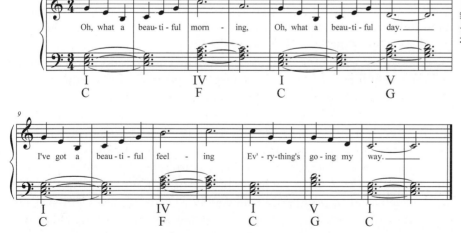

melody above, harmony below

BUILDING HARMONY

Chords are the building blocks of harmony. A **chord** is simply a group of two or more pitches that sound at the same time. When we learn to play guitar or jazz piano, we first learn mainly how to construct chords. The basic chord in

building blocks of harmony

Western music is the **triad,** so called because it consists of three pitches arranged in a very specific way. Here is a C major triad.

EXAMPLE 4–2

constructing a triad

Note that it comprises the first, third, and fifth notes of the C major scale. The distance between each of these notes is called an **interval.** C to E, spanning three letter names (C, D, E), is the interval of a third. E to G, again spanning three letter names (E, F, G), is another third. Triads always consist of two intervals of a third placed one on top of the other. Here are triads built on every note of the C major scale.

EXAMPLE 4–3

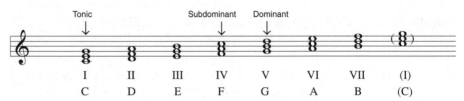

These triads provide all the basic chords necessary to harmonize a melody in C major.

Notice that each of the chords is given a Roman numeral, indicating on which note of the scale the triad is built, and that the triads built on I, IV, and V are called the tonic, subdominant, and dominant chords, respectively. We have already met the tonic* note in our discussion of melody—it is the pitch around which a tune gravitates and on which it ends. Similarly, the tonic chord, or triad, is the "home" chord of the harmony. It is the most stable and the one toward which the other chords move. The **dominant** triad, always built on the fifth note of the scale, is next in importance. Dominant triads are especially likely to move to tonic triads at the ends of musical phrases, where such a movement (V–I) helps create the strong effect of a full cadence*. The **subdominant** triad is built on the fourth note of the scale and is called the "sub"-dominant because its pitch is just below the dominant. The subdominant often moves to the dominant, which in turn moves to the tonic, creating the succession IV–V–I. A movement of chords in a purposeful fashion like this is called a **chord progression.** The individual chords in a chord progression seem to "pull" each other along, one giving way to the next, and all ultimately gravitating toward the powerful tonic harmony.

important triads

But why is it necessary for chords to change? The answer lies in the fact that the pitches of a melody continually change, sometimes moving through all the notes of a scale. But a single triadic chord can only be harmonious, or consonant, with the three notes of the scale that it contains. A tonic triad in C major, for example, can only "harmonize" with the melody notes C, E, and G (see Ex. 4–2). In order to keep the harmony consonant with the melody, then, chords must continually change. If they do not, dissonance results.

Finally, the notes of a triad need not always enter together but can be spaced out over time. Such a broken, or staggered, triad is called an **arpeggio.** The name derives from *arpa,* the Italian word for "harp," because the harp often plays the notes of a chord not together, but in succession. Arpeggios can appear either as part of the melody or, more often, in the harmony that supports a melody. An arpeggio used in an accompaniment gives the listener the sense that the harmony is more active than it really is. In Example 4–4, the beginning of "Oh, What a Beautiful Morning" is harmonized with the supporting triads spaced out, and repeated, as arpeggios (beneath the brackets). These chords are the same as in Example 4–1, but now the harmony seems more active because one note of the accompanying triad is sounding on every beat.

EXAMPLE 4–4

chords become arpeggios

CONSONANCE AND DISSONANCE

You have undoubtedly noticed, when pressing the keys of the piano at one time or another, that some combinations of keys produce a harsh, jarring sound, while others are pleasing and harmonious. The former chords are characterized by **dissonance** (pitches sounding disagreeable and unstable) and the latter by **consonance** (pitches sounding agreeable and stable) (Fig. 4–2). Generally, chords that contain pitches that are very close together, just a half or a whole step apart, sound dissonant. On the other hand, chords that involve a third, a somewhat larger interval, are usually consonant. Each of the triads built on the notes of the major scale (see Ex. 4–3), for example, contains two intervals of a third and therefore is consonant. Dissonant chords add a feeling of tension and anxiety to music; consonant ones produce a sense of rest and stability.

HEARING THE HARMONY CHANGE

The first step to listening to harmony is to focus your attention on the bass, separating it from the higher melody line. Chords are often built on the bass note, and a change in the bass from one pitch to another may signal a change in chord. Concentrating on the bass at first might not be easy. Most of us have always thought that listening to music means essentially listening to melody. Certainly, hearing melody is crucial. But the bass is next in importance, and it rules supreme in a sort of subterranean world. It carries the chords and determines where the harmony is going, more so than the higher melody. Baroque music (1600–1750) usually has a clear, driving bass line, and

FIGURE 4–2

Henri Matisse, *Violinist at the Window* (1918). In his writings on art, Matisse often spoke of the "consonance and dissonance of color."

hard rock music perhaps even more so. Next time you listen to a piece of rock, follow the electric bass line instead of the melody and lyrics. See if you don't begin to sense when the chords are changing and when you have reached a chord that feels like the home key (the tonic triad). Listening Exercise 7 will help you follow the bass line as you enjoy the famous Pachelbel Canon.

Listening Exercise 7

Hearing the Bass Line and Harmony
Johann Pachelbel, Canon in D major (c1690)
(For more on Pachelbel's Canon, see page 59)

ThomsonNOW
To take this Listening Exercise online and receive feedback or email answers to your instructor, go to *ThomsonNOW* for this chapter.

When we listen to music, most of us naturally concentrate on the highest-sounding part, which is where the melody is usually to be found. To hear harmony, however, we need to focus on the lowest-sounding line, the bass. In Johann Pachelbel's famous four-part Canon in D major, there is a canon (a round) in the upper three parts. (Canon is explained more fully in Chapter 6.) Below this canon, however, Pachelbel writes a solitary bass part moving very slowly. This bass supports the canon that unfolds above. As with most bass lines, here the lowest part establishes the foundation for the harmony (chords) above each of its pitches. In this piece, the bass enters first, and then the canon (round) gradually unfolds. Focus now on the bass and answer the following questions.

1. The bass enters first. At what point does the first violin enter?
   a. 0:00   b. 0:17   c. 0:21

2. Listen again to the beginning. How many pitches do you hear before the violin enters and the bass begins to repeat? In other words, how many pitches are there in the bass pattern?
   a. four   b. six   c. eight

3. Are all the pitches within the pattern of the bass held for the same duration?
   a. yes   b. no

4. Therefore, the rate of harmonic change in Pachelbel's Canon is what?
   a. regular   b. irregular

5. Which diagram most accurately reflects the pitches (the pattern) of the bass line?

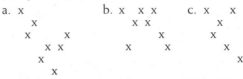

6. Listen now to more of the composition. The bass is highly repetitive as the pattern recurs again and again. Each statement of the pattern lasts approximately how long?
   a. 10 seconds   b. 15 seconds   c. 20 seconds

7. A melody, harmony, or rhythm that repeats again and again in music is called what (consult the glossary for the meanings of these terms)?
   a. a pizzicato   b. a legato
   c. a tempo   d. an ostinato

8. Now listen up to 2:02 of the recording. Does the bass pattern ever change?
   a. yes   b. no

9. From the beginning of the piece (0:00) to this point (2:02), how many times do you hear the pattern?
   a. 8   b. 10   c. 12   d. 14

10. Listen all the way to the end of the work. Does Pachelbel ever vary his bass and his harmonic pattern?
    a. yes   b. no

The continually repeating bass line in Johann Pachelbel's Canon is unusual in classical music. In most classical pieces, the bass and the resulting chords do not repeat in a regular fashion, and that makes hearing the harmonic changes difficult. Yet in popular music, sensing when the harmony changes can be easier because a succession of chord changes may repeat over and over again. Rock music of the 1950s and 1960s frequently repeats three or four chords without varying the order. Similarly, harmonic repetition occurs in the **blues,** an expressive, soulful style of singing that unfolds above repeating chord changes. Although there are several variants, the standard harmony of the blues involves just three chords—tonic, subdominant, and dominant—which spread out over twelve measures. Within the **twelve-bar blues** pat-

The Twelve-Bar Blues Harmony Then and Now

Arguably the most influential chord progression in all of American popular music is the so-called twelve-bar blues. The blues, as we shall see in Chapter 38, emerged in the late nineteenth century, among descendants of slaves of the American south, as a folk music tradition, combining elements of African-American praise songs, field hollers, and chants. In their early rural manifestations, blues songs employed varying and unpredictable harmonic progressions, featuring surprising harmonic shifts in some cases while remaining essentially static in others. During the 1920s, as the blues began to migrate from the rural south to northern cities, the twelve-bar form became increasingly common, and by the 1930s, it had emerged as the standard blues progression.

Such is the attraction of this relatively straightforward harmonic progression that it has been used widely not only throughout the history of blues music but in countless other musical genres as well. For example, the twelve-bar blues has featured prominently throughout the history of country music, from many of the songs of the first country music superstar, Jimmy Rogers (such as "Train Whistle Blues," 1930), to the "Texas Swing" style of Bob Wills and His Texas Playboys (for example, their cover of "Corrine, Corrina," 1940), to Johnny Cash's "Folsom Prison Blues" (1956). The great majority of early rock 'n' roll was based on the twelve-bar form: "Rock Around the Clock" (made famous in 1954 by Bill Haley and the Comets), "Hound Dog" (as performed by Elvis Presley in 1956), and Chuck Berry's "Johnny B. Goode" (1958) all use this same twelve-bar pattern. What is more, countless jazz "standards" are built on an embellished but easily recognizable variant of the twelve-bar blues, and the progression has long been common among rural and urban folk musicians. The British "supergroups" of the 1960s and 1970s made much use of the twelve-bar blues, as can be seen, for example, in The Beatles 1964 cover of "Johnny B. Goode," the Rolling Stones' 1969 cover of

Mississippi Delta blues singer Riley B. (B.B.) King.

© Reuters/Corbis

"Love in Vain" (composed by legendary bluesman Robert Johnson), and Led Zeppelin's "You Shook Me" (1969). The seemingly timeless appeal of this progression has continued through the 1980s and 1990s and to the present day; examples include the late blues rocker Stevie Ray Vaughn (for example, "Pride and Joy," 1983) and crossover pop singer Tracy Chapman ("Give Me One Reason," 1995). And, of course, today's vibrant blues scene—represented by such stars as Buddy Guy, Otis Rush, and B. B. King—makes frequent use of this nearly hundred-year-old chord progression.

tern, however, the chords do not sound for the same length of time. The rate of harmonic change is thus irregular. The first tonic holds for four bars, while all subsequent chords sound for just two bars. Once completed, the pattern repeats again and again, until the singer is finished.

```
Chord:    I ——————————IV————I————V———— I —————  (Repeat)
Measure:  1   2   3   4   5   6   7   8   9   10   11   12
```

To get the sound of the repeating harmony of the blues in your ear, we have created our own blues tune, "The Listening to Music Blues," in which the changing chords of the twelve-bar harmony are played by an electric keyboard.

Listening Exercise 8

Hearing Chord Changes in the Harmony
"The Listening to Music Blues"

(Intro 10)

In "The Listening to Music Blues," the left hand of the electric keyboard player holds one chord until it is time to move on to the next. Each time he stops holding and moves elsewhere, we have a new chord. Fill in the time log for the chord changes in this repeating blues harmony. At numbers 1–9, record the minute and second that a new chord appears (write 1:10, for example). Several of the correct times are already filled in to make your task easier.

Statement 1:

0:00   1. ____   2. ____   0:17   3. ____   0:21
  I   IV   I   V   IV   I

Statement 2 (melody guitar enters):

0:25   4. ____   5. ____   0:42   6. ____   0:46
  I   IV   I   V   IV   I

Statement 3:

0:50   7. ____   8. ____   1:06   9. ____   1:11
  I   IV   I   V   IV   I

10. What is the rate of harmonic change here?
     a. regular   b. irregular

Key Words

harmony (**39**)
chord (**39**)
triad (**40**)
interval (**40**)
dominant (**40**)

subdominant (**40**)
chord
  progression (**40**)
arpeggio (**40**)
dissonance (**41**)

consonance (**41**)
blues (**42**)
twelve-bar blues (**42**)

Chapter 5

Dynamics and Color

As we have seen, rhythm, melody, and harmony constitute the primary elements of music. In order for a musical composition to be conveyed to a listener, however, these abstract concepts must be translated into concrete musical sounds. This is accomplished when musical instruments and voices transform the composer's ideas about rhythm, melody, and harmony into actual sound waves. We use the terms *dynamics* and *color* to describe the particular character of these musical sounds as they are performed by the various instruments or voices.

Our response to dynamics and musical color is immediate. For example, we may be struck by a certain passage, not so much because of its pitches or rhythm, but because of a sudden, dynamic shift from very quiet to very loud, or because the melody is played by a brilliant-sounding trumpet. Dynamics and color, then, refer not so much to a musical idea itself, but instead to the way in which that musical idea is presented.

DYNAMICS

In all music, **dynamics** are the various levels of volume, loud and soft, at which sounds are produced. Dynamics work together with tone colors to affect the way we hear and react to musical sound. A high note in the clarinet has one quality—shrill and harsh—when played *fortissimo* (very loud) and quite another—vague and otherworldly—when played *pianissimo* (very soft). Figure 5–1 shows a computerized representation of the waveforms of a clarinet playing *pianissimo* and then *fortissimo*. Because they were first used by composers working in Italy, the terms for musical dynamics are traditionally written in Italian. Below are the most common terms and the musical symbols for them.

FIGURE 5–1

Computerized digital waveform of about ten seconds of sound of a clarinet playing soft and loud. The narrower the vertical lines, the softer the sound.

Term	Musical Symbol	Definition
fortissimo	*ff*	very loud
forte	*f*	loud
mezzo forte	*mf*	moderately loud
mezzo piano	*mp*	moderately soft
piano	*p*	soft
pianissimo	*pp*	very soft

louds and softs

Dynamics sometimes change abruptly, for special effects. Most common among these quick changes is the ***sforzando,*** a sudden, loud attack on one note or chord. A famous *sforzando* occurs in the second movement of Joseph Haydn's "Surprise" Symphony (1792), for example, in which the composer interrupts a soft melody with a thunderous crash on a single chord (Intro/22 at 0:33)—his intent was apparently to awaken those listeners who might have dozed off!

But changes in dynamics need not be sudden and abrupt. They can be gradual and extend over a long period of time. A gradual increase in the intensity of sound is called a crescendo, while a gradual decrease is called either a decrescendo or diminuendo.

Term	Musical Symbol	Definition
crescendo	<	growing louder
decrescendo or diminuendo	>	growing softer

changing dynamics

Ludwig van Beethoven was a master at writing long crescendos. The transition to the last movement of his Symphony No. 5 comes upon the listener like a tidal wave of sound (6 3/10 at 5:00). An equally impressive crescendo can be heard at the beginning of Richard Strauss's *Thus Spoke Zarathustra* as the full orchestra gradually enters (Intro/3). Spectacular moments such as these remind us that in music, as in marketing and communications generally, the medium (here dynamics and color) can be the message.

COLOR

Simply stated, **color** in music is the tone quality of any sound produced by a voice or an instrument. **Timbre** is another term for the tone quality of musical sound. Instruments produce sounds of different colors because they are

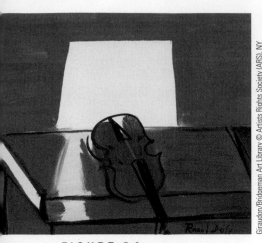

Giraudon/Bridgeman Art Library © Artists Rights Society (ARS), NY

FIGURE 5–2

We sometimes associate the sound of different instruments with particular colors. Possibly for this reason, the painter Raoul Dufy (1877–1953) called this work *Red Violin.*

constructed in different ways and of different materials. We need not understand the acoustical properties of the various instruments to appreciate that they sound different. We can all hear that the sound of a flute has a much different tone quality than does that of a trombone. Similarly, the voice of pop singer Mariah Carey has a different timbre than that of opera star Renée Fleming, even when the two produce the same pitches. Because the human voice was probably the first "instrument" to make music, it provides an appropriate starting point for our investigation of musical color.

The Voice

The human voice is an instrument of a very special sort that naturally generates sound without the aid of any kind of mechanical contrivance. It is highly expressive, in part because it can produce a wide range of sounds and do so at greatly contrasting dynamic levels.

When we sing we force air up through our vocal cords (two folds of mucous membrane within the throat), causing them to vibrate. Men's vocal cords are longer and thicker than women's, and for that reason the sound of the mature male voice is lower. (This principle is also at work with the string instruments: the longer and thicker the string, the lower the pitch.) Voices are classified by range into four principal parts. The two women's vocal parts are the **soprano** and the **alto,** and the two men's parts the **tenor** and the **bass.** The soprano is the highest voice, and the bass the lowest. When many voices join together, they form a **chorus;** the soprano, alto, tenor, and bass constitute the four standard choral parts. In addition, the area of pitch shared by the soprano and alto is sometimes designated as a separate vocal range called the **mezzo-soprano,** just as the notes adjoining the tenor and bass are said to be encompassed by the **baritone** voice.

types of voices

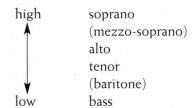

high   soprano
             (mezzo-soprano)
             alto
             tenor
             (baritone)
low   bass

The voice is capable of producing many different styles of singing: the raspy sound of a blues singer, the twang of the country balladeer, the gutsy belt of a Broadway songster, or the lyrical tones of an operatic soprano. We all try to sing, and we would like to sing well. How well we do, and what kind of sound we produce, depends on our training and our physical makeup—the lungs, vocal cords, throat, nose, and mouth are all involved in the production of vocal sound.

Musical Instruments

Musical instruments come in groups, or families. The Western symphony orchestra traditionally includes four such groups. The first is the string family, so called because sound is produced by plucking or bowing the strings of these instruments. The second and third groups are the woodwind and brass families. In both groups, music is generated by blowing air through various pipes or tubes. In the fourth group, the percussion family, sound is produced

ThomsonNOW™

For a video of the instruments of the orchestra, go to *ThomsonNOW.*

by striking a suspended membrane (a drum), a block of wood, or a piece of metal with a stick of some kind. In addition, there is a fifth group of instruments, the keyboard instruments, which are not normally part of the symphony orchestra. The organ, harpsichord, and piano are the main keyboard instruments, and they make sound by means of keys and pipes (organ) or keys and strings (harpsichord and piano). The organ is usually played alone, while the piano is most often heard either by itself or as an accompaniment to another instrument or the voice.

families of instruments

STRINGS

Generally, when we speak of string instruments in Western music, we broadly include all instruments that produce sound by means of vibrating strings: the guitar, banjo, ukulele, and the harp, as well as the violin and its close relatives, the viola, cello, and double bass. But the guitar, banjo, ukulele, and harp usually produce their sound when plucked, whereas the violin and its relatives are normally played with a bow, not just plucked. Indeed, it is their use of a bow, along with their distinctive shape, that identifies the four members of the violin group. We traditionally associate these instruments with classical music. The guitar, banjo, ukulele, and harp, on the other hand, have their origins in folk music.

VIOLIN GROUP

The violin group constituted the original core of the symphony orchestra when it was first formed during the Baroque era (1600–1750). In numbers of players, the violins, violas, cellos, and double basses still make up the largest part of any Western symphony orchestra. A large orchestra can easily include as many as a hundred members, at least sixty of whom play one of these four instruments.

The **violin** (Fig. 5–3 center; see also page 3) is chief among the string instruments. It is also the smallest—it has the shortest strings and therefore the highest pitch. Because of its high range and singing tone, it often is assigned the melody in orchestral and chamber music. The violins are usually divided into groups known as firsts and seconds. The seconds play a part slightly lower in pitch and subordinate in function to the firsts.

The sound of the violin is produced when a bow is pulled across one of four strings held tightly in place by tuning pegs at one end of the instrument and by a tailpiece at the other. The strings are slightly elevated above the wooden body by means of a supporting bridge. Different sounds or pitches are produced when a finger of the left hand shortens, or "stops," a string by pressing it against the fingerboard—again, the shorter the string, the higher the pitch. Because each of the four strings can be stopped quickly in many different places, the violin possesses both great range and agility. The strings themselves are made of either animal gut or metal wire. The singing tone of the violin, however, comes not so much from the strings as from the wooden body, known as the sound box, which amplifies and enriches the sound. The better the design, wood, glue, and varnish of the sound box, the better the tone. (For the sound of the violin, turn to (Intro)/11 at 0:00.)

FIGURE 5–3

This photo of the American group, the Brentano Quartet, shows the relative size of the violin (center), viola (left), and cello (right).

© Christian Steiner/Courtesy Brentano String Quartet

FIGURE 5–4
Double bass player Edgar Meyer.

FIGURE 5–5
The harp's unique special effect is its glissando, a rapid run up and down the strings that seems to fill the airwaves with energized sound.

The **viola** (Fig. 5–3 left) is about six inches longer than the violin, and it produces a somewhat lower sound. If the violin is the string counterpart of the soprano voice, then the viola has its parallel in the alto voice. Its tone is darker, richer, and more somber than that of the brilliant violin. (For the sound of the viola, turn to 🅘ntro/11 at 1:37.)

You can easily spot the **cello** (violoncello) in the orchestra because the player sits with the instrument placed between the legs (Fig. 5–3 right). The pitch of the cello is well below that of the viola. It can provide a low bass sound as well as a singing melody. When played in its middle range by a skilled performer, the cello is capable of producing an indescribably rich, expressive tone. (For the sound of the cello, turn to 🅘ntro/11 at 2:10.)

The **double bass** (Fig. 5–4) gives weight and power to the bass line in the orchestra. Since at first it merely doubled the notes of the cello an octave* below, it was called the double bass. As you can see, the double bass is the largest, and hence lowest-sounding, of the string instruments. Its job in the orchestra, and even in jazz bands, is to help set a solid base for the musical harmony. (For the sound of the double bass, turn to 🅘ntro/11 at 2:50.)

SPECIAL EFFECTS

The members of the violin group all generate pitches in the same way: A bow is drawn across a tight string. This produces the traditional, penetrating string sound. In addition, a number of other effects can be created by using different playing techniques.

- **vibrato:** By shaking the left hand as it stops the string, the performer can produce a sort of controlled "wobble" in the pitch. This adds richness to the tone of the string because, in fact, it creates a blend of two or more pitches. (For an example of a violin playing without vibrato and then with vibrato, turn to 🅘ntro/11 at 0:31 and at 0:51.)
- **pizzicato:** Instead of bowing the strings, the performer plucks them. With this technique, the resulting sound has a sharp attack, but it dies away quickly. (For an example of pizzicato, turn to 🅘ntro/11 at 1:13.)
- **tremolo:** The performer creates a musical "tremor" by rapidly repeating the same pitch with quick up-and-down strokes of the bow. Tremolo creates a feeling of heightened tension and excitement when played loudly, and a velvety, shimmering backdrop when performed quietly. (For an example of tremolo, turn to 🅘ntro/11 at 1:24.)
- **trill:** The performer rapidly alternates between two distinctly separate but neighboring pitches. Most instruments, not just the strings, can play trills. (For an example of a trill, turn to 🅘ntro/11 at 1:30.)
- **mute:** If a composer wants to dampen the penetrating tone of a string instrument, he or she can instruct the player to place a mute (a metal or rubber clamp) on the strings of the instrument.

HARP

Although originally a folk instrument, one found in virtually every musical culture, the **harp** (Fig. 5–5) is sometimes added to the modern symphony orchestra. Its role is to add its distinctive color to the orchestral sound and sometimes to create special effects, the most striking of which is a rapid run up or down the strings called a **glissando.** (For the sound of the harp and an example of a glissando, turn to 🅘ntro/11 at 3:35 and 3:44.)

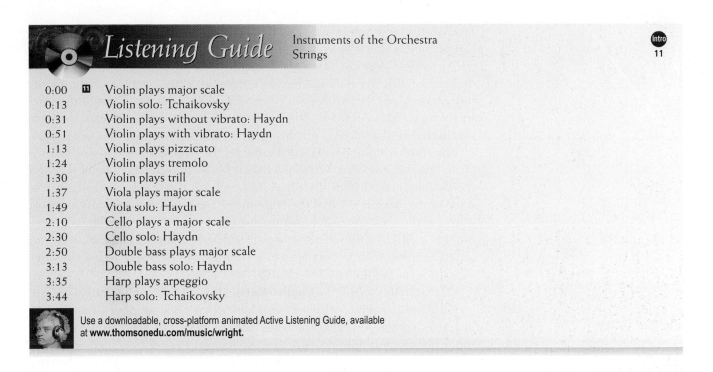

Listening Guide   Instruments of the Orchestra
Strings

Intro
11

0:00	**11**	Violin plays major scale
0:13		Violin solo: Tchaikovsky
0:31		Violin plays without vibrato: Haydn
0:51		Violin plays with vibrato: Haydn
1:13		Violin plays pizzicato
1:24		Violin plays tremolo
1:30		Violin plays trill
1:37		Viola plays major scale
1:49		Viola solo: Haydn
2:10		Cello plays a major scale
2:30		Cello solo: Haydn
2:50		Double bass plays major scale
3:13		Double bass solo: Haydn
3:35		Harp plays arpeggio
3:44		Harp solo: Tchaikovsky

Use a downloadable, cross-platform animated Active Listening Guide, available at **www.thomsonedu.com/music/wright.**

WOODWINDS

The name "woodwind" was originally given to this family of instruments because they emit sound when air is blown through a wooden tube or pipe. The pipe has holes along its length, and the player covers or uncovers these to change the pitch. Nowadays, however, some of these woodwind instruments are made entirely of metal. Flutes, for example, are constructed of silver, and sometimes of gold or even platinum. As with the violin group, there are four principal woodwind instruments in every modern symphony orchestra: flute, oboe, clarinet, and bassoon (Fig. 5–6). In addition, each of these has a close relative that is larger or smaller in size and that possesses a somewhat different timbre and range. The larger the instrument or length of pipe, the lower the sound.

The lovely, silvery tone of the **flute** is probably familiar to you. The instrument can be rich in the lower register and then light and airy on top. It is especially agile, capable of playing tones rapidly and moving quickly from one range to another. (For the sound of the flute, turn to ⊙/12 at 0:00.)

The smaller cousin of the flute is the **piccolo.** ("Piccolo" comes from the Italian *flauto piccolo*, meaning "little flute.") It can produce higher notes than any other orchestral instrument. And though very small, its sound is so shrill that it can always be heard, even when the full orchestra is playing loudly. (For the sound of the piccolo, turn to ⊙/12 at 0:38.)

The **clarinet** produces sound when the player blows against a single reed

FIGURE 5–6

(from left to right) A flute, two clarinets, an oboe, and a bassoon. The flute, clarinet, and oboe are about the same length. The bassoon is nearly twice their size.

fitted to the mouthpiece. The tone of the clarinet is an open, hollow sound. It can be mellow in its low notes, but shrill in its high ones. It also has the capacity to slide or glide smoothly between pitches, and this allows for a highly expressive style of playing. The flexibility and expressiveness of the instrument have made it a favorite with jazz musicians. (For the sound of the clarinet, turn to (Intro)/12 at 0:54.) A lower, larger version of the clarinet is the **bass clarinet.**

The **oboe** is equipped with a double reed—two reeds tied together with an air space in between. When the player blows into the instrument through the double reed, a nasal, slightly exotic sound is created. It is invariably the oboe that gives the pitch at the beginning of every symphony concert. Not only was the oboe the first nonstring instrument to be added to the orchestra, but it is a difficult instrument to tune (regulate the pitch). Thus, it's better to have the other instruments tune to it than to try to have it adjust to them. (For the sound of the oboe, turn to (Intro)/12 at 1:24.)

Related to the oboe is the **English horn.** Unfortunately, it is wrongly named, for the English horn is neither English nor a horn. It is simply a larger (hence lower-sounding) version of the oboe that originated on the continent of Europe. The English horn produces a dark, haunting sound, one that was especially favored by composers of the Romantic period (1820–1900). (For the sound of the English horn, turn to (6)5/1 at 0:00.)

The **bassoon** functions among the woodwinds much as the cello does among the strings. It can serve as a bass instrument, adding weight to the lowest sound, or it can act as a soloist in its own right. When playing moderately fast or rapid passages as a solo instrument, it has a dry, almost comic tone. (For the sound of the bassoon, turn to (Intro)/12 at 1:54.)

There is also a double bassoon, usually called the **contrabassoon.** Its sound is deep and sluggish. Indeed, the contrabassoon can play notes lower than any other orchestral instrument.

The bassoon, contrabassoon, and English horn are all double-reed instruments, just like the oboe. Their tones, therefore, may sound more vibrant, even more exotic, than those of the single-reed instruments like the clarinet and saxophone.

Strictly speaking, the single-reed **saxophone** is not a member of the symphony orchestra, though it can be added on occasion. Its sound can be mellow and expressive but also, if the player wishes, husky, even raucous. The expressiveness of the saxophone makes it a welcome member of most jazz ensembles.

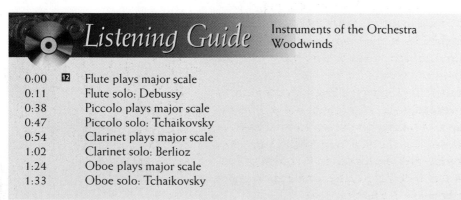

Listening Guide   Instruments of the Orchestra   (Intro)
Woodwinds   12

0:00	12	Flute plays major scale
0:11		Flute solo: Debussy
0:38		Piccolo plays major scale
0:47		Piccolo solo: Tchaikovsky
0:54		Clarinet plays major scale
1:02		Clarinet solo: Berlioz
1:24		Oboe plays major scale
1:33		Oboe solo: Tchaikovsky

1:54	Bassoon plays major scale
2:05	Bassoon solo: Stravinsky

 Use a downloadable, cross-platform animated Active Listening Guide, available at **www.thomsonedu.com/music/wright.**

BRASSES

Like the woodwind and string groups of the orchestra, the brass family consists of four primary instruments: trumpet, trombone, French horn, and tuba (Fig. 5–7). Brass players use no reeds, but instead blow into their instruments through a cup-shaped **mouthpiece** (Fig. 5–8). By adjusting valves or moving a slide, the performer can make the length of pipe on the instrument longer or shorter, and hence the pitch lower or higher.

Everyone has heard the high, bright, cutting sound of the **trumpet.** Whether on a football field or in an orchestral hall, the trumpet is an excellent solo instrument because of its agility and penetrating tone. (For the sound of the trumpet, turn to ⓘ/13 at 0:00.) The trumpet sounds forth with special brilliance at the beginning of Strauss's *Thus Spoke Zarathustra* (ⓘ/3 at 0:16). When provided with a mute (a hollow plug placed in the bell of the instrument to dampen the sound), the trumpet can produce a softer tone that blends well with other instruments. (To hear a trumpet with mute, turn to ⓘ/13 at 0:22.)

Although distantly related to the trumpet, the **trombone** (Italian for "large trumpet") plays in the middle range of the brass family. Its sound is large and full. Most important, the trombone is the only brass instrument to generate sounds by moving a slide in and out, thereby producing higher or lower pitches. Needless to say, the trombone can easily slide from pitch to pitch, sometimes for comical effect. (For the sound of the trombone, turn to ⓘ/13 at 0:35.)

The **French horn** (sometimes just called "horn") was the first brass instrument to join the orchestra, back in the late seventeenth century. Its sound is rich and mellow, yet somewhat veiled or covered. The French horn was especially popular during the Romantic period (1820–1900) because the horn's traditional association with the hunt and with Alpine mountains suggested nature, a subject dear to the hearts of the Romantics. (For the sound of the French horn, turn to ⓘ/13 at 0:59.) It is easy to confuse the sound of the French horn with that of the trombone, because both are middle-range brass instruments and have a full, majestic tone. But the sound of the trombone is somewhat clearer and more focused, and its attack more direct, than that of the French horn. (For an immediate comparison of the trombone with the French horn, turn to ⓘ/13, first at 0:45 and then at 1:17.)

The **tuba** is the largest and lowest-sounding of the brass instruments. It produces a full, though sometimes muffled, tone in its lowest notes. Like the double bass of the violin group, the tuba is most often used to set a base, or foundation, for the melody. (For the sound of the tuba, turn to ⓘ/13 at 1:39.) On occasion, the tuba itself is assigned a melodic line, as in Picture 4 of Musorgsky's *Pictures at an Exhibition* (⑥ 4/9 at 0:00.) Here, the tuba demonstrates the melodious upper range of the instrument in a lengthy solo.

Martin Reichenthal

FIGURE 5–7

Members of the Canadian Brass, with the French horn player at the left and the tuba player at the right.

FIGURE 5–8

Mouthpieces for brass instruments.

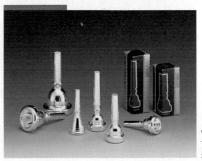

Yamaha Corp.

Listening Guide

Instruments of the Orchestra
Brasses

Intro
13

0:00	13	Trumpet plays major scale
0:09		Trumpet solo: Mouret
0:22		Trumpet solo with mute: Mouret
0:35		Trombone plays major scale
0:45		Trombone solo: Copland
0:59		French horn plays major scale
1:17		French horn solo: Copland
1:39		Tuba plays major scale
2:00		Tuba solo: Copland

Use a downloadable, cross-platform animated Active Listening Guide, available
at **www.thomsonedu.com/music/wright.**

FIGURE 5–9

Tympanist Jonathan Haas.

© Tim Wimborne/Reuters/Corbis

FIGURE 5–10

The xylophone, a fixed-pitch percussion
instrument on which can be played a fully
chromatic scale of several octaves.

PhotoDisc

PERCUSSION

Percussion instruments are those that are struck in some way, either by hitting the head of a drum with a stick or by banging or scraping a piece of metal or wood in one fashion or another. Some percussion instruments, like the timpani (kettledrums), produce a specific pitch, while others generate sound that, while precise rhythmically, has no recognizable musical pitch. It is the job of the percussion instruments to sharpen the rhythmic contour of the music. They can also add color to the sounds of other instruments and, when played loudly, can heighten the sense of climax in a piece.

The **timpani** (Fig. 5–9) is the percussion instrument most often heard in classical music. Whether struck in single, detached strokes or hit rapidly to produce a thunderlike roll, the function of the timpani is to add depth, tension, and drama to the music. Timpani usually come in pairs, one instrument tuned to the tonic* and the other to the dominant.* Playing only these pitches, the timpani feature prominently at the beginning of Strauss's *Thus Spoke Zarathustra* (Intro)/3 at 0:30).

The rat-ta-tat-tat of the **snare drum,** the dull thud of the **bass drum,** and the crashing ring of the **cymbals** are sounds well known from marching bands and jazz ensembles, as well as the classical orchestra. None of these instruments produces a specific musical tone. (To hear all three in succession, turn to (Intro)/14 at 0:11.)

The xylophone, glockenspiel, and celesta, however, are three percussion instruments that do generate specific pitches. The **xylophone** (Fig. 5–10) is a set of wooden bars that, when struck by two hard mallets, produce a dry, wooden sound. The **glockenspiel** works the same way, but the bars are made of metal so that the tone is brighter and more ringing. The **celesta,** too, produces sound when hammers strike metal bars, but the hammers are activated by keys, as in a piano; the tone of the celesta is bright and tinkling—a delightful, "celestial" sound, as the name of the instrument suggests.

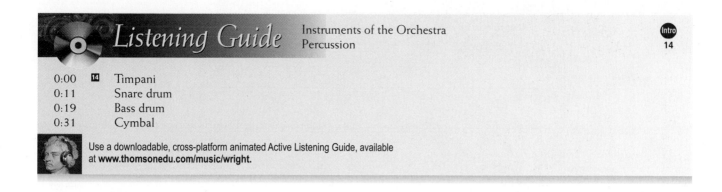

Listening Guide   Instruments of the Orchestra
Percussion

Intro
14

0:00	14	Timpani
0:11		Snare drum
0:19		Bass drum
0:31		Cymbal

Use a downloadable, cross-platform animated Active Listening Guide, available at www.thomsonedu.com/music/wright.

THE SYMPHONY ORCHESTRA

The modern Western symphony orchestra is one of the largest and certainly the most colorful of all musical ensembles. It originated in the seventeenth century and has continually grown in size since then. When at full strength, the symphony orchestra can include upward of one hundred performers and nearly thirty different instruments, from the high piping of the piccolo down to the rumble of the contrabassoon. A typical seating plan for an orchestra is given in Figure 5–11. To achieve the best balance of sound, strings are placed toward the front, and the more powerful brasses at the back. Other seating arrangements are also used, according to the special requirements of the composition to be performed.

Surprisingly, a separate conductor was not originally part of the orchestra. For the first 200 years of its existence (1600–1800), the symphony was led by

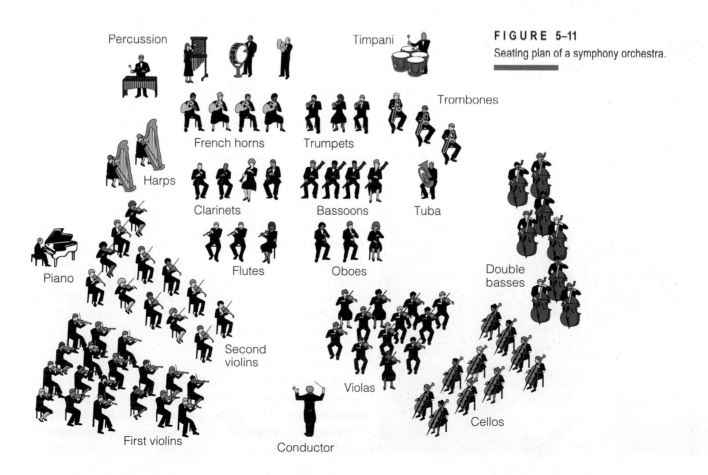

FIGURE 5–11
Seating plan of a symphony orchestra.

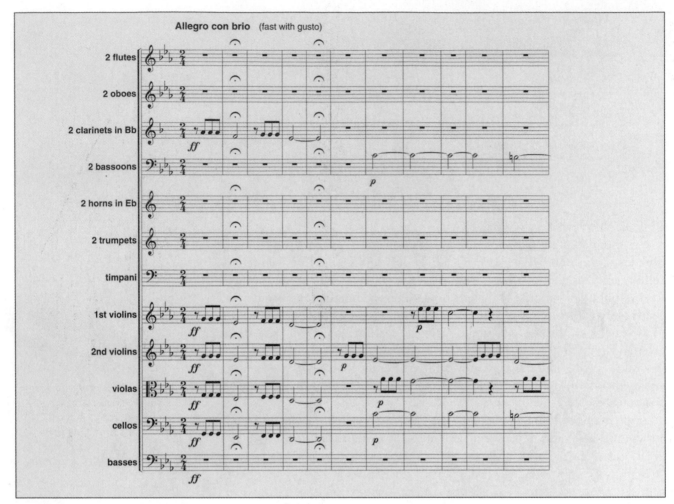

FIGURE 5–12
The orchestral score of the beginning of Beethoven's Symphony No. 5, first page, with instruments listed.

FIGURE 5–13
Esa-Pekka Salonen rehearses the Los Angeles Philharmonic.

one of the performers, either a keyboard player or the principal first violinist. By the time of Beethoven (1770–1827), however, the group had grown so large that it was thought necessary to have someone stand before it and lead, not only to keep all the players together but also to help draw out and elucidate the important musical lines. The conductor follows an **orchestral score,** a composite notation of all the instrumental parts for a particular piece. Figure 5–12 shows the orchestral score of the beginning of Beethoven's Symphony No. 5. Obviously, Beethoven had to put many, many notes on the page to achieve just a few seconds of music. It is the job of the conductor to follow the orchestral score and pick out any incorrectly played pitches and rhythms in this complicated web of instrumental sounds. To do this, the conductor must have an excellent musical ear. That's one reason the great conductors, such as Esa-Pekka Salonen (Fig. 5–13), make millions of dollars annually.

KEYBOARD INSTRUMENTS

Perhaps owing to their highly intricate mechanisms, keyboard instruments are unique to Western music, and are not found in indigenous musical cultures around the world. The pipe organ, harpsichord, and piano are the West's

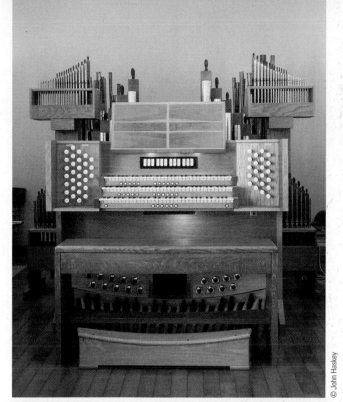

FIGURE 5–14

A three-manual (keyboard) pipe organ with only small pipes visible. Notice the stops (small circular objects on either side of the manual keyboards) and the pedal keyboard below.

FIGURE 5–15

A two-manual harpsichord built by Pascal Taskin (Paris, 1770), preserved in the Yale University Collection of Musical Instruments, New Haven, Connecticut.

principal keyboard instruments, and they originated at markedly different times. The **pipe organ** (Fig. 5–14), which traces its origins back to ancient Greece, is by far the oldest. It works according to the following principle: The player depresses a key that allows air to rush into a pipe, thereby producing sound. The pipes are arranged in separate groups according to their shape and material. Each group produces a full range of musical pitches with one special timbre (the sound of the trumpet, for example). When the organist wants to add a particular musical color to a piece, he or she simply pulls a knob, called a **stop.** The most colorful, forceful sound occurs when all the stops have been activated (thus the expression "pulling out all the stops"). The several keyboards of the organ make it possible to play several musical lines at once, each with its own timbre. There is even a keyboard for the feet! The largest fully functioning pipe organ in the world is in the Cadet Chapel of the United States Military Academy at West Point, New York. It has 270 stops and 18,408 pipes.

stops on an organ

The **harpsichord** (Fig. 5–15) was played in northern Italy as early as 1400, but it reached its heyday during the Baroque era (1600–1750). It produces sound not by means of pipes but by strings. When a key is depressed, it drives a lever upward that, in turn, forces a pick to pluck a string. The plucking creates a bright, jangling sound. Some harpsichords are equipped with two keyboards so that the player can change from one group of strings to another, each with its particular tone color and volume of sound. The harpsichord has one important shortcoming, however: The lever mechanism does not allow the performer to control the force with which the string is plucked, so each string always sounds at the same volume. (For more on the harpsichord, see page 114.)

The **piano** (Fig. 5–16) was invented in Italy around 1700, in part to overcome the dynamic limitations of the harpsichord. In a piano, strings are not plucked; they are hit by soft hammers. A lever mechanism makes it possible

FIGURE 5–16
Pianist André Watts.

ThomsonNOW
ThomsonNOW will allow you not only to hear but also to see the organ, harpsichord, and piano in action.

for the player to regulate how hard each string is struck, thus producing softs and louds (the original piano was called the *pianoforte*, the "soft-loud"). During the lifetime of Mozart (1756–1791), the piano replaced the harpsichord as the favorite domestic musical instrument. By the nineteenth century, every aspiring household had to have a piano, whether as an instrument for real musical enjoyment or as a symbol of affluence. Even today the piano stands as a domestic status symbol.

If the organ's familiar home is the church, where it is heard in association with religious services, the versatile piano is found almost everywhere. With equal success it can accompany a school chorus or an opera singer; it can harmonize with a rock band when in the hands of an Elton John or a Billy Joel; or it can become a powerful, yet expressive, solo instrument when played by a master such as André Watts. The harpsichord, on the other hand, is used mainly to re-create the music of the time of Johann Sebastian Bach (1685–1750).

You have now been introduced to the principal instruments of the Western symphony orchestra, as well as the West's three main keyboard instruments. Listening Exercises 9–11 test your ability to recognize orchestral instruments, and are graduated in difficulty.

Listening Exercise 9

Hearing the Instruments of the Orchestra
Identifying a Single Instrument

15

ThomsonNOW
To take this Listening Exercise online and receive feedback or email answers to your instructor, go to *ThomsonNOW* for this chapter.

By listening to the Intro CD, tracks 11–14, you have heard all of the principal instruments of the Western symphony orchestra. Now it is time to test your ability to identify these instruments. The Intro CD, track 15, contains excerpts of performances of ten solo instruments. Write the name of the correct instrument in the blank by choosing one from the right-hand column.

1. (0:00)   _____   Clarinet (Rimsky-Korsakov)
2. (0:14)   _____   Oboe (Tchaikovsky)
3. (0:38)   _____   Tuba (Berlioz)
4. (0:52)   _____   Bassoon (Rimsky-Korsakov)
5. (1:13)   _____   Violin (Tchaikovsky)
6. (1:30)   _____   French horn (Brahms)
7. (1:48)   _____   Flute (Tchaikovsky)
8. (2:09)   _____   Cello (Saint-Saëns)
9. (2:34)   _____   Double bass (Beethoven)
10. (2:50)   _____   Trombone (Ravel)

Listening Exercise 10

Hearing the Instruments of the Orchestra
Identifying Two Instruments

16

ThomsonNOW
To take this Listening Exercise online and receive feedback or email answers to your instructor, go to *ThomsonNOW* for this chapter.

Now things get more difficult. Can you identify two instruments playing at once, and the one that is playing in a higher range? To keep you on track, a few instruments have been filled in. Choose from among the following instruments for the remaining blanks below: violin, viola, cello, double bass, flute (heard twice), clarinet, oboe (heard twice), bassoon, trumpet, and French horn.

	First Instrument	Second Instrument	Higher Instrument
(0:00) Brahms	French horn	1. _____	2. _____
(0:40) Mahler	3. _____	4. _____	5. _____
(1:08) Lully	6. _____	clarinet	7. _____
(1:29) Bach	8. _____	bassoon	9. _____
(1:44) Bach	10. _____	11. _____	12. _____
(2:00) Telemann	13. _____	viola	14. _____
(2:27) Bartók	15. _____	16. _____	17. _____
(2:52) Bach	18. _____	19. _____	20. _____

Listening Exercise 11

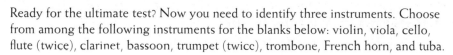

Hearing the Instruments of the Orchestra
Identifying Three Instruments

ThomsonNOW™
To take this Listening Exercise online and receive feedback or email answers to your instructor, go to *ThomsonNOW* for this chapter.

Ready for the ultimate test? Now you need to identify three instruments. Choose from among the following instruments for the blanks below: violin, viola, cello, flute (twice), clarinet, bassoon, trumpet (twice), trombone, French horn, and tuba.

	First Instrument	Second Instrument	Third Instrument
(0:00) Tchaikovsky	1. _____	French horn	2. _____
(0:18) Tchaikovsky	3. _____	4. _____	5. _____
(0:40) Lully	6. _____	bassoon	7. _____
(1:00) Bach	8. _____	French horn	9. _____
(1:44) Beethoven	10. _____	11. _____	12. _____

Finally, identify the highest and lowest sounding of the three instruments in four of the excerpts.

	Highest	Lowest
(0:40) Lully	13. _____	14. _____
(0:00) Tchaikovsky	15. _____	16. _____
(0:18) Tchaikovsky	17. _____	18. _____
(1:44) Beethoven	19. _____	20. _____

Key Words

dynamics (**45**)	tenor (**46**)	trill (**48**)
forte (**45**)	bass (**46**)	mute (**48**)
piano (**45**)	chorus (**46**)	glissando (**48**)
sforzando (**45**)	mezzo-soprano (**46**)	mouthpiece (**51**)
color (**45**)	baritone (**46**)	orchestral score (**54**)
timbre (**45**)	vibrato (**48**)	stop (**55**)
soprano (**46**)	pizzicato (**48**)	
alto (**46**)	tremolo (**48**)	

ThomsonNOW™
ThomsonNOW for *Listening to Music, 5th Edition,* and *Listening to Western Music* will assist you in understanding the content of this chapter with lesson plans generated for your specific needs. In addition, you may complete this chapter's Listening Exercises in ThomsonNOW's interactive environment, as well as download Active Listening Guides and other materials that will help you succeed in this course.

Musical Texture and Form

Texture in music is the density and disposition of the musical lines that make up a musical composition. To understand this better, picture in your mind a tapestry or some other type of woven material. The individual strands, or lines, can be dense or thin; colors can be bunched toward the center or spread out more or less evenly; the lines may have either a strong vertical or a horizontal thrust. Just as a weaver or painter can fabricate a particular texture—dense, heavy, light, or thin, with independent or interdependent strands—so, too, can the composer create similar effects with musical lines. The opening section of Richard Strauss's *Thus Spoke Zarathustra* (Intro/3) begins with the bottom range of the orchestral palette, then fills in the middle- and upper-range sounds, and concludes with the densest orchestral texture—all the instruments of the great nineteenth-century orchestra (including an organ) fill in the full sonic spectrum.

MONOPHONIC, POLYPHONIC, AND HOMOPHONIC TEXTURES

There are three primary textures in music—monophonic, polyphonic, and homophonic—depending on the number of musical lines and the way they relate to one another. Often we call these lines, or parts, voices even though they may not actually be sung.

Monophony is the easiest texture to hear. As the name "one sounding" indicates, **monophony** is a single line of music, with no accompaniment. When you sing by yourself, you are creating monophonic music. When a group of men (or of women) sing the same pitches together, they are singing in **unison.** Unison singing is monophonic singing. Even when men and women sing together, doubling pitches at the octave*, the texture is still monophonic. Monophonic texture is the sparest of all musical textures.

As you may suppose from the name "many sounding," **polyphony** requires two or more lines in the musical fabric. In addition, the term *polyphonic* implies that each of the lines will be autonomous and independent. They compete equally for the listener's attention. Usually, they move against one another, and when this happens they create what is called counterpoint. **Counterpoint** is simply the harmonious opposition of two or more independent musical lines (Fig. 6–1). Because counterpoint presupposes polyphony, the terms *contrapuntal texture* and *polyphonic texture* are often used interchangeably.

What is more, there are two types of counterpoint: free and imitative. In free counterpoint, the voices are highly independent; they may begin all together or begin separately, but they go their separate ways. Much jazz improvisation is done in free counterpoint. To hear a fine example, turn to the end of Louis Armstrong's rendition of "Willie the Weeper" (Intro/8 at 2:49).

In imitative counterpoint, on the other hand, a leading voice begins followed by one or more other voices that duplicate what the first voice pre-

FIGURE 6–1

Simultaneous Counter Composition (1929–1930), by Theo van Doesburg, comes very close to a musical definition of counterpoint: "the harmonious opposition of two or more independent [entities]."

sented. If the followers copy exactly, note for note, what the leader plays or sings, then a **canon** results. Think of "Three Blind Mice," "Are You Sleeping?," and "Row, Row, Row Your Boat," and remember how each voice enters in turn, imitating the first voice from beginning to end. These are all short canons, or rounds, a type of strictly imitative counterpoint popular since the Middle Ages. Example 6–1 shows the beginning of a brief canon for three voices.

EXAMPLE 6–1

Among the most famous canons in music is Johann Pachelbel's Canon in D major (Intro/9), written in Germany about 1690. This is not a short round like "Are You Sleeping?" but a lengthy work in which one violin begins and then two others in turn duplicate this line over the duration of four minutes. As we saw in Listening Exercise 7, in Pachelbel's Canon, a repeating bass supports the three canonic parts; the bass sounds forth during the first two measures, and then the canon begins.

EXAMPLE 6–2

Homophony means "same sounding." In this texture, the voices, or lines, move to new pitches at roughly the same time. Homophony, then, differs from polyphony in that the strands are not independent but interdependent; they proceed in a tight, interlocking fashion. As the arrows in Examples 6–1 and 6–3 show, in polyphonic texture, the musical fabric has lines with a strong linear (horizontal) thrust, whereas in homophonic texture, the fabric is marked by lines that are more vertically conceived, as blocks of accompanying chords. The most common type of homophonic texture might be called tune-plus-accompaniment. Here a melody is supported by blocks of sound called chords*.

Holiday carols, popular songs, and folk songs almost always have this sort of tune-plus-accompaniment disposition.

EXAMPLE 6–3

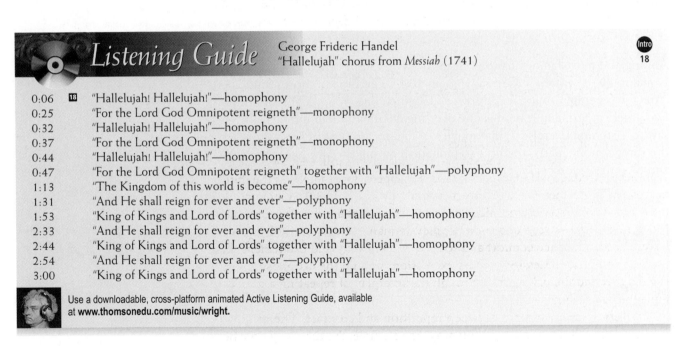

Of course, composers are not limited to just one of these three musical textures—they can switch them within a given work. To get the sound of the various textures in your ear, as well as to hear changes of texture, listen to the famous "Hallelujah" chorus from George Frideric Handel's *Messiah*. Notice how rapidly, yet smoothly, the composer moves back and forth among homophonic, polyphonic, and monophonic textures.

Listening Guide

George Frideric Handel
"Hallelujah" chorus from *Messiah* (1741)

Intro
18

0:06	18	"Hallelujah! Hallelujah!"—homophony
0:25		"For the Lord God Omnipotent reigneth"—monophony
0:32		"Hallelujah! Hallelujah!"—homophony
0:37		"For the Lord God Omnipotent reigneth"—monophony
0:44		"Hallelujah! Hallelujah!"—homophony
0:47		"For the Lord God Omnipotent reigneth" together with "Hallelujah"—polyphony
1:13		"The Kingdom of this world is become"—homophony
1:31		"And He shall reign for ever and ever"—polyphony
1:53		"King of Kings and Lord of Lords" together with "Hallelujah"—homophony
2:33		"And He shall reign for ever and ever"—polyphony
2:44		"King of Kings and Lord of Lords" together with "Hallelujah"—homophony
2:54		"And He shall reign for ever and ever"—polyphony
3:00		"King of Kings and Lord of Lords" together with "Hallelujah"—homophony

Use a downloadable, cross-platform animated Active Listening Guide, available at **www.thomsonedu.com/music/wright**.

Listening Exercise 12

Hearing Musical Textures

Intro
19

ThomsonNOW™

To take this Listening Exercise online and receive feedback or email answers to your instructor, go to *ThomsonNOW* for this chapter.

On your Intro CD, track 19, you have ten excerpts that exemplify the three basic textures of music. Monophonic texture, you will find, is easy to hear because it has only one line of music. More difficult is to differentiate between polyphonic texture and homophonic texture. Polyphonic texture embodies many active, independent lines. Homophonic texture, on the other hand, usually uses blocks of chords that accompany and support a single melody. Identify the texture of each of the excerpts by writing an M, P, or H in the appropriate blank.

1. (0:00) _____ Beethoven, Symphony No. 5, 1st movement

2. (0:09) _____ Bach, *The Art of Fugue*, Contrapunctus IX

3. (0:50) _____ Musorgsky, *Promenade* from *Pictures at an Exhibition*

4. (1:00) _____ Musorgsky, *Promenade* from *Pictures at an Exhibition*

5. (1:10) _____ Debussy, *Prelude to The Afternoon of a Faun*

6. (1:35) _____ Bach, Organ Fugue in
    G minor

7. (2:27) _____ Josquin Desprez, *Ave Maria*

8. (2:51) _____ Dvořák, Symphony No. 9,
    "From the New World,"
    2nd movement

9. (3:24) _____ Louis Armstrong, "Willie
    the Weeper"

10. (3:45) _____ Copland, "A Gift to Be
    Simple" from *Appalachian
    Spring*

FORM

Form in music is the purposeful arrangement of important musical events. In architecture, sculpture, and painting, objects are situated in physical space so as to impose a formal design. Similarly, in music, a composer places salient sonic events in an order that creates a pleasing shape as sounds pass by in time.

To create form in music, a composer employs any one of four processes: statement, repetition, contrast, or variation. In other words, important musical ideas are stated, repeated, contrasted, or varied. After the initial statement of a melody, **repetition** usually sets forth the formal guideposts within a piece, declaring each return an important musical event. Repetition is welcome because music is the most abstract of all the arts—the only one we can't actually see. Thus, instead of creating tedium or boredom, each return of a melody, or some other musical element, conveys an agreeable feeling of weight, balance, and symmetry. Because the musical material is familiar, repetition gives the listener a feeling of comfort and security.

a composer needs a plan

Contrast, on the other hand, takes us away from the familiar and into the unknown. A quiet melody in the strings can suddenly be followed by an insistent theme blasting from the French horns, as happens, for example, in the third movement of Beethoven's well-known Symphony No. 5 (❻3/9). Contrasting melodies, rhythms, textures, and moods can be used as a foil to familiar material, to provide variety, and even conflict. In many aspects of our lives, we have a need to balance comfort and security with novelty and excitement. In music, this human necessity is given expression through the juxtaposition of the familiar and the unknown—through the interplay of repeating and contrasting musical units.

Variation stands midway between repetition and contrast. The original melody returns but is altered in some way. For example, the tune may now be more complex, or new instruments may be added against it to create counterpoint. The listener has the satisfaction of hearing the familiar melody, yet is challenged to recognize in what way it has been changed.

Needless to say, memory plays an important role in hearing musical form. In architecture, painting, and sculpture, form is taken in all at once by a single glance. But in music, our memory must put the pieces together and show us the relationships. For this to happen, we must be able to recognize an exact repetition, a varied repetition, and a contrasting musical event. To help in this process, musicians have developed a simple system to visualize forms by labeling musical units with letters. The first prominent musical idea is designated **A.** Subsequent contrasting sections are labeled **B, C, D,** and so on. If the first or any other musical unit returns in varied form, then that variation is indicated by a superscript number—A^1 and B^2, for example. Subdivisions of each large musical unit are shown by lowercase letters (**a, b,** and so on). How this works will become clear in the following examples.

a listener needs to know the plan

Five Favorite Musical Forms

Most musical forms transcend epochs—they are not unique to any one period in the history of music. The five forms discussed below have been favored by composers of both popular and classical music for many hundreds of years.

STROPHIC FORM

This is the most familiar of all musical forms because our hymns, carols, folk tunes, and patriotic songs invariably make use of it. In **strophic form,** the composer sets the words of the first stanza and then uses the same entire melody for all subsequent stanzas. A good example is the Welsh holiday carol "Deck the Halls." Notice how the first phrase (**a**) of the musical unit (**A**), or stanza, is repeated:

hymns and carols

	a	Deck the halls with boughs of holly, fa, la, la, la, la, etc.
A	a	'Tis the season to be jolly, fa, la, la, la, la, etc.
	b	Don we now our gay apparel, fa, la, la, la, la, etc.
	a¹	Troll the ancient Yule-tide carol, fa, la, la, la, la, etc.

The basic musical unit, **A**, with the subdivisions **a, a, b, a¹**, is then heard four more times for each of the remaining stanzas, or strophes, of text. The overall form is thus:

$$A \qquad A \qquad A \qquad A \qquad A$$
$$a\,a\,b\,a^1 \quad a\,a\,b\,a^1 \quad a\,a\,b\,a^1 \quad a\,a\,b\,a^1 \quad a\,a\,b\,a^1$$

A famous example of strophic form can be heard in the well-known *Wiegenlied* (*Lullaby*) of Johannes Brahms. Here the same music is used for each of two strophes of text.

Listening Guide
Johannes Brahms
Lullaby (1868)

Intro
20

0:00	20	Piano introduction		
0:05		Soprano sings strophe 1	Guten Abend, gut Nacht, Mit rosen bedacht, Mit Näglein besteckt Schlupf unter die Deck': Morgen früh, wenn Gott will, Wirst du wieder gewecht.	Good evening, good night Covered with roses, Adorned with carnations, Slip under the covers. Tomorrow early, if God so wills, You will awake again.
0:50		Repeat of piano introduction		
0:56		Soprano sings strophe 2 of text to same melody	Guten Abend, gut Nacht, Von Englein bewacht, Die zeigen im Traum Dir Christkindleins Baum: Schlaf nun selig und süss, Schau im Traum's Paradies.	Good evening, good night Watched over by angels, Who in dreams show You the Christ child's tree. Now sleep blissful and sweetly, Behold Paradise in your dreams.

Use a downloadable, cross-platform animated Active Listening Guide, available at **www.thomsonedu.com/music/wright.**

THEME AND VARIATIONS

If, in the preceding example, the music of the first stanza (**A**) is altered in some way each time it returns, then **theme and variations** form is present. Additions to the melody, new chords in the supporting accompaniment, and more density in the texture are the sort of changes that might occur. The return of the basic musical unit (**A**) provides a unifying element, while the changes add variety. Theme and variations form can be visualized in the following scheme:

Statement of theme	Variation 1	Variation 2	Variation 3	Variation 4
A	$\mathbf{A^1}$	$\mathbf{A^2}$	$\mathbf{A^3}$	$\mathbf{A^4}$

When Mozart was a young man, he lived briefly in Paris, where he heard the French folk song *Ah, vous dirai-je Maman*. We know it today as *Twinkle, Twinkle, Little Star*. Upon this charming tune (**A**), he later composed a set of variations for piano, the first three of which are described in the following Listening Guide (for more on this piece, see page 200).

FIGURE 6–2
The Sydney Opera House, Australia, offers a clear example of theme and variations form applied to architecture.

Listening Guide

Wolfgang Amadeus Mozart
Variations on *Twinkle, Twinkle, Little Star* (c1781)

Intro
21

0:00	21	**A**	Tune played without ornamentation; melody above, harmony below
0:51		$\mathbf{A^1}$	Variation 1: tune above decorated with florid, fast-moving figurations
1:45		$\mathbf{A^2}$	Variation 2: tune above undecorated; florid, fast-moving figurations now in bass
2:36		$\mathbf{A^3}$	Variation 3: tune above decorated with graceful arpeggios*

Use a downloadable, cross-platform animated Active Listening Guide, available at **www.thomsonedu.com/music/wright**.

BINARY FORM

As the name indicates, **binary form** consists of two contrasting units, **A** and **B**. In length and general shape, **A** and **B** are constructed so as to balance and complement each other (Fig. 6–3). Variety is usually introduced in **B** by means of a dissimilar mood, key*, or melody. Sometimes in binary form, both **A** and **B** are immediately repeated, note for note. Musicians indicate exact repeats by means of the following sign: ‖: :‖. Thus, when binary form appears as ‖: A :‖‖: B :‖, it is performed **AABB**.

FIGURE 6–3
(far left) The essence of binary form, or **AB** form, can be seen in Barbara Hepworth's *Two Figures (Menhirs)* (1964). Here the two units of sculpture are distinctly different, yet mutually harmonious. (left) Ternary form, or **ABA** form, can clearly be seen in the architecture of the cathedral of Salzburg, Austria, where Mozart and his father frequently performed.

Joseph Haydn created a perfect example of binary form in music for the second movement of his Symphony No. 94. Here an eight-bar musical phrase (**A**) is balanced by a different but corresponding eight-bar phrase (**B**). First **A** and then **B** are repeated. Notice that the repeats involve slight alterations. In the repeat of **A**, Haydn adds a sudden *sforzando* to startle sleepy listeners. From this musical gesture the symphony derives its name: the "Surprise" Symphony. In the repeat of **B**, flutes are added to the melody to enrich it.

Listening Guide

Joseph Haydn
Symphony No. 94, the "Surprise" Symphony
Second movement, *Andante* (moving)

(Intro) 22

0:00	22	A presented by strings
0:17		A repeated with surprise *sforzando* at end
0:33		B presented by strings
0:50		B repeated with flutes added to melody

With this charming binary-form melody now in place, Haydn proceeds to compose a set of variations on it. The movement is discussed in full on page 201.

Use a downloadable, cross-platform animated Active Listening Guide, available at **www.thomsonedu.com/music/wright**.

TERNARY FORM

Ternary form in music is even more common than binary. It consists of three sections. The second is a contrasting unit, and the third is a repeat of the first—hence the formal pattern is **ABA**. As we will see (page 188), ternary form has appeared many times in the history of music. It is an especially satisfying arrangement because it is simple yet rounded and complete. It, too, sometimes uses musical repeats, first of the **A** section, then of both **B** and **A** together (‖: A :‖: B A :‖).

Listen now to the "Dance of the Reed Pipes" from Peter Tchaikovsky's famous ballet *The Nutcracker*. The **A** section is bright and cheery because it makes use of the major mode as well as silvery flutes. However, **B** is dark and low, even ominous, owing to the minor mode and the insistent ostinato* in the bass. The return of **A** is shortened because the melody is not repeated.

Listening Guide

Peter Tchaikovsky
"Dance of the Reed Pipes" from *The Nutcracker* (1891)

(Intro) 23

0:00	23	Flutes play melody above low string pizzicato*	}	
0:34		English horn and then clarinet add counterpoint		A
0:49		Melody repeats with violins now adding counterpoint		
1:20		Change to minor mode: trumpets play melody above two-note bass ostinato*		B
1:35		Violins join melody		
1:53		Return to flute melody (with violin counterpoint) in major mode		A¹

Use a downloadable, cross-platform animated Active Listening Guide, available at **www.thomsonedu.com/music/wright**.

FIGURE 6–4
The château of Chambord, France, has a formal design equivalent to **ABACABA** structure, a pattern often encountered in music in rondo form.

RONDO FORM

Rondo form involves a simple principle: a refrain (**A**) alternates with contrasting music. Usually in a rondo, there are at least two contrasting sections (**B** and **C**). Perhaps because of its simple, but pleasing design (Fig. 6–4), rondo form has been favored by musicians of every age—medieval monks, classical symphonists such as Mozart and Haydn, and even contemporary pop stars like Elton John and Sting. Although the principle of a recurring refrain is a constant, composers have written rondos in several different formal patterns, as seen below. The hallmark of each, however, is a refrain (**A**).

ABACA   ABACABA   ABACADA

You may already be familiar with a rondo composed by Jean-Joseph Mouret (1682–1738), for it is used as the theme music for *Masterpiece Theatre* on PBS-TV. Mouret was a composer at the French court during the reign of Louis XV (1715–1774), and his well-known *Rondeau* typifies the ceremonial splendor of the royal household during the Baroque era (1600–1750). Here the refrain (**A**), played by full orchestra with brilliant trumpets and drums, alternates with two contrasting ideas (**B** and **C**) to form a neatly symmetrical pattern.

Listening Guide

Jean-Joseph Mouret
Rondeau from *Suite de symphonies* (1729)

Intro
24

0:00	24	A	Refrain played by full orchestra, including trumpets and drums, and then repeated (at 0:12)
0:24		B	Quieter contrasting section played by organ
0:37		A	Refrain returns but without repeat
0:50		C	New contrasting section played by organ
1:21		A	Refrain returns and is repeated (at 1:33)

Use a downloadable, cross-platform animated Active Listening Guide, available at **www.thomsonedu.com/music/wright**.

summary

To sum up: form in music is the purposeful arrangement of important musical elements. It offers a user-friendly guide to the passage of music through time. Strophic form involves the repetition of the same short piece again and again, each time with a new text. In theme and variations form, a single idea continually returns but is varied in each presentation. Binary form involves two contrasting sections, whereas ternary form calls for statement, contrast, and return. Finally, in rondo form, a predominant theme returns at regular intervals.

Although these examples of musical form are all short, they clearly show that an internal logic and cohesiveness is at work in each piece. More complex musical forms, of course, do exist, and these give rise to longer, more complex compositions. Sonata–allegro form and fugal form are the principal ones. These we will discuss when we come to the music of the Baroque and Classical periods. In addition, there are also free musical forms, such as the fantasy and the prelude, which give free rein to the composer's imagination without tight formal restraints. These, too, we will meet in good time.

Listening Exercise 13
Identifying Musical Forms

Intro 25   **Thomson**NOW™
To take this Listening Exercise online and receive feedback or email answers to your instructor, go to *ThomsonNOW* for this chapter.

An awareness of musical form is perhaps the most important tool a listener can employ when engaging a piece of music. All music rushes by quickly. *What has happened? Where am I? What is about to come?* These questions are invariably asked, consciously or unconsciously, by every first-time listener. Recognizing the musical form can provide answers. This Listening Exercise asks you to identify the musical form of five pieces of classical music. Fill in the blanks using the appropriate letters, starting with A, for each piece, as exemplified in the preceding listening guides. For the first piece, for example, you should fill in the five blanks with three letters (A, B, and C), as the different musical sections require.

Piece 1: Purcell, theme from *Abdelazer* (later used
by Benjamin Britten as the theme of his
The Young Person's Guide to the Orchestra)
0:00 _____   0:29 _____   0:44 _____
0:59 _____   1:15 _____
Name of musical form _____

Piece 2: Handel, Minuet from *Water Music*
1:34 _____   1:47 _____
Name of musical form _____

Piece 3: Beethoven, *Für Elise*
2:04 _____   2:15 _____   2:22 _____
Name of musical form _____

Piece 4: Anonymous, Gregorian chant
2:38 _____   3:05 _____   3:32 _____
Name of musical form _____

Piece 5: Vivaldi, the "Spring" Concerto
4:03 _____   4:11 _____
Name of musical form _____

ThomsonNOW™
ThomsonNOW for *Listening to Music, 5th Edition,* and *Listening to Western Music* will assist you in understanding the content of this chapter with lesson plans generated for your specific needs. In addition, you may complete this chapter's Listening Exercises in ThomsonNOW's interactive environment, as well as download Active Listening Guides and other materials that will help you succeed in this course.

Key Words

texture (**58**)
monophony (**58**)
unison (**58**)
polyphony (**58**)

counterpoint (**58**)
canon (**59**)
homophony (**59**)
form (**61**)

repetition (**61**)
contrast (**61**)
variation (**61**)
strophic form (**62**)

Musical Style

Chapter 7

O ne of the challenges of listening to music is to evaluate what we hear. Consciously or not, we do this every day. When we turn on the car radio, for example, we often hear a piece of music, classical or popular, for the first time. Intuitively, we try to make an educated guess as to the style of the music, and perhaps the composer. Is it rap or reggae? Romantic or Baroque? Bach or Bono? With regard to classical music, identifying the style of a work, and even the composer, is an important step toward true musical enjoyment. But what is style generally (Fig. 7–1) and what, specifically, is musical style?

Style in music is the distinctive sound produced by the interaction of the elements of music: rhythm, melody, harmony, color, texture, and form. The special manner of presentation of all these elements creates a style. Every composer, like every creative artist, has a personal style, one that makes his or her work different from that of all other artists. Take a work by Mozart (1756–1791), for example. A trained listener will recognize it as a piece from the Classical period (1750–1820) because of its generally symmetrical melodies, light texture, and dynamic ebb and flow. A truly experienced ear will identify Mozart as the composer, perhaps by recognizing the sudden shifts to minor keys, the intensely chromatic melodies, or the colorful writing for the woodwinds, all hallmarks of Mozart's personal musical style.

Each period in the history of music has a musical style, too. That is, the music of one period has a common set of characteristics; the same practices and procedures appear in many, many works of that epoch. Many motets* from the Renaissance (1475–1600) exhibit short bursts of imitative counterpoint sung by voices alone, without instrumental accompaniment. A symphony* from the Romantic period (1820–1900), on the other hand, will typically exhibit long, nonimitative melodies, chromatic* harmonies, languid rhythms, and uniformly dense orchestral textures.

Historians have divided the history of music into eight style periods:

Middle Ages: 476–1475	Romantic: 1820–1900
Renaissance: 1475–1600	Impressionist: 1880–1920
Baroque: 1600–1750	Modern: 1900–1985
Classical: 1750–1820	Postmodern: 1945–present

Of course, human activity—artistic or otherwise—cannot be so neatly categorized. Historical periods, in some ways, are like the ages of humankind.

FIGURE 7–1

Portions of the East Wing of the National Gallery of Art in Washington, built in 1978 to a design by I. M. Pei, stand in contrast to the United States Capitol in the background. Pei's building, with its flat surfaces and unadorned geometric shapes, is representative of the modern style in architecture, while the Capitol reflects the neoclassical style of the eighteenth century.

National Gallery of Art, Washington/Photo: Dennis Brack/Black Star

When does an infant become a child or the child the adult? Similarly, musical styles do not change overnight; they evolve and overlap. Composers can stand midway between periods. Beethoven (1770–1827), for example, straddles the Classical and Romantic eras, being somewhat conservative in his choice of harmonies but radically progressive in his use of rhythm and form. Despite such contradictions, historians of music, like historians of art, find it useful to discuss style in terms of historical periods. This makes it possible to explore the ceaseless continuum of human creativity in terms of shorter, more manageable units.

The following Checklists of Musical Style analyze the style of each historical period in terms of the fundamental elements of music: melody, harmony, rhythm, etc. Each list is also repeated later in the book at the end of each historical period.

ThomsonNOW

ThomsonNOW for *Listening to Music, 5th Edition*, and *Listening to Western Music* will assist you in understanding the content of this chapter with lesson plans generated for your specific needs. In addition, there are comparisons of and quizzes on musical styles of all periods in the history of music in Active Listening for your Introductory CD.

Key Word

style (**67**)

Checklists of Musical Style by Periods

Middle Ages: 476–1475

Representative composers
Hildegard of Bingen
Leoninus
Perotinus
Machaut
Countess of Dia
Dufay
Binchois

Principal genres
Gregorian chant
polyphonic Mass
troubadour and *trouvère* songs
French polyphonic chanson
instrumental dance

Melody	Moves mostly by step within narrow range; rarely uses chromatic notes of the scale
Harmony	Most surviving medieval music is monophonic Gregorian chant or monophonic *troubadour* and *trouvère* songs—hence there is no harmony
	Medieval polyphony (Mass, motet, and chanson) has dissonant phrases ending with open, hollow-sounding chords
Rhythm	Gregorian chant as well as *troubadour* and *trouvère* songs sung mainly in notes of equal value without clearly marked rhythms; medieval polyphony is composed mostly in triple meter and uses repeating rhythmic patterns
Color	Mainly vocal sounds (choir or soloists); little instrumental music survives
Texture	Mostly monophonic—Gregorian chant as well as *troubadour* and *trouvère* songs are monophonic melodies
	Medieval polyphony (two, three, or four independent lines) is mainly contrapuntal
Form	Strophic form of *troubadour* and *trouvère* songs; ternary form of the Kyrie; rondo form of the French *rondeau*

Renaissance: 1475–1600

Melody — Mainly stepwise motion within moderately narrow range; still mainly diatonic, but some intense chromaticism found in madrigals from end of period

Harmony — More careful use of dissonance than in Middle Ages as the triad, a consonant chord, becomes the basic building block of harmony

Rhythm — Duple meter is now as common as triple meter; rhythm in sacred vocal music (Mass and motet) is relaxed and without strong downbeats; rhythm in secular vocal music (chanson and madrigal) and in instrumental dances is usually lively and catchy, with frequent use of syncopation

Color — Although more music for instruments alone has survived, the predominant sound remains that of unaccompanied vocal music, whether for soloists or for choir

Texture — Contrapuntal, polyphonic texture for four or five vocal lines is heard throughout Masses, motets, and madrigals, though occasional passages of chordal homophonic texture are inserted for variety

Form — Strict musical forms are not often used; most Masses, motets, madrigals, chansons, and instrumental dances are through-composed—they have no musical repetitions and hence no standard formal plan

Representative composers
Desprez
Palestrina
Byrd
Lasso
Weelkes
Dowland

Principal genres
sacred Mass and motet
secular chanson and madrigal
instrumental dance

Early and Middle Baroque: 1600–1710

Melody — Less stepwise movement, larger leaps, wider range, and more chromaticism reflect influence of virtuosic solo singing; melodic patterns idiomatic to particular musical instruments emerge; introduction of melodic sequence

Harmony — Stable, diatonic chords played by *basso continuo* support melody; clearly defined chord progressions begin to develop; tonality is reduced to major and minor keys

Rhythm — Relaxed, flexible rhythms of the Renaissance transformed into regularly repeating, driving rhythms

Color — Musical timbre becomes enormously varied as traditional instruments are perfected (e.g., harpsichord, violin, and oboe) and new combinations of voices and instruments are explored; symphony orchestra begins to take shape; sudden shifts in dynamics (terraced dynamics) reflect dramatic quality of Baroque music

Texture — Chordal, homophonic texture predominates; top and bottom lines are strongest as *basso continuo* creates powerful bass to support melody above

Form — Arias and instrumental works often make use of *basso ostinato* procedure; ritornello form emerges in the concerto grosso; binary form regulates most movements of the sonata and orchestral suite

Representative composers
Gabrieli
Monteverdi
Barbara Strozzi
Purcell
Corelli
Vivaldi

Principal genres
polychoral motet
chamber cantata
opera
sonata
concerto grosso
solo concerto
orchestral suite
French overture

Late Baroque: 1710–1750

Representative composers
Bach
Handel
Telemann
Vivaldi

Principal genres
church cantata
opera
oratorio
sonata
dance suite
concerto grosso
prelude
fugue
French overture

Melody	Grows longer, more expansive, and more asymmetrical; idiomatic instrumental style influences vocal melodies
Harmony	Functional chord progressions govern harmonic movement— harmony moves purposefully from one chord to the next; *basso continuo* continues to provide strong bass
Rhythm	Exciting, driving, energized rhythms propel the music forward with vigor; "walking" bass creates feeling of rhythmic regularity
Color	Instruments reign supreme; instrumental sounds, especially of violin, harpsichord, and organ, set musical tone for the era; one tone color used throughout a movement or large section of a movement
Texture	Homophonic texture remains important, but polyphonic texture reemerges because of growing importance of the contrapuntal fugue
Form	Binary form in sonatas and orchestral suites; *da capo* aria (ternary) form in arias; fugal procedure used in fugues

Classical: 1750–1820

Representative composers
Mozart
Haydn
Beethoven
Schubert

Principal genres
symphony
sonata
string quartet
solo concerto
opera

Melody	Short, balanced phrases create tuneful melodies; melody more influenced by vocal than instrumental style; frequent cadences produce light, airy feeling
Harmony	The rate at which chords change (harmonic rhythm) varies dramatically, creating a dynamic flux and flow; simple chordal harmonies made more active by "Alberti" bass
Rhythm	Departs from regular, driving patterns of Baroque era to become more stop-and-go; greater rhythmic variety within a single movement
Color	Orchestra grows larger; woodwind section of two flutes, oboes, clarinets, and bassoons becomes typical; piano replaces harpsichord as principal keyboard instrument
Texture	Mostly homophonic; thin bass and middle range, hence light and transparent; passages in contrapuntal style appear sparingly and mainly for contrast
Form	A few standard forms regulate much of Classical music: sonata–allegro, theme and variations, rondo, ternary (for minuets and trios), and double exposition (for solo concerto)

Romantic: 1820–1900

Representative composers
Beethoven
Schubert
Berlioz

Melody	Long, singable lines with powerful climaxes and chromatic inflections for expressiveness
Harmony	Greater use of chromaticism makes the harmony richer and more colorful; sudden shifts to remote chords for expressive

purposes; more dissonance to convey feelings of anxiety and longing

Rhythm   Rhythms are flexible, often languid, and therefore meter is sometimes not clearly articulated; tempo can fluctuate greatly (tempo *rubato*); tempo can slow to a crawl to allow for "the grand gesture"

Color   The orchestra becomes enormous, reaching upward of one hundred performers: trombone, tuba, contrabassoon, piccolo, and English horn added to the ensemble; experiments with new playing techniques for special effects; dynamics vary widely to create different levels of expression; piano becomes larger and more powerful

Texture   Predominantly homophonic but dense and rich because of larger orchestras; sustaining pedal on the piano also adds to density

Form   No new forms created; rather, traditional forms (strophic, sonata–allegro, and theme and variations, for example) used and extended in length; traditional forms also applied to new genres such as symphonic poem and art song

Mendelssohn
Robert and Clara Schumann
Chopin
Liszt
Verdi
Wagner
Bizet
Brahms
Dvořák
Tchaikovsky
Musorgsky
Mahler
Puccini

Principal genres
symphony
program symphony
symphonic poem
concert overture
opera
art song
orchestral song
solo concerto
character piece for piano
ballet music

Impressionist: 1880–1920

Melody   Varies from short dabs of sound to long, free-flowing lines; melodies are rarely tuneful or singable; they often twist and turn rapidly in undulating patterns; chromatic scale, whole tone scale, and pentatonic scale often replace usual major and minor scales

Harmony   Primarily homophonic; triad is extended to form seventh chords and ninth chords, and these frequently move in parallel motion

Rhythm   Usually free and flexible with irregular accents, making it sometimes difficult to determine meter; rhythmic ostinatos used to give feeling of stasis rather than movement

Color   More emphasis on woodwinds and brasses and less on violins as primary carriers of melody; more soloistic writing to show that the color of the instrument is as important as the melody line it plays

Texture   Can vary from thin and airy to heavy and dense; sustaining pedal of the piano often used to create wash of sound; glissandos run quickly from low to high or high to low

Form   Traditional forms involving clear-cut repetitions rarely used; composers try to develop a form unique and particular to each new musical work

Representative composers
Debussy
Ravel
Fauré

Principal genres
symphonic poem
string quartet
orchestral song
opera
character piece for piano
ballet music

Modern: 1900–1985

Representative composers
Stravinsky
Schoenberg
Berg
Webern
Bartók
Prokofiev
Shostakovich
Copland
Zwilich
Gershwin
Bernstein
Sondheim

Principal genres
symphony
solo concerto
string quartet
opera
ballet music
Broadway musical
film music

Melody	Wide-ranging disjunct lines, often chromatic and dissonant, angularity accentuated by use of octave displacement
Harmony	Highly dissonant; dissonance no longer must move to consonance but may move to another dissonance; sometimes two conflicting, but equal, tonal centers sound simultaneously (polytonality); sometimes there is no audible tonal center (atonality)
Rhythm	Vigorous, energetic rhythms; conflicting simultaneous meters (polymeter) and rhythms (polyrhythm) make for temporal complexity
Color	Color becomes agent of form and beauty in and by itself; composers seek new sounds from traditional, acoustical instruments, from electronic instruments and computers, and from noises in environment
Texture	As varied and individual as the men and women composing music
Form	A range of extremes: sonata–allegro, rondo, theme and variations benefit from Neo-classical revival; twelve-tone procedure allows for almost mathematical formal control; forms and processes of classical music, jazz, and pop music begin to influence one another in exciting new ways

Postmodern: 1945–present

Representative composers
Varèse
Cage
Glass
Reich
Partch
Adams
Tavener
Pärt
Tan

Principal genres
no common genres;
each work of art
creates a genre
unique to itself

Nearly impossible to generalize as to musical style; major stylistic trends not yet discernible

Barriers between high art and low art removed; all art judged to be of more or less equal value

Experimentation with electronic music and computer-generated sound

Previously accepted fundamentals of music, such as discrete pitches and division of octave into twelve equal pitches, often abandoned

Narrative music (goal-oriented music) rejected

Chance music permits random "happenings" and noises from the environment to shape a musical work

Introduction of visual and performance media into written musical score

Instruments from outside the tradition of Western classical music (e.g., electric guitar, sitar, kazoo) prescribed in the score

Experimentation with new notational styles within musical scores (e. g., sketches, diagrams, prose instructions)

PART II.

The Middle Ages and Renaissance, 476–1600

Historians use the term *Middle Ages* as a catchall phrase to refer to the thousand years of history between the fall of the Roman Empire (476) and the dawn of the Age of Discovery (late 1400s, exemplified by the voyages of Christopher Columbus). It was a period of monks and nuns, of knightly chivalry and brutal warfare, of sublime spirituality and deadly plagues, and of soaring cathedrals amidst abject poverty. Two institutions vied for political control: the church and the court. From our modern perspective, the medieval period appears as a vast chronological expanse dotted by outposts of dazzling architecture, stunning stained glass, and equally compelling poetry and music.

Renaissance means literally "rebirth" or "reawakening." Historians generally use the term to designate a period of intellectual and artistic flowering that

400	500	600	700	800	900	1000	1100	1200	1300	1400

MIDDLE AGES

● 476 Fall of Rome to Visigoths

Erich Lessing / Art Resource, NY

········· Hildegard of Bingen (1098–1179), musician, poet, visionary

● c530 Benedict of Nursia founds monastic order

● c1150 Beatriz of Dia and other *troubadours* flourish in southern France

● c1160 Gothic Cathedral of Notre Dame begun in Paris

● c700 *Beowulf*

Photo Researchers, Inc.

c1170–1230 Leoninus and Perotinus develop polyphony in Paris

1348–1350 Black Death

c1360 Guillaume ● de Machaut (c1300–1377) composes *Mass of Our Lady* at Reims

● 800 Charlemagne crowned Holy Roman Emperor

c1390 Geoffrey ● Chaucer (c1340–1400) writes *Canterbury Tales*

● c880 Vikings invade Western Europe

1430s Guillaume ● Dufay (c1397–1474) composes chansons for Court of Burgundy

● 1066 William the Conqueror invades England

occurred first in Italy, then in France and the Low Countries, and finally in England, during the years 1350–1600. Music historians apply the term *Renaissance* more narrowly to musical developments that occurred in those same countries during the period 1475–1600. The Renaissance was an age in which writers, poets, painters, sculptors, and architects looked back to classical Greece and Rome to find models for personal and civic expression. It was an important period for music as well. Among the most significant musical developments of the Renaissance was a newfound desire to tie musical tones closely to the given text, as well as the growth of popular (nonreligious) types of music. During the Renaissance, men and women took pride in their human accomplishments, bringing a renewed sense of confidence and vitality to the music of their everyday lives.

The British Library/The Bridgeman Art Library

1475   1500   1525   1550   1575   1600

RENAISSANCE

● 1473 Pope Sixtus IV leads
revival of Rome and
begins Sistine Chapel

● 1545 Council of Trent begins

● 1517 Martin Luther (1483–1546)
posts Ninety–five Theses

● 1486 Josquin Desprez (c1450–1521)
joins Sistine Chapel choir

● 1554 Palestrina (1525–1594)
joins Sistine Chapel choir ····▸

Fratelli Alinari/
SuperStock

● 1492 Christopher Columbus's
first voyage

● 1534 King Henry VIII of England
establishes Church of England

● 1501 Ottaviano Petrucci publishes
first book of polyphonic music (Venice)

1558–1603 Elizabeth I queen of England

Bridgeman Art Library,
London/NY

◂···● 1501–1504 Michelangelo (1475–1564)
sculpts statue of David

1599–1613
Shakespeare's plays
performed at
Globe Theater

● c1495 Leonardo da Vinci (1452–1519)
begins *Last Supper*

● 1528 Pierre Attaingnant publishes
first book of polyphonic music
north of the Alps (Paris)

1601 ●
Madrigal collection
The Triumphes of Oriana
published to honor Elizabeth I

Medieval Music, 476—1475

MUSIC IN THE MONASTERY

There were many kinds of music in the Middle Ages: songs for knights as they rode into battle, songs for men in the fields and women around the hearth, songs and dances for nobles in their castles, and chants for priests as they celebrated the Christian service in the monasteries and cathedrals. Unfortunately, most of this music, and virtually all of it emanating from the common folk, is now lost because it was never written down. Only the music of the Church is preserved in any significant quantity, because at that time only the men of the Church, and to a lesser degree the nuns, were educated. Even the nobility was largely illiterate. The reading and copying of texts was the private preserve of the rural monasteries and, somewhat later, the urban cathedrals. Musical notation as we know it today (with note heads placed on lines and spaces) began in the monasteries of Western Europe around the year 1000. Notation allowed the monks of one monastery to write down their music and send it to another monastic community.

life in the monastery

Life in a medieval monastery was rigorous. The founder of the principal monastic order, Saint Benedict (died c547), prescribed a code of conduct for the clergy and a cycle of times for worship throughout the day. The Benedictines rose at about four o'clock in the morning for their first hour of prayer (Matins), at which they sang psalms and read scripture. After a break "for the necessities of nature" the brethren returned at daybreak to sing another service in praise of the Lord. The high point of the church day was the Mass, celebrated about nine o'clock in the morning; it commemorated Christ's suffering on the cross through the ritual act of communion (see page 82). Between these religious services, the monks dispersed to farm and otherwise attend to their lands. They worked to feed their bodies, and they prayed and sang to save their souls, day after day, year after year.

Gregorian Chant

The music sung daily at the eight monastic hours of prayer and at Mass was what we today call Gregorian chant, named in honor of Pope Gregory the Great (c540–604). Ironically, Gregory wrote little, if any, of this music. Being more a church administrator than a musician, he merely decreed that certain chants should be sung on certain days of the liturgical year. Melodies for the Christian service had, of course, existed since the time of Christ's Apostles. In truth, *chant composed for fifteen centuries* what we now call **Gregorian chant** (also called **plainsong**) is really a large body of unaccompanied vocal music, setting sacred Latin texts, written for the Western (Roman Catholic) Church over the course of fifteen centuries. Churchmen and churchwomen composed chant from the time of the earliest Fathers to the Council of Trent (1545–1563), which, as we shall see, brought sweeping reforms to the Church of Rome.

Gregorian chant is like no other music. It has a timeless, otherworldly quality that arises, no doubt, because Gregorian chant has neither meter nor regular rhythms. True, some notes are longer or shorter than others, but they do not recur in obvious patterns that would allow us to clap our hands or tap our feet. Free of tension and drama, chant is far more conducive to pious reflection than to dancing. Because all voices sing together in unison*, Gregorian chant is considered monophony*, or music for one line. There is no instrumental accompaniment, nor, as a rule, are men's and women's voices mixed when performing chant. Finally, Gregorian chant has a uniform, monochromatic sound. Any contrasts that occur are of the mildest sort. Sometimes a soloist will alternate with a full choir, for example. Occasionally, a passage of **syllabic singing** (only one or two notes for each syllable of text) will give way to **melismatic singing** (many notes sung to just one syllable), as in Example 8–1.

chant is monophony

Example 8–1 shows most of a lengthy chant, *All the Ends of the Earth*, sung during Mass on Christmas Day. Created as early as the fifth century—we know not by whom—church singers passed this chant along orally from one generation to the next over the course of several centuries. Notice the absence of signs to indicate rhythm. The notes are generally of one basic value, something close to our eighth note in length. Notice also the presence of syllabic singing on the words "Viderunt" (they saw) and "jubilate" (sing joyfully) and, conversely, the melismatic singing, particularly on "Dominus" (the Lord). This melisma allowed the clergy to rejoice in the Lord by expanding vocally on his name.

EXAMPLE 8–1

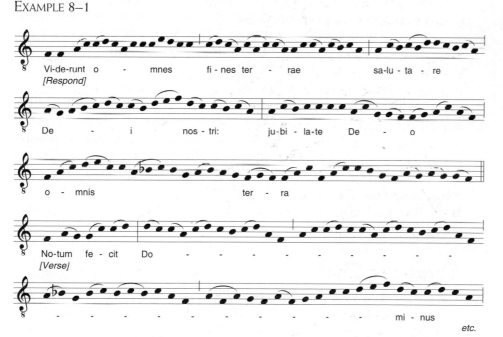

a chant for Christmas Day

All the ends of the earth have seen the salvation of our God; sing joyfully to God, all the earth.
The Lord hath made known…

 *Listening Guide*   Anonymous
Gregorian chant, *All the Ends of the Earth* (fifth century?)

 6
1/1

Texture: monophonic

0:00	▪	(soloist) Viderunt omnes (choir) fines terrae salutare Dei nostri: jubilate Deo omnis terra.	All the ends of the earth have seen the salvation of our God; sing joyfully to God, all the earth.

(continued)

1:06   (soloist) Notum fecit Dominus salutare suum: The Lord hath made known his salvation:
        ante conspectum gentium revelavit   He hath revealed his justice
        (choir) justitiam suam.   in the sight of the gentiles.

 Use a downloadable, cross-platform animated Active Listening Guide, available at **www.thomsonedu.com/music/wright**.

FIGURE 8–1

A twelfth-century illumination depicting Hildegard of Bingen receiving divine inspiration, perhaps a vision or a chant, directly from the heavens. To the right, her secretary, the monk Volmar, peeks in on her in amazement.

FIGURE 8–2

(upper frame) A vision of Hildegard revealing how a fantastic winged figure of God the Father, the Son, and the Mystical Lamb killed the serpent Satan with a blazing sword. (lower frame) Hildegard (center) receives the vision and reports it to her secretary (left). This manuscript dates from the twelfth century.

The Gregorian Chant of Hildegard of Bingen (1098–1179)

Gregorian chant was composed by churchwomen as well as churchmen. One of the most remarkable contributors to the repertoire of Gregorian chant was Hildegard of Bingen (1098–1179), from whose pen we received seventy-seven chants (Fig. 8–1). Hildegard was the tenth child of noble parents who gave her to the Church as a tithe (a donation of a tenth of one's worldly goods). She was educated by Benedictine nuns and then, at the age of fifty-two, founded her own convent near the small town of Bingen, Germany, on the west bank of the Rhine River. In the course of time, Hildegard manifested her extraordinary intellect and imagination as a playwright, poet, musician, naturalist, pharmacologist, and visionary (Fig. 8–2). Ironically, then, the first "Renaissance man" was really a medieval woman: Hildegard of Bingen.

Hildegard's *O Greenest Branch* possesses many qualities typical of her chants, and chant generally. First, it sets a starkly vivid text, which Hildegard herself created. It depicts the Virgin Mary, as the text tells us, as the most verdant branch of the tree of Jesse, through whom the heat of the sun radiates like the aroma of balm. The joyful Mary brings new life to all flora and fauna of the earth. The music gravitates around a tonal center—here the pitch G. Notice in the first stanza (Ex. 8–2) how the music starts on G, works up a fifth to the pitch D and then down an octave to the D below, and finally returning to the initial G. Notice also how *O Greenest Branch* is a predominantly stepwise melody, one without large leaps. This was, after all, choral music to be sung by the full community of musically unsophisticated nuns or monks, so it had to be easy. *O Greenest Branch* was sung at Mass; more specifically, it is a Sequentia, the sixth musical portion of the Mass (see page 83). Finally, the piece, as with most chant, has no overt rhythm or meter. The unaccompanied, monophonic line and the absence of rhythmic drive allow a restful, contemplative mood to develop. Hildegard did not see herself as an "artist" as we think of one today, but rather as a vessel through which divine revelation came to earth. Indeed, she styled herself simply as "a feather floating on the breath of God."

EXAMPLE 8–2 Hildegard of Bingen, *O Greenest Branch* (first stanza)

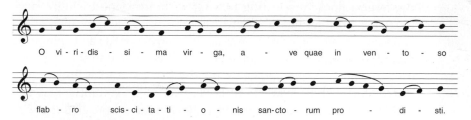

O vi - ri - dis - si - ma   vir - ga,   a - ve quae in   ven - to - so

flab - ro   scis - ci - ta - ti - o - nis   san - cto - rum   pro - - di - sti.

Listening Guide

Hildegard of Bingen
Gregorian chant, *O Greenest Branch* (c1150)

6
1/2

Texture: monophonic

Stanza 1

0:00 [2] O viridissima virga, ave
quae in ventoso flabro sciscitationis
sanctorum prodisti.

Hail, o greenest branch
who sprang forth in the airy breeze
of the prayers of the saints.

Stanza 2

0:27 Cum venit tempus,
quod tu floruisti,
in ramis tuis,
ave, ave sit tibi,
quia calor solis in te sudavit
sicut odor balsami.

So the time has come that
you flourished
in your boughs,
hail, hail to you,
because the heat of the sun radiated
in you like the aroma of balm.

Stanza 3

1:01 Nam in te floruit pulcher flos
qui odorem dedit omnibus aromatibus
quae arida erant.

For in you bloomed the beautiful
flower which scented all parched
perfumes.

Stanza 4

1:28 Et illa apparuerunt omnia
in viriditate plena.

And all things have been manifested
in their full verdure.

Stanza 5

1:46 Unde celi dederunt rorem super gramen
et omnis terra leta facta est,
quoniam viscera ipsius frumentum protulerunt
et quoniam volucres celi nidos in ipsa habuerunt.

Whence the skies set down dew on the
pasture, and all the earth was made
more joyful because her womb produced
grain, and because the birds of Heaven
built their nests in her.

Stanza 6

2:27 Deinde facta est esca hominibus
et gaudium magnum epulantium;
inde, o suavis virgo,
in te non deficit ullum gaudium.

Then the harvest was made ready for
Man, and a great rejoicing of
banqueters, because in you,
o sweet Virgin, no joy is lacking.

Stanza 7

2:59 Hec omnia Eva contempsit.
Nunc autem laus sit altissimo.

All these things Eve rejected.
Now let there be praise to you in the Highest.

Use a downloadable, cross-platform animated Active Listening Guide, available
at **www.thomsonedu.com/music/wright.**

MUSIC IN THE CATHEDRAL

Gregorian chant arose primarily in secluded monasteries and convents around
Western Europe. The future of art music within the Church, however, rested
not in rural monasteries, but rather in urban cathedrals. Every cathedral served

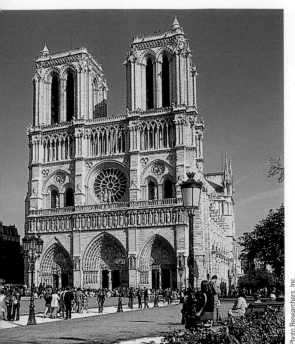

FIGURE 8–3

The cathedral of Notre Dame of Paris, begun c1160, was one of the first to be built in the new Gothic style of architecture. The polyphony of Master Leoninus and Master Peròtinus was composed as the building was being constructed.

FIGURE 8–4

A thirteenth-century manuscript preserving Leoninus's organum for Christmas, *All the Ends of the Earth.* Here, eleven four-line staves are shown. Leoninus's newly created voice is notated on each of the odd-numbered staves while the slower-moving Gregorian chant appears below it on each of the even-numbered staves.

as the "home church" of a bishop, and the bishop could minister to the largest flock by locating himself within the increasingly large urban centers. During the twelfth century, cities such as Milan, Paris, and London, among others, grew significantly, as trade and commerce increased. Much of the commercial wealth generated in the cities was used to construct splendid new cathedrals that served as both houses of worship and monuments of civic pride. So substantial was this building campaign that the period 1150–1350 is often called the "Age of the Cathedrals." Most were constructed in what we now call the Gothic style, with pointed arches, high ceiling vaults, supporting buttresses, and richly colored stained glass.

Notre Dame of Paris

Gothic architecture began in northern France, in the region that now has Paris as its capital. The cathedral of Paris (Fig. 8–3), dedicated to Notre Dame (Our Lady), was begun about 1160, yet not completed until more than a hundred years later. Throughout this period, Notre Dame was blessed with a succession of churchmen who were not only theologians and philosophers but poets and musicians as well. Foremost among these were Master Leoninus (flourished 1169–1201) and Master Perotinus, called the Great (fl. 1198–1236). Leoninus wrote a great book of religious music (called, in Latin, the *Magnus liber organi*). Perotinus revised Leoninus's book and also composed many additional pieces of his own.

Leoninus and Perotinus created a new style of composition. They wrote polyphony* (two or more voices, or lines, sounding simultaneously) and not merely monophonic (one-voice) Gregorian chant. In truth, earlier composers had written polyphony, but this earlier music rarely had voices or lines that were fully separate from the chant. The novelty of the new music arising in Paris rested in the fact that Parisian composers added one or more wholly independent voices above the existing chant. In this musical development, we see an early instance of a creative spirit breaking free of the ancient authority (the chant) of the Church.

Leoninus: Organum *All the Ends of the Earth*

To see how Leoninus added a new voice to a preexisting plainsong, we return to the chant *All the Ends of the Earth* (*Viderunt omnes;* see page 77). By adding his own musical line above the chant, Leoninus created a two-voice **organum,** the name given to early church polyphony. The old chant unfolds in the lower voice, and Leoninus's newly created line sounds on top (see Listening Guide). The organum (polyphony), sung by soloists, is actually rather brief, extending over only two words (*Viderunt omnes*). But something of importance occurs on the word *omnes*—the introduction of clearly articulated rhythms. The Notre Dame composers are important for being the first to institute a type of notation that allowed for the control of musical rhythm. Owing in part to this rhythmic complexity, Parisian organum was sung only by highly trained soloists. When the word *omnes* concludes, the solo portion of the music is at an end, as is the organum. Thereafter, the full clerical choir entered to continue and complete the remaining music in monophonic Gregorian chant.

To acquaint yourself with the unusual sound of medieval organum, try listening to this piece twice. First, listen following the Listening Guide, which

Chant at the Top of the Charts

In recent years, Gregorian chant has become all the rage. The excitement began in 1994 with the release, appropriately enough by Angel Records, of the CD *Chant*, which sold one million copies within the first two months of its appearance. That success spawned sequels, leading to the present *Chant IV* (Angel 56373). Much of the popularity of Gregorian chant can be attributed to the fact that it has stylistic traits in common with New Age music. Both project smooth, uniform, rhythmically fluid sounds that are decidedly nonassertive and nonconfrontational.

Hildegard, too, has been popularized as something of a New Age mystic. She is a fixture on the World Wide Web, where you can study her chants in the original notation, find translations of her poetry, view spectacular medieval depictions of her visions, and order the latest CDs or DVDs. A Google search will return more than 320,000 results for "Hildegard of Bingen." Most recently, her chant *O Redness of Blood* featured prominently in the score of the 2006 Academy Award–winning film *Crash*. Could the visionary nun have foreseen that this intensely spiritual person would become overtly commercial?

Angel Records/EMI

presents a graphic indication of Leoninus's added part above the preexisting chant. Then listen again, following the original thirteenth-century manuscript from Paris (Fig. 8–4). Here the upper stave of each pair of four-line staves contains Leoninus's newly created voice. It undulates while the lower voice holds the chant below. What Leoninus has fashioned here is a rather free, rhapsodic hymn in praise of the Christ child. Imagine how these new sounds struck the ear of the citizens of medieval Paris, as the music rebounded around the bare stone walls of the vast, newly constructed cathedral of Notre Dame.

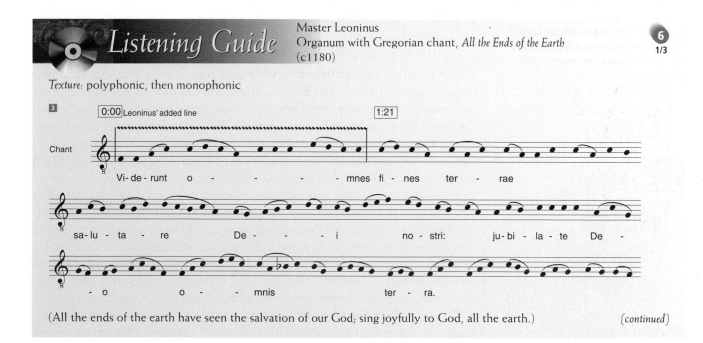

Listening Guide

Master Leoninus
Organum with Gregorian chant, *All the Ends of the Earth*
(c1180)

6
1/3

Texture: polyphonic, then monophonic

3   0:00 Leoninus' added line   1:21

Chant

Vi- de - runt o - - - mnes fi - nes ter - rae

sa- lu - ta - re De - - i no - stri: ju - bi - la - te De -

- o o - - mnis ter - ra.

(All the ends of the earth have seen the salvation of our God; sing joyfully to God, all the earth.)   *(continued)*

0:00	3	Polyphonic organum sung by soloists
1:21		Monophonic chant sung by choir

Use a downloadable, cross-platform animated Active Listening Guide, available at **www.thomsonedu.com/music/wright.**

FIGURE 8–5
Interior of the cathedral of Reims looking from floor to ceiling. The pillars carry the eye up to the ribbed vaults of the roof, creating a feeling of great upward movement, just as the Mass of Machaut, with four superimposed voices, has a new sense of verticality.

origins of the names of the voice parts

Notre Dame of Reims

Notre Dame of Paris was not the only important cathedral in northern Europe devoted to Our Lady. The city of Reims, one hundred miles east of Paris in the Champagne region of France, was graced with a monument equally large and impressive (Fig. 8–5). In the fourteenth century, it, too, benefited from the service of a poetically and musically talented churchman, Guillaume de Machaut (c1300–1377). Judging by his nearly 150 surviving works, not only was Machaut the most important composer of this day, he was equally esteemed as a lyric poet. Today, historians of literature place him on a pedestal with his slightly younger English counterpart, Geoffrey Chaucer (c1340–1400), author of the *Canterbury Tales*. Indeed, Chaucer knew and borrowed heavily from the poetic works of Machaut.

Machaut: *Mass of Our Lady*

Machaut's *Mass of Our Lady* (*Messe de Nostre Dame*) is deservedly the best-known work in the entire repertoire of medieval music. It is impressive for its length and the novel way it applies music to the texts of the **Mass**—the central and most important service of the Roman Catholic Church. Before Machaut's time, composers writing polyphony for the Mass had set only one or two sections of what is called the **Proper of the Mass** (chants whose texts changed to suit the feast day in question). Leoninus's *All the Ends of the Earth* (*Viderunt omnes*), for example, is a setting of the Gradual (see box) of the Proper of the Mass for Christmas Day.

Machaut, on the other hand, chose to set all of the chants of the **Ordinary of the Mass** (chants with unvarying texts that were sung virtually every day). Setting the Ordinary of the Mass had the obvious practical advantage that the composition could be heard more than on just one feast day of the church year. Machaut's *Mass of Our Lady*, for example, could be sung any time a Mass in honor of the Virgin Mary was celebrated. The box on the next page lists the musical portions of the Mass and the order in which they are sung. From Machaut's work onward, composing a Mass meant setting the five texts of the Ordinary (Kyrie, Gloria, Credo, Sanctus, and Agnus Dei) and finding some way to shape them into an integrated whole. Palestrina, Bach, Mozart, and Beethoven were just a few of the later composers to follow Machaut's lead and set the five parts of the Ordinary of the Mass.

To construct his Mass, Machaut added not just one but three new voices to a preexisting chant, which was sung in longer notes, as in the previous example by Leoninus. Because the men who sang the chant sustained it in long notes, they came to be called the "tenors" (from the Latin *tenere*, "to hold"). Above the tenor line, Machaut added two voices that came to be called the *superius* and the *contratenor altus*, whence we get our terms "soprano" and "alto." The voice added below the tenor was called the *contratenor bassus*, whence our term "bass." The disposition of the four voices in the musical score is evident in Example 8–3. By writing for four voices and spreading these over a range

Musical Portions of the Mass

Proper of the Mass	Ordinary of the Mass
1. Introit (an introductory chant for the entry of the celebrating clergy)	
	2. Kyrie (a petition for mercy)
	3. Gloria (a hymn of praise to the Lord)
4. Gradual (a reflective chant)	
5. Alleluia or Tract (a chant of thanksgiving or penance)	
6. Sequentia (a chant commenting on the text of the Alleluia)	
	7. Credo (a profession of faith)
8. Offertory (a chant for the offering)	
	9. Sanctus (an acclamation to the Lord)
	10. Agnus Dei (a petition for mercy and eternal peace)
11. Communion (a chant accompanying communion)	

of two and a half octaves, Machaut was able to create truly sonorous choral polyphony. Finally, note in Example 8–3 that each voice is written in rhythmic values, the tenor in slow-moving notes, and the other three voices in durations both fast and slow. By the fourteenth century, composers were able to specify rhythm and meter just as precisely as pitch.

EXAMPLE 8–3

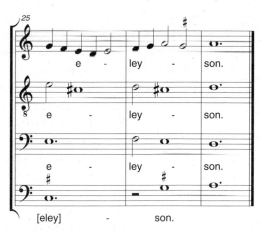

When you listen to Machaut's *Kyrie* for the first time, you will be struck by its dark, dissonant sound. This dark quality arises from the presence of exclusively male voices. Only men and choirboys were allowed to sing in medieval cathedrals. Men in falsetto voice (see page 100) or boys sang the soprano and alto parts. Sacred singing by women was confined to nunneries (for more on this point, see pages 86 and 101). The dissonant, biting sound, meanwhile, results from Machaut's use of unusual dissonances, many of which were later forbidden in Western polyphonic music. In stark contrast to these dissonances, each section of polyphony ends with an open, somewhat hollow-sounding consonant chord. These chords use only the intervals of a fifth and the octave. Such open, hollow final chords sound especially rich in buildings with very resonant, or "lively," acoustics of the sort universally found in medieval cathedrals.

distinctive sound of medieval polyphony

 **Listening Guide**   Guillaume de Machaut
Kyrie of the *Mass of Our Lady* (c1360)   **6** 1/4   **2** 1/1

Form: ternary
Texture: polyphonic and monophonic

0:00		Kyrie eleison (sung three times)	Lord have mercy upon us
2:16		Christe eleison (sung three times)	Christ have mercy upon us
3:37		Kyrie eleison (sung three times)	Lord have mercy upon us

 Use a downloadable, cross-platform animated Active Listening Guide, available
at **www.thomsonedu.com/music/wright**.

Listening Exercise 14

Machaut
Kyrie of the *Mass of Our Lady*

The *Kyrie* of the Ordinary of the Mass is a threefold petition for mercy (*Kyrie eleison* means "Lord have mercy upon
us"). In Machaut's setting, the composer makes use of preexisting monophonic chant in two ways: he sets it in the
tenor voice in long notes and builds polyphony around
it (see Ex. 8–3); and he requires that sections of the *Kyrie*
be sung in chant alone. On this recording, when the chant
alone is heard, it is sung by men in unison*. Your task
in this listing exercise is straightforward: identify which
sections are composed in four-voice polyphony and which
make use of monophonic Gregorian chant by writing
either "polyphony" or "chant" in the blanks below.

1. (0:00) Kyrie eleison: _____
2. (1:00) Kyrie eleison: _____

6 1/4   **2** 1/1   **Thomson**NOW™
To take this Listening Exercise online and
receive feedback or email answers to your
instructor, go to *ThomsonNOW* for this chapter.

3. (1:17) Kyrie eleison: _____
4. (2:16) Christe eleison: _____
5. (2:31) Christe eleison: _____
6. (3:23) Christe eleison: _____
7. (3:37) Kyrie eleison: _____
8. (4:17) Kyrie eleison: _____
9. (4:32) Kyrie eleison: _____
10. Finally, notice that each of the polyphonic sections
    takes longer to perform than the monophonic ones.
    Why is that the case?
    a. because singing the tenor in longer notes in the
       polyphony causes the music to be drawn out
    b. because the soloists singing polyphony have more
       words to sing in each section

MUSIC AT THE COURT

churchmen active at court

Outside the walls of the cathedral, there was yet another musical world, one
of popular song and dance centered at the court. Indeed, the court embraced
forms of public entertainment not permitted by church authorities. Itinerant
actors, jugglers, jesters, and animal acts all provided welcome diversions. Min-
strels wandered from castle to castle, bringing the latest tunes, along with
news and gossip. Churchmen, too, sojourned at court. Guillaume de Machaut,
for example, enjoyed a double career as cleric and courtier. He composed liturgical music for the cathedral of Reims, yet at various times in his life was employed by the king of Bohemia, the king of Navarre, and the Duke of Berry.
While it may seem strange that a clergyman like Machaut was active in worldly
affairs at court, during the Middle Ages learned churchmen were much in demand for their ability to read and write. And because of their skill with letters
and their knowledge of musical notation gained in the church, clerics were
inevitably drawn to the poetry and music of the courtly song. Indeed, most of
the polyphonic love songs emanating from the court in the late Middle Ages
were written by ordained priests.

Music at the Forefront of Science

During the Middle Ages—indeed, since the time of Plato—music was viewed not as an art but as a science. It was studied in the schools and universities along with geometry, astronomy, and arithmetic in a curriculum called the *quadrivium.* These four subjects were deemed the core sciences because each could be precisely measured. The musical interval of the octave, for example, could be demonstrated by means of two strings the lengths of which were in a 2:1 proportion; a fifth could be produced by strings with a ratio of 3:2; and so on. A separate curriculum, called the *trivium* (grammar, logic, and rhetoric), was devoted to the study of language and philosophy. These subjects together constituted the **seven liberal arts.** We draw from this ancient formulation such English expressions as "Bachelor of Arts" and "trivial"—the word-based subjects were thought far less important than music and her sister sciences.

The Middle Ages gave to Western society a gift that accounts for the near total domination of the West today in matters of science and technology: rigorous quantification. During the late Middle Ages, most important modes of human experience—the measurement of time, the calculation of the value of goods and services, the mapping of the surface of the earth, even the visual layout of a painting—came to be measured in proportional units. Around 1320, pipe organs and mechanical clocks appear in the naves of churches—shining examples of the new technology wrought by measurement. Measurement also was applied to music by means of a system of notation that regulated the two primary components of this art: sound and time (see Ex. 8–3). Pitch was determined by setting symbols higher or lower on a vertical axis. Time was controlled by creating different shapes (note shapes) and placing these symbols left to right on a horizontal axis. The larger notes were exact multiples of smaller ones, just as whole, quarter, and half notes are today. Thus by 1350, the heyday of Machaut, all the elements of modern musical notation were essentially in place. The components of music were precisely measured and manipulated far earlier than those in other areas of human activity. The musical staff was the West's first graph.

The court emerged as a center for the patronage of the arts during the years 1150–1400, as the power of the church gradually declined. Kings, dukes, counts, and lesser nobles increasingly assumed responsibility for the defense of the land and the administration of justice. The aristocratic court became a small, independent city-state, but one that could move from place to place. To enhance the ruler's prestige and show that he or she was a person of refinement and sensibility, nobles often engaged bands of trumpeters to herald an arrival, instrumentalists to provide dance music for festivals, and singers and poets to create lyric verse. Some poems were meant to be recited, but most were sung.

decline of the Church; rise of the court

Troubadours and Trouvères

Southern France was the center of this new courtly art, though it extended into northern Spain and Italy as well. The poet-musicians who flourished there were known as **troubadours** (men) and **trobairitz** (women). Both terms derived from the verb *trobar,* which meant "to find" in the vernacular tongue of medieval southern France. Thus the *troubadours* and *trobairitz* were "finders" or inventors of new modes of verbal and vocal expression. Their art was devoted mainly to the creation of songs of love that extolled the courtly ideals of faith and devotion, whether to the ideal lady, the just seigneur (lord), or the knight crusading in the Holy Land. Their songs were not in the Latin of the Church, but in the vernacular tongue: medieval Italian, Catalan, and Provençal (medieval French of the South). The origins of the *troubadours* were equally varied. Some were sons of bakers and drapers, others were members of the nobility, many were clerics living outside the Church, and not a few were women.

composed mostly love songs

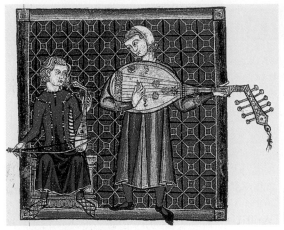

FIGURE 8–6

A thirteenth-century Spanish miniature showing a medieval fiddle (the rebec) on the left and a lute on the right. Both instruments were brought into Spain by the Arabs and then carried northward into the lands of the *troubadours* and *trouvères*.

In the Middle Ages, and later during the Renaissance (1475–1600), women were not allowed to sing in church, except in convents, owing to the early injunction of the Apostle Paul ("A woman must be silent in the church"). But at court, women often recited poetry, sang, and played musical instruments, performing on the so-called *bas* (soft) instruments like the harp, lute, rebec (medieval fiddle), and flute (Fig. 8–6). Moreover, *trobairitz* were not merely performers, but creators in their own right. One such composer was Beatriz, Countess of Dia (Fig. 8–7), who lived in southern France during the middle of the twelfth century. She was married to Count William of Poitiers but fell in love with a fellow *troubadour*, Raimbaut d'Orange (1146–1173). Her song *A chanter m'er* (*I Must Sing*) laments her failure in love, despite her self-proclaimed charms. It is composed of five strophes, or stanzas, each with seven lines of text and seven musical phrases. The seven-phrase melody displays a clear music form, **ABABCDB** (the use of letters to indicate musical form is explained on page 61). As with the chant of the Church, *troubadour* song has no clearly articulated meter and rhythm, but is sung in notes of more or less equal length.

Listening Guide

Countess of Dia
Troubadour song, I Must Sing (c1175)

6
1/5

0:00   **5**   Improvised introduction played on medieval fiddle
0:26   Solo voice enters and sings the first of five strophes

A chan - tar m'er   de   so qu'eu   no   vol - ri - a   A

Tant me ran - cur   de   lui   cui sui   a - mi - a   B

Car eu l'am mais   que nul - ha   ren   que si - a   A

Vas lui no'm val   mer - ces   ni   cor - te - zi - a   B

Ni   ma bel - tatz ni mos pretz ni   mos sens   C

Qu'a - tres - si'm   sui   en - ga - nad'   e   tra - hi - a   D

Com de-gr'es - ser   s'eu   fos   de - sa -   vi - nens.   B

(I must sing of that which I'd rather not,
So bitter do I feel toward him
Whom I love more than anything.
But with him kindness and courtliness get me nowhere,
Neither my beauty, nor my worth, nor my intelligence.
In this way am I cheated and betrayed,
Just as I would be if I were ugly.)

 Use a downloadable, cross-platform animated Active Listening Guide, available at **www.thomsonedu.com/music/wright**.

Gradually, the musical traditions created by the *troubadours* were carried to the north of France, where such composer-performers came to be called **trouvères,** and even to Germany, where they were called **Minnesingers.** Around 1300, some of the *trouvères* began to mix the traditions of the *troubadours* with the learned vocal polyphony coming from the Church. Soon churchmen such as Guillaume de Machaut (see page 82) adopted the musical forms and poetic style of the *trouvères* to fashion a new genre of music, the polyphonic **chanson** (French for "song"). The chanson is simply a love song, normally in French, for two, three, or four voices. At its best, the chanson is a small jewel of poignant lyricism.

Music at the Court of Burgundy

During the late Middle Ages, the Court of Burgundy (fl. 1364–1477) was the envy of all courts in Western Europe. Its army was the most powerful, its arts the most beautiful, and its fashions the most *à la mode.* Moreover, the Burgundian treasury was the richest, primarily because the dukes of Burgundy controlled not only the territory of Burgundy in eastern France but also parts of northern France as well as most of modern-day Belgium and Holland. Among the musicians of Burgundy (Fig. 8–8) were Gilles Binchois (c1400–1460) and Guillaume Dufay (c1397–1474), both of whom excelled at writing chansons. Although ordained priests, both moved easily between ecclesiastical and courtly circles.

The sounds that typically grace a French chanson can be heard in *Ce moys de may* (*This Month of May*) by Guillaume Dufay. (His name is pronounced with three syllables: "Doo-fah-ee" and rhymes with "mel-od-y.") In the Middle Ages, May marked the beginning of the "season of love" in which a lad might approach his lass with flowers in hopes that love would bloom. The effervescent quality of Dufay's music—created here by sprightly rhythms and a tuneful melody—suggests all the youthful optimism of spring. Medieval poets and musicians called the form of *This Month of May* a **rondeau** (rondo) because a musical refrain appears several times (on the rondo, see page 65). There are two musical sections (**a** and **b**) to which a text refrain is often set (creating **A** and **B**; see Listening Guide). Toward the end, the composer himself invites all to join the song and dance. Indeed, *This Month of May* likely was not only sung but also danced, the youthful participants moving around a circle in a traditional medieval round dance.

FIGURE 8–7

Beatriz Countess of Dia as depicted in a manuscript of *troubadour* and *trouvère* poetry.

FIGURE 8–8

Guillaume Dufay and Gilles Binchois as depicted in a manuscript copied c1440. Dufay stands next to a small organ, the quintessential instrument of the church, while Binchois holds a harp, one of the principal instruments of the court.

Listening Guide Guillaume Dufay
                   This Month of May (c1430)

1/6

Genre: chanson
Form: rondo
(Boldface shows text refrain.)

0:00		**Ce moys de may soyons lies et joyeux**	A	**This month of May be happy and gay,**	
		Et de nos cuers ostons merancolye;		**Remove melancholy from our hearts.**	
0:23		**Chantons, dansons et menons chiere lye,**	B	**Let us sing and dance and be of good cheer**	
		Por despiter ces felons envieux.		**To spite the envious low born.**	
		Plus c'onques mais chascuns soit curieux	a	More than ever before let each one strive	
		De bien servir sa maistresse jolye:		To serve his pretty mistress:	
		Ce moys de may soyons lies et joyeux	A	**This month of May be happy and gay,**	
		Et de nos cuers ostons merancolye.		**Remove melancholy from our hearts.**	
		Car la saison semont tous amoureux	a	For the season bids all lovers	
		A ce faire, poutant n' y fallons mye.		This to do, and so let us not fail.	
		Carissimi! Dufay vous en prye	b	Dearest friends, Dufay begs you,	
		Et Perinet dira de mieux en mieux.		And little Pierre will say more and more.	
2:17		**Ce moys de may soyons lies et joyeux**	A	**This month of May be happy and gay,**	
		Et de nos cuers ostons merancolye;		**Remove melancholy from our hearts.**	
2:40		**Chantons, dansons et menons chiere lye,**	B	**Let us sing and dance and be of good cheer**	
		Por despiter ces felons envieux.		**To spite the envious low born.**	

Use a downloadable, cross-platform animated Active Listening Guide, available at www.thomsonedu.com/music/wright.

Listening Exercise 15

Dufay
This Month of May

1/6

ThomsonNOW™
To take this Listening Exercise online and receive feedback or email answers to your instructor, go to *ThomsonNOW* for this chapter.

Form: rondo

Characteristic of hundreds of French chansons of the late Middle Ages, Dufay's *This Month of May* is written in *rondeau* form, the medieval version of the rondo. In all *rondeaux*, a refrain (**AB**) sounds three times, wholly or in part. The musical process of rondo, with its recurring refrain, would remain a favorite with composers for centuries (Vivaldi's famous the "Spring" Concerto from *The Seasons*, for example, makes use of it as well; see page 138). The following exercise will help you differentiate one musical section from another in Dufay's delightful *rondeau*.

1–4. Fill in the blanks indicating the time when the
      musical sections **a** and **b** return.
      A 0:00   B 0:23   a _____   A _____
      a _____   b _____   A 2:17   B 2:40

5. Which of the following is true?
   a. The capital **A** and capital **B** indicate that the voices drop out in these sections.
   b. The capital **A** and capital **B** indicate the presence of a textual and musical refrain.

6. Section **a** begins with an instrumental introduction played by a lute and a medieval fiddle. Do the instruments drop out when the voices enter?
   a. yes   b. no

7. Do the instruments also introduce section **b**?
   a. yes   b. no

8. Melismatic* singing always occurs when?
   a. at the beginning of sections **a** and **b**
   b. at the end of sections **a** and **b**

9. The beginning of section **b** is characterized by which type of musical texture?
   a. monophonic
   b. homophonic
   c. polyphonic

10. The voices singing on this recording are what?
    a. all male
    b. all female
    c. a mixture of male and female

MEDIEVAL MUSICAL INSTRUMENTS

In the late Middle Ages, the principal musical instrument of the monastery and cathedral was the pipe organ. Indeed, the organ was the only instrument admitted by church authorities. At court, however, a variety of instrumental sounds could be heard. Instruments were divided into two groups according to the amount of volume they produced. The first group was called the *hauts* (loud) instruments and included trumpet, **sackbut** (forerunner of the trombone), **shawm** (ancestor of the oboe), and the drums. Later, in the Renaissance, a **cornetto,** a curved wooden instrument sounding something like a cross between a trumpet and a clarinet, joined the *hauts* instruments. The second group was called the *bas* (soft) instruments and included flute, recorder, fiddle, psaltery, harp, and lute. Dancing was an inevitable part of courtly recreation, and for this a standard "dance band" of *hauts* instruments was required: two or three shawms, a sackbut, and perhaps a cornetto and a drum (Figs. 8–9 and 8–10). The sackbut played the dance tune in long notes while the shawms or other instruments wove ornamental lines, much like a contemporary jazz quartet in which a trumpet or saxophone improvises above the fundamental bass notes provided by the double bass or the guitar. The late fifteenth-century tune entitled *La Spagna* (*The Spanish Tune*) is typical of the dance melodies played at the court of Burgundy during the waning years of the Middle Ages.

FIGURE 8-9

A later scene, c1600, showing musicians in a procession as painted by Denis van Alsloot. The instruments are, from right to left, a sackbut, two shawms, a cornetto, another shawm, and an early bassoon.

Museo del Prado, Madrid/The Bridgeman Art Library

FIGURE 8-10

Dance scene at a wedding at a French court in the mid-fifteenth century. The musicians, who play shawms and a sackbut, are placed on high in a balcony.

Bibliothèque Nationale, Paris

Listening Guide

Anonymous
Instrumental dance tune, *The Spanish Tune* (c1470)
Set for three instruments by Heinrich Isaac (c1490)

6
1/7

Texture: Polyphonic

0:00	**7**	Drum begins
		Sackbut plays the tune in long notes in bass while shawm provides counterpoint above
0:04		Cornetto enters to add another line of counterpoint above tune
1:05		Repeat of previous music at slightly faster tempo

Use a downloadable, cross-platform animated Active Listening Guide, available at **www.thomsonedu.com/music/wright.**

Key Words

Gregorian chant (**76**)	Proper of the	*trouvère* (**87**)
plainsong (**76**)	Mass (**82**)	*Minnesinger* (**87**)
syllabic singing (**77**)	Ordinary of the	chanson (**87**)
melismatic	Mass (**82**)	*rondeau* (**87**)
singing (**77**)	seven liberal arts (**85**)	sackbut (**89**)
organum (**80**)	*troubadour* (**85**)	shawm (**89**)
Mass (**82**)	*trobairitz* (**85**)	cornetto (**89**)

Checklist of Musical Style

Representative composers
Hildegard of Bingen
Leoninus
Perotinus
Machaut
Countess of Dia
Dufay
Binchois

Principal genres
Gregorian chant
polyphonic Mass
troubadour and *trouvère* songs
French polyphonic chanson
instrumental dance

Middle Ages: 476–1475

Melody	Moves mostly by step within narrow range; rarely uses chromatic notes of the scale
Harmony	Most surviving medieval music is monophonic Gregorian chant or monophonic *troubadour* and *trouvère* songs—hence there is no harmony
	Medieval polyphony (Mass, motet, and chanson) has dissonant phrases ending with open, hollow-sounding chords
Rhythm	Gregorian chant as well as *troubadour* and *trouvère* songs sung mainly in notes of equal value without clearly marked rhythms; medieval polyphony is composed mostly in triple meter and uses repeating rhythmic patterns
Color	Mainly vocal sounds (choir or soloists); little instrumental music survives
Texture	Mostly monophonic—Gregorian chant as well as *troubadour* and *trouvère* songs are monophonic melodies
	Medieval polyphony (two, three, or four independent lines) is mainly contrapuntal
Form	Strophic form of *troubadour* and *trouvère* songs; ternary form of the Kyrie; rondo form of the French *rondeau*

An Islamic Call to Worship

During the Middle Ages, Western Europe was Christian in matters of religion. The center of the Western Latin (Catholic) Church was Rome. Much of Eastern Europe and western Asian lands, including what is now called Russia and the Ukraine, gradually came to profess the faith of the Eastern Orthodox Church, which was centered in Constantinople (now called Istanbul [Turkey]). Lands to the south of Constantinople were under the control of Arab Muslims.

But in 1453, the Muslims seized Constantinople, an event signifying the spread of their power in the eastern Mediterranean. Hostilities between followers of the Eastern Orthodox Church (Christians) and the brotherhood of Islam (Muslims) continued for centuries, and play out even today in the countries of Serbia, Bosnia, and in the region of Chechnia in Russia.

Islam is the name that all Muslims give to their religion. It is based on the teachings of the prophet Mohammed (c570–632), born in Mecca (Saudi Arabia). The revelations of Mohammed, believed to have been sent from Allah (God) to the prophet in the year 610, are collected in the **Koran.** Written in Arabic but translated into many languages, the Koran provides Muslims with direction in religious and civic duties, just as the Torah and the New Testament guide Jews and Christians, respectively.

Within a century of the death of the prophet Mohammed (632), Islam had spread from North Africa to Spain and, following the silk trade route, as far east as China. The most populous Islamic countries today, moving roughly west to east, are Egypt, Saudi Arabia, Turkey, Iraq, Iran, Afghanistan, Pakistan, (northern) India, and Indonesia. Of the great world religions today, Islam ranks second in number of adherents, as the following approximate numbers suggest: Christians (2.1 billion), Muslims (1.2 billion), Hindus (0.9 billion), and Buddhists and Chinese folk religionists (0.8 billion).

Every devout Muslim is required to worship God five times each day: just before sunrise, at noon, before sunset, just after sunset, and just after the day has closed. (In medieval monasteries in the West, Benedictine monks and nuns gathered daily for eight hours of prayer plus Mass.) Muslims may pray alone or in a house of worship called a **mosque.** On Friday, the Muslim holy day, the noon service is set for the full community in the mosque. Men pray in rows and women in rows behind them or in a separate area of the mosque. The service consists of exclamations and the recital of parts of the Koran, accompanied by prostrations of the body. No matter where in the world Muslim worshippers may be, they face in the direction of Mecca as they pray.

Christians around the world have historically summoned the faithful to the church by means of bells. Muslims, however, call the faithful to each of the five times of prayer by chanting from the tall tower of the mosque, called the **minaret** (see figure). The call to worship is named the **Adhan.** In large cities, the voice of a single cantor is linked by loudspeakers, and thus he chants the Adhan in synchronized fashion around the city. In nearly all Islamic countries, no matter what the native language, the call to worship is sung in

© Jose Fuste Raga/CORBIS

A mosque with ascending minaret in Cairo, Egypt.

Arabic, and the text (see Listening Guide following) is always the same. The melody, however, can vary according to the singing style of the cantor.

The cantor, or principal singer, of the mosque is called the **muezzin.** Some muezzins know the entire Koran by memory, and the more famous of them have recorded it (all 6,236 verses) on CDs. Among these is Turkish muezzin Hafiz Huseyin Erek. On the recording discussed below, the voice of Erek can be heard calling all Muslims to worship, just as it still can be heard today live above the houses and mosques of Istanbul, Turkey.

Islamic chant compared to Gregorian chant: Although it would be unwise to draw too much from a single example, Islamic and Gregorian chant can be instructively compared. Both are monophonic* in texture, and both avoid regular rhythms or meters. Because of this, both musics also have a floating, undulating quality to them. Here the word *arabesque* (meaning "Arab-like") can correctly be used, for the Muslim melody, like Gregorian chant, seems to twist and turn to form elaborate patterns.

There is, however, one distinctive quality of the Adhan sung by Hafiz Huseyin Erek, and this characteristic marks much of non-Western music: The performer slides between pitches. In fact, much of the musical interest and beauty of this call to worship derives from what the performer is doing between pitches, not what he does on them. By way of comparison, Gregorian chant—indeed almost all Western music—moves from one discrete pitch to the next, carefully avoiding all intermediate sounds.

Finally, it is quite possible, even likely, that when Gregorian chant was created during the Middle Ages, it sounded much like Islamic music does today—surely it, too, originally involved singing between pitches. In the course of time, we in the West, influenced by fixed-pitched keyboard instruments such as the organ and the piano, have eliminated from our melodies the microtonal sounds between pitches. Significantly, highly complex, mechanized keyboard instruments are unique to the music of the West. Such comparisons show Western music to differ fundamentally in a number of important ways from other musical practices of the world, and suggest once again that technology has played a primary role in shaping our musical tradition.

Key Words

Koran (**91**)	minaret (**91**)	muezzin (**92**)
mosque (**91**)	Adhan (**91**)	

Listening Guide

Adhan (Islamic Call to Worship)
A Timeless Islamic Chant sung by Hafiz Huseyin Erek

6
6/18

0:00	18	Phrase **a**: chant rises from first note to fifth degree of scale	Allahu Akbar. God is great.
0:06		Phrase **a** repeats with slight variation	God is great.
0:12		Phrase **b**: syllabic chant gives way to more melismatic singing in higher range	I testify that there is no God but Allah.
0:30		Phrase **b**: repeated with variation	I testify that Mohammed is his prophet.
0:53		Phrase **c**: voice rises to higher level, concludes with melismatic singing	Come to Prayer. Come to Prayer.
1:13		Phrase **c** repeats and is extended	Come to Salvation. Come to Salvation.
1:33		Phrase **a** returns	God is great.
1:39		End of phrase **b** returns	There is no God but Allah.

Use a downloadable, cross-platform animated Active Listening Guide, available at **www.thomsonedu.com/music/wright.**

Renaissance Music, 1475–1600

Historians use the term *Renaissance* to designate the period 1350–1600 during which Western Europe experienced a rebirth of interest in classical antiquity and a reawakening of interest in the fine arts generally. Music historians, however, usually apply the term more narrowly to indicate the time span from 1475 to 1600. In these years, composers began to think of themselves as independent artists, rather than servants of the Church, and music theorists rediscovered ancient Greek treatises on music, which ultimately affected the way musicians created and thought about music.

Ancient Greece and Rome, of course, were pagan, non-Christian cultures. As a result, the Renaissance, while a religious period in many ways, was decidedly more worldly, or secular, in its outlook. The surviving music of the Middle Ages is overwhelmingly religious in character (Gregorian chant and sacred polyphony). By contrast, the music of the Renaissance is about equally divided between religious music, used in worship, and secular music, serving as popular entertainment.

Renaissance more worldly in outlook

The Renaissance originated in Italy, in large measure because the manuscripts and the ruins of classical antiquity lay all around. The great Italian minds of the day believed that they could create a new and better society, not only by gazing forward but also by looking backward into history for guidance. Antiquity, they maintained, could provide a model for how a city should be run and how its citizens should behave. Greek and Roman design showed how buildings might be constructed (Fig. 9–1) and what sort of statues might be placed in them (Fig. 9–4). Similarly, Greek and Roman literature suggested how poetry should be written and public speeches composed. So, too, the ancient philosophers provided guidelines for personal behavior and a new way of thinking about the fine arts (see boxed essay).

originated in Italy

©Cameraphoto Arte Venice/Art Resource, NY

FIGURE 9–1

Andrea Palladio's Villa Rotunda (c1550) near Vicenza, Italy, clearly shows the extent to which classical architecture was reborn during the Renaissance. Elements of the ancient style include the columns with capitals, triangular pediments, and central rotunda (compare Fig. 15-1).

Music Becomes a Fine Art

Music enjoyed a new, higher estimation in the public consciousness during the Renaissance because it was now less a science, more an art. Recall that during the Middle Ages music had been grouped with three other mathematical disciplines (arithmetic, geometry, and astronomy) to form a core curriculum called the *quadrivium* (see page 85). These subjects, along with the *trivium* of grammar, logic, and rhetoric, constituted the seven liberal arts. But now a new appreciation of the so-called mechanical arts led to a whole-sale reshuffling of categories. Leonardo da Vinci himself argued that painting should be added to these seven disciplines, indeed placed at their head. So, too, poetry should join her sisters, though sculpture, because it was wrought by hard manual labor, should not. By the end of the sixteenth century, academies of painting and of music had replaced the medieval craft guilds. The expressive disciplines of poetry, painting, music, and architecture were now separated into a category of "fine arts," a worthy complement to the liberal arts and the sciences.

FIGURE 9–2

Leonardo da Vinci's *Madonna, Child, Saint Anne, and a Lamb* (c1508–1517). Notice the warm, human expression and the near-complete absence of religious symbolism, as well as the highly formalistic composition of the painting; the figures form successively larger triangles.

FIGURE 9–3

The expressive grief of the Virgin, Saint John, and Mary Magdalene mark this portion of an altarpiece painted by Mathias Grünewald (1510–1515).

Musée du Louvre, Paris/Giraudon/The Bridgeman Art Library

Musée d'Unterlinden, Colmar/The Bridgeman Art Library

The ancient Greek writers, especially Homer and Plato, had spoken of the great emotional power of music. Their stories told how music had calmed the agitated spirit or made brave the warrior. Musicians in the Renaissance eagerly embraced this notion that music could sway the emotions, and even the behavior, of listeners. Consequently, composers of the Renaissance began to develop an expanded vocabulary of musical expression. Music, they believed, should underscore and heighten the meaning of each and every phrase of the text. If the verse depicted birds soaring gracefully in the sky, the accompanying music should be in a major key and ascend into a high range; if the text lamented the pain and sorrow of sin, the music ought be in a minor key, and dark and dissonant. As a result, the Renaissance produced a greater range of musical styles, mirroring the development of the visual arts of the Renaissance, which now likewise allowed for a greater range of emotional expression. Compare, for example, the highly contrasting moods of two paintings created within a few years of one another—the peaceful serenity of Leonardo da Vinci's *Madonna, Child, Saint Anne, and a Lamb* (Fig. 9–2) and the painful intensity of Mathias Grünewald's *Saint John and the Two Marys* (Fig. 9–3).

Attending the rebirth of the arts and letters of classical antiquity was a renewed interest in humankind itself. We have come to call this enthusiastic self-interest humanism. Simply said, **humanism** is the belief that people are something more than a mere conduit for gifts descending from heaven, that they have the capacity to create many things good and beautiful, indeed, the ability to shape their own world. The culture of the Middle Ages, as we have seen, was fostered by the Church, which emphasized a collective submission to the almighty, hiding the individual human form beneath layers of clothing. The culture of the Renaissance, by contrast, rejoiced in the human form in all its fullness (Fig. 9–4). It looked outward and indulged a passion for invention and discovery.

True to the humanistic spirit, composers in the Renaissance began to think of themselves not merely as subservient churchmen, but as talented artists, and they sought credit for their musical creations. In the Middle Ages, musical compositions were usually preserved anonymously in manuscripts—the earthly creator was not considered important enough to be named. But from the mid-fifteenth century onward, the name of the composer was usually placed at the head of each piece in a music manuscript. Josquin Desprez and other Renaissance composers even went so far as to insert their own names into liturgical texts in honor of the Virgin Mary, a bold act of self-promotion. In a similar fashion, artists such as Raphael, Botticelli, and Michelangelo painted their own faces into their religious frescoes. A composition or a painting came to be viewed as a tangible record of a single individual's creative genius, and the artist was eager to "take a bow."

Moreover, these artists wanted to be paid, and paid well. Medieval craftsmen had traditionally belonged to guilds, which regulated both what type of work they could accept and what they might earn. In the Renaissance, however, this system began to break down. Now a gifted artist might vie for the highest-paying commission, just as a sought-after composer might play one patron off against another for the highest salary. Money, it seems, could "prime the pump" of creativity, leading to greater productivity. This productivity, in turn, was in some cases richly rewarded—the prolific Michelangelo left an estate worth some $10 million in terms of money today.

If artists were paid more in the Renaissance, it was because art was now thought to be more valuable. For the first time in the Christian West, there emerged the concept of a "work of art": the belief that an object serve not only as a religious symbol, but might also be a creation of purely aesthetic value and enjoyment. Music in the Renaissance was composed by proud artists who aimed to give pleasure. Their music conversed, not with eternity, but with the listener. It was judged good or bad only to the degree that it pleased fellow human beings. Music and the other arts could now be freely evaluated in the secular world for their quality, and composers and painters could be ranked according to their greatness. Artistic judgment, appreciation, and criticism entered Western thought for the first time in the humanistic Renaissance.

Bridgeman Art Library, London/NY

FIGURE 9–4

Michelangelo's giant statue of David (1501–1504) expresses the heroic nobility of man in near-perfect form. Like Leonardo da Vinci, Michelangelo made a careful study of human anatomy.

FIGURE 9–5

The only surviving portrait of Josquin Desprez.

The British Library/The Bridgeman Art Library

JOSQUIN DESPREZ (c1455–1521) AND THE RENAISSANCE MOTET

Josquin Desprez (pronounced "Josh-can Day-pray") was one of the greatest composers of the Renaissance or, indeed, of any age (Fig. 9–5). He was born somewhere near the present border between France and Belgium about 1455, and died in the same region in 1521. Yet, like so many musicians of northern France, he was attracted to Italy to pursue professional and monetary gain. Between 1484 and 1504, he worked for various dukes in Milan and Ferrara, and for the pope in his Sistine Chapel in Rome. Evidence suggests that Josquin (he was known universally just by his first name) had a temperamental, egotistical personality, one typical of many artists of the Renaissance. He would fly into a rage when singers tampered with his music; he composed only when he, not his patron, wished; and he demanded a salary twice that of composers only slightly less gifted. Yet Josquin's contemporaries recognized his genius. Castiglione (*The Book of the Courtier*, 1528) and Rabelais (*Pantagruel*, 1535) praised him. He was the favorite of Martin Luther, who said, "Josquin is master of the notes, which must express what he desires; other composers can do only what the notes dictate." Florentine humanist Cosimo Bartoli compared him to the great Michelangelo (1475–1564), who decorated the ceiling of the Sistine Chapel where Josquin had once sung (Fig. 9–6). In Bartoli's words:

a great but temperamental artist

Fratelli Alinari/SuperStock

FIGURE 9–6
Interior of the Sistine Chapel. The high altar and Michelangelo's *Last Judgment* are at the far end, the balcony for the singers, including Josquin Desprez, at the lower right. The congregants could stand and listen from the near side of the screen.

Josquin may be said to have been a prodigy of nature, as our Michelangelo Buonarroti has been in architecture, painting, and sculpture; for, as there has not thus far been anyone who in his compositions approaches Josquin, so Michelangelo, among all those who have been active in these arts, is still alone and without a peer; both Josquin and Michelangelo have opened the eyes of all those who delight in these arts or are to delight in them in the future.

Josquin composed in all of the musical genres of his day, but he excelled in writing motets, some seventy of which survive under his name. The Renaissance **motet** can be defined as a composition for a choir, setting a Latin text on a sacred subject, and intended to be sung either in a church or chapel, or at home in private devotion. While composers of the Renaissance continued to set the text of the Ordinary of the Mass*, they turned increasingly to the motet because its texts were more vivid and descriptive. Most motet texts were drawn from the Old Testament of the Bible, especially from the expressive Psalms and the mournful Lamentations. A vivid text cried out for an equally vivid musical setting, allowing the composer to fulfill a mandate of Renaissance humanism: use music to heighten the meaning of the word.

Most motets in the Renaissance, as well as most Masses for the Church, were sung **a cappella** (literally, "in the chapel"), meaning that they were performed by voices alone, without any instrumental accompaniment. (Instruments other than the organ were generally not allowed in churches during the Middle Ages and the Renaissance.) This, in part, accounts for the often serene quality of the sound of Renaissance sacred music. Indeed, the Renaissance has been called "the golden age of a cappella singing."

Josquin's motet *Ave Maria* (*Hail, Mary*) was written about 1485 when the composer was in Milan, Italy, in the service of the Duke of Milan. Composed in honor of the Virgin Mary, it employs the standard four voice parts: soprano, alto, tenor, and bass. As the motet unfolds, the listener hears the voices enter

a period of a cappella singing

in succession with the same musical motive. This process is called **imitation,** a procedure whereby one or more voices duplicate in turn the notes of a melody.

EXAMPLE 9–1

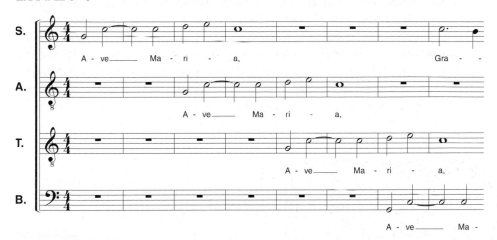

Josquin also sometimes has one pair of voices imitate another—the tenor and bass, for example, imitating what the alto and soprano have just sung.

EXAMPLE 9–2

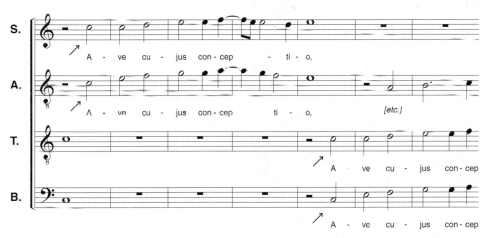

In Josquin's imitative writing, each voice is given equal opportunity to present the melodic material; thus, all four voices are of equal importance. Josquin and his contemporaries favored this texture of four equal voices in part because of its symmetry and balance. Agreeable proportions were prized not only in Renaissance music but in the arts generally during this period (see Figs. 9–1 through 9–4).

imitative writing creates balance

Because each voice enters independently, imitative writing invariably produces counterpoint*—individual voices working with and against one another in harmonious fashion. In Josquin's *Ave Maria,* sections in imitative counterpoint (polyphony*) alternate with passages of chordal writing (homophony*), achieving a variety of musical textures and, in so doing, maintaining the listener's interest.

imitative writing creates counterpoint

Josquin organizes the overall structure of *Ave Maria* in much the same manner that a humanistic orator would construct a persuasive speech or address. It begins with a salutation to the Virgin, sung in imitation. Thereafter, a key word, "Ave" ("Hail"), sparks a series of salutes to the Virgin, each making reference to one of her principal feast days during the church year (Conception, Nativity, Annunciation, Purification, and Assumption). At the end of this series of "hails" comes a final exclamation, "O Mother of God, be mindful of me. Amen." These last words are set to striking chords, with each syllable of text receiving its own chord. The chordal, homophonic treatment allows this final text to stand out with absolute clarity, again observing the principle of musical humanism: text and music must work together to persuade and move the listener. Here they must persuade the Virgin Mary as well, for she is asked to intercede on behalf of the needy soul at the hour of death.

Listening Guide

Josquin Desprez
Motet, *Ave Maria* (c1485)

6 1/8   **2** 1/2

Time	Description	Latin	English
0:00	All four voices present each two-word phrase in turn	Ave Maria, gratia plena, Dominus tecum, virgo serena.	Hail Mary, full of grace. The Lord be with you, serene Virgin.
0:46	Soprano and alto are imitated by tenor and bass; then all four voices work to peak on "laetitia" ("joy")	Ave cujus conceptio, Solemni plena gaudio, Coelestia, terrestria, Nova replet laetitia.	Hail to you whose conception, With solemn rejoicing, Fills heaven and earth With new joy.
1:20	Imitation in pairs; soprano and alto answered by tenor and bass	Ave cujus nativitas Nostra fuit solemnitas, Ut lucifer lux oriens, Verum solem praeveniens.	Hail to you whose birth Was to be our solemnity, As the rising morning star Anticipates the true sun.
1:58	More imitation by pairs of voices; soprano and alto followed by tenor and bass	Ave pia humilitas, Sine viro foecunditas, Cujus annuntiatio, Nostra fuit salvatio.	Hail pious humility, Fruitful without man, Whose annunciation Was to be our salvation.
2:26	Chordal writing; meter changes from duple to triple	Ave vera virginitas, Immaculata castitas, Cujus purificatio Nostra fuit purgatio.	Hail true virginity, Immaculate chastity, Whose purification Was to be our purgation.
3:03	Return to duple meter; soprano and alto imitated by tenor and bass	Ave praeclara omnibus Angelicis virtutibus, Cujus fuit assumptio Nostra glorificatio.	Hail shining example Of all angelic virtues, Whose assumption Was to be our glorification.
3:58	Strict chordal writing; clear presentation of text	O Mater Dei, Memento mei. Amen.	O Mother of God, Be mindful of me. Amen.

Use a downloadable, cross-platform animated Active Listening Guide, available at **www.thomsonedu.com/music/wright.**

Listening Exercise 16

6 1/8   **2** 1/2

ThomsonNOW™

To take this Listening Exercise online and receive feedback or email answers to your instructor, go to *ThomsonNOW* for this chapter.

Josquin Desprez
Ave Maria

Josquin's *Ave Maria* is a fine example of a Renaissance motet employing imitative counterpoint, the dominant musical texture for sacred music during the Renaissance. What follows is mainly an exercise in hearing the four voices unfold and identifying how Josquin clarifies the meaning of the text. On this modern recording, the soprano part is sung by women, and the alto, tenor, and bass parts by men.

1. (0:00–0:26) As the four voices enter, which texture gradually emerges?
   a. monophonic   b. polyphonic   c. homophonic
2. (0:00–0:26) What is the term for the musical procedure in which the voices replicate in turn the notes of a melody?
   a. replication   b. citation   c. imitation
3. (0:00–0:44) The opening stanza of *Ave Maria* contains eight words divided into four syntactical units (units of meaning): Ave Maria—gratia plena—dominus tecum—virgo serena. Josquin clarifies the meaning of the text by grouping the words in pairs, and he does so how?
   a. by assigning each pair of words first to the soprano and then to the other voices
   b. by assigning each pair of words first to the bass and then to the other voices
4. (0:00–0:44) In each case, what is the order in which the voices enter?
   a. soprano, tenor, alto, bass
   b. bass, tenor, alto, soprano
   c. soprano, alto, tenor, bass
5. (1:05–1:20) Now the voices work toward a joyful climax on the word "laetitia" ("joy") and Josquin expresses the meaning of this passage by writing music that does what?
   a. ascends and then descends in an excited fashion
   b. forcefully reiterates the same pitches
   c. emphatically descends to a lower tessitura
6. (1:18) Which voice joyfully sings the final "laetitia"?
   a. soprano   b. male alto   c. bass
7. (2:15–2:40) A new stanza of text appears, and the meter and texture change for the sake of variety. Which is correct?
   a. Triple-meter polyphony gives way to duple-meter homophony.
   b. Duple-meter homophony gives way to triple-meter polyphony.
   c. Duple-meter polyphony gives way to triple-meter homophony.
8. (4:23–end) The final word of the motet is "Amen," which is Hebrew for "and so be it." Josquin declaims the meaning of this word by having the voices sing what with emphasis?
   a. "A" and "men" to two different pitches
   b. "A" and "men" to the same pitches
9. Which is true throughout this motet?
   a. In the imitative sections, the soprano and alto always enter before the tenor and bass.
   b. In the imitative sections, the tenor and bass always enter before the soprano and alto.
10. Do instruments accompany the voices on this performance? If not, then what is this style of performance called?
    a. imitative   b. a cappella   c. Vatican style

THE COUNTER-REFORMATION AND PALESTRINA (1525–1594)

On October 31, 1517, an obscure Augustinian monk named Martin Luther nailed to the door of the castle church at Wittenberg, Germany, ninety-five complaints against the Roman Catholic Church—his famous ninety-five theses. With this defiant act, Luther began what has come to be called the Protestant Reformation. Luther and his fellow reformers sought to bring an end to corruption within the Roman Catholic Church: the selling of indulgences (forgiveness of sin in exchange for money), the unholy lives of leading churchmen (at least two popes admitted to having illegitimate children), and the abuse of power in church appointments (one pope rewarded the fifteen-year-old keeper of his pet monkey by making him a cardinal). By the time the Protestant Reformation had run its course, most of Germany, Switzerland, the Low Countries, and all of England, as well as parts of France, Austria, Bohemia, Poland, and Hungary, had gone over to the Protestant cause. The established Roman Catholic Church was shaken to its very foundations.

Protestant Reformation

    In response to the Protestant Reformation, the Church of Rome began to clean its own house. The cleansing applied not only to matters of spirituality and church administration but also to art, liturgy, and music. Nudity in religious paintings, musical instruments within the church, pop tunes and catchy

Male Choirs

On our recording of Palestrina's *Sanctus*, the soprano part is performed by men singing in head voice, or what is called **falsetto** voice. This is a historically authentic manner of performance. Following an early decree of the Apostle Paul, women in the Middle Ages and Renaissance were not allowed to sing in the Roman Church, except in convents. Similarly, women were not allowed to appear in public in theatrical productions within territories under strict church control. Thus, most polyphonic church choirs in the Renaissance were exclusively male, the soprano part being performed by either choirboys or adult men singing in falsetto. Beginning in 1562, however, **castratos** (castrated males) were introduced into the papal chapel, mainly as a money-saving measure. A single castrato could produce as much volume as two falsettists or three or four boys. Castrati were renowned for their power and their great lung capacity, which allowed them to execute unusually long phrases in a single breath. Surprisingly, castrati sopranos remained a hallmark of the papal chapel until 1903, when they were officially banned by Pope Pius X.

Church of St. Frediano, Lucca

All-male choir with choirboys for the soprano part as depicted in a sixteenth-century Italian fresco.

FIGURE 9–7

A portrait of Giovanni Palestrina. Palestrina was the first important composer of the Church to have been a layman rather than a member of the clergy.

Scala/Art Resource, NY

rhythms in the midst of polyphonic Masses, and married church singers—all of these "transgressions" were now deemed inappropriate to a truly pious environment.

The reform movement that promoted a more conservative and austere art within the established Church is called the **Counter-Reformation.** Its spirit was institutionalized in the **Council of Trent** (1545–1563), a congress of bishops and cardinals held in the small town of Trent in the Italian Alps. What bothered the Catholic reformers most about the church music of the day was that the incessant entry of voices in musical imitation obscured the text—excessively dense counterpoint was burying the word of the Lord. As one well-placed bishop said mockingly:

> In our times they [composers] have put all their industry and effort into the writing of imitative passages, so that while one voice says "Sanctus," another says "Sabaoth," still another says "Gloria tua," with howling, bellowing, and stammering, so that they more nearly resemble cats in January than flowers in May.

Initially, the assembled prelates considered banning music altogether from the service or limiting it to just the old, monophonic Gregorian chant. But the timely appearance of a few sacred compositions by Giovanni Pierluigi da Palestrina (1525–1594), among them his *Mass for Pope Marcellus* (1562), showed the Council that sacred polyphony for four, five, or six voices could still be written in a clear, dignified manner. For his role in maintaining a place for composed polyphony within the established Church, Palestrina came to be called "the savior of church music" (Fig. 9–7).

Female Choirs in Convents

Although public church choirs in the Middle Ages and Renaissance were all-male ensembles, there was still much opportunity for women to make music. They did so as singers and performers in secular genres, such as the chanson* and madrigal*, at court and in the home. In convents, too, women performed, yet always under the watchful eye of an outside father superior. Behind cloistered walls, the sisters sang not only Gregorian chant but also the latest polyphonic Masses and motets of Palestrina and Orlando di Lasso (c1530–1594). They, too, had old manuscripts of plainsong*, and

Nuns in the choir stalls of their convent singing a religious service, from a fifteenth-century English manuscript.

this monophonic chant they transposed into their own higher vocal range. When it came to singing polyphony, the tenor and bass parts were played on an organ while the sisters sang alto and soprano. Thus organs and organists were of primary importance in convents. Yet because almost all music teachers in this period were males, cloistered women were denied proper tutors. When a nun tried to circumvent the rules of strict segregation by gender, painful consequences might result, as Sister Angela Serafina, nun and principal musician at the monastery of San Appolinare in Milan, learned in 1571:

> Suor Angela Serafina is to be without her veil [i.e., with a bare, shaven head] for three months. She is relieved of the organist's duties, nor may she return to this position for six years. The large harpsichord is not to be kept in her room, but somewhere else in the house; nor can she play it or any other keyboard, nor sing polyphony for three years. And every Wednesday for six months she is to eat on the floor of the refectory, and ask forgiveness for the disturbance she caused, for the scandal of having fed the [male] organist inside the convent. (from Robert L. Kendrick, *Celestial Sirens*)

So extreme a punishment for such a seemingly minor offense! Yet here we see the tension inherent in the very thought that women might make music in the Catholic Church during the austere Counter-Reformation.

Palestrina (Fig. 9–7) was born in the small town of that name outside Rome and spent almost his entire professional life as a singer and composer at various churches in and around the Vatican: Saint Peter's Basilica, Saint John Lateran, Saint Mary Major, and the **Sistine Chapel,** the pope's private chapel within his Vatican apartments (see Fig. 9–6). But in 1555, Paul IV, one of the more zealous of the reforming popes, dismissed Palestrina from the Sistine Chapel because he was a married layman not conforming to the strict rule of celibacy. Later, under a new pope, Palestrina returned to papal employment at Saint Peter's, holding the titles *maestro di cappella* (master of the chapel) and ultimately *maestro compositore* (master composer).

biography of Palestrina

The *Sanctus* of Palestrina's *Missa Aeterna Christi Munera* (*Mass: Eternal Gifts of Christ*) epitomizes the musical spirit of the Counter-Reformation that then radiated from Rome. (Remember, a Sanctus is the fourth of five parts of the Ordinary of the Mass* that composers traditionally set to music; see page 83.) Palestrina's *Sanctus* unfolds slowly and deliberately with long notes gradually giving way to shorter, faster-moving ones, but without catchy rhythms or a strong beat. As is true for Gregorian chant*, the melodic lines move mainly in stepwise fashion, avoiding large leaps and chromatic turns. The sober mood is created in part by the careful use of imitative counterpoint. Each phrase of text is assigned its own motive*, which appears, in turn, in each voice. A motive used in this fashion is called a **point of imitation.** Palestrina's *Sanctus* has four points of imitation (see examples in the following Listening Guide). The first enters in the order soprano, alto, tenor, bass, and the music works to a cadence*. While the soprano and bass conclude the cadence, the alto and tenor begin the second point of imitation and so on. Palestrina was a master at sewing a cadence to the beginning of a new point of imitation. The listener experiences not only a sense of satisfaction on arrival at the cadence, but also a feeling of ongoing progress as the new point pushes forward. As you listen to the *Sanctus*, follow the diagram in the Listening Guide and see if you can hear when the voices are cadencing and when a new point of imitation begins.

sewing together points of imitation

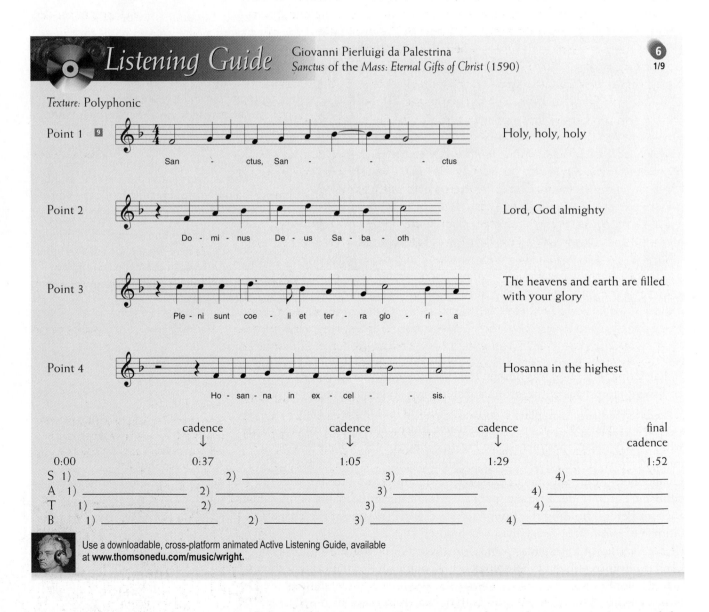

Listening Guide

Giovanni Pierluigi da Palestrina
Sanctus of the Mass: Eternal Gifts of Christ (1590)

6
1/9

Texture: Polyphonic

Point 1   San - ctus, San - - - ctus   Holy, holy, holy

Point 2   Do - mi - nus De - us Sa - ba - oth   Lord, God almighty

Point 3   Ple - ni sunt coe - li et ter - ra glo - ri - a   The heavens and earth are filled with your glory

Point 4   Ho - sa - na in ex - cel - - sis.   Hosanna in the highest

	cadence ↓		cadence ↓		cadence ↓		final cadence
0:00	0:37		1:05		1:29		1:52
S 1) _____	2) _____		3) _____		4) _____		
A 1) _____	2) _____		3) _____		4) _____		
T 1) _____	2) _____		3) _____		4) _____		
B 1) _____	2) _____		3) _____		4) _____		

Use a downloadable, cross-platform animated Active Listening Guide, available at **www.thomsonedu.com/music/wright.**

Palestrina's serene music best captures the somber, restrained spirit of the Counter-Reformation, embodying in its quiet simplicity all that Roman Catholic authority thought proper church music should be. After his death in 1594, the legend of Palestrina, "savior of church music," continued to grow.

Later composers such as Bach (*Mass in B minor,* 1733) and Mozart (*Requiem Mass,* 1791) incorporated elements of Palestrina's style into their sacred compositions. Even in our universities today, courses in counterpoint for advanced music students usually include some practice in composing in the pure, contrapuntally correct style of Palestrina. Thus the spirit of the Counter-Reformation, distilled into a set of contrapuntal rules, has continued to influence musicians long after the Renaissance came to an end.

POPULAR MUSIC IN THE RENAISSANCE

The Masses and motets of Josquin and Palestrina represent the "high" art of the Renaissance—learned music for the church. But secular, popular music flourished in the Renaissance as well. Indeed, the sixteenth century witnessed an increase in commerce and trade, and with it came a growing middle class. Though it constituted only about 6 percent of the population, the middle class was concentrated in the cities, where the new technology of music printing was beginning to flourish. Naturally, the urban middle class had different, more popular musical tastes than did the high churchmen and the nobles.

a growing middle class

In truth, there had always been popular music for the less exalted members of society. Dance music and popular songs, for example, are indigenous to all classes in all societies. But like rock musicians today, popular musicians in the Middle Ages performed without benefit of written musical notation. Most people in the Middle Ages were completely illiterate, and certainly could not read complicated music manuscripts. Written music was traditionally the private preserve of a wealthy, educated elite.

unwritten music

All this changed, however, with Johann Gutenberg's invention of printing by movable type around 1460. Printing revolutionized the world of information in the late fifteenth century no less than did the computer in the late twentieth century. Hundreds of copies of a book could be produced quickly once the type for a book had been set. The first printed book of music appeared in Venice in 1501, and to this important event can be traced the origins of the "music business" of today. The standard "press run" for a printed book of music was usually 500 copies. Mass production drastically reduced the cost of each book, putting notated music within reach of the banker, merchant, lawyer, and shopkeeper.

music printing

What is more, the new consumers lured to the market by a lower-cost product wanted a more immediately accessible sort of entertainment. They sought a simpler, more tuneful, more chordal music that they could play at home. They also preferred songs in their own vernacular tongue, not the Latin of the Church. Thus sixteenth-century printers published countless volumes of songs in Italian, Spanish, French, German, Dutch, and English.

FIGURE 9–8

Singers of a four-part madrigal during the middle of the sixteenth century. Women were very much a part of this secular, non-religious music-making.

Musée de l'Hôtel Lallemant, Bourges/The Bridgeman Art Library

The Madrigal

About 1530, a new kind of popular song arose that soon took Europe by storm: the madrigal. A **madrigal** is a piece for several solo voices (usually four or five) that sets a vernacular poem, most often about love, to music. The madrigal arose in Italy but soon spread to northern European countries. So popular did the madrigal become that by 1630 some 40,000 pieces had been printed by publishers eager to satisfy public demand. The madrigal was a truly social art, one that both men and women could enjoy (Fig. 9–8).

music depicts the text

madrigal comes to England

Of all the musical genres of the Renaissance, the madrigal best exemplifies the humanist requirement that music express the meaning of the text. In a typical madrigal, each word or phrase of poetry will receive its own musical gesture. Thus, when the madrigal text says "chase after" or "follow quickly," the music becomes fast and one voice chases after another in musical imitation*. For words such as "pain," "anguish," "death," and "cruel fate," the madrigal composer almost invariably employs a twisting chromatic* scale or a biting dissonance*. This practice of depicting the text by means of a descriptive musical gesture, whether subtly or jokingly as a musical pun, is called **word painting.** Word painting became all the rage with madrigal composers in Italy and England. Even today such musical clichés as a falling melody for "swoon" and a dissonance for "pain" are called **madrigalisms.**

The madrigal was born in Italy, but popular favor soon carried it over the Alps to Germany, Denmark, the Low Countries, and England. The first madrigals to be printed in England appeared in a 1588 publication titled *Musica transalpina* (*Music from Across the Alps*), a collection of more than fifty madrigals, mainly by Italian composers, with the texts translated into English. Soon English composers—all contemporaries of William Shakespeare (1564–1616)—were writing their own madrigals to new English poems. One of the best of the English madrigalists was Thomas Weelkes (1576–1623), an organist who spent most of his career in rural Chichester but ended his days in London, an honorary Gentleman of the Royal Chapel.

In 1601, Weelkes and twenty-three other English composers each contributed a madrigal to a collection titled *The Triumphes of Oriana*, an album of music compiled in honor of the Virgin Queen Elizabeth (1533–1603). (Oriana, a legendary British princess and maiden, was used as the poetic nickname of Queen Elizabeth.) Weelkes's contribution to *The Triumphes of Oriana* was the six-voice madrigal *As Vesta Was from Latmos Hill Descending*. Its text, likely fashioned by Weelkes himself, is a rather confused mixture of images from classical mythology: the Roman goddess Vesta, descending the Greek mountain of Latmos, spies Oriana (Elizabeth) ascending the hill; the nymphs and shepherds attending the goddess Diana desert her to sing the praises of Oriana. The sole virtue of this verse is that it provides frequent opportunity for word painting in music.

As the text commands, the music descends, ascends, runs, mingles imitatively, and offers "mirthful tunes" to the maiden queen. Elizabeth herself played lute and harpsichord, and loved to dance (Fig. 9–9). Weelkes saw fit to end his madrigal with cries of "Long live fair Oriana"—an overt example of an artist flattering a patron in Elizabethan England.

Madrigals such a Weelkes's *When Vesta Was from Latmos Hill Descending* were popular because they were fun to sing. Vocal lines were written within a comfortable range, melodies were often triadic, rhythms were catchy, and the music was full of puns. When Vesta descends the mountain, so too her music moves down the scale; when Oriana (Queen Elizabeth) ascends, her music does likewise; when Diana, the goddess of virginity, is all alone—you guessed it, we hear a solo voice! With sport like this to be had, no wonder the popularity of the madrigal endured beyond the Renaissance. Even today the madrigal remains a staple of a cappella singing groups in North American and European colleges and universities.

FIGURE 9–9

A painting believed to show Queen Elizabeth dancing with the Duke of Leicester.

© Penshurst, Kent

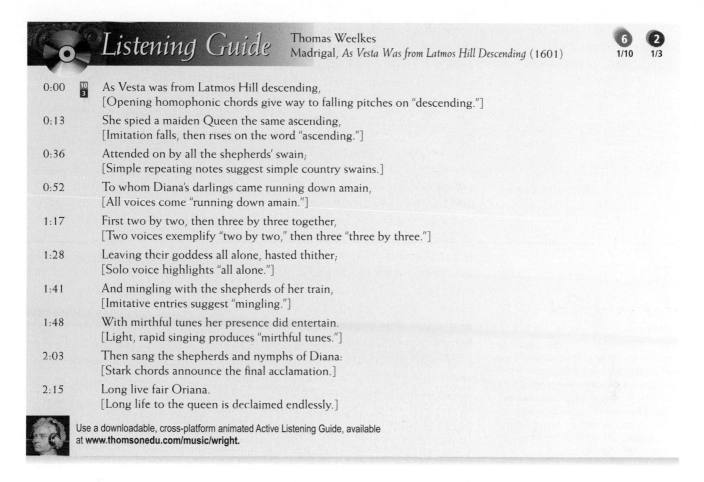

Listening Guide

Thomas Weelkes
Madrigal, *As Vesta Was from Latmos Hill Descending* (1601)

6 1/10   2 1/3

0:00   As Vesta was from Latmos Hill descending,
[Opening homophonic chords give way to falling pitches on "descending."]

0:13   She spied a maiden Queen the same ascending,
[Imitation falls, then rises on the word "ascending."]

0:36   Attended on by all the shepherds' swain;
[Simple repeating notes suggest simple country swains.]

0:52   To whom Diana's darlings came running down amain,
[All voices come "running down amain."]

1:17   First two by two, then three by three together,
[Two voices exemplify "two by two," then three "three by three."]

1:28   Leaving their goddess all alone, hasted thither;
[Solo voice highlights "all alone."]

1:41   And mingling with the shepherds of her train,
[Imitative entries suggest "mingling."]

1:48   With mirthful tunes her presence did entertain.
[Light, rapid singing produces "mirthful tunes."]

2:03   Then sang the shepherds and nymphs of Diana:
[Stark chords announce the final acclamation.]

2:15   Long live fair Oriana.
[Long life to the queen is declaimed endlessly.]

Use a downloadable, cross-platform animated Active Listening Guide, available at **www.thomsonedu.com/music/wright**.

Listening Exercise 17

Weelkes
As Vesta Was from Latmos Hill Descending

 6 1/10   2 1/3

ThomsonNOW™

To take this Listening Exercise online and receive feedback or email answers to your instructor, go to *ThomsonNOW* for this chapter.

So striking is the depiction of the text through music in the madrigal of the Renaissance that these instances of musical word painting are called madrigalisms. Often the music depicts the text by its motion (up, down, or stationary) or by its texture (polyphonic, monophonic, or homophonic). At these moments, the word painting is so obvious as to be amusing, and that makes several of the following questions rather easy to answer.

1. (0:00–0:13) The text sets the scene of this madrigal at the top of Latmos Hill, a mountain in Greek mythology. At the beginning, we hear sounds that are what?
   a. generally low with male voices predominating
   b. generally high with female voices predominating
2. (0:00–0:34) Which is true about the direction of the music for the words "descending" and "ascending"?
   a. It ascends for "descending" and descends for "ascending."
   b. There is no clear direction, and word painting is not present.
   c. It descends for "descending" and ascends for "ascending."

3. (0:36–0:47) Which is true about the music for the words "attended on"?
   a. The singers mostly repeat the same pitches, so the music sounds static.
   b. It ascends.
   c. It descends.
4. (0:58–1:13) For the word "running," what does the music do?
   a. It goes faster and ascends.
   b. It goes faster and descends.
   c. It goes slower and remains stationary in pitch.
5. (1:28–1:33) What is the texture of the music at the words "Leaving their goddess"?
   a. imitative polyphony
   b. monophony
   c. homophony
6. (1:34–1:37) What is the texture of the music at the words "all alone"?
   a. imitative polyphony
   b. monophony
   c. homophony

7. (2:03–2:10) What is the texture at the words "Then sang the shepherds"?
   a. imitative polyphony
   b. monophony
   c. homophony

8. (2:15–3:09) What is the texture at the words "Long live fair Oriana"?
   a. imitative polyphony
   b. monophony
   c. homophony

9. (2:20–end) When the bass enters with a presentation of "Long live fair Oriana," what is the nature of the musical line?

   a. The bass sings long, steady notes to emphasize the word "long."
   b. The bass sings rapid notes, joining the many acclamations of the upper voices.

10. Which of the following is true?
   a. The performance of this madrigal is a cappella with one singer to a part.
   b. The performance of this madrigal is a cappella with two singers to a part.
   c. The performance of this madrigal is not a cappella.

ThomsonNOW

ThomsonNOW for *Listening to Music, 5th Edition*, and *Listening to Western Music* will assist you in understanding the content of this chapter with lesson plans generated for your specific needs. In addition, you may complete this chapter's Listening Exercises in ThomsonNOW's interactive environment, as well as download Active Listening Guides and other materials that will help you succeed in this course.

Key Words

humanism (**94**)	Counter-	madrigal (**103**)
motet (**96**)	Reformation (**100**)	word painting (**104**)
a cappella (**96**)	Council of Trent (**100**)	madrigalism (**104**)
imitation (**97**)	Sistine Chapel (**101**)	
falsetto (**100**)	point of imitation	
castrato (**100**)	(**102**)	

Checklist of Musical Style

Representative composers
Desprez
Palestrina
Byrd
Lasso
Weelkes
Dowland

Principal genres
sacred Mass and motet
secular chanson and madrigal
instrumental dance

Renaissance: 1475–1600

Melody	Mainly stepwise motion within moderately narrow range; still mostly stepwise, but some intense chromaticism found in madrigals from end of period
Harmony	More careful use of dissonance than in Middle Ages as the triad, a consonant chord, becomes the basic building block of harmony
Rhythm	Duple meter is now as common as triple meter; rhythm in sacred vocal music (Mass and motet) is relaxed and without strong downbeats; rhythm in secular vocal music (chanson and madrigal) and in instrumental dances is usually lively and catchy, with frequent use of syncopation
Color	Although more music for instruments alone has survived, the predominant sound remains that of unaccompanied vocal music, whether for soloists or for choir

the Baroque period as it is of that of Bach and Handel at the end. During the Baroque period, several new musical genres emerge: opera, cantata, and oratorio enter the realm of vocal music, and sonata and concerto appear among the instrumental types.

| 1680 | 1690 | 1700 | 1710 | 1720 | 1730 | 1740 | 1750 |

BAROQUE

● 1685 Johann Sebastian Bach and George Frideric Handel born in Germany

● 1687 Isaac Newton publishes his masterpiece *Mathematical Principles*

● 1689 Jean-Baptiste Lully composes opera *Armide* in Paris

● c1689 Henry Purcell composes opera *Dido and Aeneas* in London

c1681–1700 Arcangelo Corelli publishes violin sonatas in Rome

c1700–1730 Antonio Vivaldi composes concertos in Venice

● 1711 Handel moves to London and writes operas

● 1723 Bach moves to Leipzig and writes cantatas

● 1741 Handel composes oratorio *Messiah*

Introduction to Baroque Art and Music

Music historians agree, with unusual unanimity, that Baroque music first appeared in northern Italy in the early seventeenth century. To be sure, around 1600, certain qualities of the Italian madrigal—virtuosic solo singing, for example—came to be emphasized in a way that created an entirely new sound. The older equal-voiced choral polyphony of the Renaissance receded in importance as a new, more flamboyant style gained in popularity. Eventually, the new style was given a new name: Baroque.

Baroque is the term used to describe the arts generally during the period 1600–1750. It is taken from the Portuguese word *barroco*, meaning a pearl of irregular shape then used in jewelry and fine decorations. Critics applied the term "Baroque" to indicate excessive ornamentation in the visual arts and a rough, bold instrumental sound in music. Thus, originally, *Baroque* had a negative connotation: it signified distortion, excess, and extravagance. Only during the twentieth century, with a new-found appreciation of the painting of Peter Paul Rubens (1577–1640) and the music of Antonio Vivaldi (1678–1741) and J. S. Bach (1685–1750), among others, has the term *Baroque* come to assume a positive meaning in Western cultural history.

FIGURES 10–1 AND 10–2

(left) The high altar at Saint Peter's Basilica, Rome, with baldachin by Gian Lorenzo Bernini. Standing more than ninety feet high, this canopy is marked by twisted columns and curving shapes, color, and movement, all typical of Baroque art. (right) Saint Peter's Square, designed by Bernini in the mid-seventeenth century. The expanse is so colossal it seems to swallow people, cars, and buses.

BAROQUE ARCHITECTURE AND MUSIC

What strikes us most when standing before a monument of Baroque design, such as the basilica of Saint Peter in Rome or the palace of Versailles outside of Paris, is that everything is constructed on the grandest scale. The plazas, buildings, colonnades, gardens, and fountains are all massive. Look at the ninety-foot-high altar canopy inside Saint Peter's, designed by Gian Lorenzo Bernini (1598–1680), and imagine how it dwarfs the priest below (Fig. 10–1).

Scala/Art Resource, NY

© Bob Krist/Corbis

Outside the basilica, a circle of colonnades forms a courtyard large enough to encompass several football fields (Fig. 10–2). Or consider the French king's palace of Versailles, constructed during the reign of Louis XIV (1643–1715), so monumental in scope that it formed a small independent city, home to several thousand court functionaries (see Fig. 12–2). *palaces and churches of great size*

The music composed for performance in such vast expanses could also be grandiose. While at first the Baroque orchestra was small, under King Louis XIV it sometimes swelled to more than eighty players. Similarly, choral works for Baroque churches sometimes required twenty-four, forty-eight, or even fifty-three separate lines or parts. These compositions for massive choral forces epitomize the grand or "colossal" Baroque.

Once the exteriors of the large Baroque palaces and churches were built, the artists of the time rushed in to fill these expanses with abundant, perhaps even excessive, decoration. It was as if the architect had created a large vacuum, and into it energetically raced the painter, sculptor, and carver to fill the void. Examine again the interior of Saint Peter's (Fig. 10–1), and notice the ornamentation on the ceiling, as well as the elaborate twists and turns of Bernini's canopy. Or consider the Austrian monastery of Saint Florian (Fig. 10–3); there are massive columns, yet the frieze connecting them is richly decorated, as is the ceiling above. Here elaborate scrolls and floral capitals add warmth and humanity to what would otherwise be a vast, cold space. *filled with decoration*

Similarly, when expressed in the music of the Baroque era, this love of energetic detail within large-scale compositions took the form of a highly ornamental melody set upon a solid chordal foundation. Sometimes the decoration almost seems to overrun the fundamental harmonic structure of the piece. Notice in Figure 10–4 the abundance of melodic flourishes in just a few measures of music for violin by Arcangelo Corelli (1653–1713). Such ornaments were equally popular with the singers of the early Baroque period, when the cult of the vocal virtuoso first emerged. *musical decoration above a solid support*

FIGURE 10–3

Church of the monastery of Saint Florian, Austria (1686–1708). The powerful pillars and arches set a strong structural framework, while the painted ceiling and heavily foliated capitals provide decoration and warmth.

Chorherrenstift St. Florian, Austria

FIGURE 10–4

Arcangelo Corelli's sonata for violin and *basso continuo*, Opus 5, No. 1. The bass provides the structural support, while the violin adds elaborate decoration above.

Yale University Music Library

FIGURE 10–5

Rubens's *The Horrors of War* (1638) is a reaction to the Thirty Years' War (1618–1648) that ravaged Europe at this time. Here Mars, the god of war (center, wearing a military helmet), is pulled to the right by Fury and to the left by a mostly naked Venus, goddess of love. Beneath these figures, the populace suffers.

BAROQUE PAINTING AND MUSIC

FIGURE 10–6

Judith Beheading Holofernes (c1615) by Artemisia Gentileschi. The grisly scene of Judith slaying the tyrant general was painted several times by Gentileschi, perhaps as a vivid way of demonstrating her abhorrence of aggressive male domination.

Many of the principles at work in Baroque architecture are also found in Baroque painting and music. Baroque canvases are usually large and colorful. Most important, they are overtly dramatic. Drama in painting is created by means of contrast: bold colors are pitted against one another; bright light is set against darkness; and lines are placed at right angles to one another, which suggests tension and energetic movement. Figure 10–5 shows Peter Paul Rubens's *The Horrors of War.* The large canvas swirls with a chaotic scene that is extravagant yet sensual, typical qualities of Baroque art. Barely visible in the right lower foreground is a woman with a broken lute, which symbolizes that harmony (music) cannot exist beside the discord of war. Figure 10–6 paints an even more horrific scene: Judith visiting retribution upon the Assyrian general Holofernes, as depicted by Artemisia Gentileschi (1593–1652). Here the play of light and dark creates a dramatic effect, the stark blue and red colors add intensity, while the head of the victim, set at a right angle to his body, suggests an unnatural motion. Baroque art sometimes delights in the pure shock value of presenting gruesome events from history or myth in a dramatic way.

Music of the Baroque is also highly dramatic. We observed in the music of the Renaissance (1475–1600) a growing awareness of the capacity of this art to sway, or affect, the emotions. This led in the early seventeenth century to an aesthetic theory called the Doctrine of Affections. The **Doctrine of Affections** held that different musical moods could and should be used to influence the emotions, or affections, of the listener. A musical setting should reinforce the intended "affection" of the text. Yet each work of Baroque art in general confines itself to one specific emotion, keeping each unit of space and expression separate and distinct from the next. There is a unity of mood in each work of art. So, too, writers about music spoke of the need to dramatize the text yet maintain a single affection—be it rage, revenge, sorrow, joy, or love—from beginning to end of a piece. Not surprisingly, the single most important new genre to emerge in the Baroque period was opera. Here the drama of the stage joined with music to form a powerful new affective medium.

CHARACTERISTICS OF BAROQUE MUSIC

Perhaps more than any period in the history of music, the Baroque (1600–1750) gave rise to a variety of musical styles, beginning with the expressive monody of Claudio Monteverdi (1567–1643) and ending with the complex polyphony of J. S. Bach (1685–1750). It also saw the introduction of many new musical genres—opera, cantata, oratorio, sonata, concerto, and suite—each of which is discussed in the following chapters. Yet despite the quick stylistic changes and all the new types of music created, two elements remain constant throughout the Baroque period: an expressive melody and a strong supporting bass.

Expressive Melody

Renaissance music, as we saw in Chapter 9, was dominated by polyphonic texture in which the voices spin out a web of imitative counterpoint. The nature and importance of each of the lines is about equal, as the following graphic suggests:

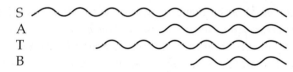

Renaissance had equal voice imitation

In early Baroque music, however, the voices are no longer equal. Rather, a polarity develops in which the musical emphasis gravitates toward the top and bottom lines:

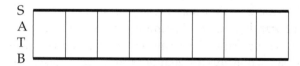

Baroque emphasizes top and bottom

Renaissance vocal music was mostly ensemble music—motets, Masses, and madrigals for groups of vocalists, even if there was only one singer on a part. In the early Baroque, however, the musical focus shifts from vocal ensemble to accompanied solo song. A choir might be a useful medium to convey the abstract religious thoughts of the multitudes, but to communicate raw human emotions, direct appeal by an individual soloist now seemed more appropriate. The new kind of solo singing was at first called **monody** (from Greek terms meaning "to sing alone"). A single singer stepped forward, accompanied by a very few supporting instruments, to project a highly charged text. Within the medium of monody, the vocal virtuoso would soon emerge, the star of the court theater and the operatic stage.

importance of accompanied solo song

The *Basso Continuo*

Monody emphasizes a solo melody, but one supported by chords springing up vertically from the bass. In simple terms, the soprano carries the melody while the bass provides a strong harmonic support. In between, the middle voices do little more than fill out the texture. If Renaissance music was conceived

Columbus Museum of Art

FIGURE 10–7

A Lady with Theorbo (c1670) by John Michael Wright. The bass strings are at the top of the instrument and off the fingerboard. The theorbo was often used to play the *basso continuo* in the seventeenth century.

polyphonically and horizontally, line by line, that of the early Baroque period is organized homophonically and vertically, chord by chord.

The bass-driven, chordal support in Baroque music is called the ***basso continuo,*** and it is played by one or more instruments. Figure 10–7 shows a woman singing to the accompaniment of a large plucked string instrument called the theorbo. This instrument has more low strings than its close cousin the lute, which allows it to not only strum chords but also play low bass notes. In the early seventeenth century, a theorbo or some other kind of bass lute often played the *basso continuo.* Figure 10–8 shows a solo violinist accompanied by two instruments: a cello-like instrument called the *viola da gamba,* which plays the bass line, and a harpsichord, which improvises chords built above that bass line. The violin performs an expressive melody while the other two instruments provide the *basso continuo.* Harpsichord and low string instrument formed the most common *basso continuo* in the Baroque period. Indeed, it is the continual tinkling of the harpsichord, in step with low sounds of a cello or *viola da gamba,* that signals the listener that the music being played comes from the Baroque. Coincidentally, the top-bottom structure of monodic singing in Baroque music is not conceptually different from the straight-ahead rock 'n' roll music of today with electric bass; in both styles, an expressive soloist sings above a rock-solid bass, while a keyboardist, building upon the bass line, improvises chords in the middle of the texture.

What chords did the Baroque harpsichordist play? These were suggested to the performer by means of **figured bass**—a numerical shorthand placed below the bass line. A player familiar with chord formations would look at the bass line such as that given in Example 10–1a and improvise chords along the lines of those given in Example 10–1b. These improvised chords, generated from the bass according to the numerical code, support a melody above. Here, too, there is a modern parallel. Figured bass is similar in intent to the numerical code found in "fake books" used by jazz pianists today that suggest which chords to play beneath the written melody.

FIGURE 10–8

Basso continuo and violin. This continuo consists of a harpsichord and a large string instrument, the *viola da gamba,* or bass viol. The viol has six strings and frets (as on a guitar), and produces a slightly darker, less brilliant sound than members of the violin family. The gambist playing here is Eva Linfield.

Barrie-Kent Photographers

EXAMPLE 10–1

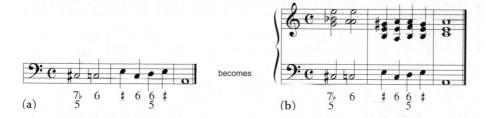

ELEMENTS OF BAROQUE MUSIC

Baroque music, as we have seen, is marked by grandeur, by passionate expression, and by drama. It is held together by a chordal framework and a strong bass line, both supplied by the *basso continuo.* These qualities can be heard in all three chronological subdivisions of Baroque music: early Baroque (1600–1660), middle Baroque (1660–1710), and late Baroque (1710–1750). In the music of the early Baroque in particular, the artistic expression of the voice and the richness of the harmony were especially intense. In the late Baroque, some of the excessively exuberant qualities of early Baroque music would be smoothed out and regularized by Bach and Handel (see Chapters 13 and 14). The following elements, however, are common to all periods of Baroque music.

exuberant quality of early Baroque music

Melody

In the Renaissance, melody was more or less all of one type. It was a direct, uncomplicated line that could be performed by either a voice or an instrument. But in early Baroque music, beginning about 1600, two different melodic styles begin to develop: a dramatic, virtuosic style in singing and a more mechanical style, full of figural repetitions, in instrumental music. Vocal melody in the Baroque is marked by quick shifts from long notes to very short ones, which creates an excited, exuberant sound. From time to time, the voice will luxuriate in a long flourish as it projects a single syllable in long melisma* (Ex. 10–2). Below are two melodies, one from Monteverdi's opera *Orfeo* at the beginning of the Baroque, and the other from Handel's oratorio *Messiah* from the end of the period.

long, luxuriant vocal lines

EXAMPLE 10–2

Tan - ta bel - lez-za il pa-ra-di - - - - - - - - - so ha se - co.
(Wherever so much beauty resides contains paradise.)

EXAMPLE 10–3

[Every valley] shall be ex - alt - - - - - - - - - - ed,

Generally, Baroque melody does not unfold in short, symmetrical units, but expands luxuriantly, and often unpredictably, over long musical phrases.

Harmony

chord progressions

Baroque harmonies are chordally conceived and tightly bound to the *basso continuo*. Composers in the early seventeenth century sometimes placed their chords in an order that sounds arbitrary to our modern ears. But as the century progressed, harmonies unfold more and more in familiar patterns, and standard harmonic progressions emerge; in other words, chord progressions* as we know them come into being. The shortest and most frequent of these is the V-I (dominant-tonic) cadence (see page 40). The advent of standard harmonic progressions like the V-I cadence gives added direction and cohesion to the music.

Attending this development is the growing importance—and eventual total domination—of the major and minor keys. These two scale patterns, major and minor, replaced the dozen or so scales (or "modes," as they were called) employed during the Renaissance and before. Moreover, as music was reduced to just two qualities of sound, the composer could play the dark minor off against the bright major, just as a painter might contrast light and dark (see Fig. 10–6), for particular effect.

Rhythm

uniform rhythms

Rhythm in Baroque music is characterized by uniformity. Just as a single mood, or affect, is carried from the beginning to the end of a piece of Baroque music, so the rhythmic patterns heard at the beginning will surface again and again, right to the end. Moreover, in Baroque music—especially instrumental music—a strong recurring beat is usually clearly audible, which pushes the music forward. This tendency toward rhythmic uniformity, clarity, and drive becomes more and more pronounced as the Baroque period proceeds. It culminates in the rhythmically propulsive music of Vivaldi and Bach.

Texture

predominantly homophonic texture

Baroque composers approached musical texture in ever-changing ways. Texture in the early Baroque is overwhelmingly homophonic, the *basso ostinato* providing a wholly chordal framework. Indeed, composers of the early seventeenth century rebelled against the predominantly polyphonic, imitative texture of the Renaissance. This initial hostility toward polyphony gradually diminished, however. In the late Baroque, composers such as Bach and Handel returned to contrapuntal writing, in part to add richness to the middle range of the standard top-bottom (soprano-bass) dominated texture.

Dynamics

sudden contrasts of dynamics

For the first time in the history of music, composers in early seventeenth-century Italy began to specify in the score the dynamic level at which they wanted their music played. The words they wrote in the music were very simple: *piano* (soft) and *forte* (loud). Sudden contrasts of dynamics were more prized than gradual crescendos and diminuendos. This practice of shifting the volume of sound suddenly from one level to another is called **terraced dynamics.** Terraced dynamics went hand in hand with clear contrasts between major and minor keys, as well as with abrupt changes in orchestration. By contrasting distinctly different dynamics, moods, and colors, composers of the Baroque created the one thing prized above all others in Baroque art: drama.

Key Words

Baroque (**110**)	monody (**113**)	terraced
Doctrine of	*basso continuo* (**114**)	dynamics (**116**)
Affections (**112**)	figured bass (**114**)	

ThomsonNOW™

ThomsonNOW for *Listening to Music, 5th Edition,* and *Listening to Western Music* will assist you in understanding the content of this chapter with lesson plans generated for your specific needs.

Early Baroque Vocal Music

Chapter

11

OPERA

Given the popularity of opera today—and the fact that there had been opera in China and Japan since the thirteenth century—it is surprising that this genre of music emerged comparatively late in the history of Western European culture. Not until around 1600 did opera appear, and its native soil was Italy.

Opera requires a union of music, drama, scenery, costumes, and often dance. It demands singers who can act or, in some cases, actors who can sing. In opera, all lines are sung, unlike in a Broadway musical, for example, in which the dialogue is spoken and only the emotional high points are sung. The text of an opera is called the **libretto** ("little book"), and it is normally written by a poet working in collaboration with the composer. Because all the text must be sung, opera creates a somewhat unnatural art. We don't usually sing to our roommate, "Get out of the bathroom, I need to get to class this morning." The advantage of communication in song, however, lies in the increased potential for expressive intensity, as the sung melody supports and amplifies the text. By combining orchestrally accompanied song, scenic design, and dramatic action to make opera, composers of the seventeenth century created for their day a genre not unlike the multimedia IMAX film of today. In opera, however, everything unfolds live on stage and in "real time."

The term *opera* literally means "work." The word was first employed in the early seventeenth century in the Italian phrase *opera drammatica in musica* ("a dramatic work set to music"). Early Baroque opera rejected the Renaissance belief that emotions could best be expressed by a group of singers gathered into a choir. The individual, not the multitude, was now deemed the best vehicle to convey heartfelt, personal feelings. From its inception, then, opera placed the solo singer at center stage. Then, as now, three laws ruled the opera house: (1) In opera, all parts of the drama are sung, mainly by soloists; (2) the major roles go to the best singers; and (3) the costs are enormous, in large measure because opera singers are the highest paid of all classical musicians.

The origins of opera can be traced to late sixteenth-century Italy—specifically, to progressive musicians and intellectuals in the cities of Florence, Mantua, and Venice (Fig. 11–1). Here, a

FIGURE 11–1

The major musical centers in northern Italy in the seventeenth century.

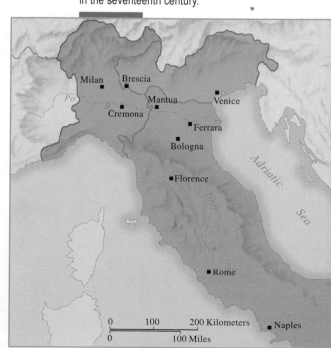

number of visionary thinkers continued to pursue a goal of late Renaissance humanism*—recapture the expressive power of ancient Greek music. Florence, in particular, was home to several outstanding musical intellectuals, including Vincenzo Galilei (1533–1591), the father of the famous astronomer Galileo Galilei (1564–1642). The elder Galilei and his followers believed that the power of Greek drama owed much to the fact that every line was sung, not spoken. In an attempt to imitate the ancient Greeks, the fathers of opera strove to create a theatrical medium in which the drama might be projected through vocal recitations sung to the plainest of accompaniments. While various composers tried their hand at this new genre in the years around 1600, it was not until 1607, with Claudio Monteverdi's *Orfeo*, that the first great opera emerged.

Claudio Monteverdi (1567–1643)

Claudio Monteverdi was a musical genius who could manifest his enormous talents equally well in a madrigal, a motet, or an opera (Fig. 11–2). He was born in the northern Italian town of Cremona in 1567 and moved to the larger city of Mantua (see Fig. 11–1) about 1590 to serve Duke Vincenzo Gonzaga as a singer and as a performer on string instruments. In 1601, Monteverdi was appointed director of music, and in this capacity he composed two operas for the court, *Orfeo* (1607) and *Ariana* (1608). But the duke failed to pay Monteverdi what he had promised. "I have never in my life suffered greater humiliation of the spirit than when I had to go and beg the treasurer for what was mine," said the composer some years later. Thus disenchanted with Mantua, Monteverdi accepted the much-coveted position of *maestro di cappella* at Saint Mark's in Venice (Fig. 11–3). Although called to Venice ostensibly to write church music for Saint Mark's, Monteverdi continued to compose opera as well. Among his important later works in this genre are *The Return of Ulysses* (1640) and *The Coronation of Poppea* (1642). He died in Venice in 1643 after thirty years of faithful service.

FIGURE 11–2

Portrait of Claudio Monteverdi by Bernardo Strozzi (1581–1644). Strozzi also painted the singer and composer Barbara Strozzi (see page 123).

FIGURE 11–3

Piazza San Marco painted by Gentile Bellini, c1500. Saint Mark's was the focal point of all religious and civic activities in Venice. In the 1630s, Venice became home to the first public opera houses.

Monteverdi's first opera—and the first important opera in the history of Western music—is his *Orfeo.* Because the aim of early opera was to reproduce elements of ancient Greek drama, it was only natural that the libretto for *Orfeo* drew from a tale found in classical Greek mythology. The leading character is Orfeo (Orpheus), the son of Apollo, the Greek god of the sun and of music. (Indeed, the very word *music* comes from the artistic muses who attended Apollo.) Orfeo, himself a demigod, finds love in the form of the beautiful Euridice, a mortal. No sooner are they married than she is killed by a poisonous snake and carried off to Hades (the ancient world's version of Hell). Orfeo vows to descend into the Underworld to rescue his beloved. This he nearly accomplishes by means of his divine musical powers, for Orfeo can make trees sway, calm savage beasts, and overcome demonic forces with the beauty of his song alone. The theme of *Orfeo,* then, is the divine power of music.

aimed to revive Greek drama

Monteverdi advances the drama in *Orfeo* mainly through **monody** (expressive solo singing to simple accompaniment), a medium thought to have approximated the singing of the ancient Greek theater. The simplest type of monody was recitative. **Recitative,** from the Italian word *recitativo* ("something recited"), is musically heightened speech, through which the plot of the opera is communicated to the audience. Because recitative attempts to mirror the natural stresses of everyday speech, it is often made up of rapidly repeating notes followed by one or two long notes at the ends of phrases, as in the following recitative from Act II of *Orfeo.*

emphasized expressive solo singing

EXAMPLE 11–1

A l'a-ma - ra no-vel-la   Ras-sem-bra l'in-fe-li - ceun mu-to sas-so
(At the bitter news the unhappy one resembled a mute stone)

Recitative in Baroque opera is accompanied only by the *basso continuo,* which consists, as we have seen, of a bass line and accompanying chords (Fig. 11–4). Such sparsely accompanied recitative is called **simple recitative** (*recitativo semplice* in Italian). (In the nineteenth century, recitative accompanied by the full orchestra, called *recitativo accompagnato,* would become the norm.) A good example of simple recitative can be heard at the beginning of the vocal excerpt from Act II of *Orfeo* discussed later in the Listening Guide.

In addition to recitative, Monteverdi made use of a more lyrical type of monody called aria. An **aria,** Italian for "song" or "ayre," is more passionate, more expansive, and more tuneful than a recitative. It also tends to have a clear meter and more regular rhythms. If a recitative tells what is happening on stage, an aria conveys what the character *feels* about those events. Similarly, whereas a recitative advances the plot, an aria usually brings the action to a halt so as to focus a spotlight on the emotional state of the singer. Finally, whereas a recitative often involves a rapid-fire delivery of text, an aria will work through text at a more leisurely pace; words are repeated to heighten their dramatic effect, and important

FIGURE 11–4

The beginning of the third act of Monteverdi's *Orfeo* (1607), from the original print of the opera. The vocal part of Orfeo is on the staff above; the slower-moving bass line of the *basso continuo* is below.

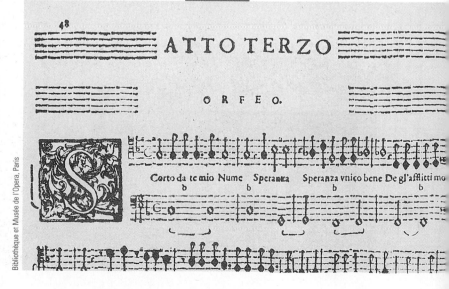

vowels are extended by means of vocal melismas*, as can be seen, for example, in Orfeo's aria "Powerful spirit."

EXAMPLE 11–2

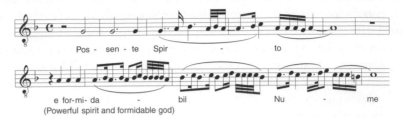

Pos - sen - te   Spir — to
e for-mi- da — bil   Nu — me
(Powerful spirit and formidable god)

FIGURE 11–5

Orfeo charms the guardians of Hades with his voice and lyre. A detail from a painting by Nicolas Poussin (1594–1665).

Bibliothèque et Musée de l'Opéra, Paris

An aria is an important, self-contained unit, both textually and musically. Whereas recitative is normally written in blank verse, an aria is usually composed in rhyming lines organized in stanzas (strophes). The text of Orfeo's aria "Powerful spirit" consists of three three-line stanzas, each with a rhyme scheme "a-b-a." Moreover, the music for each stanza begins and ends in the same key (G minor). Finally, operatic arias are nearly always accompanied not merely by the *basso continuo* but also by all or part of the orchestra. Monteverdi gives special prominence to the violins, cornettos, and harps in "Powerful spirit" to give added weight to the aria, as well as to show how music can charm even the guards of Hell (Fig. 11–5).

Recitative and aria are the two main styles of singing in Baroque opera, and in opera in general. In addition, there is a third style called arioso. **Arioso** is a manner of singing halfway between aria and recitative. It is more declamatory than an aria but has a less-rapid-fire delivery than a recitative. The lament that Orfeo sings on learning of the death of Euridice, "Thou art dead" (see Listening Guide below), is a classic example of arioso style.

Like all operas, *Orfeo* begins with a purely instrumental work that serves as a curtain raiser. Such instrumental introductions are usually called overtures, preludes, or sinfonias, but Monteverdi called his musical preamble a toccata. The term **toccata** (literally, "a touched thing") refers to an instrumental piece, for keyboard or other instruments, requiring great technical dexterity of the performers. It is, in other words, an instrumental showpiece. Here the trumpet races up and down the scale while many of the lower parts rapidly articulate repeating pitches. Monteverdi instructs that the toccata be sounded three times. Brief though it may be, this toccata is sufficiently long to suggest the richness and variety of instrumental sounds available to a composer in the early Baroque period. Its theatrical function, of course, is to call the audience to attention, to signal that the action is about to begin.

an instrumental curtain raiser

Listening Guide   Claudio Monteverdi
Orfeo (1607)
Toccata

6
1/11

0:00	11	Trumpet highlights highest part
0:28		Repeat of toccata
0:54		Repeat of toccata

Use a downloadable, cross-platform animated Active Listening Guide, available at www.thomsonedu.com/music/wright.

Although Monteverdi divided his *Orfeo* into five short acts, this ninety-minute opera was originally performed at Mantua without intermission. The first dramatic high point occurs midway through Act II, when the hero learns that his new bride, Euridice, has been claimed by the Underworld. In a heartfelt arioso, "Thou art dead," Orfeo laments his loss and vows to enter Hades to reclaim his beloved. Listen especially to the poignant conclusion in which Orfeo, by means of an ascending chromatic vocal line, bids farewell to earth, sky, and sun, and thus begins his journey to the land of the dead.

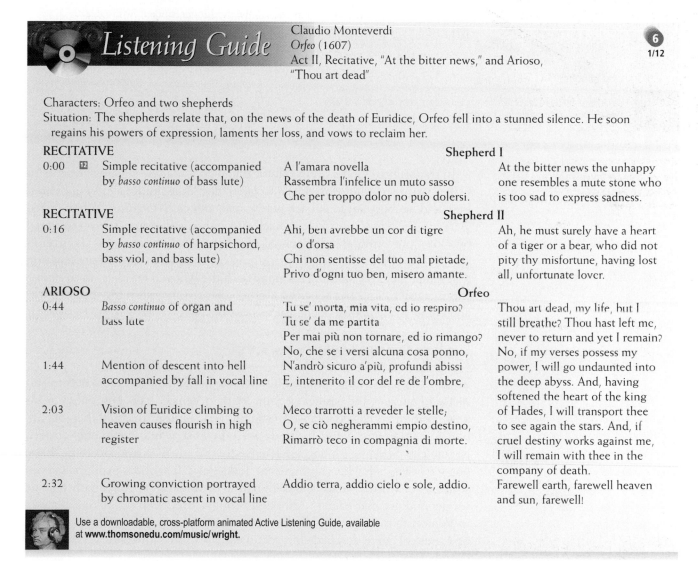

Listening Guide

Claudio Monteverdi
Orfeo (1607)
Act II, Recitative, "At the bitter news," and Arioso,
"Thou art dead"

6
1/12

Characters: Orfeo and two shepherds
Situation: The shepherds relate that, on the news of the death of Euridice, Orfeo fell into a stunned silence. He soon regains his powers of expression, laments her loss, and vows to reclaim her.

RECITATIVE   Shepherd I

0:00 [12]	Simple recitative (accompanied by *basso continuo* of bass lute)	A l'amara novella	At the bitter news the unhappy
		Rassembra l'infelice un muto sasso	one resembles a mute stone who
		Che per troppo dolor no può dolersi.	is too sad to express sadness.

RECITATIVE   Shepherd II

0:16	Simple recitative (accompanied by *basso continuo* of harpsichord, bass viol, and bass lute)	Ahi, ben avrebbe un cor di tigre o d'orsa	Ah, he must surely have a heart of a tiger or a bear, who did not
		Chi non sentisse del tuo mal pietade,	pity thy misfortune, having lost
		Privo d'ogni tuo ben, misero amante.	all, unfortunate lover.

ARIOSO   Orfeo

0:44	*Basso continuo* of organ and bass lute	Tu se' morta, mia vita, ed io respiro?	Thou art dead, my life, but I
		Tu se' da me partita	still breathe? Thou hast left me,
		Per mai più non tornare, ed io rimango?	never to return and yet I remain?
		No, che se i versi alcuna cosa ponno,	No, if my verses possess my
1:44	Mention of descent into hell accompanied by fall in vocal line	N'andrò sicuro a'più, profundi abissi	power, I will go undaunted into the deep abyss. And, having
		E, intenerito il cor del re de l'ombre,	softened the heart of the king of Hades, I will transport thee
2:03	Vision of Euridice climbing to heaven causes flourish in high register	Meco trarrotti a reveder le stelle;	to see again the stars. And, if
		O, se ciò negherammi empio destino,	cruel destiny works against me,
		Rimarrò teco in compagnia di morte.	I will remain with thee in the company of death.
2:32	Growing conviction portrayed by chromatic ascent in vocal line	Addio terra, addio cielo e sole, addio.	Farewell earth, farewell heaven and sun, farewell!

Use a downloadable, cross-platform animated Active Listening Guide, available at **www.thomsonedu.com/music/wright**.

Having descended to the shores of Hades, Orfeo now invokes all his musical powers to gain entry. In the aria "Powerful spirit," he addresses Charon, the spirit that controls access to the kingdom of the dead. Orfeo's elaborate, florid vocal style, aided by an exotic instrumental accompaniment, soon disarms the frightful guard.

Listening Guide

Claudio Monteverdi
Orfeo (1607)
Act III, Aria, "Powerful spirit" (strophes 1 and 2 only)

6
1/13

Characters: Orfeo and Charon
Situation: Orfeo pleads through his music that Charon grant passage into Hades

ARIA (Strophe 1)   Orfeo

0:00	Florid singing, joined by violin flourishes, above *basso continuo*	Possente spirto e formidabil nume, Senza cui far passaggio a l'altra riva Alma da corpo sciolta in van presume	Powerful spirit and formidable god, without whom no soul, deprived of body, may presume to pass to Hades' shore
1:35	Instrumental postlude played by *basso continuo* and two solo violins		

ARIA (Strophe 2)   Orfeo

1:57	Florid singing continues, joined now by cornettos, above *basso continuo*	Non viv'io, no, che poi di vita è priva Mia cara sposa, il cor non è più meco, E senza cor com'esser può ch'io viva?	I live no longer, since now my dear spouse is deprived of life, I have no heart within me, and without a heart how can I still be alive?
3:07	Instrumental postlude played by *basso continuo* and two solo cornettos		

Use a downloadable, cross-platform animated Active Listening Guide, available
at **www.thomsonedu.com/music/wright**.

In the original Greek myth, Pluto, the lord of Hades, releases Euridice to Orfeo with one condition: He is to have faith that she is following behind him, and he must not look back before reaching earth's surface. When Orfeo yields to the temptation to look back and embrace Euridice, she is reclaimed by Pluto forevermore. In his opera *Orfeo*, Monteverdi altered this tragic conclusion: Apollo intervenes, transforming his son Orfeo into a constellation that radiates eternal spiritual harmony with the beloved Euridice. In so doing, Monteverdi established what was to become a convention for seventeenth- and eighteenth-century opera: the *lieto fine*, or "happy ending."

CHAMBER CANTATA

Venice, a worldly city

In 1613, Claudio Monteverdi left his unrewarding job in Mantua to become director of music at the basilica of Saint Mark in Venice, Italy. Not only was his new position perhaps the most prestigious post a musician could then obtain, but Venice, a central port for trade with the East, was a remarkably cosmopolitan city. Said English traveler Thomas Coryat (c1577–1617) in 1605: "Here you see Poles, Slavs, Persians, Greeks, Turks, Jews, Christians of all the famous religions of Christendom, and each nation distinguished from another by its proper and peculiar habits." Although Monteverdi composed religious music in Venice, in this very worldly environment he also wrote opera, as well as a new musical genre that had emerged in early seventeenth-century Venice: the chamber cantata.

music for a private audience

Whereas opera was the dominant form of theatrical music during the Baroque period, the cantata became the primary genre of vocal **chamber music** (music for soloists performed in the home or a small auditorium). The word **cantata** literally means "something sung," as opposed to sonata, "something sounded" (played on a musical instrument). Because it was usually performed before a select group of listeners in a private residence, this genre is called the chamber cantata. Like opera, the seventeenth-century **chamber cantata** emphasized accompanied solo singing, and the subject matter usually concerned unrequited

Barbara Strozzi: Professional Composer

Until the twentieth century, very few women earned a living as professional composers. In the Middle Ages, for example, a few *trobairitz** wrote chansons, but to a woman, they were all members of the lesser nobility and not financially dependent on the success of their creations. So, too, a few women composed during the late Renaissance and early Baroque, but most were cloistered nuns who received their sustenance from the Church. The reason for the scarcity of independent women composers in the Baroque era is simple: only performance within the home was then thought to be an appropriate musical activity for ladies. Musical activities outside the home were not deemed proper because they smacked of "professionalism." Women did not go to university, nor did they engage in income-earning professions or trades.

There were, however, a few notable exceptions. Adriana Basile, an associate of Monteverdi at Mantua, carved out for herself a highly successful career as a virtuoso soprano, thereby laying claim to the title "the first diva." In 1678, Elena Piscopia became the first woman to receive a university degree, when she earned the title Doctor of Philosophy at the University of Padua, Italy, following a rigorous public examination carried out in Latin. We have seen the work of Artemisia Gentileschi (Fig. 10–6), a Florentine

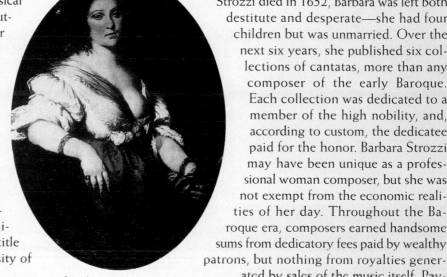

A portrait of Barbara Strozzi painted in the 1630s by Bernardo Strozzi, perhaps a relative.

Gemäldegalerie, Staatliche Kunstsammlungen, Dresden/ Erich Lessing/Art Resource, NY

painter who became the first woman to be admitted to the prestigious Accademia del Disegno and who went on to become a court painter for King Charles I of England. And to this list of illustrious women artists and intellectuals should be added the name of Barbara Strozzi.

Barbara Strozzi was a native of Venice, the illegitimate daughter of Giulio Strozzi, a man of letters who encouraged her musical development. Giulio Strozzi not only provided his daughter with lessons in composition but also organized domestic gatherings where her works could be heard. When Giulio Strozzi died in 1652, Barbara was left both destitute and desperate—she had four children but was unmarried. Over the next six years, she published six collections of cantatas, more than any composer of the early Baroque. Each collection was dedicated to a member of the high nobility, and, according to custom, the dedicatee paid for the honor. Barbara Strozzi may have been unique as a professional woman composer, but she was not exempt from the economic realities of her day. Throughout the Baroque era, composers earned handsome sums from dedicatory fees paid by wealthy patrons, but nothing from royalties generated by sales of the music itself. Payment of royalties, to both male and female composers, would not come until the twentieth century.

---

love or the heroes and heroines of ancient history and mythology. (Later, Bach would transform the secular chamber cantata into the sacred church cantata; see Chapter 13.) A typical chamber cantata lasts eight to fifteen minutes, and is usually divided into contrasting sections that alternate between recitative and aria. Although it lacks costumes and scenery, a chamber cantata might be considered a "mini-opera," but for a single soloist. The most prolific composer of chamber cantatas in the early Baroque was the Venetian Barbara Strozzi.

Barbara Strozzi (1619–1677) was steeped in the traditions of Claudio Monteverdi. Her teacher, Francesco Cavalli, was a pupil of Monteverdi, and her father, Giulio Strozzi, wrote librettos for him. The younger Strozzi excelled in composing chamber cantatas, works for solo voice and *basso continuo* that she herself could sing in the fashionable homes of Venice's elite. Her cantata *L'Amante Segreto* (*The Secret Lover*) treats the eternal subject of unrequited love. The hopeless lover is too timid to reveal her passion to the object of her desire, preferring instead to plead for a merciful death. The petition for death,

a "mini opera" for a vocal soloist

"Voglio morire" ("I want to die"), comes in the form of a brief aria accompanied by a *basso continuo*. The bass line of the *basso continuo* sounds a stepwise descent that repeats again and again.

EXAMPLE 11–3

A melody, harmony, or rhythm that repeats continually throughout a musical composition is an **ostinato.** When the repetition occurs in the bass, it is called a ***basso ostinato.*** The term *ostinato* comes from an Italian word meaning "obstinate," "stubborn," or "pig-headed." In Baroque operas and cantatas, performers often sang laments accompanied by a *basso ostinato* that descended, as here, in stepwise motion. Such a descending bass, consequently, became a symbol for grief or lamentation. Consider the title of Barbara Strozzi's aria: Could any sentiment be more lamentable than "I want to die"?

Listening Guide

Barbara Strozzi
The Secret Lover (1651)
Aria, "I want to die," Part 1

1/14

Genre: chamber cantata
Form: ostinato

0:00	*Basso continuo* begins, with *basso ostinato* played by cello
0:19	Soprano enters as *basso continuo* proceeds
0:41	*Basso ostinato* extended by one note to accommodate cadence*
0:45	*Basso continuo* alone
0:50	Soprano reenters; *basso continuo* proceeds to end

Voglio, voglio morire,	I want to die,
più tosto ch'il mio mal venga a scoprire;	rather than have my pain discovered;
ò disgrazia fatale,	oh, fatal misfortune,
quanto più miran gl'occhi il suo bel volto	the more my eyes admire his beautiful face
più tien la bocca il mio desir sepolto.	the more my mouth keeps my desire hidden.

 Use a downloadable, cross-platform animated Active Listening Guide, available at **www.thomsonedu.com/music/wright.**

Listening Exercise 18

Strozzi
"I want to die"

1/14

ThomsonNOW
To take this Listening Exercise online and receive feedback or email answers to your instructor, go to *ThomsonNOW* for this chapter.

Most early Baroque vocal music consists of arias and recitatives accompanied by a *basso continuo* and, in some cases, other instruments as well. In this recording of the

aria "I want to die," which begins Barbara Strozzi's cantata *The Secret Lover,* the continuo is played by a cello, harpsichord, and guitar. The cello plays the short bass line again and again, thereby forming a *basso ostinato*. The harpsichord and guitar fill out the texture, offering chordal support above this bass. The simplicity of this example allows both *basso continuo* and *basso ostinato* to be heard with unusual clarity.

1. (0:00–) The *basso ostinato* takes about four seconds to play. How many notes are there in the pattern?
   a. two   b. four   c. six
2. (0:00–) How many chords are there in the pattern?
   a. two   b. four   c. six
3. (0:00–0:18) At the beginning of the aria, the *basso continuo* sounds alone. How many presentations of the pattern occur before the voice enters?
   a. three   b. five   c. seven
4. (0:19–0:35) Now the voice enters and the pattern continues. Between 0:19 and 0:35, how many times is the pattern heard?
   a. three   b. five   c. seven
5. (0:36–0:43) In this passage, the *basso ostinato* suddenly changes—one or more notes are added to the bass pattern. Now how many notes are in the pattern?
   a. three   b. five   c. seven

6. (0:44–end) From here to the end of the aria, does the bass pattern ever change?
   a. yes   b. no
7. The rate of harmonic change (the amount of time between each chord) in this aria is
   a. regular.   b. irregular.

Now we focus on issues other than the *basso continuo* and the *basso ostinato*.

8. Which of the three continuo instruments improvises elaborate decorations?
   a. cello   b. harpsichord   c. guitar
9. An aria, as opposed to recitative, is usually characterized by luxuriant singing in which the voice occasionally breaks out into a melisma (one syllable sung to many notes). In this aria, when do the melismas occur?
   a. toward the beginning   b. toward the end
10. In many arias, the singer is accompanied by instruments in addition to the *basso continuo*, most often the violins. Do violins accompany the voice in this aria?
    a. yes   b. no

OPERA IN LONDON

Opera originated in Italy during the early seventeenth century. From there it spread over the Alps to German-speaking countries, to France, and eventually to England. But owing to the strong tradition of theater in England, epitomized by productions of Shakespeare's plays, opera in England, whether sung in Italian or English, had a checkered history—sometimes the English wanted to hear opera, and sometimes they did not. The first important opera written in English, Henry Purcell's *Dido and Aeneas*, dates from 1689. Chronologically, it falls outside the boundaries of the "early Baroque." But because English opera at this time was heavily influenced by earlier Italian opera, Purcell's opera belongs stylistically to the earlier period.

Henry Purcell (1659–1695)

Henry Purcell (Fig. 11–6) has been called the "greatest of all English composers." Indeed, only the late-Baroque composer George Frideric Handel (who was actually German born) and pop-songsters John Lennon and Paul McCartney can plausibly challenge Purcell for this title. Purcell was born in London, the son of one of the king's singers. In 1679, the younger Purcell obtained the position of organist at Westminster Abbey, and then, in 1682, he became organist to the king's Chapel Royal as well. But London has always been a vital theater town, and although an employee of the court, Purcell increasingly devoted his attention to works for the stage.

Purcell's *Dido and Aeneas* was among the first operas written in the English language. Yet it was apparently created not for the king's court, but for a private girls' boarding school in the London suburb of Chelsea. The girls presented one major stage production annually, something akin to the senior class play

FIGURE 11–6
Henry Purcell, by an anonymous painter.

FIGURE 11–7
A detail from the painting *The Death of Dido* by Guercino (1599–1666). The servant Belinda bends over the dying Dido, who has fallen on her formidable sword.

music emphasizes stresses in the text

of today. In *Dido and Aeneas,* they sang the numerous choruses and danced in the equally frequent dance numbers. All nine solo parts save one (the role of Aeneas) were written for female voices. The libretto* of the opera, one appropriate for a school curriculum steeped in classical Latin, is drawn from Virgil's *Aeneid.* Surely the girls had studied this epic poem in Latin class, and likely they had memorized parts of it. Surely, too, they knew the story of the soldier-of-fortune Aeneas who seduces proud Dido, queen of Carthage, but then deserts her to fulfill his destiny—sailing on to found the city of Rome. Betrayed and alone, Dido vents her feelings in an exceptionally beautiful aria, "When I am laid in earth," and then expires. In Virgil's original story, Dido stabs herself with the sword of Aeneas (Fig. 11–7). Here in Purcell's opera, she dies of a broken heart: her pain is poison enough.

Dido's final aria is introduced by a brief recitative, "Thy hand, Belinda." Normally, recitative is a business-like process that moves the action along through direct declamation. In this passage, however, recitative transcends its typically perfunctory role. Notice the remarkable way Purcell sets the English language. He understood where the accents fell in the text of his libretto, and he knew how to replicate these effectively in music. In Example 11–4, the stressed words in the text generally appear in long notes and at the beginning of each measure. Equally important, notice how the vocal line descends a full octave, passing through chromatic notes along the way. (Chromaticism* is another device composers use to signal pain and grief.) As the voice twists chromatically downward, we feel the pain of the abandoned Dido. By the end, she has slumped into the arms of her servant Belinda.

EXAMPLE 11–4

Thy hand, Be - lin - da! Dark - - ness shades me; on thy bo - som let me rest. More I would, but Death in - vades me: Death is now a wel - come guest.

a lament on a ground bass

From the recitative "Thy hand Belinda," Purcell moves imperceptibly to the climactic aria "When I am laid in earth," where Dido sings of her impending death. Because this highpoint of the opera is a lament, Purcell chooses, in the Baroque tradition, to build it upon a *basso ostinato*. English composers called the *basso ostinato* the **ground bass,** because the repeating bass provided a solid foundation, or grounding, on which an entire composition could be built. The ground bass Purcell composed for Dido's lament consists of two sections (see Listening Guide): (1) a chromatic stepwise descent over the interval of a fourth (G, F♯, F, E, E♭, D) and (2) a two-measure cadence returning to the tonic G (B♭, C, D, G).

In the libretto, Dido's lament consists of a brief one-stanza poem with an "a-b-a" rhyme scheme:

When I am laid in earth, may my wrongs create
No trouble in thy breast.
Remember me, but ah! forget my fate.

Each line of text is repeated, as are many individual words and pairs of words alike. (Such repetition of text is typical of an aria but not of recitative.) In this case, Dido's repetitions are perfectly appropriate to her emotional state—she can communicate in fragments, but cannot articulate her feelings in complete sentences. Here the listener cares less about grammatical correctness, however, and more about the emotion of the moment. No fewer than six times does Dido plead with Belinda, and with us, to remember her. And, indeed, we do remember, for this plaintive aria is one of the most moving pieces in all of opera.

repetition of text typical of the aria

Listening Guide

Henry Purcell
Dido and Aeneas (1689)
Aria, "When I am laid in earth"

1/15   1/4

Characters: Dido, queen of Carthage; Belinda, her servant
Situation: Having been deserted by her lover, Aeneas, Dido sings
  farewell to Belinda (and to all) before dying of a broken heart.

BRIEF RECITATIVE

0:00   15/4   Continuo played by large lute and cello

Thy hand, Belinda! Darkness shades me; on thy bosom let me rest. More I would—but Death invades me: Death is now a welcome guest.

ARIA (0:58)

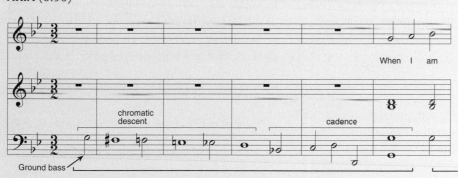

(continued)

0:58	*Basso ostinato* alone in cellos and double basses
1:10	*Basso ostinato* with voice and strings
1:27	*Basso ostinato* repeats beneath voice
1:44	*Basso ostinato* repeats beneath voice
2:02	*Basso ostinato* repeats beneath voice
2:19	*Basso ostinato* repeats beneath voice
2:37	*Basso ostinato* repeats beneath voice
2:53	*Basso ostinato* repeats beneath voice
3:10	*Basso ostinato* repeats beneath voice
3:29	*Basso ostinato* alone with strings
3:46	*Basso ostinato* alone with strings

When I am laid in earth, may my wrongs create no trouble in thy breast. Remember me, but ah! Forget my fate.

Use a downloadable, cross-platform animated Active Listening Guide, available at **www.thomsonedu.com/music/wright**.

Listening Exercise 19

Purcell
"When I am laid in earth"

6 **2**
1/15   1/4

ThomsonNOW
To take this Listening Exercise online and receive feedback or email answers to your instructor, go to *ThomsonNOW* for this chapter.

Henry Purcell begins the climactic scene of *Dido and Aeneas* with an expressive recitative and follows it with a mournful aria.

1. (0:00–0:57) Is the recitative a simple recitative (accompanied only by the instruments of the *basso continuo*) or an accompanied recitative?
   a. simple   b. accompanied

2. (0:00–0:57) What is the trajectory of the voice in this recitative?
   a. It descends to reflect the depressed spirit of Dido.
   b. It ascends to reflect Dido's exalted mood.

3. (0:58–1:09) How many statements of the *basso ostinato* sound before the voice enters?
   a. one   b. two   c. three

4. (1:10–) When the voice enters, does the rest of the orchestra (strings) enter then as well?
   a. yes   b. no

5. (1:10–2:15) How many times does the voice sing the lines "When I am laid in earth, may my wrongs create no trouble in thy breast"?
   a. once   b. twice   c. three times

6. (1:10–2:15) During this same passage, how many statements of the *basso ostinato* are performed?
   a. one   b. two   c. three   d. four

7. (2:16–3:28) How many times does the voice sing the musical phrase "Remember me, but ah! Forget my fate" and how many statements of the *basso ostinato* accompany it?
   a. once, one
   b. twice, two
   c. three times, three
   d. twice, four

8. (2:16–3:28) The emotional highpoint in this aria (and the opera) comes when the singer reaches her highest notes and loudest dynamic. When does this occur?
   a. at the first statement of "Remember me" (2:16–2:52)
   b. at the second statement of "Remember me" (2:53–3:28)

9. Which of the following, as appropriate for a lament, is true of this aria?
   a. It is in a major key and a fast tempo.
   b. It is in a minor key and a fast tempo.
   c. It is in a major key and a slow tempo.
   d. It is in a minor key and a slow tempo.

10. Dido singing a lament over a ground bass has much in common with which song?
    a. Bessie Smith singing the twelve-bar blues "Lost Your Head Blues" (see pages 43 and 420)
    b. Eminem singing the rap song "The Real Slim Shady" (see pages 20–21)

Elton John and Basso Ostinato

For an up-to-date example of ostinato bass, we can look at a modern aria-lament by a more recent English composer, Elton John. Although not built exclusively on an ostinato figure, John's song "Sorry Seems to Be the Hardest Word" (*Live in Australia*, MCA2-8022) nonetheless has one striking affinity to the aria by Purcell—it, too, makes use of a *basso ostinato*, incorporating a chromatically descending fourth as a way of setting a very, very sad text. (More recently, this song has appeared in "cover" versions by Ray Charles, Nena Tyler, and the singing group Blue.) The ostinato pattern begins on G, with a chromatically descending fourth followed by a one-measure cadence:

It's sad (so sad), it's a sad, sad situation
Bass
G   F♯   F   E

And it's getting more and more absurd
          E♭   D   F♯GAD
                         (cadence)

This *basso ostinato*, and a slightly varied form of it, is then repeated several times for this and other lines of text. Compare Elton John's bass line with Purcell's *basso ostinato* (see page 127), and note that both laments are set in the key of G minor. Was the pop artist, who studied at the Royal Academy of Music in London, inspired by the famous aria of his well-coiffured countryman (see Fig. 11–6)?

McMullen/Cozoretz Associates, Los Angeles

Elton John (Sir Reginald Dwight).

Key Words

opera (**117**)

libretto (**117**)

monody (**119**)

recitative (**119**)

simple recitative (**119**)

aria (**119**)

arioso (**120**)

toccata (**120**)

chamber music (**122**)

cantata (**122**)

chamber cantata (**122**)

ostinato (**124**)

basso ostinato (**124**)

ground bass (**126**)

ThomsonNOW™

ThomsonNOW for *Listening to Music, 5th Edition*, and *Listening to Western Music* will assist you in understanding the content of this chapter with lesson plans generated for your specific needs. In addition, you may complete this chapter's Listening Exercises in ThomsonNOW's interactive environment, as well as download Active Listening Guides and other materials that will help you succeed in this course.

Middle Baroque Instrumental Music

Chapter

12

The seventeenth century was a period in which instrumental music came to rival, and indeed surpass, vocal music in popularity. Statistics prove the point. During the Renaissance, the number of prints of vocal music outsold those of instrumental music by almost ten to one; by the end of the seventeenth century, on the other hand, instrumental publications outnumbered vocal ones by about three to one. Much of this new-found desire for instrumental music can be attributed directly to the growing popularity of the violin and other instruments of the violin family. While the violin originated around 1520 as an instrument played solely by professionals, by 1650 it had become a favorite of talented amateurs. Composers such as Corelli, Vivaldi, and (later) Bach responded to the growing demand for music for the violin and other string instruments by writing sonatas and concertos for them.

Accompanying the growth of instrumental music was the emergence of a distinctly instrumental sound. During the Renaissance, melody was all of one generic type. It was a direct, uncomplicated line that could be performed by either a voice or an instrument. Around 1600, however, instrumental and vocal styles began to diverge. Composers increasingly became aware that the Baroque trumpet, for example, could easily leap an octave, but could not run quickly up a scale and stay in tune. Accordingly, they began to write idiomatic (well-suited) music not only for voice but also for instruments so as to take advantage of their special abilities and colors. **Idiomatic writing,** then, exploits the strengths and avoids the weaknesses of particular voices and instruments.

a distinctively instrumental style

Finally, during the Baroque era the vocabulary of expressive gestures that had developed for vocal music came to be applied to instrumental music as well. Composers realized that the Doctrine of Affections (see page 112) was valid for instrumental music, too. By adopting devices used in vocal music, composers made it possible for purely instrumental music to express rage (with tremolos* and rapidly racing scales, for example), despair (as with a swooning melody above a lament bass), or a bright spring day (by such means as trills and other "chirps" high in the violins and flutes). Even without the benefit of a text, instrumental music could tell a tale or paint a scene. As we shall see, it was by means of such expressive devices that Antonio Vivaldi was able to depict all the seasons of the year.

THE BAROQUE ORCHESTRA

The symphony orchestra as we know it today had its origins in seventeenth-century Italy and France. At first, the term *orchestra* referred to the area for musicians in the ancient Greek theater, between the audience and the stage; eventually, it came to mean the musicians themselves. At the beginning of the seventeenth century, the orchestra was something of a musical "ark"—it included an impressive variety of instruments, but usually no more than one or two of each type. The small orchestra that accompanied Monteverdi's *Orfeo* (1607), for example, consisted of fourteen different instruments. By the mid-seventeenth century, however, many of the older instruments from the late Renaissance—viol, sackbut (trombone), cornetto, shawm, and theorbo—began to disappear. Into their place stepped the instruments of the violin family—violins, violas, cellos, and the related double bass. The violin family formed a core string ensemble, one that would henceforth dominate the orchestra. To this string nucleus were added woodwinds: first flute and oboes, and then bassoons, usually in pairs. Occasionally, a pair of trumpets would be included to provide extra brilliance. When trumpets appeared, so too, often did timpani*, although the parts for these drums were usually not written out but simply extemporized as the music seemed to require. Finally, by the end of the seventeenth century, a pair of French

the beginnings of the symphony orchestra

FIGURE 12–1

Detail of an orchestra playing for a Baroque opera, as seen in Pietro Domenico Olivero's *Interior of the Teatro Regio,* Turin (1740). From left to right are a bassoon, two French horns, a cello, a double bass, a harpsichord, and then violins, violas, and oboes.

horns was sometimes added to the orchestra to give it more sonic resonance. Supporting the entire ensemble was the ever-present *basso continuo,* one usually consisting of a harpsichord to provide chords and one or two low string instruments to play the bass line (Fig. 12–1). The **orchestra** for Western classical music, then, can be said to be an ensemble of musicians, organized around a core of strings, with added woodwinds and brasses, playing under a leader.

Most Baroque orchestras were small, usually with no more than twenty performers. None of the parts was doubled—no more than one instrumentalist, that is, was assigned to a single written line—until the last quarter of the seventeenth century, when it became the norm to have two, three, or four players on each of the string parts. In Italy, orchestral composers usually required four string lines: first violins, second violins, violas, and basses (played by both cellos and some form of double bass). Joining this core of approximately a dozen strings were pairs of woodwinds and brasses, along with a harpsichord. Yet while the typical Baroque orchestra had no more than twenty players, there were exceptions. At some of the more splendid courts around Europe, the orchestra might swell to as many as eighty instrumentalists for special occasions. Foremost among these was the court of French King Louis XIV.

ORCHESTRAL OVERTURE

Of all the courts of Baroque Europe, that of King Louis XIV was the most splendid. Louis styled himself the "Sun King," after Apollo, the god of the sun and of music. Outside of Paris, near the small town of Versailles, Louis built himself a palace, the largest court complex ever constructed (Fig. 12–2). There Louis not only shone forth in all his glory but also ruled absolutely: as he famously said, "I *am* the state" ("L'État, c'est moi"). His exceptionally long and authoritarian reign (1643–1715) inspired the political theory of **absolutism**—that power within the state rests totally in the hands of a king who rules by divine right. This mode of thought so dominated the Baroque era that it is sometimes also referred to as the "Age of Absolutism." Louis XIV invariably attended the operas and ballets he commanded, sitting in the front row and quietly singing along with the music.

FIGURE 12–2

This standard view of the front of Versailles gives a sense of the grandeur of the palace that King Louis XIV began there in 1669.

Jean-Baptiste Lully (1632–1687)

Music at the court of Louis XIV was directed by another domineering figure, Jean-Baptiste Lully. By birth, Lully was not French but Italian (his baptismal name was Giovanni Battista Lulli), and he had come to the French court to serve as an Italian-language tutor. But Lully could also dance, play violin, and compose. In 1661, Louis XIV appointed Lully superintendent of music of the court, and then in 1672, the king granted him a monopoly on the performance of theater music in and around Paris. Lully had become the absolute ruler of music, and he used his authoritarian powers to create the first thoroughly disciplined orchestra.

Lully established the make-up of the early orchestra

Lully built his orchestra around a nucleus of twenty-four string players arranged in five parts: six first violins, four second violins, four first violas, four second violas, and six basses. To these he added flutes, oboes, and bassoons. Lully was the first composer to require that strings and woodwinds always play together in an orchestra, though often he asked the woodwinds to do no more than double the notes of the strings. For special occasions, such as royal marriages, the ensemble could swell in size to nearly eighty. Lully selected the players, led rehearsals, and made sure they all executed the notes exactly and in strict time. If necessary, he instilled discipline by force; in one instance, he hit a violinist with his large conducting stick, and in another, he broke a violin over the owner's back. Ironically, Lully's penchant for musical discipline killed him. Late in 1686, while conducting a motet with his large conducting stick, he stabbed himself in the foot and died of gangrene a few weeks later.

a distinctive overture to operas and ballets

To gain a sense of the kind of orchestral music Jean-Baptiste Lully composed for the court of King Louis XIV, we turn to an overture that he wrote for his opera *Armide* (1686). An **overture** is an instrumental piece that precedes and thus "opens" some larger composition, such as an opera, oratorio, ballet, or suite of dances. Lully perfected what has come to be called the **French overture,** which consists of two sections. The first is set in a slow duple meter, with stately dotted rhythms suggesting a royal procession; the second is in a fast triple meter and features much imitation* among the various musical lines. Sometimes, at the end of the second section, the musical style of the first section returns briefly. If necessary, sections could be repeated to fill the time necessary for the audience, including the king, to be seated and come to attention.

Listening Guide   Jean Baptiste Lully
Overture to *Armide* (1686)

6
1/16

Genre: French overture
Form: ternary (ABA')

0:00   16   A: duple meter, slow tempo, and dotted rhythms

0:24   A repeated

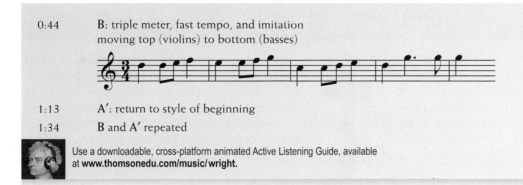

0:44   B: triple meter, fast tempo, and imitation
         moving top (violins) to bottom (basses)

1:13   A': return to style of beginning
1:34   B and A' repeated

Use a downloadable, cross-platform animated Active Listening Guide, available
at www.thomsonedu.com/music/wright.

SOLO SONATA AND TRIO SONATA

The instrumental music that Jean-Baptiste Lully composed for the French
royal court was predominantly orchestral music designed to be played by
professionals employed by the king. The growing popularity of the violin
around Europe, however, created a demand for instrumental music that talented amateurs might play in the home. This demand, in turn, encouraged
the growth of a new genre of instrumental music: the sonata.

A **sonata** is a type of instrumental chamber music* (music for the home with
just one player per part). When the term sonata originated in early sixteenth-
century Italy, it connoted "something sounded" in distinction to a cantata (see
page 122), which meant "something sung." A Baroque sonata consists of a
collection of movements*, each with its own mood and tempo, but all in the
same key. In the Baroque era, the movements usually carried such names as
"allemande," "sarabande," "gavotte," or "gigue"—all named after dances. A
Baroque sonata with dance movements was normally called a **chamber sonata**
(*sonata da camera*) and consisted of four movements with alternating tempos:
slow-fast-slow-fast.

a collection of instrumental movements

In the Baroque era, there were two types of sonatas: the solo sonata and
the trio sonata. A **solo sonata** might be written either for a solo keyboard instrument, such as the harpsichord, or for a solo melody instrument, such as
the violin, in which case three musicians were actually needed: the violinist
and the two *basso continuo* performers. A **trio sonata** consists of three musical
lines (two melody instruments plus bass). Yet here, too, the term is somewhat
misleading, for when a harpsichord joins with the bass to form the *basso continuo*, four players actually perform. The sonata originated in Italy and then
spread to the rest of Europe, in large measure through the published works of
Arcangelo Corelli.

Arcangelo Corelli (1653–1713)

The composer-virtuoso who made the Baroque solo and trio sonatas interna-
tionally popular was Arcangelo Corelli. Corelli was born in 1653 near Bologna,
Italy, then an important center for violin instruction and performance. By
1675, he had moved to Rome, where he remained for the duration of his life
as a teacher, composer, and performer on the violin (Fig. 12–3). Although
Corelli's musical output was small, consisting of only five sets of sonatas and
one of concertos, his works were widely admired. Such diverse composers as

FIGURE 12–3
Arcangelo Corelli looks placid enough
in this late seventeenth-century portrait.
But when playing the violin, according to
a contemporary, "his eyes turn red as fire,
his face becomes distorted, and his eye-
balls roll as if in agony."

Staatliche Schlösser and Gärten Berlin, Schloss Charlottenburg

The Baroque Violin

The most important string instrument in the Baroque period was the violin. The term derives from the Italian *violino* ("little viol"), from which English speakers gradually dropped the final "o" to create "violin." Unlike the viol (see Fig. 10–8), the violin has no frets and only four strings. At first the violin was something of a "low-class" instrument used by professional "bar fiddlers" to accompany dancing in inns and taverns. But the violin had two special virtues: (1) It produced a more powerful, penetrating sound than had the earlier viol; and (2) it was more versatile and expressive. Of all the instruments, the violin comes closest to the sound of the human voice in its agility, flexibility, and expressiveness. It can play a gentle lullaby with great tenderness, just as it can execute a loud fanfare with great splendor. By 1650, the members of the violin family had become the core of the Baroque orchestra.

The center of violin making during the Baroque era was, and remains today, Cremona, Italy (see Fig. 11–1). Cremonese violin makers were able to assure that one instrument was almost identical in shape to the next because they worked from wooden molds and because one craftsman passed his secrets on to the next, generation after generation. The best of the violin makers was **Antonio Stradivari** (1644–1737). Stradivari produced nearly 1,000 violins, violas, cellos, and guitars, some 600 of which survive today. In fact, Stradivari was still making violins in his last year, at the age of ninety-two. Today the best Stradivari violins each sells at auction in London or New York for as much as $4 million. Some of these violins have provocative names such as "The Messiah" and "Lady Blunt." Over the centuries, murder and intrigue have been associated with these rare instruments, as, for example, in the music-murder-mystery film *The Red Violin*.

The front of a Stradivari violin.

Victoria & Albert Museum, London/
The Bridgeman Art Library

Johann Sebastian Bach in Leipzig, François Couperin (1668–1733) in Paris, and Henry Purcell in London either borrowed his melodies directly or more generally studied and absorbed his style.

The most remarkable aspect of Corelli's music is its harmony: It sounds modern to our ears. We have heard so much classical and popular music that we have come to possess an almost subconscious sense of how a succession of chords—a harmonic progression—should sound. Corelli was the first in a long line of composers to write fully "functional" harmony, in which each chord has a specific role, or function, in the overall succession of chords. Not only does the individual chord constitute an important sound in itself, but it also prepares or leads toward the next, thereby helping to form a tightly linked chain of chords, which sounds directed and purposeful. The most basic link in the chain is the V-I (dominant-tonic) cadence (see page 40). In addition, Corelli often constructs bass lines that move upward chromatically by half step. This chromatic, stepwise motion pulls up and into the next-higher note, increasing the sense of direction and cohesiveness we feel in Corelli's music.

the beginnings of modern functional harmony

TRIO SONATA IN C MAJOR, OPUS 4, NO. 1 (1694)

The Trio Sonata in C major, Opus 4, No. 1, is a chamber sonata written by Corelli in 1694 for two violins and *basso continuo*, here played by a harpsichord and cello. Corelli called this sonata Opus 4, No. 1. (Composers frequently use **opus,** the Latin word meaning "work," to enumerate and identify their compositions; this was the first piece in Corelli's fourth published collection.) This chamber sonata is in four movements, the second and fourth of which are dance movements in binary form* (**AB**), the most common musical form for Baroque dances. No one danced, however. These movements were stylized pieces that aimed only to capture in music the spirit of the dance in question. As one musician of the day observed, they are written "for the refreshment of the ear alone."

binary form predominates

Corelli begins sonata Opus 4, No. 1 with a *preludio* (prelude), which gives the players a chance to warm up and also establishes the general musical mood of the sonata. Notice that the prelude makes use of what is called a **walking bass,** a bass that moves at a moderate, steady pace, mostly in equal note values and often stepwise up or down the scale.

EXAMPLE 12–1

The second movement, a dance called the *corrente* (from the Italian *correre*, "to run"), is rather fast and in triple meter. Here the first violin engages in a rapid dialogue with the cello. The second violin is scarcely audible as it helps fill in the chords, literally playing "second fiddle" to the first violin. The short *adagio* ("slow" movement) merely serves as a bridge that links the *corrente* with the final movement—the brisk, duple meter *allemanda* (literally, "the German dance"). This last movement, too, has a walking bass, but the tempo is so fast (*presto*) that it sounds more like a running or a sprinting bass.

Listening Guide

Arcangelo Corelli
Trio Sonata in C major, Opus 4, No. 1 (1694)

6
1/17

Ensemble: two violins, cello, and harpsichord

PRELUDE
0:00	🔢	"Walking bass" descends stepwise below dotted rhythms in violins
0:28		Cadence
0:32		Bass now moves twice as fast
0:41		Bass returns to original slow pace

CORRENTE
1:17	First violin and cello lead lively dance in triple meter
1:34	Repeat of **A**
1:49	**B** section begins with sequences in cello and violins
2:10	Rhythmic syncopation signals arrival of final cadence
2:19	Repeat of **B** including syncopation (2:40)

ADAGIO
2:53	Stationary chords in violins; only cello moves in purposeful fashion
4:05	Cadential chords prepare way to next movement

ALLEMANDA
4:25	Two violins move together above racing bass
4:46	Repeat of **A** and pause
5:07	**B** section begins with sudden shift to minor key
5:23	Moves back to tonic major key for final cadence
5:27	Repeat of **B** including final shift back to major (5:43)

 Use a downloadable, cross-platform animated Active Listening Guide, available at **www.thomsonedu.com/music/wright.**

THE BAROQUE CONCERTO

The concerto was to the Baroque era what the symphony would later become to the Classical period: the most popular and important genre of orchestral music. A Baroque concerto emphasized abrupt contrasts within a unity of mood, just as striking change between the zones of light and darkness often characterized a Baroque painting (see, for example, Fig. 10–6).

A **concerto** (from the Latin *concertare*, "to strive together") is a musical composition marked by a friendly contest or competition between a soloist and an orchestra. When only one soloist confronts the orchestra, the work is a **solo concerto.** When a small group of soloists works together, performing as a unit against the full orchestra, the piece is called a **concerto grosso.** The soloists in a concerto grosso constitute a subgroup called the **concertino** (little concert), and the full orchestra is called the **tutti** ("all" or "everybody"). A typical concerto grosso had a concertino of two or three violins and continuo. The soloists were not highly paid masters imported from afar, but rather the regular first-chair players who, when they were not serving as soloists, joined with the tutti to play the orchestral string parts. The contrast in sound between the heavy tutti and the lighter, more virtuosic concertino is the most distinctive feature of the concerto grosso.

solo concerto and concerto grosso

As written by Vivaldi and Bach, the solo concerto and the concerto grosso usually had three movements: fast, slow, fast. The serious first movement is composed in a carefully worked-out structure called ritornello form (see page 138); the second movement is invariably more lyrical and tender; while the third movement, though often using ritornello form, tends to be lighter, more dance-like, sometimes even rustic in mood. Both the solo concerto and the concerto grosso originated in Italy toward the end of the seventeenth century. Solo concertos for violin, flute, recorder, oboe, trumpet, and harpsichord were especially popular. The vogue of the concerto grosso peaked about 1730 and then all but ended about the time of Bach's death (1750). But the solo concerto continued to be cultivated during the Classical and Romantic periods, becoming increasingly a showcase in which a single soloist could display his or her technical mastery of an instrument.

FIGURE 12–4

Portrait of a violinist and composer believed by some to be the musician Antonio Vivaldi.

Antonio Vivaldi (1678–1741)

No composer was more influential, and certainly none more prolific, in the creation of the Baroque concerto than Antonio Vivaldi (Fig. 12–4). Vivaldi, like Barbara Strozzi a native of Venice, was the son of a barber and part-time musician at the basilica of Saint Mark (see Fig. 11–3). Young Vivaldi's proximity to Saint Mark's naturally brought him into contact with the clergy. Although he became a skilled performer on the violin, he also entered Holy Orders, ultimately being ordained a priest. Vivaldi's life, however, was by no means confined to the realm of the spirit: He concertized on the violin throughout Europe; he wrote and produced nearly fifty operas, which brought him a great deal of money; and he lived for fifteen years with an Italian opera star. The worldly pursuits of *il prete rosso* ("the red-haired priest") eventually provoked a response from the authorities of the Roman Catholic Church. In 1737, Vivaldi was forbidden to practice his musical artistry in papally controlled lands. This ban affected his income as well as his creativity. He died poor and obscure in 1741 in Vienna, where he had gone in search of a post at the imperial court.

The Hospice of Mercy: Convent and Concert Hall

In the early eighteenth century, there were approximately 400 girls and young women residents at the Hospice of Mercy in Venice. All received not only religious instruction but also training in academic disciplines and domestic crafts (cooking, embroidery, lace making, cotton spinning, health care, and music). Those who showed a special talent for music were placed within a core of forty young musicians, a prestigious group given special privileges and a distinctive red habit. Each day these young women studied or practiced for as much as four hours, and their musical education included tutelage in singing, ear training, and counterpoint, as well as instruction on at least two musical instruments. To guide them, music teachers such as Antonio Vivaldi were hired from outside the walls of the convent. The level of performance at the Hospice of Mercy was thought to be the highest in Venice, higher even than at the opera.

When performing publicly in the chapel of the orphanage, the members of the girls' musical corps stood on high in a special gallery, a musicians' loft, and played to the outside world through a grill. Like disembodied voices, their sounds could be heard, but their faces not fully seen. Each Sunday and religious holiday, they performed the musical parts of the Mass, and purely instrumental concertos as well. After individual pieces, the audience applauded. On Sunday afternoons, the all-female orchestra played publicly in a different room from 4 to 6 P.M. What had begun as religious music in a convent had become a public concert series.

Women musicians perform behind a grill at an eighteenth-century Venetian orphanage.

Photo Costa

From 1703 until 1740, Vivaldi worked in Venice at the *Ospedale della Pietà* (Hospice of Mercy), first as a violinist and music teacher, and then as musical director. The Hospice of Mercy was an orphanage for the care and education of young women. It was one of four such charitable institutions in Venice that accepted abandoned, mostly illegitimate girls, who, as several reports state, "otherwise would have been thrown in the canals." By 1700, music had been made to serve an important role in the religious and social life of the orphanage. Each Sunday afternoon, its orchestra of young women offered public performances for the well-to-do of Venice (see boxed essay). Also attending these concerts were foreign visitors—Venice was already a tourist city—among them a French diplomat, who wrote in 1739:

music in an orphanage for girls

> These girls are educated at the expense of the state, and they are trained solely with the purpose of excelling in music. That is why they sing like angels and play violin, flute, organ, oboe, cello, and bassoon; in short, no instrument is so big as to frighten them. They are kept like nuns in a convent. All they do is perform concerts, always in groups of about forty girls. I swear to you that there is nothing as pleasant as seeing a young and pretty nun, dressed in white, with a little pomegranate bouquet over her ears, conducting the orchestra with all the gracefulness and incredible precision one can imagine.

VIOLIN CONCERTO IN E MAJOR, OPUS 8, NO. 1, THE "SPRING" (EARLY 1700s)

During the early 1700s, Vivaldi composed literally hundreds of solo concertos for the all-female orchestras of the Hospice of Mercy in Venice. In 1725, he gathered twelve of the more colorful of these together and published them under the title "Opus 8." (This set of concertos was thus Vivaldi's eighth published work.) In addition, he called the first four of these solo concertos **The Seasons.** What Vivaldi meant by this was that each of the four concertos in turn represents the feelings, sounds, and sights of one of the four seasons of the year, beginning with spring. So that there be no ambiguity as to what sensations and events the music depicts at any given moment, Vivaldi first composed a poem (an "illustrative sonnet" as he called it) about each season. Then he placed each line of the poem at the appropriate point in the music where that particular event or feeling was to be expressed, even specifying at one point that the violins are to sound "like barking dogs." In so doing, Vivaldi showed that not only voices, but instruments as well, could create a mood and sway the emotions. Vivaldi also fashioned here a landmark in what is called instrumental program music—music that plays out a story or a series of events or moods (for more on program music, see page 275).

It is fitting that *The Seasons* begins with the bright, optimistic sounds of spring (Fig. 12–5). In fact, the "Spring" Concerto for solo violin and small orchestra is Vivaldi's best-known work. The fast first movement of this three-movement concerto is composed in **ritornello form,** a form that Vivaldi was the first to popularize. The Italian word *ritornello* means "return" or "refrain." In ritornello form, all or part of the main theme—the ritornello—returns again and again, invariably played by the tutti, or full orchestra. Between the tutti's statements of the ritornello, the soloist inserts fragments and extensions of this ritornello theme in virtuosic fashion. Much of the excitement of a Baroque concerto comes from the tension between the reaffirming ritornello played by the tutti and the fanciful flights of the soloist.

The jaunty ritornello theme of the first movement of the "Spring" Concerto has two complementary parts, the second of which returns more often than the first. Between appearances of the ritornello, Vivaldi inserts the music that represents his feelings about spring. He creates the songbirds of May by asking the violin to play rapidly and staccato* in a high register. Similarly, he depicts the sudden arrival of thunder and lightning by means of a tremolo* and shooting scales, then returns to the cheerful song of the birds. Thereafter, in the slow second movement, a vision of a flower-strewn meadow is conveyed by an expansive, tender melody in the violin. Finally, during the fast finale, a sustained droning in the lower strings invokes "the fes-

instrumental program music

FIGURE 12–5

The musician Vivaldi, the poet John Milton (1608–1674), and the painter François Boucher (1703–1770) were among the many artists of the seventeenth and eighteenth centuries to expound on the activities and feelings of the four seasons. Boucher's *The Four Seasons: Spring* captures the freshness and amorous possibilities of springtime.

tive sounds of country bagpipes." The full text of Vivaldi's "program" for the first movement of the "Spring" Concerto is given in the Listening Guide.

Vivaldi's "Spring" Concerto is marked by a stylistic trait that is often prominent in his music: melodic sequence. A **melodic sequence** is the repetition of a musical motive at successively higher or lower degrees of the scale. Example 12–2 shows a sequence from the middle of the first movement of this work. In this sequence, the motive is repeated twice, each time a step lower.

EXAMPLE 12–2

Although melodic sequence can be found in music from almost all periods, it is especially prevalent in the Baroque. It helps propel the music forward and create the energy we associate with Baroque style. However, because hearing the same melodic phrase time and again can become a tedious listening experience, Baroque composers usually follow the "three strikes and you're out" rule: the melodic unit appears, as in Example 12–2, three times, but no more.

Vivaldi composed more than 450 concertos and thus is known as "the father of the concerto." Widely admired as both a performer and composer in his day, within a few years of his death, he was largely forgotten, a victim of rapidly changing musical tastes. Not until the revival of Baroque music in the 1950s were his scores resurrected from obscure libraries and dusty archives. Now his music is loved for its freshness and vigor, its exuberance and daring. Today it can be heard in television commercials, in film scores, and as background music in Starbucks. More than 200 professional recordings have been made of *The Seasons* alone. So often is the "Spring" Concerto played that it has passed from the realm of art music into that of "classical pops."

"the father of the concerto" rescued from obscurity

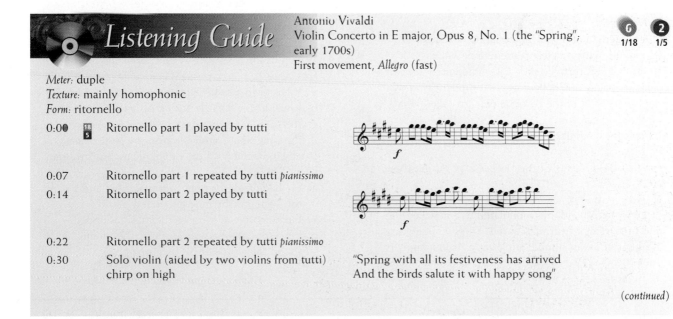

Listening Guide

Antonio Vivaldi
Violin Concerto in E major, Opus 8, No. 1 (the "Spring"; early 1700s)
First movement, *Allegro* (fast)

G 1/18   2 1/5

Meter: duple
Texture: mainly homophonic
Form: ritornello

0:00	18/5	Ritornello part 1 played by tutti
0:07		Ritornello part 1 repeated by tutti *pianissimo*
0:14		Ritornello part 2 played by tutti
0:22		Ritornello part 2 repeated by tutti *pianissimo*
0:30		Solo violin (aided by two violins from tutti) chirp on high

"Spring with all its festiveness has arrived
And the birds salute it with happy song"

(continued)

1:05	Ritornello part 2 played by tutti	
1:13	Tutti softly plays running sixteenth notes	"And the brooks, kissed by the breezes, Meanwhile flow with sweet murmurings"
1:36	Ritornello part 2 played by tutti	
1:45	Tutti plays tremolo and violins shoot up scale	"Dark clouds cover the sky Announced by bolts of lightning and thunder"
1:51	Solo violin plays agitated, broken triads while tutti continues with tremolos below	
2:11	Ritornello part 2 played by tutti	
2:19	Solo violin chirps on high, adding ascending chromatic scale and trill	"But when all has returned to quiet The birds commence to sing once again their enchanted song"
2:37	Ritornello part 1, slightly varied, played by tutti	
2:48	Solo violin plays rising sixteenth notes	
3:03	Ritornello part 2 played by tutti	

Use a downloadable, cross-platform animated Active Listening Guide, available at www.thomsonedu.com/music/wright.

Listening Exercise 20

Vivaldi
"Spring" Concerto

6 2
1/18 1/5

ThomsonNOW
To take this Listening Exercise online and receive feedback or email answers to your instructor, go to *ThomsonNOW* for this chapter.

The opening movement of Vivaldi's "Spring" Concerto is a traditional favorite with listeners everywhere, in part because its musical gestures are clear and its ritornello form straightforward.

1. Vivaldi was a virtuoso on this instrument, which dominates the sound of this concerto.
   a. organ   b. harpsichord   c. violin   d. cello
2. How would you describe the rhythmic pulse of this movement?
   a. energetic and regularly repeating patterns
   b. languid with no clear sense of a downbeat
3. (0:00–0:29) Ritornello part 1 is immediately repeated *pianissimo*, as is ritornello part 2. Abrupt shifts in dynamics, typical of the Baroque era, are called what?
   a. terraced dynamics
   b. terrain dynamics
   c. terra cotta dynamics
4. (0:30–1:04) Does the *basso continuo* play during this solo section?
   a. yes   b. no
5. (1:26–1:44) Vivaldi has modulated to a new key and brings back ritornello part 2. Does it sound at a higher or lower pitch compared to its first appearance (0:14–0:29)?
   a. higher   b. lower

6. (1:51–2:01) Is the pattern in this melodic sequence rising or falling?
   a. rising   b. falling
7. (2:11–2:18) When the ritornello returns, in what mode is it?
   a. major   b. minor
8. (2:19–2:36) During this passage and beyond, what does the cello do?
   a. It rises by step.
   b. It falls by step.
   c. It plays a pedal point* (holds one bass note).
9. Which of the following is true about the "Spring" Concerto?
   a. It has both a *basso continuo* and a *basso ostinato*.
   b. It has a *basso continuo* but no *basso ostinato*.
   c. It has a *basso ostinato* but no *basso continuo*.
   d. It has neither a *basso ostinato* nor a *basso continuo*.
10. Finally, how did Vivaldi communicate his "program" to his listeners?
    a. He had created a poem about spring, and a narrator read it as the music sounded.
    b. He held up cue cards as the music sounded.
    c. He wrote onomatopoeic music that mimicked in sound the words of his own poem.

Key Words

idiomatic writing (**130**)	solo sonata (**133**)	concerto grosso (**136**)
orchestra (**131**)	trio sonata (**133**)	concertino (**136**)
absolutism (**131**)	Antonio Stradivari (**134**)	tutti (**136**)
overture (**132**)	opus (**134**)	*The Seasons* (**138**)
French overture (**132**)	walking bass (**135**)	ritornello form (**138**)
sonata (**133**)	concerto (**136**)	melodic sequence (**139**)
chamber sonata (**133**)	solo concerto (**136**)	

Checklist of Musical Style

Early and Middle Baroque: 1600–1710

Melody	Less stepwise movement, larger leaps, wider range, and more chromaticism reflect influence of virtuosic solo singing; melodic patterns idiomatic to particular musical instruments emerge; introduction of melodic sequence
Harmony	Stable, diatonic chords played by *basso continuo* support melody; clearly defined chord progressions begin to develop; tonality reduced to major and minor keys
Rhythm	Relaxed, flexible rhythms of Renaissance transformed into regularly repeating, driving rhythms
Color	Musical timbre becomes enormously varied as traditional instruments are perfected (e.g., harpsichord, violin, oboe) and new combinations of voices and instruments are explored; symphony orchestra begins to take shape; sudden shifts in dynamics (terraced dynamics) reflect dramatic quality of Baroque music
Texture	Chordal, homophonic texture predominates; top and bottom lines are strongest as *basso continuo* creates powerful bass to support melody above
Form	Arias and instrumental works often make use of *basso ostinato* procedure; ritornello form emerges in concerto grosso; binary form regulates most movements of sonata

Representative composers
Gabrieli
Monteverdi
Barbara Strozzi
Purcell
Lully
Corelli
Vivaldi

Principal genres
polychoral motet
chamber cantata
opera
French overture
sonata
concerto grosso
solo concerto

The Late Baroque

BACH

The music of the late Baroque period (1710–1750), represented by the two great figures Johann Sebastian Bach and George Frideric Handel, stands as a high-water mark in Western musical culture. Among the marvels of late Baroque music, we might also include the works of Antonio Vivaldi, treated in the previous chapter, since some of his most distinctive concertos, such as the "Spring," were written around 1710. But late Baroque music, typified by the works of Bach and Handel, is usually characterized by great length and contrapuntal complexity. Generally, the most noteworthy compositions of Bach and Handel are large-scale works full of dramatic power, broad gestures, and, often, complex counterpoint. At the same time, they convey to the listener a sense of technical mastery—that Bach and Handel could compose with grace and skill in a variety of musical forms, techniques, and styles, building on the innovations of previous Baroque composers.

refinement rather than innovation

Earlier Baroque composers had created many new musical genres such as opera*, chamber cantata*, sonata*, solo concerto*, and concerto grosso*. The late Baroque, by contrast, is not a period of musical innovation, but one of re-finement. Bach and his contemporaries did not, in the main, invent new forms, styles, techniques, or genres, but rather gave greater weight, length, and pol-ish to those established by their musical forebears. Arcangelo Corelli (1653–1713), for example, had introduced functional harmony in his sonatas, but Bach and Handel expanded Corelli's harmonic template to create much longer, and often more compelling, works of art. Bach and Handel approached the craft of composition with unbounded self-confidence. Their music has a sense of rightness, solidity, and maturity about it. Each time we choose to listen to one of their compositions, we offer further witness to their success in bring-ing a hundred years of musical innovation to a glorious culmination.

ASPECTS OF LATE BAROQUE MUSICAL STYLE

During the years 1710–1750, Bach, Handel, and their contemporaries con-tinued to build upon the distinctive elements of musical style that appeared earlier in the Baroque era (see pages 115–116). Melody is governed by the principle of progressive development; an initial theme is set forth and then continually expanded, spun out over an ever-lengthening line. Melodies are typically long and asymmetrical, and often the notes are propelled forward by melodic sequence*, as in the following example from Handel's *Messiah.*

EXAMPLE 13–1

ex - alt - ed,

Rhythm in late Baroque music is also ruled by the principle of progressive development. A piece typically begins with one prominent rhythmic idea, and it or a complementary one continues uninterrupted to the very end of the movement, pushed along by a strong, clearly audible beat. Indeed, beat and meter are more easily recognized in late Baroque music than in the music of any other period. Thus, if a concerto by Bach or Handel seems to "chug along" with irrepressible optimism and vitality, it is usually owing to a strong beat, a clearly articulated meter, and a continually recurring rhythmic pattern.

Finally, the music of Bach and Handel is usually denser in texture than that of the early Baroque era. Recall that around 1600, composers of the early Baroque rebelled against what they perceived to be the excessively polyphonic style of Renaissance music, with its constant overlapping points of imitation* (see page 102). As a result, early Baroque music is not polyphonic, but rather homophonic, in texture. By the heyday of Bach and Handel around 1725, however, composers had returned to polyphonic writing, mainly to add richness to the middle range of what had been in the early Baroque a top-bottom (soprano–bass) dominated texture. German composers of the late Baroque were particularly fond of counterpoint, perhaps owing to their traditional love of the organ, an instrument with several keyboards, thus well suited to playing multiple polyphonic lines at once. The gradual reintegration of counterpoint into the fabric of Baroque music culminates in the rigorously contrapuntal vocal and instrumental music of J. S. Bach.

the re-introduction of polyphony

JOHANN SEBASTIAN BACH (1685–1750)

In the creations of Johann Sebastian Bach (Fig. 13–1), the music of the Baroque reaches its greatest glory. Bach was born into a musical dynasty, though one originally of common standing. For nearly 200 years, members of the Bach family served as musicians in small towns in Thuringia, a province in central Germany. Johann Sebastian was merely the most talented of the ubiquitous musical Bachs, though he himself had four sons who achieved international fame. Although he received an excellent formal education in the humanities, as a musician Bach was largely self-taught. To learn his craft, he studied, copied, and arranged the compositions of Corelli, Vivaldi, Pachelbel, and even Palestrina. He also learned to play the organ, in part by emulating others, once traveling 200 miles each way on foot to hear a great performer. Bach's first position of importance was in the town of Weimar, Germany, where he served as organist to the court beginning in 1708. It was here that he wrote many of his finest works for organ. Soon Bach became the most renowned organ virtuoso in Germany, and his improvisations on that instrument became legendary.

Of all instruments, the organ is the most suitable for playing polyphonic counterpoint. Most organs have at least two separate keyboards for the hands, in addition to one placed on the floor, which the performer plays with the feet (see Figs. 5–14 and 13–2). This gives the instrument the capacity to play several lines simultaneously. More important, each of these keyboards can be set to engage a different group (rank) of pipes, each with its own color, and thus the ear can more readily hear the individual musical lines. For these reasons, the organ is the instrument *par excellence* for playing fugues.

Fugue

Bach was the master of counterpoint, and it is rich, complex counterpoint that lies at the heart of the fugue. A fugue is a contrapuntal form and procedure

FIGURE 13–1

The only authentic portrait of Johann Sebastian Bach, painted by Elias Gottlob Haussmann in 1746. Bach holds in his hand a six-voice canon*, or round, which he created to symbolize his skill as a musical craftsman.

Saint Thomas's Church, Leipzig

FIGURE 13–2

The organ presently in the choir loft of Saint Thomas's Church, Leipzig. It was from this loft that Bach played and conducted.

that flourished during the late Baroque era. The word *fugue* itself comes from the Latin *fuga,* meaning "flight." Within a fugue, one voice presents a theme and then "flies away" as another voice enters with the same theme. The theme in a fugue is called the **subject.** At the outset, each voice presents the subject in turn, and this successive presentation is called the **exposition** of the fugue. As the voices enter, they do not imitate or pursue each other exactly—this would produce a canon* or a round such as "Row, Row, Row Your Boat" (see page 59). Rather, passages of exact imitation are interrupted by sections of free writing in which the voices more or less go their own ways. These freer sections, where the subject is not heard in its entirety, are called **episodes.** Episodes and further presentations of the subject alternate throughout the remainder of the fugue.

Fugues have been written for from two to as many as thirty-two voices, but the norm is two to five. These may be actual human voices in a chorus or choir, or they may simply be lines or parts played by a group of instruments, or even by a solo instrument like the piano, organ, or guitar, which has the capacity to play several "voices" simultaneously. Thus, a formal definition of a **fugue** might be as follows: a composition for two, three, four, or five parts played or sung by voices or instruments, which begins with a presentation of a subject in imitation in each part (exposition), continues with modulating passages of free counterpoint (episodes) and further appearances of the subject, and ends with a strong affirmation of the tonic key. Fortunately, the fugue is easier to hear than to describe: The unfolding and recurrence of one subject makes it easy to follow.

ORGAN FUGUE IN G MINOR (c1710)

Bach has left us nearly a hundred keyboard fugues, about a third of which are for organ. The organ was Bach's favorite instrument, and in his day he was known more as a performer and improviser on it than as a composer. Bach's G minor organ fugue was composed rather early in his career, sometime between 1708 and 1717, when he was in Weimar. It is written for four voices, which we will refer to as soprano, alto, tenor, and bass, and it begins with the subject appearing first in the soprano.

Example 13–2

a typical fugue subject

As fugue subjects go, this is a rather long one, but it is typical of the way Baroque composers liked to "spin out" their melodies. It sounds very solid in tonality because the subject is clearly constructed around the notes of the G minor triad (G, B♭, D), not only in the first measure but on the strong beats of the following measures as well. The subject also conveys a sense of gathering momentum. It starts moderately with quarter notes, and then seems to gain speed as eighth notes and finally sixteenth notes are introduced. This, too, is typical of fugue subjects. After the soprano introduces the subject, it is then presented, in turn, by the alto, the tenor, and the bass. The voices need not appear in any particular order; here Bach just decided to have them enter in succession from top to bottom.

FIGURE 13–3

Fugue (1925) by Josef Albers. Albers's design suggests the "constructivist" quality of the fugue, one full of repeating and reciprocal relationships. The black-and-white units seem to allude to subject and episode, respectively.

When each voice has presented the subject and joined the polyphonic complex, Bach's exposition is at an end. Now a short passage of free counterpoint follows—the first episode—which uses only bits and pieces of the subject. Then the subject returns, but in a highly unusual way: It begins in the tenor, but continues and ends in the soprano (see † in the following Listening Guide). Thereafter, Bach's G minor fugue unfolds in the usual alternation of episodes and statements of the subject. The episodes sound unsettled and convey a sense of movement, modulating from one key to another. The subject, on the other hand, doesn't modulate. It is *in* a key, here the tonic G minor, or the dominant, D minor, or some other closely related key. The tension between settled music (the subject) and unsettled music (the episodes) creates the exciting, dynamic quality of the fugue.

the subject sounds solid, the episodes unsettled

Finally, because Bach wrote many fugues for organ, they often make use of a device particularly well suited to the organ, the pedal point. A **pedal point** is a note, usually in the bass, that is sustained (or repeated) for a period of time while harmonies change around it. Such a sustaining tone in the bass derives its name, of course, from the fact that on the organ the note is sounded by a foot holding down a key on the pedal keyboard. After a pronounced pedal point and additional statements of the subject, Bach modulates back to the tonic key, G minor, for one final statement of the subject in the bass to end his fugue. Notice that, although this fugue is in a minor key, Bach puts the last chord in major. This is common in Baroque music, composers preferring the brighter, more optimistic, sound of the major mode in the final chord. Given all its complexities and the fact that it is full of reciprocating, almost mathematical relationships (Fig. 13–3), it is not surprising that the fugue has traditionally appealed to listeners with scientific interest. Fugues are music for the eye and mind, as much as for the ear and heart.

minor to major in last chord

Listening Guide

Johann Sebastian Bach
Organ Fugue in G minor (c1710)

6 1/19   **2** 1/6

Texture: polyphonic

(continued)

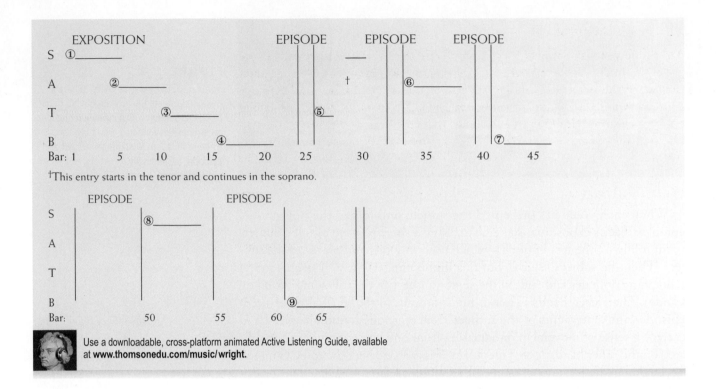

†This entry starts in the tenor and continues in the soprano.

Use a downloadable, cross-platform animated Active Listening Guide, available at **www.thomsonedu.com/music/wright.**

Listening Exercise 21

Bach
Organ Fugue in G minor

1/19   1/6

ThomsonNOW™
To take this Listening Exercise online and receive feedback or email answers to your instructor, go to *ThomsonNOW* for this chapter.

As you can see by the above diagram, Bach's Fugue in G minor is composed for four voices. In the exposition (entries 1–4) the subject appears four times, once in each voice, and it returns five times thereafter (entries 5–9). The first skill needed to enjoy a fugue is the ability to differentiate the subject from the episodes. To assure that you are hearing the presentations of the subject, questions 1–5 ask you to identify the moments at which the subject enters after the exposition. The remaining questions suggest the complexities that typically reside within a fugue.

1. Statement 5 of the subject begins at what time?
   a. 1:20   b. 1:28
2. Statement 6 of the subject begins at what time?
   a. 1:56   b. 2:04
3. Statement 7 of the subject begins at what time?
   a. 2:25   b. 2:33
4. Statement 8 of the subject begins at what time?
   a. 3:00   b. 3:09
5. Statement 9 of the subject begins at what time?
   a. 3:39   b. 3:48
6. (1:07–1:14) During this passage, as the bass plays the end of the subject, what does the soprano execute against it?

a. a pedal point
b. a descending melodic sequence
c. a trill
d. a long rising scale

7. (1:37–1:47) During this passage, what does the bass play?
   a. a pedal point
   b. a descending melodic sequence
   c. a trill
   d. a long rising scale
8. (2:18–2:27) During this passage, what does the soprano play?
   a. a pedal point
   b. a descending melodic sequence
   c. a trill
   d. a long rising scale
9. (3:33–3:42) During this passage, what does the tenor play?
   a. a pedal point
   b. a descending melodic sequence
   c. a trill
   d. a long rising scale
10. Bach intended this four-voice fugue to be played by how many performers on the organ?
    a. one   b. two   c. three   d. four

Bach's Orchestral Music

After nine years as organist in Weimar, Bach, then a young man with a wife and four children, determined to improve his station in life. In 1717, he auditioned for the position of music director at the court of Cöthen, Germany, and was awarded the post. When he returned to Weimar to collect his family and possessions, the Duke of Weimar, displeased that the composer had "jumped ship," had Bach thrown in jail for a month. (Composers before the time of Beethoven were little more than indentured servants who needed to obtain a release from one employer before entering the service of another.) When freed from jail, Bach fled to Cöthen, where he remained for six years (1717–1723).

Bach in jail for a month

At Cöthen, Bach turned his attention from organ music for the church to instrumental music for the court. It was here that he wrote the bulk of his orchestral scores, including more than a dozen solo concertos. The Prince of Cöthen had assembled something of an "all-star" orchestra, drawing many top players from the larger city of Berlin. He also ordered a large two-keyboard harpsichord from Berlin and sent Bach to fetch it. About this time, Bach began his *The Well-Tempered Clavier* (see page 156) for keyboard, and during these years, he completed six concertos of the concerto grosso* type. This set has come to be called the Brandenburg Concertos.

THE BRANDENBURG CONCERTOS (1715–1721)

In 1721, still in Cöthen, Bach began to look for yet another job in the politically more important city of Berlin—specifically, at the court of Margrave Christian Ludwig of Brandenburg. To impress the margrave, Bach gathered together a half-dozen of his best concertos and sent them to his prospective employer. Although no job offer was forthcoming, Bach's autograph manuscript survives (Fig. 13–4), and in it are found six superb examples of the concerto grosso.

concertos in hopes of a new position

The concerto grosso, as we have seen (page 136), is a three-movement work involving a musical give-and-take between a full orchestra (tutti) and a much smaller group of soloists (concertino), consisting usually of just two or three violins and continuo. In the first movement, the tutti normally plays a recurring musical theme, called the ritornello*. The soloists in the concertino play along with the tutti; but when the ritornello stops, they go on to present their own musical material in a flashy, sometimes dazzling show of technical skill. Each of the six Brandenburg Concertos calls for a different group of soloists in the concertino. Together, these works constitute an anthology of nearly all instrumental combinations known to the Baroque era.

Bach's aim in the Brandenburg Concertos was to show his ability to write challenging music for any and all instruments. A listener cannot fail to be impressed by the brilliant writing for the harpsichord in Concerto No. 5, for example. Here the full orchestra (tutti) is pitted against a concertino consisting of solo violin, flute, and, most important, harpsichord. In principle, the tutti plays the ritornello, and the soloists play motives derived from it. In practice, however, the separation between tutti and concertino is not as distinct with Bach as it had been in the earlier concertos of Vivaldi

FIGURE 13–4

The autograph manuscript of the opening of Bach's Brandenburg Concerto No. 5.

Berlin, Deutsches Staadsbibliothek

FIGURE 13–5

The Hall of Mirrors at the court of Cöthen, Germany, the hall in which most of Bach's orchestral music was performed while he resided in that town.

(see page 138). In Bach's more refined treatment of ritornello form, the line between the large (loud) ensemble and the small (soft) group of soloists is less obvious. Notice here that Bach's ritornello (see Listening Guide) possesses many characteristics of Baroque melody: It is idiomatic to the violin (having many repeated notes); it is lengthy and somewhat asymmetrical (spinning out over many measures); and it possesses a driving rhythm that propels the music forward.

While the sound of violins dominates the ritornello in this opening movement, gradually the solo harpsichord takes center stage. In fact, this work might fairly be called the first keyboard concerto. In earlier concertos, the harpsichord had appeared only as part of the *basso continuo*, not as a solo instrument. But here, toward the end of the movement, all the other instruments fall silent, leaving the harpsichord to sound alone in a lengthy section full of brilliant scales and arpeggios. Such a showy passage for soloist alone toward the end of a movement in a concerto is called a **cadenza.** One can easily imagine the great virtuoso Bach performing Brandenburg Concerto No. 5 in the Hall of Mirrors at Cöthen (Fig. 13–5), the principal concert hall of the court. There, seated at the large harpsichord he had brought from Berlin, Bach would have dazzled patron and fellow performers alike with his bravura playing.

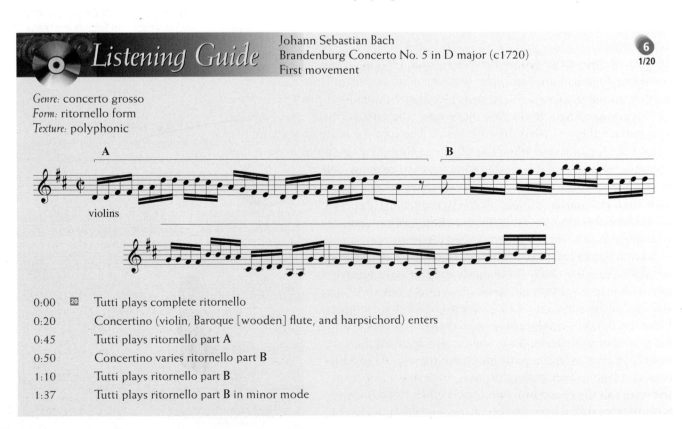

Listening Guide

Johann Sebastian Bach
Brandenburg Concerto No. 5 in D major (c1720)
First movement

6
1/20

Genre: concerto grosso
Form: ritornello form
Texture: polyphonic

violins

0:00	20	Tutti plays complete ritornello
0:20		Concertino (violin, Baroque [wooden] flute, and harpsichord) enters
0:45		Tutti plays ritornello part **A**
0:50		Concertino varies ritornello part **B**
1:10		Tutti plays ritornello part **B**
1:37		Tutti plays ritornello part **B** in minor mode

1:43	Concertino plays motives derived from ritornello, especially part **B**
2:24	Tutti plays ritornello part **B**
2:30	Concertino plays motives derived from ritornello part **B**
3:21	Cello of tutti joins concertino, plays arpeggios in descending melodic sequence*
3:50	Double bass of tutti repeats single bass pitch (pedal point)
4:08	Tutti plays ritornello part **A**
4:31	Concertino repeats much of music heard toward beginning (0:20)
4:57	Tutti plays ritornello parts **A** and **B**; sounds very solid
5:09	Concertino plays motives derived from ritornello part **B**
5:36	Tutti plays ritornello part **B**
5:43	Harpsichord plays scales that race up and down keyboard
6:22	Cadenza: long, brilliant passage for solo harpsichord
8:30	Left hand (bass) of harpsichord repeats one pitch (pedal point)
8:52	Pedal point doubled octave* lower and played *forte*
9:19	Tutti plays complete ritornello

Use a downloadable, cross-platform animated Active Listening Guide, available at **www.thomsonedu.com/music/wright.**

The fingers of the harpsichordist get a much-deserved rest in the slow second movement of Brandenburg Concerto No. 5. Now an elegiac mood envelops the music as the violin and flute engage in a quiet dialogue. The fast finale is dominated by fugal writing, a style in which Bach excelled above all other composers.

The Church Cantata

In 1723, Bach moved yet again, this time to assume the coveted position of cantor of Saint Thomas's Church and choir school in Leipzig, Germany (Fig. 13–6), a post he retained until his death in 1750. He seems to have been attracted to Leipzig, then a city of about 30,000 inhabitants, because of its excellent university where his sons might enroll at no cost.

Although prestigious, the post of cantor of the Lutheran church of Saint Thomas was not an easy one. As an employee of the town council of Leipzig, Bach was charged with superintending the liturgical music of the four principal churches of that city. He also played organ for all funerals, composed any music needed for ceremonies at the university, and sometimes taught Latin grammar to the boys at the choir school of Saint Thomas. But by far the most demanding part of his job as cantor was to provide new music for the church each Sunday and religious holiday, a total of about sixty days a year. In so doing, Bach brought an important genre of music, the church cantata, to the highest point of its development.

Like the opera, the sonata, and the concerto, the cantata first appeared in Italy during the seventeenth century in the form we call the chamber cantata* (see page 122). Typically written for a solo singer and small accompanying orchestra,

FIGURE 13–6

Leipzig, Saint Thomas's Church (center) and choir school (left) from an engraving of 1723, the year in which Bach moved to the city. Bach's large family occupied several floors of the choir school.

© Bettmann/Corbis

FIGURE 13-7

Looking across the parishioner's pews and toward the high altar at Saint Thomas's Church, Leipzig, as it was in the mid-nineteenth century. The pulpit for the sermon is at the right. In Bach's day, nearly 2,500 people would crowd into the church.

Saint Thomas's Church, Leipzig

*cantata follows the Gospel
and precedes the sermon*

the chamber cantata treated subjects of love or history and was performed in the home. During the early eighteenth century, however, composers in Germany increasingly came to see the cantata as an appropriate vehicle for religious music in the church. Bach and his contemporaries created the **church cantata,** a multimovement sacred work including arias, ariosos, and recitatives, performed by vocal soloists, a chorus, and a small accompanying orchestra. The church cantata became the musical core of the Sunday service of the Lutheran Church, the protestant religion that then dominated spiritual life in German-speaking lands.

In Bach's time, Saint Thomas's Church in Leipzig (Fig. 13–7) celebrated a Sunday Mass, as prescribed by Martin Luther (1483–1546) nearly two centuries earlier. The service began at seven o'clock in the morning and lasted nearly four hours. The musical high point, the cantata, came after the reading of the Gospel and provided a commentary on the Gospel text, allowing the congregation to meditate on the word of the Lord. The preacher then delivered an hour-long sermon, which also expounded on the scriptural theme of the day. Bach wrote almost 300 cantatas (five annual cycles) for the citizens of Leipzig, though only about 200 of these survive. His musical forces consisted of about a dozen men and boy singers from the Saint Thomas choir school (see Fig. 13–6) and an equal number of instrumentalists from the university and town. The ensemble was placed in a choir loft above the west door (see Fig. 13–2), and Bach himself conducted the group, beating time with a roll of paper.

WACHET AUF, RUFT UNS DIE STIMME (Awake, a Voice Is Calling, 1731)
Bach was a devoted husband, a loving father to twenty children in all, and a respected burgher of Leipzig. Yet above all he was a religious man who composed not only for self-expression but also for the greater glory of God. His cantata *Awake, a Voice Is Calling* reveals his abiding faith in the religious traditions of his German Lutheran community. Bach composed it in 1731 for a service on a Sunday immediately before the beginning of Advent (four Sundays before Christmas). The text of the cantata announces the coming of a bridegroom toward his hopeful bride. Christ is the groom. A group of ten virgins, whose story is recounted in the Gospel of Matthew (25:1–13), symbolizes the bride and the entire community. Here is the Gospel of Matthew as it was read to the congregation at Saint Thomas's Church immediately before Bach's cantata was performed:

Then shall the kingdom of heaven be likened unto ten virgins, which took their lamps, and went forth to meet the bridegroom. And five of them were wise, and five were foolish. They that were foolish took their lamps, but took no oil with them. . . . And at midnight there was a cry made, Behold, the bridegroom cometh; go ye out to meet him. Then all those virgins arose, and trimmed their lamps. And the foolish said unto the wise, Give us of your oil; for our lamps are gone out. But the wise answered, saying, Not so; lest there be not enough for us and you: but go ye rather to them that sell, and buy for yourselves. And while they went to buy, the bridegroom came; and they that were ready went in with him to the marriage:

What Did Mrs. Bach Do?

Actually, there were two Mrs. Bachs. The first, Maria Barbara, died suddenly in 1720, leaving the composer with four young children. The second, Anna Magdalena, he married in 1722, and she would bear him thirteen more. Anna Magdalena Bach was a professional singer, earning about as much as her new husband at the court of Cöthen. But when the family moved to Leipzig and the Saint Thomas Church, Anna Magdalena curtailed her professional activities. Women did not perform publicly in the Lutheran Church at this time; the difficult soprano lines in Bach's religious works were sung by choirboys. Consequently, Anna Magdalena put her musical skills to work as manager of what might be called "Bach Inc."

For almost every Sunday throughout the year, J. S. Bach was required to produce a cantata, about twenty to twenty-five minutes of new music, week after week, year after year. Writing the music was only part of the high-pressure task. Rehearsals had to be set and music learned by the next Sunday. But composing and rehearsing paled in comparison to the amount of time needed to copy all the parts—these were the days before photocopy machines and software programs to notate music. Each of the approximately twelve independent lines of the full score had to be copied, entirely by hand, for each new cantata, along with sufficient copies (parts) for all the singers and players. For this, Bach turned to the members of his household—namely, his wife and children (both sons and daughters), as well as the nephews, and other fee-paying private students who resided in the cantor's quarters at the Saint Thomas school (see Fig. 13–6). In 1731, the year he composed the cantata *Awake, a Voice Is Calling*, the roof was taken off the building and two more stories added to accommodate the Bach family and its "music industry."

When Bach died in 1750, he left his most valuable assets (his musical scores) to his eldest sons. The performing parts to many of his cantatas, however, he left to his wife with the expectation that she would rent or sell them in the course of time—her old-age pension in the days before social security. In the end, however, the income from these cantata manuscripts did not prove sufficient, and Anna Magdalena Bach finished her days in 1760 as a ward of the city of Leipzig.

and the door was shut. . . . Watch therefore, for ye know neither the day nor the hour wherein the Son of man cometh.

The message to every good Lutheran of Leipzig was clear: Get your spiritual house in order so as to receive the coming Christ. Thus Bach's cantatas were intended not as concert pieces but as religious instruction for his community—sermons in music.

The cantata *Awake, a Voice Is Calling* is made up of a succession of seven independent movements. Those for chorus provide a structural framework, coming at the beginning, the middle, and the end. They make use of the three stanzas of text of a sixteenth-century Lutheran hymn, *Awake, a Voice Is Calling*, from which this cantata derives its name. The text of the recitatives and arias, on the other hand, is a patchwork of biblical quotations cobbled together by a contemporary of Bach's. Thus the chorus sings the verses of the traditional hymn, while the soloists present the biblical excerpts in the recitatives and arias. Notice how the structure of the cantata creates a formal symmetry: recitative–aria pairs surround the central choral movement, and are preceded and followed in turn by a chorus.

a solid, symmetrical structure

Movement:						
1	2	3	4	5	6	7
Chorus chorale 1st stanza	Recitative	Aria (duet)	Chorus chorale 2nd stanza	Recitative	Aria (duet)	Chorus chorale 3rd stanza

FIGURE 13–8

Like the opening chorus of Bach's cantata *Awake, a Voice Is Calling*, Tiepolo's *Vision of Saint Clement* projects three distinct levels of activity: the Trinity on high, angels in the middle, and Pope Clement I, Christ's vicar on earth, at the bottom.

Awake, a Voice Is Calling is a built upon a **chorale,** a spiritual melody or religious folksong of the Lutheran Church—what other denominations would simply call a hymn. Most chorale tunes were centuries old by Bach's time and belonged to the religious tradition of the community; most Lutherans knew these melodies by heart. Chorales are easy to sing because they have clear-cut phrases and a steady beat with one syllable of text per note. The structure of the chorale tune *Awake, a Voice Is Calling* is typical of this genre (see the Listening Guide); the music unfolds in **AAB** form, and the seven musical phrases are allocated in the following way: A(1,2,3) A(1,2,3) B(4–7,3). The last phrase of section **A** returns at the end of **B** to round out the melody.

Of the seven movements of the cantata *Awake, a Voice Is Calling,* the most remarkable is the first, a gigantic chorale fantasy that displays a polyphonic mastery exceptional even for Bach. Here Bach creates a multidimensional spectacle surrounding the coming of Christ. First the orchestra announces Christ's arrival by means of a three-part ritornello* that conveys a sense of growing anticipation. Part **a** of the ritornello, with its dotted rhythm, suggests a steady march; part **b,** with its strong downbeat and then syncopations, imparts a tugging urgency; part **c,** with its rapid sixteenth notes, implies an unrestrained race toward the object of desire (Christ). Now the chorale melody enters high in the sopranos, the voice of tradition, perhaps the voice of God. In long, steady notes placed squarely on downbeats, it calls the people to prepare themselves to receive God's Son. Beneath this the voices of the people—the altos, tenors, and basses—scurry in rapid counterpoint, excited by the call to meet their savior. Lowest of all is the bass of the *basso continuo.* It plods along, sometimes in a dotted pattern, sometimes in rapid eighth notes, but mostly in regularly recurring quarter notes falling on the beat. In sum, the opening movement of *Awake, a Voice Is Calling* is the musical equivalent of a great religious painting in which the canvas is energized by several superimposed levels of activity (see Fig. 13–8). The enormous complexity of a movement such as this shows why musicians, then and now, view Bach as the greatest contrapuntalist who ever lived.

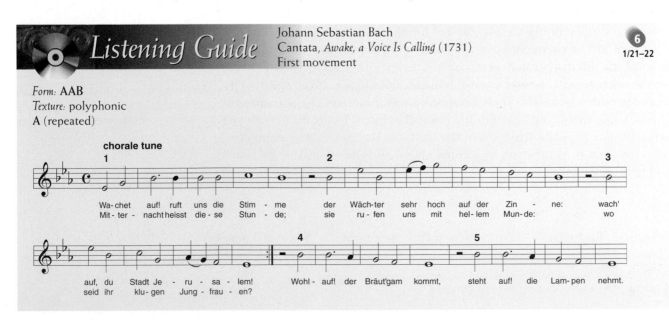

Listening Guide

Johann Sebastian Bach
Cantata, *Awake, a Voice Is Calling* (1731)
First movement

6
1/21–22

Form: **AAB**
Texture: polyphonic
A (repeated)

chorale tune

1   2   3

Wa-chet auf! ruft uns die Stim - me   der Wäch-ter sehr hoch auf der Zin - ne: wach'
Mit - ter - nacht heisst die - se Stun - de;   sie ru - fen uns mit hel - lem Mun-de: wo

4   5

auf, du Stadt Je - ru - sa - lem!   Wohl - auf! der Bräut'gam kommt, steht auf! die Lam-pen nehmt.
seid ihr klu - gen Jung - frau - en?

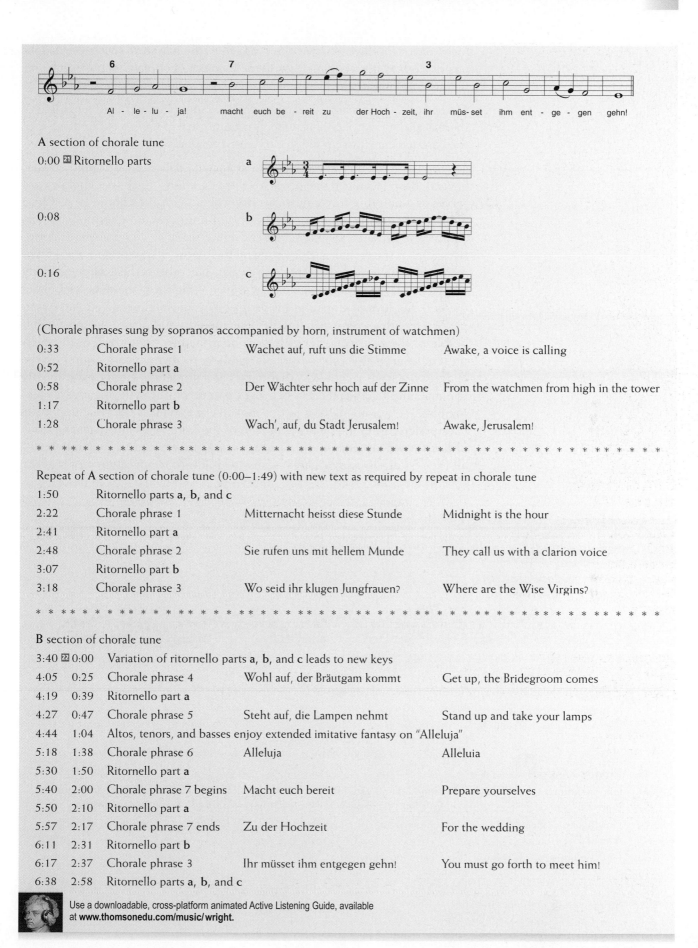

Al - le - lu - ja!   macht euch be - reit zu   der Hoch - zeit, ihr müs - set   ihm ent - ge - gen gehn!

A section of chorale tune

0:00 🎵 Ritornello parts   a

0:08   b

0:16   c

(Chorale phrases sung by sopranos accompanied by horn, instrument of watchmen)

0:33	Chorale phrase 1	Wachet auf, ruft uns die Stimme	Awake, a voice is calling
0:52	Ritornello part **a**		
0:58	Chorale phrase 2	Der Wächter sehr hoch auf der Zinne	From the watchmen from high in the tower
1:17	Ritornello part **b**		
1:28	Chorale phrase 3	Wach', auf, du Stadt Jerusalem!	Awake, Jerusalem!

* *

Repeat of **A** section of chorale tune (0:00–1:49) with new text as required by repeat in chorale tune

1:50	Ritornello parts **a**, **b**, and **c**		
2:22	Chorale phrase 1	Mitternacht heisst diese Stunde	Midnight is the hour
2:41	Ritornello part **a**		
2:48	Chorale phrase 2	Sie rufen uns mit hellem Munde	They call us with a clarion voice
3:07	Ritornello part **b**		
3:18	Chorale phrase 3	Wo seid ihr klugen Jungfrauen?	Where are the Wise Virgins?

* *

B section of chorale tune

3:40	🎵 0:00	Variation of ritornello parts **a**, **b**, and **c** leads to new keys	
4:05	0:25	Chorale phrase 4	Wohl auf, der Bräutgam kommt	Get up, the Bridegroom comes
4:19	0:39	Ritornello part **a**		
4:27	0:47	Chorale phrase 5	Steht auf, die Lampen nehmt	Stand up and take your lamps
4:44	1:04	Altos, tenors, and basses enjoy extended imitative fantasy on "Alleluja"	
5:18	1:38	Chorale phrase 6	Alleluja	Alleluia
5:30	1:50	Ritornello part **a**		
5:40	2:00	Chorale phrase 7 begins	Macht euch bereit	Prepare yourselves
5:50	2:10	Ritornello part **a**		
5:57	2:17	Chorale phrase 7 ends	Zu der Hochzeit	For the wedding
6:11	2:31	Ritornello part **b**		
6:17	2:37	Chorale phrase 3	Ihr müsset ihm entgegen gehn!	You must go forth to meet him!
6:38	2:58	Ritornello parts **a**, **b**, and **c**		

Use a downloadable, cross-platform animated Active Listening Guide, available at **www.thomsonedu.com/music/wright**.

Movement 2.   In this recitative, the Evangelist (the narrator) invites the daughters of Zion to the wedding feast; there is no use of chorale tune. In Bach's religious vocal music, the Evangelist is invariably sung by a tenor.

Movement 3.   In this aria (duet) between the Soul (soprano) and Jesus (bass), there is also no use of chorale tune. It is traditional in German sacred music of the Baroque era to assign the role of Christ to a bass.

Movement 4.   For this meeting of Christ and the daughters of Zion (true believers), Bach fashioned one of his loveliest creations. Again the chorale tune serves as a unifying force, now carrying stanza 2 of the chorale text. Once more Bach constructs a musical tapestry for chorus and orchestra, but a less complex one than the first movement. Here we hear only two central motives. One is the chorale melody sung by the tenors, who represent the watchmen calling on Jerusalem (Leipzig) to awake. The other is the exquisite melody played by all the violins and violas in unison—their togetherness symbolizes the unifying love of Christ for his people. This unison line is a perfect example of a lengthy, ever-expanding Baroque melody, and one of the most memorable of the entire era. Beneath it we hear the measured tread of the ever-present *basso continuo.* The bass plays regularly recurring quarter notes on the beat. As we have seen, a bass that moves at a moderate, steady pace, mostly in equal note values and often stepwise up or down the scale, is called a walking bass*. The walking bass in this movement enhances the meaning of the text, underscoring the steady approach of the Lord. This movement was one of Bach's own favorites and the only cantata movement that he published—all the rest of his Leipzig cantata music was left in handwritten scores at the time of his death.

Bach's favorite cantata movement

Listening Guide

Johann Sebastian Bach
Awake, a Voice Is Calling
Fourth movement

6 2/1   **2** 1/7

Form: **AAB**
Texture: polyphonic

Time		German	English
0:00 1/7	Violins and violas play flowing melody above walking bass		
	(Chorale phrases sung by the tenors)		
0:43	Chorale phrases 1, 2, and 3	Zion hört die Wächter singen,	Zion hears the watchmen singing
		Das Herz tut ihr vor Freuden springen,	Her heart fills with joy
		Sie wachet und steht eilend auf.	She awakes and quickly rises.
1:12	Flowing string melody repeated		
1:55	Chorale phrases 1, 2, and 3 repeated	Ihr Freund kommt vom Himmel prächtig,	Her splendid friend arrives from Heaven
		Von Gnaden stark, von Wahrheit mächtig,	Mighty in grace, strong in truth
2:24	Flowing string melody repeated	Ihr Licht wird hell, ihr Stern geht auf.	Her light grows bright, her star arises.
2:51	Chorale phrases 4, 5, and 6	Nun komm, du werte Kron,	Now come, you worthy crown
		Herr Jesu, Gottes Sohn!	Lord, Jesus, Son of God!
		Hosanna!	Hosanna!
3:09	String melody continues in minor		

3:33	Chorale phrases 7 and 3	Wir folgen all	We will follow all
		Zum Freudensaal	to the banquet hall
		Und halten mit das Abendmahl.	And share in the Lord's supper.
4:00	String melody concludes movement		

 Use a downloadable, cross-platform animated Active Listening Guide, available at **www.thomsonedu.com/music/wright**.

Listening Exercise 22

Bach
Awake, a Voice Is Calling

6   2
2/1   1/7

ThomsonNOW™
To take this Listening Exercise online and receive feedback or email answers to your instructor, go to *ThomsonNOW* for this chapter.

The most famous section of Bach's cantata *Awake, a Voice Is Calling* is in the middle (fourth) movement. Here the composer creates for the strings a lovely melody to be used as a counterpoint to the chorale tune. Let us begin by considering the string melody and its accompaniment, and then the chorale.

1. (0:00–0:42) How many musical lines or parts do you hear at the beginning of the movement?
   a. one   b. two   c. three

2. (0:00–0:42) A bass that plods along in equal note values moving in predominantly stepwise motion is called what?
   a. a *basso continuo*
   b. a walking bass
   c. a *basso ostinato*

3. (0:00–0:42) The basses (double basses and cellos) play only quarter notes on the beat until they begin to move more quickly in eighth notes. Where does that change to eighth notes begin?
   a. 0:10   b. 0:18   c. 0:26   d. 0:34

4. (0:43) When the chorale tune enters, how is it sung?
   a. in four-part harmony
   b. in unison by the sopranos
   c. in unison by the tenors

5. (0:43–1:11) Bach sets the chorale tune in notes that are which?
   a. longer (and hence sound slower) than those of the strings
   b. shorter (and hence sound faster) than those of the strings

6. (0:43–1:11) Throughout this section, which is true?
   a. The chorale tune is in the middle of the texture, strings at the top, and double basses and cellos at the bottom.
   b. The chorale tune is at the top of the texture, strings in the middle, and double basses and cellos at the bottom.

7. (1:12–2:50 repeat of section A of the movement) Do the relative positions of the string melody and the chorale tune change during this repeat?
   a. yes   b. no

8. (2:51–end) Which is true about the nature of the string melody during the B section?
   a. Sometimes it repeats phrases from the A section.
   b. It is an entirely new melody.

9. At any time throughout this movement, is the three-line texture (bass, choral tune, string melody) augmented by the addition of woodwinds and brasses?
   a. Yes; Bach adds these instruments to create a grand climax.
   b. No; once Bach decides upon his three-strand texture, he maintains it rigorously to the end.

10. Why do you suppose this piece remains one of the most famous works in the repertoire of classical music?
   a. The lilting string melody has clear-cut phrases yet continually presses forward.
   b. The strong bass and lyrical melody provide a rock-solid framework.
   c. Bach ingeniously combines this beautiful melody with a preexisting chorale tune.
   d. All of the above.

Movement 5. In this recitative for Christ (bass), there is no use of chorale tune. Christ invites the anguished Soul to find comfort in Him.

Movement 6. In this aria (duet) for bass and soprano, again there is no use of chorale tune. This is a strict *da capo* aria (see page 164) in which Christ and the Soul sing a passionate love duet. A religious man who did not compose operas, Bach most closely approaches the world of the theater in this beautiful duet.

Movement 7.   Bach's cantatas usually end with a simple four-voice homophonic setting of the last stanza of the chorale tune. In his closing movements, he always places the chorale melody in the soprano part, harmonizing and supporting it with the other three voices below. The instruments of the orchestra have no line of their own and merely double the four vocal parts. But more important, the members of the congregation join in the singing of the chorale melody. At that moment, all of the spiritual energy of Leipzig was concentrated into this one emphatic declaration of belief. The coming Christ reveals to all true believers a vision of life in the celestial kingdom.

Listening Guide

Johann Sebastian Bach
Awake, a Voice Is Calling
Seventh and last movement

6
2/2

Form: **AAB**
Texture: homophonic

0:00	2	Gloria sei dir gesungen (phrase 1)	May Glory be sung to you
		Mit Menschen und englischen Zungen (phrase 2)	With the tongues of man and the angels
		Mit Harfen und mit Zimbeln schon. (phrase 3)	And harps and cymbals too.
0:38		Von zwölf Perlen sind die Pforten, (phrase 1)	The gates are of twelve pearls,
		An deiner Stadt, wir sind Konsorten (phrase 2)	In your city we are consorts
		Der Engel hoch um deiner Thron. (phrase 3)	Of the angels high above your throne.
1:16		Kein Aug hat je gespürt, (phrase 4)	No eye has ever seen,
		Kein Ohr hat je gehört (phrase 5)	No ear has ever heard
		Solche Freude. (phrase 6)	Such joy.
		Des sind wir froh, (phrase 7)	Let us therefore rejoice,
		Io, io!	Io, io!
		Ewig in dulci jubilo. (phrase 3)	Eternally in sweet jubilation.

Use a downloadable, cross-platform animated Active Listening Guide, available at **www.thomsonedu.com/music/wright**.

In the last decade of his life, Bach gradually withdrew from the world to dwell in the contrapuntal realm of his own mind. He finished the best-known of his large-scale contrapuntal projects, ***The Well-Tempered Clavier*** (1720–1742), a "clavier" simply being a general term for keyboard instruments. (It is called "Well-Tempered," or "Well-Tuned," because Bach was grad-

Bach's Bones

When Bach died in 1750, the music of "the old wig," as one of his sons irreverently referred to him, was soon forgotten. His style was thought to be too old-fashioned, with its heavy reliance on traditional chorale tunes and dense counterpoint. Bach was buried in a distant parish church. Not until nearly a hundred years after his death did the citizens of Leipzig come to discover that they had once had in their midst a genius—perhaps the greatest composer of all time! A statue of Bach was then placed before Saint Thomas's Church, and a stained glass window with the composer's likeness was set within the church. Most strange of all, in 1895, Bach's corpse was unearthed. His skull was examined to see if it was unusual in size (it was not), and his skeleton photographed. Ultimately, Bach's bones were reinterred, but now at the high altar of Saint Thomas's Church (see Fig. 13–7). A patron saint of music had been created. Today thousands of pilgrims come each year to this shrine to pay homage to the great man and hear his music.

Bach's bones.

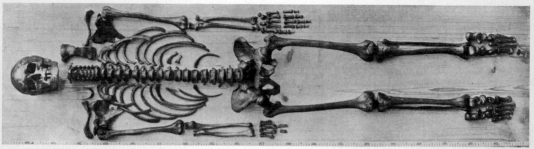

"Gesammtansicht des Bach-Skeletts" In: W. His, Anatomische Forschungen über Johann Sebastian Bach's Gebeine und Antlitz S. Leipzig: S. Hirzel, 1895.

ually adopting a keyboard in which all the half steps were equidistant in pitch, something that had not been universally true before this time.) *The Well-Tempered Clavier* consists of two sets of twenty-four preludes and fugues. The **prelude** is a short preparatory piece that sets a mood and serves as a technical warm-up for the player before the fugue. In both sets of twenty-four, there is one prelude and fugue in each of the twelve major and twelve minor keys. Today every serious pianist around the world "cuts his or her teeth" on what is affectionately known as the "WTC."

Bach's last project was the *The Art of Fugue* (1742–1750), an encyclopedic treatment of all known contrapuntal procedures set forth in nineteen canons and fugues. The final fugue, one in which Bach combines four related subjects, was broken off by his death in 1750. **The Art of Fugue** was thus Bach's valedictory statement of a musical form he brought to supreme mastery. It remains a fitting testimony to this composer's stylistic integrity, grand design, and superhuman craftsmanship.

two large contrapuntal projects

Key Words

subject (**144**)	pedal point (**145**)	*The Well-Tempered*
exposition (**144**)	cadenza (**148**)	*Clavier* (**156**)
episode (**144**)	church cantata (**150**)	prelude (**157**)
fugue (**144**)	chorale (**152**)	*The Art of Fugue* (**157**)

ThomsonNOW™

ThomsonNOW for *Listening to Music*, 5th Edition, and *Listening to Western Music* will assist you in understanding the content of this chapter with lesson plans generated for your specific needs. In addition, you may complete this chapter's Listening Exercises in ThomsonNOW's interactive environment, as well as download Active Listening Guides and other materials that will help you succeed in this course.

The Late Baroque
HANDEL

Bach and Handel were born in the same year, 1685, in small towns in central Germany. Other than that commonality, however, their careers could not have been more different. While Bach spent his life confined to towns in the region of his birth, the cosmopolitan Handel traveled the world—from Rome, to Venice, to Hamburg, to Amsterdam, to London, to Dublin. If Bach was most at home playing organ fugues and conducting church cantatas from the choir loft, Handel was a man of the public theater, by training and temperament a composer of opera. And if Bach fell into virtual obscurity at the end of his life, retreating into a world of esoteric counterpoint, Handel's stature only grew larger on the international stage. He became during his lifetime the most famous composer in Europe and a treasured national institution in England.

GEORGE FRIDERIC HANDEL (1685–1759)

George Frideric Handel was born in the town of Halle, Germany, in 1685, and died in London in 1759 (Fig. 14–1). Although his father had decreed a program of study in law, the young Handel managed to cultivate his intense interest in music, sometimes secretly in the attic. At the age of eighteen, he left for the city of Hamburg, where he took a job as second violinist in the public opera (he was later promoted to continuo harpsichordist). But since the musical world around 1700 was dominated by things Italian, he set off for Italy to learn his trade and broaden his horizons. He moved between Florence and Venice, where he wrote operas, and Rome, where he composed mainly chamber cantatas. In 1710, Handel returned to North Germany to accept the post of chapel master to the Elector of Hanover, but on the condition that he be given an immediate leave of absence to visit London. Although he made one final voyage back to his employer in Hanover in 1711 and many subsequent visits to the Continent, Handel conveniently "forgot" about his obligation to the Hanoverian court. London became the site of his musical activity and the place where he won fame and fortune.

London in the early eighteenth century was the largest city in Europe, boasting a population of 500,000. It was also the capital city of a country in the process of forming an empire for international trade and commerce. London may not have possessed the rich cultural heritage of Rome or Paris, but it offered opportunity for financial gain. As the eighteenth-century saying went: "In France and Italy there is something to learn, but in London there is something to earn."

Handel soon found employment in the homes of the aristocracy and became the music tutor to the English royal family. As fate would have it, his continental employer, the Elector of Hanover, became King George I of England in 1714, when the Hanoverians acceded to the throne on the extinction of the Stuart line. Fortunately for Handel, the new king bore his truant musician no grudge, and he was called on frequently to compose festival music to entertain the court or mark its progress.

FIGURE 14–1

Thomas Hudson's 1749 portrait of Handel with the score of *Messiah* visible in the composer's left hand. Handel had a quick temper, could swear in four languages, and liked to eat.

akg-images

For these events, Handel produced such works as *Water Music* (1717), *Music for the Royal Fireworks* (1749), and the Coronation Service (1727) for King George II and Queen Caroline, parts of which have been used at the coronation of every English monarch since its first hearing.

Handel and the Orchestral Dance Suite

WATER MUSIC (1717)

The English royal family, which has historically had a problem with its image, has sometimes given concerts of popular music to win favor with the public, as Queen Elizabeth II did recently at Buckingham Palace. Handel's *Water Music* was created for another royally sponsored bit of image-building. In 1717, King George I, a direct ancestor of the present queen, was an unpopular monarch. He refused to speak a word of English, preferring his native German. He fought with his son, the Prince of Wales, even banning him from court. His subjects considered George dimwitted, "an honest blockhead," as one contemporary put it.

To improve his standing in the eyes of his subjects, the king's ministers planned a program of public entertainments, including an evening of music on the Thames River for the lords of Parliament and the lesser people of London (Fig. 14–2). Thus, on July 17, 1717, the king and his court left London, accompanied by a small armada of boats, and progressed up the Thames to the strains of Handel's orchestral music. An eyewitness describes this nautical parade in detail:

> About eight in the evening the King repaired to his barge, into which were admitted the Duchess of Bolton, Countess Godolphin, Madam de Kilmansech (the king's mistress), Mrs. Were and the Earl of Orkney, the Gentleman of the Bedchamber in Waiting. Next to the King's barge was that of the musicians, about 50 in number, who played on all kinds of instruments, to wit trumpets, horns, hautboys [oboes], bassoons, German flutes, French flutes [recorders], violins and basses; but there were no singers. The music had been composed specially by the famous Handel, a native of Halle [Germany], and His Majesty's principal Court Composer. His

Water Music: music to polish the royal image

National Gallery, Prague/Bridgeman-Giraudon/Art Resource, NY

FIGURE 14–2

View of London, Saint Paul's Cathedral, and the Thames River by Canaletto (1697–1768). Notice the large barges. Crafts such as these could have easily accommodated the fifty musicians reported to have played behind the king as he moved upstream in 1717, listening to Handel's *Water Music*.

Majesty so greatly approved of the music that he caused it to be repeated three times in all, although each performance lasted an hour—namely twice before and once after supper. The evening weather was all that could be desired for the festivity, the number of barges and above all of boats filled with people desirous of hearing the music was beyond counting.

The score played for King George and the crowd of music lovers moving on the Thames River was, of course, Handel's *Water Music*. *Water Music* belongs to a genre called the **dance suite**: a collection of dances, usually from four to seven in number, all in one key and for one group of instruments, be it full orchestra, trio, or solo. (The term derives from the French word *suite*, meaning a succession of pieces.) Listeners usually did not dance to the music of a suite; these were stylized, abstract dances intended only for the ear. But it was the job of the composer to bring each one to life, to make it recognizable to the audience by incorporating the salient elements of rhythm and style of each particular dance. Among the dances found in a typical late-Baroque suite are the allemande (literally, "the German dance"; a moderate or brisk, stately dance in duple meter), the saraband (a slow, sensual dance of Spanish origin in triple meter), and the minuet (a moderate, elegant dance in triple meter).

a succession of dances in binary form

Almost all dances of the Baroque period were composed in one musical form: binary form (**AB**), the two sections of which could be repeated. Normally, **A** takes the movement from tonic to dominant, while **B** brings it back home to the tonic. Some dance movements are followed by a second, complementary dance, as the minuet is followed by a trio (**CD**). In such cases, the first dance should be repeated after the second, thereby creating a large-scale ternary arrangement: **AB|CD|AB**. What make the dance movements of *Water Music* so enjoyable and easy to comprehend are their arresting themes and formal clarity. Notice in the Minuet and Trio how Handel asks the French horns and trumpets first to announce both the **A** and **B** sections before passing this material on to the woodwinds and then the full orchestra.

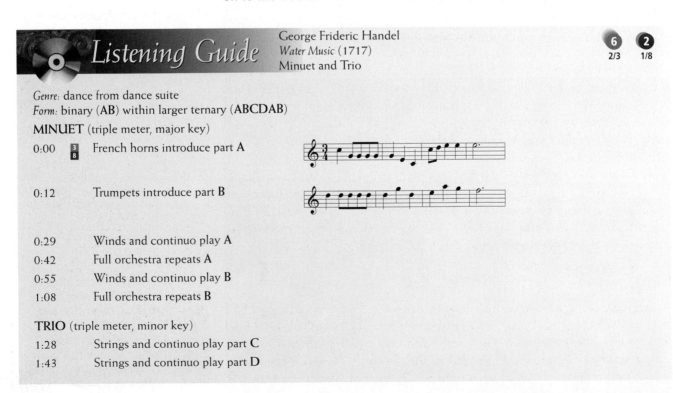

Listening Guide

George Frideric Handel
Water Music (1717)
Minuet and Trio

6   2
2/3   1/8

Genre: dance from dance suite
Form: binary (**AB**) within larger ternary (**ABCDAB**)

MINUET (triple meter, major key)

0:00   [3/8]   French horns introduce part **A**

0:12   Trumpets introduce part **B**

0:29   Winds and continuo play **A**
0:42   Full orchestra repeats **A**
0:55   Winds and continuo play **B**
1:08   Full orchestra repeats **B**

TRIO (triple meter, minor key)
1:28   Strings and continuo play part **C**
1:43   Strings and continuo play part **D**

MINUET

2:19	Full orchestra plays **A**
2:31	Full orchestra plays **B**

Use a downloadable, cross-platform animated Active Listening Guide, available at **www.thomsonedu.com/music/wright**.

Handel and Opera

George Frideric Handel emigrated from Germany to England in 1710 not for the chance to entertain the king, and certainly not for the cuisine or the climate. Rather, he went to London to make money producing Italian opera. With the rare exception of a work such as Purcell's *Dido and Aeneas* (see page 125), there was no opera in London at this time. English audiences preferred spoken plays, with an occasional musical interlude. Handel aimed to change this. London audiences, he reasoned, were daily growing more wealthy and cosmopolitan, and would welcome the "high art" form provided by Italian opera. Guaranteeing himself a healthy share of the profits, Handel participated in the formation of an opera company, the Royal Academy of Music. He composed the music, engaged high-paid soloists from Italy, led the rehearsals, and conducted the finished product from the harpsichord in the orchestra pit.

Handel brings Italian opera to London

The type of Italian opera Handel produced in London is called ***opera seria*** (literally, serious, as opposed to comic, opera), a style that then dominated the operatic stage throughout continental Europe. The librettos* of *opera seria* are usually derived from historical events or mythology, and they chronicle the triumphs and tragedies of kings and queens, gods and goddesses. Much of the action occurs off stage and is reported in the form of recitatives. The principal characters react to these events by means of arias that express stock emotions—hope, anger, hate, frenzy, and despair, to name a few. In Handel's day, the leading male roles were sung by castrati* (castrated males with the vocal range of a female); Baroque audiences associated high social standing on stage with a high voice, male or female. From 1710 until 1728, Handel had great artistic and some financial success, producing two dozen examples of Italian *opera seria*. Foremost among these was *Giulio Cesare* (*Julius Caesar*, 1724), a recasting of the story of Caesar's conquest of the army of Egypt, and Cleopatra's romantic conquest of Caesar (Fig. 14–3).

But opera is a notoriously risky business, and in 1728, Handel's Royal Academy of Music went bankrupt, a victim of the exorbitant fees paid the star singers and the unpredictable tastes of the opera-going public. Handel continued to write operas into the early 1740s, but he increasingly turned his attention to a musical genre similar in construction to opera: oratorio.

Handel and Oratorio

An **oratorio** is literally "something sung in an oratory," an oratory being a hall or chapel used specifically for prayer and sometimes prayer with music. Thus, the oratorio as it first appeared in seventeenth-century Italy was an extended musical setting of a sacred text intended for the spiritual edification of the faithful and performed in a special hall or chapel. By the time it reached Handel's

FIGURE 14–3

Title page of an early English edition of Handel's opera *Julius Caesar*. The musicians form a *basso continuo*.

The Theatrical Quality of Baroque Art

A striking feature of much Baroque art is its theatrical quality. Drama in the arts is created by conflict, by forces that move in opposition, and yet at the same time are so positioned as to project a satisfying wholeness. In late-Baroque music, the competing musical units are generally lengthy and unchanging in mood, with large, clearly defined blocks of sound placed in opposition.

By the early 1700s, Bach and Handel could make music theatrical by drawing on the many opposing styles, textures, colors, and performing groups available to them. For example, voices could be set against instruments, soloists against orchestra, a tutti* against a concertino*, and a fugal chorus against a homophonic one. This same theatrical equilibrium is apparent in the visual arts of the late Baroque, as can be seen, for example, in Giambattista Tiepolo's *The Triumph of Nobility and Virtue over Ignorance*. Here, two large-scale units contrast in position (high and low) and color (white and black). Yet the artist creates a grand spatial harmony because the two units have approximately the same mass and because intersecting diagonal lines within each unit pull with equal force. There is energy, movement, spec-tacle, and grandeur—theatricality—yet there is formal control. Such are the important qualities of late Baroque art, expressed in Handel's choruses and Tiepolo's paintings alike.

The Norton Simon Museum, Pasadena

The Triumph of Nobility and Virtue over Ignorance (c1740)
by Giambattista Tiepolo (1692–1770).

---

hands, however, the oratorio had become in most ways nothing but an unstaged opera with a religious subject.

Both Baroque oratorio and opera begin with an overture*, are divided into acts, and are composed primarily of recitatives and arias. Both genres are also long, usually lasting two to three hours. But there are a few important differences between opera and oratorio, aside from the obvious fact that oratorio treats a religious subject. Oratorio, being a quasi-religious genre, is performed in a church, a theater, or a concert hall, but makes no use of acting, staging, or costumes. Because the subject matter is almost always sacred, there is more of an opportunity for moralizing, a dramatic function best performed by a chorus. Thus the chorus assumes greater importance in an oratorio. It sometimes serves as a narrator, but more often functions, like the chorus in ancient Greek drama, as the voice of the people commenting on the action that has transpired.

By the 1730s, oratorio appeared to Handel as an attractive alternative to the increasingly unprofitable opera in London. He could do away with the irascible and expensive castrati and prima donnas. He no longer had to pay for elaborate sets and costumes. He could draw on the ancient English love of choral music, a tradition that extended well back into the Middle Ages. And

oratorio and opera compared

he could exploit a new, untapped market—the faithful of the Puritan, Methodist, and growing evangelical sects in England who had viewed the pleasures of foreign opera with distrust and even contempt. And in contrast to the Italian opera, the oratorio was sung in English, contributing further to the appeal of the genre to a large segment of English society.

MESSIAH (1741)

Beginning in 1732 and continuing over a twenty-year period, Handel wrote upward of twenty oratorios. The most famous of these is his *Messiah*, composed in the astonishingly short period of three-and-a-half weeks during the summer of 1741. It was first performed in Dublin, Ireland, the following April as part of a charity benefit, with Handel conducting. Having heard the dress rehearsal, the local press waxed enthusiastic about the new oratorio, saying that it "far surpasses anything of that Nature, which has been performed in this or any other Kingdom." Such a large crowd was expected for the work of the famous Handel that ladies were urged not to wear hoopskirts and gentlemen were admonished to leave their swords at home. In this way, an audience of 700 could be squeezed into a hall of only 600 seats.

Messiah premiered in Dublin

Buoyed by his artistic and financial success in Dublin, Handel took *Messiah* back to London, made minor alterations, and performed it in Covent Garden Theater. In 1750, he offered *Messiah* again, this time in the chapel of the Foundling Hospital, an orphanage in London (Fig. 14–4), and again there was much popular acclaim for Handel, as well as profit for charity. This was the first time one of his oratorios was sung in a religious setting rather than a theater or a concert hall. The annual repetition of *Messiah* in the Foundling Hospital chapel during Handel's lifetime and long after did much to convince the public that his oratorios were essentially religious music to be performed in church.

In a general way, *Messiah* tells the story of the life of Christ. It is divided into three parts (instead of three acts): (I) the prophecy of His coming and

FIGURE 14–4

The chapel of the Foundling Hospital, London, where *Messiah* was performed annually for the benefit of the orphans. Handel himself designed and donated the organ seen at the back of the hall.

British Library, London

His Incarnation; (II) His Passion and Resurrection, and the triumph of the Gospel; and (III) reflections on the Christian victory over death. Most of Handel's oratorios recount the heroic deeds of characters from the Old Testament; *Messiah* is exceptional because the subject comes from the New Testament, though much of the libretto is drawn directly from both the Old and New Testaments. There is neither plot action nor "characters" in the dramatic sense. The music consists of fifty-three numbers: nineteen choruses, sixteen solo arias, sixteen recitatives, and two purely instrumental pieces.

There are many beautiful and stirring arias in *Messiah*, including "Ev'ry valley shall be exalted," "O thou that tellest good tidings to Zion," and "Rejoice greatly, O daughter of Zion." Significantly, "Rejoice greatly, O daughter of Zion" is on the same topic as Bach's cantata *Awake, a Voice Is Calling* (see page 151): It tells of the joy felt by all true believers, here personified by the daughter of Zion, at the coming of the Messiah.

da capo *aria*

Handel composed "Rejoice greatly, O daughter of Zion" in the form of a modified *da capo* aria. The **da capo aria,** which originated in Italian opera, has two musical sections, **A** and **B**, with the second usually contrasting in key and mood. When the singer reaches the end of part **B**, he or she is instructed by the words "da capo" to "take it from the top" and thus repeat **A**, note for note. What results is **ABA**, another example of ternary form* in music. Composers such as Handel and Bach sometimes change **A** when it returns so as to achieve variety. A modified *da capo* aria (**ABA'**) is thus created. Such a modification is usually effected to allow the soloist to build to a final climax by means of embellishment and vocal virtuosity. At the end of "Rejoice greatly, O daughter of Zion," for example, what was a relatively easy passage of simple stepwise motion at the end of **A** is transformed into a more difficult, and dramatic, series of leaps of octaves and sevenths in **A'**.

EXAMPLE 14–1

be- hold, thy King cometh un - to thee   be- hold, thy King cometh un- to thee, be- hold, thy King

Examples of *da capo* form and modified *da capo* form abound in arias in both oratorio and opera of the late Baroque era. Indeed, the line of distinction between these two Baroque musical genres, between the sacred oratorio and the profane opera, was a thin one. Although the text of "Rejoice greatly, O daughter of Zion" comes from scripture (Zech. 9:9–10), the daredevil style of singing has its origins in the more worldly opera house.

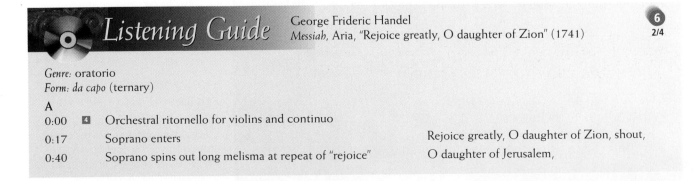

Listening Guide

George Frideric Handel
Messiah, Aria, "Rejoice greatly, O daughter of Zion" (1741)

6
2/4

Genre: oratorio
Form: da capo (ternary)

A

0:00	⁴	Orchestral ritornello for violins and continuo	
0:17		Soprano enters	Rejoice greatly, O daughter of Zion, shout,
0:40		Soprano spins out long melisma at repeat of "rejoice"	O daughter of Jerusalem,

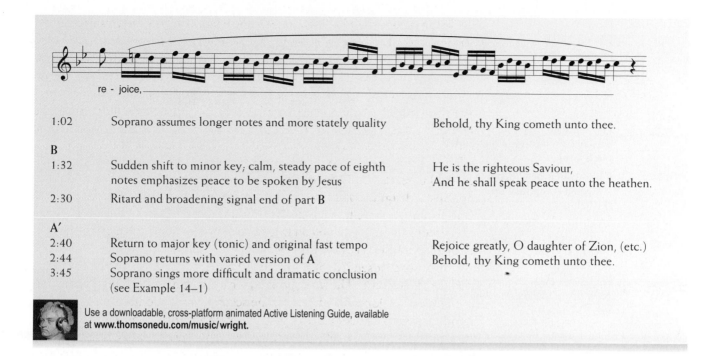

re - joice,

1:02	Soprano assumes longer notes and more stately quality	Behold, thy King cometh unto thee.
B		
1:32	Sudden shift to minor key; calm, steady pace of eighth notes emphasizes peace to be spoken by Jesus	He is the righteous Saviour, And he shall speak peace unto the heathen.
2:30	Ritard and broadening signal end of part **B**	
A'		
2:40	Return to major key (tonic) and original fast tempo	Rejoice greatly, O daughter of Zion, (etc.)
2:44	Soprano returns with varied version of **A**	Behold, thy King cometh unto thee.
3:45	Soprano sings more difficult and dramatic conclusion (see Example 14–1)	

Use a downloadable, cross-platform animated Active Listening Guide, available at **www.thomsonedu.com/music/wright**.

Despite the bravura quality of the arias, the true glory of *Messiah* is to be found in its choruses. Handel is arguably the finest composer for chorus who ever lived. As a world traveler with an unsurpassed ear, he absorbed a variety of musical styles from throughout Europe: in Germany, he acquired knowledge of the fugue and the Lutheran chorale; in Italy, he immersed himself in the styles of the oratorio and the chamber cantata; and during his years in England, he became familiar with the idioms of the English church anthem (essentially an extended motet). Most important, having spent a lifetime in the opera theater, Handel had a flair for the dramatic.

Handel's choruses

Nowhere is Handel's choral mastery more evident than in the justly famous "Hallelujah" chorus that concludes Part II of *Messiah*. Here a variety of choral styles are displayed in quick succession: chordal, unison, chorale, fugal, and fugal and chordal together. The opening word "Hallelujah" recurs throughout as a powerful refrain, yet each new phrase of text generates its own distinct musical idea. The vivid phrases speak directly to the listener, making the audience feel like a participant in the drama. So moved was King George II when he first heard the great opening chords, as the story goes, that he rose to his feet in admiration, thereby establishing the tradition of the audience standing for the "Hallelujah" chorus—for no one sat while the king stood. Indeed, this movement would serve well as a royal coronation march, though in *Messiah*, of course, it is Christ the King who is being crowned.

"Hallelujah" chorus

Listening Guide   George Frideric Handel
Messiah, "Hallelujah" chorus (1741)

Intro
18

Genre: oratorio
Form: through composed

0:00   Brief string introduction

(continued)

Time	Description	Text / Music
0:06	Chorus enters with two salient motives:	

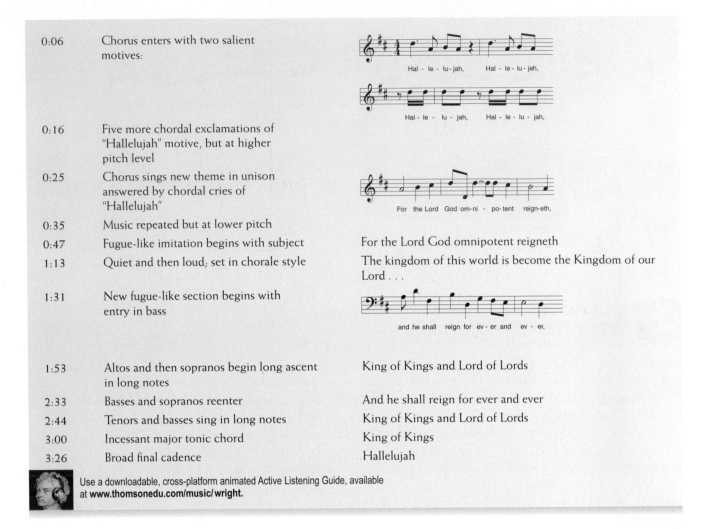

Hal - le - lu - jah, Hal - le - lu - jah,

Hal - le - lu - jah, Hal - le - lu - jah,

| 0:16 | Five more chordal exclamations of "Hallelujah" motive, but at higher pitch level | |
| 0:25 | Chorus sings new theme in unison answered by chordal cries of "Hallelujah" | |

For the Lord God om-ni - po-tent reign-eth,

0:35	Music repeated but at lower pitch	
0:47	Fugue-like imitation begins with subject	For the Lord God omnipotent reigneth
1:13	Quiet and then loud; set in chorale style	The kingdom of this world is become the Kingdom of our Lord . . .
1:31	New fugue-like section begins with entry in bass	

and he shall reign for ev - er and ev - er,

1:53	Altos and then sopranos begin long ascent in long notes	King of Kings and Lord of Lords
2:33	Basses and sopranos reenter	And he shall reign for ever and ever
2:44	Tenors and basses sing in long notes	King of Kings and Lord of Lords
3:00	Incessant major tonic chord	King of Kings
3:26	Broad final cadence	Hallelujah

 Use a downloadable, cross-platform animated Active Listening Guide, available at **www.thomsonedu.com/music/wright.**

Listening Exercise 23

Handel
Messiah, "Hallelujah" chorus

Intro 18

ThomsonNOW™
To take this Listening Exercise online and receive feedback or email answers to your instructor, go to *ThomsonNOW* for this chapter.

As a man of the theater, Handel was the master of the dramatic gesture. Sometimes, as we shall see, he would even insert a "thundering silence" for special effect. This exercise asks you to hear the frequent changes of texture in the "Hallelujah" chorus. It is by means of striking textural changes that Handel creates the grand effects of this classical favorite.

1. (0:06–0:24) In what kind of musical texture do the voices sing when they enter with "Hallelujah"?
   a. monophonic   b. homophonic   c. polyphonic
2. (0:25–0:30; "For the Lord God omnipotent reigneth") As the chorus sings in unison and the violins double (play the same line as) their part, what kind of texture is created?
   a. monophonic   b. homophonic   c. polyphonic

3. (0:47–1:12; "For the Lord God omnipotent reigneth") Now we have a passage of imitative, contrapuntal writing in which a subject is presented in succession in the voices. In what order do the voices enter with this subject?
   a. soprano, alto, male voices
   b. alto, male voices, soprano
   c. soprano, male voices, alto
4. (1:31–1:52; "And he shall reign for ever and ever") Again, Handel offers a passage of imitative writing, with a new subject. In what order do the voices enter?
   a. bass, tenor, soprano, alto
   b. bass, alto, tenor, soprano
   c. bass, tenor, alto, soprano
   d. bass, soprano, alto, tenor

5. Polyphonic passages such as this (1:31–1:52) most closely approximate the style and musical texture found where?
   a. in a Gregorian chant
   b. in a chorale tune
   c. in a fugue

6. (2:06–2:30) What are the sopranos doing here on "King of Kings and Lord of Lords"?
   a. rising in an arpeggio
   b. rising by leap
   c. rising by step

7. (2:54–end) What brass instruments, associated with kings through history, sound forth here along with "King of Kings"?
   a. trombones b. trumpets c. tubas

8. (3:22–3:24) In a brilliant stroke, Handel sets off and highlights the final statement of "Hallelujah" (and the final cadence) by inserting a new kind of texture. Which is correct?
   a. He inserts a homophonic brass fanfare.
   b. He inserts the texture of silence.

9. Which correctly identifies the ways in which *our modern recording* of the "Hallelujah" chorus differs from the performance practices of Handel's time (see paragraph below)?
   a. An orchestra has been added to support what was only a chorus in Handel's original.
   b. The chorus is much larger, and women sing the alto and soprano chorus parts.
   c. Castrati would have been used in Handel's original chorus.

10. What is it that creates the drama and grandeur in this choral movement?
    a. a very clear setting of the English text (with the music emphasizing the stressed words)
    b. the skillful use of a variety of textures and styles
    c. the concentration of all voices and instruments on a few simple musical gestures
    d. all of the above

The "Hallelujah" chorus is a strikingly effective work mainly because the large choral force creates a sense of heavenly power and strength. In fact, however, Handel's chorus for the original Dublin *Messiah* was much smaller than those used today. It included about four singers on the alto, tenor, and bass parts and six choirboys singing the soprano (Fig. 14–5). The orchestra was equally slight. For the Foundling Hospital performances of the 1750s, however, the orchestra grew to thirty-five players. Then, in the course of the

FIGURE 14–5

Eighteenth-century London was a place of biting satire. Here, in William Hogarth's *The Oratorio Singer* (1732), the chorus of an oratorio is the object of parody. But there is an element of truth here: the chorus for the first performance of *Messiah*, for example, numbered about sixteen males, with choirboys (front row) taking the soprano part. Women, however, sang soprano and alto for the vocal solos.

Yale Center for British Art, Paul Mellon Collection

next hundred years, the chorus progressively swelled to as many as 4,000 with a balancing orchestra of 500 in what were billed as "Festivals of the People" in honor of Handel.

And just as there was a continual increase in the performing forces for his *Messiah,* so too Handel's fortune and reputation grew. Toward the end of his life, he occupied a squire's house in the center of London; bought paintings, including a large and "indeed excellent" Rembrandt; and, on his death, left an enormous estate of nearly 20,000 pounds, as the newspapers of the day were quick to report. More than 3,000 persons attended his funeral in Westminster Abbey on April 20, 1759, and a sculpture of the composer holding an aria from *Messiah* was erected above his grave and is still visible today (Fig. 14–6). As a memento of Handel's music, *Messiah* was an apt choice, for it is still performed each year at Christmas and Easter by countless amateur and professional groups throughout the world.

FIGURE 14–6

Handel's funeral monument at Westminster Abbey. The composer holds the aria "I know that my Redeemer liveth" from *Messiah.* When Handel was buried, the gravedigger left room to cram in another body immediately adjacent. That space was later filled by the corpse of Charles Dickens.

Bridgeman Art Library, London/NY

Key Words

dance suite (**160**)	oratorio (**161**)
opera seria (**161**)	*da capo* aria (**164**)

Checklist of Musical Style

Representative composers
Bach
Handel
Telemann
Vivaldi

Late Baroque: 1710–1750

Melody	Grows longer, more expansive, and more asymmetrical; idiomatic instrumental style influences vocal melodies
Harmony	Functional chord progressions govern harmonic movement—harmony moves purposefully from one chord to next; *basso continuo* continues to provide strong bass

Rhythm	Exciting, driving, energized rhythms propel music forward with vigor; "walking" bass creates feeling of rhythmic regularity	*Principal genres* church cantata opera
Color	Instruments reign supreme; instrumental sounds, especially of violin, harpsichord, and organ, set musical tone for era; one tone color used throughout movement or large section of movement	French overture oratorio sonata dance suite
Texture	Homophonic texture remains important, but polyphonic texture reemerges because of growing importance of contrapuntal fugue	concerto grosso prelude fugue
Form	Binary form in sonatas and dance suites; *da capo* aria (ternary) form in arias; fugal procedure used in fugue	

PART IV

The Classical Period, 1750–1820

During the years 1750–1820, music manifested a style called "Classicism," often termed "Neoclassicism" in the other fine arts. In art and architecture, for example, Neoclassicism aimed to reinstitute the aesthetic values of the ancient Greeks and Romans by incorporating balance and harmonious proportions while avoiding ornate decoration, all leading to a feeling of quiet grace and noble simplicity. When expressed in music, these same tendencies

1750	1755	1760	1765	1770	1775	1780	1785

CLASSICAL

1756–1763 Seven Years War (French and Indian War)

● 1759 Voltaire publishes Enlightenment novel *Candide*

● 1761 Joseph Haydn takes first job at Esterházy court

● 1762 Rousseau publishes outline for just government in *The Social Contract*

1763–1766 Mozart family tours and performs around Western Europe

● 1776 American Declaration of Independence signed in Philadelphia

● 1781 Mozart moves to Vienna and composes operas, symphonies, concertos, and quartets

appeared as balanced phrases, lucid textures, and clear, easily audible musical forms. Although composers in cities such as Milan, Paris, and London all wrote symphonies and sonatas with these qualities, the music of this period is often referred to as the "Viennese Classical style." Vienna, Austria, was the capital city of the Holy Roman Empire and the most active center of Classical music in Central Europe. The three principal composers of the classical era—Joseph Haydn (1732–1809), Wolfgang Amadeus Mozart (1756–1791), and Ludwig van Beethoven (1770–1827)—chose to make Vienna their home because of the city's vibrant musical life. In many ways, Mozart and Haydn created the Classical style while Beethoven extended it. The majority of the works of Beethoven fall within the time frame of the Classical era, but they also sometimes exhibit stylistic characteristics of the succeeding Romantic period.

| 1790 | 1795 | 1800 | 1805 | 1810 | 1815 | 1820 | 1825 |

CLASSICAL

● 1789 French Revolution begins

1791–1795 Haydn composes his "London" Symphonies

● 1792 Ludwig van Beethoven moves from Bonn to Vienna

● 1796 Napoleon invades Austrian Empire

● 1797 Haydn composes *The Emperor's Hymn* as act of patriotism

● 1803 Beethoven writes his "Eroica" Symphony

● 1815 Napoleon defeated at Waterloo

● 1824 Beethoven composes his ninth and last symphony

Chapter 15

Classical Style

Classical as a musical term has two separate, though related, meanings. We use the word *classical* to signify the "serious" or "art" music of the West as distinguished from folk music, popular music, jazz, and the traditional music of various ethnic cultures. We call this music "classical" because there is something about the excellence of its form and style that makes it enduring, just as a finely crafted watch or a vintage automobile may be said to be a "classic" because it has a timeless beauty. Yet in the same breath we may refer to "Classical" music (now with a capital C), and by this we mean the music of a specific historical period, 1750–1820, a period of the great works of Haydn and Mozart and the early masterpieces of Beethoven. The creations of these artists have become so identified in the public mind with musical proportion, balance, and formal correctness—with standards of musical excellence—that this comparatively brief period has given its name to all music of lasting aesthetic worth.

"Classical" derives from the Latin *classicus*, meaning "something of the first rank or highest quality." To the men and women of the eighteenth century, no art, architecture, philosophy, or political institutions were more admirable, virtuous, and worthy of emulation than those of ancient Greece and Rome. Other periods in Western history also have been inspired by classical antiquity—the Renaissance heavily (see Fig. 9–1), the early Baroque less so, and the twentieth century to some degree—but no period more than the eighteenth century. This fascination with antiquity is evident, for example, in the enthusiasm surrounding the discovery of the ruins of Pompeii (1748) and the publication of Edward Gibbon's *Decline and Fall of the Roman Empire* (1788).

The eighteenth century was also the period during which young English aristocrats made the "grand tour" of Italy and carted back to their country estates Roman statues, columns, and parts of entire villas. Classical architecture, with its formal control of space, geometric shapes, balance, and symmetrical design, became the only style thought worthy for domestic and state buildings of consequence. European palaces, opera houses, theaters, and country homes all made use of it. Thomas Jefferson also traveled to Italy in these years while American ambassador to France, and later brought Classical design to the United States (Figs. 15–1 and 15–2). Our nation's capitol, many state capitols, and countless other governmental and university buildings abound with the well-proportioned columns, porticos, and rotundas of the Classical style.

FIGURES 15–1 AND 15–2

(top) The second-century Pantheon in Rome. (bottom) The library of the University of Virginia, designed by Thomas Jefferson in the late eighteenth century. Jefferson had visited Rome and studied the ancient ruins while serving as ambassador to France (1784–1789). The portico, with columns and triangular pediment, and the central rotunda are all elements of Classical style in architecture.

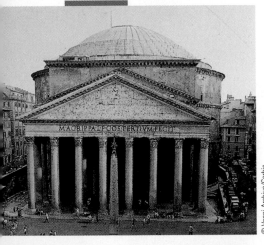

THE ENLIGHTENMENT

The Classical era in music, art, and architecture coincides with the period in philosophy and letters called the **Enlightenment.** During the Enlightenment, also referred to as the Age of Reason, thinkers gave free rein to the pursuit of truth and the discovery of natural laws. This is the era that saw the rise of a natural religion called Deism, the belief that a Creator made the world, set it in motion, and has left it alone ever since. This is also the age of such scientific

172

advances as the discovery of electricity and the invention of the steam engine. The first *Encyclopedia Britannica* appeared in 1771 and the French *Encyclopédie* between 1751 and 1772, a twenty-four volume set whose authors discarded traditional religious convictions and superstitions in favor of more rational scientific, philosophical, and political beliefs. In France the encyclopedists Voltaire (1694–1778) and Jean-Jacques Rousseau (1712–1778) espoused the principles of social justice, equality, religious tolerance, and freedom of speech. These Enlightenment ideals subsequently became fundamental to democratic government and were enshrined in the American Constitution.

Needless to say, the notion that all persons are created equal and should enjoy full political freedom put the thinkers of the Enlightenment on a collision course with the defenders of the existing social order. The old political structure had been built on the superstitions of the Church, the privileges of the nobility, and the divine right of kings. Voltaire attacked the habits and prerogatives of both clergy and aristocracy, and championed middle-class virtues: honesty, common sense, and hard work. The extravagant gestures and powdered wig of the frivolous courtier were easy targets for his pen. A more natural appearance, one appropriate to a tradesman, merchant, or manufacturer, now became the paradigm (Fig. 15–3). Spurred on by economic self-interest and the principles of the Enlightenment philosophers, an expanding, more confident middle class in France and America rebelled against the monarchy and its supporters. The Age of Reason gave way to the Age of Revolution.

FIGURE 15–3

Thomas Jefferson, by the French sculptor Houdon, done in 1789, the year of the French Revolution.

MUSIC AND SOCIAL CHANGE: COMIC OPERA

Music was affected by these profound social changes, and in some ways, it helped to precipitate them. A new form of opera, comic opera, proved to be a powerful vehicle for social reform. Opera in the Baroque period had been dominated by *opera seria** (see page 161). It was beautiful, grandiose, somewhat stiff, and expensive to mount. Portraying the deeds of mythological gods and goddesses, and historical emperors and kings, it glorified the deeds of the aristocracy. By contrast, the new **comic opera,** called *opera buffa* in Italy, championed middle-class values. It made use of everyday characters and situations; it typically employed spoken dialogue and simple songs in place of recitatives and *da capo** arias; and it was liberally spiced with sight gags, slapstick comedy, and bawdy humor. The librettos, such as they were, either poked fun at the nobility for its pomposity and incompetence or criticized it for being heartless.

middle-class characters
middle-class values

Like seditious pamphlets, comic operas appeared across Europe; among them were John Gay's *The Beggar's Opera* (1728) in England, Giovanni Pergolesi's *La serva padrona* (*The Maid Made Master*, 1733) in Italy, and Rousseau's *Le Devin du village* (*The Village Soothsayer*, 1752) in France. Even composers of greater stature were seduced by the charms of this more middle-class entertainment. Mozart, who was treated poorly by the nobility during his adult life, set one libretto *Le nozze di Figaro* (*The Marriage of Figaro*, 1786), in which a barber and a maid outsmart a count and hold him up to public ridicule, and another, *Don Giovanni* (1787), in which the villain is a leading nobleman of the town. The nobility took seriously the threat that such works posed to the established social order; indeed, the play that served as the basis for Mozart's *Figaro* was initially banned by French King Louis XVI. By the time of the French Revolution (1789), comic opera, a rebellious upstart, had nearly driven the established *opera seria* off the eighteenth-century stage.

PUBLIC CONCERTS

The social changes of the eighteenth century, in turn, affected who listened to classical music. In an earlier day, the average citizen might hear sacred vocal music in a church, and that was about all. But by mid-century, the book-keeper, physician, cloth merchant, and stock trader collectively had enough disposable income to organize and patronize their own concerts. In Paris, then a city of 450,000, one could attend "the best concerts every day with complete freedom." The most successful Parisian concert series was the *Concert spirituel* (founded in 1725), the West's first standing orchestra with a regular schedule of performances, all open to the public. The *Concert spirituel* advertised its performances by means of flyers distributed in the streets. To make its offerings accessible to several strata of society, it also instituted a two-tiered price scheme for subscription tickets (four *livres* for boxes and two *livres* for the pit; roughly $200 and $100 in today's money). Children under fifteen were admitted for half price. Thus we can trace to the middle of the eighteenth century the tradition of middle-class citizens paying an admission fee and attending a public performance. The institution of the "concert," as we know it today, dates from this time.

In London, entrepreneurs offered concerts in the Vauxhall Gardens, an eighteenth-century amusement park drawing as many as 4,500 paying visitors daily. Here symphonies could be heard inside in the orchestra room, or outside, when the weather was fine. When Leopold Mozart took his young son Wolfgang to concerts there in 1764, he was surprised to see that the audience was not segregated by class. Likewise in Vienna, the Burgtheater (City Theater) opened in 1759 to any and all paying customers, as long as they were properly dressed and properly behaved. Although the nobility still occupied the best seats (Fig. 15–4), the doors of the concert hall were now open to the general public, fostering a leveling between classes with respect to all the fine arts. The middle class was seizing control of high culture from the aristocracy. Classical music was becoming public entertainment.

THE ADVENT OF THE PIANO

The newly affluent middle class wished not only to listen to music but also to play it. Most of this music-making was centered in the home and around an instrument that first entered public consciousness in the Classical period: the piano. Invented in Italy about 1700, the piano gradually replaced the harpsi-chord as the keyboard instrument of preference (Fig. 15–5)—and with good reason, for the piano could play at more than one dynamic level (hence the original name **pianoforte,** "soft-loud"). Compared with the harpsichord, the piano could produce gradual dynamic changes, more subtle contrasts, and—ultimately—more power.

Those who played this new domestic instrument were mostly amateurs, and the great majority of these were women. A smattering of French, an eye for

FIGURE 15–4

A performance at the Burgtheater in Vienna in 1785. The nobility occupied the front-most seats on the floor, but the area behind (to the left of) the partition was open to all. So, too, in the galleries, the aristocracy bought boxes low and close to the stage, while commoners occupied higher rungs, as well as the standing room in the fourth gallery. Ticket prices depended, then as now, on proximity to the performers.

Kunsthistorisches Museum, Vienna/The Bridgeman Art Library

needlepoint, and some skill at the piano—these were signs of status and gentility that rendered a young woman suitable for marriage. For the nonprofessional woman to play in the home, however, a simpler, more homophonic style of keyboard music was needed, one that would not tax the presumed technical limitations of the female performer. The spirit of democracy may have been in the air, but this was still very much a sexist age. It was assumed that ladies would not wish, as one publication said, "to bother their pretty little heads with counterpoint and harmony," but would be content with a tuneful melody and a few rudimentary chords to flesh it out. Collections such as *Keyboard Pieces for Ladies* (1768) were directed at these new musical consumers.

ELEMENTS OF CLASSICAL STYLE

Much has been written about the Classical style in music: its quiet grace, noble simplicity, purity, and serenity. It is certainly "classical" in the sense that emphasis is placed on formal clarity, order, and balance. Compared with the relentless, often grandiose sound of the Baroque, Classical music is lighter in tone, more natural, yet less predictable. It is even capable of humor and surprise, as when Joseph Haydn explodes with a thunderous chord in a quiet passage in his "Surprise" Symphony (1791). But what in precise musical terms creates the levity, grace, clarity, and balance characteristic of Classical music?

Melody

Perhaps the first thing that strikes the listener about the music of Haydn or Mozart is that the theme is often tuneful, catchy, even singable. Not only are melodies simple and short, but the phrases tend to be organized in antecedent–consequent*, or "question–answer," pairs. (Think of the first two phrases of *Twinkle, Twinkle Little Star*, a folksong set by Mozart.) Indeed, antecedent-consequent phrases appear in significant number for the first time in the history of music during the Classical period. The melody usually progresses by playing out these short phrases in symmetrical groups of two, three, four, eight, twelve, or sixteen bars. The brevity of the phrase and frequent cadences allow for ample light and air to penetrate the melodic line.

Below is the theme from the second movement of Mozart's Piano Concerto in C major (1785). It is composed of two three-bar phrases—an antecedent and a consequent phrase. The melody is light and airy, yet perfectly balanced. It is also singable and quite memorable—indeed, it has been turned into a popular movie theme (the "love song" from *Elvira Madigan*). Contrast this to the long, asymmetrical melodies of the Baroque that were often instrumental in character (see pages 115, 142, and 148).

symmetrical phrases

EXAMPLE 15–1

FIGURE 15–5
Marie Antoinette, in 1770 at the age of fifteen, seated at an early piano. In 1774, this Austrian princess became queen of France, but in 1793, at the height of French Revolution, she was beheaded.

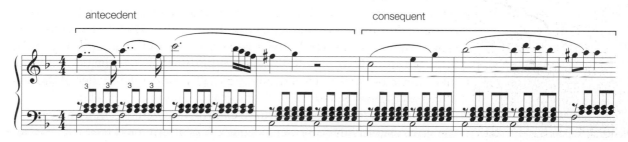

Harmony

flexible harmonic rhythm

After about 1750, all classical music assumed a more homophonic, less polyphonic character. The new tuneful melody was supported by a simple harmony. In the preceding example, only two chords, tonic and dominant, support Mozart's lovely melody. The heavy *basso continuo* of the Baroque era has disappeared entirely. The bass still generates the harmony, but it does not always move in the regular, constant fashion typified by the Baroque walking bass*. Rather, the bass might sit on the bottom of one chord for several beats, even several measures, then move rapidly, and then stop again. Thus, the rate at which chords change—the "harmonic rhythm" as it is called—is much more fluid and flexible with Classical composers.

Alberti bass

To avoid a feeling of inactivity when the harmony is static, Classical composers invented new patterns for accompaniment. Sometimes, as in Example 15–1, they simply repeat the accompanying chord in a uniform triplet rhythm. More common is the pattern called the **Alberti bass,** named after the minor Italian keyboard composer Domenico Alberti (1710–1740), who popularized this figure. Instead of playing the pitches of a chord all together, the performer spreads them out to provide a continual stream of sound. Mozart used an Alberti bass at the beginning of his famous C major piano sonata (1788).

EXAMPLE 15–2

The Alberti pattern serves essentially the same function as the modern "boogie-woogie" bass. It provides an illusion of harmonic activity for those moments when, in fact, the harmony is stationary.

Rhythm

Rhythm, too, is more flexible in the hands of Haydn and Mozart than it had been in the music of the Baroque era, animating the stop-and-go character of Classical melody and harmony. Rapid motion may be followed by repose and then further quick movement, but there is little of the driving, perpetual motion of Baroque musical rhythm.

Texture

light texture

Musical texture was also transformed in the latter half of the eighteenth century, mainly because composers began to concentrate less on writing dense counterpoint and more on creating charming melodies. No longer are independent polyphonic lines superimposed, layer upon layer, as in a Baroque fugue of Bach or a polyphonic chorus of Handel. This lessening of counterpoint made for a lighter, more transparent sound, especially in the middle range of the texture. Mozart, after a study of Bach and Handel in the early 1780s, infused his symphonies, quartets, and concertos with greater polyphonic content, but this seems to have caused the pleasure-loving Viennese to think his music too dense!

Classical Style in Painting

Painting of the late eighteenth century is often termed "Neoclassical," because it draws heavily on the themes and styles of classical antiquity. Many of the major artists of the day traveled to Rome between 1760 and 1790 to study the architecture, sculpture, and frescoes that remained in the Roman forum and elsewhere around the city. They incorporated into their works not only the style and ornament of Roman dress but also the clarity, simplicity, and formal balance inherent in ancient classical design. The Englishwoman Angelica Kauffmann (1741–1807) was one of the Neoclassical painters who had journeyed to Rome. By studying Roman art, Kauffmann was also studying Greek art, for the Romans had been heavily influenced by the Greeks in matters of artistic style.

Angelica Kauffmann's The Artist in the Character of Design Listening to the Inspiration of Poetry (1782).

© Mary Evans Picture Library/The Image Works

Kauffmann's painting *The Artist [Angelica Kauffmann] in the Character of Design Listening to the Inspiration of Poetry* shows a pair of balanced figures in Roman costume: Design on the left and Poetry on the right. Poetry is crowned with the laurel wreath of the Roman poet laureate. In addition, each figure holds a symbol of her art: Design a drawing board and Poetry a lyre. To their left are two columns, which similarly invoke a feeling of antiquity and, at the same time, balance the two women. Nowhere to be found are secondary figures, who might clutter the scene. Our eyes focus solely on Design and Poetry. The simplicity, balance, and static quality of the painting create a feeling of calm, serenity, and repose, sentiments often felt in Classical music as well.

THE DRAMATIC QUALITY OF CLASSICAL MUSIC

What is perhaps most revolutionary in the music of Haydn, Mozart, and their younger contemporary, Beethoven, is its capacity for rapid change and endless fluctuation. Recall that in earlier times a work by Purcell, Corelli, Vivaldi, or Bach would establish one "affect," or mood, to be rigidly maintained from beginning to end—the rhythm, melody, and harmony all progressing in a continuous, uninterrupted flow. Such a uniform approach to expression is part of the "single-mindedness" of Baroque art. Now, with Haydn, Mozart, and the young Beethoven, the mood of a piece might change radically within a few short phrases. An energetic theme in rapid notes may be followed by a second one that is slow, lyrical, and tender. Similarly, textures might change quickly from light and airy to dense and more contrapuntal, adding tension and excitement. For the first time, composers began to call for crescendos and diminuendos, a gradual increase or lessening of the dynamic level, so that the volume of sound might continually fluctuate. When skilled orchestras made use of this technique, audiences were fascinated and rose to their feet. Keyboard players, too, now took up the crescendo and diminuendo, assuming that the new, multidynamic piano was at hand in place of the older, less flexible harpsichord. These rapid changes in mood, texture, color, and dynamics give to Classical music a new sense of urgency and drama. The listener feels a

frequent changes of mood

FIGURE 15–6

Baritone Kyle Ketelsen singing the role of Figaro in a recent production of Mozart's *The Marriage of Figaro* at the New York City Opera.

constant flux and flow, not unlike the continual swings of mood we experience in daily life.

An Example of Classical Style

To experience the essence of the Classical style in music, let us turn to an aria from Mozart's comic opera *The Marriage of Figaro* (1786). Recall that the libretto* of this opera was taken from a revolutionary play that criticized the aristocracy (see page 173). It was Mozart's idea to set this play to music, and he retained in his opera most of the socially incendiary ideas from the play.

Social tension is immediately apparent at the beginning of the opera. The main character is Figaro (Fig. 15–6), a clever, mostly honest barber and manservant who outwits his lord, the philandering, mostly dishonest Count Almaviva. We first meet Figaro as he discovers that he and his betrothed, Susanna, have been assigned a bedroom next to the Count's. The Count wishes to exercise his ancient *droit de seigneur*—the lord's claim to sexual favors from the servant's fiancée. Figaro responds with a short aria "Se vuol ballare" ("If you want to dance"). Here he calls the Count by the diminutive "Contino," translated roughly as "Count, you little twerp," and vows to outwit his master.

Example 15–3 shows the simplicity, clarity, and balance typical of the Classical style. The texture is light and homophonic—really only supporting chords—as if Figaro were accompanying himself on the guitar. The melody begins with a four-bar phrase that immediately repeats at a higher level of pitch. Formally, the aria consists of four sections: **A**, **B**, **C**, and **D**, with a return to **A** at the end. Section **A** has five four-bar phrases, and so do sections **B** and **C**, while section **D** has twice that number. Although the sections are connected by a measure or two of purely instrumental musical, the vocal sections of this aria thus have the proportions 20 + 20 + 20 + 40 + 20, a balanced arrangement indeed.

EXAMPLE 15–3

(If you want to dance, Count, you little twerp . . .)

The dynamic quality of Classical music—its capacity to encompass changes of mood—is also evident in Figaro's "If you want to dance." Figaro begins in a calm, measured manner, but the more he thinks about the Count's lechery and treachery, the more anxious he becomes. Musically, we hear Figaro's agitation grow throughout sections **A**, **B**, **C**, and **D**, each gaining in intensity. Only at the end does the barber regain his composure, as signaled by the return of **A**. Mozart casts the aria "If you want to dance" within the context of a dance—specifically, the courtly minuet. Here dance serves as a metaphor for the ways of life—if the Count wants to "dance" (fool around), Figaro, the servant, will call the tune.

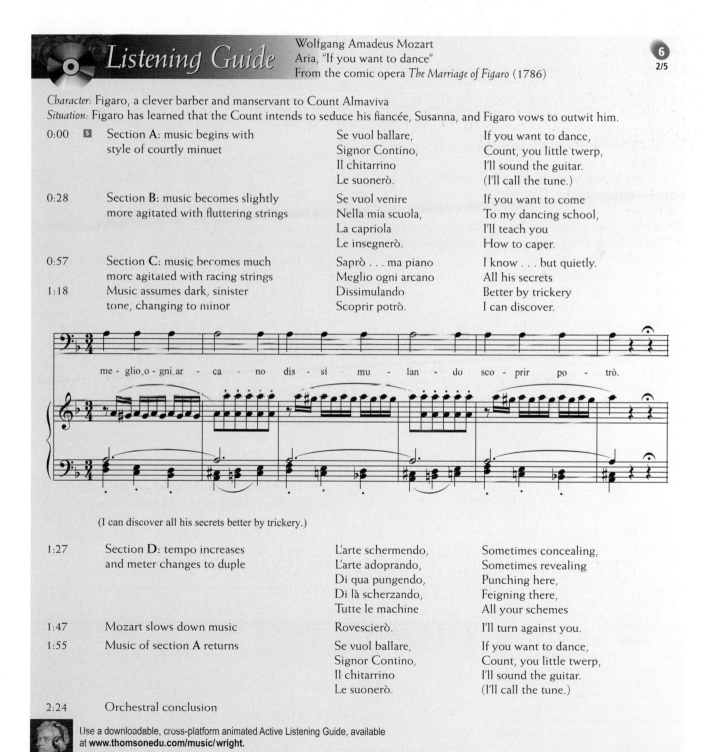

Listening Guide

Wolfgang Amadeus Mozart
Aria, "If you want to dance"
From the comic opera *The Marriage of Figaro* (1786)

6
2/5

Character: Figaro, a clever barber and manservant to Count Almaviva
Situation: Figaro has learned that the Count intends to seduce his fiancée, Susanna, and Figaro vows to outwit him.

0:00	**5**	Section **A**: music begins with style of courtly minuet	Se vuol ballare, Signor Contino, Il chitarrino Le suonerò.	If you want to dance, Count, you little twerp, I'll sound the guitar. (I'll call the tune.)
0:28		Section **B**: music becomes slightly more agitated with fluttering strings	Se vuol venire Nella mia scuola, La capriola Le insegnerò.	If you want to come To my dancing school, I'll teach you How to caper.
0:57		Section **C**: music becomes much more agitated with racing strings	Saprò . . . ma piano Meglio ogni arcano	I know . . . but quietly. All his secrets
1:18		Music assumes dark, sinister tone, changing to minor	Dissimulando Scoprir potrò.	Better by trickery I can discover.

me - glio_o-gni_ar - ca - no dis - si - mu - lan - do sco - prir po - trò.

(I can discover all his secrets better by trickery.)

1:27	Section **D**: tempo increases and meter changes to duple	L'arte schermendo, L'arte adoprando, Di qua pungendo, Di là scherzando, Tutte le machine	Sometimes concealing, Sometimes revealing Punching here, Feigning there, All your schemes
1:47	Mozart slows down music	Rovescierò.	I'll turn against you.
1:55	Music of section **A** returns	Se vuol ballare, Signor Contino, Il chitarrino Le suonerò.	If you want to dance, Count, you little twerp, I'll sound the guitar. (I'll call the tune.)
2:24	Orchestral conclusion		

Use a downloadable, cross-platform animated Active Listening Guide, available at **www.thomsonedu.com/music/wright.**

Listening Exercise 24

Mozart
"If you want to dance"

ThomsonNOW™
To take this Listening Exercise online and receive feedback or email answers to your instructor, go to *ThomsonNOW* for this chapter.

At the beginning of the aria "If you want to dance," Figaro appears to be a well-balanced, honest, if simple, fellow (section **A**). But as he thinks about the skills he will need to foil the Count's designs, Figaro reveals a more impetuous, sinister side (sections **B**, **C**, and **D**). This exercise asks you to focus on the ways tension and dramatic intensity can be set loose within what is essentially a balanced, foursquare framework typical of Classical style.

1. (0:00–0:27) What are the meter and tempo at the beginning of the aria?
   a. duple and moderate as is appropriate for a stately, courtly minuet
   b. triple and moderate as is appropriate for a stately, courtly minuet

2. (0:00–0:27) What aspect of the accompaniment conveys the light texture of Classical music, suggesting, perhaps, that Figaro might be accompanying himself on a guitar?
   a. The strings play tremolo.
   b. The strings play vibrato.
   c. The strings play pizzicato.

3. (0:28–0:56) Section **B** has a balanced phrase structure similar to section **A**, but how does Mozart suggest that Figaro is becoming agitated?
   a. He adds a quivering accompaniment in the strings, and Figaro sings more loudly.
   b. He adds a trill in the French horns, and Figaro sings more softly.

4. (0:57–1:07) In section **C**, Figaro's agitation grows as Mozart does what?
   a. employs shorter note values that give the sense that music is going faster
   b. inserts a rising scale in rapid notes
   c. begins each statement of the scale on a successively higher pitch (rising melodic sequence)
   d. all of the above

5. (1:08–1:13) How does Mozart suggest that Figaro will have to carry out his schemes quietly?
   a. The music becomes quiet on the word *piano* (quiet) and falls in pitch.
   b. The music becomes quiet on the word *piano* (quiet) and rises in pitch.

6. (1:18–1:26) How does Mozart suggest that Figaro will have to be tricky and slippery (see musical example in Listening Guide)?
   a. While Figaro repeats one pitch, the orchestra turns to minor and slides chromatically.
   b. While the orchestra repeats one pitch, Figaro turns to minor and slides chromatically.

7. (1:27–1:46) In section **D**, Figaro's mind seems to race as he contemplates the skills he will need to outfox the Count. What in the libretto at this point may have caused Mozart to rush along in five-note musical phrases?
   a. The poetry of section **D** has five lines and the rhyme scheme "a, b, c, d, e."
   b. The poetry of section **D** begins with five-syllable lines, all rhyming with "o."

8. (1:47–1:52) How does Mozart slow the music to suggest that Figaro is regaining his composure?
   a. He writes in a retard* and then a fermata*.
   b. He writes in a diminuendo* and a fugato*.

9. (2:23–end) Does the purely instrumental conclusion make use of antecedent–consequent phrase structure?
   a. yes   b. no

10. Finally, how does Mozart underscore through music the drama inherent in this scene?
    a. He contrasts major and minor tonalities.
    b. He contrasts diatonic and chromatic writing.
    c. He has Figaro sing at a moderate tempo at the beginning and end but fast in the middle.
    d. He has Figaro sing both very loudly and very softly as the situation demands.
    e. All of the above.

ThomsonNOW™
ThomsonNOW for *Listening to Music, 5th Edition,* and *Listening to Western Music* will assist you in understanding the content of this chapter with lesson plans generated for your specific needs. In addition, you may complete this chapter's Listening Exercise in *ThomsonNOW*'s interactive environment, as well as download Active Listening Guides and other materials that will help you succeed in this course.

Key Words

Enlightenment (172)
comic opera (173)

opera buffa (173)
pianoforte (174)

Alberti bass (176)

Classical Composers
HAYDN AND MOZART

We tend to think of the music of the Classical era as the work of just three composers: Haydn, Mozart, and Beethoven. There were, of course, others. At the very beginning of the Classical period, Haydn was greatly influenced by Carl Philipp Emanuel Bach, then residing in Berlin, just as Mozart was by this Bach's half-brother Johann Christian Bach, living in London. (Both Bachs were sons of Baroque master J. S. Bach.) In the 1790s, the symphonies of Mozart were not as well known in Paris and London as those of Haydn's pupil, Ignace Pleyel. Mozart once played a piano competition against Muzio Clementi, whose sonatas are still studied by beginning pianists today. Haydn's younger brother Michael, who worked in Salzburg, composed a Symphony in G (1783) that was long thought (mistakenly) to be Mozart's. As this confusion suggests, there were other musicians in Europe during the Classical era whose compositional skills were not so much less than those of the three great masters. The best compositions of Haydn, Mozart, and Beethoven, however, reached a level all their own.

VIENNA: A CITY OF MUSIC

The careers of Haydn, Mozart, and Beethoven culminated in Vienna, Austria. (Because Beethoven's life extended into the early Romantic period, his biography and music will be considered separately in Chapter 21.) So closely are these composers, along with the young Franz Schubert, associated with Vienna that they are sometimes referred to as the "Viennese School," and their music that of the "Viennese Classical style."

Vienna was then the capital of the old Holy Roman Empire, a huge expanse covering much of Western and Central Europe (Fig. 16–1). In 1790, the heyday of Haydn and Mozart, Vienna had a population of 215,000, which made it the fourth-largest city in Europe, after London, Paris, and Naples. Vienna served as the administrative center for portions of modern-day Germany, Italy, Croatia, Bosnia, Serbia, Slovakia, Poland, Czech Republic, and Hungary, in addition to all of Austria. It was bordered to the east by vast agricultural lands, with no other large city

FIGURE 16–1

A map of eighteenth-century Europe showing the Holy Roman Empire and the principal musical cities, including Vienna, Austria.

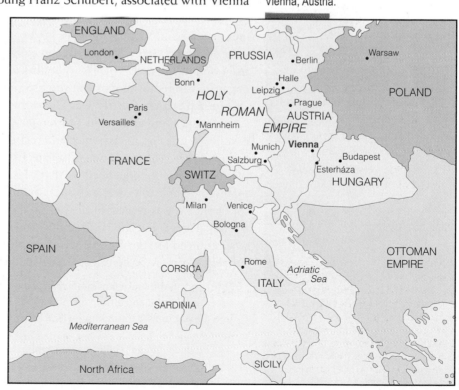

Precision Graphics

aristocracy gravitates to Vienna

for hundreds of miles. The landowning aristocracy from even as far away as Russia congregated in Vienna, especially during the long winter months when there was little agricultural work to be supervised. The nobles patronized music, often enjoying it together with middle-class citizens at public concerts. There were theaters for German and Italian opera, concerts in the streets on fine summer nights, and ballroom dances where as many as 4,000 persons might sway to a minuet or a waltz by Mozart or Beethoven.

composers do likewise

With so much musical patronage to offer, Vienna attracted musicians from throughout Europe. Haydn moved there from Lower Austria, Mozart from Upper Austria, his rival Antonio Salieri from Italy, and Beethoven from Bonn, Germany. Later, in the nineteenth century, in addition to native-born Franz Schubert, outsiders such as Anton Bruckner, Johannes Brahms, and Gustav Mahler spent many of their most productive years there. Even today Vienna remains the capital of a nation (Austria) that spends nearly as much money on its state opera as it does on national defense.

FRANZ JOSEPH HAYDN (1732–1809)

Joseph Haydn was the first of the great composers to move to Vienna, and his life offers something of a "rags-to-riches" story (Fig. 16–2). Haydn was born in 1732 in a farmhouse in Rohrau, Austria, about twenty-five miles east of Vienna. His father, a wheelwright, played the harp but could not read music. When the choir director of Saint Stephen's Cathedral in Vienna happened to be scouting for talent in the provinces, he heard the boy soprano Haydn sing and, impressed by his musicianship, brought him back to the cathedral in Vienna. Here Haydn remained as a choirboy, studying the rudiments of composition and learning to play the violin and keyboard. After nearly ten years of service, his voice broke and he was abruptly dismissed. For most of the 1750s, Haydn eked out a "wretched existence," as he called it, working as a freelance musician around Vienna. He gave keyboard lessons, accompanied singers, and sang or played violin or organ at three churches each Sunday, moving quickly from one to the next. In 1761, Haydn's years of struggle ended when he was engaged as director of music at the Esterházy court.

The **Esterházy family** was the richest and most influential among the German-speaking aristocrats of Hungary, with extensive landholdings southeast of Vienna and a passionate interest in music. At the family seat at Esterháza (see Fig. 16–1), Prince Nikolaus Esterházy (1714–1790) constructed a palace (Fig. 16–3) influenced by that of King Louis XIV at Versailles. Here he maintained an orchestra, a chapel for singing religious music, and a theater for opera. As was typical of the period, Prince Nikolaus engaged Haydn to be a musical servant at the court and wear servants' dress (see Fig. 16–2). Haydn was required to sign a contract of employment, one that suggests the subservient place of the composer in eighteenth-century society:

> [He] and all the musicians shall appear in uniform, and the said Joseph Haydn shall take care that he and all the members of the orchestra follow the instructions given, and appear in white stocking, white linen, powdered, and with either a pigtail or a tiewig. . . .
>
> The said [Haydn] shall be under obligation to compose such music as his Serene Highness may command, and neither to communicate such compositions to any other person, nor to allow them to be copied, but he shall retain them for the

FIGURE 16–2

Portrait of Joseph Haydn (c1762–1763) wearing a wig and the blue livery of the Esterházy court.

With the kind permission of Professor Daniel Heartz

absolute use of his Highness, and not compose for any other person without the knowledge and permission of his Highness.

Haydn was thus prohibited from circulating his music without the express permission of his patron. But somehow his symphonies, quartets, and sonatas began to make their way to Vienna and other foreign capitals. In the 1770s, they surfaced in Amsterdam, London, and Paris in "pirated" editions. Since there was no international copyright in those years, a publisher might simply print a work from a copyist's score without the composer's knowledge or consent. When Haydn signed another contract with Prince Nikolaus in 1779, there was no such "exclusive use" provision, and he began to sell his works to various publishers, sometimes consigning the same piece to two or three at the same time!

For a period of nearly thirty years, Haydn served Nikolaus Esterházy, writing symphonies and divertimentos* for evening entertainment, operas for the court theater, and string trios in which the prince himself might participate. When Nikolaus died in 1790, the Esterházy orchestra was dismissed in favor of a smaller, military band. Haydn retained his title as court composer as well as his full salary, but he was now free to travel as he wished. After settling briefly in Vienna, he journeyed to London, where he had been engaged at a substantial fee to compose and conduct. From this commission resulted the twelve **London Symphonies** (Nos. 93–104), which were first performed in the Hanover Square Rooms (see Fig. 18–3), a large public concert hall built in part with capital supplied by Johann Christian Bach, old Bach's youngest son. Haydn stayed in London during 1791–1792 and returned again for the concert season in 1794–1795. He was presented to the king and queen, received the honorary degree of doctor of music at Oxford, and was generally accorded the status of a visiting celebrity, as a letter written within a fortnight of his arrival attests:

> Everyone wants to know me. I had to dine out six times up to now, and if I wanted, I could have an invitation every day; but first I must consider my health and second my work. Except for the nobility, I admit no callers 'til 2 o'clock in the afternoon.

In the summer of 1795, Haydn returned from London to Vienna a wealthy man. From his activities in London, he had netted 24,000 Austrian gulden, the equivalent of more than twenty years' salary at the Esterházy court. In his last years, Haydn composed mostly religious works, including a handful of Masses for chorus and orchestra, and two oratorios, *The Creation* (1798) and *The Seasons* (1801)—it seems he had been deeply impressed by the performances of Handel's oratorios he had heard while in England. When he died on May 31, 1809, at the age of seventy-seven, he was the most respected composer in Europe.

Haydn's long life, commitment to duty, and unflagging industry resulted in an impressive number of musical compositions: 104 symphonies, about 70 string quartets, nearly a dozen operas, 52 piano sonatas, 14 Masses, and 2 oratorios. He began composing before the death of Bach (1750) and did not put

© magno/Gerhard Trumler/Getty Images

FIGURE 16–3

The palace of the Esterházy family southeast of Vienna, where Joseph Haydn lived until 1790. It was modeled on the grand French palace of Versailles, west of Paris.

Haydn, a celebrity in London

down his pen until about the time Beethoven set to work on his Fifth Symphony (1808). Thus, Haydn not only witnessed but, more than any other composer, helped to create the mature Classical style.

Despite his accomplishments, Haydn did not rebel against the modest station assigned to him in traditional eighteenth-century society: "I have associated with emperors, kings, and many great people," he said, "and I have heard many flattering things from them, but I would not live in familiar relations with such persons; I prefer to be close to people of my own standing." And though keenly aware of his own musical gifts, he was quick to recognize talent in others, especially Mozart: "Friends often flatter me that I have some genius, but he [Mozart] stood far above me."

WOLFGANG AMADEUS MOZART (1756–1791)

Indeed who, except possibly Bach, could match Mozart's diversity, breadth of expression, and perfect formal control? Wolfgang Amadeus Mozart (Fig. 16–4) was born in 1756 in the mountain town of **Salzburg,** Austria, then a city of about 20,000 residents. His father, **Leopold Mozart,** was a violinist in the orchestra of the archbishop of Salzburg and the author of a best-selling introduction to playing the violin. Leopold was quick to recognize the musical gifts of his son, who by the age of six was playing the piano, violin, and organ as well as composing. In 1762, the Mozart family coached off to Vienna, where Wolfgang and his older sister Nannerl displayed their musical wares before Empress Maria Theresa (1717–1780). They then embarked on a three-year tour of Northern Europe that included extended stops in Munich, Brussels, Paris, London, Amsterdam, and Geneva (Fig. 16–5). In London, Wolfgang sat on the knee of Johann Christian Bach (1735–1782) and improvised a fugue. And here, at the age of eight, he heard his first two symphonies performed. Eventually, the Mozarts made their way back to Salzburg. But in 1768, they were off again to Vienna, where the now twelve-year-old Wolfgang staged a production of his first opera, *Bastien und Bastienne,* in the home of the famous Dr. Franz Anton Mesmer (1733–1815), the inventor of the theory of animal magnetism (hence, "to mesmerize"). The next year father and son visited the major cities of Italy, including Rome, where, on 8 July 1770, the pope dubbed Wolfgang a Knight of the Golden Spur (Fig. 16–6). Although the aim of all this globe-trotting was to acquire fame and fortune, the result was that Mozart, unlike Haydn, was exposed at an early age to a wealth of musical styles—French Baroque, English choral, German polyphonic, and Italian vocal. His extraordinarily keen ear absorbed them all, and ultimately they increased the breadth and substance of his music.

A period of relative stability followed: For much of the 1770s, Mozart resided in Salzburg,

FIGURE 16–4 AND 16–5

(top) An unfinished portrait of Mozart painted by his brother-in-law Joseph Lange during 1789–1790. (bottom) The child Mozart at the keyboard, with his sister Nannerl and his father Leopold, in Paris in 1764 during their three-year tour of Europe.

Mozart Museum, Salzburg/Alinari/The Bridgeman Art Library

The British Library, London/The Bridgeman Art Library

What's a Genius? Was Mozart a Musical Genius?

The notion of "genius" likely involves at least two types of special qualities. Some people are clearly creative geniuses. They have the capacity to think "outside the box"—to formulate intellectual constructs or works of art that are so original, compelling, and visionary as to make some extraordinary contribution to human civilization. So measured, the poet Shakespeare, the painter Michelangelo, and the scientist Isaac Newton would clearly qualify as geniuses. Other persons are what might be designated cognitive geniuses. They have the ability to process or manipulate information with incredible facility. Those who can do large sums in their heads, who have photographic memories, or who have absolute musical pitch can be called cognitive geniuses. By any criteria, Mozart was both a creative and a cognitive genius.

Although Mozart may not have been the most precocious child composer in the history of music—that honor would likely go to Schubert or Mendelssohn—once he reached the age of twenty-two, he tossed off one masterpiece after another with frightening frequency. Moreover, Mozart's prodigious cognitive skills are legendary. As a child, he could identify the notes played in any chord, judge the pitch of an instrument within a quarter of a tone, or pick out a wrong note in a musical score while crawling on his back across a table. At the age of fourteen, he heard a motet sung in the Sistine Chapel in Rome and wrote it down by memory, note for note. This motet was about two minutes long and in several voices. How much music can we remember on first hearing—four or five seconds of the melody? Obviously Mozart could store and process a great deal of music in his "mind's ear." And not just music but other sounds as well! Mozart was a superb mimic, and he learned to speak several foreign languages almost upon first hearing. Little wonder that the great German poet Goethe (1749–1832) referred to him as "the human incarnation of a divine force of creation."

But with the gifts of genius came disorders of personality—geniuses are rarely "normal." Mozart fidgeted constantly with both hands and feet, and his mouth filled the air with childish jokes and puns. Until the age of ten or so, he was terrified by the sound of the trumpet, and out-of-tune instruments brought physical pain to his ears (was he mildly autistic?). Mozart's numerous apartments in Vienna were messy, indeed chaotic. He often both ate and composed in bed. Never did he attend a school or receive a systematic education beyond the art of music, though his letters reveal him to be highly intelligent. Mozart owned few books and read fewer. His almost sole interest, indeed obsession, was music. When possessed by this muse, he became oblivious of the growing chaos around him. Ironically, his inner world of music, judging from the works he created, was all balance, order, and perfection.

where he served as organist, violinist, and composer to the archbishop. But the reigning archbishop, Colloredo, was a stern, frugal man who had little sympathy for Mozart, genius or not (the composer referred to him as the "Archboobie"). Mozart was given a place in the orchestra, a small salary, and his board. Like the musicians at the court of Esterházy, those at Salzburg ate with the cooks and valets. For a Knight of the Golden Spur who had played for kings and queens across Europe, this was humble fare indeed, and Mozart chafed under this system of aristocratic patronage. After several unpleasant scenes in the spring of 1781, the twenty-five-year-old composer cut himself free of the archbishop and determined to make his living as a freelance musician in Vienna.

Mozart chose Vienna partly because of the city's rich musical life and partly because it was a comfortable distance from his overbearing father. In a letter to his sister written in the spring of 1782, Wolfgang spells out his daily regimen in the Austrian capital:

> My hair is always done by six o'clock in the morning and by seven I am fully dressed. I then compose until nine. From nine to one I give lessons. Then I lunch, unless I am invited to some house where they lunch at two or even three o'clock. . . . I can never work before five or six o'clock in the evening, and even then I am often prevented by a concert. If I am not prevented, I compose until nine. Then I go to my dear Constanze.

FIGURES 16–6

Young Mozart proudly wearing the collar of a Knight of the Order of the Golden Spur, an honor conferred upon him for his musical skills by Pope Clement XIV in July 1770.

Mozart Museum, Salzburg/The Bridgeman Art Library

Mozart and Amadeus

Perhaps you have seen the extraordinary film *Amadeus* (1985), based on a play by Peter Schaffer, and wondered if the Mozart portrayed there bore any relation to the real Mozart. The answer is, in a few ways, yes; in most ways, no. To be sure, Mozart's lifestyle was chaotic, he had expensive tastes, and he was often downright silly in his behavior. Yet there is no hint of drunkenness in the contemporary documents; he had an excellent, if erratic income; and his childish behavior, according to his brother-in-law Joseph Lange, was the way in which he released excess tension built up during concentrated periods of creative activity. Mozart did not die poor. Indeed, his income from two major operas in 1791 and the famous Requiem Mass made his last year one of his most lucrative. Nor was he abandoned to suffer a pauper's funeral. He received the same sort of burial (placed in a common grave) as 85 percent of the upper-middle-class in Vienna at that time. Nor, finally, was Mozart poisoned by his principal rival in Vienna, the composer **Antonio Salieri** (1750–1825). Salieri, court composer to Emperor Joseph II and his two successors, was a universally respected, if not supremely gifted, musician who later went on to become, at various times, the teacher of Beethoven,

Schubert, Liszt, and even one of Mozart's two sons. Salieri may have been a mediocre composer, but he was no murderer.

If *Amadeus* offers an inaccurate portrayal of Mozart, its central point, nonetheless, poses an intriguing question: What does a mediocre or even somewhat gifted person (Salieri) do when faced with an absolute genius (Mozart)?

© 1964 The Saul Zaentz Company

A scene from Amadeus. *Mozart did, in fact, keep a billiard table in his bedroom.*

Against the advice of his father, Wolfgang married his "dear Constanze" (Weber) in the summer of 1782. But, alas, she was as romantic and impractical as he, though less given to streaks of hard work. In addition to his composing, teaching, and performing, Mozart now found time to study the music of Bach and Handel, play chamber music with his friend Joseph Haydn, and join the **Freemasons.** Although still very much a practicing Catholic, he was attracted to this fraternity of the Enlightenment because of its belief in tolerance and universal brotherhood. His opera, *Die Zauberflöte* (*The Magic Flute*, 1791), is viewed by many as a hymn in praise of Masonic ideals.

The years 1785–1787 witnessed the peak of Mozart's success and the creation of many of his greatest works. He had a full complement of pupils, played several concerts a week, and enjoyed lucrative commissions as a composer. Piano concertos, string quartets, and symphonies flowed from his pen, as did his two greatest Italian operas, *The Marriage of Figaro* and *Don Giovanni.*

nobility deserts Mozart

But *Don Giovanni*, a huge success when first performed in Prague in 1787, was little appreciated when mounted in Vienna in the spring of 1788. "The opera is divine, perhaps even more beautiful than *Figaro*," declared Emperor Joseph II, "but no food for the teeth of my Viennese." Mozart's music was no longer in vogue with the nobility. The elite failed to subscribe to his concerts, and his aristocratic pupils began to dwindle. His style was thought to be too dense, too intense, and too dissonant. One publisher warned him: "Write in a more popular style or else I cannot print or pay for more of your music."

In his last year (1791), despite declining health, Mozart was still capable of creating the greatest sort of masterpieces. He composed a superb clarinet concerto and *The Magic Flute*, and began work on a Requiem Mass, one he was never to finish (it was completed by a pupil, Franz Süssmayr). Mozart died on December 5, 1791, at the age of thirty-five. The precise reason for his death has never been determined, though rheumatic fever and kidney failure, made worse by needless blood-letting, are the most likely causes. No single event in the history of music is more regrettable than the premature loss of Mozart. What he would have given to the world had he enjoyed the long life of a Handel or a Haydn!

successes of his last year

Key Words

Vienna (**181**)   Salzburg (**184**)
Esterházy family (**182**)   Leopold Mozart (**184**)
London Symphonies   Antonio Salieri (**186**)
  (**183**)   Freemasons (**186**)

Classical Forms
TERNARY AND SONATA–ALLEGRO

Chapter 17

How did composers of the Classical period reconcile the Classical principles of order and balance with their urge to create a more dramatic style of music—music with more contrast in volume, color, and tempo? They did so, in a word, by means of form. In the Classical period, more than any other, a small number of forms—ternary, sonata–allegro, rondo, and theme and variations—regulated nearly all art music. At the same time, none of these forms was unique to the Classical period. Ternary form can be found in the earliest examples of Gregorian chant* and in the Baroque *da capo* aria. The rondo had its origins in the popular dances of the Middle Ages, and its repetitive structure has made it attractive to such diverse musicians as Mozart, Beethoven, Elton John, and Sting (see boxed essay on page 206). Only sonata–allegro form actually came into being in the Classical period. It dominated musical structure during the time of Mozart and Haydn, and remained a potent force in the works of most composers of the Romantic era (1820–1900) and in the creations of some twentieth-century musicians as well. Thus, the forms discussed in this chapter should be thought of not as belonging to the Classical period alone, but in the broader meaning of "classical music." With the single exception of sonata–allegro form, all recur in eras and genres throughout the history of Western music.

TERNARY FORM

Ternary structure is a simple arrangement (**ABA**) that can serve as a useful introduction to the more complex sonata–allegro form discussed later in this chapter. Classical composers favored **ternary form** for its simplicity and directness. Everyone is familiar with the tune *Twinkle, Twinkle, Little Star* (also the tune of *Baa, Baa, Black Sheep* and *A, B, C, D, E, F, G*). Less known is the fact that the tune originated as a French folksong, *Ah, vous dirai-je, Maman (Ah, Let Me Tell You, Mama)*. Wolfgang Amadeus Mozart came to know the melody when he toured France as a youth, and composed a setting for keyboard.

EXAMPLE 17–1

Notice that both units (**A** and **BA**) are repeated (see repeat sign ⦂‖). Observe also that **A** is in the tonic, **B** emphasizes a contrasting key (here the dominant), and the returning **A** is again in the tonic (these harmonies are indicated by the roman numerals I and V). If a piece in ternary form is in a minor key, the

FIGURE 17–1

A ball at the Redoutensaal in the emperor's palace in Vienna, c1800. Mozart, Haydn, and, later, Beethoven composed minuets and "German dances" for these events, which sometimes attracted nearly 4,000 fee-paying dancers. The orchestra can be seen in the gallery at the left.

Museum der Stadt Wien

FIGURE 17–2

Couples in the late eighteenth century dancing the stately minuet. In some areas of Europe at this time, women were forbidden to dance the minuet because it was thought to involve excessive body contact!

contrasting **B** section is usually in what is called the **relative major.**[†] Needless to say, most pieces in ternary form are more complex than *Twinkle, Twinkle.* Most have more contrast of melody, key, and/or mood between the **B** section and the surrounding units of **A**.[‡]

Minuet and Trio

The most common use of ternary form in the Classical period is found in the minuet and trio. Strictly speaking, the **minuet** is not a form, but rather a genre of dance featuring a moderate tempo and constant triple meter (Fig. 17–2). It first appeared at the French royal court early in the reign of King Louis XIV (1643–1715). Most minuets in the Baroque era were in binary form (**AB**), but by 1770, the dance was usually composed in ternary form and grouped with a second minuet possessing a much lighter texture. Because this second minuet had originally been played by only three instruments, it was called the **trio,** a name that persisted into the nineteenth century, no matter how many instrumental lines were required. Once the trio was finished, convention dictated that there be a return to the first minuet, now performed without repeats. Since the trio also was composed in ternary form, an **ABA** pattern was heard three times in succession. (In the following, the **ABA** structure of the trio is represented by **CDC**, to distinguish it from the minuet.) And, since the trio was different from the surrounding minuet, the entire minuet–trio–minuet movement formed an **ABA** arrangement:

minuet, an elegant dance

$$
\begin{array}{ccc}
\textbf{A (minuet)} & \textbf{B (trio)} & \textbf{A (minuet)} \\
\lVert\colon A \colon\rVert\colon BA \colon\rVert & \lVert\colon C \colon\rVert\colon DC \colon\rVert & \textbf{ABA}
\end{array}
$$

[†]Relative keys are keys that share the same key signature—E♭ major and C minor (both with three flats), for example.

[‡]Note for instructors: on the designation "ternary form" for this and other pieces, see the "Acknowledgments" in the Preface of this book.

Mozart's A Little Night Music

Mozart's *Eine kleine Nachtmusik* (*A Little Night Music*), written in the summer of 1787, is among his most popular works. It is a **serenade,** a light, multimovement piece for strings alone or small orchestra, one intended for public entertainment and often performed outdoors. Although we do not know the precise occasion for which Mozart composed it, we might well imagine *A Little Night Music* providing the musical backdrop for a torch-lit party in a formal Viennese garden. The *Menuetto* appears as the third of four movements in this serenade, and is a model of grace and concision.

EXAMPLE 17–2

formal symmetry

As you can see, the **B** section is only four measures long, and the return to **A** does not reproduce the full eight bars of the original but only the last four—thus, this pattern might be viewed as **ABA′**. In the trio that follows, a lighter texture is created as the first violin plays a solo melody quietly above a soft accompaniment in the lower strings. The **D** section of the trio is distinguished by a *forte* stepwise run up and down the scale, and then the quiet melody of **C** returns to complete the ternary form. Finally, the minuet appears once again, but now without repeats.

Listening Guide

Wolfgang Amadeus Mozart
Serenade, *A Little Night Music* (1787)
Third movement, Minuet and Trio

6 2/9   **2** 1/12

Form: ternary

MINUET		Form	Number of bars
0:00 ⁹⁄₁₂	Strong violin melody with active bass	A	8
0:10	Repeat of **A**		
0:20	Softer violin scales	B	4
0:26	Return of violin melody	A'	4
0:30	Repeat of **B** and **A'**		
TRIO			
0:41	Soft, stepwise melody in violins	C	8
0:52	Repeat of **C**		
1:03	Louder violins	D	4
1:09	Return of soft stepwise melody	C	8
1:20	Repeat of **D** and **C**		
MINUET			
1:37	Return of **A**	A	8
1:48	Return of **B**	B	4
1:54	Return of violin melody **A'**	A'	4

Use a downloadable, cross-platform animated Active Listening Guide, available at **www.thomsonedu.com/music/wright.**

We have said that Classical music is symmetrical and proportional. Note here how both minuet and trio are balanced by a return of the opening music (**A** and **C**) and how all the sections are either four or eight bars in length.

If Mozart's *Menuetto* represents the minuet in its most succinct form, the minuet of Haydn's Symphony No. 94 (the "Surprise" Symphony) offers a more typically symphonic presentation of this ternary design. The form is considerably extended, in part because Haydn was writing for a full orchestra rather than the small string ensemble of Mozart's serenade. (It is axiomatic in music that the larger the performing force, the more extended the musical form.) But keeping the model of Mozart's simple ternary minuet in our ears, we can easily follow Haydn's more expansive formal plan.

Listening Guide

Franz Joseph Haydn
Symphony No. 94, the "Surprise" Symphony (1791)
Third movement, Minuet and Trio

6 2/10

Form: ternary

MINUET [ ] = repeats		Form
0:00 ⑩	Rollicking dance in triple meter begins	A
0:19	Repeat of **A**	

(continued)

0:40	[1:33]	Imitation and lighter texture	B
0:50	[1:43]	Strong harmonic movement	
0:58	[1:51]	Bass sits on dominant note	
1:05	[1:59]	Return of **A**	A′
1:13	[2:07]	Pause on dominant chord	
1:23	[2:17]	Gentle rocking over tonic pedal point*	

TRIO

2:27		Light descending scales for violins and bassoon	C
2:37		Repeat of **C**	
2:46	[3:08]	Two-voice counterpoint for 1st and 2nd violins	D
2:58	[3:21]	Bassoon reentry signals return of **C**	C

MINUET

3:30		Return to minuet	A
3:51		Return of **B**	B
4:16		Return of **A**	A′

Use a downloadable, cross-platform animated Active Listening Guide, available at **www.thomsonedu.com/music/wright**.

SONATA–ALLEGRO FORM

Sonata–allegro form is at once the most complex and most satisfying of music forms. As mentioned previously, it is also the only form to originate during the Classical period (1750–1820). It came into being around 1750 as a means of incorporating more drama and conflict into a single movement of music. Like a great play, a movement in sonata–allegro form has the potential for dramatic presentation, conflict, and resolution. Sonata–allegro form would continue to serve composers into the Romantic period and beyond, and thus, every serious listener of classical music should have a solid understanding of it.

a dramatic form

We should keep in mind, however, the distinction between the general term *sonata* and the more specific *sonata–allegro form*—that is, between the multi-movement genre, the sonata, and the single-movement form, sonata–allegro. The sonata genre in the Classical period generally designates a composition either for solo piano or for a melody instrument with piano accompaniment. The typical Classical sonata comprises three movements: fast-slow-fast. Several other Classical genres are not called "sonatas," and are typically composed in four movements: fast-slow-minuet-fast. When such a sequence of movements is composed for string quartet or quintet, for example, it is simply called a "string quartet" or "string quintet," and when intended for full orchestra, it is called a "symphony."

"sonata" contrasted with "sonata-allegro form"

Although all of these Classical genres comprise multiple movements, the movements themselves can make use of any one of several musical forms. The form of the first movement is almost invariably composed in what is called **sonata–allegro form.** The first half of the term ("sonata") derives, obviously, from the fact that most sonatas feature this form in their first movement, while the second ("allegro") refers to the standard practice of setting this first movement to a fast tempo. Although the slow second movements and fast finales of Classical compositions are sometimes written in sonata–allegro form as well, they often make use of other forms, such as rondo or theme and variations (both discussed in Chapter 18). If there are four movements, the third is usually a minuet with trio, and thus in ternary form. To make sense of this, consider the movements and forms of Mozart's *A Little Night Music* and Haydn's Symphony No. 94:

Mozart, *A Little Night Music* (1787)

Fast	Slow	Minuet and Trio	Fast
(sonata–allegro)	(rondo)	(ternary)	(rondo)

typical uses of musical forms by movement

Haydn, Symphony No. 94 (1791)

Fast	Slow	Minuet and Trio	Fast
(sonata–allegro)	(theme and variations)	(ternary)	(sonata–allegro)

The Shape of Sonata–Allegro Form

To get a sense of what might happen in a typical first movement of a sonata, string quartet, symphony, or serenade, look at the diagram below. As with all models of this sort, this one is an ideal, an abstraction of what commonly occurs in sonata–allegro form. It is not a blueprint for any composition. Composers have exhibited countless individual solutions to the task of writing in this and every other form. Yet such a model can be of great use to the listener because it gives a clear picture of what we might expect to hear. Ultimately, once we have embraced the form and are familiar with its workings, we will take as much delight in having our musical expectations foiled or delayed as in having them fulfilled.

a blueprint outlining the form

SONATA-ALLEGRO FORM

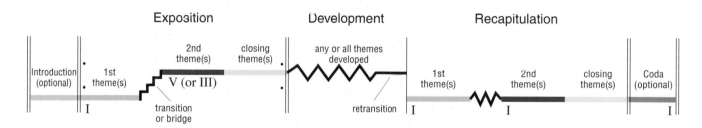

In its broad outline, sonata–allegro form looks much like ternary form. It consists of an **ABA** plan, with the **B** section providing contrast in mood, key, and thematic treatment. The initial **A** in sonata–allegro form is called the exposition, the **B** the development, and the return to **A** the recapitulation. In the early Classical period, the exposition (**A**) and the development and recapitulation (**BA**) were each repeated, as in ternary form. But Haydn and Mozart eventually dropped the repeat of the development and recapitulation, and composers of the Romantic period gradually dispensed with the repeat of the exposition. Let's examine each of these sections in turn and learn what we are likely to hear.

EXPOSITION

presentation

In the **exposition,** the composer presents the main themes of the movement. It begins with the first theme (or group of themes) and is always in the tonic key. Next comes the **transition,** or **bridge** as it is sometimes called, which carries the music from the tonic to the dominant (from tonic to relative major if the movement is in a minor key) and prepares for the arrival of the second theme. Often the transition is composed of rapid figural patterns—scales, arpeggios*, and melodic sequences*—that convey a feeling of motion. The second theme typically contrasts in mood with the first; if the first is rapid and assertive, the second may be more languid and lyrical. The exposition usually concludes with a closing theme (or group of themes), often simply oscillating between dominant and tonic chords. The static harmony at this point signals that the exposition is nearing its end. After the final cadence, the exposition is repeated in full.

DEVELOPMENT

confrontation

If sonata–allegro is a dramatic musical form, most of the drama is heard in the **development.** As the name indicates, a further working out, or developing, of the thematic material occurs here. The themes can be extended or varied, or reduced to just a few notes, to their very musical essence. Dramatic confrontation might occur, as when more than one theme sounds simultaneously. Sometimes the composer will demonstrate the contrapuntal possibilities lurking within a theme by using it as the subject of a brief fugue*. (A fugue within a movement of a sonata is called a **fugato.**) Not only are developments dramatic, they are often unstable harmonically, as the music typically modulates rapidly from one key to the next. Only toward the end of the development, in the passage called the **retransition,** is tonal order restored, often by means of a pedal point* on the dominant note. When the dominant chord (V) finally gives way to the tonic (I), the recapitulation begins.

RECAPITULATION

resolution

After the turmoil of the development, the listener greets the return of the first theme and the tonic key of the exposition with welcome relief. Though the **recapitulation** is not an exact, note-for-note repetition of the exposition, it nonetheless presents the same musical events in the same order. The only change that regularly occurs in this restatement is the rewriting of the transition, or bridge. Because the movement must end in the tonic, the bridge must not modulate to the dominant (or relative major) as before, but must stay at home in the tonic key. Thus, the recapitulation imparts to the listener not only a feeling of return to familiar surroundings but also an increased sense of harmonic stability, as all themes are now heard in the tonic key.

The following two elements are optional to sonata–allegro form.

INTRODUCTION

About half the mature symphonies of Haydn and Mozart have brief introductions before the exposition begins. (That the introduction is not part of the exposition is shown by the fact that it is never repeated.) These are, without exception, slow and stately, and usually filled with ominous or puzzling chords designed to get the listener wondering what sort of musical excursion he or she is about to undertake.

CODA

As the name **coda** (Italian for "tail") indicates, this is a section added to the end of the movement. Like tails, codas can be long or short. Haydn and Mozart wrote relatively short codas in which a motive might simply be repeated again and again in conjunction with repeating dominant-tonic chords. Beethoven, however, was inclined to compose lengthy codas, sometimes introducing new themes even at the end of the movement. But no matter how long the coda, most will end with a final passage of dominant-tonic chords played over and over, all intended to create a grand effect and announce to the listener that the movement is at an end—the harmony is no longer moving forward. The longer this final cadence*, the greater the feeling of conclusion.

FIGURE 17–3

The Mozart family (1781) with Wolfgang and his sister playing four-hands at the keyboard, his father with violin, and a portrait of his deceased mother on the wall.

Hearing Sonata–Allegro Form

Given its central place in the music of Mozart and Haydn, and later in that of Beethoven, Schubert, Brahms, and Mahler, among others, sonata–allegro is perhaps the most important of all musical forms in the Western tradition. But it is also the most complex and the most difficult for the listener to follow. A sonata–allegro movement tends to be long, lasting anywhere from four minutes in a simple composition from the Classical period, to twenty minutes or more in a full-blown movement of the Romantic era.

How does one tame this musical beast? First, be sure to memorize the diagram of sonata–allegro form given on page 193. Next, sharpen your ability to grasp and remember melodies. (If necessary, return to Chapter 3 and practice some melodic graphing by redoing Listening Exercise 3.) Finally, think carefully about the four distinctive styles of writing found in sonata–allegro form: thematic, transitional, developmental, and cadential. A thematic passage has a clearly recognizable theme, often a singable tune. The transition is full of motion, with melodic sequences* and rapid chord changes. The development sounds harmonically active, is full of counterpoint, and makes use of a recognizable theme (or themes), albeit either extended in length or reduced to short motives. Finally, a cadential passage, coming at the end of a section or the end of the piece, sounds repetitious because the same chords are heard again and again in a harmony that seems to have stopped moving forward. Each of these four styles has a specific function within sonata–allegro form: to state, to move, to develop, or to conclude.

four functional styles within sonata-allegro form

To test our ability to follow along in a movement composed in sonata–allegro form, we turn to the first movement of Mozart's *A Little Night Music*. The following Listening Guide is not typical of this book. It is unusually lengthy so as to lead you through the difficult process of hearing sonata–allegro form. First, read the description in the center column; then listen to the music, stopping where indicated to rehear each of the principal sections of the form. Likely this movement, one of the favorites in the classical repertoire, will seem like an old friend. Its sophisticated sounds have been used as background music in countless radio and TV commercials to suggest that the product is "high end"— we associate expensive items with Classical elegance.

 Wolfgang Amadeus Mozart
A Little Night Music (1787)
First movement, *Allegro* (fast)

2/6–8 1/9–11

Genre: serenade
Form: sonata–allegro

FIRST THEME GROUP [ ] = repeats

0:00 [6/9] [1:37] The movement opens aggressively with a leaping, fanfare-like motive. It then moves on to a more confined, pressing melody with sixteenth notes agitating beneath, and ends with a relaxed, stepwise descent down the G major scale, which is repeated with light ornamentation.

STOP: LISTEN TO THE FIRST THEME GROUP AGAIN

TRANSITION

0:30 [2:08] This starts with two quick turns and then races up the scale in repeating sixteenth notes. The bass is at first static, but when it finally moves, it does so with great urgency, pushing the modulation forward to a cadence. The stage is then cleared by a brief pause, allowing the listener an "unobstructed view" of the new theme that is about to enter.

0:30 Rapid scales
0:40 Bass moves
0:45 Cadence and pause

STOP: LISTEN TO THE TRANSITION AGAIN

SECOND THEME

0:48 [2:26] With its *piano* dynamic level and separating rests, the second theme sounds soft and delicate. It is soon overtaken by a light, somewhat humorous closing theme.

STOP: LISTEN TO THE SECOND THEME AGAIN

CLOSING THEME

1:01 [2:39] The light quality of this melody is produced by its repeating note and the simple rocking of dominant-to-tonic harmony below. Toward the end, more substance is added when the music turns *forte*, and counterpoint appears in the bass. The bass's closing theme is then repeated, and a few cadential chords are tacked on to bring the exposition to an end.

1:09 Loud; counterpoint in bass
1:14 Closing theme repeated
1:33 Cadential chords

STOP: LISTEN TO THE CLOSING SECTION AGAIN

1:37–3:14   The exposition is now repeated.

DEVELOPMENT

3:15 [7/10] 0:00 Just about anything can happen in a development, so the listener had best be on guard. Mozart begins with the fanfare-like first theme again in unison, as if this were yet another statement of the exposition! But abruptly the theme is altered and the tonal center slides up to a new key. Now the closing theme is heard, but soon it, too, begins to slide tonally, down through several keys that sound increasingly remote and bizarre. From this arises a unison scale (all parts move up stepwise together) in a dark-sounding minor key. The dominant note is held, first on top in the violins and then in the bass (0:33). This is the retransition. The mode changes from dark

0:00 First theme developed
0:05 Quick modulation
0:10 Closing theme developed
0:17 More modulations
0:26 Rising scale in unison
0:33 Retransition: held note (dominant) in violins and then bass

minor to bright major, and the first theme returns forcefully in the tonic key, signaling the beginning of the recapitulation.

STOP: LISTEN TO THE DEVELOPMENT AGAIN

RECAPITULATION

3:52		0:00	It is this "double return" of both the tonic key and the first theme that makes the arrival of this and all recapitulations so satisfying. We expect the recapitulation to more or less duplicate the exposition, and this one holds true to form. The only change comes, as usual, in the transition, or bridge, where the modulation to the dominant is simply omitted—there's no need to modulate to the dominant since tradition demands that the second theme and the closing theme appear in the tonic.	0:00 Loud return of first theme 0:31 Transition much abbreviated 0:46 Second theme 0:59 Closing theme 1:13 Closing theme repeated 1:31 Cadential chords

CODA

5:26   1:34   After the cadential chords that ended the exposition are heard again, a brief coda begins. It makes use of a fanfare motive that strongly resembles that of the opening theme, but this one is supported below by a pounding tonic chord that drives home the feeling that the movement has come to an appropriate end.

Use a downloadable, cross-platform animated Active Listening Guide, available at **www.thomsonedu.com/music/wright**.

What we have just heard is an example of sonata–allegro form in miniature. Rarely has this design been produced in less time, or space, and almost never as artfully.

In the Classical era, sonatas, quartets, symphonies, and serenades typically began with a movement in sonata–allegro form. So, too, did operas. That is, a Classical opera often commenced with an overture*, performed by full orchestra, composed in sonata–allegro form. A case in point is Mozart's overture to *Don Giovanni* (1787), which amply demonstrates the drama inherent in sonata–allegro form. (The full opera will be discussed in Chapter 20.) Mozart begins this overture with a slow introduction in a minor key that incorporates some of the musical motives we hear later in the opera. This slow, ominous beginning soon changes to a fast tempo and a major key at the start of the exposition. Because this is an overture to an opera, and not a symphony, the exposition is not repeated.

Listening Guide   Wolfgang Amadeus Mozart
Overture to the opera *Don Giovanni* (1787)

2/20–22

Genre: opera overture
Form: sonata–allegro

INTRODUCTION

0:00   **20**   Slow, sinister chords give way to twisting chromaticism, and finally, writhing scales, all of which suggest the evil nature of Don Giovanni

(continued)

EXPOSITION

1:56	First theme moves ahead rapidly	
2:20	Transition starts with a scalar theme presented in melodic sequence*	
2:30	Continues with unstable chords that build tension	
2:35	Transition ends with a strong cadence	
2:41	Second theme marked by a scalar descent and "birdlike fluttering" in woodwinds	
3:00	Light closing theme	
3:20 21 0:00	**DEVELOPMENT** (material discussed in the following Listening Exercise)	
4:27 22 0:00	**RECAPITULATION** (material discussed in the following Listening Exercise)	
5:46 1:19	**CODA** There are no loud cadential chords to produce a "big bang" ending for this overture. Rather, Mozart writes an orchestral fadeout designed to coincide with the raising of the curtain and the beginning of the first scene in the opera.	

Use a downloadable, cross-platform animated Active Listening Guide, available at **www.thomsonedu.com/music/wright**.

A discussion of another Classical movement in sonata–allegro form (Mozart's Symphony No. 40 in G minor, first movement) can be found on pages 210–212, along with a Listening Guide and Listening Exercise.

Listening Exercise 25

Mozart
Overture, *Don Giovanni*

2/20–22 **Thomson**NOW™
To take this Listening Exercise online and receive feedback or email answers to your instructor, go to *ThomsonNOW* for this chapter.

The sections of the exposition were identified in the above Listening Guide to allow you to become familiar with the main themes of the movement. Here, beginning with the development and continuing through the recapitulation and brief coda, you are asked a series of questions that relate to the unfolding of sonata–allegro form.

Development

1. (0:00–0:19) Which theme is used at the beginning of 21 the development?
   a. first theme   b. second theme   c. closing theme
2. (0:11–0:19) This same theme is heard in the woodwinds in which guise?
   a. as a chorale
   b. as a cadence
   c. in counterpoint (overlapping imitation)
3. (0:20) Which theme enters?
   a. first theme   b. second theme   c. closing theme

4. (0:26) How does Mozart effect a change in theme?
   a. He switches from major to minor mode.
   b. He switches from minor to major mode.
5. (0:34) Which theme now returns?
   a. first theme   b. second theme   c. closing theme
6. (1:00–1:06) Retransition: In this section, is the harmony active or static?
   a. The double basses and timpani are moving to different pitches, and the harmony is active.
   b. The double basses and timpani are just repeating one pitch, and the harmony is static.

Recapitulation (return of first theme and tonic key)

7. (0:22) Which material returns here?
22 a. first theme   b. transition   c. second theme
8. (0:41) Which material returns here?
   a. transition   b. second theme   c. closing theme

9. (1:19) A brief coda begins here as the curtain rises. A reminiscence of which theme is heard as the main melodic material (1:19–1:25)?
   a. first theme   b. second theme   c. closing theme
10. Reflect upon your experience with the concerto grosso, which often uses ritornello form (see page 138), and the fugue, which uses fugal form (see page 144). Which musical form requires the listener to keep track of many separate and distinctive themes?
    a. ritornello form
    b. fugal form
    c. sonata–allegro form

Key Words

ternary form (**188**)	sonata–allegro form (**192**)	development (**194**)
relative major (**189**)	exposition (**194**)	fugato (**194**)
minuet (**189**)	transition (bridge) (**194**)	retransition (**194**)
trio (**189**)		recapitulation (**194**)
serenade (**190**)		coda (**195**)

ThomsonNOW™

ThomsonNOW for *Listening to Music, 5th Edition,* and *Listening to Western Music* will assist you in understanding the content of this chapter with lesson plans generated for your specific needs. In addition, you may complete this chapter's Listening Exercise in ThomsonNOW's interactive environment, as well as download Active Listening Guides and other materials that will help you succeed in this course.

Classical Forms
THEME AND VARIATIONS, RONDO

Chapter 18

In addition to sonata–allegro and ternary, there were other important musical forms during the Classical period, most notably theme and variations, and rondo. Both of these forms are relatively simple and straightforward, usually emphasizing just one theme, in contrast to the multiplicity of themes present in sonata–allegro form. A composition in theme and variations or rondo form may exist as a movement within a multimovement sonata or symphony, or it may stand alone as a one-movement, independent piece.

THEME AND VARIATIONS

The principle of **theme and variations** is one common to many artistic media. For example, in the contemporary sculpture by Donald Judd shown in Figure 18–1, we see a single object (a horizontal stripe of black Plexiglass) arranged in six different positions. In music, the object of variation is most often the melody, although other musical parameters—harmony, mode, meter, and so on—can be varied as well. For theme and variations to be effective, the theme must be clearly stated and easily grasped. Traditionally, composers have chosen to vary well-known melodies—folksongs, popular tunes, and favorite arias, for example. Patriotic songs have always seemed especially apt for musical variation. Those so treated include *God Preserve Franz the Emperor* (Haydn), *God Save the King* (Beethoven), *Rule Britannia* (Beethoven), and later *Yankee Doodle* (Vieuxtemps) and *America* (Ives). Such tunes are popular, in part, because they are simple, and this, too, is an advantage for the composer. Melodies that are spare and uncluttered can more easily be dressed in new musical clothing.

FIGURE 18–1
Donald Judd, Untitled, 1984

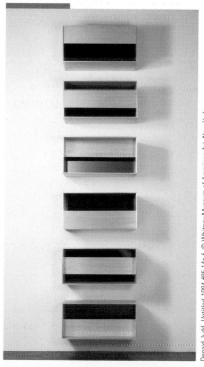

Originale di A. Mozardt

Mozarteum, Salzburg

FIGURE 18–2

The autograph manuscript of Mozart's variations on *Twinkle, Twinkle, Little Star* (c1781), beginning with the theme and first three variations. Notice how the texture is very thin at the beginning, but becomes thicker as ornamentation is added to the theme in the variations.

Variation can be affected in either of two ways: (1) by changing the primary theme itself, or (2) by changing the context around that theme (the accompaniment). The accompaniment can be modified, for example, by adding new figural or contrapuntal embellishment. Changing the theme itself, a more radical transformation, is accomplished by alterations to the theme's melodic or rhythmic profile. Sometimes, these two techniques are used simultaneously.

The two examples that follow—one by Mozart and one by Haydn—illustrate a number of techniques for altering or embellishing a melody. The primary task of the listener, of course, is to keep track of the tune throughout its various permutations.

Mozart: Variations on *Twinkle, Twinkle, Little Star* (c1781)

In the Classical period, it was common for a composer-pianist to improvise in concert a set of variations on a well-known tune, perhaps one requested by the audience. Contemporary reports tell us that Mozart was especially skilled in this art of spontaneous variation. In the early 1780s, Mozart wrote down a set of such improvised variations built on the French folksong *Ah, vous dirai-je, Maman*, which we know as *Twinkle, Twinkle, Little Star* (Fig. 18–2). With a tune as well known as this, it is easy to follow the melody as it is increasingly ornamented and altered in the course of twelve variations. (Only the first eight bars of the theme are given here; for the complete melody, see page 188; the music through the first three variations can be heard on (intro)/21.)

EXAMPLE 18–1a: *Twinkle, Twinkle, Little Star,* Basic Theme (0:00)

Variation 1 ornaments the theme and almost buries it beneath an avalanche of sixteenth notes. Would you know that *Twinkle, Twinkle* lurks herein (see the asterisks) if you did not have the tune securely in your ear?

EXAMPLE 18–1b: Variation 1 (0:51)

In variation 2 the rushing ornamentation is transferred to the bass, and the theme surfaces again rather clearly in the upper voice.

EXAMPLE 18–1c: Variation 2 (1:45)

In variation 3, triplets* in the right hand alter the theme, which is now only recognizable by its general contour.

EXAMPLE 8–1d: Variation 3 (2:36)

After the same technique has been applied to the bass (variation 4), a thematic alteration again occurs in variation 5. Here the rhythm of the melody is "jazzed up" by placing part of it off the beat, in syncopated fashion.

EXAMPLE 18–1e: Variation 5

Of the remaining seven variations, some change the tune to minor, while others add Bach-like counterpoint against it. The final variation presents this duple-meter folk tune reworked into a triple-meter waltz! Yet throughout all of Mozart's magical embroidery, the theme remains clearly audible, so well ingrained is *Twinkle, Twinkle* in our musical memory.

Haydn: Symphony No. 94 (the "Surprise" Symphony, 1792), Second movement

Joseph Haydn (1732–1809) was the first composer to take theme and variations form and use it for a movement within a symphony. To be sure, Haydn was an innovative composer—he could "surprise" or "shock" like no other composer of the Classical period. In his "Surprise" Symphony, the shock comes in the form of a sudden *fortissimo* chord inserted, as we shall see, in the second movement in the middle of an otherwise serene theme. When Haydn's

FIGURE 18–3

The Hanover Square Rooms in London, the hall in which Haydn's "Surprise" Symphony was first performed in 1792. Designed for an audience of 800 to 900, nearly 1,500 crowded in for the performances of these London Symphonies*.

Symphony No. 94 was first heard in London in 1792, the audience cheered this second movement and demanded its immediate repetition (Fig. 18–3). Ever since, this surprising movement has been Haydn's most celebrated composition.

The famous opening melody of the second movement (*Andante*) is written in binary form (**AB**), and to this simple sixteen-bar theme Haydn adds four variations. Notice how the beginning of the theme is shaped by laying out in succession the notes of a tonic triad (**I**) and then a dominant chord (**V**) in C major (see the first notated example in the Listening Guide). The triadic nature of the tune accounts for its folksong-like quality and makes it easy to remember during the variations that follow. These first eight bars (**A**) are stated and then repeated quietly. And just when all is ending peacefully, the full orchestra comes crashing in with a *fortissimo* chord, as if to shock the drowsy listener back to attention. What better way to show off the latent dynamic power of the larger Classical orchestra? The surprise *fortissimo* chord is a dominant chord that leads into the **B** section of the theme (second example in the Listening Guide), another eight-bar phrase, which is also repeated but with added flute and oboe accompaniment. With the simple yet highly attractive binary theme now in place, Haydn proceeds to compose four variations on it, adding a superb coda at the end.

a surprising chord

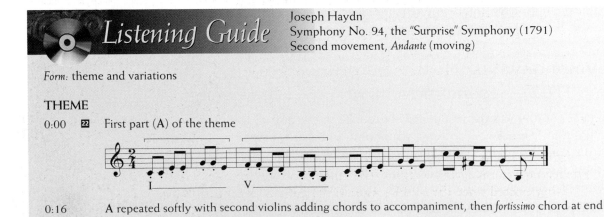

Listening Guide

Joseph Haydn
Symphony No. 94, the "Surprise" Symphony (1791)
Second movement, *Andante* (moving)

(Intro 22)

Form: theme and variations

THEME

0:00   **22**   First part (A) of the theme

0:16   A repeated softly with second violins adding chords to accompaniment, then *fortissimo* chord at end

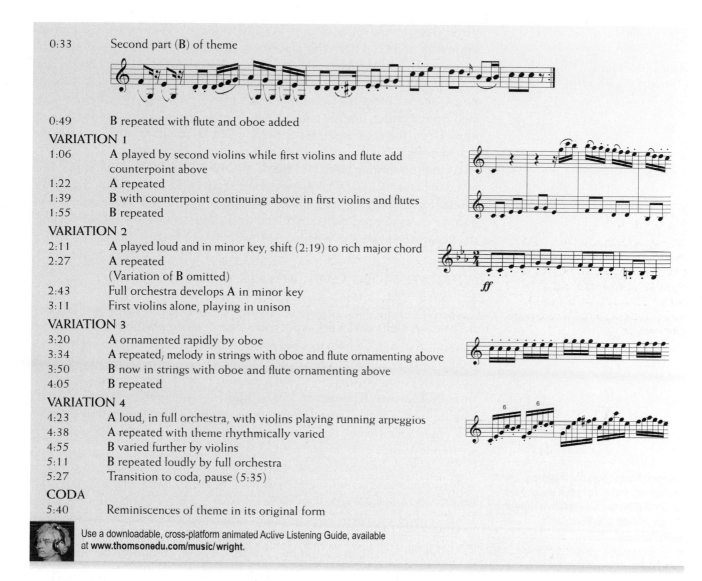

0:33   Second part (**B**) of theme

0:49   **B** repeated with flute and oboe added

VARIATION 1

1:06   **A** played by second violins while first violins and flute add
         counterpoint above
1:22   **A** repeated
1:39   **B** with counterpoint continuing above in first violins and flutes
1:55   **B** repeated

VARIATION 2

2:11   **A** played loud and in minor key, shift (2:19) to rich major chord
2:27   **A** repeated
         (Variation of **B** omitted)
2:43   Full orchestra develops **A** in minor key
3:11   First violins alone, playing in unison

VARIATION 3

3:20   **A** ornamented rapidly by oboe
3:34   **A** repeated; melody in strings with oboe and flute ornamenting above
3:50   **B** now in strings with oboe and flute ornamenting above
4:05   **B** repeated

VARIATION 4

4:23   **A** loud, in full orchestra, with violins playing running arpeggios
4:38   **A** repeated with theme rhythmically varied
4:55   **B** varied further by violins
5:11   **B** repeated loudly by full orchestra
5:27   Transition to coda, pause (5:35)

CODA

5:40   Reminiscences of theme in its original form

Use a downloadable, cross-platform animated Active Listening Guide, available
at **www.thomsonedu.com/music/wright**.

After listening to this movement by Haydn, you can understand that hearing theme and variations form requires listening to discrete units of music. Each block (variation) is marked by some new treatment of the theme. In the Classical period, all the units are usually the same size, that is, have the same number of measures. The variations become progressively more complicated as more ornamentation and transformation are applied, but each unit remains the same length (similar to Fig. 18–1). The addition of a coda after the last variation gives extra weight to the end, so the listener feels that the set of variations has reached an appropriate conclusion. If such extra bars were not appended, the audience would be left hanging, expecting yet another variation to begin.

RONDO FORM

Of all musical forms, the rondo is perhaps the easiest to hear, because a single, unvaried theme (the refrain) returns again and again. The rondo is also one of the oldest forms, having existed since the Middle Ages in the guise of the vocal *rondeau** (see page 87) and since the Baroque era in the ritornello* form of the concerto (see page 138). A true Classical **rondo** must have at least

FIGURE 18–4

A portrait of Joseph Haydn at work. His left hand is trying an idea at the keyboard while his right is ready to write it down. Haydn said about his compositional process: "I sat down at the keyboard and began to improvise. Once I had seized upon an idea, my whole effort was to develop and sustain it."

music with a refrain

three statements of the refrain (**A**) and at least two contrasting sections (at least **B** and **C**). Often the placement of the refrain creates symmetrical patterns such as **ABACA**, **ABACABA**, or even **ABACADA**. Haydn and Mozart infused the rondo with musical processes found in sonata–allegro form—specifically, transitional and developmental writing. They thereby created a more elastic, flexible rondo "environment" in which the refrain (**A**) and, more often, the contrasting sections (**B**, **C**, or **D**) might develop and expand dramatically.

As in the following piece by Mozart, the rondo is typically light, quick, and jovial in nature. Classical composers most often chose the rondo form for the **finale** (Italian for "end") of a sonata, quartet, or symphony. The carefree tune and the easily grasped digressions lend to the rondo finale an "upbeat" feeling, the musical equivalent of a happy ending.

Mozart: Horn Concerto in E♭ major (1786), K. 495, Third movement (finale)

In his short lifetime Mozart wrote more than 650 compositions, an enormous amount of music. To help us keep track of them, a musicologist in the nineteenth century, Ludwig von Köchel, published a list of Mozart's works in approximate chronological order, and even today we identify Mozart's compositions by a **Köchel (K) number.** This is especially handy in the case of Mozart's four concertos for the French horn, three of which he composed in E♭: How else could we differentiate them without a number? Thus, the concerto in E♭ written in Vienna in 1786 is identified as K. 495.

The fact that Mozart wrote three of his four horn concertos in E♭ major tells us something about the French horn in the Classical era. It was a "natural" horn (one without valves or keys), and it was set to play in only a few tonal centers, usually in keys with flats (Fig. 18–5). Because the French horn then had no valves or mechanical keys, it also had difficulty playing a fully chromatic scale in tune. For that reason, composers wrote for the horn what it could play easily: repeated notes, as well as triads* spun out as arpeggios*.

Mozart conceived all four of his horn concertos with one performer in mind, Joseph Leutgeb (1732–1811). Mozart had grown up with Leutgeb in Salzburg and counted him among his best friends, one at whom he could poke fun. Thus the inscription to the first horn concerto in E♭ (K. 417) reads: "Wolfgang Amadé Mozart has taken pity on Leutgeb, ass, ox, and fool." All four horn concertos by Mozart end with a movement in rondo form. The horn had something of a light-hearted, playful sound in Mozart's day, one well suited to the similarly light-hearted, playful quality of the Classical rondo.

FIGURE 18–5

A natural French horn of the late eighteenth century, the sort of horn that would have been used in the Classical orchestras of Mozart, Haydn, and Beethoven.

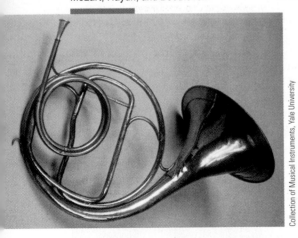

Collection of Musical Instruments, Yale University

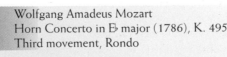

Listening Guide

Wolfgang Amadeus Mozart
Horn Concerto in E♭ major (1786), K. 495
Third movement, Rondo

 6
2/11

 2
1/13

Form: rondo

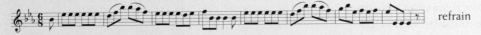

refrain

0:00		A played by French horn	A (refrain)
0:08		A repeated by orchestra	
0:15		B part 1: triad spun out as arpeggios	
0:35		B part 2: circling arpeggios	B
0:45		B part 3: rising arpeggio	
0:56		Transition back to A	
1:03		A played by French horn	A
1:11		A repeated by orchestra	
1:18		C new theme played in a minor key	C
1:34		Rising melodic sequence is then balanced by	
1:46		Falling melodic sequence	
1:55		A played by French horn	A
2:02		A repeated by orchestra	
2:10		B part 1 developed	B
2:26		B part 2 developed	
2:35		B part 3 ends with *fortissimo*	
2:54		A played by horn	A
3:00		Orchestra begins to repeat A but then launches into	
3:02		Coda: reminiscences of A and descending arpeggios	Coda

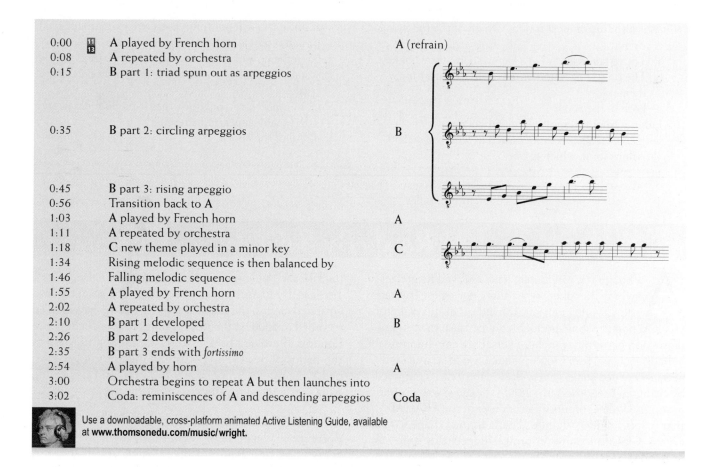

Use a downloadable, cross-platform animated Active Listening Guide, available at www.thomsonedu.com/music/wright.

Listening Exercise 26

Mozart
Horn Concerto in E♭ major

 6 **2**
2/11 1/13

ThomsonNOW
To take this Listening Exercise online and receive feedback or email answers to your instructor, go to *ThomsonNOW* for this chapter.

The key to hearing rondo form is to recognize the refrain and know when it has returned. Sometimes it is useful to make a simple melodic graph (as in Question 1) to help differentiate between the refrain and the contrasting material.

1. Which of the three melodic graphs most closely approximates the beginning of the refrain (**A**)?

    a.   xxxxx   b.   x   c. xxxxxx
      xxx   xx   x   x
        x   x
        x   x

2. (0:00–0:07) Judging from the refrain at the beginning of this movement (and all the motives given in the musical examples above), which of the following is true?

    a. The natural French horn can play scales easily but not repeated pitches or triads.
    b. The natural French horn can play repeated pitches and triads easily but not scales.

3. (0:00–0:07) Listen again to the beginning. Which is true?

    a. The French horn is accompanied quietly by strings.
    b. The French horn plays entirely by itself at the beginning.

4. (0:08–0:14) When the orchestra repeats the refrain, does the French horn play along?

    a. yes   b. no

5. (0:15) The first part of contrasting theme **B** enters here. Which melodic graph in Question 1 above does it most closely approximate?

    a. a   b. b   c. c

6. (1:18) The first part of contrasting theme **C** enters here. Which melodic graph in Question 1 above does it most closely approximate?

    a. a   b. b   c. c

Finally:

7. How many times in all does the French horn play the refrain in this rondo form movement?

    a. three times   c. five times
    b. four times   d. six times

8. Although Mozart provides no tempo marking for this finale, he intended it to be performed (as performed on this recording) at which tempo?

    a. *lento*   b. *adagio*   c. *allegro*

(continued)

9. As is also true of most rondos, which of the following is correct?
   a. The refrain is always in a happy-sounding major key.
   b. The only shift to minor occurs in a contrasting theme.
   c. Both of the above
10. Judging from this movement and your experience with sonata–allegro form, as well as with theme and variations form, which is true?

   a. In sonata–allegro form, there are many themes, and often no one theme predominates.
   b. In theme and variations form, there is usually only one theme, but it is continually ornamented and altered.
   c. In rondo form, only one theme predominates, and it usually appears unaltered.
   d. All of the above.

A Rondo By Sting

Although the rondo may have enjoyed its greatest favor in the sphere of art music during the Baroque and Classical periods, it lived on in the realm of folk and popular song, undoubtedly because the refrain–digression pattern has such universal appeal. Traditional ballads such as "Tom Dooley" make use of it, and so do more recent pop songs. "Every Breath You Take," composed by Sting and recorded in 1983 by his new-wave supergroup the Police, produces a rondo pattern (**ABACABA**) that in its symmetrical, indeed palindromic, shape would do any Classical composer proud. Indeed, this song has now been around for more than twenty years and has become something of a classic itself, reborn as the title track of the Police's greatest-hits compilation *Every Breath You Take: The Classics* (A & M Records). The song has also crossed over into the classical-pop repertoire, having been recorded in 2000 by the Royal Philharmonic Orchestra of London. It crossed back in 2002, becoming hip-hop in the hands of Sean "Puffy" Combs. According to Wikipedia, the rondo "Every Breath You Take" still earns Sting $2,000 per day in royalties.

Every breath you take	Every single day	
Every move you make	Every word you say	
Every bond you break	Every game you play	A
Every step you take	Every night you stay	
I'll be watching you.	I'll be watching you.	

O can't you see, you belong to me?
How my poor heart aches, with every step you take.　　B

Every move you make
Every vow you break
Every smile you fake　　　　　　　　　　　　A
Every claim you stake
I'll be watching you

Since you've gone I've been lost without a trace
I dream at night I can only see your face
I look around but it's you I can't replace　　　C
I feel so cold and I long for your embrace
I keep crying baby, baby please.

Instrumental interlude (no text) to **A** music,　　A

O can't you see, you belong to me? . . . (etc.)　　B

Every move you make . . . (etc.)　　　　　　　A

Coda (fade out)

Sting (Gordon Sumner).

Photofest

FORM, MOOD, AND THE LISTENER'S EXPECTATIONS

The audience of the late eighteenth century brought to the concert hall certain expectations, not only about the structure but also about the mood of the music that they would hear. Listeners had a notion of what the form, tempo, and general character would be of each movement of a sonata, quartet, or symphony. For the Classical period, we might summarize these as follows:

	Movement			
	1	**2**	**3**	**4**
Tempo:	Fast	Slow	Lively	Fast
Form:	Sonata–allegro	Large ternary, theme and variations, or rondo	Minuet and trio in ternary form	Sonata–allegro, theme and variations, or rondo
Mood:	Serious and substantive despite fast tempo	Lyrical and tender	Usually light and elegant, sometimes spirited	Bright, light-hearted, sometimes humorous

Ludwig van Beethoven (1770–1827) and later composers of the Romantic era (1820–1900) modified somewhat this conventional format—the third movement, for example, was often treated as a boisterous scherzo (see page 214) rather than an elegant minuet. Yet the Classical model was well established in the minds of subsequent listeners. Succeeding generations not only wanted to hear "new" music but were delighted to return to the tried and-true works of Haydn, Mozart, and their later contemporary Beethoven. Perhaps owing to the pleasing melodies and balanced structures of their sonatas, quartets, and symphonies, the works of the Classical Viennese masters came to form the nucleus of the "canon" (standard musical repertoire) of Western Classical music.

lasting influence of Classical music

Key Words

theme and variations **(199)**

rondo **(203)**
finale **(204)**

Köchel (K) number **(204)**

Classical Genres
INSTRUMENTAL MUSIC

In music the general term *genre* refers to that special quality of musical style, performing medium, and even place of performance that we associate with one class or type of music. The string quartet is a genre of music just as is the country music ballad, the twelve-bar blues piece, the military march, and even the rap song. When we listen to a piece of music, we come armed with expectations as to how it will sound, how long it will last, and how we should behave. We may even go to a special place—an opera house or a bar—and dress a certain way—in tuxedo and earrings or black leather jacket and nose rings, for example. It all depends on the genre of music we expect to hear. In simplest terms, then, a musical genre is a general type of music.

In the age of Mozart, there were five main genres of secular art music: the symphony, string quartet, sonata, concerto, and opera. Opera, of course, had been around since the early Baroque era. The sonata and concerto, too, had existed during the Baroque, but underwent such change at the hands of Haydn and Mozart that each became essentially a new genre. The symphony and string quartet were entirely new to the Classical period, created in no small part by Haydn.

THE SYMPHONY AND THE SYMPHONY ORCHESTRA

During the Classical era, the symphony became the preeminent genre of instrumental music. The fact that Haydn composed so many (104), and Mozart (given his short life) an even more astonishing number (41), shows that the symphony had become, and would remain, a staple of concert life.

origins of symphony

The symphony traces its origins to the late-seventeenth-century Italian opera overture called the **sinfonia** ("a harmonious sounding together"). Around 1700, the typical Italian *sinfonia* was a one-movement instrumental work in three sections: fast-slow-fast. Soon, Italian musicians and foreigners alike took the *sinfonia* out of the opera house and expanded it into three separate and distinct movements. A fourth movement, the minuet, was inserted by composers north of the Alps beginning in the 1740s. Thus, by midcentury the **symphony** had emerged as a major instrumental genre and assumed its familiar four-movement format: fast-slow-minuet-fast.

symphony tied to large, public concert halls

The public favor that the symphony came to enjoy was tied to progressive social changes that swept Europe during the Enlightenment, including the appearance of public concerts (see page 174). The center of musical life in such cities as London, Paris, and, to a lesser degree, Vienna gradually shifted from the aristocratic court to the newly constructed or refurbished public concert hall. Among these halls were the Hanover Square Rooms in London (see Fig. 18–3), where Haydn's London Symphonies* premiered, and the Burgtheater (City Theater) in Vienna (Fig. 19–1), where many of Mozart's symphonies and concertos were first heard. All but a few of Haydn's last twenty symphonies were composed for public performance in Paris and London, and Mozart wrote no symphonies for a court patron during the last ten years of his life. His famous G minor symphony (1788) was apparently first performed in

Museum der Stadt Wien

FIGURE 19–1

The interior of the Burgtheater, which could accommodate an audience of about 700. Not only were works of Mozart and Haydn performed here, but Beethoven also made his Viennese debut in this theater on March 29, 1795, at a benefit concert for Mozart's widow. For another interior view, see Figure 15–4.

a casino in Vienna—that's where the people were and that's where the money was to be found.

The audience at these public concerts in the capital cities of Europe increasingly came to hear the symphony and the large ensemble that played it. A symphony usually opened and closed each concert. Indeed, so closely did the genre of the symphony come to be linked with the performing force called the "orchestra," that the instrumental group came to be called a "symphony orchestra."

The Classical Symphony Orchestra

As the place of performance of the symphony orchestra moved from the private salon to the public auditorium, the size of both orchestra and audience increased. During the 1760s and 1770s, the orchestra at the court of Haydn's patron, Prince Nikolaus Esterházy, was never larger than twenty-five, and the audience at court was often only the prince and his staff (Fig 19–2). But when Haydn went to London in 1791, his orchestra and audiences alike were much larger. By 1795, Haydn's orchestra had more than doubled in size, now consisting of some sixty players. He conducted his London Symphonies* in the public Hanover Square Rooms, which typically held 800–900 people but sometimes more—for one concert in the spring of 1792, nearly 1,500 eager patrons crowded the hall.

Mozart's experience in Vienna was similar. For the public concerts he mounted in the Burgtheater in the mid-1780s, he engaged an orchestra of 35–40 players. But in a letter of 1781, he mentions an orchestra of 80 instrumentalists including 40 violins, 10 violas,

FIGURE 19–2

A watercolor of 1775 shows Haydn leading the small orchestra at the court of the Esterházy princes during a performance of a comic opera. The composer is seated at the keyboard, surrounded by the cellos. The higher strings and woodwinds are seated in two rows at the desk.

Deutsches Theatermuseum, Munich/The Bridgeman Art Library

8 cellos, and 10 double-basses. While this was an exceptional ensemble brought together for a special benefit concert, it shows that at times a very large group could be assembled. It also reveals that a large number of string players could be assigned to play just one string part—as many as 20 might "double" each other on the first violin line, for example.

To balance the growth in the string section, and to increase the variety of color in the orchestra, more winds were added. Now, instead of just one oboe or one bassoon, there were usually pairs. And a new woodwind, the clarinet, was welcomed into the orchestra. Mozart was especially fond of the clarinet and introduced it into his symphonies as early as 1778. Moreover, Mozart began to write independent lines for his woodwinds, not being satisfied with simply using them to double the string parts, as often happened in Baroque scores. Independent woodwind lines added not only color but also contrapuntal density to the orchestral fabric. By the 1790s, a typical symphony orchestra in a large European city might include the instrumentalists listed below. Compared to the Baroque orchestra, this ensemble of up to forty players was larger, more colorful, and more flexible.

woodwinds become numerous and important

Strings: 1st violins, 2nd violins, violas, cellos, double basses; about 27 players in all
Woodwinds: 2 flutes, 2 oboes, 2 clarinets, 2 bassoons
Brasses: 2 French horns, 2 trumpets (for festive pieces)
Percussion: 2 timpani (for festive pieces)

Mozart: Symphony No. 40 in G minor (1788), K. 550

Mozart's celebrated symphony in G minor requires all the full instrumental sound and disciplined playing the late-eighteenth-century orchestra could muster. This is not a festive composition (hence no trumpets and drums), but rather an intensely brooding work that suggests tragedy and despair. While we might be tempted to associate the minor key and despondent mood with a specific event in Mozart's life, apparently no such causal relationship exists. This was one of three symphonies, his last three, that Mozart produced in the incredibly short span of six weeks during the summer of 1788, and the other two are sunny, optimistic works. Rather than responding to a particular disappointment, it is more likely that Mozart invoked the tragic muse in this G minor symphony by drawing on a lifetime of disappointments and a premonition—as his letters attest—of an early death (Fig. 19–3).

FIRST MOVEMENT (*MOLTO ALLEGRO*)

Exposition   Although Mozart begins his G minor symphony with a textbook example of Classical phrase structure (four-bar antecedent, four-bar consequent phrases), an unusual sense of urgency is created by the repeating, insistent eighth-note figure at the beginning. This urgent motive is immediately grasped by the listener and becomes the most memorable theme in the work. Embedded in the motive is a falling half step* (here E♭ to D), an interval used throughout the history of music to denote pain and suffering.

The New Market in Vienna, as painted in 1759. The building on the right housed the city casino, and it was here that Mozart's G minor symphony was apparently first performed in 1788. Even today famous musicians, such as Luciano Pavarotti, perform in casinos—that's where the money is!

Kunsthistorisches Museum, Vienna

EXAMPLE 19–1

Not so quickly seized, but still contributing equally to the sense of urgency, is the accelerating rate of harmonic change. At the outset, chords are set beneath the melody at an interval of one chord every four measures, then one every two bars, then one every measure, then two chords per measure, and finally four. Thus, the "harmonic rhythm" is moving sixteen times faster at the end of this section than at the start. This is how Mozart creates the drive and urgency we all feel yet may be unable to explain. After this quickening start, the first theme begins once again, but soon veers off its previous course, initiating the transition. Transitions are filled with motion, especially running scales, and this one is no exception. What is unusual is that a new motive is inserted, one so distinctive that we might call it a "transition theme" (see the example in the following Listening Guide). As if to reciprocate for an extra theme here, Mozart dispenses with one toward the end of the exposition, at the point where we would expect a closing theme to appear. Instead, as closing material he uses the persistent motive and rhythm from the beginning of the first theme, which rather nicely rounds off the exposition. Finally, a single, isolated chord is heard, one that first leads back to a repeat of the exposition, and then, after the second statement of the exposition, launches into the development.

accelerating harmonic rhythm

Development   In the development, Mozart employs only the first theme (and then only the first four bars), but subjects it to a variety of musical treatments. First he carries it through several distantly related keys, next shapes it into a fugue subject for use in a fugato*, then sets it as a descending melodic sequence, and finally inverts the direction of the half-step* motive.

EXAMPLE 19–2

manipulation of the motive

The retransition* is suddenly interrupted by *sforzandi* (loud attacks). But soon a dominant pedal point* is heard in the bassoons, and above it the flute and clarinets begin to cascade down to the tonic pitch. This use of colorful, solo woodwinds in the retransition is a hallmark of Mozart's symphonic style.

Recapitulation   As expected, the recapitulation offers the themes in the same order in which they appeared in the exposition. But now the transition theme, which Mozart has left untouched since its initial appearance, receives extended treatment, creating something akin to a second development section as it pushes through one new key after another, only to end up back in the original tonic minor. When the lyrical second theme finally reappears, now in the minor mode, its mood is somber and plaintive. Because the repeating figure of the first theme rounds off the recapitulation by way of a closing theme, only the briefest coda is needed to end this passionate, haunting movement.

Listening Guide

Wolfgang Amadeus Mozart
Symphony No. 40 in G minor (1788), K. 550
First movement, *Molto allegro* (very fast)

6 2/12–14   **2** 1/14–16

Form: sonata–allegro

EXPOSITION   [ ] = repeat

0:00	[1:53]	Urgent, insistent first theme
0:21	[2:15]	First theme begins to repeat but is cut short
0:30	[2:23]	Transition
0:36	[2:28]	Rapid, ascending scales
0:44	[2:38]	Strong cadence ending transition, pause to clear air
0:47	[2:41]	Lyrical second theme, major key contributes to brighter mood
0:56	[2:50]	Second theme repeated with new orchestration
1:09	[3:02]	Crescendo leads to closing material (taken from first theme); abrupt stop

DEVELOPMENT

3:49	0:00	First theme modulates through several distant keys
4:05	0:16	First theme used as fugue subject in fugato in basses and then violins
4:45	0:38	First theme reduced to just opening motive
5:03	0:58	*Sforzandi* (loud attacks) give way to retransition*
5:12	1:07	Retransition: dominant pedal point* in bassoons as music cascades downward

RECAPITULATION

4:59	0:00	First theme returns
5:19	0:20	First theme begins to repeat but is cut off by transition
5:29	0:30	Transition theme returns but is greatly extended
5:55	0:56	Rapid, ascending scales
6:06	1:07	Cadence and pause
6:09	1:10	Second theme now in (tonic) minor
6:19	1:20	Second theme repeated with new orchestration
6:32	1:33	Return of crescendo, which leads to closing material (taken from first theme)

CODA

7:13	2:14	Begins with rising chromatic scale
7:20	2:21	Opening motive returns, then three final chords

Use a downloadable, cross-platform animated Active Listening Guide, available at www.thomsonedu.com/music/wright.

Listening Exercise 27

Mozart
Symphony No. 40 in G minor

6 2/12–14   **2** 1/14–16

ThomsonNOW™
To take this Listening Exercise online and receive feedback or email answers to your instructor, go to *ThomsonNOW* for this chapter.

As mentioned, Mozart was the first composer to integrate colorful writing for independent woodwinds, including the

clarinet, into his symphonic scores. Yet the strings remained the core of the Classical symphony orchestra. The following exercise asks you to consider the relationship between woodwinds and strings in one of Mozart's most famous symphonic movements.

0:00–1:52 Exposition
1. Which instruments begin by playing the haunting melody?
   a. cellos b. clarinets c. violins
2. When do the woodwinds first enter?
   a. 0:00 b. 0:14 c. 0:24
3. (0:37–0:45) What do the French horns do in this transition, something that is typical of the horns in orchestras during the Classical period?
   a. They stand out by playing independent solo melodies as in a horn concerto.
   b. They add "background" resonance by repeating one or two pitches.
4. (0:47–1:04) Which is true about the orchestration of the second theme?
   a. The strings begin with the theme, and then the woodwinds take it over.
   b. The woodwinds begin with the theme, and then the strings take it over.
5. (1:22–1:32) Echoes of the first theme close the exposition. Which woodwind instrument plays a main motive of the first theme?
   a. French horn b. clarinet c. bassoon d. oboe

1:53–3:45 Repeat of exposition
6. (0:00–0:39) Which family of instruments dominates the first section of the development?
   a. strings b. brasses c. woodwinds

7. (1:07–1:13) Which family of instruments dominates the end of the development, the retransition?
   a. strings b. brasses c. woodwinds
8. (0:00–0:09) At the beginning of the recapitulation, Mozart reorchestrates his score (compare the exposition, 0:00–0:10). Which of the following is true?
   a. The melody is now assigned to the woodwinds.
   b. A flute plays a new contrapuntal line against the melody.
   c. A bassoon plays a new contrapuntal line against the melody.
9. (1:10–1:33) Which is true about Mozart's re-orchestration of the second theme?
   a. The strings begin with the theme, and then the woodwinds take it over.
   b. The woodwinds begin with the theme, and the strings take it over.
10. In sum, which of the following is true about this movement (and Mozart's symphonies generally)?
    a. The violins introduce all themes, the woodwinds add color and counterpoint, and the brasses play sustaining pitches in the background.
    b. The woodwinds introduce all themes, the violins add color and counterpoint, and the brasses play sustaining pitches in the background.
    c. The brasses introduce all themes, the woodwinds add color and counterpoint, and the violins play sustaining pitches in the background.

SECOND MOVEMENT (*ANDANTE*)

After the feverish excitement of the opening movement, the slow, lyrical *Andante* comes as a welcome change of pace. What makes this movement exceptionally beautiful is the extraordinary interplay between the light and dark colors of the woodwinds against the constant tone of the strings. If there is no thematic contrast and confrontation here, there is, nonetheless, heartfelt expression brought about by Mozart's masterful use of orchestral color.

THIRD MOVEMENT (*MINUETTO: ALLEGRETTO*)

We expect the aristocratic minuet to provide elegant, graceful dance music. But much to our surprise, Mozart returns to the intense, somber mood of the opening movement. This he does, in part, by choosing to write in the tonic minor key—a rare minuet in minor.

FOURTH MOVEMENT (*ALLEGRO ASSAI*)

The finale starts with an ascending "rocket" that explodes in a rapid, *forte* flourish—and only carefully rehearsed string playing can bring off the brilliant effect of this opening gesture. The contrasting second theme of this sonata-allegro form movement is typically Mozartean in its grace and charm, a proper foil to the explosive opening melody. Midway through the development, musical compression takes hold: There is no retransition, only a pregnant pause before the recapitulation; the return dispenses with the repeats built into the first theme; and a coda is omitted. This musical foreshortening at the end produces the same psychological effect experienced at the very beginning of the symphony—a feeling of urgency and acceleration.

THE STRING QUARTET

The symphony is the ideal genre for the public concert hall, for it aims to please a large listening public. The string quartet, on the other hand, typifies chamber music—music for the small concert hall, for the private chamber, or, often, just for the enjoyment of the performers themselves. Unlike the symphony, which might have a dozen violinists joining on the first violin line, the **string quartet** has only one player per part: first violinist, second violinist, violist, and cellist (Fig. 19–4). Moreover, there is no conductor. All performers function equally and communicate directly among themselves. No wonder the German poet Johann Wolfgang von Goethe (1749–1832) compared the string quartet to a conversation among four intelligent people. All chamber music, whether for string quartet, solo piano or violin, wind quintet, or even string octet, employs just one player on a part. Of these chamber media, the string quartet is historically the most important.

chamber music: one player per part

Joseph Haydn is rightly called "the father of the string quartet." In the 1760s and 1770s, he took the Baroque trio sonata and made it into something new. He removed the old *basso continuo* and replaced it with a more melodically active bass played by an agile cello alone. And he enriched the middle of the texture by adding a viola, playing immediately above the cello. If the Baroque trio sonata had a "top- and bottom-heavy" texture, the newer Classical string quartet shows a texture covered evenly by four instruments, each of which participates more or less equally in a give-and-take of theme and motive.

The string quartet, of course, is not only a performing force but also a musical genre. The Classical string quartet has four movements that are identical to those of the Classical symphony: fast-slow-minuet-fast. Moreover, in a set of quartets he wrote in 1772, Haydn dubbed each minuet a **scherzo** (Italian for "joke"), aptly characterizing the high-spirited style of playing intended for this third movement.

both a performing force and a genre

It was the chance to play string quartets together that gave rise to a lasting friendship between Haydn and Mozart. During 1784–1785, the two men met in Vienna, sometimes at the home of an aristocrat, sometimes in Mozart's

FIGURE 19–4

A representation of a string quartet at the end of the eighteenth century. The string quartet was at first an ensemble for playing chamber music in the home. Not until 1804 did a string quartet appear in a public concert in Vienna, and not until 1814 in Paris.

own apartment. In their quartet, Haydn played first violin, and Mozart viola. As a result of this experience, Mozart was inspired to dedicate a set of his best works in this genre to the older master, which he published in 1785 (Fig. 19–5). Yet in this convivial, domestic music-making, Haydn and Mozart merely joined in the fashion of the day. For whether in Vienna, Paris, or London, aristocrats and members of the well-to-do middle class were encouraged to play quartets with friends as well as to engage professional musicians to entertain their guests.

Haydn: Opus 76, No. 3, the "Emperor" Quartet (1797)

Haydn's "Emperor" Quartet, written in Vienna during the summer of 1797, numbers among the best works of the string quartet genre. It is known as the "Emperor" because it makes liberal use of *The Emperor's Hymn*, a melody that Haydn composed in response to the military and political events of his day.

In 1796, the armies of Napoleon invaded the Austrian Empire, which ignited a firestorm of patriotism in Vienna, the Austrian capital. But the Austrians were at a musical disadvantage: The French now had the *Marseillaise*, and the English had their *God Save the King*, but the Austrians had no national anthem. To this end, the ministers of state approached Haydn, who quickly fashioned one to the text "Gott erhalte Franz den Kaiser" ("God preserve Franz the Emperor"), in honor of the reigning Austrian Emperor Franz II (Fig. 19–6). Called *The Emperor's Hymn*, it was first sung in theaters throughout the Austrian realm on the emperor's birthday, February 12, 1797. Later that year, Haydn took the tune and worked it into a string quartet.

In truth, when Haydn fashioned quartet Opus 76, No. 3, he made use of his imperial hymn mainly in the slow, second movement, where it serves as the basis of a theme and variations set. The theme (see the example in the following Listening Guide) is first presented by the first violin and harmonized in simple chords. Four variations follow in which the theme is ornamented but never altered. All four instruments are given equal opportunity to hold forth with the tune. Even the cello, more flexible and lyrical than the double bass of the orchestra, can participate as an equal partner. Example 19–3 shows how in the Classical string quartet the melodic profile of each of the lines is more or less the same, a far cry from the melody/walking-bass* polarity that typified the earlier Baroque trio sonata.

H storisches Museum der Stadt Wien

FIGURES 19–5 AND 19–6

(top) Title page of six string quartets by Mozart dedicated to Haydn (1785). Mozart offers them to Haydn as "six children," asking Haydn to be their "father, guide, and friend." (bottom) Franz II (1765–1835), last Holy Roman Emperor, first Emperor of Austria. Haydn composed *The Emperor's Hymn* in his honor.

EXAMPLE 19–3

Listening Guide

Joseph Haydn
String Quartet, Opus 76, No. 3, the "Emperor" Quartet (1797)
Second movement, *Poco adagio cantabile* (rather slow, song-like)

2/15–16   1/17–18

Form: theme and variations

THEME

(repeat)

(repeat)

0:00   [15/17]   Theme played slowly in first violin; lower three parts provide chordal accompaniment

VARIATION 1

1:19   Theme in second violin while first violin ornaments above

VARIATION 2

2:27   Theme in cello while other three instruments provide counterpoint against it

VARIATION 3

3:45   [16/18]   0:00   Theme in viola; other three instruments enter gradually

VARIATION 4

4:58   1:13   Theme returns to first violin, but now accompaniment is more contrapuntal than chordal

 Use a downloadable, cross-platform animated Active Listening Guide, available
at **www.thomsonedu.com/music/wright**.

Listening Exercise 28

Haydn
"Emperor" Quartet

2/15–16   1/17–18

ThomsonNOW
To take this Listening Exercise online and
receive feedback or email answers to your
instructor, go to *ThomsonNOW* for this chapter.

As a chamber music genre, the musical style of the string
quartet is different from that of a symphony. Generally,
the first violin shares the melody more with the other instruments, and that is certainly true in this movement in
theme and variations form.

1. First, how many performers play on each of the four
   parts comprising a string quartet?
   a. one   b. two   c. three   d. four

2. 0:00–1:18   **Theme**
   [15/17]   Listen to the theme. Why does it sound so secure and
   firm—an appropriate musical vehicle to represent a
   national identity?
   a. because all the notes are the same length
   b. because the theme starts low and ends high
   c. because each phrase is the same length and each
      ends on a dominant or tonic note

1:19–2:26   **Variation 1**

3. The second violin has the theme while the first violin rapidly ornaments above. Do the viola and cello (the lowest two instruments) play at all during this variation?
   a. yes   b. no

2:27–3:44   **Variation 2**

4. The cello has the theme in this variation. Would you say the instrument is playing in the higher or the lower part of its range? (Listen especially to the last section of the melody.)
   a. higher   b. lower

0:00–1:12   **Variation 3**

5. The viola has the melody but is gradually joined by the other instruments. Which instrument is the last to enter in this variation?
   a. first violin   b. second violin   c. cello

6. The musical texture in this variation is what?
   a. homophonic (chordal)
   b. polyphonic (contrapuntal)

1:13–1:45   **Variation 4**

7. The theme now returns to the first violin. When the violin repeats the first phrase of the melody, it does so where?

a. at the same pitch level
b. an octave higher
c. an octave lower

2:31–end   **A brief coda**

8. What does the cello do for much of the coda (2:31–end)?
   a. plays an arpeggio
   b. repeats a melodic sequence*
   c. sustains a pedal point*

9. In what way does Haydn conclude the movement?
   a. He has the players execute a "fadeout" by means of a ritard* and diminuendo*.
   b. He has the players accelerate for a *fortissimo* climax.

10. Finally, how does Haydn approach the process of writing a movement in theme and variations form here?
   a. He alters the pitches and rhythms of the theme.
   b. He keeps the theme intact, but ornaments it and adds counterpoint.
   c. He both alters the theme and adds ornaments around it.

The popularity of *The Emperor's Hymn* did not end with the defeat of Napoleon in 1815 or the death of Emperor Franz II in 1835. So alluring is Haydn's melody that with altered text it became a Protestant hymn (*Glorious Things of Thee Are Spoken*), as well as the national anthem of Austria (1853) and Germany (1922). It was also Haydn's own favorite piece, and he played a piano arrangement of it daily. In fact, *The Emperor's Hymn* was the last music Haydn played before he died in the early hours of May 31, 1809.

THE SONATA

The **sonata** was another important genre of chamber music that flourished during the Classical period. No longer was it a succession of four or five dance movements, as was usually the case during the Baroque era (see page 133). Now the sonata was a work in three movements (fast-slow-fast), each of which might make use of one or another of the forms favored by Classical composers: sonata–allegro, ternary, rondo, or theme and variations.

The sonata came to enjoy great popularity during the Classical period. According to publishers' inventories from the end of the eighteenth century, more sonatas were printed than any other type of music. The explanation for this sudden vogue is tied to the equally sudden popularity of the piano. Indeed, the word "sonata" has become so closely associated with the piano that unless otherwise qualified as "violin sonata," "cello sonata," or the like, we usually assume that "sonata" refers to a three-movement work for piano.

Who played this flood of new sonatas for the piano? Amateur musicians, mostly women, who practiced and performed for polite society in the comfort of their own homes. (Oddly, men in this period usually played not the piano but string instruments such as the violin or cello.) As we have seen (page 174),

the piano sonata

piano sonatas for women

in Mozart's time, the ability to play the piano, to do fancy needlework, and to utter a few selected words of French were thought by male-dominated society all that was necessary to be a cultured young lady. To teach the musical handicraft, instructors were needed. Mozart, Haydn, and Beethoven all served as piano teachers in fashionable circles early in their careers. The piano sonatas they composed for their many pupils were not intended to be played in the public concert halls. Sonatas were to provide students with material that they might practice to develop technique and that they might play as musical entertainment in the home. Even among the thirty-two splendid piano sonatas that Beethoven composed, only one was ever performed at a public concert in Vienna during his lifetime.

(An example of a Classical piano sonata by Beethoven, his *"Pathétique"* Sonata, is found on ❻3/1–3 and ❷1/19–21. It is discussed in detail on pages 232–235.)

THE CONCERTO

solo concerto offers technical display

With the genre of the concerto, we leave the salon or private chamber and return to the public concert hall. The Classical concerto, like the symphony, was a large-scale, three-movement work for instrumental soloist and orchestra intended for a public audience. While the symphony might have provided the greatest musical substance at a concert, audiences were often lured to the hall by the prospect of hearing a virtuoso performer play a concerto. Then as now, audiences were fascinated with personal virtuosity and all the derring-do that a stunning technical display might bring. Gone was the Baroque tradition of the concerto grosso*, in which a group of soloists (concertino*) stepped forward from the full orchestra (tutti*) and then receded back into it. From this point forward, the concerto was a **solo concerto,** usually for piano but sometimes for violin, cello, French horn, trumpet, or woodwind. In the new concerto, the soloist commanded all the audience's attention.

Development of the concerto for solo piano and orchestra had begun with the two sons of J. S. Bach—Carl Philipp Emanuel and Johann Christian, the latter living in London. The London Bach, as he was called, experimented with the piano concerto in connection with a series of public concerts he gave in both London and Paris during the 1760s and 1770s. Inspired by this example, the fifteen-year-old Mozart orchestrated some of this Bach's piano sonatas, turning them into fledgling piano concertos. But credit for the creation of the mature Classical piano concerto must go to Mozart alone. Just as Haydn can be fairly said to have created the string quartet, so Mozart can be considered the father of the modern piano concerto.

Mozart composed twenty-three original piano concertos, more than any other important composer in history. He wrote most of these after he moved to Vienna in 1781, when he no longer had an annual salary and thus needed to earn a living. The Viennese were eager to hear brilliant passagework and dazzling displays of keyboard virtuosity. The piano concerto was for Mozart the perfect vehicle for such a display. At each of the public concerts he produced, Mozart offered one or two of his latest concertos. But he had to do more: He was responsible for renting the hall (see Fig. 19–1), hiring the orchestra, leading rehearsals, attracting an audience, and selling tickets from his apartment (Fig. 19–7)—all this in addition to composing the music and appearing as solo virtuoso. But when all went well, Mozart could make a killing, as a music journal of March 22, 1783, reported:

FIGURE 19–7

One of the few surviving tickets to a concert given by Mozart in Vienna. These were sold in advance, not from a ticket agency, but from Mozart's own apartment!

Today the celebrated Chevalier Mozart gave a musical concert for his own benefit at the Burgtheater in which pieces of his own music, which was already very popular, were performed. The concert was honored by the presence of an extraordinarily large audience and the two new concertos and other fantasies which Mr. Mozart played on the Forte Piano were received with the loudest approval. Our Monarch [Emperor Joseph II], who contrary to his custom honored the entire concert with his presence, joined in the applause of the public so heartily that one can think of no similar example. The proceeds of the concert are estimated at sixteen hundred gulden.

Mozart plays two concertos before the emperor

Sixteen hundred gulden was the equivalent of about $140,000 today, and more than five times the annual salary of Mozart's father. With a take such as this, young Mozart could, at least for a time, indulge his expensive tastes.

Mozart: Piano Concerto in A major (1786), K. 488

We derive our term "concerto" from the Italian word *concertare*. It means above all else "to strive together," but it also resonates with a sense of "to struggle against." In a piano concerto, the piano and orchestra engage in a spirited give-and-take of thematic material—the piano, perhaps more than any instrument, can compete on an equal footing with the orchestra (Fig. 19–8). Mozart may have composed his Piano Concerto in A major of 1786 for one of his star pupils, Barbara Ployer (see boxed essay).

FIRST MOVEMENT (*ALLEGRO*)

As with all of Mozart's concertos, this one is in three movements (there is never a minuet or scherzo in a concerto). And, as is invariably the case, the first movement is written in sonata–allegro form. Here, however, it is modified to meet the special demands and opportunities of the concerto. What results is **double exposition form,** an extension of sonata–allegro form in which the orchestra plays one exposition and the soloist then plays another. First, the orchestra presents the first, second, and closing themes, all in the tonic key. Then, the soloist enters and, with orchestral assistance, offers the piano's version of the same material, but modulating to the dominant before the second theme. After the piano expands the closing theme, part of the first theme group returns, a throwback to the ritornello* principle of the old Baroque concerto grosso.

Then a surprise: just when we expect this second exposition to end, Mozart inserts a lyrical new melody played by the strings. This is another feature of the Classical concerto—a melody held back for last-minute presentation, a way of keeping the listener "on guard" during the second exposition.

FIGURE 19–8

Mozart's piano, preserved in the house of his birth in Salzburg, Austria. The keyboard spans only five octaves, and the black-and-white color scheme of the keys is reversed, both typical features of the late-eighteenth-century piano. Mozart purchased the instrument in 1784, two years before he composed his A major piano concerto.

Mozart Museum, Archive, Salzburg

DOUBLE EXPOSITION FORM

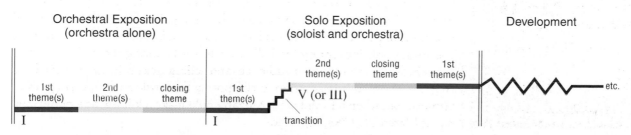

Orchestral Exposition (orchestra alone)	Solo Exposition (soloist and orchestra)	Development

Barbara Ployer: Concert Pianist

In 1781, Mozart broke from his patron, the Archbishop of Salzburg, to establish himself as a freelance musician in Vienna. To earn a living, he took on a small number of piano students whom he visited daily for their lessons. Most of these were young women, and for the more talented of them, he composed piano sonatas and concertos. Among the best was Barbara Ployer (1765–1811), the daughter of an old and wealthy acquaintance from Salzburg. In 1784, Mozart composed his Piano Concerto in G major (K. 453) for Fraulein Ployer, "who paid me handsomely," as Mozart said in a letter to his father. When it came time to perform the work, Mozart attended the concert and brought along another composer, Giovanni Paisiello (1740–1816), to show off both his star pupil and his new concerto. Mozart's Piano Concerto in A major (K. 488) is similarly believed to have been composed for Ployer.

Engraving by Johann Rudolf Holzhalb, 1777. Reproduced with the kind permission of Oxford University Press.

A young woman performs a keyboard concerto in 1777.

cadenza: chance for solo razzle-dazzle

The development here is concerned exclusively with exploiting the new theme that appeared at the end of the second exposition. The recapitulation compresses the two expositions into one, presenting the themes in the same order as before but now all in the tonic key. Finally, toward the end of the movement, the orchestra suddenly stops its forward motion and comes to rest on a single chord for several moments. Using this chord as a point of departure, the pianist plunges headlong into a flight of virtuosic fancy called a "cadenza." In a **cadenza,** the soloist, playing alone, mixes rapid runs, arpeggios, and snippets of previously heard themes into a fantasy-like improvisation. Indeed, Mozart didn't write down this cadenza when he first performed it, but improvised it on the spot, just as in our own century a talented jazz musician might improvise an extended solo. After a minute or so of this virtuosic dazzle, the pianist plays a trill*, a signal to the orchestra that it is time for it to reenter the competition. From here to the end, the orchestra holds forth, making use of the original closing theme. There is much to follow in the Listening Guide for this movement in double exposition form, but the glorious music of Mozart will amply reward the attentive listener.

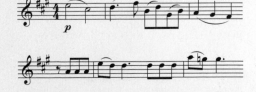

Listening Guide

Wolfgang Amadeus Mozart
Piano Concerto in A major (1786)
First movement, *Allegro* (fast)

6

2/17–19

EXPOSITION 1 (orchestra)

0:00	17	Strings present first theme, part **a**
0:16		Woodwinds repeat first theme, part **a**
0:34		Full orchestra presents first theme, part **b**

0:56	Strings present second theme, part **a**
1:12	Woodwinds repeat second theme, part **a**
1:27	Strings present second theme, part **b**
1:32	Strings present closing theme, part **a**
1:57	Woodwinds present closing theme, part **b**

EXPOSITION 2 (piano and orchestra)

2:07	Piano enters with first theme, part **a**
2:35	Orchestra plays first theme, part **b**
3:05	Piano plays second theme, part **a**
3:20	Woodwinds repeat second theme, part **a**
3:36	Piano plays and ornaments second theme, part **b**
3:41	Piano and orchestra in dialogue play closing theme, part **a**
4:15	Piano trill heralds return of first theme, part **b**
4:29	Strings quietly offer lyrical new theme

DEVELOPMENT

4:54	18	0:00	Woodwinds transform new theme as piano interjects scales and then arpeggios
5:25		0:31	Woodwinds offer new theme in imitative counterpoint
5:37		0:43	Pedal point on dominant note in low strings signals beginning of retransition
5:50		0:56	Piano takes over dominant pedal point
6:07		1:13	Piano flourish above sustained dominant chord leads to recapitulation

RECAPITULATION

6:17	19	0:00	Orchestra plays first theme, part **a**
6:31		0:14	Piano repeats first theme, part **a**
6:45		0:28	Orchestra plays first theme, part **b**
6:54		0:37	Scales in piano signal beginning of transition
7:13		0:56	Piano plays second theme, now in tonic, part **a**
7:28		1:11	Woodwinds repeat second theme, part **a**
7:43		1:26	Piano plays second theme, part **b**
7:48		1:31	Piano and orchestra divide closing theme, part **a**
8:15		1:58	Piano plays new theme
8:28		2:11	Woodwinds play new theme while piano offers scales and arpeggios against it
8:54		2:37	Trill in piano announces return of first theme, part **b**
9:21		3:04	Orchestra stops and holds chord
9:25		3:08	Cadenza for piano
10:36		4:19	Trill signals reentry of orchestra
10:47		4:30	Orchestra plays closing theme, parts **a** and **b**
11:05		4:48	Final cadential chords

Use a downloadable, cross-platform animated Active Listening Guide, available at **www.thomsonedu.com/music/wright.**

SECOND MOVEMENT (*ANDANTE*)

The essence of this movement rests in Mozart's exquisitely crafted lines and coloristic harmonies. This is the only work the Viennese master ever wrote in the remote key of F♯ minor, and the daring harmonic changes it contains prefigure those of the Romantic era. Musicians who have lived with Mozart's music from childhood to old age continue to be profoundly moved by this extraordinary movement. It is at once sublimely beautiful and distantly remote, its ending as cold and desolate as death itself.

THIRD MOVEMENT (*PRESTO*)

The sublime pessimism of the *Andante* is suddenly shattered by a boisterous rondo refrain in the piano. As Mozart was well aware, this movement, not the previous slow one, had the kind of music the fun-loving Viennese would pay to hear. And in this rondo his subscribers got more than they bargained for; the soloist and orchestra do not simply "speak in turn," but rather banter back and forth in the most playful and pleasing way. "Anything you can do, I can do better," "No you can't," "Yes I can," the antagonists seem to say. In Mozart's contest between interactive forces, there is no winner—except the listener.

"Anything you can do, I can do better."

ThomsonNOW™

ThomsonNOW for *Listening to Music, 5th Edition,* and *Listening to Western Music* will assist you in understanding the content of this chapter with lesson plans generated for your specific needs. In addition, you may complete this chapter's Listening Exercises in ThomsonNOW's interactive environment, as well as download Active Listening Guides and other materials that will help you succeed in this course.

Key Words

sinfonia (**208**)	scherzo (**214**)	double exposition
symphony (**208**)	sonata (**217**)	form (**219**)
string quartet (**214**)	solo concerto (**218**)	cadenza (**220**)

Chapter 20

Classical Genres
VOCAL MUSIC

Vocal music in the Classical era was both sacred and secular in nature. Chief among the genres of sacred music was the polyphonic Catholic Mass, a musical setting of the five parts of the Ordinary* (Kyrie, Gloria, Credo, Sanctus, and Agnus dei). The most important of the late-eighteenth-century Masses are perhaps the half dozen written by Haydn, beginning in 1796, and Mozart's final composition, his unfinished Requiem Mass (1791). Beethoven composed only two Masses, the more important being his massive *Missa Solemnis* (1822). Haydn and Beethoven perpetuated the oratorio tradition developed by Handel, but the church cantata, which Bach had perfected in the late Baroque period, all but disappeared. But while Mass and oratorio were important in the Classical era, their impact was overshadowed by the power of opera. The public remained enamored of opera because, in addition to beautiful music, it offered all the glamour and excitement of the theater.

CLASSICAL OPERA

Opera is drama, yes, but drama propelled by music. In the Classical period, opera maintained the essential features it had developed during the Baroque era. It still began with an overture, was divided into two or three acts, and made use of a succession of arias and recitatives, along with an occasional choral number. And, of course, it still was performed in a theater large enough to accommodate both an orchestra and elaborate stage sets.

features of opera

Opera in the eighteenth century was marked by the rise of comic opera*, a powerful voice for social change during the Enlightenment (see page 173). The statue-like gods, goddesses, emperors, and queens of the old Baroque *opera seria* gradually departed the stage, making room for more natural, realistic characters drawn from everyday life. Where Baroque opera had once posed magnificently, Classical opera moves fluidly. Arias and recitatives flow easily from one to another, and the mood of the music changes rapidly to reflect the quick-moving, often comic, events on stage.

easy flow of comic opera

Comic opera introduces a new element into the opera house, the **vocal ensemble,** which allows the plot to unfold more quickly. Instead of waiting for each character to sing successively, three or more characters can express their own particular emotions simultaneously. One might sing of her love, another of his fear, another of her outrage, while a fourth pokes fun at the other three. Composers often placed vocal ensembles at the ends of acts to help spark a rousing conclusion, one in which all the principals might appear on stage. The vocal ensemble typifies the more democratic spirit, and better dramatic pacing, of the late eighteenth century.

Mozart: master of vocal ensemble

MOZART AND OPERA

The master of Classical opera, and of the vocal ensemble in particular, was Wolfgang Amadeus Mozart. While Haydn wrote more than a dozen operas and conducted others (see Fig. 19–2), he lacked Mozart's instinct for what was effective in the theater and what was not. Beethoven wrote only one opera, *Fidelio*, and he labored mightily over it, working through several revisions in the course of nearly ten years. Neither Haydn nor Beethoven had Mozart's proclivity for quick changes in mood and color, nor his capacity for equally quick exchanges in musical dialogue, of the sort we witnessed in his piano concertos (see page 219). Mozart's music is inherently theatrical and perfectly suited to the genre of opera.

Mozart's music naturally suited to opera

Mozart wrote Italian *opera seria* of the old Baroque sort as well as German comic opera, which was called *Singspiel*. Like a Broadway musical, a ***Singspiel*** is made up of spoken dialogue (instead of recitative) and songs. Mozart's best work of this type is *Die Zauberflöte* (*The Magic Flute*, 1791). But Mozart also wrote Italian comic operas. These include his masterpieces *Le nozze di Figaro* (*The Marriage of Figaro*, 1786), *Don Giovanni* (1787), and *Così fan tutte* (*Thus Do They All*, 1790), all three with text (libretto) by Lorenzo da Ponte (see boxed essay).

Mozart: *Don Giovanni* (1787), K. 527

Don Giovanni has been called not only Mozart's greatest opera, but also the greatest opera ever written. It tells the tale of an amoral philanderer, a Don

Lorenzo da Ponte: Librettist to Mozart

Mozart's principal librettist during the 1780s was **Lorenzo da Ponte,** whose own life was more fantastic than the theatrical characters he created. Born in northern Italy of Jewish parents, he received his only formal education in a Catholic seminary. He became a teacher of Italian and Latin literature and then an ordained priest, but was banned from his native Venice for his democratic thinking, libertine lifestyle, and sexual escapades. Having made his way to Vienna in 1781, he was introduced to Emperor Joseph II by the imperial court composer Antonio Salieri (see page 186). Da Ponte became the official court librettist ("Poet to the Imperial Theaters"), and both Salieri and Mozart made use of his talents. But when Joseph died in 1790 and Mozart the following year, da Ponte's

Lorenzo da Ponte (1749–1838).
Unidentified artist, portrait of Lorenzo da Ponte.
Courtesy Columbia University in the City of New York

fortunes in Vienna declined. After passing time with another famous Venetian adventurer, Giacomo Casanova (1725–1798), da Ponte made his way to London, where he opened a bookstore. But da Ponte was soon charged with shady financial dealings, and in 1805 he stole away from London for America, one step ahead of his creditors. After a brief stop in New York, he established himself in Sunbury, Pennsylvania, as a trader, distiller, and occasional gunrunner during the War of 1812. Eventually, he gave this up and returned to New York, becoming the first professor of Italian literature at Columbia University in 1825. The high point of his final years came in May 1826, when he helped bring *Don Giovanni* to the stage in New York, the first opera by Mozart to be performed in America.

Juan, who seduces and murders his way across Europe before being pursued and finally dragged down to hell by the ghost of a man whom he has killed. Since the seducer and mocker of public law and morality is a nobleman, *Don Giovanni* is implicitly critical of the aristocracy, and Mozart and da Ponte danced quickly to stay one step ahead of the imperial censor before production. Mozart's opera was first performed on October 29, 1787, in Prague, Czech Republic, a city in which his music was especially popular. As fate would have it, the most notorious Don Juan of the eighteenth century, Giacomo Casanova (1725–1798), was in the audience that first night in Prague. It turns out that he had a small hand in helping his friend da Ponte shape the libretto.

an opera critical of nobility

The overture to *Don Giovanni*, as we have seen (❻2/20–22; Listening Exercise 25), is a fine example of sonata–allegro form. It begins with a slow introduction that incorporates several themes or motives important later in the opera. Just as an author postpones writing a preface until after a book is finished, so a composer typically saves the overture for the end of the creative process. In this way, the overture can not only prefigure important themes in the opera but also characterize the overall tone of the work. Mozart, as was his tendency, postponed much of the writing of *Don Giovanni* until the last minute, and the overture was not completed until the night before the premiere, the copyist's ink still wet on the pages as the music was handed to the orchestra.

overture

As the last strains of the overture die away, the curtain rises on the comic figure Leporello, Don Giovanni's faithful, though reluctant, servant. Leporello has been keeping a nocturnal vigil outside the house of Donna Anna while his master is inside attempting to satisfy his sexual appetite. Grumbling as he paces back and forth, Leporello sings about how he would gladly trade places with the fortunate aristocrat ("I would like to play the gentleman"; ⑥2/23). Immediately, Mozart works to establish Leporello's musical character: He sets this opening aria in F major, a traditional key for the pastoral in music, showing that Leporello is a rustic fellow; he gives him a narrow vocal range without fancy chromaticism; and he has him sing quick repeated notes, almost as if he were stuttering. This last technique, called "patter song," is a stock device used to depict low-caste, inarticulate characters in comic opera.

character depiction through music

As Leporello concludes his complaint, the masked Don Giovanni rushes on stage, chased by the virtuous Donna Anna. Here the strings rush up the scale and the music modulates up a fourth (at 1:32) to signify that we are now dealing with the highborn. The victim of Don Giovanni's unwanted sexual advances, Donna Anna wants her assailant captured and unmasked. While the gentleman and lady carry on a musical tug-of-war in long notes above, the cowering Leporello patters away fearfully below. This excellent example of vocal ensemble* makes clear the conflicting emotions of each party.

Now Donna Anna's father, the Commandant, enters to challenge Don Giovanni. The listener senses that this bodes ill—there is a troubling tremolo* in the strings, and the music shifts from major to minor mode (2:50). Our fear is immediately confirmed as the Don, first refusing to duel, draws his sword and attacks the aging Commandant. In the brief exchange of steel, Mozart depicts the rising tension by means of ascending chromatic scales and tight, tense chords (3:32). At the very moment Don Giovanni's sword pierces the Commandant, the action stops and the orchestra sustains on a painful **diminished chord** (3:44)—a chord comprised entirely of minor thirds. Mozart then clears the air of discord with a simple texture and accompaniment as Don Giovanni and Leporello gaze in horror on the dying Commandant.

a duel set to music

In this vocal ensemble, three very different sentiments are conveyed simultaneously: surprise and satisfaction (Don Giovanni), the desire to flee (Leporello), and the pain of a violent death (Commandant). At the end, the listener can feel the Commandant expire, his life sinking away through the slow descent of a chromatic scale (4:52). In its intensity and compression, only the opening scene of Shakespeare's *King Lear* rivals the beginning of *Don Giovanni*.

an intense vocal ensemble

Listening Guide

Wolfgang Amadeus Mozart
Opera, *Don Giovanni* (1787), K. 527
Act I, Scene 1

6
2/23

Characters: Don Giovanni, a rakish lord; Leporello, his servant; Donna Anna, a virtuous noblewoman; the Commandant, her father, a retired military man

ARIA

Leporello

0:00	23	The pacing Leporello grumbles as he awaits his master Don Giovanni	Notte e giorno faticar, per chi nulla sa gradi, piova e il vento sopportar, mangiar male e mal dormir. Voglio far il gentilumo e non volgio più servir . . .	On the go from morn 'til night for one who shows no appreciation, sustaining wind and rain, without proper food or sleep. I would like to play the gentleman and no more a servant be . . .

(Leporello continues in this vein.)

1:32	Violins rush up scale and music modulates upward as Don Giovanni and Donna Anna rush in

(continued)

ENSEMBLE (TRIO)

1:38	Donna Anna tries to hold and unmask Don Giovanni while Leporello cowers on side	

Donna Anna

Non sperar, se non m'uccidi, ch'io ti lasci fuggir mai'.	Do not hope you can escape unless you kill me.

Don Giovanni

Donna folle, indarno gridi, chi son io tu non saprai.	Crazy lady, you scream in vain, you will never know who I am.

Leporello

Che tumulto, oh ciel, che gridi il padron in nuovi guai.	What a racket, heavens, what screams, my master in a new scrape.

Donna Anna

Gente! Servi! Al traditore! Scellerato!	Everyone! Help! Catch the traitor! Scoundrel!

Don Giovanni

Taci et trema al mio furore! Sconsigliata!	Shut up and get out of my way! Fool!

Leporello

Sta a veder che il malandrino mi fara recipitar. . . .	We will see if this malefactor will be the ruin of me. . . .

(The trio continues in this manner with liberal repeats of text and music.)

2:50	String tremolo and shift from major to minor as the Commandant enters	

ENSEMBLE (TRIO)

	The Commandant comes forward to fight; Don Giovanni first refuses, then duels; Leporello tries to flee	

Commandant

Lasciala, indegno! Battiti meco!	Let her go, villain! Fight with me!

Don Giovanni

Va! non mi degno di pugnar teco!	Away, I wouldn't deign to fight with you!

Commandant

Così pretendi da me fuggir!	So you think you can get away thus?

Leporello (aside)

Potessi almeno di qua partir!	If I could only get out of here.

Don Giovanni

Misero! attendi se vuoi morir!	You old fool! Get ready then, if you wish to die!

3:32	Musical duel (running scales and tense diminished chords)	
3:44	Climax on intense diminished chord (the Commandant falls mortally wounded), then pause	

ENSEMBLE (TRIO)

3:50	Don Giovanni and Leporello look on dying Commandant; "ticking" sound in strings freezes time	

Commandant

Ah, soccorso! son tradito. L'assassino m'ha ferito, e dal seno palpitante sento l'anima partir.	Ah, I'm wounded, betrayed The assassin has run me through, and from my heaving breast I feel my soul depart.

Don Giovanni

Ah, gia cade il sciagurato, affannoso e agonizzante, gia del seno palpitante Veggo l'anima partir.	Ah, already the old fool falls, gasping and writhing in pain, and from his heaving breast I can see his soul depart.

	Leporello
Qual misfatto! qual eccesso!	What a horrible thing, how stupid!
Entro il sen dallo spavento	I can feel within my breast
palpitar il cor mi sento.	my heart pounding from fear.
Io non so che far, che dir.	I don't know what to say or do.

4:52   Slow, chromatic descent as last
         breath seeps out of the Commandant

 Use a downloadable, cross-platform animated Active Listening Guide, available at **www.thomsonedu.com/music/wright**.

When we next meet the unrepentent Don Giovanni, he is in pursuit of the country girl Zerlina. She is the betrothed of another peasant, Masetto, and the two are to be married the next day. Don Giovanni quickly dismisses Masetto and turns his charm on the naïve Zerlina. First, he tries verbal persuasion carried off in simple recitative* (the harpsichord is still used to accompany simple recitatives in Classical opera, a vestige of the older Baroque practice). Zerlina, he says, is too lovely for a country bumpkin like Masetto. Her beauty demands a higher state: She will become his wife.

Simple recitative now gives way to more passionate expression in the charming duet "Là ci darem la mano" ("Give me your hand, o fairest") (Fig. 20–1). During this duet, Don Giovanni persuades Zerlina to extend her hand (and the prospect of a good deal more). He begins with a seductive melody (**A**) cast squarely in the Classical mold of two, four-bar antecedent–consequent phrases (see the following Listening Guide). Zerlina repeats and extends this, but still sings alone and untouched. The Don becomes more insistent in a new phrase (**B**), and Zerlina, in turn, becomes flustered, as her quick sixteenth notes reveal. The initial melody (**A**) returns, but is now sung together by the two principals, their voices intertwining—musical union accompanies the act of physical touching that occurs on stage. Finally, as if to further affirm this coupling through music, Mozart adds a concluding section (**C**) in which the two characters skip off, arm in arm ("Let's go, my treasure"), their voices linked together, mainly in parallel-moving thirds to show unity of feeling and purpose. These are the means by which a skilled composer like Mozart can underscore, through music, the drama unfolding on the stage.

FIGURE 20–1

Don Giovanni (Thomas Hampson) and Zerlina (Marie McLaughlin) sing the duet "Là ci darem la mano" from *Don Giovanni*. It has been called "the most perfect duet of seduction imaginable."

 **Listening Guide**   Wolfgang Amadeus Mozart
Opera, *Don Giovanni* (1787), K. 527
Act I, Scene 7

6
2/24

Characters: Don Giovanni and the peasant girl Zerlina

Situation: Don Giovanni tries, and apparently succeeds, in the seduction of Zerlina.

RECITATIVE   **Don Giovanni**

0:00 [24] Alfin siam liberati, Zerlinetta gentil,   At last, gentle Zerlina,
            da quel sioccone.   we are free of that clown.
            Che ne dite, mio ben,   And say, my love, didn't
            sò far pulito?   I handle it well?

(continued)

Zerlina

Signore, è mio marito.

Sir, he is my fiancé.

Don Giovanni

Chi? Colui?
Vi par che un onest'uomo,
un nobil cavalier, qual io mi vanto,
possa soffrir che quel visetto d'oro,
quel viso inzuccherato
da un bifolcaccio vil sia strapazzato?

Who? Him?
Do you think that an honorable
man, a noble cavalier as I
believe I am, could let such a
golden face, such a sweet
beauty, be profaned by that
clumsy oaf?

Zerlina

Ma, signor, io gli diedi
parola di sposarlo.

But sir, I have already given
my word to marry him.

Don Giovanni

Tal parola non vale un zero.
Voi non siete fatta per esser paesana;
un altra sorte vi procuran quegli
occhi bricconcelli, quei labretti si
belli, quelle dituccia candide e
odorose, par me toccar giuncata e
fiutar rose.

Such a promise counts for
nothing. You were not made
to be a peasant girl, a higher
fate is in store for those
mischievous eyes, those beautiful
lips, those milky, perfumed
hands, so soft to touch,
scented with roses.

Zerlina

Ah! . . . Non vorrei . . .

Ah! . . . I do not wish . . .

Don Giovanni

Che non vorreste?

What don't you wish?

Zerlina

Alfine ingannata restar.
Io sò che raro colle donne voi
altri cavalieri siete onesti e sinceri.

In the end to be deceived.
I know that rarely are you
noblemen honest and
sincere with women.

Don Giovanni

Eh, un'impostura della gente plebea!
La nobiltà ha dipinta negli occhi
l'onestà. Orsù, non perdiam tempo;
in questo istante io ti voglio sponsar.

A vile slander of the low
classes. Nobility can be
seen in honest eyes. Now
let's not waste time. I
will marry you immediately.

Zerlina

Voi?

You?

Don Giovanni

Certo, io. Quell casinetto è mio.
Soli saremo, e là, gioiello mio,
ci sposeremo.

Certainly I. That villa
over there is mine. We
will be alone, and there, my
little jewel, we will be married.

ARIA (DUET)

A

1:45

Don Giovanni

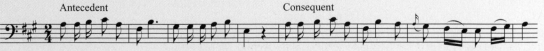

Antecedent   Consequent

Là ci da-rem la mano, là mi di-rai di sì; ve-di, non è lon-ta-no, par-tiam, ben mio, da qui.

	Là ci darem la mano,	Give me your hand, o fairest,
	là mi dirai di sì.	whisper a gentle "yes."
	Vedi, non è lontano:	See, it's not far,
	partiam, ben mio, da qui.	let's go, my love.

Zerlina

2:03	Vorrei, e non vorrei,	I'd like to but yet I would not.
	mi trema un poco il cor;	My heart will not be still.
	felice, è ver, sarei,	Tis true I would be happy,
	ma può burlarmi ancor.	yet he may deceive me still.

B

Don Giovanni

Vie - ni, mio bel di - let - to!

2:26	Vieni, mio bel diletto!	Come with me, my pretty!

Zerlina

Mi fa pietà Masetto!	May Masetto take pity!

Don Giovanni

Io cangierò tua sorte!	I will change your fate!

Zerlina

Presto, non son più forte.	Quick then, I can no longer resist.

A'

2:51　Repeat of first eight lines, but with Don Giovanni's and Zerlina's parts moving closer together

B'

3:14　Repeat of next four lines

C

3:42　Change of meter to dance-like $\frac{6}{8}$ as principals skip off together

Together

(Zerlina)
An - diam, an-diam, mio be-ne, a ri-sto-rar le pe-ne d'un' in - no - cen-te a - mor!

(Don Giovanni)
An - diam, an-diam, mio be-ne, a ri-sto-rar le pe-ne d'un' in - no - cen-te a - mor!

	Andiam, andiam mio bene,	Let's go, let's go, my treasure,
	a ristorar le pene	to soothe the pangs
	d'un innocente amor!	of innocent love.

Use a downloadable, cross-platform animated Active Listening Guide, available at **www.thomsonedu.com/music/wright**.

In the end, the frightful ghost of the dead Commandant confronts Don Giovanni and orders him to repent. Ever defiant, Don Giovanni cries, "No, no," and is dragged down to Hell to the sounds of Mozart's most demonic music. It is the admixture of divine beauty and sinister power that makes *Don Giovanni* a masterpiece of the highest order.

ThomsonNOW

ThomsonNOW for *Listening to Music, 5th Edition*, and *Listening to Western Music* will assist you in understanding the content of this chapter with lesson plans generated for your specific needs. In addition, you may download Active Listening Guides and other materials that will help you succeed in this course.

Key Words

vocal ensemble (**223**)	Lorenzo da Ponte	diminished chord
Singspiel (**223**)	(**224**)	(**225**)
Don Giovanni (**223**)		

Beethoven
BRIDGE TO ROMANTICISM

Chapter 21

FIGURE 21–1

A somewhat glamorized portrait of 1819 showing Ludwig van Beethoven at work on his *Missa Solemnis*. In reality, Beethoven had a pock-marked face and was usually unshaven.

Beethoven Haus, Bonn/The Bridgeman Art Library

No composer looms larger as an iconic figure than Ludwig van Beethoven (1770–1827). When we think of the image of the "musician as artist," most likely it is the angry, defiant, disheveled Beethoven (Fig. 21–1) who comes to mind. Is it not the bust of Beethoven, rather than the elegant Mozart or the stalwart Bach, that sits atop Schroeder's piano in the comic strip *Peanuts*? Is it not Beethoven who is the namesake of nearly a dozen popular kids' films (*Beethoven*, *Beethoven's 2nd*, and *Beethoven Lives Upstairs*, for example). And, is it not Beethoven's Fifth Symphony that, in a 2005 episode of *The Simpsons*, inaugurates Springfield's new concert hall? Such observations are not mere trivialities. Beethoven is deeply ingrained in our popular culture.

Even in his own day, Beethoven had a cult-like following, embraced as both mad genius and popular hero. Oblivious to the world, he walked about Vienna humming and scribbling music in a notebook. When he died in March 1827, 20,000 people turned out for the funeral. Schools closed, and the army mobilized to control the huge crowd.

BEETHOVEN'S MUSIC

Today Beethoven's music continues to enjoy great popular favor. Statistics show that his symphonies, sonatas, and quartets are performed in concert and on radio more than those of any other classical composer. These works are tender but powerful, sometimes carefully controlled, sometimes exploding with musical violence. And just as Beethoven the composer struggled to overcome personal adversity—his growing deafness—so his music imparts a feeling of struggle and ultimate victory. It has a sense of rightness, even morality, about it. It elevates and inspires the listener, and for that reason it has an immediate and universal appeal.

Historians divide Beethoven's music into three periods: early, middle, and late. In many regards, his work belongs to the tradition of the Classical Viennese style. Beethoven employs Classical genres (symphony, sonata, concerto, string quartet, and opera) and Classical forms (sonata–allegro, rondo, and theme and variations). Yet even in compositions from his early period, Beethoven projects a new spirit in his music, one that foreshadows the musical style of the Romantic era (1820–1900). An intense, lyrical expression is heard in his slow movements, while his allegros abound with striking themes, pounding rhythms, and startling dynamic contrasts. Although Beethoven largely stays within the bounds of Classical forms, he pushes their confines to the breaking point, so great is his urge for personal expression. Though a pupil of Haydn and a lifelong admirer of Mozart, he nevertheless elevated music to new heights of eloquence and dramatic power. For this reason, he can rightly be called the prophet of Romantic music.

Beethoven's three musical periods

THE EARLY YEARS (1770–1802)

Like Bach and Mozart before him, Beethoven came from a family of musicians. His father and grandfather were performers at the court at Bonn, Germany, on the Rhine River, where Beethoven was born on December 17, 1770. Seeing great musical talent in his young son, Beethoven's father, a violent, alcoholic man, forcibly made him practice at the keyboard at all hours, day and night. Soon he tried to exploit his son as a child prodigy, a second Mozart, telling the world that the diminutive boy was a year or two younger than he actually was. After an abortive attempt to study with Mozart in Vienna in 1787, Beethoven moved there for good in 1792, a year after Mozart's death. As one of his financial backers said at the time, "You are going to Vienna in fulfillment of your long-frustrated wishes . . . you will receive the spirit of Mozart from the hands of Haydn."

early years in Bonn

When Beethoven arrived in Vienna, he not only took composition lessons from Joseph Haydn, but also bought new clothes, located a wigmaker, and found a dancing instructor. His aim was to gain an entrée into the homes of the wealthy of the Austrian capital. And this he soon achieved, owing not to his woeful social skills, but to his phenomenal ability as a pianist.

Beethoven played the piano louder, more forcefully, and even more violently than anyone the Viennese nobility had ever heard. He possessed an extraordinary technique—even if he did hit occasional wrong notes—and this he put to good use, especially in his fanciful improvisations. As a contemporary witness observed: "He knew how to produce such an impression on every listener that frequently there was not a single dry eye, while many broke out into loud sobs, for there was a certain magic in his expression."

extraordinary pianist

The aristocracy was captivated. One patron put a string quartet at Beethoven's disposal, another made it possible for the composer to experiment with a small orchestra, and all showered him with gifts. He acquired well-to-do pupils; he sold his compositions ("I state my price and they pay," he said with pride in 1801); and he requested and eventually received an annuity from three noblemen so that he could work undisturbed. The text of this arrangement includes the following lines:

Beethoven's genius supported by aristocracy

> It is recognized that only a person who is as free as possible from all cares can consecrate himself to his craft. He can only produce these great and sublime works which ennoble Art if they form his sole pursuit, to the exclusion of all unnecessary obligations. The undersigned have therefore taken the decision to ensure that Herr Ludwig van Beethoven's situation shall not be embarrassed by his most necessary requirements, nor shall his powerful genius be hampered.

What a contrast between Beethoven's contract and the one signed by Haydn four decades earlier (see page 182)! Music was no longer merely a craft and the composer a servant. It had now become an exalted Art, and the great creator a Genius who must be protected and nurtured—a new, Romantic notion of the value of music. Beethoven did his best to encourage this belief in the exalted mission of the composer as artist. He would not stand at the beck and call of a master. When one patron demanded that he play for a visiting French general, Beethoven stormed out of the salon and responded by letter: "Prince, what you are, you are through the accident of birth. What I am, I am through my own efforts. There have been many princes and there will be thousands more. But there is only one Beethoven!"

Piano Sonata, Opus 13, the *"Pathétique"* Sonata (1799)

The bold originality in Beethoven's music can be heard in one of his most celebrated compositions, the **"Pathétique" Sonata.** A Classical sonata*, as we have seen, is a multimovement work for solo instrument or solo instrument with keyboard accompaniment. That Beethoven himself supplied the title *"Pathétique"* ("Plaintive") for this solo piano sonata suggests the passion and pathos he felt within it. Its great drama and intensity derive in large part from the juxtaposition of extremes. There are extremes of dynamics (from *fortissimo* to *pianissimo*), tempo (*grave* to *presto*), and range (from very high to very low). The piece also requires of the pianist more technical skill and stamina than had any piano sonata of Mozart or Haydn. Displaying his virtuosity, Beethoven frequently performed the *"Pathétique"* in the homes and palaces of the Viennese aristocracy.

FIRST MOVEMENT

crashing chords and quiet lyricism

Contemporaries recount how Beethoven the pianist played with "superhuman" speed and force, and how he banged the keys so hard on one occasion that he broke six strings. The crashing C minor chord that opens the *"Pathétique"* Sonata suggests Beethoven's sometimes violent approach to the instrument. After this startling opening gesture, Beethoven the dramatist continues by juxtaposing music of wildly differing moods: the *sforzando* chord is immediately followed by quiet lyricism, only to be interrupted by another chordal thunderbolt. This slow introduction is probably a written-out version of the sort of improvisation at the piano that gained Beethoven great fame in Vienna. The introduction leads to a racing first theme that rises impetuously in the right hand. The sense of anxiety the listener feels is amplified by the bass, where the left hand of the pianist plays broken octaves (the alternation of two tones an octave apart) reminiscent of the rumble of distant thunder.

EXAMPLE 21–1

The remainder of the movement now plays out as a contest between the impetuous, racing themes and the stormy chords. But while there is much passion and intensity here, there is also Classical formal control. The crashing chords come back at the beginning of both the development and the coda in this sonata–allegro form movement. Thus the chords set firm formal boundaries and thereby prevent the racing theme from flying out of control. Beethoven's music often conveys a feeling of struggle: Classical forms gave Beethoven something to struggle against.

Listening Guide

Ludwig van Beethoven
Piano Sonata, Opus 13, the *"Pathétique"* Sonata (1799)
First movement, *Grave; Allegro di molto e con brio*
(grave; very fast and with gusto)

3/1–3   1/19–21

Form: sonata–allegro

INTRODUCTION

0:00   Crashing chords alternate with softer, more lyrical ones
0:46   Softer chords continually cut off by crashing chords below
1:10   Melody builds to climax and then rapid descent

EXPOSITION [ ] = repeats

1:41   [3:14]   Rising agitated melody in right hand against broken octaves in left (first theme)

1:59   [3:34]   Transition modulates to new key, thinner texture
2:11   [3:44]   Bass, followed by treble, initiates "call and response" (second theme)·

2:39   [4:12]   Right and left hands race in opposite directions (closing theme, part 1)
2:58   [4:31]   Rapid scales in right hand above simple chords in left (closing theme, part 2)
3:04   [4:37]   Reminiscence of first theme
[3:14–4:47]   Repeat of exposition

(continued)

DEVELOPMENT

4:48	0:00	Crashing chords and softer chords from introduction
5:32	0:44	First theme extended and varied
6:09	1:21	Rapid twisting descent played by right hand leads to recapitulation

RECAPITULATION

6:15	0:00	Rising agitated melody in right hand (first theme)
6:25	0:10	Transition
6:35	0:20	Call and response between bass and treble (second theme)
6:59	0:44	Hands move rapidly in opposite directions (closing theme, part 1)
7:18	1:03	Scale runs in right hand (closing theme, part 2)
7:24	1:09	Reminiscence of first theme

CODA

7:35	1:20	Recall of chords from the introduction
8:14	1:59	Reminiscence of first theme leads to drive to final cadence

Use a downloadable, cross-platform animated Active Listening Guide, available at www.thomsonedu.com/music/wright.

Listening Exercise 29

Beethoven
"Pathétique" Sonata

3/1–3   1/19–21

ThomsonNOW™
To take this Listening Exercise online and receive feedback or email answers to your instructor, go to *ThomsonNOW* for this chapter.

0:00–1:40   **Introduction**
1. The introduction conveys an unsettled, uncertain feeling. What, specifically, does Beethoven *not* do to create this mood?
   a. He puts very loud and very soft sounds in close proximity.
   b. He contrasts high and low ranges of the piano.
   c. He starts with happy major chords and moves to sad minor ones.
   d. He contrasts slow chords with racing descents.
2. (1:36–1:39) The end of the introduction is marked by a long descent. Which hand of the pianist plays this descent?
   a. right hand   b. left hand

1:41–3:13   **Exposition**
3. (1:33–1:53) The descent gives way to the first theme (1:41) and the tempo changes. Which statement is true?
   a. A fast tempo gives way to a slower one.
   b. A fast tempo gives way to an even faster one.
   c. *Grave* (very slow) gives way to *allegro con brio* (fast with gusto).
4. A rumbling broken-octave bass had accompanied the agitated first theme (1:41–1:58). Now here in the transition (1:59–2:09), can these menacing broken octaves still be heard in the bass?
   a. yes   b. no

5. (1:59–2:05) Transitions involve a movement from one theme and key to another. This one effects motion through the use of what?
   a. rising monophony
   b. rising melodic sequence
   c. rising monotony
6. (3:07–3:13) The final cadence of the exposition is marked by a thick texture. How is this created?
   a. The left hand alternates chords in the top and middle ranges while the right plays ascending broken chords.
   b. The right hand alternates chords in the top and middle ranges while the left plays descending broken octaves.

3:14–4:47 Now comes the repeat of the exposition. As you listen, check your answers to questions 4–6.

0:00–1:26   **Development**
7. (0:27–0:52) The development begins with a return to the chords of the introduction and then proceeds with the first theme. Which statement is true about the tempo in this passage?
   a. The music accelerates and then becomes progressively slower.
   b. The music gets progressively slower, almost stopping, and then suddenly becomes fast.
   c. The music proceeds at a moderate pace and then suddenly becomes fast.

8. (1:21–1:26) Does the left hand (bass) rest during the rapid twisting descent at the end of the development? In other words, is this a solo for the right hand?
   a. yes   b. no

0:00–1:19 🎵 **Recapitulation**
1:20–2:09 **Coda**

9. (2:03–2:09) How does this movement end?
   a. with the closing theme
   b. with a soft fadeout
   c. with the crashing chords of the introduction

10. Notice the blazing speed with which the pianist Vladimir Ashkenazy plays the *allegro* portions of this piece. In a piano sonata such as Beethoven's *"Pathétique"*—and indeed in most music—the rapidly moving pitches are concentrated in one range of auditory frequency and the slower pitches in another. (There is an acoustical reason for this, because pitches "clear" more rapidly in this range, allowing others to be quickly added without creating a muddle.) The greatest abundance of rapid pitches are found where?
   a. in the top range played by pianist's left hand
   b. in the top range played by pianist's right hand
   c. in the bottom range played by pianist's left hand
   d. in the bottom range played by pianist's right hand

SECOND MOVEMENT

Eyewitnesses who heard Beethoven at the piano remarked on the "legato" quality of his playing, and contrasted it with Mozart's lighter, more staccato style. Beethoven himself said in 1796 that "one can sing on the piano, so long as one has feeling." We can hear Beethoven sing through the legato melodic line that dominates the slow second movement of the *"Pathétique"* Sonata. Indeed, the expression mark he gave to the movement is *cantabile* (songful). The singing quality of the melody seems to have appealed to pop star Billy Joel, who borrowed this theme for the refrain of his song "This Night" on the album *Innocent Man* (SONY ASIN:B00000DCHG).

THIRD MOVEMENT

A comparison of the second and third movements of the *"Pathétique"* Sonata will show that musical form does not determine musical mood. Although both the *Adagio* and the fast finale are in rondo form, the first is a lyrical hymn, and the latter a passionate, but slightly comical, chase. The finale has hints of the crashing chords and stark contrasts of the first movement, but the earlier violence and impetuosity have been softened into a mood of impassioned playfulness.

The eighteenth-century piano sonata had been essentially private music of a modest sort—music a composer-teacher like Mozart or Haydn would write for a talented amateur pupil to be played in the home. Beethoven took the modest, private piano sonata and infused it with the technical bravura of the public stage. The louder sound, wider range, and greater length of Beethoven's thirty-two piano sonatas made them appropriate for the increasingly large concert halls—and pianos—of the nineteenth century. Beginning in the Romantic period, Beethoven's piano sonatas became a staple of the professional pianist's repertoire, and so they remain today.

from private salon to public concert hall

Beethoven Becomes Deaf

Beethoven cut a strange, eccentric figure as he wandered the streets of Vienna, sometimes humming, sometimes mumbling, and sometimes jotting on music paper. Adding to the difficulties of his somewhat unstable personality was the fact that he was gradually going deaf—a serious handicap for any person, but a tragic condition for a musician (see boxed essay). Can you imagine a blind painter?

Music and Suffering

Can contented, mentally stable people write great music? Bach, Haydn, and Mendelssohn were three apparently "normal" persons whose compositions are numbered among the finest within the Western tradition. On the other hand, the biographies of Handel, Berlioz, and Robert Schumann suggests that each suffered from bipolar disorder (Schumann actually died

A fanciful, yet in many ways accurate, depiction of Beethoven in the midst of creative chaos. The illustrator has assembled many objects from Beethoven's daily life, including his ear-trumpet (left) to correct his growing deafness..

British Library, London, Collection Stefan Zweig

in a mental institution). Mozart, who had a superhuman capacity for musical memory, may at the same time have been mildly autistic. But in truth, no compelling evidence has appeared to suggest a direct link between mental imbalance or suffering and musical creativity.

The Western conception of the "suffering artist" arose in part with Beethoven, who was perceived by his contemporaries as an unhappy, misanthropic man. Indeed, Beethoven had much to be unhappy about: an abusive father, the early death of his mother, continuing failure in love (he never married), and chronic ill health (he suffered from lead poisoning). But Beethoven did, nonetheless, write superb music for all to hear. With Beethoven in mind, people in the nineteenth century began to equate personal misery with artistic creativity. This Romantic ideal—the composer as social misfit who suffers for art—has endured down to the present day and is an article of faith among fans of rock musicians who died young. Jimi Hendrix, Jim Morrison, and Kurt Cobain, three tragic figures who enjoy cult status today, do so in part because of a simple equation: they suffered and died for their art; therefore, they must have been great artists. Needless to say, this Romantic ideal would have come as a surprise to such pre-Romantic composers as Haydn and Mozart, who loved music but were simply trying to earn a living at it.

Beethoven first complained about his hearing and a ringing in his ears in the late 1790s, and he suffered considerable anguish and depression. His growing deafness did not stop him from composing—Beethoven possessed an exceptional "inner ear" and could compose even without the ability to hear external sound. However, his condition caused him to retreat even further from society and all but ended his career as a pianist, since he could no longer gauge how hard to press the keys. By late 1802, Beethoven recognized that he would ultimately suffer a total loss of hearing. In despair, he wrote his last will and testament, today called the **Heiligenstadt Testament** after the Viennese suburb in which he penned it. In this confessional document for posterity, the composer admits he considered suicide: "I would have ended my life; it was only *my art* that held me back." Beethoven emerged from this personal crisis with renewed resolve to fulfill his artistic destiny—he would now "seize Fate by the throat."

a cry of despair

THE "HEROIC" PERIOD (1803–1813)

It was in this resurgent, defiant mood that Beethoven entered what we call his **"heroic" period** of composition (1803–1813; also simply termed his "middle period"). His works became longer, more assertive, and full of grand gestures.

Simple, often triadic, themes predominate, and these are repeated, sometime incessantly, as the music swells to majestic proportions. When these themes are played *forte* and given over to the brass instruments, a heroic, triumphant sound results.

Beethoven wrote nine symphonies in all, six of them during his "heroic" period. These symphonies are few in number in part because they are so much longer and more complex than those of Mozart or Haydn. They set the standard for the epic symphony of the nineteenth century. Most noteworthy are the "Eroica" (Third), the famous Fifth Symphony, the Sixth (called the "Pastoral" because it evokes the ambiance of the Austrian countryside), the Seventh, and the monumental Ninth. In these, Beethoven introduces new orchestral colors by bringing new instruments into the symphony orchestra: the trombone (Symphony Nos. 5, 6, and 9), the contrabassoon (Symphony Nos. 5 and 9), the piccolo (Symphony Nos. 5, 6, and 9), and even the human voice (Symphony No. 9).

Symphony No. 3 in E♭ major ("Eroica") (1803)

As its title suggests, Beethoven's **"Eroica" ("Heroic") Symphony** epitomizes the grandiose, heroic style. More than any other single orchestral work, it changed the historical direction of the symphony. Its length, some forty-five minutes, is nearly twice that of a typical symphony by his teacher Haydn. It assaults the ear with startling rhythmic effects and chord changes that were shocking to early-nineteenth-century listeners. Most novel for Beethoven, the work has biographical content, for the hero of the "Eroica" Symphony, at least originally, was Napoleon Bonaparte.

Austria and the German states were at war with France in the early nineteenth century. Yet German-speaking Beethoven was much taken with the enemy's revolutionary call for liberty, equality, and fraternity. Napoleon Bonaparte became his hero, and the composer dedicated his third symphony to him, writing on the title page "intitolata Bonaparte." But when news that Napoleon had declared himself emperor reached Beethoven, he flew into a rage, saying, "Now he, too, will trample on all the rights of man and indulge his ambition." Taking up a knife, he scratched so violently to erase Bonaparte's name from the title page that he left a hole in the paper (Fig. 21–2). When the work was published, Napoleon's name had been removed in favor of the more general title "Heroic Symphony: To Celebrate the Memory of a Great Man" (Fig. 21–3). Beethoven was not an imperialist, he was a revolutionary.

Symphony No. 5 in C minor (1808)

At the center of Beethoven's symphonic output stands his remarkable Symphony No. 5 (see also pages 7–8). Its novelty rests in the way the composer conveys a sense of psychological progression over the course of four movements. An imaginative listener might perceive the following sequence of events: (1) a fateful encounter with elemental forces, (2) a period of quiet soul-searching, followed by (3) a further wrestling

FIGURE 21–2 AND 21–3

(top) The title page of the autograph of Beethoven's "Eroica" Symphony: *Sinfonia grande intitolata Bonaparte*. Note the hole where Beethoven took a knife and scratched out the name "Bonaparte." (bottom) As a young officer, Napoleon Bonaparte seized control of the government of France in 1799. He established a new form of republican government that emphasized the revolutionary ideals of liberty, equality, and humanity. After Napoleon elevated himself to emperor in 1804, Beethoven changed the title of his Symphony No. 3 from "Bonaparte" to "Eroica." The portrait by Jacques-Louis David shows the newly crowned Napoleon in full imperial regalia. Liberator had become oppressor.

with the elements, and, finally, (4) a triumphant victory over the forces of Fate. Beethoven himself is said to have remarked with regard to the famous opening motive of the symphony: "There Fate knocks at the door!"

The rhythm of the opening—perhaps the best-known moment in all of classical music—animates the entire symphony. Not only does it dominate the opening *Allegro*, but it reappears in varied form in the three later movements as well, binding the symphony into a unified whole.

EXAMPLE 21–2

a persistent rhythmic motive

first movement

second movement

third movement

fourth movement

FIRST MOVEMENT

At the very outset, the listener is jolted to attention, forced to sit up and take notice by a sudden explosion of sound. And what an odd beginning to a symphony—a blast of three short notes and a long one, followed by the same three shorts and a long, all now a step lower. The movement can't quite get going. It starts and stops, then seems to lurch forward and gather momentum. And where is the melody? This three-shorts-and-a-long pattern is more a motive or musical cell than a melody. Yet it is striking by virtue of its power and compactness. As the movement unfolds, the actual pitches of the motive prove to be of secondary importance. Beethoven is obsessed with its rhythm. He wants to demonstrate the enormous latent force that lurks within even the simplest rhythmic cell, waiting to be unleashed by a composer who understands the secrets of rhythmic energy.

To control the sometimes violent forces that will emerge, the musical processes unfold within the traditional confines of sonata–allegro form. The basic four-note motive provides all the musical material for the first theme area.

EXAMPLE 21–3

a famous beginning

ff

The brief transition played by a solo French horn is only six notes long and is formed simply by adding two notes to the end of the basic four-note motive. As expected, the transition moves the tonality from the tonic (C minor) to the relative major* (E♭ major).

EXAMPLE 21–4

The second theme offers a moment of escape from the rush of the "fate" motive, but even here the pattern of three shorts and a long lurks underneath in the low strings.

EXAMPLE 21–5

The closing theme, too, is none other than the motive once again, now presented in a somewhat different guise.

EXAMPLE 21–6

In the development, the opening motive returns, recapturing, and even surpassing, the force it had at the beginning. It soon takes on different melodic forms, as it is tossed back and forth between instruments, though the rhythmic shape remains constant.

EXAMPLE 21–7

manipulation of the motive

As the motive rises, so does the musical tension. A powerful rhythmic climax ensues and then gives way to a brief imitative passage. Soon Beethoven reduces the six-note motive of the transition to merely two notes, and then just one, passing these figures around *pianissimo* between the strings and winds.

EXAMPLE 21–8

the motive reduced to its essence

Beethoven was a master of the process of thematic condensation—stripping away all extraneous material to get to the core of a musical idea. Here, in this mysterious *pianissimo* passage, he presents the irreducible minimum of his motive: a single note. In the midst of this quiet, the original four-note motive tries to reassert itself *fortissimo*, yet at first cannot do so. Its explosive force, however, cannot be held back. A thunderous return of the opening chords signals the beginning of the recapitulation.

Although the recapitulation offers a repeat of the events of the exposition, Beethoven has one surprise in store. No sooner has the motive regained its momentum than an oboe interjects a tender, languid, and wholly unexpected solo.

A deviation from the usual path of sonata–allegro form, this brief oboe cadenza* allows for a momentary release of excess energy. The recapitulation then resumes its expected course.

a lengthy coda

What is not expected is the enormous coda that follows. It is even longer than the exposition! A new form of the motive appears, and it, too, is subjected to development. In fact, this coda constitutes essentially a second development section, so great is Beethoven's single urge to exploit the latent power of this one simple musical idea.

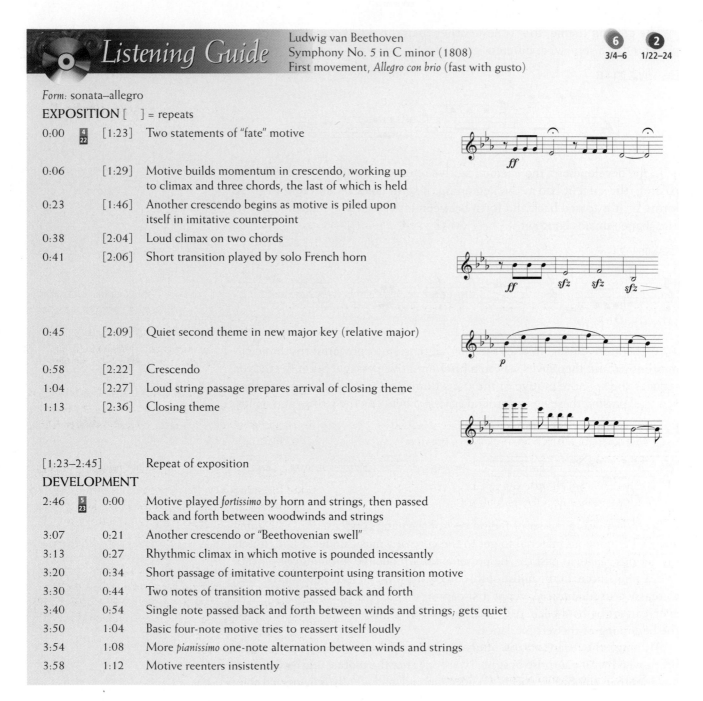

Listening Guide

Ludwig van Beethoven
Symphony No. 5 in C minor (1808)
First movement, *Allegro con brio* (fast with gusto)

6 **2**
3/4–6 1/22–24

Form: sonata–allegro

EXPOSITION [ ] = repeats

0:00	4/22	[1:23]	Two statements of "fate" motive
0:06		[1:29]	Motive builds momentum in crescendo, working up to climax and three chords, the last of which is held
0:23		[1:46]	Another crescendo begins as motive is piled upon itself in imitative counterpoint
0:38		[2:04]	Loud climax on two chords
0:41		[2:06]	Short transition played by solo French horn
0:45		[2:09]	Quiet second theme in new major key (relative major)
0:58		[2:22]	Crescendo
1:04		[2:27]	Loud string passage prepares arrival of closing theme
1:13		[2:36]	Closing theme

[1:23–2:45]	Repeat of exposition

DEVELOPMENT

2:46	5/23	0:00	Motive played *fortissimo* by horn and strings, then passed back and forth between woodwinds and strings
3:07		0:21	Another crescendo or "Beethovenian swell"
3:13		0:27	Rhythmic climax in which motive is pounded incessantly
3:20		0:34	Short passage of imitative counterpoint using transition motive
3:30		0:44	Two notes of transition motive passed back and forth
3:40		0:54	Single note passed back and forth between winds and strings; gets quiet
3:50		1:04	Basic four-note motive tries to reassert itself loudly
3:54		1:08	More *pianissimo* one-note alternation between winds and strings
3:58		1:12	Motive reenters insistently

RECAPITULATION

4:04		0:00	Return of motive
4:10		0:06	Motive gathers momentum and cadences with three chords
4:20		0:16	Unexpected oboe solo
4:36		0:32	Motive returns and moves hurriedly to climax
4:56		0:52	Transition now played by bassoon instead of horn
4:59		0:55	Quiet second theme with timpani now playing rhythm of motive
5:15		1:11	Crescendo leading to closing theme
5:32		1:28	Closing theme

CODA

5:40	1:36	Motive pounded *fortissimo* on one note, then again step higher
5:53	1:49	Imitative counterpoint
6:07	2:03	Rising quarter notes form new four-note pattern
6:19	2:15	New four-note pattern alternates between strings and woodwinds
6:39	2:35	Pounding on single note, then motive as at beginning
6:53	2:49	Succession of I–V–I chords brings movement to abrupt end

Use a downloadable, cross-platform animated Active Listening Guide, available at www.thomsonedu.com/music/wright.

Listening Exercise 30

Beethoven
Symphony No. 5 in C minor

6 **2**
3/4–6   1/22–24

ThomsonNOW
To take this Listening Exercise online and receive feedback or email answers to your instructor, go to *ThomsonNOW* for this chapter.

The first movement of Beethoven's Symphony No. 5 is perhaps the most famous movement in all of classical music. The following questions are designed to show how Beethoven honored, but sometimes broke with, the usual Classical treatment of sonata–allegro form.

1. (0:00–0:30) Which instruments carry the four-note motive and its immediate repetitions?
   a. woodwinds
   b. brasses
   c. strings
   d. percussion
2. (0:41–0:44) The French horn plays a short transition in which Beethoven does what?
   a. prefixes two long notes to the basic rhythm of the first theme
   b. appends two long notes to the basic rhythm of the first theme
   c. repeats the rhythm of the first theme
3. (0:45–0:51) Normally in a movement in sonata–allegro form in a minor key, the second theme in the exposition appears in the major mode. Does Beethoven honor that tradition?
   a. yes   b. no
4. (1:13–1:28) Similarly, in a movement in sonata–allegro form in a minor key, the exposition will normally end in a major key and go back to the minor key for the beginning of the repeat of the exposition. Does Beethoven move from major back to minor here?
   a. yes   b. no
5. Consider now the length of the exposition and compare it to other movements in sonata–allegro form previously studied (see pages 196, 197, 212, and 233). In his Symphony No. 5, Beethoven has constructed an exposition that is what?
   a. similar to the norm in length
   b. remarkably long
   c. remarkably short

0:00–1:17   **Development**

6. (0:27–0:33) Consider the rhythmic climax in which the motive is pounded incessantly. This climax occurs where in the movement?
    a. in the first third
    b. in the exact middle
    c. in the last third

7. (1:12–1:17) At the end of the development, the orchestra insistently repeats the motive, and then the recapitulation begins. Beethoven helps announce the recapitulation by using which dynamic level?
    a. *fortissimo*   b. *piano*   b. *pianissimo*

8. (0:16–0:31) A solo oboe suddenly interrupts the recapitulation. Was this oboe "cadenza" in the exposition?
    a. yes   b. no

9. (0:55–1:04) If Beethoven's treatment of sonata–allegro form honors tradition, he will bring the second theme back in the minor mode. Does the second theme, in fact, come back in minor?
    a. yes   b. no

10. Finally, how does Beethoven deviate in this movement from tradition in his treatment of Classical sonata–allegro form?
    a. He fails to honor the traditional key format for a sonata–allegro movement in minor.
    b. He interrupts the recapitulation with an instrumental "cadenza."
    c. He shifts much of the weight of the movement from the exposition to the coda.
    d. All of the above.

SECOND MOVEMENT

After the pounding we have experienced in the explosive first movement, the calm of the noble *Andante* comes as a welcome change of pace. The mood is at first serene, and the melody is expansive—in contrast to the four-note motive of the first movement, the opening theme here runs on for twenty-two measures. The musical form is also a familiar one: theme and variations*. But this is not the simple, easily audible theme and variations of Haydn and Mozart (see pages 199–203). There are two themes: the first lyrical and serene, played mostly by the strings; and the second quiet, then triumphant, played mostly by the brasses. By means of this "double" theme and variations, Beethoven demonstrates his ability to add length and complexity to a standard Classical form (Fig. 21–4). He also shows how it is possible to contrast within one movement two starkly opposed expressive domains—the intensely lyrical (theme 1) and the brilliantly heroic (theme 2).

a double theme and variations

FIGURE 21–4

Original autograph of Beethoven at work on the second movement of his Symphony No. 5. The many corrections in different-colored inks and red pencil suggest the turmoil and constant evolution involved in Beethoven's creative process.

Deutsche Staats, Berlin

*Listening Guide* Ludwig van Beethoven
Symphony No. 5 in C minor (1808)
Second movement, *Andante con moto* (progressing with movement)

Form: theme and variations

THEMES

0:00	7	Violas and cellos play beginning of theme 1

0:24	Woodwinds play middle of theme 1

0:38	Violins play end of theme 1

0:54	Clarinets, bassoons, and violins play theme 2

1:16	Brasses play theme 2 in fanfare style
1:34	Mysterious *pianissimo*

VARIATION 1

2:01	Violas and cellos vary beginning of theme 1 by adding sixteenth notes

2:24	Woodwinds play middle of theme 1
2:34	Strings play end of theme 1
2:53	Clarinets, bassoons, and violins play theme 2
3:14	Brasses return with fanfare (theme 2)
3:32	More of mysterious *pianissimo*

VARIATION 2

4:00	8	0:00	Violas and cellos overlay beginning of theme 1 with rapidly moving ornamentation

4:36	0:36	Pounding repeated chords with theme below in cellos and basses
4:53	0:53	Rising scales lead to fermata (hold)
5:12	1:12	Woodwinds play fragments of beginning of theme 1
5:54	1:54	Fanfare (theme 2) now returns in full orchestra
6:43	2:43	Woodwinds play beginning of theme 1 detached and in minor key

VARIATION 3

7:23	3:23	Violins play beginning of theme 1 *fortissimo*
7:48	3:48	Woodwinds play middle of theme 1
7:58	3:58	Strings play end of theme 1

(continued)

CODA		
8:12	4:12	Tempo quickens as bassoons play reminiscence of beginning of theme 1
8:28	4:28	Violins play reminiscence of theme 2
8:37	4:37	Woodwinds play middle of theme 1
8:48	4:48	Strings play end of theme 1
9:09	5:09	Ends with repetitions of rhythm of very first measure of movement

 Use a downloadable, cross-platform animated Active Listening Guide, available at **www.thomsonedu.com/music/wright.**

THIRD MOVEMENT

In the Classical period, the third movement of a symphony or quartet was usually a graceful minuet and trio (see page 189). Haydn and his pupil Beethoven wanted to infuse this third movement with more life and energy, so they often wrote a faster, more rollicking piece and called it a scherzo*, meaning "joke." And while there is nothing particularly humorous about the mysterious and sometimes threatening sound of the scherzo of Beethoven's Symphony No. 5, it is certainly far removed from the elegant world of the courtly minuet.

The formal plan of Beethoven's scherzo, **ABA'**, derives from the ternary form of the minuet, as does its triple meter. The scherzo, **A**, is in the tonic key of C minor, while the trio, **B,** is in C major. The conflict of major and minor, dark and light, is one of several that are resolved in the course of this four-movement symphony (Fig. 21–5).

FIGURE 21–5

Interior of the Theater-an-der-Wien, Vienna, where Beethoven's Symphony No. 5 received its premiere on December 22, 1808. This all-Beethoven concert lasted four hours, from 6:30 until 10:30 P.M., and presented eight new works, including his Symphony No. 5. During the performance of the symphony, the orchestra sometimes halted because of the difficulties in playing Beethoven's radically new music.

Museum der Stadt Wien

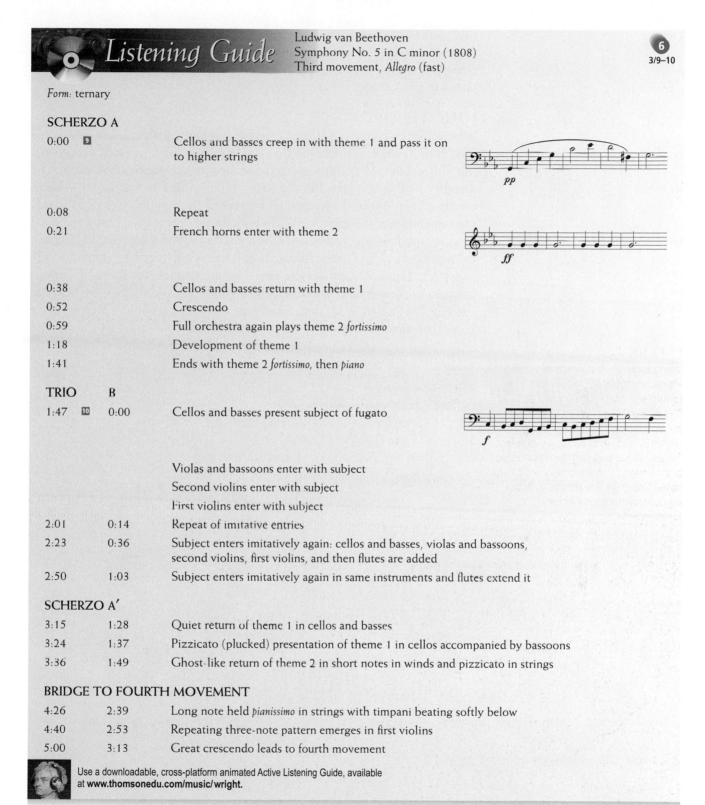

Listening Guide

Ludwig van Beethoven
Symphony No. 5 in C minor (1808)
Third movement, *Allegro* (fast)

6
3/9–10

Form: ternary

SCHERZO A

0:00	**9**	Cellos and basses creep in with theme 1 and pass it on to higher strings
0:08		Repeat
0:21		French horns enter with theme 2
0:38		Cellos and basses return with theme 1
0:52		Crescendo
0:59		Full orchestra again plays theme 2 *fortissimo*
1:18		Development of theme 1
1:41		Ends with theme 2 *fortissimo*, then *piano*

TRIO   B

1:47	**10**	0:00	Cellos and basses present subject of fugato
			Violas and bassoons enter with subject
			Second violins enter with subject
			First violins enter with subject
2:01		0:14	Repeat of imitative entries
2:23		0:36	Subject enters imitatively again: cellos and basses, violas and bassoons, second violins, first violins, and then flutes are added
2:50		1:03	Subject enters imitatively again in same instruments and flutes extend it

SCHERZO A′

3:15	1:28	Quiet return of theme 1 in cellos and basses
3:24	1:37	Pizzicato (plucked) presentation of theme 1 in cellos accompanied by bassoons
3:36	1:49	Ghost-like return of theme 2 in short notes in winds and pizzicato in strings

BRIDGE TO FOURTH MOVEMENT

4:26	2:39	Long note held *pianissimo* in strings with timpani beating softly below
4:40	2:53	Repeating three-note pattern emerges in first violins
5:00	3:13	Great crescendo leads to fourth movement

Use a downloadable, cross-platform animated Active Listening Guide, available at **www.thomsonedu.com/music/wright**.

Now, a stroke of genius on Beethoven's part: He links the third and fourth movements by means of a musical bridge. Holding a single pitch as quietly as possible, the violins create an eerie sound, while the timpani beats menacingly in the background. A three-note motive grows from the violins and is repeated over and over as a wave of sound begins to swell from the orchestra. With enormous force, the wave finally crashes down, and from it emerges the triumphant beginning of the fourth movement—one of the most thrilling moments in all of music.

FOURTH MOVEMENT

new instruments for added sonority

When Beethoven arrived at the finale, he was faced with a nearly impossible task: how to write a conclusion that would relieve the tension of the preceding musical events yet provide an appropriate, substantive balance to the weighty first movement. He did so by fashioning a monumental work in sonata–allegro form, the longest movement of the symphony, and by bringing some unusual forces into play. To bulk up his orchestra, Beethoven added three trombones, a contrabassoon (low bassoon), and a piccolo (high flute), the first time any of these instruments had been called for in a symphony. He also wrote big, bold, and in most cases, triadic themes, assigning these most often to the powerful brasses. In these instruments and themes, we hear the "heroic" Beethoven at his best. The finale projects a feeling of affirmation, a sense that superhuman will has triumphed over adversity.

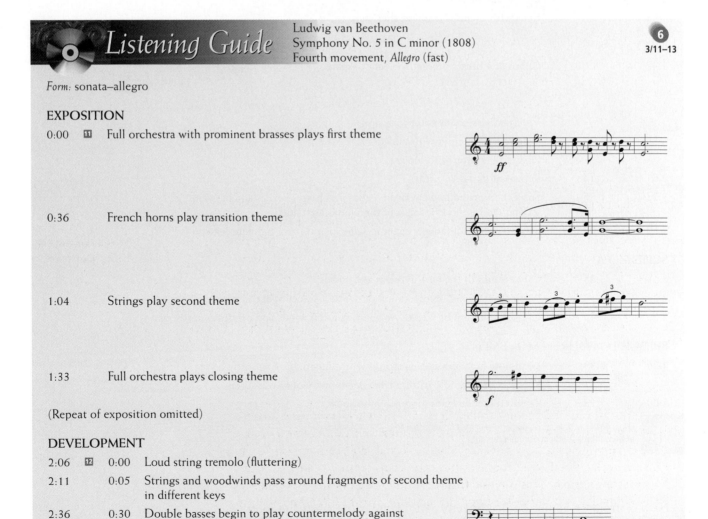

Listening Guide

Ludwig van Beethoven
Symphony No. 5 in C minor (1808)
Fourth movement, *Allegro* (fast)

6
3/11–13

Form: sonata–allegro

EXPOSITION

0:00   11   Full orchestra with prominent brasses plays first theme

0:36   French horns play transition theme

1:04   Strings play second theme

1:33   Full orchestra plays closing theme

(Repeat of exposition omitted)

DEVELOPMENT

2:06   12   0:00   Loud string tremolo (fluttering)

2:11   0:05   Strings and woodwinds pass around fragments of second theme in different keys

2:36   0:30   Double basses begin to play countermelody against second theme

2:46	0:40	Trombones play countermelody
3:13	1:07	Woodwinds and brasses play countermelody above dominant pedal point in cellos and basses
3:30	1:24	Climax and pause on dominant triad
3:48	1:42	Ghost-like theme from scherzo (third movement) with four-note rhythm

RECAPITULATION

4:17	▣	0:00	Full orchestra plays first theme *fortissimo*
4:54		0:37	French horns play transition theme
5:26		1:09	Strings play second theme
5:54		1:37	Woodwinds play closing theme

CODA

6:26	2:09	Violins play second theme
6:37	2:20	Brasses and woodwinds play countermelody from development
6:50	2:33	V–I, V–I chords sound like final cadence
6:59	2:42	Bassoons, French horns, flutes, clarinets, and then piccolo continue with transition theme
7:27	3:10	Trill high in piccolo
7:50	3:33	Tempo changes to *presto* (very fast)
8:14	3:57	Brasses recall first theme, now twice as fast
8:21	4:04	V–I, V–I cadence followed by pounding tonic chord

Use a downloadable, cross-platform animated Active Listening Guide, available at **www.thomsonedu.com/music/wright.**

Beethoven's Symphony No. 5 reveals his genius in a paradox: From minimal material (the basic cell), he derives maximum sonority. Climaxes are achieved by incessantly repeating the cell-like motive. Long crescendos swell like tidal waves of sound. Wildly different moods are accommodated within a single movement. In the quiet string music of the *Andante* (second movement), for example, we are never far from a heroic brass fanfare. Everywhere there is a feeling of raw, elemental power propelled by the newly enlarged orchestra. Beethoven was the first to recognize that massive sound could be a potent psychological weapon. No wonder that during World War II (1939–1945) both sides, Fascist as well as Allied, used the music of this symphony to symbolize "Victory."[†]

from minimal material, maximum sonority

THE FINAL YEARS (1814–1827)

By 1814, Beethoven had become totally deaf and had withdrawn almost completely from society (Fig. 21–6). His music, too, took on a more remote, inaccessible quality, placing heavy demands on performer and audience alike. In these late works, Beethoven requires the listener to connect musical ideas over long spans of time. This is music that seems intended not for the audience of Beethoven's day, but rather for future generations. Most of Beethoven's late works are piano sonatas and string quartets—intimate, introspective chamber

[†]In Morse code, short–short–short–long is the letter "V," as in "Victory."

music. But two pieces, the Mass in D (*Missa Solemnis*, 1823) and the Symphony No. 9 (1824), are large-scale compositions for full orchestra and chorus. In these works for larger forces, Beethoven strives once again to communicate directly to a broad spectrum of humanity.

Beethoven's Symphony No. 9, his last, was the first symphony in the history of music to include a chorus. Here the composer's need for expression was so great that the instruments of the orchestra alone were no longer sufficient. Something more was necessary: text and voices. The text, *An die Freude* (**Ode to Joy**) by poet Friedrich von Schiller, is a hymn in honor of universal brotherhood, a theme that had been important to Beethoven since his earliest years. Beethoven worked on the melody for this poem, on and off, for nearly twenty years. (The melody and text are given on page 30; the melody serves as the basis of Listening Exercise 5 and can be heard on ⓘ/7.)

Ultimately, Beethoven brought his setting of *Ode to Joy* into the last movement of his last symphony, where it provides a theme for a magnificent set of variations. For twenty-five minutes, the music marches toward a grand climax. Beethoven pushes the voices to sing louder and louder, higher and higher, faster than they can enunciate the text. The instrumentalists, too, are driven by the *presto* tempo to go so quickly they can scarcely play the notes. All performers strain to exceed the limits of their physical abilities and accomplish the impossible. The sound is not so much beautiful as it is overwhelming, for the chorus and orchestra speak with one exalted voice. Their message is Beethoven's message: Art will unify all humanity.

EPILOGUE: BEETHOVEN AND THE NINETEENTH CENTURY

The figure of Beethoven towered over all the arts during the nineteenth century. He had shown how personal expression might expand the confines of Classical form with astonishingly powerful results. He had given music "the grand gesture," stunning effects like the crashing introduction of the *"Pathétique"* Sonata or the gigantic crescendo leading to the finale of the Fifth Symphony. He had shown that pure sound—sound divorced from melody and rhythm—could be glorious in and of itself. At once he had made music both grandiose and intensely lyrical. His works became the standard against which composers of the Romantic era measured their worth. The cover of this book shows poet, novelist, playwright, performer, and composer all turning in reverence toward the bust of Beethoven (see also Fig. 30–2).

Beethoven, larger than life, gazes down from Olympian heights, a monument to all that is noble and sublime in art.

Original lost

FIGURE 21–6

Beethoven walking in the rain, as sketched in Vienna c1823. The composer cut an odd figure. He would repeatedly stop to record an idea in his music sketchbook as he hummed or howled in an off-key voice. In 1821, Beethoven was mistakenly arrested as a tramp.

The Cobbe Collection Trust, UK/The Bridgeman Art Library

FIGURE 21–7

A drawing of the deceased Beethoven sketched on the morning of March 28, 1827, the day after the composer's death. It was made by Josef Danhauser, the same artist who painted the group portrait that appears on the cover of this book.

Key Words

"Pathetique" Sonata (**232**)
Heiligenstadt Testament (**236**)
"heroic" period (middle period) (**236**)
"Eroica" ("Heroic") Symphony (**237**)
Ode to Joy (**248**)

ThomsonNOW™

ThomsonNOW for *Listening to Music, 5th Edition,* and *Listening to Western Music* will assist you in understanding the content of this chapter with lesson plans generated for your specific needs. In addition, you may complete this chapter's Listening Exercises in ThomsonNOW's interactive environment, as well as download Active Listening Guides and other materials that will help you succeed in this course.

ThomsonNOW™

For comparisons and quizzes on the musical style of the Classical era, see Active Listening at **www.thomson.edu.com/music/wright** and *ThomsonNow.*

Checklist of Musical Style

Classical: 1750–1820

Melody	Short, balanced phrases create tuneful melodies; melody more influenced by vocal than instrumental style; frequent cadences produce light, airy feeling
Harmony	Rate at which chords change (harmonic rhythm) varies dramatically, creating dynamic flux and flow; simple chordal harmonies made more active by "Alberti" bass
Rhythm	Departs from regular, driving patterns of Baroque era to become more stop-and-go; greater rhythmic variety within single movement
Color	Orchestra grows larger; woodwind section of two flutes, oboes, clarinets, and bassoons becomes typical; piano replaces harpsichord as principal keyboard instrument
Texture	Mostly homophonic; thin bass and middle range, hence light and transparent; passages in contrapuntal style appear sparingly and mainly for contrast
Form	A few standard forms regulate much of Classical music: sonata–allegro, theme and variations, rondo, ternary (for minuets and trios), and double exposition (for solo concerto)

Representative composers
Mozart
Haydn
Beethoven
Schubert

Principal genres
symphony
sonata
string quartet
solo concerto
opera

PART V

Romanticism, 1820—1900

The Romantic era was a period in which artists aspired to go beyond the mundane, to the world of the imagination and the world of dreams. Belief in rational inquiry, an article of faith of the Enlightenment, began to wane. Reason gave way to passion, and objective evaluation to subjective emotion. The Romantics began to see the sublime in art and, most sublime of all, in nature herself. Poets, painters, and musicians depicted surging rivers and thunderous storms in their respective media. Love, too, became an important theme; indeed, from the word *romance* we derive the term *romantic*. But the Romantic vision also had its dark side, and these same artists expressed a fascination with the occult, the supernatural, and the macabre. This was not only the age of Felix Mendelssohn's playful *Overture to a Midsummer Night's Dream* but also of Mary Shelley's chilling *Frankenstein*.

What is music? To critic Charles Burney, writing in 1776, music was "an innocent luxury, unnecessary, indeed, to our existence." But to Beethoven,

1820	1825	1830	1835	1840	1845	1850	1855	1860

ROMANTICISM

● 1818 Mary Shelley writes *Frankenstein*

● 1826 Felix Mendelssohn composes *Overture to A Midsummer Night's Dream*

Giraudon/Art Resource, NY

●----- 1830 Revolution of 1830 in Europe

● 1830 Hector Berlioz composes *Symphonie fantastique*

● 1831 Victor Hugo writes *The Hunchback of Notre Dame*

● 1845 Edgar Allen Poe writes poem "The Raven"

● 1848 Revolution of 1848 in Europe

● 1848 Karl Marx writes *The Communist Manifesto*

Bayerisches National Museum, Munich

● 1853 Giuseppe Verdi compos opera *La traviata*

1853–1876 Richard Wagner

writing in 1812, music was the most important of the arts "that would raise men to the level of gods." Clearly, the very concept of music—its purpose and meaning—had undergone a sea change in these thirty-six years. No longer seen merely as entertainment, music now could point the way to previously unexplored realms of the spirit. Beethoven led the way, and many others—Berlioz, Wagner, and Brahms among them—followed in his footsteps. When German author E. T. A. Hoffmann wrote that Beethoven's Fifth Symphony "releases the flood gates of fear, of terror, of horror, of pain, and arouses that longing for the eternal which is the essence of Romanticism," he prophesied for much Romantic music to come.

Tate Gallery/Art Resource

| 1860 | 1865 | 1870 | 1875 | 1880 | 1885 | 1890 | 1895 | 1900 |

ROMANTICISM

- 1860s Otto von Bismarck forges modern state of Germany

- 1861 Final unification of Italy with Rome as its capital

1861–1865 American Civil War

- 1869 Opening of Suez Canal

1870–1871 Franco–Prussian War

Museum der Stadt Wien

- 1876 Johannes Brahms premiers first of his four symphonies

- 1880 Peter Tchaikovsky revises symphonic poem *Romeo and Juliet*

- 1889 Eiffel Tower completed

-
1898
Spanish-American War

works on his cycle *Ring of the Nibelung*

Chapter 22

Introduction to Romanticism

The mature music of Beethoven, with its powerful crescendos, pounding chords, and grand gestures, announces the arrival of the Romantic era in music. The transition from musical Classicism to Romanticism in the early nineteenth century coincides with similar stylistic changes in the novels, plays, poetry, and paintings of the period. In all the arts, revolutionary sentiments were in the air: a new desire for liberty, bold action, passionate feeling, and individual expression. Just as the impatient Beethoven finally cast off the wig and powdered hair of the eighteenth century, many other Romantic artists gradually cast aside the formal constraints of the older Classical style.

ROMANTIC INSPIRATION, ROMANTIC CREATIVITY

Romanticism is often defined as a revolt against the Classical adherence to reason, rules, forms, and traditions. Whereas artists of the eighteenth century sought to achieve unity, order, and a balance of form and content, those of the nineteenth century sought self-expression, striving to communicate with passion no matter what imbalance might result. If Classical artists had drawn inspiration from the monuments of ancient Greece and Rome, those of the Romantic era looked to the human imagination and the wonders of nature. The Romantic artist exalted instinctive feelings—not those of the masses, but individual, personal ones. As the American Romantic poet Walt Whitman said, "I celebrate myself, and sing myself."

If a single feeling or sentiment pervaded the Romantic era, it was love. Indeed, "romance" is at the very heart of the word *Romantic*. The loves of Romeo and Juliet (Fig. 22–1), and Tristan and Isolde, for example, captured the public's imagination in the Romantic era. The endless pursuit of love, the search for the unattainable, became an obsession that, when expressed as music, produced the sounds of longing and yearning heard in so much of Romantic music.

Yet love was only one of several emotions dear to the Romantics. Despair, frenzy, and heavenly exaltation were others expressed in music and poetry. Just how the range of expression was broadened in Romantic music can be seen in the "expression marks" that came into being at this time: *espressivo* (expressively), *dolente* (sadly), *presto furioso* (fast and furiously), *con forza e passione* (with force and passion), *misterioso* (mysteriously), and *maestoso* (majestically). Not only do these directives explain to the performer how a passage ought to be played, they also reveal what the composer wished to express in the music.

Romantic musicians eloquently expressed their feelings about nature (Fig. 22–2). As Beethoven proclaimed in 1821, "I perform most faithfully the duties that Humanity, God, and Nature enjoin upon me." In his "Pastoral" Symphony (Symphony No. 6), the first important Romantic "nature piece," Beethoven seeks to capture both nature's tranquil beauty and its destructive fury. Schubert's "Trout" Quintet, Schumann's *Forest Scenes,* and Strauss's "Alpine" Symphony are just a few of the many musical works that continue the tradition.

FIGURE 22–1

The Balcony Scene of Romeo and Juliet (1845) by Eugène Delacroix typifies the nineteenth-century fascination with love and with Shakespeare. Berlioz sought to capture the spirit of the play in a five-movement program symphony (*Roméo et Juliette,* 1839); Tchaikovsky tried to do so in a one-movement symphonic poem (*Romeo and Juliet,* 1880).

Private collection

FIGURE 22–2

Man and Woman Gazing at the Moon,
by German Romantic artist Casper David
Friedrich (1774–1840).

Associated with this desire to be at one with nature was a passion for travel, what the Germans called a *Wanderlust*. Far-off places and people fired the Romantic imagination. The German composer Felix Mendelssohn (1809–1847) journeyed to Italy, Scotland, and the Hebrides Islands to find inspiration for his symphonies and overtures. The English poet Lord Byron sailed to Greece and Turkey and infused his art with a sense of travel and adventure (see boxed essay).

THE MUSICIAN AS "ARTIST," MUSIC AS "ART"

With the Romantic era came the idea that music was something more than mere entertainment and the composer was more than a hired employee. Bach had been a municipal civil servant, devoted and dutiful, to the town of Leipzig. Haydn and Mozart served, and were treated, as domestics in the homes of the great lords of Europe. But Beethoven began to break the chains of submission. He was the first to demand, and receive, the respect and admiration due a great creative spirit. Ultimately, Franz Liszt and Richard Wagner, as much through their literary works as their musical compositions, caused the public to view the artist as a sort of demigod, a prophet able to inspire the audience through the creation of music that was both morally uplifting and beautiful. "To the artist is entrusted the upbringing of mankind," said Liszt. Never was the position of the creative musician loftier than in the mid-nineteenth century.

the artist as prophet to the world

Just as the musician was elevated from servant to artist, so the music he or she produced was transformed from entertainment to art. Classical music had been created for the immediate gratification of patron and audience, with little thought given to its lasting value. With the mature Beethoven and the early Romantics, this attitude began to change. Symphonies, quartets, and piano sonatas sprang to life, not to give immediate pleasure to listeners, but to gratify a deep-seated creative urge within the composer. They became extensions of

Lord Byron's Childe Harold's Pilgrimage

The English poet George Gordon, Lord Byron (1788–1824), was the epitome of the Romantic hero: dashing, passionate, self-absorbed, idealistic, and guilt-ridden (he had had an affair with his half-sister). "He is mad, bad, and dangerous to know," said one of his lovers. Byron climbed the Swiss Alps, swam the Hellespont (separating Europe from Asia Minor), and died, at age thirty-six, fighting for Greek independence from Turkish rule. His *Childe Harold's Pilgrimage*, part autobiography and part poetic travelogue, is the fruit of his travels around Europe and Asia Minor between 1809 and 1817. Typical of the Romantics, Byron found creative stimulus in all that was foreign and in the delights of nature. He condenses into poetic verse what he saw, heard, and felt:

> There is a pleasure in the pathless woods;
> There is a rapture on the lonely shore;
> There is society, where none intrudes,
> By the deep sea, and music is its roar:
> I love not man the less, but Nature more.

(*Childe Harold's Pilgrimage*, canto iv, stanza 178; 1817)

A portrait of the English poet Lord Byron in the dress of an Albanian adventurer. Another portrait of Byron can faintly be seen hanging on the wall in the painting on the cover of this book.

National Portrait Gallery, London/The Bridgeman Art Library

---

art for art's sake

the artist's inner personality. These works might not be understood by the creator's contemporaries, as was true of the late piano sonatas of Beethoven and the orchestral works of Hector Berlioz, for example, but they would be understood by posterity, by future generations of listeners. The idea of "art for art's sake"—art free of all immediate functional concerns—was born of the Romantic spirit.

The new exalted position of the composer and his art soon brought a more serious tone to the concert hall. Prior to 1800, a concert was as much a social event as a musical experience. People talked, drank, ate, played cards, flirted, and wandered about. Dogs ran freely on the ground floor, and armed guards roamed the theater to maintain at least some order. When people turned to the music, they were loud and demonstrative. They hummed along with the melody and tapped the beat to the music they liked. If a performance went well, people applauded, not only at the ends of the pieces but also between movements. Sometimes they demanded an immediate encore; other times they hissed their disapproval.

the concert hall becomes silent

Around 1840, however, a sudden hush came over the concert hall. With the revered figure of the Romantic artist-composer now before them, the members of the audience sat in respectful silence. A listener not distracted socially became a listener engaged emotionally. More was expected of the audience, because symphonies and sonatas were longer and more complex. But the audience, in turn, expected more from the music: not just entertainment but an emotionally satisfying encounter that would leave the attentive person exhausted yet somehow purified and uplifted by the artistic experience. The cover of this book, a painting of 1840, suggests how the Romantic imagination wrapped even secular music in a sacred aura. We see a temple of art: the artists are the congregants, Liszt (center) the high priest, the piano the altar, and Beethoven the god.

Romantic Ideals and Today's Concert Hall

Romanticism has kept its grip on the Western imagination. Belief in the artist as hero, reverence toward the work of art as an object of moral inspiration, and the expectations of silence and even formal dress at a concert—all of these attitudes developed in the early Romantic period. What is more, the notion that a particular group of pieces should get repeated hearings gained currency at this time. Prior to 1800, almost all music was disposable music: It was written as entertainment for the moment and was then forgotten. But the generation following Beethoven began to see his best symphonies, concertos, and quartets, as well as those of Mozart and Haydn, as worthy of continued performance and preservation. These and the best works of succeeding generations came to constitute a "canon" of music—a body of music possessing attributes of unity, expression, and form that should be continually revisited. Such masterpieces, as they were correctly viewed, came to form the core of today's concert repertoire. Thus what we think about the composer, how we view the work of art, what we can expect to hear at a concert, and even how we behave during the performance are not eternal ideals, with us since time immemorial, but are instead values created during the Romantic period. In many respects, the attitudes about art and music that arose in the early nineteenth century still govern our thinking today.

a core repertoire for the concert hall

THE STYLE OF ROMANTIC MUSIC

The Romantic spirit rebelled against Classical ideals in ways that allow us to generalize these two artistic movements in terms of opposites: rational against irrational, intellect opposed to heart, conformity versus originality, and the masses in contradistinction to the individual. Yet in purely musical terms, the works of the Romantic composers represent not so much a *revolution* against Classical ideals as an *evolution* beyond them. The Classical genres of the symphony, concerto, string quartet, piano sonata, and opera remain fashionable, though somewhat altered in shape, throughout the nineteenth century. The symphony now grows in length, embodying the widest possible range of expression, while the concerto becomes increasingly virtuosic, as a heroic soloist does battle against an orchestral mass. The Romantics introduced no new musical forms and only two new genres: the art song (see Chapter 23) and the symphonic poem (see Chapter 30). Instead, Romantic composers took the musical materials received from Haydn, Mozart, and the young Beethoven and made them more intensely expressive, more personal, more colorful, and in some cases, more bizarre.

greater length, greater virtuosity

Romantic Melody

The Romantic period witnessed the apotheosis of melody. Melodies became broad, powerful streams of sound intended to sweep the listener away. They went beyond the neat symmetrical units (two plus two, four plus four) inherent in the Classical style, becoming longer, rhythmically more flexible and more irregular in shape. At the same time, Romantic melodies continued a trend

the popular quality of Romantic melody

that had developed in the late eighteenth century, in which themes became vocal in conception, more singable or "lyrical." Countless melodies of Schubert, Chopin, and Tchaikovsky have been turned into popular songs and movie themes—Romantic music is perfectly suited for the romance of film—because these melodies are so profoundly expressive. They sigh, lament, grow, and wax ecstatic. They start haltingly and then build to a grandiose climax, sublime and triumphant. Example 22–1 shows the well-known love theme from Tchaikovsky's *Romeo and Juliet*. As the brackets show, it rises and falls, only to rise higher again, a total of seven times, on the way to a *fortissimo* climax. (The melody can be heard on ❻ 4/16 at 3:08)

EXAMPLE 22–1

Colorful Harmony

Part of the emotional intensity of Romantic music was generated by a new, more colorful harmony. Classical music had, in the main, made use of chords built upon only the seven notes of the major or minor scale. Romantic composers went further by creating **chromatic harmony,** constructing chords on the five additional notes (the chromatic notes) within the full twelve-note chromatic scale. This gave more colors to their harmonic palette, allowing the rich, lush sounds we associate with Romantic music. Chromatic harmony made it possible to glide smoothly to chords only a half step away, and to slide progressively away from the tonic key, moving, for example, from a C major tonic (with no sharps or flats) to some tonally far-off, exotic land of six or seven sharps or flats.

chromatic harmony

bold chord changes

Chromatic harmony likewise encouraged bold chordal shifts—a chord with three sharps might be followed immediately by one with six flats, for example. The striking sound that results from these unusual juxtapositions is harmonious with music that seeks to express a wider range of feeling.

Finally, nineteenth-century composers instilled their music with a "romantic" feeling by means of new and striking dissonances. Dissonant notes in the Romantic era were not only more numerous but were held longer as well. Because dissonance always wants to move, or resolve, to consonance, the delay of the resolution produces a feeling of anxiety, longing, and searching, all sentiments appropriate to music that often deals with the subject of love.

dissonance longs for consonance

All three of these qualities of Romantic harmony—chromatic harmony, bold chordal shifts, and prolonged dissonance—can be heard in Frédéric Chopin's Nocturne in C♯ minor (1835). Neither you nor the author can take in all the music given in the following three examples simply by looking at them. (To hear them, turn to ❻ 3/23 and ❷ 2/5.) We can, however, visualize here some of the music's inner workings—first the bold harmonic shift from a chord with four sharps to one with four flats, then the chromaticism, and finally the prolonged dissonance. In this way, we may begin to understand, when hearing the rich, sensuous sound of Romantic music, how it is created.

EXAMPLE 22–2: bold harmonic shift at 2:48

EXAMPLE 22–3: chromatic harmony at 3:24

EXAMPLE 22–4: prolonged dissonance at 5:01

Romantic Tempo: *Rubato*

In keeping with an age that glorified personal freedom and tolerated eccentric behavior, tempo in Romantic music was cut loose from the restraints of a regular beat. The watchword here was *rubato* (literally "robbed"), an expression mark for the performer written into the score by the composer. A performer playing tempo **rubato** "stole" some time here and gave it back there, moving faster or slower so as to effect an intensely personal performance. The free approach to tempo was often reinforced by fluctuating dynamic levels—ritards were executed with diminuendos*, and accelerations with crescendos*—as a way of explaining, even exaggerating, the flow of the music. Whatever excesses might result could be excused under license of artistic freedom.

a flexible tempo

Romantic Forms: Monumental and Miniature

The musical forms that had earlier served Haydn and Mozart continued to satisfy the needs of the nineteenth-century composer. Sonata–allegro form, in particular, remained useful because its flexible format could accommodate any number of individual solutions. What developed, then, was not a rush to invent new forms but a trend to extend the existing ones. As composers laid out broad and sweeping melodies, indulged in gigantic crescendos, and reveled in the luxurious sound of the enlarged orchestra, the length of individual movements increased dramatically. Mozart's G minor symphony (1788) lasts about twenty minutes, depending on the tempo of the performance. But Berlioz's *Symphonie fantastique* (1830) takes nearly fifty-five minutes, and Mahler's Symphony No. 2 (1894) nearly an hour and a half. Perhaps the longest of all musical works is Richard Wagner's four-opera *Ring* cycle (1853–1876), which continues some seventeen hours during the course of four evenings. In these extended visions, the Romantic composer seems to echo the words of the novelist Jean Paul Richter: "Romanticism is beauty without bounds—the beautiful infinite."

lengthy symphonies

Yet, paradoxically, Romantic composers were fascinated by miniature forms as well. In works of only a brief minute or two, they tried to capture the essence of a single mood, sentiment, or emotion. Such a miniature was called a **character piece.** It was usually written for the piano and often made use of simple binary (**AB**) or ternary (**ABA**) form. Because the character piece passes by in a twinkling of an eye, it was sometimes given a whimsical title, such as bagatelle (a trifle), humoresque, arabesque, musical moment, caprice, romance, intermezzo, or impromptu. Schubert, Schumann, Chopin, Liszt, Brahms, and Tchaikovsky all enjoyed creating these musical miniatures, perhaps as antidotes to their lengthy symphonies and concertos.

short character pieces

EXPRESSIVE TONE COLORS, GREATER SIZE, GREATER VOLUME

Perhaps the most striking aspects of Romantic music are the color and sheer volume of the sound. Sometimes all thematic and harmonic movement stops, and nothing but pure sound remains. Appropriate to an age that indulged in wild mood swings, Romantic composers prescribed greater dynamic extremes. Whereas the range in Classical music extended only from *pp* (*pianissimo*) to *ff* (*fortissimo*), now exaggerated "hyper-marks" such as *pppp* and *ffff* appear. To create sounds as loud as *ffff*, a larger orchestra or a bigger piano was needed. Composers demanded, and received, musical forces equal to the task of expressing the emotional extremes, changing moods, and extravagant gestures of the Romantic spirit.

FIGURE 22–3
A modern French horn with valves, an invention of the 1820s. The valves allowed the performer to engage different lengths of tubing instantly, and thereby play a fully chromatic scale.

The Romantic Orchestra

The Romantic era overlapped with the Industrial Revolution, which brought not only mass-produced goods but also new musical instruments. The wood of the flute was replaced by silver, and the instrument was supplied with a new fingering mechanism that added to its agility and made it easier to play in tune. Similarly, the trumpet and French horn were provided with valves that improved technical facility and accuracy of pitch in all keys (Fig. 22–3). These brass instruments were now capable of playing intricate, chromatic melodies, as well as providing the traditional backdrop of sonic support for the rest of the orchestra. The French horn, in particular, became an object of special affection during the Romantic period. Its rich, dark tone and its traditional association with the hunt—and by extension, nature— made it the Romantic instrument par excellence. Composers often called on a solo horn to express something mysterious or distant.

Besides improvements to existing instruments, several new instruments were added to the symphony orchestra during the nineteenth century (Fig. 22–4). We have seen how Beethoven brought the piccolo (a high flute), the trombone, and the contrabassoon (a bass bassoon) into the orchestra in his famous Symphony No. 5 (1808). In 1830, Hector Berlioz went even further, requiring an ophicleide* (an early form of the tuba), an English horn* (a low-pitched oboe), a cornet*, and two harps

Victoria & Albert Museum, London/Art Resource, NY

FIGURE 22–4

A large orchestra depicted at Covent Garden Theater, London, in 1846. The conductor stands toward the middle, baton in hand, with strings to his right and woodwinds, brass, and percussion to his left. It was typical in this period to put all or part of the orchestra on risers to allow the sound to project more fully.

in his *Symphonie fantastique*. Berlioz, the embodiment of the Romantic spirit, had a typically grandiose notion of what the ideal symphony orchestra should contain. He wanted no fewer than 467 instruments including 120 violins, 40 violas, 45 cellos, 35 double basses, and 30 harps. Such a gigantic instrumental force was never actually assembled, but Berlioz's utopian vision indicates the direction in which Romantic composers were headed. By the second half of the nineteenth century, orchestras with nearly a hundred players were not uncommon. Compare, for example, the number and variety of instruments required for a typical eighteenth-century performance of Mozart's G minor symphony with the symphony orchestra needed for Berlioz's *Symphonie fantastique*, and that required for Gustav Mahler's Symphony No. 1 (see box). By the end of the nineteenth century, the symphony orchestra had become, in almost all ways, the ensemble of instruments that we see today.

Our reaction to the Romantic orchestra today, however, is very different from the response in the nineteenth century. Our modern ears have been desensitized by an overexposure to electronically amplified sound. But imagine the impact of an orchestra of a hundred players before the days of amplification. Apart from the military cannon and the steam engine, the nineteenth-century orchestra produced the loudest sonic level of any human contrivance. The big sound—and the big contrasts—of the nineteenth-century orchestra were new and startling, and audiences packed ever-larger concert halls to hear them.

greater impact in the nineteenth century

The Conductor

Naturally, someone was needed to coordinate the efforts of the enlarged orchestra. Previously, in the days of Bach and Mozart, the orchestra had been led from within, either by the keyboard player of the *basso continuo** gesturing with his head and hands, or by the chief violinist directing with his bow. When

The Growth of the Symphony Orchestra

Mozart (1788)
Symphony in G minor

1 flute
2 oboes
2 clarinets
2 bassoons
2 French horns
1st violins (8)†
2nd violins (8)
violas (4)
cellos (4)
double basses (3)

Total: 36

Berlioz (1830)
Symphonie fantastique

1 piccolo
2 flutes
2 oboes
1 English horn
2 B♭ clarinets
1 E♭ clarinet
4 bassoons
4 French horns
2 trumpets
2 cornets
3 trombones
2 ophicleides (tubas)
1st violins (15)†
2nd violins (14)
violas (8)
cellos (12)
double basses (8)
2 harps
timpani
bass drum
snare drum
cymbals and bells

Total: 89

Mahler (1889)
Symphony No. 1

3 piccolos
4 flutes
4 oboes
1 English horn
4 B♭ clarinets
2 E♭ clarinets
1 bass clarinet
3 bassoons
1 contrabassoon
7 French horns
5 trumpets
4 trombones
1 tuba
1st violins (20)†
2nd violins (18)
violas (14)
cellos (12)
double basses (8)
1 harp
timpani (2 players)
bass drum
triangle, cymbals
tam-tam

Total: 119

Wien Museum, Karlsplatz/Erich Lessing/Art Resource, NY

A satirical engraving suggesting the public's impression of Berlioz conducting his vastly enlarged symphony orchestra.

†Number of string players estimated according to standards of the period.

a leader needed for the ever-larger orchestra

Beethoven played and conducted his piano concertos, he did so seated at his instrument. When he led one of his symphonies, especially toward the end of his life, he stood before the orchestra, back to the audience, waving his hands. In 1820, the composer Louis Spohr became the first to use a wooden baton to lead the orchestra. Other objects were used as well, including a rolled-up piece of paper (Fig. 22–5), a violin bow, and sometimes even a handkerchief. As symphony orchestras became larger and symphonic scores more complex, every orchestral ensemble needed a leader to keep it from falling apart during performance. In the course of the nineteenth century, this leader evolved from a mere time-beater into an interpreter, and sometimes a dictator, of the musical score. The modern conductor had arrived.

The Virtuoso

Appropriate for an era that glorified the individual, the nineteenth century was the age of the solo **virtuoso.** Of course, there had been instrumental virtuosos before—Bach on the organ and Mozart on the piano, to name just two—but now, many musicians began to expend enormous energy striving to raise their performing skills to an unprecedented height. Pianists and violinists in particular spent long hours practicing technical exercises—arpeggios, tremolos, trills, and scales played in thirds, sixths, and octaves—to develop wizard-like hand speed on their instrument. Naturally, some of what they played for the public was lacking in musical substance, tasteless showpieces designed to appeal immediately to the audiences that packed the ever-larger concert halls. Pianists even developed tricks to make it appear they had more than two hands (see Fig. 25–6). Franz Liszt (1811–1886) sometimes played at the keyboard with a lighted cigar between his fingers. The Italian Niccolò Paganini (1782–1840) secretly tuned the four strings of his violin in ways that would allow him to negotiate with ease extraordinarily difficult passages (Figs. 22–6 and 22–7). If one of his strings broke, he could play with just three; if three broke, he continued apace with just one. So great was his celebrity that Paganini's picture appeared on napkins, ties, pipes, billiard cues, and powder boxes. As a composer later remarked, "The attraction of the virtuoso is like that of the circus performer; there's always the hope that something disastrous will happen." The daredevil quality of Paganini's virtuosic music can be seen in Example 22–5, which looks something like a roller coaster. Fortunately, as we shall see, some of these performing daredevils were also gifted composers.

FIGURE 22–5

Silhouette of composer Carl Maria von Weber conducting with a rolled sheet of music so as to highlight the movement of his hand.

© Bettmann/Corbis

FIGURE 22–6 AND 22–7

(left) Niccolò Paganini. (below) *Paganini and the Witches*, a lithograph by an unknown artist. Paganini's extraordinary powers on the violin led some to believe that he had made a deal with the devil. The highest string of his violin was said to be made of the intestine of his mistress, whom he had murdered with his own hands. None of this was true, and Paganini filed several libel suits to reclaim his honor.

CORBIS

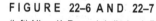

EXAMPLE 22–5: Paganini, Caprice, Opus 1, No. 5

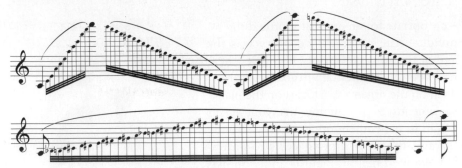

CODA

While this introduction to musical Romanticism treats the major developments of the nineteenth century, there were others. The increased attention paid to literature in the Romantic era inspired new musical genres: the art song (*Lied*), the program symphony, and the related symphonic poem. The technological innovations that fostered the development of the large symphony orchestra also led to the fabrication of a much larger and more powerful piano, as well as a musical literature specifically for it. Finally, political events, which led to the creation of modern nations such as Germany and Italy, caused musical reverberations in the form of new, nationalistic musical styles. All of these developments—the art song, program music, the Romantic piano, and musical nationalism—will be discussed in the following chapters.

Listening Exercise 31
Comparing Orchestral Works of the Classical and Romantic Periods

ThomsonNOW
To take this Listening Exercise online and receive feedback or email answers to your instructor, go to *ThomsonNOW* for this chapter.

The transition from the Classical to the Romantic period witnessed an enormous change in musical style. To appreciate the extent of this musical transformation, let us compare two orchestral works: the first movement of Mozart's Symphony No. 40 in G minor (1788) (⑥ 2/12–14 and ❷ 1/14–16) and the finale of Hector Berlioz's *Symphonie fantastique* (1830) (⑥ 3/17–18 and ❷ 2/3–4). Listen to the first four minutes of each work and answer the following questions indicating "M" for Mozart or "B" for Berlioz. If you need help, consult the Listening Guides on pages 212 and 281.

1. Which composer begins with a clear-cut pair of four-bar antecedent–consequent phrases? _____
2. Which composer begins with pure musical atmosphere, much as in a score for a modern-day motion picture? _____
3. Which composer exhibits greater "mood swings," in which the music oscillates between louds and softs, high pitches and low pitches? _____

4. Which composer designates a brass instrument and a percussion instrument to play the melody? _____
5. Which composer requires a large, colorful orchestra? _____
6. Which composer requires the violins to present all themes at first appearance? _____
7. Which composer maintains a steady beat throughout (to which you can tap your foot)? _____
8. Which composer maintains a constant tempo throughout (to which you can easily set and maintain a conducting pattern)? _____
9. Accordingly, the work of which composer is more likely to need a conductor during performance, owing to the lack of a clearly audible beat and consistent tempo? _____
10. Which composer drew inspiration for his symphony from events outside of music? _____

Key Words

chromatic   *rubato* (**257**)   virtuoso (**261**)
 harmony (**256**) character piece (**258**)

Early Romantic Music
THE ART SONG

Chapter
23

The decade 1803–1813 was perhaps the most auspicious in the history of Western music. In this short span of time were born the composers Hector Berlioz (1803), Felix Mendelssohn (1809), Frédéric Chopin (1810), Robert Schumann (1810), Franz Liszt (1811), Giuseppe Verdi (1813), and Richard Wagner (1813). Add to these the shining figure of Franz Schubert (born 1797) and this brilliant galaxy of Romantic musical geniuses is complete. We call them Romantics because they were part of—indeed, they created—the Romantic movement in music. But with the possible exception of Mendelssohn, they were very unconventional people. Their lives typify all that we have come to associate with the Romantic spirit: self-expression, passion, excess, the love of nature and literature, as well as a certain selfishness, irresponsibility, and even a bit of lunacy. Not only did they create great art, but life, and how they lived it, also became an art.

THE ART SONG

One of the hallmarks of the Romantic era was a quickening interest in literature, and especially poetry. Indeed, never were word and tone more closely allied than during the Romantic era. The Romantic poets viewed music as the truest and purest of all the arts, owing to the abstract quality of sound. Composers, in turn, found musical resonance in the poetry of the day and transformed it into song, believing that music could intensify poetic sentiments by expressing things that words alone could not.

 Songs inspired by great poetry have appeared throughout human history. But the near frenzy of poetic activity in the nineteenth century inspired Romantic composers to set poems to music with increasing frequency. The English Romantic poets William Wordsworth, John Keats, Percy Bysshe Shelley, and Lord Byron (see page 254), who burst onto the scene in the early 1800s, had German counterparts not only in the great Johann von Goethe but also in the younger Romantics Joseph von Eichendorff (1788–1857) and Heinrich Heine (1797–1856). Literally thousands of odes, sonnets, ballads, and romances poured from their pens, and many were quickly set as songs by young Romantic composers. In so doing, these musicians popularized a genre called the **art song**—a song for solo voice and piano accompaniment with high artistic aspirations. Because the art song was cultivated most intensely in

poetry and music intimately linked

German-speaking lands, it is also called the **Lied** (plural **Lieder**), German for "song." Although many composers wrote art songs, none had greater success in the genre than Franz Schubert. His special talent was to fashion music that captured both the spirit and the detail of the text, creating a sensitive mood painting in which the voice, and especially the accompanying piano, expresses every nuance of the poem. Schubert said, "When one has a good poem the music comes easily, melodies just flow, so that composing is a real joy."

Franz Schubert (1797–1828)

Franz Schubert was born in Vienna in 1797. Among the great Viennese masters—Haydn, Mozart, Beethoven, Schubert, Brahms, and Mahler—only he was native-born to the city. Schubert's father was a schoolteacher, and the son, too, was groomed for that profession. Yet the boy's obvious musical talent made it imperative that he also have music lessons, so his father taught him to play the violin, and his older brother the piano. At the age of eleven, Schubert was admitted as a choirboy in the emperor's chapel (the group today is called the Vienna Boys Choir). Proximity to the royal palace brought young Schubert into contact with Antonio Salieri, erstwhile rival of Mozart and still imperial court composer (see page 186). Schubert began to study composition with Salieri in 1810 and was soon composing his own musical works at an astonishing rate.

After his voice changed in 1812, young Franz left the court chapel and enrolled in a teacher's college. He had been spared compulsory military service because he was below the minimum height of five feet and his sight was so poor he was compelled to wear the spectacles now familiar from his portraits (Fig. 23–1). By 1815, he had become a teacher at his father's primary school. But he found teaching demanding and tedious, and so after three unpleasant years, Schubert quit his "day job" to give himself over wholly to music.

"You lucky fellow, I really envy you! You live a life of sweet, precious freedom, can give free rein to your musical genius, can express your thoughts in any way you like." This was Schubert's brother's view of the composer's newfound freedom. But as many Romantics would find, the reality was harsher than the ideal. Aside from some small income he earned from the sale of a few songs, he lacked financial support. Schubert, unlike Beethoven, kept no company with aristocrats and thus received no patronage from them. Instead, he lived a bohemian life, helped along by the generosity of his friends, with whom he often lodged when he was broke. He spent his mornings passionately composing music, passed his afternoons in cafés discussing literature and politics, and often spent his evenings performing his songs and dances for friends and admirers.

As Schubert was reaching artistic maturity, the era of the great aristocratic salon was drawing to an end, its role as a primary venue for artistic expression replaced by the middle-class parlor or living room. Here, in less formal surroundings, groups of men and women with a common interest in music, the novel, drama, or poetry would meet to read and discuss the latest developments in these arts. The gatherings at which Schubert appeared, and at which only his compositions were played, were called

FIGURE 23–1 AND 23–2

(top) Franz Schubert. (bottom) A small, private assembly known as a Schubertiad, named after the composer, at which artists presented their works. The singer before the piano is Johann Vogl, accompanied by Schubert at the piano.

Museum der Stadt Wien/The Bridgeman Art Library

Schubertiads by his friends. It was in small, purely private assemblies such as these (Fig. 23–2), not in large public concerts, that most of his best songs were first performed.

In 1822, disaster befell the composer: He contracted syphilis, a venereal disease tantamount to a death sentence before the discovery of antibiotics. His lyrical Symphony in B minor of that year, appropriately called the "Unfinished Symphony," was left incomplete. (The second theme of the first movement of this work provides an aural backdrop to several sections of Steven Spielberg's 2002 film *Minority Report.*) Yet during the years that preceded his premature death in 1828, Schubert created some of his greatest works: the song cycles *Die schöne Müllerin* (*The Pretty Maid of the Mill*, 1823) and *Winterreise* (*Winter Journey*, 1827), the "Wanderer" Fantasy for piano (1822), and the great C major symphony (1828). When Beethoven died in 1827, Schubert served as a torchbearer at the funeral. The next year, he too was dead, the youngest of the great composers. The epitaph for his tombstone reads: "The art of music here entombed a rich treasure, but even fairer hopes."

Schubert's song cycles

In his brief life of thirty-one years, Franz Schubert wrote eight symphonies, fifteen string quartets, twenty-one piano sonatas, seven Masses for chorus and orchestra, and four operas—a sizable oeuvre by any standard. Yet in his day Schubert was known almost exclusively as a writer of art songs (*Lieder*). Indeed, he composed more than 600 works in this genre, many of them minor masterpieces. In a few cases, Schubert chose to set several texts together in a series. In so doing, he created what is called a **song cycle**—a tightly structured group of individual songs that tell a story or treat a single theme. *The Pretty Maid of the Mill* (twenty songs) and *Winter Journey* (twenty-four songs), both of which relate the sad consequences of unrequited love, are Schubert's two great song cycles.

ERLKING (1815)

To gain an idea of Schubert's extraordinary musical talent, we need only listen to his song *Erlkönig* (*Erlking*), written when he was just seventeen. The text itself is a ballad—a dramatic story told alternately in narrative verse and dialogue—from the pen of the famous poet Goethe. It relates the tale of the evil King of the Elves and his malevolent seduction of a young boy. Legend had it that whosoever was touched by the King of the Elves would die. This tale typifies the dark Romantic fascination with the supernatural and the macabre, which is evinced most famously in Mary Shelley's *Frankenstein* (1818).

According to a friend's account, Schubert was reading a book of Goethe's poetry, pacing back and forth in his room. Suddenly, he sprang to the piano and, as fast as he could write, set Goethe's entire ballad to music. From there Schubert and his friend hastened to the composer's college to play it for a few kindred spirits. In his lifetime, *Erlking* became Schubert's best-known song, and one of only a few that brought him any money.

The opening line of the poem sets the sinister nocturnal scene: "Who rides so late through night and wind?" With his feverish son cradled in his arms, a father rides at breakneck speed to an inn to save the child (Fig. 23–3). Schubert captures both the general sense of terror in the scene and the detail of the galloping horse; he creates an accompanying figure in the piano that pounds on relentlessly just as fast as the pianist can make it go (Ex. 23–1).

FIGURE 23–3

The ballad of the Erlking depicted by Schubert's close friend Moritz von Schwind. The artist had heard Schubert perform the song at many Schubertiads.

akg-images

EXAMPLE 23–1

The specter of death, the Erlking, beckons gently to the boy. He does so in seductively sweet tones, in a melody with the gentle lilt and folksy accompaniment of a popular tune.

EXAMPLE 23–2

(Thou dearest boy, come go with me!)

The frightened boy cries out to his father in an agitated line that culminates in a tense, chromatic ascent.

EXAMPLE 23–3

(Dear father, my father, say, did'st thou not hear the Erlking whisper promises in my ear?)

This cry is heard again and again in the course of the song, each time at a successively higher pitch and with increasingly dissonant harmonies. In this way the music mirrors the boy's growing terror. The father tries to calm him in low tones that are steady, stable, and repetitive. The Erlking at first charms in sweet, consonant tones, but then threatens in dissonant ones, as seduction gives way to abduction. Thus each of the three characters of the story is portrayed with distinct musical qualities. This is musical characterization at its finest; the melody and accompaniment not only support the text but also intensify and enrich it. Suddenly, the end is reached: the hand of the Erlking (Death) has touched his victim. Anxiety gives way to sorrow as the narrator announces in increasingly somber (minor) tones: "But in his arms, his child was dead!"

Listening Guide

Franz Schubert
Art song, *Erlking* (1815)

6 **2**
3/14 1/25

Form: through-composed

0:00	14 25	Piano introduction: pounding triplets in right hand and ominous minor-mode motive in left	

Narrator

0:22		Wer reitet so spät durch Nacht und Wind? Es ist der Vater mit seinem Kind. Er hat den Knaben wohl in dem Arm, er fasst ihn sicher, er hält ihn warm.	Who rides so late through night so wild? A loving father with his child. He clasps his boy close with his arm, He holds him tightly and keeps him warm.

Father

0:56		Mein Sohn, was birgst du so bang dein Gesicht?	My son, what makes you hide your face in fear?

Son

1:04	With agitated leaps	Siehst, Vater, du den Erlkönig nicht? Den Erlenkönig mit Kron' und Schweif?	Father don't you see the Erlking— the Erlking with crown and shroud?

Father

1:20	In low, calming tones	Mein Sohn, es ist ein Nebelstreif.	My son, it's only some streak of mist.

Erlking

1:30	With seductive melody in major key	Du liebes Kind, komm, geh' mit mir! gar schöne Spiele spiel' ich mit dir; manch' bunte Blumen sind an dem Strand, meine Mutter hat manch' gülden Gewand.	You dear child, come along with me! I'll play some very fine games with you; where varied blossoms are on meadows fair and my mother has golden garments to wear.

Son

1:55	Tension depicted by tight chromatic movement in voice	Mein Vater, mein Vater und hörest du nicht, was Erlenkönig mir leise verspricht?	My father, my father, do you not hear how the Erlking whispers promises in my ear?

Father

2:08	In low, steady pitches	Sei ruhig, bleibe ruhig, mein Kind, in dürren Blättern säuselt der Wind.	Be calm, stay calm, my child, Through wither'd leaves the wind blows wild.

(continued)

		Erlking	
2:18	With a happy, lilting tune in major key	Willst, feiner Knabe, du mit mir geh'n? Meine Töchter sollen dich warten schön, meine Töchter führen den nächtlichen Reih'n, und wiegen und tanzen und singen dich ein.	My handsome young lad, will you come with me? My beauteous daughters wait for you, With them you would join in the dance every night, and they will rock and dance and sing you to sleep.
		Son	
2:36	Same intense chromatic notes as before, but now a step higher; minor key	Mein Vater, mein Vater, und siehst du nicht dort Erlkönigs Töchter am düstern Ort?	My Father, my father, don't you see at all the Erlking's daughters over there in the dusk?
		Father	
2:49	Low register, but more leaps (agitation) than before	Mein Sohn, mein Sohn, ich seh' es genau, es scheinen die alten Weiden so grau.	My son, my son, the form you there see, is only the aging gray willow tree.
		Erlking	
3:07	His music is no longer seductive but now threatening and in minor key	Ich liebe dich, mich reizt deine schöne Gestalt; und bist du nicht willig, so brauch' ich Gewalt.	I love you, I'm charmed by your fine appearance; And if you're not willing, I'll seize you by force!
		Son	
3:18	Piercing cries in highest range	Mein Vater, mein Vater jetzt fasst er mich an! Erlkönig hat mir ein Leids gethan!	My father, my father, now he's got me, the Erlking has seized me by his trick.
		Narrator	
3:32	With rising and then falling line	Dem Vater grausets; er reitet geschwind, er hält in den Armen das ächzende Kind. Erreicht den Hof mit Müh und Noth:	The father shudders, he rides headlong, holding the groaning child in his arms. He reaches the inn with toil and dread,
3:52	Piano slows and then stops, recitative	in seinen Armen das Kind war todt!	but in his arms, his child was dead!

Use a downloadable, cross-platform animated Active Listening Guide, available at www.thomsonedu.com/music/wright.

Listening Exercise 32

Schubert
Erlking

3/14   1/25

ThomsonNOW
To take this Listening Exercise online and receive feedback or email answers to your instructor, go to *ThomsonNOW* for this chapter.

Schubert was a master at bringing to life the essential characters and sentiments of the poetry he set to music. This exercise suggests how he used two very basic musical elements, a shift in mode and a change in the accompaniment, to intensify Goethe's dramatic ballad *Erlking*.

1. (0:00–0:22) The opening section presents rapidly repeating notes in the right hand of the accompanist and an ominous motive below in the left. In which mode is the introduction written?

    a. major   b. minor

2. (1:30–1:52) When the Erlking enters, is the ominous motive still heard in the accompaniment?
   a. yes   b. no
3. (1:30–1:52) In which mode does the Erlking sing?
   a. major   b. minor
4. (1:55–2:06) As the son reenters, what happens in the piano accompaniment?
   a. Rapidly repeating notes return in the accompanist's right hand, and the mode shifts from major to minor.
   b. Rapidly repeating notes return in the accompanist's left hand, and the mode shifts from minor to major.
5. (2:18–2:34) For the second appearance of the Erlking, which is true?
   a. Arpeggios replace the rapidly repeating notes in the right hand, and the mode is major.
   b. The rapidly repeating notes in the right hand continue, and the mode is minor.
6. (3:07–3:17) For the third and final appearance of the Erlking, which is true?

a. The accompaniment pattern changes to arpeggios in the right hand, and the mode remains a happy major throughout.
b. The repeating notes in the right hand continue, and toward the end, the mode changes abruptly from major to minor.
7. (3:52–4:00) How does Schubert tell us that the galloping horse has arrived at the inn?
   a. The piano accompaniment gradually retards and then comes to a stop.
   b. The piano accompaniment stops abruptly.
8. (4:06–4:13) How does Schubert emphatically emphasize that the child has died and that there will be no happy ending?
   a. He writes an abrupt V–I cadence in a major key.
   b. He writes an abrupt V–I cadence in a minor key.
9. Excluding the narrator, how many characters are portrayed in Schubert's *Erlking*?
   a. one   b. two   c. three
10. How many voices actually sing the *Lied* in performance?
    a. one   b. two   c. three   d. four

Just as the tension in Goethe's poem rises incessantly, from the beginning to the very end, Schubert's music unfolds continually, without significant repetition. Such a musical composition featuring ever-changing melodic and harmonic material is called **through-composed,** and Schubert's *Erlking*, accordingly, is termed a through-composed art song. For texts that do not tell a story or project a series of changing moods, however, **strophic form** is often preferred. Here a single poetic mood is maintained from one stanza, or strophe, of the text to the next. Accordingly, the same music is repeated for each strophe, as in a hymn or a folksong. Schubert used strophic form, for example, when setting a prayer found in Sir Walter Scott's *The Lady of the Lake*. The result was his immortal *Ave Maria* (1825), a song in which the music for each of three strophes is identical, note for note.

Robert Schumann (1810–1856)

While some art songs, such as Schubert's *Erlking*, were musical arrangements of dramatic ballads, most were settings of lyrical love poems. The subject of love dominates not only Schubert's *Lieder* but also those of Robert and Clara Schumann (Fig. 23–4), whose conjugal life story is itself something of an ode to love.

Robert Schumann was born not to music but to literature. His father was a novelist who introduced him to Romantic poetry and the ancient classics. But the father died young, and Robert's mother determined that her son should study law. Reluctantly, Schumann matriculated at the University of Heidelberg, but he attended not a single class, preferring to pass the time with poetry and music. In 1830, Schumann moved, with his mother's grudging consent, to Leipzig to study piano, determined to become a virtuoso. But after two years of lessons with the eminent Friedrich Wieck (1785–1873)—during which he practiced seven hours a day—all he had to show for his labors was

FIGURE 23–4

Robert and Clara Schumann in 1850, from an engraving constructed from an early photograph.

© Bettmann/Corbis

a permanently damaged right hand. His career as a virtuoso now frustrated, Schumann directed his creative energies to musical composition. He also founded a new musical periodical, the *Neue Zeitschrift für Musik* (*New Journal of Music*). Using this journal as a pulpit, Schumann became an advocate for new music within the German Romantic movement, championing the works of such "radical" young composers as Berlioz, Chopin, Mendelssohn, and Brahms.

love for Clara inspires songs

While studying piano in the Leipzig home of Friedrich Wieck, Schumann met and fell in love with Wieck's beautiful and talented daughter Clara. Her father vehemently opposed the union, however, and Robert perforce began a legal battle to win Clara's hand. One of Wieck's objections was that Schumann could not support himself, let alone a wife. Inspired by his love of Clara, and perhaps motivated to show that he could earn a living, Schumann turned to writing art songs, then probably the most marketable of musical genres. In 1840, Robert won a legal victory over Clara's father, enabling the couple to marry. That same year, Schumann composed nearly 125 *Lieder*, including settings of poems by major Romantic poets such as Byron, Goethe, and Friedrich Rückert, as well as a few by Shakespeare. Some he grouped into song cycles* such as the now-famous *Dichterliebe* (*Poet's Love*) and *Frauenliebe und –leben* (*Women in Love and Life*). In this same year, he gathered twenty-six of these art songs into a wedding book for Clara, and titled the collection *Myrten* (*Myrtles*, flowers traditionally given the bride on her wedding day). Schumann had the collection published on September 12, 1840, the day he and Clara were married, the dedication reading "Robert Schumann . . . To his beloved wife."

a strophic song in ternary form

The real dedication to Clara, however, comes in the opening song, which is titled "Widmung" ("Dedication"). Here the composer sets an effusive love poem by the Romantic poet Joseph von Eichendorff, which begins, "You are my soul, you are my heart." The poem is short, consisting of only two stanzas, and the song is similarly brief. To create formal unity, Schumann brings back the first of the two strophes at the end, varying slightly the music, and thereby creates a familiar ternary form (**ABA'**). Perhaps most remarkable are the transitions from one stanza to the next, each of which employs chromatic harmony*. At the end of strophe 1, an E♭ slides upward to an E♮, and a chord with four flats (A♭ major) goes directly to one with four sharps (E major), as can be seen in Example 23–4; when strophe 2 yields to the return of strophe 1, the process is reversed. Such rich, striking harmonic shifts are typical not only of the art song but of much Romantic music.

EXAMPLE 23–4

(...buried my sorrow. You are the quiet,)

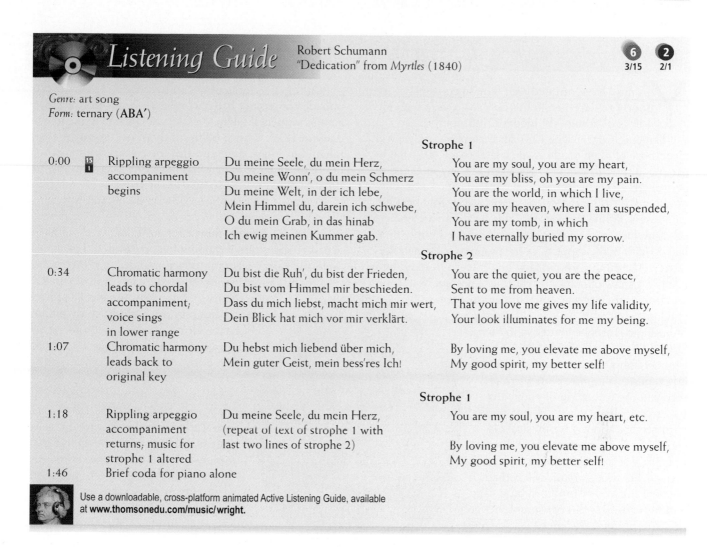

Listening Guide

Robert Schumann
"Dedication" from *Myrtles* (1840)

6 **2**
3/15 2/1

Genre: art song
Form: ternary (**ABA'**)

Strophe 1

0:00	Rippling arpeggio accompaniment begins	Du meine Seele, du mein Herz,	You are my soul, you are my heart,
		Du meine Wonn', o du mein Schmerz	You are my bliss, oh you are my pain.
		Du meine Welt, in der ich lebe,	You are the world, in which I live,
		Mein Himmel du, darein ich schwebe,	You are my heaven, where I am suspended,
		O du mein Grab, in das hinab	You are my tomb, in which
		Ich ewig meinen Kummer gab.	I have eternally buried my sorrow.

Strophe 2

0:34	Chromatic harmony leads to chordal accompaniment; voice sings in lower range	Du bist die Ruh', du bist der Frieden,	You are the quiet, you are the peace,
		Du bist vom Himmel mir beschieden.	Sent to me from heaven.
		Dass du mich liebst, macht mich mir wert,	That you love me gives my life validity,
		Dein Blick hat mich vor mir verklärt.	Your look illuminates for me my being.
1:07	Chromatic harmony leads back to original key	Du hebst mich liebend über mich,	By loving me, you elevate me above myself,
		Mein guter Geist, mein bess'res Ich!	My good spirit, my better self!

Strophe 1

1:18	Rippling arpeggio accompaniment returns; music for strophe 1 altered	Du meine Seele, du mein Herz, (repeat of text of strophe 1 with last two lines of strophe 2)	You are my soul, you are my heart, etc.
			By loving me, you elevate me above myself,
			My good spirit, my better self!
1:46	Brief coda for piano alone		

Use a downloadable, cross-platform animated Active Listening Guide, available at **www.thomsonedu.com/music/wright.**

Clara Wieck Schumann (1819–1896)

Unlike her husband, Robert, a gifted composer but failed performer, Clara Wieck Schumann was one of the great piano virtuosos of the nineteenth century (see Fig. 23–4). A child prodigy, she made her debut at the age of eleven in the famous Gewandhaus (see Figs. 24–6 and 24–7) in Leipzig, Germany, the city of her birth. She then undertook a concert tour of Europe during which she impressed and befriended several important composers of the Romantic era, including Mendelssohn, Berlioz, Chopin, and Liszt. In Austria, the emperor named her "Royal and Imperial Chamber Virtuosa"—the first time that official title had been given to a Protestant, a teenager, or a woman.

a child prodigy

When she married Robert Schumann in 1840, Clara was an international star, and Robert an unknown. Nevertheless, she took up the dual roles of wife to Robert and mother to the eight children she soon bore him (one died in infancy). She, too, tried her hand at musical composition, writing mostly art songs and character pieces* for piano. But despite her unmistakable talent as a composer, Clara was ambivalent about the capacity of women, herself included, to excel as creative artists (see boxed essay). As her children grew more numerous, her compositions became fewer. Clara's most productive period as a composer of art songs coincided with the very early years of marriage to Robert.

Where Were the Women?

You may have noticed that female composers are poorly represented in this book. We have seen the works of some—Hildegard of Bingen (page 78) and Barbara Strozzi (page 123), for example—and we will meet those of Ellen Taaffe Zwilich later (page 401). But in general, although women have been actively engaged as performers of secular music since the Middle Ages, only rarely, prior to the twentieth century, did they become composers. While the causes of this condition are numerous, one factor stands out above all others: People then had no faith in the capacity, or the propriety, of female creativity. Although a young lady might learn to play the piano in a show of domestic refinement, a woman's function in society was defined as nurturer of children (preferably male) and handmaiden of husband. Fanny Mendelssohn Hensel (1805–1847), the gifted sister of Felix Mendelssohn, was fifteen and considering music as a profession when she received the following directive in a letter from her father: "What you wrote to me about your musical occupations, and in comparison to those of Felix, was rightly thought and expressed. But though music will perhaps become his profession, for you it can and must only be an ornament, never the core of your existence. . . . You must become more steady and collected, and prepare yourself for your real calling, the only calling for a young woman—the state of a housewife."

Fanny Mendelssohn in 1829.
Mary Evans Picture Library/The Image Works

With no encouragement to become a creative force outside the home, little wonder that self-doubt arose among women of talent. As Clara Schumann wrote in her diary in 1839: "I once believed that I possessed creative talent, but I have given up this idea; a woman must not desire to compose. There has never yet been one able to do it. Should I expect to be that one?"

Composing a symphony or a string quartet is a complex process requiring years of schooling in harmony, counterpoint, and instrumentation. Women did not have access to such formal training in composition. For example, the Paris Conservatory was founded in 1793 but did not admit women into the classes in advanced music theory and composition until almost a century later. Women might study piano, but according to a decree of the 1820s they were to enter and leave by a separate door. (Similarly, women painters were not admitted to the state-sponsored Academy of Fine Arts in Paris until 1897. Even then they were barred from nude anatomy classes, instruction crucial to the figural arts, because their presence was thought "morally inappropriate.") Only in those exceptional cases in which a daughter received an intense musical education at home, as did Fanny Mendelssohn and Clara Schumann, did a woman have a fighting chance to become a musical creator.

a Lied in modified strophic form

Clara's "Liebst du um Schönheit" ("If You Love for Beauty"), like her husband's "Dedication" from his *Myrtles*, sets a love poem by Eichendorff, making for a worthwhile comparison between the two *Lieder*. The verse Clara chose comprises four playful stanzas, which set forth three reasons the singer should *not* be loved—not for beauty, youth, or money (all three of which Clara actually possessed)—but one for which she *should* be loved—for love alone. Although the melodic and accompanimental figures presented in the first strophe prevail in the subsequent ones, Clara varies the musical setting on each occasion, producing **modified strophic form,** which in this case can be represented as AA'A"A'''. Example 25-3 shows the melody of strophe 1 and how it is modified in strophe 2. The ever-evolving music gives this art song its remarkable freshness. Did Clara equal or surpass Robert as a composer of *Lieder*? You be the judge.

EXAMPLE 23–5

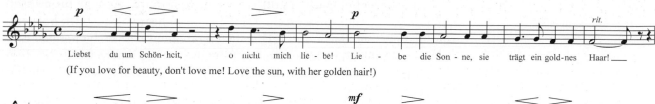

Liebst du um Schön- heit, o nicht mich lie - be! Lie - be die Son - ne, sie trägt ein gold-nes Haar!___
(If you love for beauty, don't love me! Love the sun, with her golden hair!)

Liebst du um Ju - gend, o nicht mich lie - be! Lie-be den Früh - ling der jung ist je - des Jahr!
(If you love for youth, don't love me! Love the spring, which is young each year!)

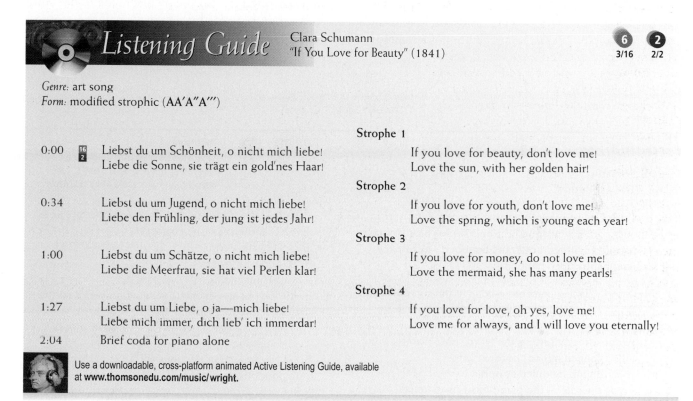

Listening Guide

Clara Schumann
"If You Love for Beauty" (1841)

6 | 3/16   2 | 2/2

Genre: art song
Form: modified strophic (**AA'A"A'''**)

Strophe 1

| 0:00 | Liebst du um Schönheit, o nicht mich liebe!
Liebe die Sonne, sie trägt ein gold'nes Haar! | If you love for beauty, don't love me!
Love the sun, with her golden hair! |

Strophe 2

| 0:34 | Liebst du um Jugend, o nicht mich liebe!
Liebe den Frühling, der jung ist jedes Jahr! | If you love for youth, don't love me!
Love the spring, which is young each year! |

Strophe 3

| 1:00 | Liebst du um Schätze, o nicht mich liebe!
Liebe die Meerfrau, sie hat viel Perlen klar! | If you love for money, do not love me!
Love the mermaid, she has many pearls! |

Strophe 4

| 1:27 | Liebst du um Liebe, o ja—mich liebe!
Liebe mich immer, dich lieb' ich immerdar! | If you love for love, oh yes, love me!
Love me for always, and I will love you eternally! |
| 2:04 | Brief coda for piano alone | |

Use a downloadable, cross-platform animated Active Listening Guide, available at **www.thomsonedu.com/music/wright**.

(For a cumulative Listening Exercise, see the end of this chapter.)

Lives of Tragedy and Fidelity

Robert Schumann was something of a "streak" composer. During the 1830s, he wrote music for solo piano almost exclusively: sonatas, variations, and character pieces. In 1840, he composed almost nothing but art songs. In 1841, he wrote two of his four symphonies, and in 1842, he turned his attention to chamber music, which culminated in a highly regarded piano quintet. The year 1845 saw the composition of the brilliant Piano Concerto in A minor, but after that his creative output diminished.

Robert a "streak" composer

From his earliest years, Robert Schumann had been afflicted with what psychiatrists now call bipolar disorder (likely exacerbated by doses of arsenic he had taken as a young man to cure a case of syphilis). His moods

Robert's mental instability

swung from nervous euphoria to suicidal depression; in some years, he produced a torrent of music, in others, virtually nothing. As time progressed, Schumann's condition worsened. He began to hear voices, both heavenly and hellish, and one morning, pursued by demons within, he jumped off a bridge into the Rhine River. Nearby fishermen pulled him to safety, but from then on, by his own request, he was confined to an asylum, where he died of dementia in 1856.

united in death

Clara Schumann outlived Robert by forty years. She raised the children, and to pay the bills, she resumed her career as a touring piano virtuoso. Dressed in mourning black, she played across Europe into the 1890s. After Robert's death, Clara never composed again and never remarried. Proving that life sometimes imitates art, Clara remained true to the pledge made in her song "If you love for beauty." Today they rest side by side in a small cemetery in Bonn, Germany, two souls exemplifying the spirit of the Romantic age.

Listening Exercise 33

Clara Schumann
"If You Love for Beauty"

3/16   2/2

ThomsonNOW
To take this Listening Exercise online and receive feedback or email answers to your instructor, go to *ThomsonNOW* for this chapter.

This exercise first asks you to answer three specific questions about Clara Schumann's "If You Love for Beauty" and then to consider it in light of Franz Schubert's *Erlking* and Robert Schumann's "Dedication."

1. How does Clara Schumann indulge in the sort of word painting* employed throughout by Franz Schubert?
   a. by composing a brief coda for piano solo
   b. by consistently setting the word "not" ("*nichts*") with a sudden minor chord
   c. by writing in modified strophic form
2. Where is the role of the piano most pronounced?
   a. in strophe 1   b. in strophe 2   c. in strophe 4
3. In the brief coda, does the music draw from the vocal melody heard previously?
   a. yes, because this provides thematic unity to the work
   b. no, because cadential "filler" is needed to end the piece

Now the comparison of art songs by three masters of this genre.

4. Which composer was the youngest at the time he or she wrote his or her song, and which the oldest?
   a. Schubert; R. Schumann
   b. R. Schumann; C. Schumann
   c. C. Schumann; Schubert

5. Which of the three songs is dramatic in nature and involves more than one character?
   a. Schubert's
   b. R. Schumann's
   c. C. Schumann's
6. In the case of the dramatic song, why does it sound dramatic and not lyrical?
   a. There is a single continuous feeling, or mood, throughout.
   b. There are several sections with distinctly contrasting moods.
7. Judging from these songs, was it a convention of the *Lied* to begin and end with the piano alone?
   a. yes   b. no
8. Judging from these songs, lyric poems are often set in which form?
   a. strophic or modified strophic
   b. through-composed
9. Which of the songs is through-composed?
   a. Schubert's
   b. R. Schumann's
   c. C. Schumann's
10. Judging from these three songs, which is your favorite composer? (There is no "correct" answer, but think about the reasons for your preference.)
    a. Schubert
    b. R. Schumann
    c. C. Schumann

Key Words

art song **(263)**   song cycle **(265)**   strophic form **(269)**
Lied (pl. *Lieder*) **(264)**   through-composed   modified strophic
Schubertiad **(265)**   **(269)**   form **(272)**

Early Romantic Music
PROGRAM MUSIC

Chapter
24

The Romantic love of literature stimulated interest not only in the art song but also in program music. Indeed, the nineteenth century can fairly be called the "century of program music." True, there had been earlier isolated examples of program music, in Vivaldi's *The Seasons,* for example (see page 138). But Romantic composers believed that music could be more than pure, abstract sound—that music alone (without a text) could tell a story.

Program music is instrumental music, usually written for symphony orchestra, that seeks to re-create in sound the events and emotions portrayed in some extramusical source: a story, legend, play, novel, or even historical event. The theory of program music rests on the obvious fact that specific musical gestures can evoke particular feelings and associations. A lyrical melody may recall memories of love, harshly dissonant chords might imply conflict, or a sudden trumpet call may suggest the arrival of the hero, for example. By stringing together such musical gestures in a convincing sequence, a composer might tell a story through music. Program music is fully harmonious with the strongly literary spirit of the nineteenth century.

Some Romantic composers, notably Johannes Brahms (1833–1897), resisted the allure of program music and continued to write what came to be called **absolute music**—symphonies, sonatas, quartets, and other instrumental music without extramusical or programmatic references. Most others, however, desiring to convey a clear, coherent message, took advantage of the more overtly narrative character of program music. In 1850, Franz Liszt, a leading advocate of program music, said that a program gave the composer a "means by which to protect the listener against a wrong poetical interpretation and to direct his attention to the poetical idea of the whole." Three of the predominant genres of program music—the program symphony, dramatic overture, and concert overture—were created simply by applying programs to the previously abstract genres of the symphony and overture. A fourth, the symphonic poem, was entirely new to the nineteenth century.

types of program music

- **Program symphony:** a symphony with the usual three, four, or five movements, which together depict a succession of specific events or scenes drawn from an extramusical story or event. Examples include Berlioz's *Symphonie fantastique* (1830) and Liszt's "Faust" Symphony (1857).

- **Dramatic overture** (to an opera or a play): a one-movement work, usually in sonata–allegro form, that encapsulates in music the essential dramatic events of an opera or play. Many overtures became audience favorites and are today performed at concerts without the opera or play. Examples include Rossini's overture to his opera *William Tell* (1829) and Mendelssohn's *Overture* (1826) to Shakespeare's play *A Midsummer Night's Dream*.

- **Concert overture** (similar to the dramatic overture but *not* designed to precede an opera or play): a one-movement work of programmatic content originally intended for the concert hall. Examples include Tchaikovsky's *The 1812 Overture* (1882) and Mendelssohn's *Hebrides Overture* (1830).

- **Symphonic poem** (also called the **tone poem**): a one-movement work for orchestra that gives musical expression to the emotions and events associated with a story, play, political event, or personal experience. Examples include Tchaikovsky's *Romeo and Juliet* (1869; revised 1880), Musorgsky' *Night on Bald Mountain* (1867), and Strauss's *Thus Spoke Zarathustra* (1896). In fact, there is little difference between the symphonic poem and the concert overture: both are one-movement orchestral works with programmatic content intended for the concert hall.

Two of the best composers of descriptive music were Hector Berlioz and Felix Mendelssohn.

HECTOR BERLIOZ (1803–1869)

Hector Berlioz was one of the most original figures in the history of music (Fig. 24–1). He was born in 1803 near the mountain city of Grenoble, France, the son of a local doctor. As a youth, Berlioz studied mainly the sciences and ancient Roman literature. Although local tutors taught him to play the flute and guitar, he had no systematic training in music theory or composition and little exposure to the music of the great masters. Among the major composers of the nineteenth century, he was the only one without fluency at the keyboard. He never studied piano and could do no more than bang out a few chords; yet he would become one of the greatest orchestrators of all time.

At the age of seventeen, Berlioz was sent off to Paris to study medicine, his father's profession. For two years he pursued a program in the physical sciences, earning a degree in 1821. But Berlioz found the dissecting table repulsive and the allure of the opera house and concert hall irresistible. After a period of soul searching, and the inevitable falling-out with his parents over the choice of a career, he vowed to become "no doctor or apothecary but a great composer."

His dismayed father immediately cut off his living stipend, leaving young Berlioz to ponder how he might support himself while studying composition at the Paris Conservatory (the French national school of music). Other composers had relied on teaching as a means to earn a regular income, but Berlioz, with no particular skill at any instrument, was not qualified to give music lessons. Instead, he turned to music criticism, writing reviews and articles for literary journals. Berlioz was the first composer to earn a livelihood as a music critic, and it was criticism, not composition, that remained his primary source of income for the rest of his life.

FIGURE 24–1

Hector Berlioz at the age of twenty-nine.

Scala/Art Resource, NY

Perhaps it was inevitable that Berlioz would turn to writing about music, for in his mind, there was always a connection between music and the written word. As a young man, he read Lord Byron's *Childe Harold's Pilgrimage* (see page 254) and Goethe's *Faust*, works that inspired his viola concerto *Harold in Italy* (1834) and his dramatic symphony *The Damnation of Faust* (1846). But of all literary influences, none was greater than that of Shakespeare.

Shakespeare's dramas first burst upon the literary scene of continental Europe early in the nineteenth century. For Berlioz, the experience was life altering: "Shakespeare, coming upon me unawares, struck me like a thunderbolt. The lightning flash of that discovery revealed to me at a stroke the whole heaven of art." Berlioz devoured Shakespeare's plays and based musical compositions on four of them: *The Tempest, King Lear, Hamlet,* and *Romeo and Juliet.* The best-known of Berlioz's tributes to the Bard, *Romeo and Juliet,* is a five-movement program symphony* in which a chorus and solo voices intermittently paraphrase Shakespeare's own words. The common denominator in the art of Shakespeare and Berlioz is range of expression. Just as no dramatist before Shakespeare had portrayed the full spectrum of human emotions on the stage, so no composer before Berlioz undertook to create the widest range of moods through sound.

To depict wild swings of mood musically, Berlioz called for enormous orchestral and choral forces—hundreds and hundreds of performers (see page 260 and Figure 24–2). He also experimented with new instruments: the **ophicleide** (an early form of the tuba), the **English horn** (a low oboe), the harp (an ancient instrument now brought into the symphony orchestra for the first time), the **cornet** (a brass instrument with valves, borrowed from the military band), and even the newly invented saxophone. In 1843, he wrote a treatise on musical instruments, one still used today as a textbook in orchestration classes at music conservatories around the world.

Berlioz's approach to musical form was equally iconoclastic and forward looking; he rarely used such standard forms as sonata–allegro or theme and variations. His French compatriots called his compositions "bizarre" and "monstrous," and thought him something of a madman. Subscribing to the adage "No man is a prophet in his own land," Berlioz took his progressive music to London, Vienna, Prague, and even Moscow, introducing such works as *Symphonie fantastique, Damnation of Faust,* and *Romeo et Juliet.* He died in Paris in 1869, isolated and embittered, the little recognition he received in his native France having come too late to boost his career or self-esteem.

Berlioz and Shakespeare

new instruments

Symphonie fantastique (1830)

Berlioz's most celebrated work, then and now, is his *Symphonie fantastique,* perhaps the single most radical example of musical Romanticism. Its form and orchestration are revolutionary. But what is more, it tells in music a vivid story and, as such, is the first complete program symphony*. The story surrounding the creation of the descriptive program of the work is as fascinating as the piece itself.

In 1827, a troupe of English actors came to Paris to present Shakespeare's *Hamlet* and *Romeo and Juliet.* Berlioz, of course, had read some of Shakespeare's plays in French translation, but he was eager to see these works performed on stage. Though he understood little English, he was overwhelmed by what he saw. The human insights, touching beauty, and onstage action in Shakespeare's work far surpassed the virtues found in traditional French theater. Not only

FIGURE 24–2

A caricature of Berlioz conducting in mid-nineteenth-century Paris, in what became known as "monster concerts" because of the huge forces the composer required. Berlioz would have liked several hundred performers for the premiere of his *Symphonie fantastique* in 1830, but the printed program suggests that he had to settle for about one hundred.

Private Collection/Archives Charmet/The Bridgeman Art Library

FIGURE 24–3

The actress Harriet Smithson became an obsession for Berlioz and the source of inspiration for his *Symphonie fantastique*. Eventually, Berlioz did meet and marry Smithson. Today they lie side by side in the cemetery of Montmartre in Paris.

was Berlioz smitten by Shakespeare, but he also fell in love with the leading lady who played Ophelia to Hamlet and Juliet to Romeo, one Harriet Smithson (Fig. 24–3). Like a lovesick adolescent, Berlioz swooned at her sight and wrote such violently passionate letters that the frightened starlet refused even to meet the student composer. Eventually, his ardor cooled—for a time he even became engaged to someone else. But the experience of an all-consuming love, the despair of rejection, and the vision of darkness and possible death furnished the stimulus—and story line—for an unusually imaginative symphony.

Berlioz composed his *Symphonie fantastique* in five movements instead of the usual four, an arrangement that may have been inspired by Shakespeare's use of a five-act format. Movements 1 and 5 balance each other in length and substance, as do 2 and 4, leaving the leisurely third movement as the center of the work. But symmetry is not the only element holding the symphony together. Berlioz creates a single melody that reappears as a unifying force, movement after movement, a total of eight times during the symphony. This melody, which represents the protagonist's beloved within the story, became, like Harriet Smithson, the composer's obsession. Berlioz called this musical fixation his ***idée fixe*** ("fixed idea"). As the protagonist's feelings about the beloved change from movement to movement, so the *idée fixe* is transformed. The composer alters the pitches slightly and assigns the theme to different instruments, each of which adds its own tone color and feeling. To make sure the listener knows what these feelings are, Berlioz prepared a written program to be read as the music was performed. It tells the story of unrequited love, attempted suicide, imaginary murder, and hellish revenge.

FIRST MOVEMENT: REVERIES, PASSIONS

> Program: A young musician . . . sees for the first time a woman who embodies all the charms of the ideal being he has imagined in his dreams. . . . The subject of the first movement is the passage from this state of melancholy reverie, interrupted by a few moments of joy, to that of delirious passion, with movements of fury, jealousy, and its return to tenderness, tears, and religious consolation.

A slow introduction ("this state of melancholy reverie") prepares the way for the first vision of the beloved, who is represented by the first appearance of the main theme, the *idée fixe*.

EXAMPLE 24–1

The movement unfolds in something akin to sonata–allegro form. The "recapitulation," however, does not so much repeat the *idée fixe* as it does transform the melody to reflect the artist's feelings of sorrow and tenderness.

SECOND MOVEMENT: A BALL

> The artist finds himself . . . in the midst of the tumult of a party.

idée fixe *transformed*

A lilting waltz now begins, but it is interrupted by the unexpected appearance of the *idée fixe*, its rhythm changed to accommodate the triple meter of the waltz. Four harps add a graceful accompaniment when the waltz returns, and toward the end, there is even a lovely solo for cornet. The sequence of waltz–*idée fixe*–waltz creates ternary form.

THIRD MOVEMENT: SCENE IN THE COUNTRY

> Finding himself one evening in the country, the artist hears in the distance two shepherds piping. . . . He reflects upon his isolation and hopes that soon he will no longer be alone.

The dialogue between the shepherds is presented by an English horn and an oboe, the latter played offstage to give the effect of a distant response. The unexpected appearance of the *idée fixe* in the woodwinds suggests that the artist has hopes of winning his beloved. But has she falsely encouraged him? The shepherd's tune recurs, but the oboe doesn't respond. To the lonely petition of the English horn, we now hear only the empty rumble of distant thunder in the timpani. The call for love goes unanswered.

FOURTH MOVEMENT: MARCH TO THE SCAFFOLD

> Having realized that his love goes unrecognized, the artist poisons himself with opium. The dose of the narcotic, too weak to kill him, plunges him into a sleep accompanied by the most horrible visions. He dreams that he has killed the one he loved, that he is condemned, led to the scaffold, and now witnesses his own execution.

This drug-induced nightmare centers on the march to the scaffold where the artist is to be executed. The steady beat of the low strings and the muffled bass drum sound the steps of the procession. Near the end the image of the beloved returns in the clarinet, only to be suddenly cut off by a *fortissimo* crash by the full orchestra. The guillotine has fallen.

FIFTH MOVEMENT: DREAM OF THE WITCHES' SABBATH

> He sees himself at the witches' sabbath surrounded by a troop of frightful shadows, sorcerers, and monsters of all sorts, gathered for his funeral. Strange noises, groans, bursts of laughter, distant cries echoed by others. The beloved melody returns again, but it has lost its noble, modest character and is now only base, trivial, and grotesque. An outburst of joy at her arrival; she joins in the devilish orgy.

In this monstrous finale, Berlioz creates his personal vision of hell (Fig. 24–4). A crowd of witches and other ghouls is summoned to dance around the corpse of the artist on its way to the inferno. Eerie sounds are produced by the strings, using mutes, and by the high woodwinds and French horn, playing glissandos*. A piercing clarinet enters with a horrid parody of the *idée fixe* as Harriet Smithson, now in the frightful garb of a wicked old hag, comes on stage.

Museo Lazaro Galdiano, Madrid/Giraudon/The Bridgeman Art Library

FIGURE 24–4

Witches' Sabbath by Francisco de Goya (1746–1828) bears the same title as the finale of Berlioz's *Symphonie fantastique*. Both create images of the bizarre and macabre so dear to the hearts of Romantic artists.

EXAMPLE 24–2

She is greeted by a joyous *fortissimo* outburst by the full assembly as all proceed to dance to the now perverted *idée fixe*. Suddenly, the music becomes ominously quiet and, in one of the most strikingly original moments in all of classical music, great Gothic church bells are heard. Against this solemn backdrop sounds the burial hymn of the medieval Church, the **Dies irae,** played by ophicleides (tubas) and bassoons. (In more recent years, the *Dies irae* has

Dies irae: a chant from the medieval church

been used to signal doom and gloom in three "horror" films: *Nightmare Before Christmas, Sleeping with the Enemy,* and *The Shining*.)

EXAMPLE 24–3

[Di - es   i - rae di - es   il - la sol - vet   sae - clum   in   fa - vil - la]
[Day of anger, day of wrath, on which the ages will be changed to ash]

Not only is the orchestration sensational, the musical symbolism is sacrilegious. Just as the painter Goya parodies the Catholic Mass in his *Witches' Sabbath*—making babies serve as communion wafers (see Fig. 24–4)—so Berlioz creates a mockery of one of the most venerable Gregorian chants of the Catholic Church. First, the *Dies irae* is played by the horns twice as fast (a process called rhythmic **diminution**). Then the sacred melody is transformed into a jazzed-up dance tune played by a shrill, high clarinet, the entire scene now becoming a blasphemous black mass.

Dies irae distorted

EXAMPLE 24–4

As the ceremony proceeds, the witches begin to dance. But they do so in a strange way: they enter one by one and create a fugato*, a fugal passage within a symphonic movement. This successive entry of more and more voices, or dancing witches, creates the effect of a growing tumult around the corpse of the artist.

EXAMPLE 24–5

A climax is reached as the witches' theme, or subject, played by the strings, as well as the *Dies irae* melody, played by the brasses and woodwinds, sound together in different keys, a bizarre example of **double counterpoint.** Stranger still is the sound that follows, for Berlioz instructs the violins to play *col legno* (with the wood)—to strike the strings, not with the usual front of the bow, but with the wooden back, creating a noise evocative of the crackling of hellfire.

col legno: a strange effect

To the audience that first heard the *Symphonie fantastique* on December 5, 1830, all of this must have seemed incomprehensible: new instruments, novel playing effects, simultaneous melodies in different keys, and a form that is not traditional, like sonata–allegro or rondo, but grows out of the events in a soap-opera-like program. But it all works. Here is a rare example in the history of ideas in which a creator thinks "outside the box" of conventional art; yet he does so in a way that produces a wholly integrated, unified, and ultimately satisfying work. The separate effects may be revolutionary and momentarily shocking, but they are consistent and logical among themselves when sub-

creating "outside the box"

The Real End of the Program

I n Berlioz's programmatic *Symphonie fantastique*, art imitates life—he constructs a musical narrative to mirror events (real and imagined) in his young life. But how did the story of Berlioz and his beloved Harriet Smithson really end? In truth, Berlioz did meet and marry Harriet, but the two lived miserably together ever after. He complained about her increasing weight, she about his infidelities. Harriet died in 1854 and was buried in a small graveyard in Paris. In 1864, that cemetery was to be closed and the remains of all the deceased transferred to a new, larger burial ground. It fell to widower Berlioz to remove Harriet's corpse to the new cemetery, as he recounts in his memoirs:

> One dark, gloomy morning I set forth alone for the sad spot. A municipal officer was waiting, to be present at the disinterment. The grave had already been opened, and on my arrival the

The Parisian painter Eugène Delacroix's depiction of the graveyard scene in Hamlet *(1829).*

gravedigger jumped in. The coffin was still entire, though it had been ten years underground; the lid alone was injured by the damp. The man, instead of lifting it out, tore away the rotten lid, which cracked with a hideous noise, and brought the contents of the coffin to light. He then bent down, took up the crowned, decayed head of the poor *Ophelia*—and laid it in a new coffin awaiting it at the edge of the grave. Then, bending down a second time, he lifted with difficulty the headless trunk and limbs—a blackish mass to which the shroud still adhered, resembling a heap of pitch in a damp sack. I remember the dull sound . . . and the odor. (Hector Berlioz, *Memoirs*)

Berlioz had begun by playing Romeo to Harriet's Juliet, and ended by playing Hamlet to her Ophelia. He cast his music, and his life, in terms of Shakespearean drama.

Musée du Louvre/Erich Lessing/Art Resource, NY

sumed in the total artistic concept. Had Berlioz never written another note of music, he would still be justly famous for this single masterpiece of Romantic invention.

Listening Guide

Hector Berlioz
Symphonie fantastique (1830)
Fifth movement, Dream of the Witches' Sabbath

6 3/17–18   **2** 2/3–4

Genre: program symphony

0:00	**17/3**	"Strange noises, groans, bursts of laughter, distant cries" high and low
1:28		Grotesquely transformed *idée fixe* in shrill clarinet
1:36		Joyful, *fortissimo* outburst by full orchestra welcoming now-ugly beloved
1:46		Witches begin to dance to newly grotesque *idée fixe*, bassoons add raucous counterpoint (1:55)
2:39		Sinister transition
2:59		Funeral bells sound
3:26		*Dies irae* heard in tubas and bassoons

(continued)

3:48		French horns and trombones play *Dies irae* twice as fast
3:58		Woodwinds pervert *Dies irae* chant
4:04		*Dies irae*, its diminution, and its perversion continue
4:30		Tubas and bassoons play *Dies irae* with bass drum reverberation
5:04		Introduction to witches' dance; crescendo
5:21		Witches' dance (fugato) begins with four entries of subject

5:47	**18/4**	0:00	Fugal episode
6:08		0:21	Three more entries of subject
6:24		0:37	More strange sounds and cries (transition out of fugato)
7:02		1:19	Fragments of the *Dies irae*
7:23		1:36	Witches' dance (fugue subject) grows to rapid climax, then *fortissimo* syncopation (2:04)
8:08		2:21	Witches' dance and *Dies irae* combined; trumpets now added
8:37		2:50	Violins use wooden back of bow (*col legno**) to produce crackling sound
8:57		3:10	*Fortissimo* chords
9:15		3:28	Fleeting recall of *Dies irae*
9:33		3:46	More chords with striking harmonic shift
9:37		3:50	Final cadential fanfare

Use a downloadable, cross-platform animated Active Listening Guide, available at **www.thomsonedu.com/music/wright**.

Listening Exercise 34

Berlioz
Symphonie fantastique

3/17–18   2/3–4

ThomsonNOW™
To take this Listening Exercise online and receive feedback or email answers to your instructor, go to *ThomsonNOW* for this chapter.

Imagine that you were among the audience in Paris on December 5, 1830, when Berlioz's *Symphonie fantastique* was first performed. If you had been a dedicated concertgoer up to that time, you might have heard one or two of the latest symphonies of Beethoven. This would have been the extent of your exposure to "radical" new music. How would you have reacted? The following set of questions asks you to focus upon several aspects of orchestration and form in this astonishingly original work.

1. (0:00–0:23) The opening moments sound eerie because the high strings create "special effects" by means of special string techniques. What two distinctive string techniques are employed?
   a. first pizzicato, then tremolo
   b. first tremolo, then pizzicato
   c. first tremolo, then ostinato

2. (1:28–1:36) The *idée fixe* returns, now transformed. The passage sounds weird because of Berlioz's unusual orchestration. What do you hear?
   a. *idée fixe* in high clarinet against pounding bass drum
   b. *idée fixe* in oboe against pounding timpani

3. (3:26–3:47) Among the instruments that introduce the *Dies irae* is one that Berlioz introduced into the symphony orchestra. Which is it?
   a. piccolo   b. tuba   c. cornet   d. high clarinet

4. (3:48–3:58) The French horns now play the *Dies irae* melody twice as fast as before. What is this sort of reduction in duration in music called?
   a. augmentation   b. diminution
   c. contraction   d. discount

5. (5:21–5:46) Now the fugato begins. Its structure is made clear, in part, because the composer cuts off the subject each time so as to announce the next entry. He does this by means of a burst of syncopated chords in the brasses. How many times does this occur?
   a. twice   b. three times   c. four times

6. (1:17–1:31) Which instruments play a reminiscence of the *Dies irae* chant?
   a. cellos and double basses   b. bells   c. tubas

7. (2:21–2:42) Now the *Dies irae* and the witches' dance (fugue subject) are heard simultaneously. How are they orchestrated?

a. *Dies irae* in violins, witches' dance in trumpets
b. *Dies irae* in trumpets, witches' dance in violins

8. (2:21–2:42) When two independent themes or motives sound simultaneously, what process results?
  a. multiple counterpoint
  b. double counterpoint
  c. double play

9. (2:50–3:04) As the strings produce the crackling sound by playing *col legno* (with the wood of the bow and not the horsehair), a melody is heard in the woodwinds. Which is it?

a. the witches' dance (fugue subject)
b. the *idée fixe*
c. the *Dies irae* chant

10. Having now heard a piece of Romantic program music, do you think it is advantageous to have a program? What might be a *disadvantage* of listening to music for which there is a program?
  a. While it is easier to follow the composer's intent, your imagination is restricted; there is only one way to hear the music.
  b. It is easier to get lost with program music than it is with absolute music.

FELIX MENDELSSOHN (1809–1847)

Berlioz was a child of the Romantic age: He tried suicide at least twice, ran around Italy with a gang of bandits (in imitation of Lord Byron), and married an image, an ideal of a woman, with disastrous consequences. Felix Mendelssohn (Fig. 24–5) was an altogether different personality, anything but the stereotype of the rebellious, self-absorbed, struggling artist.

Mendelssohn was born in 1809 into a prosperous, indeed wealthy, Jewish family. His father was a banker, and his grandfather, Moses Mendelssohn (1726–1786), was a noted philosopher. At the family home in Berlin, young Felix had every advantage: He studied languages, literature, and philosophy with private tutors, as well as painting, dancing, riding, and even gymnastics. In 1816, Mendelssohn's parents had their four children baptized Christians, partly so they might enjoy full legal equality and move freely in all social circles. Indeed, their home became a gathering place for artists and intellectuals of all sorts: the poet Heine, the philosopher Hegel, and the geographer Humboldt (discoverer of the Humboldt current) were all frequent guests. Because Felix had shown extraordinary musical talent, he was not only given piano lessons but also provided with a small orchestra on Sunday afternoons to try out his youthful compositions. At the age of sixteen, he composed a masterpiece, his octet for strings. The next year (1826) witnessed an equally astonishing work, the *Overture to A Midsummer Night's Dream*. Mendelssohn was even more precocious as a composer than either Mozart or Schubert.

Taking advantage of his privileged station in life, Mendelssohn spent the years 1829–1835 traveling across Europe to discover its natural beauty and to meet the great artists of the day. He walked across most of Switzerland, sketching and painting as he went. He met Goethe in Weimar; Berlioz in Rome; Liszt, Chopin, and the painter Delacroix (see Fig. 25–1) in Paris; and the novelist Sir Walter Scott near Edinburgh. These itinerant years ended in the spring of 1835 when he was appointed musical director of the **Gewandhaus Orchestra** in Leipzig, Germany (Figs. 24–6 and 24–7). Mendelssohn led this ensemble for a dozen years, from 1835 until 1847, when he died prematurely of a stroke at the age of thirty-eight.

During his tenure in Leipzig, Felix Mendelssohn changed the very purpose of the symphony orchestra. He established the modern notion that a symphony exists not only to promote contemporary music but also to preserve a

a privileged upbringing

FIGURE 24–5
Felix Mendelssohn in 1829 at the age of twenty.

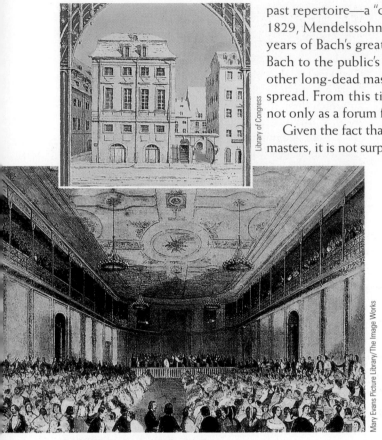

FIGURE 24–6 AND 24–7

(top) Exterior of the Gewandhaus in Leipzig, Germany, as depicted by Felix Mendelssohn. In addition to being a musician and composer and speaking four languages fluently, Mendelssohn was a gifted painter, his preferred medium being watercolor. (bottom) A concert in progress, c1840, in the Gewandhaus, the hall where Mendelssohn, Liszt, Berlioz, and Clara and Robert Schumann frequently performed.

recreating Shakespeare's play in music

past repertoire—a "canon" of musical masterpieces (see page 255). In Berlin in 1829, Mendelssohn had mounted the first performance in almost a hundred years of Bach's great *St. Matthew Passion*, thereby bringing the long-forgotten Bach to the public's attention. Now in Leipzig, he programmed the works of other long-dead masters, among them Handel, Haydn, and Mozart. The idea spread. From this time forward, a concert by a symphony orchestra served not only as a forum for new or recent works but also as a museum for old ones.

Given the fact that Mendelssohn revived the music of the eighteenth-century masters, it is not surprising that his own compositions are the most conservative, the most "classical," of the great Romantic composers. His harmonies are colorful but not revolutionary; his orchestration distinctive but not shocking—a light, dancing string sound is his hallmark; and his use of form is traditional, as seen in his heavy reliance on sonata–allegro form. Never does he indulge in startling outbursts of sound. The classical ideals of unity, grace, and formal balance predominate.

What, then, makes Mendelssohn a musical Romantic? Program music. Nature, travel, and literature provided stimuli for many of his creations. A trip to Italy in 1830–1831 gave rise to his "Italian" Symphony, just as a lengthy sojourn in Scotland a year earlier had planted the seeds for the "Scottish" Symphony. On this same northern voyage, he visited the windswept Hebrides Islands and soon captured the spirit of the churning sea and rocky coast in his *Hebrides Overture* (1830). Mendelssohn commented on the difficulty he faced when trying to harness a raging ocean within the confines of sonata–allegro form: "The whole development section smells more of counterpoint than of blubber, gulls, and salted cod."

As to literary influences, he heard the voices of Goethe and Shakespeare most clearly. To Goethe's *Faust* the composer owed the inspiration for the scherzo of his early Octet (1825) and several later orchestral works. And to Shakespeare, of course, can be traced the genesis of the music for *A Midsummer Night's Dream*.

Overture to *A Midsummer Night's Dream* (1826)

Mendelssohn began to compose, or "to dream *A Midsummer Night's Dream*," as he says, during July 1826, when he was an impressionable youth of seventeen. His aim was to transform the romantic fantasy of Shakespeare's play into an independent dramatic overture. Some years later, in 1843, he was commissioned by the king of Prussia to create **incidental music** (musical interludes inserted within the performance) for a production of the play planned for Berlin. Among these incidental pieces is his famous *Wedding March*—originally written to accompany the marriage of the characters Theseus and Hippolyta, but now traditionally played at weddings as the recessional march.

To enter fully into the enchanted world of Mendelssohn's *Overture to A Midsummer Night's Dream*, we must know something of the play—the program that inspired it (Fig. 24–8). The drama unfolds mostly in an enchanted forest on a midsummer evening. There are three separate groups of characters: the fairies, foremost among whom is Puck; pairs of lovers living under the rule of Duke Theseus; and a group of common craftsmen, led by the ass-like Bottom. Separate and distinct musical styles make the various characters identifiable and their interaction easy to hear. At the same time, the music unfolds in sonata–allegro form—typical of Mendelssohn the "classical Romantic." There is a slow four-chord introduction, a first theme (the dancing fairy music), a transition (royal music of the court of Duke Theseus), a second theme (the lovers' music), and a closing theme group (the craftsmen's music and hunting calls). The fairies dominate the development section, and in the coda (or epilogue), they have the last word, just as in Shakespeare's play. Mendelssohn's own thoughts best describe the ending: "After everything has been satisfactorily settled and the principal players have joyfully left the stage, the fairies follow them, bless the house, and disappear with the dawn. So ends the play, and so, too, my overture."

FIGURE 24-8

Oberon, Titania, and Puck with Fairies Dancing, a depiction of a scene from Shakespeare's *A Midsummer Night's Dream* by the English artist and poet William Blake (1757–1827).

Listening Guide

Felix Mendelssohn
Overture to A Midsummer Night's Dream (1826)

6
3/19–21

Genre: dramatic overture
Form: sonata–allegro

	Program	Musical Events
EXPOSITION		
0:00 ⑲	Introduction to enchantment	Four sustained chords in winds (introduction)
0:20	Fairies' music	Rapid, light, staccato notes in violins (first theme)
1:04	Duke Theseus and his court	Full orchestra *fortissimo* (transition)
1:34		Fairies' music mixes into transition
2:08	Lovers' music	Quiet melody in woodwinds, and strings grows more passionate (second theme)
3:00	Bottom's music	Raucous motive sounds like braying of donkey (closing theme, part 1)
3:22	Hunting calls of regal party	Fanfares in brasses and woodwinds (closing theme, part 2)

(continued)

DEVELOPMENT

3:46	20	0:00	Fairies' music developed	Music of fairies (first theme) worked out in different keys
4:22		0:36	French horn blasts	
4:52		1:06	Fairies' music extended	String pizzicato and string tremolo
5:27		1:41	Lysander and Hermia sleep	Ritard, soft string sound, music seems to come to stop

RECAPITULATION

5:52	21	0:00	Return to enchantment	Four introductory chords return
6:14		0:22	Fairies' music	Dancing fairies' music returns (first theme), but transition is eliminated
6:58		1:06	Lovers' music	Lyrical melody in woodwinds and strings (second theme) as before
7:47		1:55	Bottom's music	Again raucous *fortissimo* music of ass (closing theme, part 1)
8:52		3:00	Royal hunting party	Fanfares (closing theme, part 2) serve as ending to recapitulation

CODA

9:16		3:24	Epilogue by fairy Puck	Light, quick music of fairies; toward end, Duke Theseus and four opening chords recalled

 Use a downloadable, cross-platform animated Active Listening Guide, available at **www.thomsonedu.com/music/wright.**

Key Words

program music (**275**)
absolute music (**275**)
program symphony (**275**)
dramatic overture (**276**)
concert overture (**276**)

symphonic (tone) poem (**276**)
ophicleide (**277**)
English horn (**277**)
cornet (**277**)
idée fixe (**278**)
Dies irae (**279**)

diminution (**280**)
double counterpoint (**280**)
col legno (**280**)
Gewandhaus Orchestra (**283**)
incidental music (**284**)

Chapter 25

Early Romantic Music
PIANO MUSIC

Just as the symphony orchestra grew in size and power during the nineteenth century, so too did the piano, propelled by the new technology of the Industrial Revolution. While still encased in an exterior wooden "shell," the piano's internal frame, previously wooden as well, was now made of cast iron, allowing for greater tension on the strings. This cast-iron frame supported thicker steel strings, which greatly increased the volume of sound and allowed the pianist to pound away on the keyboard without breaking the strings. (Recall that Beethoven's forceful playing had been known to wreak havoc on the older wooden-frame pianos—see Chapter 21.) But not only could the Romantic piano support louder and more aggressive playing, it also facilitated a gentler, more lyrical style as well; its hammers were covered with felt, which allowed the instrument to "sing" with a mellow tone, in contrast to the "ping" of the pianos of Mozart's day. Like the growing nineteenth-century orchestra, the piano could now produce both a very loud sound (*fortissimo*) and a very soft one (*pianissimo*). The instrument's range increased as well: whereas the piano in the 1790s encompassed five octaves, it spanned seven by the 1840s. By mid-century, the piano was equipped with two pedals, operated by the performer's feet. On the right side was the **sustaining pedal,** which enabled strings to continue to sound after the performer had lifted his or her hand from the corresponding keys. On the left was the **soft pedal,** which softened the dynamic level by shifting the position of the hammers relative to the strings. Finally, in the 1850s, the Steinway company of New York began **cross-stringing** the piano, overlaying the lowest-sounding strings across those of the middle register, and thereby producing a richer, more homogeneous sound. By the mid-nineteenth century, all the essential features of the modern piano were in place—the essential design of the piano has not changed in 150 years.

greater size and complexity of the piano

As the piano grew larger and more expressive, it became something of a home entertainment center, a place where the family could gather to play and sing before the days of television and electronic entertainment. Every aspiring middle-class home had to have a piano, both for family enjoyment and as a status symbol—the "high art" instrument in the parlor signified to visitors that they had entered a "cultured" home. Parents made sure their children, especially the girls, received lessons, and publishers, eager to profit from the vogue for the piano, turned out reams of sheet music for pianists of all skill levels.

the piano: symbol of a cultured home

Spurred by the sudden popularity of the piano, a host of virtuoso performers set upon the concert halls of Europe with fingers blazing. What they played was often more a display of technical fireworks—rapid octaves, racing chromatic scales, thundering chords—than of musical substance. Happily, however, several of the greatest piano virtuosos of the nineteenth century were also gifted composers.

FIGURE 25–1

A superbly Romantic portrait of Chopin by Eugène Delacroix. It was originally painted with Chopin next to George Sand (see Fig. 25–2). But in 1870, a vandal slashed the double portrait, thereby (unintentionally) creating two canvases.

FRÉDÉRIC CHOPIN (1810–1849)

In the compositions of Frédéric Chopin (Fig. 25–1), the piano and its music have their most perfect union. This "poet of the piano," as he was called, was born near Warsaw, Poland, of a French father and a Polish mother. The father taught at an elite secondary school for the sons of Polish nobility, and it was there that Frédéric not only gained an excellent general education but acquired aristocratic friends and tastes as well. He then moved on to the newly founded Warsaw Conservatory, where, between 1826 and 1829, he concentrated on the study of piano and composition. It was during this period that he composed his first major work, a brilliant set of variations for piano and orchestra on Mozart's duet "Là ci darem la mano" ("Give me your hand") from *Don Giovanni* (on the duet, see page 227). After this success, Warsaw seemed too small, too provincial, for a young man of Chopin's musical talents. So, in 1830, he departed to seek his fortune in Vienna and Paris. The next year

FIGURE 25-2

Novelist Aurore Dudevant (George Sand) by Eugène Delacroix. Both the painter Delacroix and the composer Chopin often stayed at her summer estate in Nohant in the south of France.

Poland's fight for freedom was crushed by Russian troops, and Chopin never returned to his homeland.

After an unsuccessful year in Vienna, the twenty-one-year-old Chopin arrived in Paris in September 1831. His inaugural concerts caught Parisians' fancy, and his imaginative playing soon became the stuff of legends. But Chopin was not cut out for the life of the public virtuoso. He was introverted, physically slight, and somewhat sickly. Consequently, he chose to play at private *musicales* (musical evenings) in the homes of the aristocracy and to give lessons for a fee only the very rich could afford. "I have been introduced all around the highest circles," he said within a year of his arrival. "I hobnob with ambassadors, princes, and ministers. I can't imagine what miracle is responsible for all this since I really haven't done anything to bring it about."

In October 1836, Chopin met Baroness Aurore Dudevant (1803–1876), a writer who under the pen name of **George Sand** poured forth a steady stream of Romantic novels roughly akin to our Silhouette Romances (Fig. 25–2). Sand, a bisexual, was an ardent individualist with a predeliction for men's clothing and cigars (see cover and Fig. 25–2). Six years Chopin's senior, she became his lover and protector. Many of the composer's best works were written at Nohant, her summer residence 150 miles south of Paris. After their relationship ended in 1847, Chopin undertook a taxing concert tour of England and Scotland. While this improved his depleted finances, it weakened his delicate health. He died in Paris of tuberculosis at the age of thirty-nine.

Mazurka in B♭ major, Opus 7, No. 1 (1832)

Although Frédéric Chopin spent most of his adult life in France, he maintained strong emotional ties to Poland, and his compositions frequently drew upon musical idioms of his native land. Indeed, the expatriate composer became something of a national hero in Poland, his music embraced as a way of preserving a national heritage.

mazurka: a folk dance from Poland

As a youth, Chopin had vacationed with his family in the Polish countryside, where he was introduced to such traditional Polish dances as the mazurka and the polonaise. The **mazurka** is a fast dance in triple meter with an accent on the second beat. Its melody draws on native folk tunes, some of them of Jewish ancestry, and its harmony suggests the static droning of a village bagpipe. Chopin's Mazurka in B♭ major begins much like a triple-meter waltz, except that the strong accent often falls on beat 2, not beat 1. Yet midway through (in section **C**), the mode switches from major to minor, a strange scale enters in the melody, and a drone appears in the accompanying bass. We have been transported from the world of the Parisian salon to a Polish village, from the familiar to the foreign. In Chopin's day, these mazurkas were experienced as music or as dance: the Parisians listened, the Poles danced.

 *Listening Guide*   Frédéric Chopin
Mazurka in B♭ major, Opus 7, No. 1 (1832)

6

3/22

Form: **ABACA** (with repeats)

0:00	22	Rapid dance with triple-meter accompaniment and accent on second beat (**A**)
0:16		Repeat of **A**
0:34		Lyrical interlude (**B**)

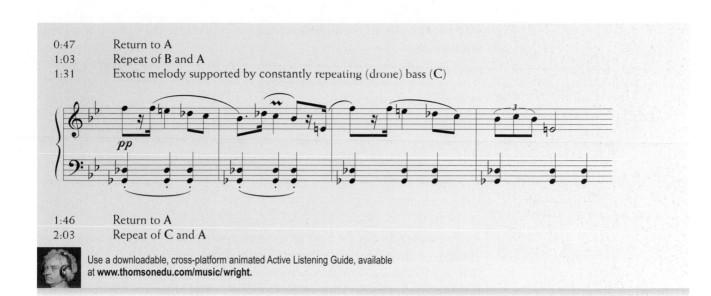

Chopin was a rarity among Romantic composers—he wrote only for the piano or ensemble pieces (including songs) in which he made the piano figure prominently. His works for solo piano include—in addition to his mazurkas and polonaise—three piano sonatas, a set of twenty-four preludes (brief character pieces, one in each of the major and minor keys), twenty-four etudes (technical studies), and twenty-one nocturnes. Far better than the other genres for piano, the dream-like nocturnes embody the essence of musical Romanticism.

Nocturne in C♯ minor, Opus 27, No. 1 (1835)

A **nocturne** (night piece) is a slow, dreamy genre of piano music that came into favor in the 1820s and 1830s. It suggests moonlit nights, romantic longing, and a certain painful melancholy, all evoked through bittersweet melodies and softly strumming harmonies. To set a nocturnal mood in his Nocturne in C♯ minor, Chopin begins with a tonic C♯ minor chord spun out as an arpeggio in the bass, like a harp played in the moonlight. The melody (**A**) enters in minor but immediately turns to major, by means of an added sharp. As the opening melody repeats again and again in the course of the work, so too the harmony shifts expressively, bending back and forth from minor to major, from dark to light. This twisting of mode is one way that the composer creates the "bittersweet" feeling.

dreamy piano music

EXAMPLE 25–1

Soon the opening melody breaks off and a more passionate, agitated mood takes hold. A new theme (**B**) enters and the tempo increases. The bass now begins a long, mostly chromatic ascent. Here Chopin joins a long list of composers who have employed rising chromaticism to create a feeling of anxiety and rising tension.

EXAMPLE 25–2

A climax is reached at the peak of this line, emphasized by a remarkable chord change—a chord with four sharps is immediately followed by one with four flats (see Ex. 22–2). As mentioned earlier (page 257), the sudden juxtaposition of such distant chords creates bold harmonic shifts of the sort favored by Romantic composers as they strove to fashion a new, more colorful harmonic language. Now a third melody (**C**) enters, which eventually gives way to **A** by means of a descending, recitative-like passage.

The return to **A** is especially rich and satisfying, as the harp-like accompaniment and plaintive melody seem to rise from the depths of the fading bass. Chopin's simple formal plan is now clear: statement-digression-return, each section with its own evocative atmosphere. The "lyrical expressive" (**A**) gives way to the "passionately anxious" (**B** and **C**), which yields to the initial lyricism (**A**). The returning **A** is extended by means of an exquisite little coda. At the very end, a painful dissonance sounds and then resolves to consonance (5:07–5:12), as the fears of the nocturnal world dissolve into a heavenly major realm. As the German poet Heine said of Chopin: "He hails from the land of Mozart, Raphael, and Goethe. His true home is in the realm of Poetry."

Listening Guide

Frédéric Chopin
Nocturne in C♯ minor, Opus 27, No. 1 (1835)

6 **2**
3/23 2/5

Form: **ABCA**

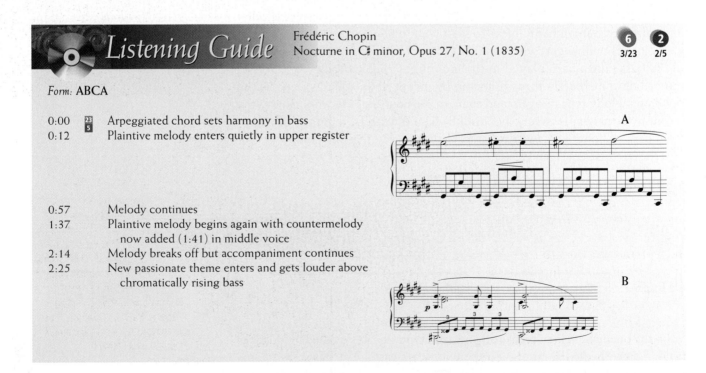

0:00	23 5	Arpeggiated chord sets harmony in bass
0:12		Plaintive melody enters quietly in upper register
0:57		Melody continues
1:37		Plaintive melody begins again with countermelody now added (1:41) in middle voice
2:14		Melody breaks off but accompaniment continues
2:25		New passionate theme enters and gets louder above chromatically rising bass

2:52	Bold harmonic shift from four sharps to four flats	
3:00	Passionate theme continues and rises	
3:12	New, more heroic melody enters	C
3:25	Very loud repeated chords, then fermata (hold)	
3:30	Loud, recitative-like passage descends deep into bass	
3:42	Arpeggiated accompaniment, then plaintive melody reemerges	A
4:33	Coda, entirely in the major mode	Coda
5:07	Dissonance resolves to consonance (5:12)	

Use a downloadable, cross-platform animated Active Listening Guide, available at **www.thomsonedu.com/music/wright**.

FRANZ LISZT (1811–1886)

Franz Liszt was not merely a musician, he was a phenomenon, perhaps the most flamboyant artistic personality of the entire nineteenth century. Handsome, supremely talented, and equally self-confident, he strutted across the stage as the musical sex symbol of the Romantic era (Fig. 25–3). But he could also play the piano, and like no other.

Franz Liszt was born in Hungary of German-speaking parents. In 1822, his ambitious father took him to Vienna and then Paris to be the next child prodigy, the latest musical *Wunderkind*. But his father died suddenly, and the young pianist's career languished. Liszt's life took a dramatic turn on April 20, 1832, however, when he attended a concert given by the great violin virtuoso Niccolò Paganini (see page 261). "What a man, what a violin, what an artist! Oh, God, what pain and suffering, what torment in those four strings." Liszt vowed to bring Paganini's technical virtuosity to the piano. Practicing four to five hours a day—unusual dedication for a prodigy—he taught himself to play on the piano what had never been played before: tremolos, leaps, double trills, glissandos, simultaneous octaves in both hands, all at breathtaking speed. When he returned to the stage for his own concerts, he overwhelmed the audience. He had become the greatest pianist of his time, and perhaps of all time.

In 1833, Liszt's life took another unexpected turn. He met the Countess Marie d'Agoult (see cover and Fig. 25–4) and decided to give up the life of the performing artist in exchange for domestic security. Although she was already married and the mother of two children, she and Liszt eloped, first to Switzerland and then to Italy. Residing in these countries for four years, the couple had three children of their own. (Their youngest daughter would become the wife of Richard Wagner; see Fig. 27–3, page 306.)

Beginning in 1839, and continuing until 1847, Liszt once more took to the road as a touring

FIGURE 25–3
The charismatic Franz Liszt, the preeminent pianist of the Romantic era.

FIGURE 25–4
Countess Marie d'Agoult in 1843. She was a novelist in her own right, and some of the tracts on music that appeared under Liszt's name were probably penned by her. Like many female writers of the day, including George Sand and George Eliot, she wrote under a masculine *nom de plume*, Daniel Stern.

Lebrecht Music & Arts/The Image Works

FIGURE 25–5

Lisztomania, as depicted in 1842. A recital by Liszt was likely to create the sort of sensation that a concert by a rock star might generate today. Women fought for a lock of his hair, a broken string from his piano, or a shred of his velvet gloves.

FIGURE 25–6

The aged Liszt, still dazzling audiences and destroying pianos. As a critic of the day said of his slash and burn technique, "He is as much a piano slayer as a piano player."

Mary Evans Picture Library/The Image Works

virtuoso. He played more than a thousand concerts: from Ireland to Turkey, from Sweden to Spain, from Portugal to Russia. Everywhere he went the handsome pianist was greeted with the sort of mass hysteria today reserved for rock stars. Audiences of 3,000 crowded into the larger halls (Fig. 25–5). Women tried to rip off his silk scarf and white gloves, and fought for a lock of his hair. **Lisztomania** swept across Europe.

Despite their obvious sensationalism, Liszt's concerts in the 1840s established the format of our modern-day piano **recital.** He was the first to play entire programs from memory (not reading from music). He was the first to place the piano parallel with the line of the stage so that neither his back nor full face, but rather his extraordinary side profile, was visible to the audience. He was the first to perform on the stage alone—up to that point concerts traditionally had included numerous performers on the program. At first, these solo appearances were called "soliloquies," and then "recitals," suggesting they were something akin to personal dramatic recitations. As Liszt modestly said in his adopted French, *"Le concert, c'est moi!"*

But Liszt was a complex man with many facets to his personality. He thought of himself not only as a showman-pianist but also as a serious composer. So, in 1847, he suddenly quit the lucrative concert circuit and settled in Weimar, Germany, to serve the ducal court as music director and composer-in-residence. Here he concentrated on writing orchestral music. All told, he composed a dozen symphonic poems*, as well as two program symphonies* and three piano concertos. In 1861, Liszt again surprised the world: he moved to Rome, entered Holy Orders in the Roman Catholic Church, and took up residence in the Vatican! "Abbé Liszt," as the composer now styled himself, had replaced Don Juan. While in Rome, Liszt wrote the bulk of his sixty religious works including two oratorios. He died at the age of seventy-five in Bayreuth, Germany, where he had gone to hear the latest opera of his son-in-law, Richard Wagner.

Despite Liszt's interest in religious music and programmatic works for orchestra, his reputation as a composer rests primarily upon his sensational piano music, particularly for his *Hungarian Rhapsodies.* Liszt had large hands and unusually long fingers with very little web-like connective tissue between them (Fig. 25–6), which allowed him to make wide stretches with relative ease. He could play a melody in octaves when others could play only the single notes of the line. If others might execute a passage in octaves, Liszt could dash it off in more impressive-sounding tenths (octave plus third). So he wrote daredevil music full of virtuosic display.

To build sufficient technique to tackle Liszt's difficult showpieces, performers practiced a musical genre called the "etude." An **etude** is a short, one-movement composition designed to improve one or more aspects of a performer's technique (fast scales, more rapid note repetition, surer leaps, and so on). Before 1840, dozens of composers had published books of technical exercises that became the cornerstone of piano instruction for the burgeoning middle class. Chopin and Liszt took this development one step further. They added beautifully crafted melodies and unusual textures to what previously had been merely mind-numbing finger work, thereby demonstrating that an etude might embody artistry as well as mechanics.

Liszt's most difficult pieces of this sort are his twelve *Transcendental Etudes* (1851). As the title suggests, these works require transcendent, indeed superhuman, technical skill. Ironically, these etudes by Liszt are not useful studies for the average pianist—they are so difficult that the performer must already be a virtuoso to play them! As composer and critic Robert Schumann said, "The *Transcendental Etudes* are studies in storm and dread designed to be performed by, at most, ten or twelve players in the world."

superhuman technical skill required

Transcendental Etude No. 8, "Wilde Jagd" ("Wild Hunt"; 1851)

Even today, rare is the pianist who will attempt Liszt's *Transcendental Etudes* in concert. Among the most technically difficult of the twelve is "Wilde Jagd" ("Wild Hunt"). The title suggests a nocturnal chase in a supernatural forest of the sort often evoked in German Romantic literature. The similarly "supernatural" demands placed on the pianist are intended to develop skill in playing broken octaves in the left hand and simultaneous chromatic runs in both hands (Ex. 25–3). Occasionally, a lyrical melody shines forth in the dark forest of digital dangers. In these moments, the pianist must project the expressive melody while keeping the difficult accompaniment up to tempo, performing simultaneously the roles of poet and technical virtuoso. In Liszt's most challenging etudes and rhapsodies, we experience the most technically demanding music ever composed for piano.

etude presents specific technical challenges

EXAMPLE 25–3

Listening Guide

Franz Liszt
Transcendental Etude No. 8, "Wild Hunt" (1851)

6
4/1

Genre: etude

0:00   **1**   Racing octaves followed by crashing chords with "short-long" rhythm

Presto furioso

fff

fff

0:44   Simultaneous chromatic scales in both hands (see Ex. 25–3)
0:52   Racing octaves and crashing chords return
1:37   "Short-long" rhythm transformed into folk-like tune
2:28   Lyrical melody appears in top of right hand (soprano line)

pp

2:44   Lyrical melody moved octave higher
3:24   Lyrical melody set to more complex accompaniment and grows in intensity
3:59   Racing octaves and crashing chords return and are developed harmonically
5:32   Lyrical melody returns
5:52   Lyrical melody rises in melodic sequence* to climax
6:03   Arpeggios ascend and then crashing chords descend to end

Use a downloadable, cross-platform animated Active Listening Guide, available
at **www.thomsonedu.com/music/wright**.

Key Words

sustaining pedal **(287)**   George Sand **(288)**   Lisztomania **(292)**
soft pedal **(287)**   mazurka **(288)**   recital **(292)**
cross-stringing **(287)**   nocturne **(289)**   etude **(292)**

Romantic Opera
ITALY

The nineteenth century is often called the "golden age of opera." It is the century of Rossini, Bellini, Verdi, Wagner, Bizet, and Puccini. True, there had been great opera composers before—Monteverdi, Handel, and Mozart, to name just three. But the nineteenth century saw the creation of much of the "core" repertoire of today. Presently, about two-thirds of the productions of the leading opera companies—the Metropolitan Opera in New York and La Scala in Milan, for example—are works created during the years 1820–1900.

Italy, of course, is the home of opera. The Italian language, with its evenly spaced, open vowels, is perfectly suited for singing, and the people of Italy seem to have an innate love of melody. Beginning around 1600, the first operas were created in Florence, Rome, Venice, and Mantua (see Chapter 11). For nearly two centuries, Italian opera dominated the international stage. When Handel wrote operas for London in the 1720s, for example, he composed Italian operas (see Chapter 14), as did Mozart when he created musical theater for the courts of Germany and Austria in the 1770s and 1780s (see Chapter 20).

Italy: the home of opera

In the early nineteenth century, the primacy of Italian opera was maintained almost single-handedly by Gioachino Rossini (1792–1868). Surprising as it may seem today, Rossini was the most celebrated composer in Europe during the 1820s, far exceeding even Beethoven in fame. He owed this public favor in large measure to the genre he chose: opera was then the most popular form of musical entertainment. More than the symphony, string quartet, or any other musical genre of the time, opera captured the popular imagination in much the way that cinema does today.

Gioachino Rossini

Rossini brought to a glorious close the eighteenth-century tradition of comic opera, or *opera buffa* (see page 173). Catchy, oft-repeating melodies, vivacious rhythms, and rollicking crescendos were his trademarks. His best-known comic opera, *The Barber of Seville,* has never disappeared from the operatic stage since it first appeared in 1816. Even casual music lovers know a little of this enduring work in the form of the "Figaro, Figaro, Figaro" call from the opening aria for the resourceful barber, Figaro. Rossini could also write in a more serious style, as exemplified in his last opera, *William Tell* (1829). This stormy drama, too, has achieved a measure of immortality, the overture providing the theme music for the radio and film character of the Lone Ranger.

The Barber of Seville and William Tell

ITALIAN BEL CANTO OPERA

Whereas German operatic composers would come to emphasize the dramatic power and instrumental color of the orchestra, Italians after Rossini increasingly focused their energies on melodies for the solo voice—on the art of beautiful singing, or **bel canto.** The two most gifted of the early creators of *bel canto* opera were Gaetano Donizetti (1797–1848) and Vincenzo Bellini (1801–1835). In their works, the orchestra merely provides a simple harmonic support for the soaring, sometimes divinely beautiful, lines of the voice. Look at the opening of the famous aria "Casta diva" from Bellini's *Norma* (1831), in which the heroine sings a prayer to a distant moon goddess (Ex. 26–1). Here

FIGURE 26–1

The reigning opera diva Renée Fleming of Rochester, New York, specializes in *bel canto* opera.

295

the orchestra functions like a giant guitar. Simple chords are fleshed out as arpeggios by the strings while an even simpler bass line is plucked below. All of the musical interest is in the rapturous sound of the human voice. One Italian newspaper of the day declared, "In the theatrical arts it is said that three things are required: action, action, action; likewise, three things are demanded for music: voice, voice, voice."

EXAMPLE 26–1

Ca - sta Di - va, ca - sta Di - va, che i - nar-

(Chaste goddess, who does bathe in silver light these hallowed, ancient trees)

gen - ti que - ste sa - cre, que - ste sa - cre, que - ste sa - cre anti - che pian - te,

Not surprisingly, by placing such importance on the voices of the leading singers, *bel canto* opera fostered a star system among the cast. Usually, it was the lyric soprano—heroine and **prima donna** (first lady)—who held the most exalted position in the operatic firmament. By the 1880s, she would also be called a **diva,** which, as in the aria "Casta diva," means "goddess." Indeed, the diva and her beautiful voice would rule Italian *bel canto* opera throughout the nineteenth century and even down to the present day (Fig. 26–1).

GIUSEPPE VERDI (1813–1901)

The name Giuseppe Verdi is virtually synonymous with Italian opera. For six decades, from the time of *Nabucco* in 1842 until *Falstaff* in 1893, Verdi had almost no rival for the affections of the opera-loving public in Italy and throughout Europe. Even today the best-loved of his twenty-six operas are more readily available—in opera houses, in TV productions, and on videotape and DVD—than those of any other composer.

Verdi was born near Busseto in northern Italy in 1813, the son of a tavern-keeper. He was apparently no musical prodigy, for at the age of eighteen, he was rejected for admission to the Conservatory of Music in Milan because he was already too old and his piano technique faulty. But Verdi stayed on in Milan to study composition. He returned to Busseto in 1835 to serve as the town's bandmaster, and then four years later went back to Milan to earn his livelihood as a composer.

To be a composer in nineteenth-century Italy was to be a composer of opera. Verdi's first, *Oberto*, was produced at the famous **La Scala** Opera House in Milan (Fig. 26–2) in 1839, and it achieved a modicum of success. But his

Nabucco of 1842 was a popular triumph, receiving an unprecedented fifty-seven performances at La Scala in that year alone. Through subsequent productions in other theaters, Verdi's reputation quickly spread throughout Italy, the rest of Europe, and even to North and South America. His career had been launched.

The text, or libretto*, of *Nabucco*, as well as most of Verdi's other operas of the 1840s, is covertly political (Fig. 26–3). It concerns the suppression of a people (in this case, the Jews) by a cruel foreign power (the Babylonians). By analogy, Verdi thus called attention to the plight of the Italian people, who were then ruled in large measure by the Austrians. Verdi had become a spirited Italian patriot. Normally, we do not think of music as expressing political ideas, but because opera was an important part of Italian mass culture, it could suborn political revolution. Verdi's soloists and choruses (the voice of the people) sang such fiery words as "You may have the universe, so long as I keep Italy" and "Long live Italy! A sacred pact binds all her sons." Partly through such patriotic music and partly by accident, Verdi became a leader in the **Risorgimento,** the movement for a united Italy free of foreign domination. By handy coincidence, the letters of the composer's last name produced an acronym for **V**ittorio **E**manuele **R**e **d**'Italia (King Victor Emanuel being the people's choice for the throne of a united Kingdom of Italy). Thus, cries of "Viva, Verdi!" echoed throughout Italy in hopes of unification. In 1861, after that goal had been largely achieved, Verdi was elected to the country's first parliament, and later, in 1874, to its senate.

But the path to national unity was not an easy one for the Italians. During the 1850s, Verdi became disillusioned with politics and turned his attention from national aspirations to personal drama. In quick order he composed a trio of works without which no opera house today could function: *Rigoletto* (1851), *La traviata* (1853), and *Il trovatore* (1853). For most of the early-to-mid-1850s, Verdi lived away from Milan, residing in Paris or traveling throughout Europe to oversee the production of his increasingly numerous works. He called these years of toil and intense productivity "my years as a galley slave."

On his return to his homeland in 1857, the pace of Verdi's opera production slackened. He composed only when the subject was of interest or the fee so substantial he couldn't refuse. His opera *Aida* (1871), commissioned to celebrate the opening of the Suez Canal, brought him the astonishing fee of 150,000 francs (about $670,000 in 2007). Verdi had become wealthy, and he retired to his estate in northern Italy to lead the life of a country squire—or so he thought.

But like a performer who feels he owes the audience more, or has something more to prove to himself, Verdi returned to the theater for two final encores: *Otello* (1887) and *Falstaff* (1893), both exceptionally well-crafted operas based on dramas of Shakespeare. The latter work was written when the composer was on the threshold of eighty, a feat without parallel in music history or the annals

Museo Teatro alla Scala, Milan/Scala/Art Resource, NY

FIGURES 26–2 AND 26–3

(top) La Scala Opera House about 1830. Verdi's first four and last two operas had their premieres at La Scala, then as now the foremost opera house in Italy. (bottom) Verdi's longtime mistress, and ultimately his wife, Giuseppina Strepponi (1815–1897), holding the score of his early opera *Nabucco*. She was instrumental in getting this and other operas by Verdi produced at La Scala in Milan.

Bridgeman Art Library, London/NY

of the dramatic stage. He died peacefully at his country home in 1901, a much-respected national institution.

Verdi's Dramaturgy and Musical Style

When the curtain goes up on a Verdi opera, the listener will find elements of dramaturgy—construction of the drama—and musical style that are unique to this composer. For Giuseppe Verdi, conflict was at the root of every emotion, and he expressed conflict, whether personal or national, by juxtaposing self-contained, clearly contrasting units of music. A rousing march, a patriotic chorus, a passionate recitative, and a lyrical aria follow in quick succession. The composer aims not at musical and dramatic subtlety but rather at banner headlines of emotion. The emotional states of the characters are so clearly depicted, sometimes exaggerated, that the drama comes perilously close to melodrama, with its excess of sentimentality and sensationalism. But it is never dull. There is action, passion, and intensity, all the things that give an opera mass appeal. In 1854, Verdi said, "There is one thing the public will not tolerate in the theater: boredom."

emotional states vividly created

How does Verdi generate this feeling of intense passion and nonstop action? He does so by creating a new kind of recitative and a new style of aria. As before, recitative still narrates the action, and arias still express the characters' emotional states. But Verdi replaces simple recitative*, accompanied only by *basso continuo* (see page 114), with orchestrally accompanied **recitativo accompagnato.** This allows the action to flow smoothly from orchestrally accompanied aria to orchestrally accompanied recitative and back without a jarring change of texture. As for the aria, Verdi brings to it a new intensity.

Yes, he is a composer squarely in the tradition of Italian *bel canto* opera. He focuses his attention on the solo voice and on a lyrical, beautiful vocal line. Indeed, no composer had a greater gift for writing simple, memorable melodies that the audience could whistle on the way out of the theater. Yet Verdi also adds intensity and passion to these arias by pushing the singers to the upper reaches of their range. The tenor is asked to sing up to the B above middle C, while the soprano must sing two octaves (or even higher!) above middle C. The thrilling moments in which the hero (the tenor) or the heroine (the soprano) go right to the top are literally the high points of any Verdi opera.

La traviata (1853)

We may measure the high intensity and passion in Verdi's operas by listening to a portion of his *La traviata* (1853). *La traviata* literally means "The Woman Gone Astray" (Fig. 26–4). It tells the story of the sickly Violetta Valery, a courtesan, or "kept woman," who resists and then succumbs to the love of a new suitor, the young Alfredo Germont. For a while, the couple retires from Paris to lead a quiet life in the country. But without explanation Violetta deserts Alfredo, in truth so that her scandalous reputation will not bring disgrace on his respectable family. The hot-tempered Alfredo now publicly insults Violetta, fights a duel with her new "protector,"

FIGURE 26–4

A photograph of Giuseppe Verdi on an early published score of his opera *La traviata*.

EDIZIONE POPOLARE DELLE OPERE DI G·VERDI

LA TRAVIATA

G·RICORDI&C EDITORI·MILANO

Nuova Arti Grafiche Ricordi, Milan

and is banished from France. When the nature of Violetta's sacrifice is revealed, Alfredo rushes back to Paris. But it is too late. She is dying of tuberculosis—her fate dictated by an operatic convention that requires the heroine to sing one last show-stopping aria and then expire.

Verdi based the libretto of *La traviata* on a play that he had seen in Paris in 1852 called *Camille,* by Alexandre Dumas the younger. (His father, Alexandre Dumas senior, wrote *The Count of Monte Cristo* and *The Three Musketeers.* (See the cover of this book; the gentleman farthest to the left is Dumas Sr.) *Camille* tells the story of the real-life figure, Marie Duplessis (Fig. 26–5), the mistress of the playwright Dumas and, for a short time, of the composer-pianist Franz Liszt as well. Marie served as the model for Violetta in Dumas's play and, a year later, for the same character in Verdi's opera *La traviata.* Like many in this period, Marie died young of tuberculosis, at the age of twenty-three.

We join *La traviata* toward the end of the first act. A gala party is in progress in a fashionable Parisian salon, and here the dashing Alfredo has finally managed to cut Violetta away from the crowd to profess his love to her. He does so in the aria "Un dì felice" ("One Happy Day"), which is lovely, yet somber in tone. The seriousness of Alfredo's intent is underscored by the slow, square, even plodding accompaniment in the orchestra. When Violetta enters she is supported by the same accompaniment, but the mood of the aria changes radically, becoming light and carefree. Witness Verdi's direct musical characterization at work: Alfredo's slow melody with a hint of minor is replaced by Violetta's flighty sound of high, rapidly moving notes. Eventually, the two join together: he below, somberly proclaiming the mysteries of love; she above, making light of them. What started as a solo aria has become a duet, the voices—and hands—of the principals now intertwined. Once again, music enhances drama by replicating in its own language the action on stage.

Lebrecht Music & Arts/The Image Works

FIGURE 26–5

Marie Duplessis. The end of her brief, scandalous life is the subject of Giuseppe Verdi's opera *La traviata.* So notorious had she become by the time of her death at the age of twenty-three that Charles Dickens said, "You would have thought her passing was a question of the death of a hero or a Joan of Arc."

Listening Guide

Giuseppe Verdi
La traviata (1853)
Act I, Scene 4

6
4/2

Characters: Alfredo, a young man of good standing; Violetta, a kept woman leading a wanton life in Paris
Situation: a party in a Parisian salon around 1850; Alfredo professes his love to Violetta, who at first rejects him.

ARIA

0:00 [2]		**Alfredo (tenor)**	
		Un dì felice, eterea,	One happy day,
		Mi balaneste innante,	you appeared to me.
		E da quel dì tremante	And from this day, trembling,
		Vissi d'ignoto amor.	I have lived in that
		Di quell'amor ch'è palpito	unspoken love, in that love
	Shift to minor	Dell'universo intero,	which animates the world,
		Misterioso, altero,	mysterious, proud, pain
		Croce e delizia al cor.	and delight to the heart.
		Violetta (soprano)	
1:22	Violetta changes aria to lighter mood through faster tempo and shorter notes	Ah, se ciò è ver, fuggitemi.	If that's true, leave me.
		Solo amistade io v'offro;	Only friendship I offer you.
		Amar non so, nè soffro	I don't know how to love
		Un cosi eroico amore.	or suffer such a heroic love.
		Io sono franca, ingenua;	I'm being honest and sincere.
		Altra cercar dovete;	You must find another.
		Non arduo troverete	It won't be difficult.
		Dimenticarmi allor.	Just leave me.

(continued)

| (DUET)
1:46 | Alfredo and Violetta together
in rapturous duet | Oh amore!
Misterioso, altero,
Croce e delizia al cor.

Non arduo troverete
Dimenticarmi allor. | **Alfredo**
Oh love!
mysterious, proud, pain
and delight to the heart.
Violetta
It won't be difficult.
Just leave me. |
| 2:48 | Exuberant vocal flourishes for both | "Ah" | "Ah" |

Use a downloadable, cross-platform animated Active Listening Guide, available at **www.thomsonedu.com/music/wright**.

FIGURE 26–6

The great Australian soprano Joan Sutherland singing the role of Violetta, and tenor Luciano Pavarotti as Alfredo, in Verdi's *La traviata*.

Beth Bergman

Alfredo kisses Violetta's hand and departs, leaving her alone on stage to ponder her future. She reveals, in a slow strophic aria, "Ah fors'è lui" ("Ah, perhaps he's the one"), that Alfredo may be the lover she has long desired. But Violetta abruptly rejects the whole idea as impossible. Forget love, she says in an impassioned accompanied recitative*: "Folly! Folly! What sort of crazy dream is this!" Recitative leads naturally to aria, and here follows "Sempre libera" ("Always free"), one of the great show arias for soprano voice. It allows Violetta to declare forcefully her resolve to remain free of love's entanglements. This aria, too, helps define through music the character of the heroine—the extraordinary, carefree flourishes on the word "pleasure," for example, reinforce her "live-for-the-moment" approach to life. Violetta's declaration of independence is momentarily broken by the distant voice of Alfredo, who again sings of the mysterious powers of love. This, too, Violetta brushes aside as she emphatically repeats her pledge always to be free.

Verdi has moved quickly from slow aria, to recitative, to fast-concluding aria. Such a three-movement unit is a dramatic convention of Italian opera called a **scena** (a scenic plan made up of diverse movements). So, too, the fast aria at the end of the scena has a name, "cabaletta." A **cabaletta** is a fast-concluding aria in which the increased speed of the music allows one or more soloists to race off stage at the end of a scene or act. Here Violetta, vowing to remain free, dashes off as the curtain falls to end Act I. But, of course, our heroine does not remain free—she falls fatally in love with Alfredo, as Acts II and III reveal. Listen now to the final scene of Act I of Verdi's *La traviata*. You will have the pleasure of hearing two of the greatest voices of the twentieth century, Joan Sutherland (soprano) and Luciano Pavarotti (tenor) (Fig. 26–6).

Listening Guide

Giuseppe Verdi
La traviata (1853)
Act I, Scene 6

 6 2
4/3–4 2/6

Characters: Violetta and Alfredo (outside her window)
Situation: Violetta at first believes Alfredo to be the passionate love she has long sought, but then rejects this notion, vowing to remain free.

ARIA

First Strophe

0:00	3	Soprano sings first phrase	Ah, fors'è lui che l'anima Solinga ne' tumulti	Ah, perhaps he's the one whom my lonely heart
0:33		First phrase repeated	Godea sovente pingere De' suoi colori occulti.	delighted often to paint with vague, mysterious colors.
0:56		Voice rises up in melodic sequence	Lui, che modesto e vigile	He who, so modest and attentive

1:24	Return of Alfredo's major-key refrain from previous aria	All'egre sogli ascese,	during my illness, waited
		E nuova febbre accese	and with youthful fervor
		Destandomi all'amor!	aroused me again to love!
		A quell'amor ch'è palpito	To that love which
		Dell'universo intero,	animates the universe,
		Misterioso, altero,	mysterious, proud, pain
		Croce e delizia al cor.	and delight to the heart.

Second Strophe

2:26	Return of first phrase	A me, fanciulla, un candido	To me, a girl, this was
		E trepido desire,	an innocent, anxious desire,
2:51	First phrase repeated	Quest'effgiò dolcissimo	this sweet vision,
		Signor dell'avvenire.	lord of things to come.
3:15	Voice rises up in melodic sequence	Quando ne' cieli il raggio	When in the heavens I saw
		Di sua beltà vedea	rays of his beauty
		E tutta me pascea	I fed myself completely
		Di quel divino error.	on that divine error.
3:42	Return of Alfredo's major-key refrain from previous aria	Sentia che amore è il palpito	I felt that love which
		Dell'universo intero,	animates the universe,
		Misterioso altero,	mysterious, proud, pain
4:16	Highly ornamental final cadence with lengthy trill	Croce e delizia al cor.	and delight to the heart.

RECITATIVE

				Violetta
0:00	4 6	Accompanied by orchestra	Follie! Follie! delirio	Folly! Folly! What sort of
			vano è questo!	crazy dream is this!
			Povera donna, sola,	Poor woman, alone,
			abbandonata, in questo	abandoned in this
			popoloso deserto che	populated desert that
			appellano Parigi.	they call Paris.
			Che spero or più?	What hope have I?
			Che far degg'io?	What can I do?
0:49		Flights of vocal fancy as she thinks of pleasure	Gioir!	Pleasure!
			Di voluttà ne' vortici perir!	Perish in a whirl of indulgence!
			Gioir!	Pleasure!
1:05		Introduction to cabaletta		

CABALETTA

			Violetta
1:16		Sempre libera degg'io	Always free I must remain
		Folleggiare di gioia	to reel from pleasure
		in gioia,	to pleasure,
		Vo' che scorra il viver mio	running my life along the
		Pei sentieri del piacer.	paths of joy.
		Nasca il giorno,	From dawn
		o il giorno muoia,	to dusk
		Sempre lieta ne' ritrovi,	I'm always happy finding
		A diletti sempre nuovi	new delights that make
		Dee volare il mio pensier.	my spirit soar.

			Alfredo
2:01	Echoes of his previous aria	Amor è palpito	Love that animates
		dell'universo,	the world,
		misterioso, altero,	mysterious, proud, pain
		croce e delizia al cor.	and delight to the heart.

			Violetta
2:48	Extravagant flourishes	Follie! Follie!	Folly! Folly!
		Gioir! Gioir!	Pleasure! Pleasure!

CABALETTA returns

3:17	This time even more brilliant in its showy, superficial style	Sempre libera . . .	Always free . . .

 Use a downloadable, cross-platform animated Active Listening Guide, available at **www.thomsonedu.com/music/wright**.

Listening Exercise 35

Verdi
La traviata

4/3–4   2/6

ThomsonNOW
To take this Listening Exercise online and receive feedback or email answers to your instructor, go to *ThomsonNOW* for this chapter.

The following questions illuminate the way in which Giuseppe Verdi, working within the tradition of Italian *bel canto* opera, makes the voice the center of attention. While Verdi from time to time pauses to allow the singers a luxuriant moment of vocal virtuosity, he nonetheless pushes the opera forward at a rapid pace.

1. (0:00–1:00) What are the meter and the mode at the beginning of this aria?
   a. duple and minor   b. triple and minor
   c. duple and major   d. triple and major

2. (0:12–0:33) What does the orchestra do while Violetta (soprano) sings?
   a. provides simple imitative polyphony
   b. provides simple chordal homophony

3. (1:24–2:11) Here Violetta sings the expansive "love" refrain introduced previously by Alfredo. The orchestra now functions as "big guitar" in its accompaniment. How does Verdi create this effect?
   a. Strings play tremolo chords and the flute plays arpeggios.
   b. Strings play vibrato chords and the flute plays arpeggios.
   c. Strings play pizzicato chords and the clarinet plays arpeggios.

4. (2:26–5:32) Violetta now sings the second strophe of her aria. When the expansive "love" refrain returns (3:42–4:36), does the orchestra still produce the "big guitar" effect?
   a. yes   b. no

5. (4:45–5:28) Toward the end of the second strophe, Violetta ornaments her melodic line to give it more interest the second time around. How do we know we are securely in the realm of *bel canto* opera during this passage?
   a. The soprano sings while the orchestra remains silent for more than thirty seconds.
   b. The voice soars above the "big guitar" effect in the accompaniment.

6. (0:00–0:22) This passage, in which Violetta expresses her fear of being a woman alone and abandoned in the "populated desert" of Paris, is a good example of what?
   a. simple recitative
   b. *secco* recitative
   c. *recitativo accompagnato*

7. After some vocal fireworks on the word "gioir" (pleasure), Violetta launches into her brilliant cabaletta "Sempre libera" ("Always free"; 1:16). What characteristic identifies this as a cabaletta?
   a. It is a fast concluding aria that Violetta will use to exit the stage.
   b. The soprano sings in a vocal range called the cabaletta.

8. (3:00–3:15) Again Violetta vows to dedicate herself to a life of pleasure ("gioir"). What does the orchestra do during this vocal flourish?
   a. merely plays chordal homophony
   b. creates the "big-guitar" effect
   c. nothing

9. Now Violetta repeats "Always free" (3:17), swearing to remain free of the snares of love. Where does the vocal high point of "Always free" occur—that is, where does the soprano go to the top of her range?
   a. at the end of the first strophe of the aria (1:57–2:01)
   b. at the end of the second strophe of the aria (4:34–4:49)

10. Consider now all the portions of *La traviata* you have heard, beginning with the aria "One happy day" and ending with the cabaletta "Always free." What can we conclude about this Italian *bel canto* opera?
    a. It is very much an "instrumentalist's" opera focusing on the orchestra.
    b. It is very much a "singer's" opera focusing on the soprano voice.
    c. It is very much a "singer's" opera focusing on the tenor voice.

ThomsonNOW

ThomsonNOW for *Listening to Music, 5th Edition,* and *Listening to Western Music* will assist you in understanding the content of this chapter with lesson plans generated for your specific needs. In addition, you may complete this chapter's Listening Exercise in ThomsonNOW's interactive environment, as well as download Active Listening Guides and other materials that will help you succeed in this course.

Key Words

bel canto (295)
prima donna (296)
diva (296)
La Scala (296)

Risorgimento (297)
recitativo
    accompagnato (298)
scena (300)

cabaletta (300)

Romantic Opera
GERMANY

Before 1820, opera was mainly an Italian affair. It was first created in Italy around 1600 and then, over the next two hundred years, was exported to all parts of Europe. With the onset of the nineteenth century, however, other people, driven by an emerging sense of national pride, developed idiomatic opera in their native tongues. Although Italian opera remained the dominant style, it now had to share the stage, not only with traditional French opera but also with the newer forms of Russian, Czech, and especially German opera.

Before the nineteenth century, German opera was of minor importance. Native opera in German-speaking lands went by the name *Singspiel*. A **Singspiel** (singing play) is a musical comedy or light musical drama that has, by sheer coincidence, many elements in common with our present-day Broadway musical: plenty of topical humor, tuneful solo songs, energetic choral numbers, and spoken dialogue instead of sung recitative. Mozart, in *The Magic Flute* (1791), and Beethoven, in his only opera, *Fidelio* (1805), tried to bring greater seriousness and unity to the *Singspiel* genre. A somewhat younger contemporary of Beethoven, Carl Maria von Weber (1786–1826), likewise attempted to develop a tradition of serious German opera distinct from the Italian style. His *The Magic Bullet* (1821) makes use of German folk songs, or folk-like melodies, as well as a libretto that delights in the supernatural. The German passion for horror subjects and supernatural tales in the Romantic period can be seen in other works, such as Heinrich Marschner's *The Vampire* (1828) and Richard Wagner's *The Flying Dutchman* (1844).

a Singspiel has much in common with a Broadway musical

RICHARD WAGNER (1813–1883)

The composer who realized the dream of a distinct, national German operatic tradition was Richard Wagner (Fig. 27–1), a titanic figure in Western cultural history. Wagner was not merely a composer; he was also a philosopher, politician, propagandist, and ardent advocate for his own vision of dramatic music. Not only did he compose operas of monumental scope, he produced a large number of theoretical writings. So controversial are his theories and his art that Wagner has become for some an object of almost religious admiration, and for others, particularly because of his anti-Semitism, the most detested composer in the history of Western music. For Wagner, opera was the perfect form of artistic expression, and the opera composer was something of a religious prophet who revealed to his "congregation" (his audience) the wonders of the musical world.

To be sure, Wagner's music is often inspiring. It contains moments of grandeur unmatched by any other composer. His influence on musical style in the late nineteenth century was enormous. Yet his reception by the musical public at large, then and now, has been divided. Some listeners are left cold, believing the music to be long-winded and the operatic plots devoid of realistic human drama. Others are immediately converted to adoring Wagnerites at the first sound of the heroic themes and powerful orchestral climaxes.

Who was this controversial artist who has stirred such mixed feelings within the musical public for more than a century? Richard Wagner was born in Leipzig,

FIGURE 27–1
Richard Wagner in a photograph of 1871.

Germany. Although he studied with the music director of the Saint Thomas Church (where Bach had worked), he was largely self-taught in musical matters. After a succession of jobs as opera director in several small German towns, Wagner moved to Paris in 1839 in hopes of seeing his first opera produced there. But instead of meeting acclaim in Paris, as had Liszt and Chopin before him, Wagner was greeted with thundering indifference. No one could be persuaded to produce his work. Reduced to poverty, he spent a brief stint in debtor's prison.

early career

When Wagner's big break came, it was not in Paris but back in his native Germany, in the city of Dresden. His opera *Rienzi* was given a hearing there in 1842, and Wagner was soon offered the post of director of the Dresden Opera. During the next six years, he created three additional German Romantic operas for the Dresden stage: *The Flying Dutchman* (1844), *Tannhäuser* (1845), and *Lohengrin* (1848). In the aftermath of the political revolution that swept much of Europe in 1848, Wagner was forced to flee Dresden, though in truth he took flight as much to avoid his creditors as to escape any repressive government.

Wagner found a safe haven in Switzerland, which was to be his home, on and off, for the next dozen years. Exiled now from the major opera houses in Germany, he began to imagine a complex of music dramas on a vast and unprecedented scale. What he ultimately created was *Der Ring des Nibelungen* (*The Ring of the Nibelung*), a set of four operas intended to be performed during the course of four successive evenings. *Das Rheingold*, the first, lasts 2½ hours; *Die Walküre* and *Siegfried* each run nearly 4½ hours; while the finale, *Götterdämmerung* (*Twilight of the Gods*), goes on for no less than 5½ hours.

Unlike the great majority of composers throughout music history, Wagner wrote not only the music but also the librettos for his operas. For his four-part **Ring cycle,** he fashioned a single continuous epic by drawing on tales from German mythology. The scene is set in the smoky mists of primeval time, in a land of gods, river nymphs, dwarfs, giants, dragons, and sword-wielding heroes. In many ways, Wagner's *Ring of the Nibelung* is similar to J. R. R. Tolkien's trilogy *The Lord of the Rings* (published in 1954 and 1955; film version, 2001, 2002, and 2003). Both are multipart sagas based on Nordic mythology, both are overrun with fantastic creatures (goblins, wizards, and dragons), and both revolve around a much-coveted ring, which seems to offer its possessor unparalleled power, but which also carries a dark, sinister curse.

the Ring *cycle and its plot*

But Wagner viewed his *Ring* cycle not as a timeless fairy tale but rather as a timely allegory exploring the themes of power, greed, honor, bravery, and race in nineteenth-century German society. At that time, bravery, power, and national identity were themes with special resonance in Germany, which was then in the process of becoming a unified nation. The German philosopher Friedrich Nietzsche (1844–1900), for a time a friend and confidant of Wagner, modeled his superhero, or superman (see also page 10), on Wagner's heroic character Siegfried in the *Ring*. In the twentieth century, Adolf Hitler exploited Wagnerian symbolism to foster the notion of a superior German race, fortifying, for example, a Siegfried Line on the Western Front during World War II.

an allegory of events in German history

Not surprisingly, publishers and producers were at first reluctant to print or mount the operas of Wagner's *Ring*, given their massive scope and fantastic subject matter. They would, however, pay well for the rights to the composer's more traditional works. So, in the midst of his labors on the *Ring* cycle, the often penurious Wagner interrupted the project for a period of years to create *Tristan und Isolde* (1865) and *Die Meistersinger von Nürnberg* (*The Mastersingers of*

Nuremberg, 1868). But these, too, were long and not easy to produce. The bulky scores piled up on his desk.

In 1864, Wagner was rescued from his plight by King Ludwig II of Bavaria, who paid off his debts, gave him an annual allowance, encouraged him to complete the *Ring* tetralogy, and helped him to build a special theater where his giant operas could be mounted according to the composer's own specifications (Fig. 27–2). This opera house, or Festival Theater as Wagner called it, was constructed at Bayreuth, a small town between Munich and Leipzig in southern Germany. The first **Bayreuth Festival** took place in August 1876 with three successive performances of the entire *Ring* cycle. Following Wagner's death in 1883, his remains were interred on the grounds of the Wagner villa in Bayreuth. To this day, the Bayreuth Festival continues to stage the music dramas of Wagner—and only Wagner. Each summer thousands of opera lovers make the pilgrimage to this theatrical shrine to one of art's most determined, and ruthless, visionaries.

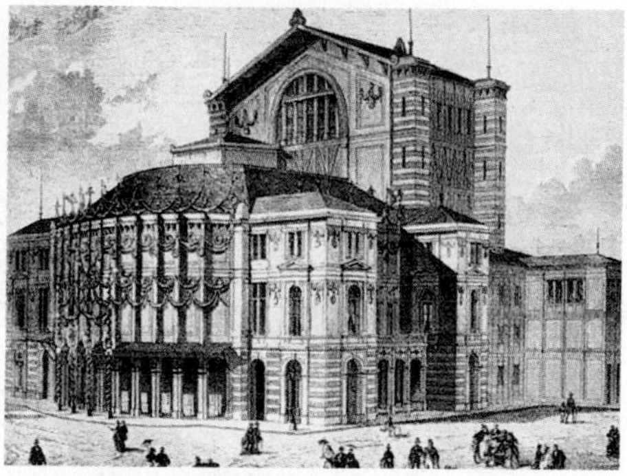

FIGURE 27–2
Bayreuth Festival Theater, an opera house built especially to produce the music dramas of Richard Wagner—and only Wagner.

Wagner's "Music Dramas"

With few exceptions, Wagner composed for the theater, ignoring such concert hall genres as the symphony and concerto. He did not call his creations operas, however, but "music dramas." A **music drama** for Wagner was a musical work for the stage in which all the arts—poetry, music, acting, mime, dance, and scenic design—function as a harmonious ensemble. Such an artistic union Wagner referred to as a ***Gesamtkunstwerk*** ("total art work"). Thus combined, the unified force of the arts would generate more realistic drama. No longer would the dramatic action grind to a halt in order to spotlight the vocal flourishes of a soloist, as often happened in Italian opera.

music dramas as total works of art

Indeed, Wagner's music drama differs from conventional Italian opera in several important ways. First, Wagner did away with the traditional "numbers" opera—a string of separate units such as aria, recitative, duet, and the like. Instead, he wrote a seamless flow of undifferentiated solo singing and declamation, what is called "endless melody." Second, he removed ensemble singing almost entirely; duets, trios, choruses, and full-cast finales became extremely rare. Finally, Wagner banished the tuneful aria to the wings. He avoids melodic repetition, symmetry, and regular cadences—all things that can make a tune "catchy"—in favor of long-flowing, nonrepetitive, not particularly song-like lines. As the tuneful aria decreases in importance, the role of the orchestra increases.

a seamless flow producing "endless melody"

With Wagner, the orchestra is everything. It sounds forth the main musical themes, develops and exploits them, and thereby "plays out" the drama through pure instrumental music. On stage, the words and actions of the singers give the audience supplementary clues as to what the musical drama in the orchestra is all about. In the 1850s, Wagner drank deeply of the philosophy of Arthur Schopenhauer (1788–1860), who wrote that "music expresses the innermost basis of the world, the essence behind appearances." In music drama, what happens on the stage is the appearance; what happens in the orchestra represents the deeper reality, the true drama.

the real drama is in the orchestra

As had Beethoven and Berlioz before him, Wagner continued to expand the size of the orchestra. The orchestra he requires for the *Ring* cycle is massive, especially with regard to the brasses: four trumpets, four trombones, eight horns (four of whom double on tuba), and a contra-bass. Perhaps most remarkable, the score calls for six harps!

A bigger orchestra demanded, in turn, more forceful singers. To be heard above an orchestra of nearly a hundred players, a large, specially trained voice was needed, the so-called Wagnerian tenor and Wagnerian soprano. The voice that typically dominates the operatic stage today—with its powerful sound and wide vibrato—first developed in Wagner's music dramas.

Tristan und Isolde (1865)

Wagner began to compose *Tristan und Isolde* during 1857 when living in Switzerland and supported in part by a wealthy patron, Otto Wesendonck. Although still married, the composer began an affair with Wesendonck's wife, Mathilde—so fully did Wagner the man live his life as Wagner the artist that it was impossible for him to create an opera dealing with passionate love without being passionately in love himself. By 1864, Wagner had made his way to Munich to prepare for the first production of the now finished *Tristan*. Having long since forgotten both Mathilde and his wife, he now fell in love with Cosima von Bülow (Fig. 27–3), the wife of the man scheduled to conduct *Tristan*. Cosima was the illegitimate daughter of Franz Liszt and Marie d'Agoult (see Figs. 25–3 and 25–4), and she and Wagner soon produced three illegitimate children of their own. The first of these, a daughter born on the first day of rehearsals for *Tristan*, was christened Isolde.

FIGURE 27–3

Cosima Wagner (daughter of Franz Liszt and Marie d'Agoult), Richard Wagner, and Liszt at Wagner's villa in Bayreuth in 1880. At the right is a young admirer of Wagner, Hans von Wolzogen, who first coined the term *leitmotif*.

The story of *Tristan und Isolde* comes from the medieval legends of King Arthur's England (Fig. 27–4). Briefly, it is the tale of the love between Isolde, an Irish princess, and Tristan, a knight in the service of King Mark of Cornwall (England). Their love, however, is both illicit and ill-fated. Isolde has mistakenly consumed a love potion, which channels her passion away from her lawful husband (King Mark) to Tristan. Despairing of any happy union with Isolde in this world, Tristan allows himself to be mortally wounded in combat and sails off to his native Brittany to die. Isolde pursues him but arrives just in time to have him expire in her arms. Knowing that their union will only be consummated through death, Isolde sings her ***Liebestod*** (*Love-Death*), an ecstatic vision of their love beyond the grave, and then she, too, expires next to her lover's body. This was the sort of all-consuming, sacrificial love so dear to the hearts of Romantic artists.

the plot of Tristan

Wagner begins *Tristan*, not with a rousing, self-contained overture, but with a simple yet beautiful prelude that sets the general tone of the drama and leads directly to the raising of the curtain. The prelude opens with a plaintive call in the cellos, answered by one in the woodwinds. Each is not so much a lengthy theme as it is a short, pregnant motive. Wagner's disciples called each a **leitmotif** (signature-tune), a brief, distinctive unit of music designed to represent a character, object, or idea, which returns repeatedly in order to facilitate the progress of the drama. Wagner's leitmotifs are usually not sung but rather are

leitmotifs (signature tunes)

played in the orchestra. In this way, an element of the subconscious can be introduced into the drama: the orchestra can give a sense of what a character is thinking even when he or she is singing about something else. By developing, extending, varying, contrasting, and resolving these representational leitmotifs, Wagner is able to play out the essence of the drama almost without recourse to his singers.

Leitmotifs in *Tristan* are associated mainly with feelings rather than concrete objects or persons. Typical are the leitmotifs representing "Longing," "Desire," and "Ecstasy."

EXAMPLE 27–1

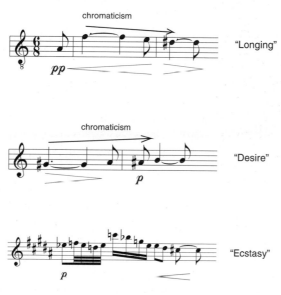

"Longing"

"Desire"

"Ecstasy"

FIGURE 27–4

Original costume designs for the premiere of Wagner's *Tristan und Isolde*, June 1865.

Notice how both the "Longing" and "Desire" motifs involve chromatic lines, the first descending, the second ascending (see arrows). This sort of linear chromatic motion made it easy for the composer to wind continually through many different keys, not stopping long enough to establish any one as a home base, or tonic*. Indeed, Wagner's intense chromatic harmony* loosened the feeling of key and eventually led to the collapse of tonality as the main organizing force in Western music, as we shall see (page 377). Here he uses twisting chromatic lines for a specific expressive purpose—to convey a sense of the anxiety and pain to be felt by the ill-fated lovers.

As you listen to the final scene of *Tristan*, you can feel Wagner trying to draw you into his all-enveloping world of love, longing, desire, and death. Here Isolde cradles the body of the dead Tristan and prepares to share his fate. As she sings her justly famous *Liebestod*, four leitmotifs sound forth, each heard previously in the opera. They frequently appear in melodic sequences*, usually moving upward so as to convey a sense of continual longing and rising tension. Cadences are avoided, thereby increasing the restless mood. Dissonances are placed at points of climax to heighten the feeling of pain and anguish. At the end, the music reaches one last, glorious climax (4:42) and hereafter all is consonance and reduced movement—Isolde has joined Tristan in the world beyond. First, listen to the *Liebestod*, concentrating on the leitmotifs as they are presented by the voice and, to a greater degree, the orchestra. Then listen once more, this time just drinking in, like a love potion, all of Wagner's divinely inspired sound. If there is such a thing as a transcendental experience in Romantic music, you will find it here.

Tristan ends with Isolde's Liebestod

Leitmotifs in Star Wars

The technique of the leitmotif, as developed by Richard Wagner, has been borrowed by many composers of Hollywood film music. To name just one: John Williams, the creator of the music for George Lucas's *Star Wars* series. When Williams wrote the music for *Star Wars*, *The Empire Strikes Back*, and *The Return of the Jedi*, he composed for each main character (and theme or force) a particular musical motive. Below are two of Williams's leitmotifs, the first signifying the hero Luke Skywalker, the second (merely an insistent rhythm) symbolizing the evil Darth Vader.

Like Wagner, Williams sets these leading motives in the orchestra, and thereby tells the audience what the character is thinking or what the future may hold. When young Luke is confined to his uncle's farm, for example, we learn that greater things await him: The orchestra plays the heroic Force leitmotif in the background. In fact, *Star Wars* has more than just leitmotifs in common with Wagner's music dramas. Both Wagner and Lucas started with a core of three dramas and added a fourth as a preface or "prequel" (*Das Rheingold* was prefixed to the *Ring* and *The Phantom Menace* to *Star Wars*). Lucas, of course, has added two further episodes to his saga, bringing his total to six, but the leitmotifs remain the same. Both Wagner's cycle and Lucas's saga play out a series of epic battles between larger-than-life heroes and villains, mythical forces for good and evil, warring throughout cosmic time.

Luke's Theme

Darth Vader's Theme

Listening Guide

Richard Wagner
Liebestod, from *Tristan und Isolde* (1865)

6   2
4/5   2/7

Characters: the lovers Tristan and Isolde
Situation: Tristan's castle in Brittany; Isolde cradles Tristan in her arms as she prepares to join him in death.

0:00	[5/7]	Isolde, gazing at Tristan, slowly sings "Love-Death" leitmotif, which is then taken up by orchestra		

Mild und leise wie er lächelt,		Oh how tenderly and gently he smiles
Wie das Auge hold er öffnet—		As he opens his eyes—
Seht ihr, Freunde? Seht ihr's nicht?		Do you see, Friends, don't you see it?
Immer lichter wie er leuchtet,		Ever brighter, how he shines,
Stern-umstrahlet hoch sich hebt?		Glowing in starlight raised on high?

1:07	Orchestra continues with "Love-Death" motif as singer goes her own way	Seht ihr's nicht?	Do you not see it?
		Wie das Herz ihm mutig schwillt,	How his heart proudly swells,
		Voll und hehr im Busen ihm quillt?	Full and brave beating in his breast?

1:37	"Ecstasy" leitmotif enters, not in voice, but in high woodwinds and then violins	

2:17	Reappearance of ascending, chromatic "Desire" motif from Prelude	Wie den Lippen, wonnig mild Süsser Atem sanft entweht— Freunde! Seht! Fühlt und seht ihr's nicht?	How from his lips, blissfully tender, Sweet breath gently flutters— Do you not see, Friends? Don't you feel and see it?

(musical notation, key signature with sharps, marked p)

2:26	"Love-Death" motif returns in voice and orchestra, followed by "Ecstasy" motif and then "Desire" motif in voice	Höre ich nur diese Weise Die so wundervoll und leise, Wonne klagend, alles sagend, Mild versöhnend aus ihm tönend, In mich dringet, auf sich schwinget, Hold erhallend um mich klinget?	Do I alone hear this melody Which, so wonderfully and gently, Moaning bliss, expressing all, Gently forgiving, sounding from within Pierces me, soars upwards, Blessedly echoing all around me?
3:33	"Transcendent Bliss" leitmotif appears in violins		

(musical notation, marked f and p)

3:53	Tension increases as "Desire" motif rises by chromatic steps in orchestra	Heller schallend, mich umwallend, Sind es Wellen sanfter Lüfte? Sind es Wolken wonniger Düfte Wie sie schwellen, mich umrauschen, Soll ich atmen, soll ich lauschen? Soll ich schlürfen, untertauchen? Süss in Düften mich verhauchen? In dem wogenden Schwall, in dem tönenden Schall.	Resounding clearly all around me, Are they waves of gentle air? Are they clouds of delightful fragrance? As they swell and envelop me, Should I breathe, should I listen? Should I sip them, plunge beneath them? Breathe my last in such sweet fragrance? In the growing swell, the surging sound.
4:42	Glorious climax with "Transcendent Bliss" motif shining forth in orchestra	In des Welt-Atems wehendem All— Ertrinken, versinken— Unbewusst— Höchste Lust!	In the vastness of the world's spirit To drown, sink down— Unconscious— Supreme bliss!

Orchestra then fades away into silence as curtain descends

Use a downloadable, cross-platform animated Active Listening Guide, available at www.thomsonedu.com/music/wright.

Listening Exercise 36

Wagner
Liebestod from *Tristan und Isolde*

6   2
4/5   2/7

ThomsonNOW
To take this Listening Exercise online and receive feedback or email answers to your instructor, go to *ThomsonNOW* for this chapter.

Isolde's *Liebestod,* which brings *Tristan und Isolde* to a glorious conclusion, is written for soprano voice—indeed, for a dramatic Wagnerian soprano. But even this powerful voice cannot always be clearly heard above Wagner's large, surging orchestra. Imagine a Verdi opera in which the hero or heroine could not be heard! As some of the following questions suggest, there are several ways in which the German music dramas of Wagner differ from the Italian operas of Verdi.

1. Does the orchestra establish a clear "um-pah" (duple-meter) or "um-pah-pah" (triple meter) accompaniment in the *Liebestod?*
   a. yes   b. no
2. When the soprano sings the "Ecstasy" leitmotif (2:48–3:11), she does so to rather square poetry—lines of 4 + 4 syllables with internal rhyme. (Try saying the German to yourself.)

Wonne klagend,	Moaning bliss,
alles sagend,	expressing all,
Mild versöhnend	Gently forgiving,
aus ihm tönend	sounding from within

What is the course of the soprano line during this couplet?

a. It rises.   b. It rises in a melodic sequence.

c. It falls.   d. It falls in a melodic sequence.

3. Immediately afterwards (3:12–3:30), the music rises toward a climax to reflect the sentiment of the next couplet:

In mich dringet,	Pierces me,
auf sich schwinget,	soars upwards,
Hold erhallend um	Blessedly echoing
mich klinget?	all around me?

How is this rising tension brought about in the music?

a. Tremolos are played by the strings.

b. There is a gradual crescendo.

c. The voice rises up chromatically.

d. All of the above.

4. (3:53–4:42) Wagner now builds to a final climax with the "Desire" leitmotif churning in the orchestra. But along the way, on the word *"lauschen"* (4:17, "listen"), he suddenly changes dynamics. To which does he change?

a. *fortissimo*   b. *pianissimo*

5. (5:05–5:39) The great climax has been reached. How does Wagner now musically depict the final words of Isolde "to drown, to sink down, unconscious—supreme bliss"?

a. The vocal line continually falls.

b. The vocal line falls, then soars up and holds a note.

c. The vocal line soars up, then falls.

6. Which leitmotif is heard softly in the oboes (at 5:59) immediately before the final chord?

a. "Ecstasy"

b. "Transcendent Bliss"

c. "Desire"

7. (5:05–6:26) In this passage, Wagner brings us to the end of the opera. The nature of the music changes to suggest a feeling of winding down. Which one of the following does *not* occur?

a. The tempo of the music appears to get slower.

b. The "Transcendent Bliss" leitmotif no longer rises upward.

c. The orchestra drives toward its own *fortissimo* climax.

d. The dynamic level gradually changes from loud to soft.

8. Who has the "last word"—that is, who is heard at the very end of the *Liebestod*?

a. the orchestra   b. the voice

9. Which musical force could be omitted without serious loss to the overall effect of the piece?

a. the orchestra   b. the voice

10. Which of the following is true about the *Liebestod*?

a. Wagner places tremendous demands on the singer, in part because the voice has no pauses of more than three seconds until she ceases at 5:20.

b. Although Wagner places tremendous demands on the singer, requiring mostly *fortissimo* singing, he nonetheless builds in several "breaks" (rests) of about 10 seconds duration along the way.

Key Words

Singspiel (303)	music drama (305)	leitmotif (306)
Ring cycle (304)	*Gesamtkunstwerk* (305)	
Bayreuth Festival (305)	*Liebestod* (306)	

Nineteenth-Century Realistic Opera

Romantic opera, both Italian and German, typically concludes with an ending in which the lovers are eternally united, if not in this world, then in the one beyond. Moreover, the stage is populated by larger-than-life characters or by the well-to-do, people of leisure untroubled by mundane concerns or financial worries. During the second half of the nineteenth century, however, a contrasting type of opera developed in Europe, one more in tune with the social truths of the day. It is called **realistic opera,** because the subject matter treats issues of everyday life in a realistic way. Poverty, physical abuse, industrial exploitation, and crime—afflictions of the lower classes in particular—are presented on stage for all to see. In realistic opera, rarely is there a happy ending.

Realistic opera reflected the social, scientific, and artistic developments of the nineteenth century, which saw the worst effects of the industrial revolution, including oppressive factory conditions resulting in widespread social disintegration. The nineteenth century also witnessed the emergence of the theory of evolution, first popularized in Charles Darwin's *On the Origin of Species* (1859), which posits a "dog-eat-dog" world in which only the fittest survive. Painters such as J.-F. Millet (1814–1875) and the young Vincent van Gogh (1853–1890) captured on canvas the life of the downtrodden (Fig. 28–1), as did writers Charles Dickens (1812–1870) and Emile Zola (1840–1902) in their realistic novels. The aim of these artists was to transform the mundane and the commonplace into art, to find the poetic and mystical in even the most ordinary aspects of human experience.

realism in nineteenth-century science and art

Reflecting a similar intent, the plots of realistic operas embrace the gritty side of life. In Bizet's *Carmen* (1875), the heroine is a knife-wielding gypsy girl who works in a cigarette factory; in Leoncavallo's *Pagliacci* (1892), a jealous

FIGURE 28–1

Vincent van Gogh, *The Potato Eaters* (1886). During his youth, van Gogh chose to live and work in the coal-mining region of eastern Belgium. This grim painting records his impressions of life within a mining family and the evening meal of potatoes and tea.

Van Gogh Museum, Amsterdam/Art Resource, NY

clown stabs his wife to death; and in Puccini's *Tosca* (1892), an abused singer murders the chief of police. If traditional Romantic opera is usually sentimental and idealistic, nineteenth-century realistic opera is sensational and usually pessimistic.

GEORGES BIZET'S CARMEN (1875)

The first important realistic opera is Georges Bizet's *Carmen* (1875). Bizet (1838–1875), who spent his short life entirely in Paris, was primarily an opera composer, and *Carmen* is his masterpiece. Set in nineteenth-century Spain, *Carmen* centers on a sensual young gypsy woman known only as Carmen (Fig. 28–2). This sexually assertive, willful woman holds the populace in her sway. By means of her alluring dance and song, she seduces a naïve army corporal, Don José. Falling hopelessly in love, Don José deserts his military post, "marries" Carmen, and takes up with her gypsy bandit friends. But Carmen, who refuses to belong to any man, soon abandons Don José to give herself to the handsome bullfighter Escamillo. Having lost all for nothing, the humiliated Don José stabs Carmen to death in a bloody ending.

the plot of Carmen

This violent conclusion highlights the stark realism of *Carmen*. The heroine is a woman of easy virtue available to every man, albeit on her own terms. She lives for the moment, surrounded by social outcasts (gypsies), prostitutes, and bandits. All this was shocking stuff for the refined Parisian audiences of Bizet's day. During the first rehearsals in 1875, the women of the chorus threatened to strike because they were asked to smoke and fight on stage. Critics called the libretto "obscene." Bizet's producers asked him to tone down the more lurid aspects of the drama (especially the bloody ending)—to make it more acceptable as family entertainment—but he refused.

FIGURE 28–2
Sally Burgess sings the seductive role of Carmen in a 1998 production by the English National Opera.

Carmen is full of alluring melodies including the well-known Toreador Song and the even more beloved Habanera. In fashioning these tunes, Bizet borrowed phrases from several Spanish popular songs, folksongs, and **flamenco** melodies (songs of southern Spain infused with gypsy elements). The Habanera, which introduces the character Carmen, makes use of a then-popular Spanish song.

Literally, **Habanera** means "the thing from Havana." Musically, it is a type of dance-song that developed in Spanish-controlled Cuba during the early nineteenth century. African and Latin influences on its musical style can perhaps be seen in the descending chromatic scale, and certainly in the static harmony (the downbeat of every measure is a D in the bass), as well as in the insistent, repetitive rhythm [♩♪♪ | ♪♪♪]. The infectious rhythm of the Habanera gives it its irresistible quality—we all want to get up and join the dance. But the Habanera is a sensual dance, like its later descendant the tango, and this sensual quality contributes greatly to Carmen's seductive aura.

The structure of Bizet's Habanera is straightforward. At first, Carmen sings a descending chromatic line of four 4-bar phrases ("Love is like an elusive bird"). By their nature, highly chromatic melodies often seem to have no tonal center. This one, too, is musically noncommittal and slippery, just as Carmen herself is both ambiguous and evasive. The chorus immediately repeats the chromatic melody, but now Carmen voluptuously glides above it, singing the single word "*L'amour*" ("Love"). As her voice soars, like the elusive bird of love, the tonality shifts from minor to major. To this is then added a refrain ("Love is like a gypsy child") in which the melody alternates between a major triad

Carmen *from Flop to Hip-Hop*

At its premiere in Paris on March 3, 1875, *Carmen* was a flop—the realistic subject matter was thought too degrading. Despondent over this poor reception, composer Georges Bizet suffered a fatal heart attack exactly ninety days later.

As the nineteenth century unfolded and theatrical subjects became increasingly realistic, however, the appeal of *Carmen* grew. Now arguably the world's most popular opera, *Carmen* has been recorded many times and has been transformed into nearly twenty films, including an early silent one of 1915 and an Academy Award–winning production of 1984. In addition, the most popular melo-

dies of *Carmen* serve as background music in countless TV commercials and cartoons. In an early episode of *The Simpsons*, for example, the family goes to the opera where it hears—what else?—*Carmen*, and Bart and Homer sing along. *Carmen* has also been refashioned into an African opera set in Senegal (*Karmen Gei*, 2001), an African-American Broadway musical (*Carmen Jones*, 1954), and an MTV special (*Carmen: A Hip Hopera*, starring Beyoncé Knowles, 2001). Not surprisingly for a realistic opera, *Carmen* is a work that transcends race and class, and that quality accounts in part for its lasting popularity.

and a minor one. Against this refrain, the chorus shouts, "Watch out!" warning of Carmen's destructive qualities. This same structure—a chromatically descending melody, followed by a triadic refrain with choral shouts—then repeats. Bizet wanted this Habanera to establish the character of Carmen as a sensual enchantress. In every way, the music *is* Carmen. And like Carmen, once this seductive melody has us in its spell, it will never let go.

Listening Guide　Georges Bizet
Habanera from the opera *Carmen* (1875)

6
4/6

Situation: The scantily clad gypsy woman Carmen, exuding an almost primeval sexuality, dances before Don José, soldiers, and other gypsies.

0:00　6　Bass ostinato with Habanera rhythm; minor mode
0:06　　Carmen enters with enticing descending melody

(continued)

L'amour est un oiseau rebelle	Love is like an elusive bird,
Que nul ne peut apprivoiser;	That cannot be tamed;
Et c'est bien en vain qu'on l'appelle,	You call it in vain
S'il lui convient de refuser.	If it decides to refuse.
Rien n'y fait, menace ou prière,	Neither threat nor prayer will prevail;
L'un parle bien, l'autre se tait;	One man talks a lot, the other is silent;
Et c'est l'autre que je préfère	And it's the latter I prefer,
Il n'a rien dit; mais il me plaît.	He hasn't said a word, but he pleases me.

0:38 Change to major mode; chorus repeats melody; Carmen soars above on word "Love"
0:53 Carmen sings refrain

L'amour est enfant de Bohème,	Love is like a gypsy child,
Il n'a jamais connu de loi,	Who has never known constraint,
Si tu ne m'aimes pas, je t'aime;	If I love you, and you don't love me,
Si je t'aime, prends garde à toi!	Watch out!

1:09 Chorus shouts "Watch out!"
1:32 Chorus sings refrain with Carmen

Second stanza

2:09 Bass ostinato with Habanera rhythm
2:17 Carmen enters with enticing chromatic melody

L'oiseau que tu croyais surprendre	The bird you thought you'd surprised
Battit de l'aile et s'envola;	Beat its wings and flew away;
L'amour est loin, tu peux l'attendre;	Love is far away, but expect it;
Tu ne l'attends plus, il est là!	You don't expect it, but there it is!
Tout autour de toi, vite,	All around you, quick!
Il vient, s'en va, puis il revient;	It comes, it goes, and then it returns;
Tu crois le tenir, il t'évite;	You think you've trapped it, it escapes;
Tu crois l'éviter, il te tient!	You think you've escaped it, it traps you!

2:50 Change to major mode; chorus repeats melody; Carmen soars above on word "Love"
3:05 Carmen, chorus (3:41), and then Carmen (3:58) again sing refrain

 Use a downloadable, cross-platform animated Active Listening Guide, available
at **www.thomsonedu.com/music/wright**.

Listening Exercise 37

Bizet
Habanera from *Carmen*

6
4/6

ThomsonNOW
To take this Listening Exercise online and
receive feedback or email answers to your
instructor, go to *ThomsonNOW* for this chapter.

The enduring popularity of Bizet's *Carmen* can be explained in part by its sensational plot, socially diverse characters, captivating melodies, and rousing choruses, as the following questions suggest.

1. (0:00–0:37) Which sensual dance has the same rhythmic pattern as the Habanera?
   a. the flamenco
   b. the fandango
   c. the tango

2. (0:00–0:37) The sultry mood of the beginning is created in part by the presence of which mode?
   a. major   b. minor

3. (0:06–0:10) What type of scale does the elusive Carmen execute when she first begins to sing?
   a. major   b. minor   c. chromatic

4. (0:20–0:30) How do we sense that Carmen is a sensual creature?

a. The singer does not move from one exact pitch to the next but slides upward between pitches.
b. The singer shakes an exotic percussion instrument called the castanet.
c. The singer recalls her earlier days as a cigar maker in Havana.

5. (0:38–0:54) When the chorus enters, it sings what?
   a. a flamenco tune   b. a gypsy melody
   c. the melody just sung by Carmen

6. (0:53–1:32) Carmen now sings the refrain. What is the mode of the refrain?
   a. major   b. minor

7. (2:09–end) Consider the second stanza of the Habanera. Which is true?
   a. It is essentially the same in content and length as the first stanza.
   b. It offers an elaborate variation of the first stanza.

8. Accordingly, what is the form of this Habanera?
   a. strophic
   b. theme and variations
   c. through-composed
9. Which of the following cultures is *not* represented in Bizet's Habanera?
   a. French   b. Spanish   c. gypsy
   d. English   e. Cuban

10. What likely makes Bizet's Habanera such a successful number?
    a. It possesses not one, but two seductive melodies, one major, the other minor.
    b. It combines the beauty of an aria with the power of a chorus.
    c. Despite the sometimes soaring vocal lines, it is firmly grounded on an ostinato bass.
    d. All of the above.

GIACOMO PUCCINI'S LA BOHÈME (1896)

Italian realistic opera of the late nineteenth century goes by its own special name, **verismo opera** (*verismo* is Italian for "realism"). Yet while it enjoys a separate name, *verismo* opera in Italy was little different than realistic opera elsewhere. Although many Italian composers wrote *verismo* operas, by far the best known today is Giacomo Puccini, who also created early-twentieth-century exotic operas (see Chapter 32).

Giacomo Puccini (1858–1924) was the scion of four generations of musicians from the northern Italian town of Lucca (Fig. 28–3). His father and his grandfather had both written operas, and his forebears before them had composed religious music for the local cathedral. But Puccini was no child prodigy. For a decade following his graduation from the Milan Conservatory, he lived in poverty as he struggled to develop a distinctive operatic style. Not until the age of thirty-five did he score his first triumph, the *verismo* opera *Manon Lescaut* (1893). Thereafter, successes came in quick order: *La bohème* (1896), *Tosca* (1900), and *Madama Butterfly* (1904). Growing famous, wealthy, and a bit complacent, Puccini worked less and less frequently. His last, and many believe his best, opera, *Turandot* (see Chapter 32), was left unfinished at the time of his death from throat cancer in 1924.

Puccini's best-known opera—indeed the most famous of all *verismo* operas—is *La bohème* (*Bohemian Life*, 1896). The realism of *La bohème* rests in the setting and characters: the principals are bohemians—unconventional artists living in abject poverty. The hero, Rodolfo (a poet), and his pals Schaunard (a musician), Colline (a philosopher), and Marcello (a painter), inhabit an unheated attic on the Left Bank of Paris. The heroine, Mimi, their neighbor, is a poor, tubercular seamstress. Rodolfo and Mimi meet and fall in love. He grows obsessively jealous while she becomes progressively ill. They separate for a time, only to return to each other's arms immediately before Mimi's death. If this sounds familiar, there may be a reason: the Pulitzer Prize–winning musical *Rent* (1996, produced as a motion picture in 2005) is a modern adaptation of this bohemian tale, but here the protagonist dies of AIDS in Greenwich Village, rather than of tuberculosis in Paris.

In truth, there is not much of a plot to *La bohème*, nor is there much character development. Instead, the glorious sound of the human voice carries the day. Puccini continues the nineteenth-century tendency to lessen the distinction between recitative and aria. His solos typically start syllabically (no more than one note per syllable), as if the character is beginning a conversation. Gradually, the voice grows in intensity and becomes more expansive, with the strings doubling the melody to add warmth and expression. When Rodolfo,

FIGURE 28–3
Giacomo Puccini.

for example, sings of Mimi's frozen little hand in the aria "Che gelida man-
ina," we move imperceptibly from recitative to aria, gradually transcending
the squalor of the Left Bank garret and soaring to a better world far beyond.
The contrast between the dreary stage setting and the transcendental beauty
of the music is the great paradox of realistic opera.

Listening Guide

Giacomo Puccini
La bohème (1896)
Aria, "Ah, what a frozen little hand"

6
4/7

Characters: the poor poet Rodolfo and the equally impoverished seamstress Mimi
Situation: Mimi has knocked on Rodolfo's door to ask for a light for her candle. Charmed by the lovely stranger, he naturally obliges. The wind again blows out Mimi's candle, and amidst the confusion she drops her key. As the two search for it
in the darkness, Rodolfo by chance touches her hand and, then holding it, seizes the moment to tell her about himself and
his hopes.

0:00	**7**	Rodolfo begins conversationally, much like in recitative	Che gelida manina se la lasci riscaldar. Cercar che giova? Al buio non si trova. Ma per fortuna è una notte di luna, e qui la luna l'abbiamo vicina.	Ah, what a frozen little hand, let me warm it up. What's the good of searching? We won't find it in the dark. But by good luck there is moonlight tonight, and here we have the moon nearby.

(Mimi tries to withdraw her hand)

1:03		Voice increases in range, volume, and intensity	Aspetti, signorina, le dirò con due parole chi son, e che faccio, come vivo. Vuole? Chi son? Sono un poeta. Che cosa faccio? Scrivo. E come vivo? Vivo!	Wait, young lady, I will tell you in two words who I am and what I do, how I live. Would you like this? Who am I? I'm a poet. What do I do? I write. How do I live? I live!

(Rodolfo proceeds to explain who he is and what he does)

1:52		Return to conversational style	In povertà mia lieta scialo da gran signore rime et inni d'amore. Per sogni et per chimere e per castelli in aria, l'anima ho milionaria.	In my delightful poverty I grandiosely scatter rhymes and songs of love. Through dreams and reveries and through castles in the air, I have the soul of a millionaire.
2:30		Voice grows more expansive with longer notes and higher range; orchestra doubles voice in unison	Talor dal mio forziere ruban tutti i gioelli due ladri: gli occhi belli. V'entrar con voi pur ora, ed i miei sogni usati e i bei sogni miei tosto si dileguar! Ma il furto non m'accora,	Sometimes from the strongbox two thieves steal all the jewels: two pretty eyes. They came in with you just now and my usual dreams, my lovely dreams vanish at once! But the theft doesn't bother me
3:24		Orchestra sounds melody alone; then is joined by voice for climactic high note "hope"	poichè v'ha preso stanza la speranza!	because their place has been taken by hope!

(As music diminishes, Rodolfo asks for a response from Mimi)

			Or che mi conoscete, parlate voi, deh! parlate. Chi siete? Vi piaccia dir!	Now that you know who I am, Tell me about yourself, speak. Who are you? Please speak.

 Use a downloadable, cross-platform animated Active Listening Guide, available
at **www.thomsonedu.com/music/wright**.

ThomsonNOW™

ThomsonNOW for *Listening to Music, 5th Edition*, and *Listening to Western Music* will assist you in understanding the content of this chapter with lesson plans generated for your specific needs. In addition, you may complete this chapter's Listening Exercise in ThomsonNOW's interactive environment, as well as download Active Listening Guides and other materials that will help you succeed in this course.

Key Words

realistic opera (311)   Habanera (312)

flamenco (312)   *verismo* opera (315)

Music and Nationalism

Chapter
29

Music does not exist in isolation. As we have seen with realistic opera (Chapter 28), it is often influenced by contemporary social, scientific, and artistic developments. So, too, music can be affected by politics. The nineteenth century was a period in which various European ethnic groups sought to free themselves from foreign domination. During the 1820s and 1830s, the Greeks fought to throw off the rule of the Ottoman Turks, the Poles worked (unsuccessfully) to end control by the Russians, and the Belgians broke free from the Dutch. Simultaneously, lands previously divided into small states became unified nations. In 1861, Italy, once a patchwork of city-states controlled by Austria and Spain, achieved full independence and unification, with Rome as its capital. Ten years later, a German nation, under the political leadership of Chancellor Otto von Bismarck (1815–1898), was formally recognized. Smaller groups, such as the Czechs, Hungarians, Poles, and Finns, sought to break free from more powerful nations, such as Germany, Austria, and Russia. These groups likewise exhibited pride in their national traditions, each highlighting its cultural individuality through artistic expression.

wars of independence

Owing to its emotive power, music naturally gave voice to ethnic and linguistic distinction, a process called **musical nationalism.** A flood of national anthems, native dances, protest songs, and victory symphonies gave musical expression to the rising tide of nationalism. *The Star Spangled Banner*, the *Marseillaise* (French national anthem), and *Italian Brothers, Italy Has Arisen* (Italian national anthem) were all products of revolution and patriotic zeal. National color in music was communicated by means of indigenous folk elements— folksongs, native scales, dance rhythms, and local instrumental sounds. It could also be conveyed by the use of national subjects—the life of a national hero, for example—as the program for a symphonic poem* or the libretto for an opera. Among musical compositions with overtly nationalistic titles are *Hungarian Rhapsodies* (Liszt), *Russian Easter Overture* (Nikolai Rimsky-Korsakov), *Slavonic Dances* (Antonin Dvořák), and *Finlandia* (Jean Sibelius).

indigenous musical elements create musical nationalism

FIGURE 29-1
Modest Musorgsky.

Tretyakov Gallery, Moscow/The Bridgeman Art Library

RUSSIAN NATIONALISM: MODEST MUSORGSKY (1839–1881)

Russia was one of the first countries to develop its own national style of art music, one distinct and separate from the traditions of German orchestral music and Italian and German opera. An early use of Russian subject matter can be found in Mikhail Glinka's opera *A Life for the Tsar* (1836). Glinka's nationalist spirit was passed to a group of young composers whom contemporaries dubbed "The Mighty Handful" or, less grandiosely, the **Russian Five:** Alexander Borodin (1833–1887), César Cui (1835–1918), Mily Balakirev (1837–1910), Nikolai Rimsky-Korsakov (1844–1908), and Modest Musorgsky (1839–1881). They dedicated themselves to writing Russian music, free of Western influence, for the Russian people. Of these, the most original and least Western in musical style was Musorgsky (Fig. 29–1).

As with most members of the "Russian Five," Musorgsky did not at first seem destined for a career in music. He was trained to be a military officer, and for a period of four years was commissioned in the Russian army. He resigned his appointment in 1858 in favor of a minor post as a civil servant and more free time to indulge his avocation, musical composition. The next year he said, "I have been a cosmopolitan, but now there's been some sort of regeneration. Everything Russian is becoming dear to me." Unfortunately, his brief, chaotic life was marked by increasing poverty, depression, and alcoholism. During his few periods of creative productivity, Musorgsky managed to compile a small *oeuvre*, which includes a boldly inventive symphonic poem, *Night on Bald Mountain* (1867); an imaginative set of miniatures for piano, *Pictures at an Exhibition* (1874); and an operatic masterpiece, *Boris Godunov* (1874), based on the life of a popular sixteenth-century Russian tsar. Many of Musorgsky's works were left unfinished at the time of his death in 1881.

Pictures at an Exhibition (1874)

a musical walk through a picture gallery

The genesis of *Pictures at an Exhibition* can be traced to the death of Musorgsky's close friend, the Russian painter and architect Victor Hartmann, who had died suddenly of a heart attack in 1873. As a memorial to Hartmann, an exhibition of his paintings and drawings was mounted in Moscow the next year. Musorgsky was inspired to capture the spirit of Hartmann's works in a series of ten short pieces for piano. To provide unity within the sequence of musical pictures, the composer hit on the idea of incorporating a recurring interlude, which he called "Promenade." This gave the listener the impression of enjoying a leisurely stroll through a gallery, moving from one of Hartmann's paintings to the next each time the Promenade music was heard. Though originally composed as a work for piano, the imaginative sounds of the ten musical pictures begged for orchestration, a task that several composers later undertook.

from piano to orchestra

Pictures at an Exhibition is best known today in the brilliantly orchestrated version by Maurice Ravel, completed in 1922.

PROMENADE

Here the composer projects himself, and by extension the listener, as wandering through an exposition of Hartmann paintings. Immediately, we are transported musically into a world of purely Russian art. The tempo is marked

"Fast but resolute, in the Russian manner"; the meter is irregular, as in a folk dance, with alternating five- and six-beat measures; and the melody is built on a folk-influenced **pentatonic scale,** which uses only five notes instead of the usual Western scale of seven, here B♭, C, D, F, and G.

EXAMPLE 29–1

Allegro guisto, nel modo russico

Now begins a musical depiction of ten paintings. We focus our gaze on numbers 4, 6, and 10.

PICTURE 4: *POLISH OX-CART*

Hartmann's scene is a view of a rickety ox-cart seen lumbering down a dirt road. The rocking of the cart is suggested by a two-note ostinato*. Notice in this brief composition how music can project a sense of time and movement in a way that a painting cannot. In Musorgsky's setting, the viewer remains stationary as the cart appears in the distance (*pp*), moves closer and closer by means of a crescendo (reaching *fff*), and slowly disappears as the orchestra is gradually reduced to playing *ppp*. In addition, Musorgsky was aware of an important acoustical phenomenon: larger sound waves (and hence lower pitches) travel farther than shorter waves (higher pitches). (This is why we hear the bass drum and tubas of an approaching marching band long before we hear the higher trumpets and clarinets.) Thus, in *Polish Ox-Cart*, Musorgsky begins and ends with the very lowest sounds (orchestrated with tuba and double basses), to give the impression that the sound comes from a distance and then disappears again into the distance.

PICTURE 6: *SAMUEL GOLDENBERG AND SCHMUYLE: TWO JEWS, RICH AND POOR*

As the title suggests, we are looking here at a pair of Hartmann's drawings, both of which are reproduced (Figs. 29–2 and 29–3). One Jew (Goldenberg) gazes forward confidently; the other (Schmuyle) displays an attitude of despair. They might just as well be two Christians or two Muslims—what counts here is social status, not religion. The oriental quality of Musorgsky's musical setting, however, makes clear that the two hail from Eastern Europe. In particular, the augmented

FIGURE 29–2 AND 29–3

(top) Victor Hartmann, pencil drawing, *A Rich Jew.* The subject wears a comfortable fur skull cap, the symbol of his religion. (bottom) Victor Hartmann, pencil and watercolor, *A Poor Jew.* The subject sits downcast, a sack containing his worldly possessions placed nearby. Musorgsky created appropriately downcast music to characterize this figure.

RIA Novosti/The Bridgeman Art Library

RIA Novosti/The Bridgeman Art Library

FIGURE 29–4

Victor Hartmann's vision *The Great Gate of Kiev*, which inspired the last of the musical paintings in Musorgsky's *Pictures at an Exhibition*. Note the bells in the tower, a motif that is featured prominently at the very end of Musorgsky's musical evocation of this design.

second (here Db-E), which Musorgsky associates with Goldenberg, recalls the Eastern European folk music genre of Jewish klezmer*.

PICTURE 10: *THE GREAT GATE OF KIEV*

The stimulus for the majestic conclusion to *Pictures at an Exhibition* was Hartmann's design for a new and grandiose gate to the ancient city of Kiev, then part of Russia. Musorgsky arranges his thematic material to give the impression of a parade passing beneath the giant gate, in what is tantamount to rondo form (here **ABABCA**). The majestic vision of the gate (**A**) alternates with religious music for a procession of Russian pilgrims (**B**), and even the composer-viewer walks beneath the gate as the Promenade theme (**C**) appears, before a final return to a panoramic view of the gate (**A**), now with Hartmann's bells ringing triumphantly.

In this climactic final tableau, Ravel's setting for full orchestra is able to give more powerful expression to all of the local color and grandeur inherent in Musorgsky's original music for piano, just as Musorgsky's musical creation is a more powerful artistic statement than was Hartmann's original design (Fig. 29–4).

Listening Guide

Modest Musorgsky
Pictures at an Exhibition (1874)
(orchestrated by Maurice Ravel, 1922)

6 4/8–11   **2** 2/8–9

PROMENADE

0:00	**8**	Solo trumpet begins *Promenade* theme
0:08		Full brasses respond
0:15		Trumpet and full brasses continue to alternate
0:30		Full strings, and then woodwinds and brasses enter
1:22		Brasses briefly restate *Promenade* theme

PICTURE 4: POLISH OX-CART

0:00	**9**	Solo tuba plays Ox-Cart melody against backdrop of two-note ostinato
0:51		Strings, and full orchestra join in
1:33		Full orchestra plays Ox-Cart theme (note rattle of tambourine)
1:54		Tuba returns with Ox-Cart theme
2:24		Diminuendo and fadeout

PICTURE 6: SAMUEL GOLDENBERG AND SCHMUYLE: TWO JEWS, RICH AND POOR

0:00	**10**	Strings in unison play imposing music of Goldenberg

0:45		Trumpet (with mute), accompanied by woodwinds, plays trembling music of Schmuyle
1:23		Strings loudly interject the music of Goldenberg
1:51		Music of Schmuyle slithers away in strings

PICTURE 10: THE GREAT GATE OF KIEV

0:00		A	Gate theme in full brasses
1:05		B	Pilgrims' hymn sounds in woodwind choir
1:35		A	Gate theme in brasses, with running scales in strings
2:10		B	Pilgrims' reappear in woodwinds
2:42		X	Exotic sounds
3:21		C	Promenade theme returns in trumpet
3:59		A	Gate theme in full glory, with bells added toward end

 Use a downloadable, cross-platform animated Active Listening Guide, available at **www.thomsonedu.com/music/wright**.

Listening Exercise 38

Musorgsky
Pictures at an Exhibition

ThomsonNOW
To take this Listening Exercise online and receive feedback or email answers to your instructor, go to *ThomsonNOW* for this chapter.

6   2
4/8–11   2/8–9

For *Pictures at an Exhibition*, the exercise is limited to *Promenade* and *The Great Gate of Kiev*, both of which are available on the 2CD set and the 6CD set.

Promenade

1. (0:00–0:14) Throughout *Promenade*, the meter is irregular, which is typical of Eastern European folk music. What is correct regarding the beginning?
   a. The trumpet plays for eleven beats, and the full brasses respond for twenty-two beats.
   b. The trumpet plays for twenty-two beats, and the full brasses for twenty-two beats.
   c. The trumpet plays for eleven beats, and the full brasses for eleven beats.

2. (0:15–0:29) There are two complementary musical phrases. Which is true of each?
   a. The trumpet plays the first eleven beats, and the brasses the next eleven.
   b. The trumpet plays the first seven beats, and the brasses join for the next four.

3. (0:00–0:29) How would you describe the musical texture here?
   a. A monophonic trumpet is followed by polyphonic brass choir.
   b. A monophonic trumpet is followed by a homophonic brass choir.

4. (0:50–1:02) The irregular meter continues as the larger orchestra plays. Which of the following is true about the metrical groups in this section? (Compare 0:50–0:57 with 0:58–1:02.)
   a. Units of two beats are followed by units of three.
   b. Units of three beats are followed by units of two.

5. (1:21–end) Which is true about the ending of *Promenade*?
   a. A phrase of eleven beats is followed by a phrase of nine.
   b. A phrase of nine beats is followed by a phrase of eleven.

The Great Gate of Kiev

6. (0:00–1:04) How would you describe the mode and texture at the beginning?
   a. major and polyphonic
   b. major and homophonic
   c. minor and polyphonic
   d. minor and homophonic

7. (0:00–1:04) Tap your foot to the music and try conducting, first with a duple-meter pattern and then with a triple-meter one. Which of the following is true?
   a. The music has a regular duple meter.
   b. The music has a regular triple meter.
   c. The music continues the irregular meter of *Promenade*.

8. (2:42–3:19) Exotic sounds, similar to those of Eastern music, are suggested in this passage. Which is *not* one of them?
   a. a Chinese erhu* playing the melody
   b. the sound of a gong and cymbals
   c. a shimmering tremolo in the strings
   d. a static harmony that repeats in four-beat cycles

9. (5:00–end) To give the conclusion a feeling of majesty, what happens?
   a. The full orchestra plays and the tempo slows.
   b. The full orchestra drives quickly and triumphantly to the end.

10. (5:00–end) Why do percussive sounds simulating bells appear so prominently at the end?
    a. In the nineteenth century, church bells were rung at moments of national rejoicing.
    b. In the nineteenth century, a ringing bell signaled the closing of the picture gallery.

CZECH NATIONALISM: ANTONÍN DVOŘÁK (1841–1904)

In the nineteenth century, Russia, with its huge army, was capable of dominating its neighbors. The Czechs, on the other hand, were a much smaller ethnic group surrounded, and often controlled, by foreigners (Fig. 29–5). The country we today call The Czech Republic, comprising the provinces of Bohemia and Moravia, has had an unstable past. At various times in its history, this territory has been united to a land to the east called Slovakia, originally settled by the **Slavs,** an ethnic group found throughout much of Eastern Europe. While most Czechs today have a mixture of Germanic and Slavic blood, their language, Czech, is a Slavic language. Much of their cultural heritage, including Antonín Dvořák's *Slavonic Dances,* is also Slavic.

a musical "late bloomer"

Antonín Dvořák (his name is pronounced "Dah-vor-shock") is a classic case of the "late bloomer"; or, perhaps more accurately, his talent was late to be recognized, owing to the comparative obscurity of the minority culture to which he belonged. The son of a butcher, Dvořák spent the first twenty years of his adult life as a freelance musician in Prague, where he cobbled together a living as a violist and organist, playing in dance bands, opera orchestras, and in church. Yet all the while he composed tirelessly—operas, symphonies,

FIGURE 29–5

The Czech Republic.

string quartets, and songs, almost all of which went unheard. When recognition came, it was thanks to the intervention of the composer Johannes Brahms, who encouraged the German music publisher Fritz Simrock to print some of Dvořák's music. Knowing that Brahms's *Hungarian Dances* had been a commercial success, Simrock commissioned from Dvořák a collection of eight piano pieces called *Slavonic Dances* (1878). To the astonishment of both publisher and composer, these caught on like wildfire. Almost overnight, Dvořák became known across Europe.

Simrock's firm got rich from Dvořák's *Slavonic Dances*, though the composer received only the equivalent of two months income. (There were no artists' royalties at this time; the composer or author simply sold the work for a flat fee to the publisher, who took all risks and kept all revenues.) What Dvořák did receive from this publication was recognition. Commissions from various orchestras and conductors now poured in. During the 1880s, his symphonies, string quartets, and choral works were heard in London, Berlin, Vienna, Dresden, Leipzig, Moscow, Budapest, and even Cincinnati, which then had a large Czech population. In 1892, Dvořák came to New York, for the equivalent of an annual salary of $700,000 today, to direct the National Conservatory of Music. While in America he composed his "American" Quartet and his Symphony No. 9, "From the New World." He died in Prague in 1904, a Czech national hero.

Slavonic Dances bring recognition

Among Dvořák's nationalistic compositions are his two sets of *Slavonic Dances* (1878 and 1886), *Slavonic Rhapsodies* (1879), and *Moravian Duets* (1875). In his *Slavonic Dances*, Dvořák captures in music the spirit of several indigenous Czech dances, including the furiant and the *skočná* (jump dance), as well as dances from neighboring Germany and Poland, specifically the polka and mazurka* (see page 228). The **furiant** is a fast folk dance in which duple and triple meter alternate. Dvořák wrote several furiants, including one in his Symphony No. 6 and one in his Piano Quintet in A major. In the first set of *Slavonic Dances*, the furiant appears as the last of eight dances where it provides a rousing conclusion. Although barred in $\frac{3}{4}$, here three groups of two beats consistently precede two groups of three beats (see Ex. 29–2). The prominence of the B♮ in the score (bar 5) signals a sudden shift from minor to major mode. Again, irregular meter, as well as the constant alternation of major and minor modes, are hallmarks of Eastern European folk music. Capitalizing on the instant success of the *Slavonic Dances*, Dvořák arranged them for orchestra, and, as with *Pictures at an Exhibition*, this more colorful orchestral version is the one most often performed today.

a suite of folk dances

EXAMPLE 29–2

Listening Guide   Antonín Dvořák
Furiant from *Slavonic Dances*, Opus 46 (1876)

6
4/12

Genre: dance from dance suite arranged for orchestra
Form: ternary with coda

0:00   12   Energetic dance alternating duple and triple meter
as well as minor and major mode

1:21   Contrasting quiet section with
slow tempo, clear triple meter,
and major mode

1:54   Energetic dance returns

3:07   Coda: bold harmonic shifts; reminisence of contrasting slow section; final recall of opening

 Use a downloadable, cross-platform animated Active Listening Guide, available
at www.thomsonedu.com/music/wright.

Key Words

musical nationalism (317)	Russian Five (318)	Slavs (322)
	pentatonic scale (319)	furiant (323)

Late Romantic Orchestral Music

Chapter 30

During the last decades of the nineteenth century, orchestral music—especially German orchestral music—came increasingly to dominate the European musical scene. The continued growth in the number and variety of instruments made listening to a live symphony orchestra the most powerful aesthetic experience that a citizen of the late nineteenth century could enjoy. As the orchestra expanded, so too did the hall in which it performed. The period 1870–1910 was a golden age for the construction of large concert halls, not only in Europe but also in the United States. Auditoriums constructed during this period, such as the Musikverein (1870) in Vienna and Carnegie Hall (1893) in New York, remain the finest ever built, especially with regard to their excellent acoustics.

As the symphony orchestra grew in size, the genres of music it performed became more numerous. The vogue for program music, as we have seen, resulted in the program symphony* and the symphonic poem*. At the same time, the orchestra appropriated the art song*, transporting it from the parlor to the concert hall, so that now the singer of a *Lied* was often accompanied not merely by a piano but by a full orchestra. Finally, the symphony itself grew ever longer and more complex, a direct response to the increased number and variety of instruments. Let us review briefly the history of the symphony during the nineteenth century.

THE LATE ROMANTIC SYMPHONY

The four-movement symphony originated during the Classical period (1750–1820), principally in the orchestral works of Haydn and Mozart, and remained a favorite with audiences throughout the nineteenth century, except in Italy (obsessed as it was with opera). Symphonic composers in the Romantic period generally continued to follow the four-movement format inherited from their Classical forebears—(1) fast, (2) slow, (3) minuet or scherzo, (4) fast. Yet throughout the nineteenth century, the length of movements got progressively longer. Perhaps as a consequence, composers wrote fewer symphonies. Schumann and Brahms composed only four, Mendelssohn five, Tchaikovsky six, and Dvořák, Bruckner, and Mahler each nine. No one approached the 40-odd symphonies of Mozart, to say nothing of the 104 of Haydn.

composers write fewer but longer symphonies

For a Romantic composer contemplating the creation of a symphony or concerto, no figure loomed larger than Beethoven. Wagner asked why anyone after Beethoven bothered to write symphonies at all, given the dramatic impact of Beethoven's Third, Fifth, and Ninth. Wagner himself wrote only one, Verdi none. Some composers, notably Berlioz and Liszt, turned to a completely different sort of symphony, the program symphony*, in which an external scenario determined the nature and order of the musical events. But these works often lacked the force, internal unity, and compelling logic of Beethoven's symphonies. It was not until the late Romantic period, nearly fifty years after the death of Beethoven, that someone came forth to claim the title of successor to Beethoven the symphonist. That figure was Johannes Brahms.

the legacy of Beethoven

Johannes Brahms (1833–1897)

Brahms was born in the north German port city of Hamburg in 1833 (Fig. 30–1). He was given the Latin name Johannes to distinguish him from his father Johann, a street musician and "beer-hall" fiddler. Although Johannes's formal education never went beyond primary school, his father saw to it that he received the best training on the piano and in music theory. He was fed a heavy diet of the great masters: Bach's *The Well-Tempered Clavier* (see page 156), Beethoven's piano sonatas, and Haydn's chamber music. While he studied these works by day, by night he earned money playing out-of-tune pianos in "stimulation bars" on the Hamburg waterfront. To get his hands on better instruments, he practiced daily in the showrooms of local piano stores.

Brahms first caught the public's attention in 1853, when Robert Schumann published a highly laudatory article proclaiming him to be a musical Messiah, the heir apparent of the legacy of Haydn, Mozart, and Beethoven. Brahms, in turn, embraced Robert and his wife Clara (see Fig. 23–4), as his musical mentors. After Robert was confined to a mental institution, Brahms became Clara's confidant, and his respect and affection for her ripened into love, despite the

FIGURE 30–1

Johannes Brahms in his early thirties. Said an observer of the time, "The broad chest, the Herculean shoulders, the powerful head, which he threw back energetically when playing—all betrayed an artistic personality replete with the spirit of true genius."

Brahms moves to Vienna

a conservative composer in a conservative city

fact that she was fourteen years his senior. Whether owing to his unconsummated love for Clara or other reasons, Brahms remained a bachelor all his life.

Disappointed first in love and then in his attempt to gain a conducting position in his native Hamburg, Brahms moved to Vienna in 1862. He supported his modest lifestyle—very "un-Wagnerian," he called it—by performing and conducting. His fame as a composer increased dramatically in 1868 with performances of his *German Requiem*, which was soon sold to amateur choruses around the world. In this same year, he composed what is today perhaps his best-known piece, the simple, yet beautiful art song known among English speakers as "Brahms's Lullaby" (see page 62). Honorary degrees from Cambridge University (1876) and Breslau University (1879) attested to his growing stature. After Wagner's death in 1883, Brahms was generally considered the greatest living German composer. His own death, from liver cancer, came in the spring of 1897. He was buried in the central cemetery of Vienna, thirty feet from the graves of Beethoven and Schubert.

Vienna was (and remains) a very conservative city, fiercely protective of its rich cultural heritage. That Brahms should choose it as his place of residence is not surprising—Vienna had been the home of Haydn, Mozart, Beethoven, and Schubert, and the conservative Brahms found inspiration in the music of these past masters (Fig. 30–2). Again and again he returned to traditional genres, such as the symphony, concerto, quartet, and sonata, and to conventional forms, such as sonata–allegro and theme and variations. The symphony orchestra Brahms required was modest in size, no larger than the one Beethoven had called for in his Symphony No. 9. Most telling, Brahms composed no program music. Instead, he chose to write **absolute music,** chamber sonatas, symphonies, and concertos without narrative intent. The music of Brahms unfolds as patterns of pure sound within the tight confines of traditional forms. While Brahms could write lovely Romantic melodies, he was at heart a contrapun-

FIGURE 30–2

Brahms's composing room in Vienna. On the wall, looking down on the piano, is a bust of Beethoven. The spirit of Beethoven loomed large over the entire nineteenth century (see also the cover) and over Brahms in particular.

talist, a "developer" in the tradition of Bach and Beethoven. Indeed, he was to be dubbed the last of the famous "three B's": Bach, Beethoven, and Brahms.

Symphony No. 2 in D major (1877)

In 1870, Brahms wrote, "I shall never compose a symphony! You have no idea how the likes of us feel when we hear the tramp of a giant like him behind us." "That giant," of course, was Beethoven, and Brahms, like other nineteenth-century composers, was terrified by the prospect of competing with his revered predecessor. But Brahms did go on to write a symphony—indeed, four of them, first performed, in turn, in 1876, 1877, 1883, and 1885. Following the Classical tradition, each has four movements.

Among Brahms's symphonies, the second is by far the most radiant, lyrical, and "romantic" in tone. Brahms composed it during the summer of 1877 while vacationing in the lake region of southern Austria, where pastoral melodies, he said, were "so abundant one had to be careful not to step on them." The relaxed quality of the symphony is epitomized by the third movement. Here the mood is akin to a leisurely peasants' dance in a summer meadow, though one that unfolds within the ternary form of a traditional scherzo with a repeated trio. Adding to the rustic feel is the continually changing metrical grouping, evocative of an Eastern European folk dance (see page 323). Moreover, the composer enhances the light, dance-like quality of the trio by requiring the performers to play **staccato**—he places dots above the notes that instruct the players to hold each pitch for only the shortest possible time. So popular was this third movement at the premiere of the symphony in Vienna on December 30, 1877, that the audience immediately demanded its encore—unlike now, earlier audiences clapped between movements of a symphony.

Brahms's most "romantic" symphony

folk elements

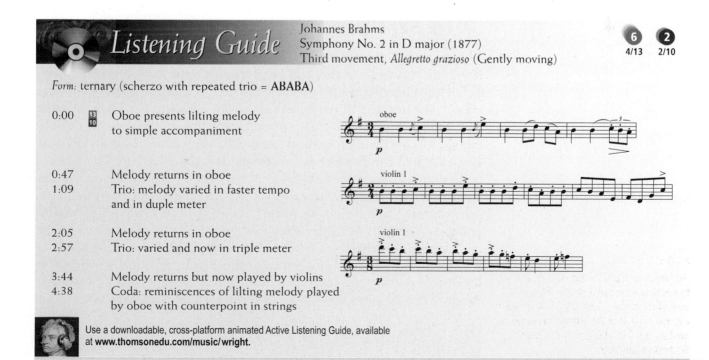

Listening Guide

Johannes Brahms
Symphony No. 2 in D major (1877)
Third movement, *Allegretto grazioso* (Gently moving)

6 4/13   2 2/10

Form: ternary (scherzo with repeated trio = **ABABA**)

0:00	13 10	Oboe presents lilting melody to simple accompaniment
0:47		Melody returns in oboe
1:09		Trio: melody varied in faster tempo and in duple meter
2:05		Melody returns in oboe
2:57		Trio: varied and now in triple meter
3:44		Melody returns but now played by violins
4:38		Coda: reminiscences of lilting melody played by oboe with counterpoint in strings

Listening Exercise 39

Brahms
Symphony No. 2 in D major

6   **2**
4/13   2/10

ThomsonNOW
To take this Listening Exercise online and
receive feedback or email answers to your
instructor, go to *ThomsonNOW* for this chapter.

Contemporary critics were quick to point out that Brahms's
Symphony No. 2 (1877) had many of the same characteristics as Beethoven's Symphony No. 6, called the "Pastoral"
(1808). Indeed, in many ways, the departed Beethoven
served as Brahms's musical mentor from the grave. The
following questions emphasize the means by which
Brahms conveys a relaxed, rural feeling in this third movement of his own, most pastoral symphony.

1. (0:00–0:23) Which string technique is used in the
   accompaniment to create a light, airy sound?
   a. tremolo   b. vibrato   c. pizzicato
2. (0:24–0:42) Which instrument, traditionally associated with the outdoors, enters in the background?
   a. trumpet   b. tuba
   c. French horn   d. harp
3. (1:01–1:08) In this passage, the mode of the
   piece changes, causing a shift in mood. Which
   is correct?
   a. It changes from major to minor.
   b. It changes from minor to major.
4. (1:09) As we enter the trio, the music becomes fast
   and light. Which technique contributes to the feeling
   of lightness?
   a. pizzicato   b. staccato   c. vibrato

5. (1:58–2:05) Here Brahms skillfully fuses the trio to
   the return of the lilting melody. When the oboe returns (2:01), has the scherzo theme disappeared?
   a. yes   b. no
6. (2:13–2:22) Now the melody reenters, but Brahms
   has rewritten the return by creating a solo in the
   background for which bucolic instrument?
   a. clarinet   b. trumpet   c. French horn
7. (2:36–2:56) This passage is a fine example of what?
   a. retard   b. accelerando   c. crescendo
8. (2:57–3:13) In this varied presentation of the trio, the
   meter sounds uncertain because there is much what?
   a. orchestral procrastination
   b. rhythmic syncopation
   c. temporal elevation
9. The return of the lilting melody (3:44) sounds especially lush and "romantic" because Brahms has now
   assigned it to which instrument(s)?
   a. violins   b. oboe   c. French horn
10. The feeling of lyrical repose that characterizes this
    movement is felt most clearly where?
    a. in the lilting melody, which has a predominantly
       triple meter
    b. in the slower trio, which is marked by metrical
       inconsistency

THE SYMPHONIC POEM

types of program music

The desire for music to express a narrative program through sound alone
lay at the very heart of the creative process of most Romantic composers.
While the conservative Brahms held fast to the Classical ideal of absolute
music*, the majority of the Romantics wrote either program music (music
that told a tale without a text) or opera (music that followed the text of a libretto). No instrumental medium could tell a story more colorfully than the
ever-enlarging symphony orchestra. By mid-nineteenth century, four types of
orchestral program music had emerged (see pages 275–276): the multimovement program symphony* and the one-movement dramatic overture*, concert overture*, and symphonic poem*. As we have seen, the program symphony is exemplified by Berlioz's *Symphonie fantastique* and the dramatic
overture by Mendelssohn's *Overture to A Midsummer Night's Dream*. The genres of
the concert overture and symphonic poem, which are virtually identical in
length and purpose, are best experienced in the works of Peter Tchaikovsky,
the most prolific composer of late-nineteenth-century program music.

Peter Tchaikovsky (1840–1893)

Tchaikovsky was born in 1840 into an upper-middle-class family in provincial
Russia (Fig. 30–3). He showed a keen ear for music in his earliest years, and

by the age of six could speak fluent French and German. (An excellent musical ear and a capacity to learn foreign languages often go hand in hand—both involve processing patterns of sound.) As to his career, his parents determined that law would provide the easiest path to success. Thus, young Tchaikovsky spent seven years, 1852–1859, at the School of Jurisprudence in St. Petersburg and four more years as a clerk in the Ministry of Justice. Then, like Robert Schumann before him, he realized that it was music, not law, that fired his imagination. He made his way to the St. Petersburg Conservatory of Music, from which he was graduated in 1866. That same year, he went to the newly formed Moscow Conservatory, where he assumed the position of professor of harmony and musical composition.

In truth, it was not his official position in Moscow that supported Tchaikovsky during most of his mature years, but rather a private arrangement with an eccentric patroness, Madame Nadezhda von Meck (Fig. 30–4). This wealthy, music-loving widow furnished him an annual income of 6000 rubles on the condition that she and the composer never meet—a requirement not always easily fulfilled, since the two sometimes resided at the same summer estate. In addition to this annuity, in 1881, Tsar Alexander III awarded Tchaikovsky an annual pension of 3000 rubles in recognition of his importance to Russian cultural life. Being a man of independent means meant that Tchaikovsky not only was able to travel extensively in Western Europe, and even to America, but also could enjoy the freedom he found so necessary to creative activity.

Tchaikovsky's creative output touched every genre of nineteenth-century music: opera, song, string quartet, piano sonata, concerto, symphony, and symphonic poem. It is, however, his large-scale works for orchestra that have best stood the test of time. His extravagant concert overture, *The 1812 Overture* (1882), which commemorates the Russian defeat of Napoleon in 1812, is heard in the United States on the Fourth of July, with Tchaikovsky's musical pyrotechnics usually followed by fireworks in the night sky. Indeed, Tchaikovsky's musical strengths—colorful instrumentations, sweeping melodies, dramatic contrasts, and grand gestures—could only be fully expressed by a large symphony orchestra. Not surprisingly, he also achieved unparalleled success as a composer of orchestral music for ballet, a type of music in which short bursts of colorful sounds and evocative rhythms are necessary to create distinct moods for each new scene. His *Swan Lake* (1876), *Sleeping Beauty* (1889), and *Nutcracker* (1892) are the most popular works in the entire repertoire of grand Romantic ballet, beloved by young and old alike.

Despite his considerable popular success, Tchaikovsky's life was not a happy one. He was a manic-depressive, a neurotic, and a hypochondriac. He was also a homosexual, and this during a time when there was little sympathy for homosexuality or awareness of its biological causes. He died suddenly in 1893, at the age of fifty-three, after drinking unboiled water during an epidemic of cholera.

Symphonic Poem, *Romeo and Juliet* (1869; revised 1880)

Tchaikovsky was at his best when writing illustrative music for large orchestra, whether program music or music for ballet. He termed his most overtly programmatic works "overture," "overture fantasy," or "symphonic fantasy." Today we group all of these in the general category of **symphonic poem,** a title suggesting the literary flavor of these one-movement, programmatic pieces.

FIGURE 30–3
Peter Tchaikovsky.

FIGURE 30–4
Nadezhda von Meck was the widow of an engineer who made a fortune constructing the first railroads in Russia during the 1860s and 1870s. She used her money, in part, to support composers such as Tchaikovsky and, later, Claude Debussy.

Tchaikovsky, like Berlioz and Mendelssohn before him, found that Shakespeare's plays provided the richest source of extramusical inspiration. Of his three symphonic poems based on the works of Shakespeare—*Romeo and Juliet* (1869; revised 1880), *The Tempest* (1877), and *Hamlet* (1888)—the best is *Romeo and Juliet.*

the spirit but not the letter of Shakespeare's play

In *Romeo and Juliet,* Tchaikovsky aimed to capture the spirit, not the letter, of Shakespeare's play, and thus he crafted a free, not literal, representation of the principal dramatic events of the play. In fact, the composer distills these into just three musical themes: the compassionate music of the kindly Friar Laurence, whose plan to unite the lovers goes fatally awry; the fighting music, which represents the feud between the Capulets and Montagues; and the love theme, which expresses the passion of Romeo and Juliet. Most importantly, whereas Shakespeare's drama unfolds as a continuous linear process, Tchaikovsky sets his themes within the confines of sonata–allegro form, which gives the music a recursive shape: presentation, confrontation, reiteration.

The introduction begins with the music of Friar Laurence and concludes with a succession of mysterious chords strummed on a harp, as if Friar Laurence, like a medieval bard, were about to narrate a long tragic tale. When the exposition begins, we hear angry percussive music, racing strings, and syncopated cymbal crashes, suggesting that we have entered the violent world of the Capulets and Montagues. Soon the fighting subsides and the love theme emerges, precisely where we would expect a lyrical second theme to appear in sonata–allegro form. As appropriate for a pair of lovers, the love theme is in two parts (Exs. 30–1 and 30–2), each of which grows and becomes more passionate when pushed upward in ascending melodic sequences.

a two-part love theme

EXAMPLE 30–1 (love theme part 1)

EXAMPLE 30–2 (love theme part 2)

The brief development section pits the feuding families against the increasingly adamant pleas of Friar Laurence. The recapitulation, true to sonata form, begins with the feud music but moves quickly to an expanded, more ecstatic presentation of the love theme (part 2 first, then part 1), which is eventually cut off by a noisy return of the feuding clans. The beginning of the dramatic coda is announced by a foreboding *fortissimo* roll on the timpani. As we hear the steady drumbeats of a funeral procession and fragments of the broken love theme, we know that Romeo and Juliet are dead. A celestial, hymn-like passage (a transformation of the love theme) suggests that the lovers have been united above, a feeling confirmed by the return of the love theme in high violins. There only remains to bring the curtain down on the story of the star-crossed lovers, which Tchaikovsky does with seven *fortissimo* hammer-strokes for full orchestra, all on the tonic chord.

Shakespeare wrote *Romeo and Juliet* as a tragedy: "For never was a story of more woe / Than this of Juliet and her Romeo," say the final lines of the play. By incorporating a "celestial conclusion" into his coda—a hymn-like choir of angelic woodwinds followed by the transcendent love theme on high in the violins—Tchaikovsky has changed the final import of the play. True child of the Romantic age, he suggests that the love-death of Romeo and Juliet was, in fact, not a tragedy but a spiritual triumph.

Tchaikovsky turns tragedy to spiritual triumph

Listening Guide

Peter Tchaikovsky
Romeo and Juliet (1869; revised 1880)

6
4/14–17

Genre: symphonic poem
Form: sonata–allegro

INTRODUCTION

0:00 **14**	Friar Laurence theme sounding organ-like in woodwinds	
0:36	Anguished, dissonant sound in strings and French horn	
1:25	Harp alternates with flute solo and woodwinds	
2:07	Friar Laurence theme returns with new accompaniment	
2:34	Anguished sound returns in strings with French horn	
3:23	Harp strumming returns	
3:56	Timpani roll and string tremolos build tension; hints of Friar Laurence theme in woodwinds	
4:31	Anguished sound again returns, then yields to crescendo on repeating tonic chord	

EXPOSITION

5:01 **15**	0:00	Feud theme in agitated minor; angry rhythmic motive in woodwinds, racing scales in strings	
5:48	0:47	Crashing syncopations (with cymbal) running against scales	
6:19	1:18	Gentle transition, with release of tension, to second theme	
6:57	1:56	Love theme (part 1) played quietly by English horn and viola	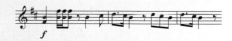
7:13	2:12	Love theme (part 2) played quietly by strings with mutes	
7:51	2:50	Love theme (part 1) returns with growing ardor in high woodwinds while French horn plays counterpoint against it	
8:51	3:50	Lyrical closing section in which cellos and English horn engage in dialogue against backdrop of gently plucked chords in harp	

DEVELOPMENT

9:52 **16**	0:00	Feud theme against which horn soon plays Friar Laurence theme
10:11	0:19	String syncopations, again against Friar Laurence theme
10:38	0:46	Feud theme and Friar Laurence theme continue in opposition
11:23	1:31	Cymbal crashes signal climax of development as trumpet blares forth with Friar Laurence theme

(continued)

RECAPITULATION

11:58	2:06	Feud theme in woodwinds and brasses against racing strings
12:21	2:29	Love theme (part 2) softly in woodwinds
13:00	3:08	Love theme (part 1) sounds ecstatically with all its inherent force and sweep
13:41	3:49	Love theme begins again in strings, with counterpoint in brasses
14:01	4:09	Fragments of love theme in strings, then brasses
14:28	4:36	Love theme begins again but is cut off by feud theme; syncopated cymbal crashes
14:43	4:51	Feud theme and Friar Laurence theme build to a climax
15:43	5:51	Timpani roll announces coda

CODA

15:52	🔟	0:00	Timpani beats funeral march while strings play fragments of love theme
16:38		0:46	Love theme (part 2) transformed into sound of heavenly chorale played by woodwinds
17:43		1:51	Transcendent love theme sounds from on high in violins
18:18		2:26	Timpani roll and final chords

Use a downloadable, cross-platform animated Active Listening Guide, available at **www.thomsonedu.com/music/wright.**

THE ORCHESTRAL SONG

We began our discussion of Romantic music with an art song by Franz Schubert (page 265), and we end it with an orchestral song by Gustav Mahler. These pieces serve as appropriate "bookends" for our investigation of musical Romanticism, for the nineteenth century was marked by an exceptionally strong union between music and poetry. Poetry had the power to communicate feelings of love, grief, pain, or longing, and these typically Romantic sentiments were intensified when set to music.

an orchestrally accompanied song

Given the growing importance of the orchestra, it was only a matter of time before the genres of art song and symphony began to interact and influence each other, producing something new: the orchestral song. In its simplest form, the **orchestral song** (or **orchestral *Lied***) was an art song in which the full orchestra replaced the piano as the medium of accompaniment. Yet because the orchestra could supply more color and add a greater number of contrapuntal lines, the orchestral song grew to be longer, denser, and more complex than the piano-accompanied art song. Berlioz, Brahms, and Wagner all experimented with the orchestral *Lied* in various ways, but not until Gustav Mahler did this hybrid musical genre reach maturity.

Gustav Mahler (1860–1911)

Gustav Mahler (Fig. 30–5) was born in 1860 into a middle-class Jewish family in Bohemia, then part of the Austrian Empire but now encompassed by The Czech Republic (see Fig. 29–5). At the age of fifteen, he was admitted to the prestigious Vienna Conservatory of Music, where he studied musical composition and conducting. Mahler felt that his mission in life was to conduct—to interpret—the works of the masters ("to suffer for my great masters," as he put it). Like most young conductors, he began his career in provincial towns, grad-

trained as a conductor

ually working his way to larger and more important musical centers. His itinerary as resident conductor took him, among other places, to Kassel (1883–1884), Prague (1885–1886), Leipzig (1886–1888), Budapest (1888–1891), Hamburg (1891–1897), and finally back to Vienna.

In May 1897, Mahler returned triumphantly to his adopted city as director of the Vienna Court Opera, a position Mozart had once coveted. The next year he also assumed directorship of the Vienna Philharmonic, then and now one of the world's great orchestras. But Mahler was a demanding autocrat—a musical tyrant—in search of an artistic ideal. That he drove himself as hard as he pushed others was little comfort to the singers and instrumentalists who had to endure his wrath during rehearsals. After ten stormy but artistically successful seasons (1897–1907), Mahler was dismissed from the Vienna Opera. About this time, he accepted an offer from New York to take charge of the Metropolitan Opera, and eventually, he conducted the New York Philharmonic as well. Here, too, there was both acclaim and controversy. And here, too, at least at the Met, his contract was not renewed after two years, though he stayed on longer, until February 1911, with the Philharmonic. He died in Vienna in May 1911 of a lingering streptococcal infection that had attacked his weak heart—a sad end to an obsessive and somewhat tormented life.

FIGURE 30-5
Gustav Mahler.

CORBIS/Bettmann

Mahler is unique among composers in that as a mature artist he wrote only orchestral songs and symphonies. These he managed to create during the summers when freed of his conducting duties. His five orchestral song cycles* typically contain settings of four, five, or six poems by a single author. *Kindertotenlieder* (*Songs on the Death of Children*, 1901–1904), for example, is a collection of five songs for voice and orchestra to words by Friedrich Rückert (1788–1866). They express the poet's overwhelming grief at the loss of two young children to scarlet fever. By tragic coincidence, no sooner had Mahler finished setting Rückert's painfully personal memorials than his own eldest daughter died of scarlet fever at the age of four, a loss from which the highly sensitive composer never recovered.

When Mahler wrote for the symphony, he did something unusual: he borrowed from his own songs. The single-movement songs served as a musical repository, or vault, to which the composer could return for inspiration while wrestling with the problems of a large, multimovement work for orchestra. Mahler's First Symphony (1889), though entirely instrumental, makes use of melodies already present in his song cycle *Lieder eines fahrenden Gesellen* (*Songs of a Wayfaring Lad*, 1885). His Second (1894), Third (1896), and Fourth (1901) symphonies incorporate various portions of the *Wonderhorn Songs* (1892–1899) as solo vocal parts within the symphony. Symphonies Five (1902) and Six (1904) are again purely instrumental, but once more incorporate preexisting melodies, in this case from *Songs on the Death of Children* and *Five Rückert Songs* (1901–1902). Altogether Mahler wrote nine symphonies, seven of which make use of his own orchestral *Lieder* or other preexisting vocal music.

songs influence symphonies

But to Mahler a symphony was much more than just an extended orchestral *Lied*. "The symphony is the world; it must embrace everything," he once said. And so he tried to embrace every sort of music within it. There are folk dances, popular songs, military marches, off-stage bands, bugle calls, and even

all-embracing symphonies

FIGURE 30–6

A cartoon of Mahler conducting his "Symphony of a Thousand" in 1910. A German caption says that there is no audience because everyone is needed on stage.

Gregorian chant* at various points in his symphonies. What results is a collage of sound on the grandest scale, one achieved, in part, by employing massive forces and a greatly extended sense of time. Mahler's Symphony No. 2, for example, calls for ten horns and eight trumpets, and lasts an hour and a half. And the first performance of his Symphony No. 8 in Munich in 1910 involved 858 singers and 171 instrumentalists! With good reason, it has been nicknamed the "Symphony of a Thousand" (Fig. 30–6).

Gustav Mahler was the last in the long line of great German symphonists that extends back through Brahms, Schubert, and Beethoven to Mozart and, ultimately, to Haydn. What had begun as a modest instrumental genre with a limited emotional range had grown in the course of the nineteenth century into a monumental structure, the musical equivalent, in Mahler's view, of the entire cosmos.

Orchestral Song, *I am Lost to the World*, from the *Five Rückert Songs* (1901–1902)

It is the everyday world, not the grand cosmos, that concerns Mahler in his setting of Friedrich Rückert's *Ich bin der Welt abhanden gekommen (I Am Lost to the World)*. Rückert, as we have seen, was a German Romantic poet whose verse was set by Schubert, as well as both Robert and Clara Schumann. During the summers of 1901 and 1902, Mahler chose to set five of the many hundreds of poems by Rückert, five poems that express in various ways the composer's outlook on life and on art.

an artist withdraws into the realm of music

I Am Lost to the World speaks of the artist's growing remoteness from the travails of everyday life and withdrawal into a private, heavenly world of music, here signified by the final word *Lied* (song). Although the poem has three stanzas, Mahler chose not a strophic setting*, but a through-composed* one. The first strophe sets the mood of the song as a mournful English horn begins to play a halting melody, one then picked up and extended by the voice. The second stanza moves to a faster tempo and more rapid declamation in the voice, as if the mundane world should be quickly left behind. The final strophe returns to a slow tempo. It also sets the notes of the bass on the beat and on the roots of triads*, all of which help project a settled, satisfied feeling—the self-absorbed poet-composer has withdrawn into the peaceful world of art. Toward the end, Mahler shows how music has the capacity to sum up in a few brief sounds the entire progress of the poem, the movement from the dissonance of the world to the peace of the inner self. First, the strings (❻5/2 at 2:44) play an extended dissonance (F against E♭), which resolves to a consonance (E♭ against E♭), and this is repeated at the very end (❻5/2 at 3:00) by the English horn, "dying out expressively" as the composer requests. The desire to escape from this dissonant world into the consonant realm of art has been fulfilled.

dissonance seeks resolution

I Am Lost to the World has been called Mahler's best orchestral *Lied*. That he made use of some of this same music in the beautiful slow movement of his Symphony No. 5 suggests that these musical ideas were important to him and express, as he said at the time, "his very self." Both song and symphony have a certain world-weariness about them, as if Mahler had a premonition that both his own life and the Romantic era were coming to an end.

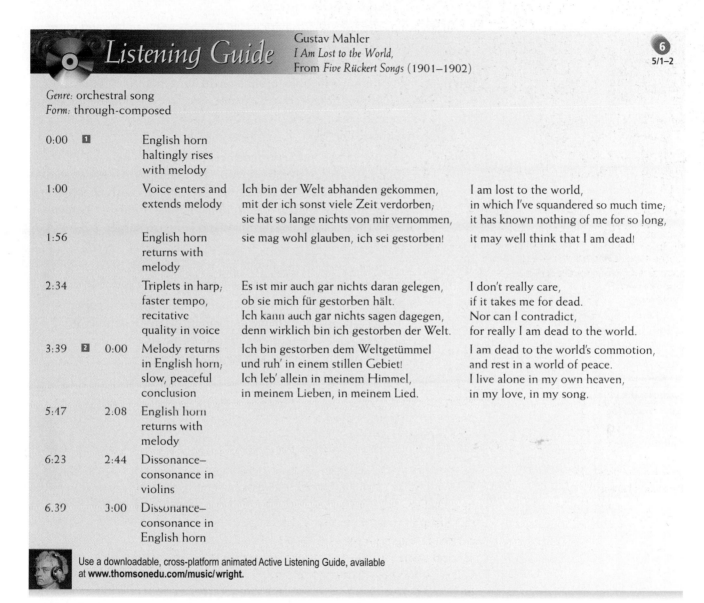

Listening Guide

Gustav Mahler
I Am Lost to the World,
From *Five Rückert Songs* (1901–1902)

6
5/1–2

Genre: orchestral song
Form: through-composed

0:00	**1**		English horn haltingly rises with melody		
1:00			Voice enters and extends melody	Ich bin der Welt abhanden gekommen, mit der ich sonst viele Zeit verdorben; sie hat so lange nichts von mir vernommen,	I am lost to the world, in which I've squandered so much time; it has known nothing of me for so long,
1:56			English horn returns with melody	sie mag wohl glauben, ich sei gestorben!	it may well think that I am dead!
2:34			Triplets in harp; faster tempo, recitative quality in voice	Es ist mir auch gar nichts daran gelegen, ob sie mich für gestorben hält. Ich kann auch gar nichts sagen dagegen, denn wirklich bin ich gestorben der Welt.	I don't really care, if it takes me for dead. Nor can I contradict, for really I am dead to the world.
3:39	**2**	0:00	Melody returns in English horn; slow, peaceful conclusion	Ich bin gestorben dem Weltgetümmel und ruh' in einem stillen Gebiet! Ich leb' allein in meinem Himmel, in meinem Lieben, in meinem Lied.	I am dead to the world's commotion, and rest in a world of peace. I live alone in my own heaven, in my love, in my song.
5:47		2:08	English horn returns with melody		
6:23		2:44	Dissonance–consonance in violins		
6:39		3:00	Dissonance–consonance in English horn		

Use a downloadable, cross-platform animated Active Listening Guide, available at **www.thomsonedu.com/music/wright**.

Key Words

absolute music (**326**)
staccato (**327**)
symphonic
   poem (**329**)

orchestral song
   (orchestral *Lied*)
   (**332**)

ThomsonNOW™

ThomsonNOW for *Listening to Music*, 5th Edition, and *Listening to Western Music* will assist you in understanding the content of this chapter with lesson plans generated for your specific needs. In addition, you may complete this chapter's Listening Exercise in ThomsonNOW's interactive environment, as well as download Active Listening Guides and other materials that will help you succeed in this course.

ThomsonNOW™
For comparisons and quizzes on the musical style of the Romantic era, see Active Listening at **www.thomson.edu.com/music/wright** and ThomsonNow.

Representative composers
Beethoven
Schubert
Berlioz
Mendelssohn
Robert Schumann
Clara Schumann
Chopin
Liszt
Verdi
Wagner
Bizet
Brahms
Dvořák
Tchaikovsky
Musorgsky
Mahler
Puccini

Principal genres
symphony
program symphony
symphonic poem
concert overture
opera
art song
orchestral song
solo concerto
character piece for piano
ballet music

Checklist of Musical Style

Romantic: 1820–1900

Melody	Long, singable lines with powerful climaxes and chromatic inflections for expressiveness
Harmony	Greater use of chromaticism makes harmony richer and more colorful; sudden shifts to remote chords for expressive purposes; more dissonance conveys feelings of anxiety and longing
Rhythm	Rhythms are flexible, often languid, and therefore meter is sometimes not clearly articulated; tempo can fluctuate greatly (tempo *rubato*); tempo can slow to crawl to allow for "grand gesture"
Color	Orchestra becomes enormous, reaching more than one hundred performers: trombone, tuba, contrabassoon, piccolo, and English horn added to ensemble; experiments with new playing techniques for special effects; dynamics vary widely to create different levels of expression; piano becomes larger and more powerful
Texture	Predominantly homophonic but dense and rich because of larger orchestra; sustaining pedal on piano also adds to density
Form	No new forms created; instead, traditional forms (strophic, sonata–allegro, and theme and variations, for example) used and extended in length; traditional forms also applied to new genres such as art song and symphonic poem

PART
VI

Modern and Postmodern
Art Music, 1880–Present

31 *Impressionism*

32 *Exoticism*

33 *Modernism in Music
   and the Arts*

34 *Early-Twentieth-
   Century Modernism*

35 *Russian and Eastern
   European Modernism*

36 *Three American Voices*

37 *Postmodernism*

Human activity, artistic or otherwise, never occurs within tidy chronological units. Historical periods overlap, and different styles coexist in time. Setting the dates of "modernism" and "postmodernism" is a particularly difficult task. Until recently, historians have usually referred to "modern" music simply as "twentieth-century" music. But modern musical idioms appeared in some Impressionist music of the late nineteenth century, while aspects of musical Romanticism extended well into the twentieth century. Similarly, "postmodernism" may have begun as early as the 1930s and continues to develop during our own times. Recognizing, then, that the terms "modern" and "postmodern" together connote a large, multifaceted musical period, what are a few of the characteristics that mark this epoch?

At the beginning of the twentieth century, composers increasingly turned against the warm sentimentality characteristic of much of nineteenth-century

| 1880 | 1890 | 1900 | 1910 | 1920 | 1930 | 1940 |

MODERN AND POSTMODERN

Musée d'Orsay, Paris/Erich Lessing/Art Resource, NY

Hermitage Museum, St. Petersburg, Russia/AGE FotoStock/SuperStock © Succession H. Matisse, Paris/Artists Rights Society (ARS), NY

• 1894 Claude Debussy composes *Prelude to The Afternoon of a Faun*

• 1907 Pablo Picasso paints *Les Demoiselles d'Avignon*

1908–1914 Charles Ives composes
Three Places in New England

• 1912 Arnold Schoenberg composes
Moonstruck Pierrot

• 1913 Igor Stravinsky composes
The Rite of Spring

1914–1918 World War I

• 1917 Sergey Prokofiev composes
Classical Symphony

• 1924 Joseph Stalin takes
control of Soviet government

• 1929 Crash of
American stock market

1929–1941 Great Depression

• 1937
Dmitri Shostakovich composes
Symphony No. 5

1939–1945
World War II

music, replacing this Romantic aesthetic with a harsh, percussive, impersonal sound. Melodies become more angular, and harmonies more dissonant. Simultaneously, the massive compositions of the late Romantic period—perhaps best represented by Gustav Mahler's *Symphony of a Thousand* (1906)—yield to smaller, less extravagant works. The abstract, impersonal quality of modern music is most clearly evident in Arnold Schoenberg's rigid twelve-tone music. In the 1960s, a reaction against the formalism of Schoenberg and his disciples contributed to the increasing popularity of musical postmodernism, which allowed for a diversity of musical genres—electronic music and chance music, for example—performed in unconventional ways. If modernism turned against traditional musical styles, postmodernism, which continues today, often dispenses entirely with conventional musical forms and processes.

1950   1960   1970   1980   1990   2000   2010

MODERN AND POSTMODERN

- 1944 Aaron Copland composes ballet *Appalachian Spring*

- 1945 Atomic bombs dropped on Hiroshima and Nagasaki

- 1945 Béla Bartók composes *Concerto for Orchestra*

1950–1952 Korean War

- 1958 Edgard Varèse composes *Poème électronique* for World's Fair

- 1963 John F. Kennedy assassinated

1963–1973 Vietnam War

- 1985 Ellen Zwilich composes *Concerto Grosso 1985*

- 1986 John Adams composes *Short Ride in a Fast Machine*

- 1991 Fall of Berlin Wall; end of Cold War

- 2000 Tan Dun records score for film *Crouching Tiger, Hidden Dragon*

Impressionism

Romantic music reached its apogee during the late nineteenth century in the grandiose works of Wagner, Tchaikovsky, Brahms, and Mahler. But by 1900, this German-dominated musical empire had started to weaken. Some composers outside the mainstream of Romanticism challenged the validity of the predominantly German style, epitomized by the music of Wagner. Not surprisingly, the most powerful anti-German sentiment was felt in France. (France and Germany went to war in 1870 and would do so again in 1914.) Having first embraced Wagner's music during the 1870s and 1880s, the French avant-garde had, by the 1890s, turned against it. The French began to ridicule the sentimentality of Romanticism in general and the grandiose structures of the Germans in particular. German music was said to be too heavy, too pretentious, and too bombastic, like one of Wagner's Nordic giants. Meaningful expression, it was believed, might be communicated in more subtle ways, in something other than sheer volume of sound and epic length.

IMPRESSIONISM IN PAINTING AND MUSIC

The movement that arose in France in opposition to German Romantic music has been given the name **Impressionism** (Fig. 31–1). We are, of course, more familiar with this term as a designation for a school of late-nineteenth-century painters working in and around Paris including Claude Monet (1840–1903), Auguste Renoir (1841–1919), Edgar Degas (1834–1917), Camille Pissarro (1830–1903), and the American Mary Cassatt (1844–1926). Impressionist painters were not overtly anti-German like their musical counterparts. There was no need to be, because the well-established tradition of French painting was widely considered superior to the German one (see Figs. 12–5 and 25–1). Instead, Monet and his colleagues rebelled against the traditional academic style of their native France. When the French Academy of Fine Arts refused to allow the progressive painters to show their canvases at the official Salon in the early 1870s, they mounted their own exhibition. In the uproar that followed, the artists were disparagingly called "impressionists" for the seemingly imprecise quality of their art. The painters accepted the name, partly as an act of defiance against the establishment, and soon the term was universally adopted.

It is ironic that French Impressionism, which once generated such controversy, is now the most popular of all artistic styles. Indeed, judging by museum attendance and re-

FIGURE 31–1
The painting that gave its name to an epoch, Claude Monet's *Impression: Sunrise*, was exhibited at the first group exhibition organized by Monet, Renoir, Degas, and Pissarro in Paris in 1874. The ships, rowboats, and other elements in the early morning light are more suggested than fully drawn. Said the critic Louis Leroy derisively of this painting at the time, "Wallpaper in its most embryonic state is more finished than that seascape."

Musée Marmottan, Paris/SuperStock

productions sold, there is an almost limitless enthusiasm for the art of Monet, Degas, Renoir, and their associates—precisely the paintings that the artists' contemporaries mocked and jeered. But what is it about the Impressionist style that had initially caused such a furor?

The Impressionists were the first to turn against photographic realism in painting. Instead, they tried to re-create the impression that an object produced upon the senses in a single, fleeting moment. The key here is light: the Impressionists saw the world as awash in vibrant rays of light and sought to capture the aura that light-bathed objects created in the eyes of the beholder. To accomplish this, they covered their canvases with small, dab-like brushstrokes in which light was broken down into spots of color, thereby creating a sense of movement and fluidity. Shapes are not clearly defined but blurred, more suggested than delineated. Minor details disappear. Sunlight is everywhere and everything shimmers (Fig. 31–2).

As impressions and sensations became paramount for these painters, not surprisingly, they showed an intensified interest in music. What art form is more elusive and suggestive? What medium allows the receiver—the listener—more freedom to interpret the sensations he or she perceives? Painters began to speak in musical terms. Paul Gauguin (1848–1903) referred to the harmonies of line and color as the "music of painting," and Vincent van Gogh (1853–1890) suggested "using color as the music of tones." Paul Cézanne (1839–1906) painted an "overture" in homage to Wagner, while James Whistler (1844–1903), an American who worked in Paris in the 1860s and 1880s, created "nocturnes" and "symphonies." The painters envied the musicians' good fortune to work in a medium that changes continually—rather than one that required the artist to seize the moment and fix it on canvas.

For their part, musicians found inspiration in the visual arts. Claude Debussy, whose work most consistently displayed the Impressionist style in music, was delighted to be grouped with the Impressionist painters. "You do me great honor by calling me a pupil of Claude Monet," he told a friend in 1916. Debussy gave various collections of his compositions such artistic titles as *Sketches*, *Images*, and *Prints*. Rare are the moments in history when the aesthetic aims of painters and musicians were as closely allied.

Musée d'Orsay, Paris/Giraudon/The Bridgeman Art Library

FIGURE 31–2

Claude Monet, *Woman with Umbrella* (1886). The Impressionist canvas is not a finished surface in the traditional sense. Rather, the painter breaks down light into separate dabs of color and juxtaposes them for the viewer's eye to reassemble. Here bold brushstrokes convey an astonishing sense of movement, freshness, and sparkling light.

CLAUDE DEBUSSY (1862–1918)

Debussy (Fig. 31–3) was born in 1862 into a modest family living in a small town outside Paris. Since neither of his parents was musical, it came as a surprise when their son demonstrated talent at the keyboard. At the age of ten, he was sent to the Paris Conservatory for lessons in piano, composition, and music theory. Owing to his skill as a performer, he was soon engaged for summer work in the household of Nadezhda von Meck, a wealthy patroness of the arts and the principal supporter of Tchaikovsky (see Fig. 30–4). This employment took him, in turn, to Italy, Russia, and Vienna. In 1884, he won the Prix de Rome, an official prize in composition funded by the French

not from a musical family

FIGURE 31-3
Claude Debussy at the age of twenty-four.

government, one that required a three-year stay in Rome. But Debussy was not happy in the Eternal City. He preferred Paris, with its bistros, cafes, and bohemian ambience.

Returning to Paris more or less permanently in 1887, the young Frenchman continued to study his craft and to search for his own independent voice as a composer. He had some minor successes, and yet, as he said, in 1893, "There are still things that I am not able to do—create masterpieces, for example." But the next year, in 1894, he did just that. With the completion of *Prélude à l'Après-midi d'un Faune* (*Prelude to The Afternoon of a Faun*), he gave to the public what has become his most enduring orchestral work. Debussy's later compositions, including his opera *Pelléas et Mélisande* (1902), the symphonic poem *La Mer* (*The Sea*, 1905), and his two books of *Preludes* for piano, met with less popular favor. Critics complained that Debussy's works were lacking in form, melody, and forward motion.

Today, in hindsight, we see in these works the beginnings of modernism. Debussy hated what he called the German "developmental agenda" and wrote no symphonies. He replaced the warm strings and heavy low brasses of the Romantic orchestra with a variety of woodwinds, which often dominate his textures. He began to separate color (instrumental sound) from line (traditional melody), and then to luxuriate in color alone. Illness and the outbreak of World War I in 1914 brought Debussy's innovations to a halt. He died of cancer in the spring of 1918 while the guns of the German army were shelling Paris from the north.

FIGURE 31-4

The poet Stéphane Mallarmé, author of *The Afternoon of a Faun*, as painted by the great predecessor of the Impressionists, Edouard Manet (1832–1883). Mallarmé was a friend and artistic mentor of the composer Debussy.

Prelude to The Afternoon of a Faun (1894)

Debussy spent more of his time in the company of poets and painters than with musicians. His orchestral *Prelude to The Afternoon of a Faun*, in fact, was written to precede a stage reading of the poem *The Afternoon of a Faun* by his friend and mentor Stéphane Mallarmé (Fig. 31–4).

Mallarmé was the spiritual leader of a group of versifiers in *fin-de-siècle* Paris called the **Symbolists,** poets whose aesthetic aims were in harmony with those of the Impressionist painters. They worked to create a poetic style in which the literal *meaning* of the word was less important than its *sound* and the associations that that sound might produce. Said Mallarmé, "To name an object is to destroy its poetic enjoyment; the aim is to suggest the object."

Symbolism is certainly at the heart of Mallarmé's evocative *The Afternoon of a Faun*, which applies suggestive language to an ancient Greek theme. The faun of Mallarmé's poem is not a young deer but a satyr (a mythological beast that is half man, half goat), who spends his days in lustful pursuit of the nymphs of the forest. On this afternoon, we see the faun, exhausted from the morning's escapades, reclining on the forest floor in the still air of the midday heat. He contemplates future conquests while piping listlessly on his flute.

The following passage suggests the dream-like mood, vague and elusive, that Debussy sought to re-create in his musical setting:

> No murmur of water in the woodland scene,
> Bathed only in the sounds of my flute.
> And the only breeze, except for my two pipes,
> Blows itself empty long before
> It can scatter the sound in an arid rain.
> On a horizon unmoved by a ripple
> This sound, visible and serene,
> Mounts to the heavens, an inspired wisp.

a Symbolist poem

Debussy, who did not compose linear, narrative programmatic music in the tradition of Berlioz or Tchaikovsky, made no effort to follow Mallarmé's poem closely. As he said at the time of the first performance in December 1894, "My *Prelude* is really a sequence of mood paintings, throughout which the desire and dreams of the Faun move in the heat of the midday sun." When Mallarmé heard the music, he, in turn, said the following about Debussy's musical response to the poem: "I never expected anything like it. The music prolongs the emotion of my poem and paints its scenery more passionately than colors could."

Significantly, both musician and poet refer to *Prelude to The Afternoon of a Faun* in terms of painting (Fig. 31–5). But how does one create a painting in music? Here a tableau is depicted by using the distinctive colors of the instruments, especially the woodwinds, to evoke vibrant moods and sensations. The flute has one timbre, the oboe another, the clarinet yet a third. Debussy has said, in effect, let us focus on the sound-producing capacity of the instruments, let us see what new shades can be elicited from them, let us try new registers, let us try new combinations. Thus a solo flute begins in its lowest register (the pipes of the faun), followed by a harp glissando*, then dabs of color from the French horn. These tonal impressions swirl, dissolve, and form again, but seem not to progress. As with the poetic language of the Symbolists, in Debussy's musical syntax, units of meaning can come irregularly. There are no repeating rhythms or discernible meters to push the music forward. All is languid beauty, a music that is utterly original and shockingly sensual.

music paints a poem

FIGURE 31–5

Mallarmé's *The Afternoon of a Faun* created something of a sensation among late-nineteenth-century French artists. This painting by Ker-Xavier Roussel (1867–1944) is just one of several such representations of the faun surrounded by woodland nymphs.

Musée du Petit Palais, Paris

Listening Guide

Claude Debussy
Prelude to The Afternoon of a Faun (1894)

6 **2**
5/3–4 2/11–12

Genre: symphonic poem
Form: ternary

A

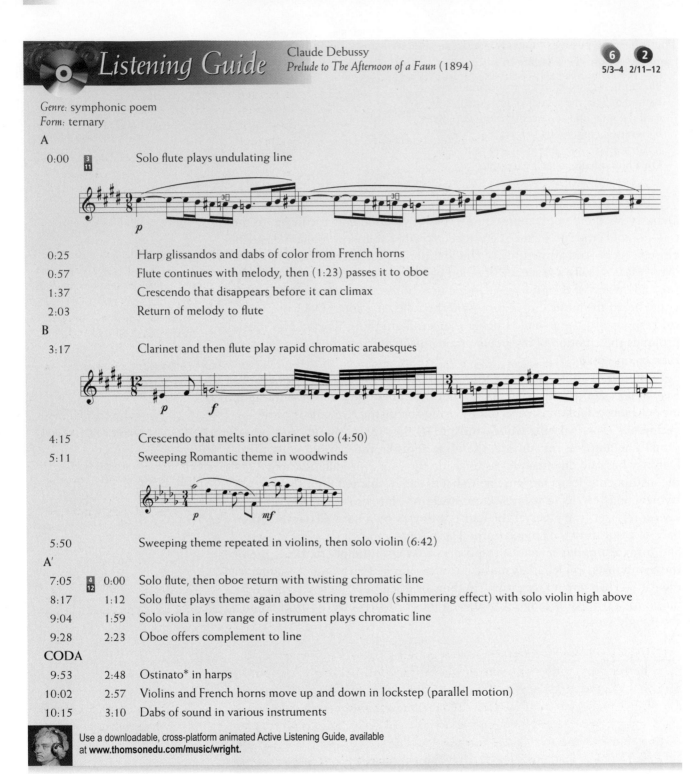

0:00   **3/11**   Solo flute plays undulating line

0:25   Harp glissandos and dabs of color from French horns
0:57   Flute continues with melody, then (1:23) passes it to oboe
1:37   Crescendo that disappears before it can climax
2:03   Return of melody to flute

B

3:17   Clarinet and then flute play rapid chromatic arabesques

4:15   Crescendo that melts into clarinet solo (4:50)
5:11   Sweeping Romantic theme in woodwinds

5:50   Sweeping theme repeated in violins, then solo violin (6:42)

A′

7:05   **4/12**   0:00   Solo flute, then oboe return with twisting chromatic line
8:17   1:12   Solo flute plays theme again above string tremolo (shimmering effect) with solo violin high above
9:04   1:59   Solo viola in low range of instrument plays chromatic line
9:28   2:23   Oboe offers complement to line

CODA

9:53   2:48   Ostinato* in harps
10:02   2:57   Violins and French horns move up and down in lockstep (parallel motion)
10:15   3:10   Dabs of sound in various instruments

Use a downloadable, cross-platform animated Active Listening Guide, available
at **www.thomsonedu.com/music/wright**.

Listening Exercise 40

Debussy
Prelude to The Afternoon of a Faun

6 **2**
5/3–4 2/11–12

To take this Listening Exercise online and
receive feedback or email answers to your
instructor, go to *ThomsonNOW* for this chapter.

Debussy, as we have seen, was a master of generating new
sonorities, as well as creating new, discontinuous orchestrations. The following questions, therefore, pertain
mainly to issues of color and orchestration.

1. (0:00–0:23) Which of the following is true about the beginning of this piece?
   a. The texture is polyphonic, the meter is clear, and the melody has chromaticism.
   b. The texture is monophonic, the meter is vague, and the melody has chromaticism.
   c. The texture is homophonic, the meter is clear, and the melody does not have chromaticism.
2. (0:57–1:22) The flute returns with the opening line, but now the strings quietly shimmer behind it. Which string technique creates this shimmering effect?
   a. pizzicato   b. obligato   c. tremolo
3. (1:37–2:02) By repeating a motive as it fades away, Debussy avoids any large climax of the sort beloved by Romantic composers. In restating this motive continuously, on the same pitches, Debussy is employing what?
   a. an ostinato
   b. a walking bass
   c. an arpeggio
4. (1:37–2:02) Which dynamic marking does Debussy use to create this feeling of evasion and anticlimax?
   a. crescendo–diminuendo
   b. diminuendo–crescendo
5. (2:03, 2:18, 2:40, and 0:00) When the flute returns with the twisting chromatic line, which instrument provides a colorful background?
   a. English horn
   b. harp
   c. French horn
6. What helps to create a background "wash of sound"? (This is particularly clear at 0:00–0:16.)
   a. pedal points
   b. chromatic scales
   c. arpeggios
7. (3:21–3:46) Which is a correct description of the music at this point?
   a. The violins sweep forward with a sensuous melody based on a whole-tone scale.
   b. Various instruments dart in and out with tiny motives, creating colorful sonorities but a discontinuous texture.
8. (5:50–6:35) In this beautiful passage, Debussy comes closest to re-creating the lush sentimentality more typical of Romantic than Impressionist music. Which statement is *not* correct?
   a. There is a solo for French horn and then violin at the beginning.
   b. There is a long, sweeping, rhythmically free melody.
   c. The melody is played expressively by the violins.
9. A passage with a prominent flute is stated (0:00–0:29) and then repeated at a lower pitch (0:33–1:04), now featuring an oboe. What happens to the texture and orchestration in the course of each of these two passages?
   a. Polyphonic texture and discontinuous orchestration give way to homophonic texture and unchanging orchestration.
   b. Homophonic texture and unchanging orchestration give way to polyphonic texture and discontinuous orchestration.
10. In a typical orchestral work of the Classical or Romantic periods it is usually the violins that present most themes. In Debussy's Impressionist *Prelude*, however, the instruments of which family introduce most melodic motives?
    a. strings
    b. brasses
    c. woodwinds
    d. percussion

Debussy's voluptuous *Prelude* creates an entirely new world of musical aesthetics, one very different from the German Romantic school of Mendelssohn, Wagner, and Brahms. Where a composer in the German Romantic tradition asserts a strongly profiled theme, a French Impressionist like Debussy instead insinuates a tiny motive. In place of clear meters and regular rhythms, the Impressionist favors constantly shifting accents that obscure the pulse. Rather than working toward a thunderous climax and a strong cadence, the Impressionist prefers to avoid a climax by placing a diminuendo before the cadence, thereby creating an anticlimax. Instead of marching purposefully along a well-directed harmonic progression, the Impressionist chooses to sit on a single static harmony and let the colorful instruments work their magic. Most important, instead of using musical color to reinforce the musical theme, the Impressionist prefers to call on the instruments to demonstrate their sonorities *independent* of theme. In the music of Debussy and the Impressionists, then, beautiful sonorities are allowed simply to exist without having to progress thematically to some distant goal.

German Romantic and French Impressionist music contrasted

National Gallery, London/The Bridgeman Art Library

FIGURE 31–6
In Edgar Degas's *Combing of the Hair* (c1896) the lines of the objects are sometimes only vaguely sketched, and the intense orange color runs beyond the boundaries of the lines.

Debussy separates color from line

All this was radically modern. Think back to the orchestral music of Beethoven, Brahms, and Tchaikovsky. In these earlier works, new themes are generally introduced by a new instrument or group of instruments. Instrumental color thus reinforces and gives profile to the theme. With Debussy, on the other hand, instruments enter with a distinct color, but with no easily discernible theme. Thus, color and texture begin to replace melody as the primary agents in the creation of musical form. Debussy's approach was adopted by the revolutionary figures of twentieth-century music—among them Charles Ives, Edgard Varèse, and John Cage (see Chapters 36 and 37)—who often generate musical form through colors and textures, rather than through thematic development. Not coincidentally, during the peak of Debussy's career (around the turn of the twentieth century), the Impressionist painters began to separate color from line as well (Fig. 31–6).

Preludes for Piano (1910, 1913)

piano pieces with evocative titles

Debussy's last and most far-reaching attempt at descriptive writing in music is found in the two books of *Preludes* for piano that he published in 1910 and 1913. Here the challenge to create musical impressions was all the greater, for the piano has a more limited musical palette than the multicolor orchestra. The evocative titles of some of these short pieces allude to their mysterious qualities: *Steps in the Snow, The Sunken Cathedral, What the West Wind Saw,* and *Sounds and Perfumes Swirl in the Night Air.*

Voiles (Sails), from the first book of *Preludes* of 1910, takes us to the sea (Fig. 31–7). As we hear a fluid descent, mostly in parallel motion*, we imagine sails flapping listlessly in the breeze. The hazy, languid atmosphere is created in part by the special scale Debussy employs, the **whole-tone scale,** one in which all the pitches are a whole step apart.

FIGURE 31–7
Claude Monet's *Sailboats* (1874). The rocking of the boats is suggested by the exaggerated reflections on the water.

EXAMPLE 31–1

whole-tone scale

Because in the whole-tone scale each note is the same distance from its neighbor, no one pitch is heard as the tonal center—all pitches seem equally important. The composer can stop on any note of the scale, and it will sound no more central, or final, than any other note. The music floats without a tonal anchor. Then, as if impelled by a puff of wind, the boats seem to rock on the now-rippling waters. Debussy creates this gentle rocking sensation by inserting a four-note ostinato* into the texture. Frequently employed by Impressionist composers, ostinatos help account for the often static, restful feeling in the harmony. By definition, ostinatos involve repetition rather than dramatic movement.

EXAMPLE 31–2

ostinatos return

A new ostinato now appears in the upper register (right hand), while a succession of four-note chords sounds in the middle register (left hand). Notice that all four notes of each chord consistently move in what is called parallel motion. In **parallel motion,** all parts move together, locked in step, in the same direction.

EXAMPLE 31–3

parallel motion   left hand

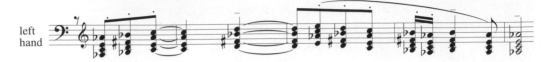

Parallel motion is the antithesis of counterpoint, the traditional musical technique in which two or more lines usually move in directions opposite to one another. Parallel motion was an innovation of Debussy, and it was one way he expressed his opposition to the German school of Wagner and Brahms, so heavily steeped in counterpoint.

Suddenly, a gust of wind seems to shake the ships as the pianist races up the scale in a harp-like glissando*. This scale, however, is different from the preceding whole-tone one. It is a pentatonic scale*. There are only five notes within each octave, here the five notes corresponding to the black keys on the piano. We have seen before that the pentatonic scale is often found in folk music (see page 319). Debussy first encountered it in the Southeast Asian music he heard at the Paris World's Fair of 1889.

EXAMPLE 31–4

pentatonic scale

Following this energized whirl around the pentatonic scale, the seascape regains its placid demeanor with the return of the whole-tone scale and, ultimately, the descending parallel thirds with which the piece began. At the end, Debussy directs the pianist to push down and hold the sustaining pedal (the right-most of the three pedals). Once the sustaining pedal is pressed and held, all notes sounded thereafter will blur into a vague haze, similar to the hazes and mists that envelop many Impressionist paintings (see Fig. 31–1).

Listening Guide   Claude Debussy
Voiles (Sails), from *Preludes,* Book I (1910)

6
5/5

Form: ternary

0:00	5	Descending parallel thirds using whole-tone scale
0:12		Bass pedal point* enters
1:11		Ostinato enters in middle register

1:38	Ostinato moves into top register; chords move in parallel motion in middle register
2:14	Harp-like glissandos using pentatonic scale
2:28	Chords moving in parallel motion above pedal point
2:51	Glissandos now employing whole-tone scale
3:36	Descending thirds return
3:57	Glissandos blur through use of sustaining pedal

 Use a downloadable, cross-platform animated Active Listening Guide, available at **www.thomsonedu.com/music/wright.**

Key Words

| Impressionism (340) | whole-tone scale | parallel motion (348) |
| Symbolists (342) | (346) | |

Checklist of Musical Style

Impressionist: 1880–1920

Melody	Varies from short dabs of sound to long, free-flowing lines; melodies are rarely tuneful or singable; they often twist and turn rapidly in undulating patterns; chromatic scale, whole-tone scale, and pentatonic scale often replace usual major and minor scales	*Representative composers* Debussy Ravel Fauré
Harmony	Primarily homophonic; triad is extended to form seventh chords and ninth chords, and these frequently move in parallel motion	*Principal genres* symphonic poem string quartet
Rhythm	Usually free and flexible with irregular accents, making it sometimes difficult to determine meter; rhythmic ostinatos used to give feeling of stasis rather than movement	orchestral song opera character piece for piano ballet music
Color	More emphasis on woodwinds and brasses and less on violins as primary carriers of melody; more soloistic writing to show that color of instrument is as important as the melody line it plays	
Texture	Can vary from thin and airy to heavy and dense; sustaining pedal of piano often used to create wash of sound; glissandos run quickly from low to high or high to low	
Form	Traditional forms involving clear-cut repetitions rarely used; composers try to develop form unique and particular to each new musical work	

CULTURAL
CONTEXT

An Orchestra from Bali, Indonesia

In 1889, Claude Debussy, then an impressionable young man of twenty-six, paid several visits to the *Exposition universelle* (World's Fair) organized in Paris next to the newly constructed Eiffel Tower. There he not only saw newfangled inventions like electric lighting and electric-powered elevators but also gained exposure to the cultures of the Far East. He saw a Cambodian pagoda that seems to have been the inspiration for a later piano piece called *Pagodes* (*Pagodas*, 1903). And he heard a colorful gamelan* orchestra, as he recalled to a friend some years later: "Do you not remember the Javanese (Indonesian) music that was capable of expressing every nuance of meaning, even unmentionable shades, and makes our tonic and dominant sounds seem weak and empty?" This experience encouraged Debussy to incorporate in his own music the sounds of the East: ostinatos, sta-

tic harmonies, pentatonic and whole-tone scales, and shimmering surfaces. It also suggested to him that music did not always have to progress toward a goal—instead, it might simply exist for the moment.

The gamelan orchestra (see below) forms an important part of the musical culture of several Southeast Asian countries, and nowhere is it more prominent than in Indonesia. Although sections of the country were devastated by the catastrophic tsunami of 2004, Indonesia's population has grown to 260 million, making it the fourth largest country on earth. Toward the center of this vast archipelago is the is-

The Cambodian pagoda at the World's Fair in Paris in 1889. Here Debussy heard the music of Cambodia, China, Thailand, and Indonesia, and he began to formulate a musical aesthetic different from the prevailing German symphonic tradition.

Indonesian gamelan at the 1889 World's Fair.

Photo collection Sirot

Mary Evans Picture Library

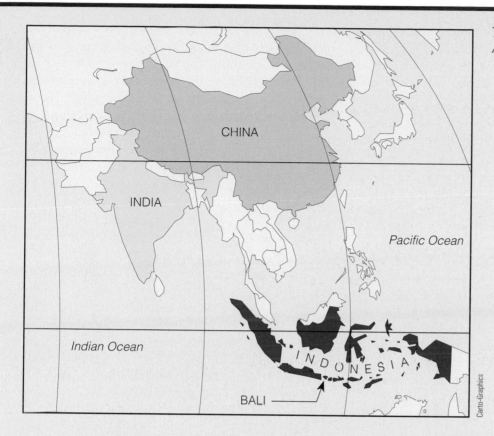

The subcontinent of Asia, Southeast Asia, and the Pacific Rim.

land of **Bali,** a land of swaying palm trees, fertile fields, and hundreds of small villages, each with its own vital and distinctive musical tradition. For the more than 2 million inhabitants of Bali, music is an integral part of their daily lives, for it is intimately connected with religion and folklore. Hindu deities and local spirits must be honored daily in the temple and in the home. The most important ceremonies are celebrated to the accompaniment of the music performed by a gamelan.

A **gamelan** is a collection of as many as twenty-five different musical instruments that, when played together, make up an orchestra. However, the ensemble sounds very unlike our Western orchestra, for the dominant instrumental family of the gamelan is not the strings but the percussion: **metallophones** (xylophone-like instruments with bronze keys struck by hammers; see figure, right), tuned gongs, gong-chimes, cymbals, and drums, along with an occasional flute. So, too, the gamelan employs a different approach to generating musical lines. In the Western orchestra, a single instrument is responsible for providing a melody or countermelody, or creating a single instrumental color. In gamelan music, however, players of several instruments continually contribute

A Balinese gamelan with gongs (first row) and metallophones (second and third rows).

bits of music that, when taken together, form a composite line of distinctive color. In Example 31–5, notice how the parts are interlocking and mutually interdependent. They are also often repetitious, creating both rhythmic and melodic ostinatos.

EXAMPLE 31–5

Baris is a traditional Balinese composition used to accompany a solo dance—one portraying a warrior-in-training. The dancer's taut, upright posture, darting eye movements, and cautious forays around the stage create a tense and exciting mood. Every so often, the dancer initiates bolder, more aggressive turns and steps, which are interpreted as cues by the lead drummer. The gamelan responds to the gestures of the dance with crashing chords and sudden breaks. In this recording of *Baris*, the many interdependent musical parts are demonstrated at a slow tempo. After a drum introduction, a set of three gongs creates an eight-beat rhythmic cycle. Thereafter, the various metallophones* and drums enter one-by-one to state, or elaborate upon, the eight-note cycle four times. Each four-cycle unit is separated from the preceding one by an "empty" cycle, one in which the gongs alone sound. The Listening Guide contains a bewildering variety of names for the Indonesian musical instruments, names we need not remember. Nevertheless, the great number of instruments and the variety of their sounds show that the Balinese orchestra—though producing a completely different sound from our Western symphony orchestra—is every bit as complex and colorful.

Listening Guide

Baris for Balinese Gamelan
Prepared by ethnomusicologist Michael Tenzer
Recorded July 1989 in Denpasar, Bali, with students of the
Indonesian Arts Academy

6
6/19

Genre: gamelan music

0:00	19	Introduction to *kendang* (two-headed drums)
0:12		Full ensemble enters for introductory phrase
0:23		Gongs *kempur* (midrange gong) and *kempli* (muted, small gong) lay foundation for rhythmic cycle
0:42		*Ugal* (lead metallophone) plays basic eight-note melody, one note per beat
1:00		Two *pemade* and two *kantilan* (metallophones) play *ugal*'s melody with repeated pitches
1:19		Two more *pemade* and *kantilan* play complementary part
1:38		All *pemade* and *kantilan* plus *ugal* play together
1:56		Two *calung* (metallophones) play simplified version of *ugal* melody
2:13		Two deep-tone *jegogan* (metallophones) play further simplified version
2:32		Several *reyong* (tiny gongs) play rhythmically more complex version of melody
2:51		Other *reyong* gongs respond
3:10		Together, whole *reyong* interlocks to create swift variant of *ugal* melody
3:28		First *kendang* (two-headed drum) plays rhythm composed to accompany melody
3:48		Second *kendang* plays complementary rhythm

4:04	Two *kendang* interlock
4:27	Conclusion: all instruments reenter in growing wave of sound
4:52	Cue from drums heralds *ritardando* and final cycle

 Use a downloadable, cross-platform animated Active Listening Guide, available at **www.thomsonedu.com/music/wright.**

Key Words

Bali (351)   gamelan (351)   metallophone (351)

Exoticism

One of the magical qualities of music is its capacity to carry us to distant lands. Far-off places can be experienced in our minds, if only through the strange and mysterious sounds we associate with them. In the eighteenth century, composers like Mozart and Haydn sometimes imitated the sounds of the Turkish military band, evoking the exotic East by using such Turkish percussion instruments as cymbals and triangles, and often making this effect explicit with the performance indication "alla Turca" ("in the Turkish style"). In the nineteenth century, Georges Bizet took his audience to then "exotic" Spain in his opera *Carmen* (see page 312). Composers at the turn of the twentieth century especially delighted in the sounds of the Far East, as is evident in Claude Debussy's musical reaction to the gamelan orchestra he heard at the World's Fair in Paris in 1889.

Debussy's contemporaries were similarly attracted to the "exotic other." The painter Claude Monet decorated his home in Giverny, France, not with his own canvases or those of fellow Impressionists, but instead with prints and watercolors from Japan. The influence of these Japanese paintings is readily apparent in Monet's startling portrait of his wife in traditional Japanese costume (Fig. 32–1). Modernists like Pablo Picasso (1881–1973) and Georges Braque (1882–1963) began collecting African art in Paris during the years 1905–1908. Some historians believe that the Cubist movement in painting (see page 366) was born of Picasso's interest in African sculpture and ceremonial masks.

Although there had been many sporadic contacts made by Western explorers since the Middle Ages, Western society's real love affair with the culture of the East began in earnest in the eighteenth century, when the British India Company gained a monopoly on trade with China. A vogue for the art objects and fashions of China—collectively called **Chinoiserie**—swept the West and stimulated the importation, or imitation, of consumer products such as porcelain dishware (still called "china"), vases, wallpaper, silks, tea, and even opium. In 1853, the American naval officer Matthew Perry arrived in Japan, and in 1868, Japan ended a long period of isolation, allowing Western merchants access to Japanese markets. Now, it seemed, all things Japanese were fashionable, both in clothing and furniture and in the decorative and fine arts. American, French, Dutch, and German painters commenced to adopt the Japanese style. Such flat blocks of color and two-dimensional planes, as seen in Vincent van Gogh's *The Blooming Plum Tree* (Fig. 32–2), show that this interest in the "oriental" hastened the appearance of modern abstract art.

But how did exoticism express itself in music? Briefly, musical **exoticism** was communicated by any sounds drawn from outside the traditional Western European musical experience. A non-Western scale or harmony, a folk rhythm, or a musical instrument like the erhu* or gong* all could signal the exotic. So, too, might a foreign subject (program) for a symphonic poem, or a libretto for an opera.

FIGURE 32–1

Claude Monet, *La Japonaise (Madame Camille Monet in Japanese Costume,* 1876). America and Europe began to show an enthusiasm for things Japanese after the opening of trade with Japan in the 1850s. Fashionable Parisian women wore kimonos and furnished their homes with oriental furniture, prints, and *objets d'art.*

THE EXOTIC OF CHINA: PUCCINI'S TURANDOT (1924)

One composer drawn to the music and culture of distant lands at the turn of the twentieth century was Giacomo Puccini (1858–1924). We met Puccini in Chapter 28 in his capacity as composer of important *verismo** operas, such as *La bohème* (1896) and *Tosca* (1900). During the last two decades of his life, however, Puccini based his operas on foreign subjects. The first was *Madama Butterfly* (1904), set in Japan; the next, *The Girl of the Golden West* (1910), set in America's Wild West (for Puccini, the American West was as exotic as the Japanese East); and the last, *Turandot* (1924), set in China. In all three operas, Puccini endeavored to infuse ethnic authenticity by incorporating local musical color.

Although not as well known as *La bohème*, Puccini's last opera, *Turandot*, is surely not only his best but also one of the best in the entire operatic repertoire. The libretto is based on an Eastern fairy tale that first appeared in a collection of stories called *1001 Arabian Nights*. Princess Turandot, daughter of the emperor of China, has sworn to wed only a suitor of royal blood, one able to solve three riddles that she has devised. Should a suitor fail, he will lose his head. But Turandot has made the riddles impossible to answer, believing she has no interest in love or marriage. Calaf, son of the deposed king Timur, proves successful where all others have failed. In the end, he offers to release Turandot from her vow, but she acknowledges that she has loved Calaf from the first moment. The success of the opera comes not from the unfolding of this fantastical story, but from the spectacular choruses, stunning arias, and abundant local color Puccini built into the tale.

At the outset of *Turandot*, we are greeted by a barrage of strange sounds. Percussive dissonances—a sure sign of Western musical modernism—assault our ears, but so, too, do several non-Western elements. A xylophone and a gong, both Asian instruments, project prominently from the orchestra, and the harmony is static, as is often the case in Eastern music. When the harmony finally moves, it does so by means of musical parallelism*—specifically, by parallel fifths (the in-step movement of the same interval, one spanning a distance of five letter names). Example 32–1 presents a composite of the parallel fifths that appear in the orchestral harmony.

FIGURE 32–2
Vincent van Gogh, *The Blooming Plum Tree*. With its "oriental" flat blocks of color and two-dimensional planes, it presaged modern abstract art.

Bildarchiv Preussischer Kulturbesitz/Art Resource, NY

non-Western sounds

EXAMPLE 32–1

Parallel fifths historically have been used by Western composers as a symbol for the "primitive" in music. Not only was the earliest written polyphony in the West fashioned in parallel fifths, such fifths also appear in the music of different ethnic groups around the world, ranging from the Hunan Chinese, to the American Pueblo Indians, to the Wasukuma tribe of East Africa. Parallel motion is the antithesis of contrary motion, which lies at the heart of

parallel motion: a symbol of the "primitive"

ethnic stereotyping through music

traditional Western European art music. To signify something non-Western—to suggest the "other" or the "primitive"—a composer might simply write parallel fifths. (Hollywood film composers of the mid-twentieth century knew this, and whenever there appeared on the screen a junk sailing into Hong Kong harbor or a band of Indians coming over a hill out west, parallel fifths would sound in the score.) This was ethnic stereotyping through music. The parallel fifths at the beginning of *Turandot* tell us that we have been musically transported somewhere else, but where?

the plot of Turandot

The text of the opening recitative confirms that we are in China. With the words "Popolo di Pekino!" ("People of Peking" [Beijing]), a mandarin (high court official) announces that yet another of Turandot's suitors, having failed to answer the three riddles, will be decapitated. In this opening scene, the parallel fifths unfold ever so slowly in the harmony, almost unheard. The sense of the exotic is projected more explicitly by the sounds of the xylophone and gong, as well as by the piercing tones of the upper woodwinds, orchestrated to sound like bamboo flutes.

Listening Guide

Giacomo Puccini
"People of Peking" from *Turandot* (1924)
(beginning only)

6
5/6

Situation: As the curtain rises, a mandarin reiterates the law that any suitor for the hand of Turandot must solve the three riddles she has devised. The Prince of Persia, having failed to do so, must lose his head.

0:00	**6**	Orchestral flourish, then single, dissonant chord, played *fortissimo*	
0:30		Mandarin announces the law as harmony below slowly changes in parallel fifths	Popolo di Pekino! La legge è questa: Turandot la Pura sposa sarà di chi, di sangue regio, spieghi i tre enigmi ch'ella proporrà. Ma chi affronta il cimento e vinto resta, porga alla scure la superba testa!	People of Peking This is the law: Turandot the Pure will marry the person of royal blood who solves the three riddles she posed. But if he should fail in this test, he must submit his superb head to the sword!
1:16		Crowd exclaims	Ah! Ah!	Ah! Ah!

 Use a downloadable, cross-platform animated Active Listening Guide, available at **www.thomsonedu.com/music/wright**.

Next we met the hero of the opera, Calaf; his aged father, Timur; and the father's faithful servant girl, Liù. Calaf announces that he will try to win the hand of Turandot. Liù, knowing the fatal consequences of failure, tries to dissuade him. Her aria "Signore, ascolta!" ("Lord, please listen!") incorporates another non-Western symbol, the familiar pentatonic scale (see also pages 319 and 348), here using the pitches G♭, A♭, B♭, D♭, E♭, (G♭). Puccini has chosen for this through-composed aria the key of G♭ major, one in which the pentatonic scale falls naturally on all five of the black keys of the piano.

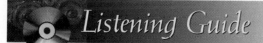

Situation: The servant Liù tries to dissuade Calif from pursuing Turandot, knowing that failure will result in his death, as well as the exile of herself and Calif's father.

Si - gno-re,a - scol - ta!   Ah,   si - gno-re,a - scol - ta   Liù non reg-ge più!___ Si_spez-za_il cuor! Ahi - mè, ahi-mè,

0:00 **7** Melody unfolds quietly along pitches of pentatonic scale	Signore, ascolta! Ah, signore, ascolta! Liù non regge più, si spezza il cuor! Ahimè, quanto cammino col tuo nome nell'anima, col nome tuo sulle labbra!	Lord, please listen! Ah, lord, please listen! Liù can bear it no longer, her heart is breaking! Alas, how much wandering with only your name to support her, with only your name on her lips!
1:01 Second strophe of text; melody continues to grow expansively	Ma se il tuo destino, doman sarà deciso, noi morrem sulla strada dell'esilio. Ei perderà suo figlio . . . io l'ombra d'un sorriso. Liù non regge più! Ah!	But if your fate is decided tomorrow, we will die on the road of exile. He will have lost his only son . . . and the remembrance of a smile. Liù can bear it no longer. Ah!

 Use a downloadable, cross-platform animated Active Listening Guide, available at **www.thomsonedu.com/music/wright**.

Moving the action from the streets of Beijing inside to the imperial palace, Act II of *Turandot* opens with a scene of comic relief. Three servants of the court—Puccini's equivalent of the Three Stooges—chatter away about the current, troubled state of affairs. They are Ping, Pang, and Pong, and their dress and gestures are as stereotypical as their names (Fig. 32–3). Here Puccini's depiction of local color is so heavy that it borders on parody, the uninformed Westerner's view of "the comical Chinaman." Not only the typical

Puccini's equivalent of the Three Stooges

© Clive Barda/ArenaPAL/Topham/The Image Works

FIGURE 32–3
Ping, Pang, and Pong, Puccini's caricature of Chinese civil servants, from *Turandot*.

non-Western scales—Ping makes use of the whole-tone* scale, while Pang and Pong adopt the pentatonic*—but also the excessively square rhythms and static ostinato in the orchestra contribute to Puccini's caricature. Moreover, Pang and Pong's accompaniment is formed by an additive process in which many different instruments separately contribute small amounts of sound, as happens in the Eastern gamelan* orchestra.

EXAMPLE 32–2

Listening Guide

Giacomo Puccini
"Hello, Pang! Hello, Pong!" from *Turandot* (1924)
(beginning only)

6
5/8

Situation: Three comical court servants, Ping, Pang, and Pong, complain about the troubled state of affairs in China; they don't know whether to prepare a wedding or a funeral.

0:00	8	Above ostinato, Ping comments on confusion at court	Olà, Pang! Olà, Pong! Poiché il funesto gong desta la reggia e desta la città, siam pronti ad ogni evento: se lo straniero vince, per le nozze e s'egli perde, per seppellimento.	Hello, Pang! Hello, Pong! Since the fateful gong has awakened both the court and the city, we are ready for any event: if the stranger wins, for a wedding, and if he loses, for a burial.
0:30		Pang and Pong sing pentatonic melody above gamelan-like accompaniment	Io prepare le nozze, ed io le esequie, le rosse lanterne di festa, le bianche lanterne di lutto (etc.)	I shall prepare the wedding, and I the funeral, the red lanterns of rejoicing, the white lanterns of mourning. (etc.)

 Use a downloadable, cross-platform animated Active Listening Guide, available at www.thomsonedu.com/music/wright.

Puccini's allocation of local color—parallel fifths, exotic instruments, additive accompaniments, and pentatonic and whole-tone scales—is not haphazard. The lower-caste characters always project the most local color. On the other side, characters of royal blood, such as Calaf and Turandot, sing sweeping arias with long lines and powerful climaxes, always within conventional Western major or minor scales. Thus, not only does Puccini's musical setting stereotype the Chinese in general, it also separates the opera's characters according to class.

THE EXOTIC OF SPAIN: RAVEL'S BOLERO (1928)

While not as distant as China, Spain was nonetheless considered an exotic place for Northern Europeans in the late-nineteenth and early-twentieth centuries. The culture of southern Spain in particular, only thirty miles distant from the tip of North Africa, offered the mysterious allure of the Near East. As the French poet Victor Hugo (1802–1885) said, "Spain is still the Orient; Spain is half African, and Africa is half Asiatic." French composers, perhaps even more than the poets and painters, created art with a would-be-Spanish character. Claude Debussy composed an orchestral piece (*Ibéria*, 1908) and a piano work ("Evening in Grenada," 1902) using Spanish melodies. Maurice Ravel wrote his first orchestral work (*Spanish Rhapsody*, 1907) and his last ballet (*Bolero*, 1928), as well as an opera (*The Spanish Hour*, 1911), on Spanish subjects. Yet neither Debussy nor Ravel ever set foot in Spain. In art, the evocative powers of the imagination are often a more potent force than mundane reality.

Spain: an exotic land

A friend of Maurice Ravel (1875–1937) once said about him, "He was the eternal traveler who never went there." Indeed, Ravel spent almost all of his life in Paris, a modest music teacher and composer earning a modest living. Only through his music did he journey to Spain, Arabia, ancient Greece, and the Far East—all lands he sought to evoke through the exotic-sounding elements he brought into his music.

Ravel's life of the imagination

Yet there was one exception to Ravel's life of the imagination. In 1928, he embarked on a four-month tour of the United States. He heard jazz in Harlem with American composer George Gershwin (1898–1937), had breakfast in Hollywood with comedian Charlie Chaplin (1889–1977), and visited Niagara Falls and the Grand Canyon. Having performed and conducted his music in twenty-five American cities, Ravel returned to Paris with what was then the enormous sum of $27,000, financially secure for the final decade of his life.

The first work Ravel undertook upon his return to Paris was the composition of a new, modern-style ballet titled *Bolero*. A **bolero** is a sultry Spanish dance in a slow tempo and triple meter. For the first performance in Paris, on November 22, 1928, Ravel intended the stage to be set to represent the interior of a Spanish inn. A single large table sits in the center of the stage, and above it hangs a huge chandelier that casts both bright light and dark shadows upon the colorful scene below. Around the room, male dancers sit listlessly, seemingly unaware of the presence

FIGURE 32–4
John Singer Sargent (1856–1925), *El Jaleo: Spanish Dancer*. Sargent was an American expatriate painter who got caught up in the European enthusiasm for all things Spanish during the late nineteenth century.

© Burstein Collection/Corbis

of a single female dancer, a seductive gypsy reminiscent of Carmen (see page 312). But as the gypsy mounts the table and begins to move with increasing passion, the men, one by one, join in her enticing dance. With growing abandon, the entire company begins to sway to the hypnotic music, moving inexorably toward a frenzied climax.

a rhythmic, harmonic, and melodic ostinato

The opening sound of *Bolero* is that of a snare drum*, which stands in for the Spanish castanets carried by the ballerina. The drum's rhythmic pattern is only two measures long, but it repeats over and over, for nearly fourteen minutes. While the drum moves along implacably, a few string instruments pluck quietly in the background, providing a harmonic accompaniment and establishing a clear triple meter. Soon a flute enters with a soft, enchanting melody. Ravel later recalled that this theme had come to him one day while working at the piano, inspired, he said, by the Spanish folksongs his Basque mother used to sing to him. The melody actually appears in two contrasting guises. One (**A**, Ex. 32–3) is rhythmically square and in C major; the other (**B**, Ex. 32–4) is more syncopated and is written in a scale closely related to minor. Both versions of the melody are sixteen measures long, and they, too, repeat again and again, according to this arrangement: **AABBAABB** (etc.) **AB.**

EXAMPLE 32–3

EXAMPLE 32–4

Most of the audience that first night in Paris cheered Ravel and his new work, but at least one woman yelled, "He's mad!" What excited the passions of the crowd was that Ravel had written a work with only a single two-part melody repeated over and over. Ravel himself was ambivalent about his creation: "I have written only one masterpiece. That is the *Bolero*. Unfortunately, it contains no music." What Ravel meant by this paradoxical statement is that the piece contains little in the way of traditional, Western European music; in *Bolero*, Ravel fails to present a theme and then develop and contrast it over a long span of time, as might Beethoven or Brahms. Ravel's music goes nowhere; it simply repeats, getting louder and louder as more instruments enter and the texture becomes denser. As with much Impressionist music, non-Western music, and twentieth-century modernist music, Ravel creates new colors and textures, but does not develop melody in the conventional, nineteenth-century European manner.

a gigantic crescendo

Finally, after nearly fourteen minutes of repetition and growing tension, the melody rises to a higher pitch level. This shift breaks the hypnotic spell, and soon the work comes to a crashing conclusion with dissonant chords.

Listening Guide

Maurice Ravel
Bolero (1928)

6
5/9–11

Genre: **ballet**
Form: **AABBAABB** etc.

0:00	9		Snare drum and low strings begin two-measure rhythmic ostinatos
0:10			Flute enters quietly with melody **A**
0:55			Clarinet presents melody **A**
1:42			Bassoon enters with melody **B**, harp added to accompaniment
2:29			High clarinet presents melody **B**
3:08			Bassoon joins with snare drum in playing rhythmic ostinato
3:13			Low oboe plays melody **A**
4:00			Trumpet (with mute) and flute together play melody **A**
4:45			Saxophone plays melody **B**
5:32			High saxophone repeats melody **B**
6:18	10	0:00	Two flutes, French horn, and celesta (keyboard instrument that produces sound like a bell) together play melody **A**
7:03		0:45	Several woodwind instruments play melody **A**
7:48		1:30	Trombone plays melody **B**
8:33		2:15	Woodwinds and French horn play melody **B** loudly
9:13		2:55	Timpani added to accompaniment
9:19	11	0:00	First violins and woodwinds play melody **A**
10:03		0:44	First and second violins and woodwinds play melody **A**
10:48		1:29	Violins, woodwinds, and trumpets play melody **B**
11:33		2:14	Violins, violas, cellos, woodwinds, and trumpets play melody **B**
12:19		3:00	Melody **A** played mainly by first violins, trumpets, and piccolos
13:07		3:48	Same instruments, now with trombone added, play melody **B**
13:46		4:27	Musical climax: melody **B** moves to higher pitches and is extended
14:06		4:47	Melody settles back down to original pitch level
14:11		4:52	End: no melody, just rhythmic ostinato and cymbal crashes

Use a downloadable, cross-platform animated Active Listening Guide, available at **www.thomsonedu.com/music/wright**.

Listening Exercise 41

Ravel
Bolero

It would be interesting to know your reaction to Ravel's highly unusual music for the ballet *Bolero*. Are you bored by it? Do you think Ravel was lazy, taking the "easy way out" after having hit upon a good melody? Are you inspired to learn to dance the bolero? Do you experience a growing sense of exhilaration, even power, as the sound swells? No matter, the following questions are more technical, and several deal with issues of the exotic in music.

1. (0:10–0:54) Listen to the first statement of the melody. At the end, there is an interlude during which the melody is absent. For how many measures in $\frac{3}{4}$ time does the interlude last?
   a. one
   b. two
   c. three
   d. four

2. (0:55–3:59) Listen now to several statements of the melody. Does the musical interlude return after each one?
   a. yes
   b. no

3. (4:45) Is the saxophone usually part of the Western symphony orchestra? Did we hear it in the music of Brahms and Tchaikovsky, for example?
   a. yes
   b. no

4. (1:30–2:07) The trombone is the only instrument of the orchestra to have a slide. In this performance, does the sound of the trombone slide audibly between pitches?
   a. yes
   b. no

5. (0:00) When the violins enter, how many do you hear?
   a. two or three
   b. the entire violin section

6. (3:48) Although many instruments are playing the melody here, they are playing the same pitches (or pitches an octave higher or lower). What is this called?
   a. playing in unison
   b. playing in full cadence
   c. playing in imitation

7. (4:27) Music that changes pitch level to a new key with a new tonic has undergone what?
   a. an augmentation
   b. a diminution
   c. a retransition
   d. a modulation

8. Which statement below is true?
   a. Ravel requires a large, traditional Western orchestra to play his vision of a Spanish dance.
   b. Ravel requires a large Western orchestra but augments it with Eastern-sounding gong, erhu, xylophone, and bamboo-flute.
   c. Ravel requires a few Western instruments, but the orchestra is essentially that of an Eastern gamelan.

9. Which of the following is *not* an aspect of exoticism, or the "foreign," in *Bolero*?
   a. a Spanish-influenced melody
   b. ostinatos
   c. crashing, dissonant final chords

10. Which of the following musical symbols correctly represents the shape, or form, of *Bolero*?
    a. <
    b. >
    c. <>

Key Words

Chinoiserie (354)   exoticism (354)   bolero (359)

Indigenous Music from Mexico: Mariachi Music

Beginning in the fifteenth century, Spanish culture spread across the globe, eastward around Africa and westward to the Americas. Spanish music and dance migrated with the explorers, ultimately blending with local customs and yielding such hybrid genres as the Cuban Habanera* (dance of Havana; see page 312), the Argentine tango*, and Mexican mariachi music.

Mariachi music is an exuberant popular music that enjoys great favor today in Mexico and parts of the southwestern United States. It originated in the western Mexican state of Jalisco (also the birthplace of Tequila), and then spread east to Mexico City and north to California, Arizona, New Mexico, and Texas. The first mariachi were itinerant performers who wandered from one hacienda (large ranch) to another as a group. The term **mariachi** thus denotes a performing ensemble—like the words "orchestra" in the West and "gamelan" in the East—but one that generates a particularly Mexican sound.

Mariachi music reflects the diverse musical history of Mexico. Some of its influences can be traced to Spanish music of the sixteenth century, but strains of indigenous Mexican folk music and even African music can be heard as well. The instrumental core of mariachi music is formed by string instruments brought to Mexico by the Spanish: violins, guitars, and the harp. During the early twentieth century, trumpets were added, and the harp was replaced, or supplemented, by a large bass guitar, called the **guitarrón** (see figure). The standard mariachi band of today thus includes as many as six to eight violins, two trumpets, and two or three guitars, including a guitarrón. Many pieces also require a singer, and for these the instruments either alternate with the soloist or simply provide an accompaniment.

Two factors create the distinctive sound of mariachi music: (1) the disposition of the instruments and (2) the rhythms. The sweet-sounding violins, often playing in "close harmony" at the interval of a third, alternate with the brilliant-sounding trumpets in pre-

Mariachi Cobre

Courtesy Mariachi Cobre

senting the melody. The guitars provide the supporting accompaniment and, equally important, set the rhythms. Rhythm in mariachi music is both strong and disruptive. At first, the players set a clear meter, either duple or triple, only to upset it suddenly by heavy and continuous syncopation that temporarily sets up a conflicting meter. It is this metrical uncertainty that creates the genre's exciting, infectious mood. Originally, mariachi music was not merely played and sung, but also danced, with the dancers driving the heels of their shoes or boots into a wooden floor to emphasize the rhythmic patterns and metrical shifts.

A brief example of mariachi music can be heard in the traditional tune "El burro," an amusing piece in which the instruments occasionally mimic the sounds of a burro, or donkey. The primary beat here unfolds at a very fast tempo in triple meter. Often, however, this triple pattern is obscured by syncopation. Twice (at 1:21 and 1:46) the syncopation is consistently applied so that bars *written* in triple meter actually *sound* as a succession of measures in duple meter. When three bars of duple meter replace two bars of triple, as in Example 32–5, the phenomenon is known as **hemiola.** Hemiola is a constant feature of mariachi music and of classical music as well.

EXAMPLE 32–5

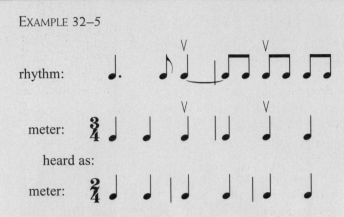

The ensemble performing "El burro" is Mariachi Cobre, which was first formed in Tucson, Arizona, in 1971, and continues to perform today from California to Florida. Although "El burro" was arranged and written down in the 1930s by Silvestre Vargas and Rubin Fuentes, it is a traditional song; its musical fabric is a patchwork of phrases widely found in unwritten Mexican popular music. There are no Bachs or Beethovens in the world of mariachi. This is folk music that derives from the heart of all people of Mexican origin. The spirited, exuberant cries—***gritos***—often heard in a performance form part of the experience.

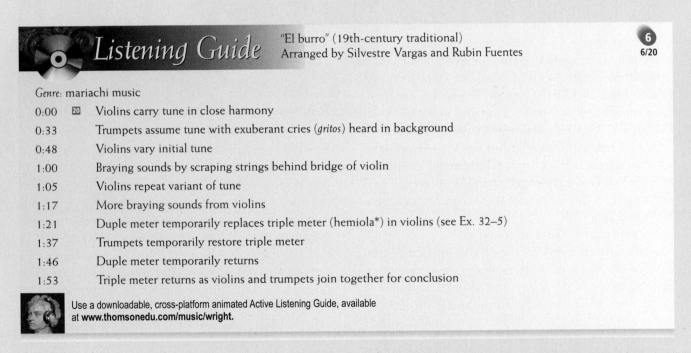

Listening Guide

"El burro" (19th-century traditional)
Arranged by Silvestre Vargas and Rubin Fuentes

6

6/20

Genre: mariachi music

0:00 20 Violins carry tune in close harmony

0:33 Trumpets assume tune with exuberant cries (*gritos*) heard in background

0:48 Violins vary initial tune

1:00 Braying sounds by scraping strings behind bridge of violin

1:05 Violins repeat variant of tune

1:17 More braying sounds from violins

1:21 Duple meter temporarily replaces triple meter (hemiola*) in violins (see Ex. 32–5)

1:37 Trumpets temporarily restore triple meter

1:46 Duple meter temporarily returns

1:53 Triple meter returns as violins and trumpets join together for conclusion

Use a downloadable, cross-platform animated Active Listening Guide, available at **www.thomsonedu.com/music/wright**.

Today mariachi music is performed at weddings, baptisms, birthdays, and various other social gatherings at which a good time is to be had. Equally important, in the southwestern United States, mariachi enjoys a growing place in the formal school curriculum, replacing chorus and marching band as a music elective. More than 500 public schools in this region now have classes in mariachi as a way of teaching the fundamentals of music, as well as maintaining an important part of the Mexican cultural heritage.

Key Words

mariachi (**363**)   hemiola (**363**)

guitarrón (**363**)   *grito* (**364**)

Modernism in Music and the Arts

The twentieth century might best be called the Age of Extremes. On the one hand, the era was marked by unspeakable tragedies, including two world wars; the systematic extermination of millions of people; the use of chemical, biological, and atomic weapons; and brutal acts of terrorism. On the other hand, scientific advances significantly improved both the quality and length of human life. Such medical advances as antibiotics, organ transplants, and laser surgery have saved countless lives. The automobile and airplane have profoundly changed the way we travel, offering quick access to virtually the whole world. And important technological innovations—first radio and television, then computers and the Internet—have revolutionized the dissemination of information.

Technological progress has also affected our musical culture. The twentieth century saw steady advances in recording and playback technology, with the respective inventions of the LP record, magnetic tape, compact disc, and MP3 file, which have made popular and classical music alike available to ever-larger segments of the population. These advances, however, have not come without a cost, arguably having discouraged musical education and music-making in the home: Why learn to play an instrument, one might wonder, when you can much more easily hear music on a CD player or iPod?

MODERNISM: AN ANTI-ROMANTIC MOVEMENT

The first half of the twentieth century was a particularly horrific time. In World War I (1914–1918), 9 million soldiers were killed on the battlefields. Shocked by the carnage, intellectuals turned away from the predominantly idealistic, sentimental aesthetics of Romanticism—how could one think of love and beauty in the face of wholesale destruction? For writers, painters, and composers alike, disjunction, anxiety, and even hysteria became valid artistic sentiments that reflected the realities of the day.

an aesthetic of disjunction, anxiety, and even hysteria

Musicians of the early twentieth century did not ignore the traditions of classical music. They retained, for example, the genres of opera, ballet, symphony, concerto, and string quartet. The most progressive composers, however, radically transformed the elements of expression *within* these genres, creating new kinds of melody, harmony, rhythm, and tone color.

Radical experimentation in music began quietly enough in the music of the Impressionists—specifically, in Claude Debussy's early separation of color from line (see page 346). But as World War I approached, a crescendo of protest could be heard in the music of the avant-garde. The progressives renounced the notion that music should be beautiful, pleasing, and expressive or that it should delight or comfort the listener. Instead, they resorted to distorting traditional musical practice, sometimes violently, with the intention of shocking their audiences. Their compositions often achieved the intended effect: Arnold Schoenberg's early experiments with dissonance were received at first with hoots by a hostile public in Vienna in 1913; and Igor Stravinsky's

from Romantic mists to harsh reality

FIGURE 33–1

One of the first statements of Cubist art, Picasso's *Les Demoiselles d'Avignon* (1907). The ladies of the evening are depicted by means of geometric shapes on a flat, two-dimensional plane. Like much avant-garde music of the time, Cubist paintings reject the emotionalism and decorative appeal of nineteenth-century art.

dissonant chords and pounding rhythms caused a riot at the first performance of *Le Sacre du printemps* (*The Rite of Spring*) in Paris that same year. Such avant-garde composers sought to shake their listeners out of a state of complacency, to yank them out of the Romantic mists and back to harsh reality.

One can see clear parallels between the music and the visual art of this period: early-twentieth-century painters also introduced radical distortions into their works, similarly offending middle-class sensibilities. The increasingly angular melody and discontinuous rhythm of the new music found analogous expression in an artistic style called **Cubism.** In a Cubist painting, the artist fractures and dislocates formal reality into geometrical blocks and planes, as in the famous *Les Demoiselles d'Avignon* (Fig. 33–1), created in 1907 by Pablo Picasso (1881–1973), where the female form has been recast into angular interlocking shapes. Picasso seems to have found his musical counterpart in Stravinsky—the two friends admired each other's works and occasionally collaborated artistically. Schoenberg, a talented painter himself, found artistic camaraderie in the works of the German Expressionist painters (see pages 378–379), who so distorted formal reality that objects in their paintings were sometimes barely recognizable. To compare a Cubist painting with an Expressionist one: whereas we can easily recognize the women in Picasso's *Les Demoiselles d'Avignon* (see Fig. 33–1), the performers and audience in Wassily Kandinsky's *Concert* (1911) (Fig. 33–2) are much more difficult to discern. Just as traditional (singable) melody disappeared from early modernist music, so, too, the conventional figure vanished from avant-garde painting (Fig. 33–3).

FIGURE 33–2

Wassily Kandinsky's *Impression III (Concert)* (1911). Kandinsky was one of the founders of the Expressionist movement, which was centered in Vienna and Munich. This painting of an audience at a concert does not depict the concert so much as a psychological state—the audience's reaction to the concert.

FIGURE 33–3
The angularity and disjointed quality of much early-twentieth-century melody can also be seen in contemporary painting. In Picasso's *Three Musicians* (1921), for example, the figures are fractured and out of alignment. Compare the disjunct melody of Arnold Schoenberg given in Example 33–1.

EARLY-TWENTIETH-CENTURY MUSICAL STYLE

The early twentieth century was a period of stylistic diversity and conflict. During these years, Gustav Mahler continued to write his massive symphonies in a predominantly Romantic idiom (see Chapter 30), while Claude Debussy composed in the Impressionist style (see Chapter 31), an early French fore-runner of modernism. At the same time, the most progressive composers of art music turned to radical, indeed shocking, new ways of expressing melody, harmony, rhythm, and tone color.

Melody: More Angularity and Chromaticism

Unlike the melodies of the Romantic period, many of which are song-like in style and therefore easily sung and remembered, there are very few themes in twentieth-century music that the listener goes away humming. In fact, melody per se is less important to the avant-garde composer than is a pulsating rhythm, an unusual texture, or a new sonority. If Romantic melody was gen-erally smooth, diatonic*, and conjunct* in motion (moving more by steps than by leaps), early-twentieth-century melody tends to be fragmented, chro-matic*, and angular. The young avant-garde composers went to great lengths to *avoid* writing conjunct, stepwise lines. Rather than moving up a half-step from C to D♭, for example, they were wont to jump down a major seventh to the D♭ an octave below. Avoiding a simple interval for a more distant one an

asymmetrical, angular themes

octave above or below is called **octave displacement;** it is a feature of modern music. So, too, is the heavy use of chromaticism. In the following example by Arnold Schoenberg (1874–1951), notice how the melody makes large leaps where it might more easily move by steps and also how several sharps and flats are introduced to produce a highly chromatic line.

EXAMPLE 33–1

octave displacement

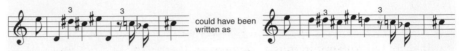

Harmony: The "Emancipation of Dissonance," New Chords, New Systems

Ever since the late Middle Ages, the basic building block of Western music had been the triad, a consonant, three-note chord (see page 40). A composer might introduce dissonance (a nontriad tone) for variety and tension, yet the rules of consonant harmony required that a dissonance pitch move (resolve) immediately to a consonant one. During the late Romantic period, however, composers like Richard Wagner (1813–1883) began to enrich their music with more and more chromaticism. By the first decade of the twentieth century, composers such as Arnold Schoenberg were using so much dissonance that the triad had all but disappeared. Schoenberg famously referred to this development as "the emancipation of dissonance," meaning that dissonance was now liberated from the requirement that it move to a consonance. At first, audiences rebelled when they heard Schoenberg's dissonance-filled scores, but the composer ultimately succeeded in "raising the bar" for what the ear might stand and preparing listeners for a much higher level of dissonance in both classical and popular music. Indeed, the work of Schoenberg and like-minded composers paved the way, albeit indirectly, for the heavy dissonances of today's progressive jazz and the often dissonant "metal" styles of Metallica, Slipknot, and others.

the "emancipation of dissonance"

Early-twentieth-century composers created dissonance not only by obscuring or distorting the traditional triad but also by introducing new chords. One technique for creating new chords was the superimposition of more thirds above the consonant triad. In this way were produced not only the **seventh chord** (a seventh chord spans seven letters of the scale, from A to G, for example) but also the **ninth chord** and the **eleventh chord.** The more thirds that were added on top of the basic triad, the more dissonant the sound of the chord.

EXAMPLE 33–2

new chords

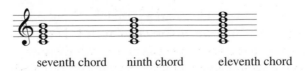

seventh chord   ninth chord   eleventh chord

The ultimate new chord was the **tone cluster,** the simultaneous sounding of a number of pitches only a whole step or a half step apart. Example 33–3 shows a tone cluster created by the American modernist Charles Ives

(1874–1954). But you, too, can create this high-dissonance chord simply by striking a group of adjacent keys on the piano with the fist or forearm. Try it.

EXAMPLE 33–3

tone clusters

Chromatic dissonance, new chords, and tone clusters all weakened the traditional role of tonality in music. Remember that triads had belonged to an interlocking system (key) and that each moved progressively toward a tonic (see page 40). As the triad disappeared, so, too, did the feeling of a key and the pull of a tonic. What were composers to do without triads, keys, and tonality, all of which had provided a structural framework for music? Simply said, they invented new systems to give structure to music. As we shall see, Igor Stravinsky anchored much of his music in long ostinatos*, while Arnold Schoenberg invented an entirely new type of musical structure called the twelve-tone* method.

abandoning the triad and keys

Rhythm: New Asymmetrical Rhythms and Irregular Meters

Most art music before the twentieth century, as well as most of our pop and rock music down to the present day, is built on regular patterns of duple ($\frac{2}{4}$), triple ($\frac{3}{4}$), or quadruple ($\frac{4}{4}$) meter. Romantic music of the previous generation of composers had many qualities to recommend it: direct expression, broad themes, powerful climaxes, and moments of tender lyricism, to name several. But only rarely was Romantic music carried along by an exciting, vital rhythm, staying instead within the comfortable confines of regular accents and duple or triple meter.

At the turn of the twentieth century, composers of art music began to rebel against the rhythmic and metric regularity that had governed most of nineteenth-century music. Musicians such as Stravinsky and Béla Bartók began to write music in which syncopations and measures with odd numbers of beats made it all but impossible for the listener to feel regular metrical patterns. Accents moved from one pulse to another, and meters changed from measure to measure. In abandoning the traditional structures of regular rhythms and consistent meters, these composers mirrored the techniques of modern poets like Gertrude Stein (1874–1946) and T. S. Eliot (1888–1965), who dispensed with traditional poetic meters and repeating accents in favor of free verse.

Tone Color: New Sounds from New Sources

Twentieth-century composers created a brave new world of sound. This came about in large part because many musicians were dissatisfied with the string-dominated tone of the Romantic symphony orchestra. The string sound, with its lush vibrato, was thought to be too gentle, perhaps too mushy and sentimental, for the harsh realities of the modern world. So the strings, which had traditionally carried the melody, relinquished this role to the sharper, crisper woodwinds. Instead of playing a sweeping melody, the violinists might now be called on to beat on the strings with the wooden part of the bow or to take

FIGURE 33–4
Lines of varying lengths can be seen as analogous to measures of different lengths caused by changing meters. Theo van Doesburg's *Rhythms of a Russian Dance* (1918) was surely inspired by the Russian sounds of Igor Stravinsky's *The Rite of Spring* (1913).

a preference for percussion

their hands and strike the instrument on its sound box. This preference for percussive effects over lyrical melody was also expressed in the new importance assigned the instruments of the percussion family. Entire pieces were written for percussion instruments alone. Instruments such as the xylophone*, glockenspiel*, and celesta* were added to the group (see page 52), and objects that produced an unfixed pitch, like the cowbell, brake drum, and police siren, were also heard on occasion. Finally, the piano, which in the Romantic era had been favored for its lyrical "singing" tone, came to be used as an orchestral instrument prized for the percussive way in which the hammers could be made to strike the strings.

Introducing new instruments, or having traditional instruments make new sounds by means of novel playing techniques, was an important innovation. But a more radical development came about as composers began to think of musical color as a wholly independent expressive element. During the Classical and Romantic periods, sounds of different colors were used mainly as a way to demarcate themes, and thus to articulate the form of a composition. The second theme in sonata–allegro form, for example, was often assigned to a new instrument, thereby emphasizing for listeners that a new theme had entered. The use of tone color as a servant of melody came to an end at the turn of the twentieth century, when Claude Debussy began to use color, independent of melody, to give form to a work. But Debussy's innovation was carried to radical lengths by later composers such as Charles Ives (1874–1954), Edgard Varèse (1883–1965), and John Cage (1912–1992), whose works sometimes seem to do nothing but progress from bright tones spaced far apart to dark tones densely grouped. These compositions may have no melody or harmony as traditionally conceived, but instead only clusters or streams of sounds with changing colors. This approach to color and line is, of course, similar to the one taken by avant-garde painters of the early twentieth century, who deconstructed recognizable figures in order to emphasize the emotive power of pure color (Fig. 33–5). The bold recognition that color alone can elicit a strong emotional response from the listener or viewer was arguably the most significant development in the history of early modern music and painting.

FIGURE 33–5

In his *The Piano Lesson* (1916), Henri Matisse allows the color gray to take over the canvas, moving into the space occupied by the seated teacher, the piano, and the student. The emotionally neutral mass of gray conveys to the viewer a sense of apathy, and even boredom—all of the joy has been removed from playing the piano!

Digital Image © The Museum of Modern Art/Licensed by Scala/Art Resource, NY/
© Succession H. Matisse, Paris, Artists Rights Society (ARS), New York

Key Words

Cubism (**366**)	seventh chord (**368**)	tone cluster (**368**)
octave displacement (**368**)	ninth chord (**368**)	
	eleventh chord (**368**)	

Early-Twentieth-Century Modernism

Among the composers of the early twentieth century, Igor Stravinsky and Arnold Schoenberg stand out both for the excellence of their compositions and for their lasting influence upon the trajectory of Western musical history. Each of these figures composed masterpieces still performed by orchestras today, and each had his own vision as to the direction modernist art should take. Schoenberg ultimately developed what is called the twelve-tone* system of composition, while Stravinsky, after perfecting flamboyant modernist ballet, moved on to a more restrained idiom called Neo-classicism.

IGOR STRAVINSKY (1882–1974)

For three-quarters of the twentieth century, Igor Stravinsky personified the cultural pluralism and stylistic diversity of cutting-edge art music (Fig. 34–1). He created masterpieces in many different genres: opera, ballet, symphony, concerto, church Mass, and cantata. His versatility was such that he could write a ballet for baby elephants (*Circus Polka*, 1942) just as easily as he could set to music a Greek classical drama (*Oedipus Rex*, 1927). Throughout his long life he traveled with the fashionable set of high art. Although reared in St. Petersburg, he later lived in Paris, Venice, Lausanne, New York, and Hollywood. Forced to become an expatriate by the Russian Revolution (1917), he took French citizenship in 1934, and then, having moved to the United States at the outbreak of World War II, he became an American citizen in 1945. He counted among his friends the painter Pablo Picasso (1881–1973), the novelist Aldous Huxley (1894–1963), and the poet T. S. Eliot (1888–1965). On his eightieth birthday, in 1962, he was honored by President John F. Kennedy at the White House and, later in the same year, by Russian Premier Nikita Khrushchev in the Kremlin. He died in New York in 1971 at the age of eighty-eight.

Stravinsky rose to international fame as a composer of ballet music. In 1908, his early scores caught the attention of Sergei Diaghilev (1872–1929), the legendary **impresario** (producer) of Russian opera and ballet (Fig. 34–2). Diaghilev wanted to bring modern Russian ballet to Paris, at that time the artistic capital of the world. So he formed a dance company, called the **Ballets russes** (Russian Ballets), and hired, over the course of time, the most progressive artists he could find: Pablo Picasso and Henri Matisse for scenic designs (see Figs. 33–1, 33–3, and 33–5) and Claude Debussy, Maurice Ravel, and Stravinsky, among others, as composers. Stravinsky soon became the principal composer of the company, and the *Ballets russes* became the focus of his musical activity for the next ten years. Accordingly, the decade 1910–1920 has become known as Stravinsky's Russian ballet period.

With the onset of World War I and the concurrent disappearance of large symphony orchestras in Europe, Stravinsky, along with others, developed a style called Neo-classicism* (see Chapter 35), which emphasized classical forms and smaller ensembles. Stravinsky's Neo-classical period extended from

FIGURE 34–1
Igor Stravinsky.

FIGURE 34–2
Sergei Diaghilev in New York in 1916.

1920 until 1951, when he adopted the twelve-tone technique of Arnold Schoenberg, which he continued to pursue until his death.

Although Stravinsky's style continually evolved over the course of nearly seventy years, a recognizable "Stravinsky sound" is always evident. In simple terms, his music is lean, clean, and cool. Stravinsky's instrumental colors are not "homogenized" sounds, as when the winds and strings together join on a single line, but rather distinctly separate colors. While his orchestra is sometimes large, he downplays the warm strings, preferring instead the tones of piercing winds and brittle percussion. Thus, while his orchestral scores are often opulent, they are rarely lush or sentimental. Most important, rhythm is the vital element in Stravinsky's compositional style. His beat is strong, but often metrically irregular, and he builds complexity by requiring independent meters and rhythms to sound simultaneously (see below). Many of these stylistic traits can be heard in his most famous work, *The Rite of Spring*, a watershed of early musical modernism.

FIGURES 34–3 AND 34–4
(top) In 1909, Henri Matisse painted the first of two canvases titled *Dance*. Here he achieves a raw primitive power by exaggerating a few basic lines and employing a few cool tones. Two years later, he created an even more intense vision of the same scene. (bottom) In *Dance* (1911), Matisse uses greater angularity and more intense colors, and thereby inspires a more intense reaction to this later version of a primitive dance scene.

Le Sacre du Printemps (The Rite of Spring, 1913)

Igor Stravinsky composed three important early ballet scores for Diaghilev's dance company: *The Firebird* (1910), *Petrushka* (1911), and *The Rite of Spring* (1913). All are built upon Russian folk tales—a legacy of musical nationalism*—and all make use of the large, colorful orchestra of the late nineteenth century. Yet the choreography for these Russian ballets is not the elegant, graceful ballet in the Romantic tradition, the sort that we associate with Tchaikovsky's *Swan Lake* (1877) and *The Nutcracker* (1892). These are modern dances with angular poses and abrupt, jerky motions (see Figs. 34–3 and 34–4). To inspire this dance in the modern style, Stravinsky composed rhythms and chords that explode with a primordial force.

Although *The Rite of Spring* has been called *the great masterpiece of modern music, at its premiere it provoked not admiration but a riot of dissent. This premiere, the most notorious in the history of Western music, took place on an unusually hot evening, May 29, 1913, at the newly built Théâtre Champs-Élysées in Paris. With the very first sounds of the orchestra, many in the packed theater voiced, shouted, and hissed their displeasure. Some, feigning auditory pain, yelled for a doctor, others for two. There were arguments and flying fists as opponents and partisans warred over this Russian brand of modern art. To restore calm, the curtain was lowered momentarily and the house lights were turned on and off. All in vain. The musicians still could not be heard, and consequently, the dancers had difficulty following the pulse of the music. The disorder was experienced firsthand by a visiting critic of the *New York Press*, who reported as follows:

> I was sitting in a box in which I had rented one seat. Three ladies sat in front of me and a young man occupied the place behind me. He stood up during the course of the ballet to enable himself to see more clearly. The intense excitement under which he was laboring, thanks to the potent force of the music, betrayed itself presently when he began to beat rhythmically on the top of my head with his fists. My emotion was so great that I did not feel the blows for some time. They were perfectly synchronized with the beat of the music!

a violent premiere

In truth, the violent reaction to *The Rite of Spring* was in part a response to the modernist choreography, which sought to obliterate any trace of classical ballet: the dance was just as "primitive" as Stravinsky's musical score. But what aspects, specifically, of Stravinsky's music shocked so many in the audience that night?

PERCUSSIVE ORCHESTRA

First, there is a new percussive—one might say "heavy metal"—approach to the orchestra. The percussion section is enlarged to include four timpani, a triangle, a tambourine, a guiro*, cymbals, antique cymbals, a bass drum, and a tam-tam*. Even the string family, the traditional provider of warmth and richness in the symphony orchestra, is required to play percussively, attacking the strings with repeated down-bows at seemingly random moments of accent. Instead of warm, lush sounds, we hear bright, brittle, almost brutal ones pounded out by percussion, heavy woodwinds, and brasses.

warm, lush sounds yield to bright, brittle ones

IRREGULAR ACCENTS

Stravinsky intensifies the effect of his harsh, metallic sounds by placing them where they are not expected, on unaccented beats, thereby creating explosive syncopations. Notice in the following example, the famous beginning of "Augurs of Spring," how the strings accent (>) the second, fourth, and then first pulses of subsequent four-pulse measures. In this way, Stravinsky destroys ordinary 1-2-3-4- meter and forces us to hear, in succession, groups of 4, 5, 2, 6, 3, 4, and 5 pulses—a conductor's nightmare!

EXAMPLE 34–1

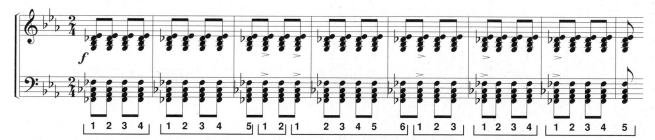

POLYMETER

The rhythm of *The Rite of Spring* is complex because Stravinsky often superimposes two or more different meters simultaneously. Notice in Example 34–2 that the oboe plays in $\frac{6}{8}$ time, the E♭ clarinet plays in $\frac{7}{8}$, while the B♭ clarinet is in $\frac{5}{8}$. This is an example of **polymeter**—two or more meters sounding simultaneously.

EXAMPLE 34–2

POLYRHYTHM

Not only do individual parts often play separate meters, but they also sometimes project two or more independent rhythms simultaneously. Look at the reduced score given in Example 34–3. Every instrument seems to be doing its own thing! In fact, six distinct rhythms can be heard, offering a good example of **polyrhythm**—the simultaneous sounding of two or more rhythms.

EXAMPLE 34–3

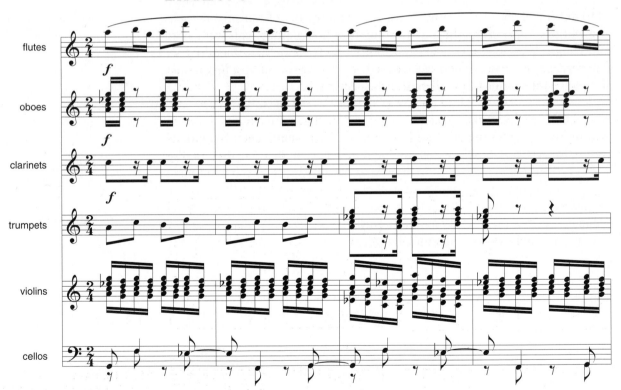

OSTINATO FIGURES

Notice also in Example 34–3 that most of the instruments play the same motive over and over at the same pitch level. Such a repeating figure, as we have seen, is called an ostinato*. In this instance, we hear multiple ostinatos. Stravinsky was not the first twentieth-century composer to use ostinatos extensively—Debussy had done so earlier in his Impressionist scores (see page 347). But Stravinsky employs them more often and for longer spans than had his predecessors. In *The Rite of Spring*, ostinatos give the music its incessant, driving quality, especially in the sections with fast tempos.

DISSONANT POLYCHORDS

The harsh, biting sound that is heard throughout much of *The Rite of Spring* is often created by two triads*, or a triad and a seventh chord* sounding at once. What results is a **polychord** — the simultaneous sounding of one triad or seventh chord with another (Fig. 34–5). When the individual chords of a polychord are only a whole step* or a half step* apart, the result is especially dissonant. In Example 34–4, the passage from the beginning of "Augurs of Spring," a seventh chord* built on E♭ is played simultaneously with a major triad built on F♭.

EXAMPLE 34–4

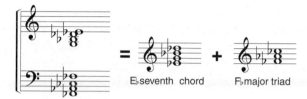

E♭ seventh chord   F♭ major triad

Stravinsky's dissonant polychord

THE PLOT

The plot of *The Rite of Spring* is suggested by its subtitle: *Pictures of Pagan Russia*. Part 1, "The Kiss of the Earth," depicts the springtime rituals of primitive Slavic tribes. In Part 2, "The Sacrifice," a virgin dances herself to death as an offering to the god of spring. Before the curtain rises on Part 1, the orchestra plays an Introduction. This music unfolds gradually but inexorably, from soft to loud, and from one line to many, suggesting the flora and fauna of the earth coming to life with the beginning of spring. The first scene, "Augurs of Spring," features jarring, almost brutal accents (see Ex. 34–1) and pounding

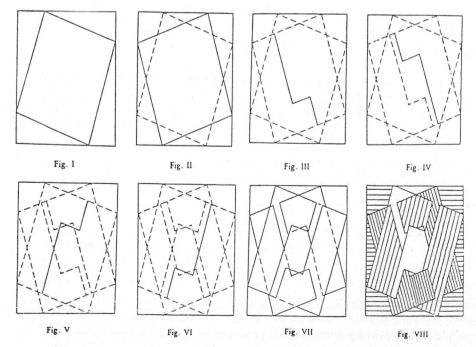

Fig. I   Fig. II   Fig. III   Fig. IV

Fig. V   Fig. VI   Fig. VII   Fig. VIII

FIGURE 34–5

In his *Schemes of Painting* (1922), the artist Albert Gleizes demonstrates that a Cubist work could be created by rotating a figure or line against itself, and then again and again until visual dissonance results. Similarly, a polychord is created by placing two or more triads or seventh chords off center and against one another, thereby creating musical dissonance.

an influence of folk music

dissonance (see Ex. 34–4). Yet there are also lyrical, almost sensuous moments in the score, especially when Stravinsky incorporates folksongs, whether quoting authentic Russian songs or (more commonly) composing his own melodies within this folk idiom. Despite the folkloric element, the bulk of the composition came from within. As Stravinsky declared, "I had only my ears to guide me. I heard and I wrote what I heard. I am the vessel through which *The Rite of Spring* passed."

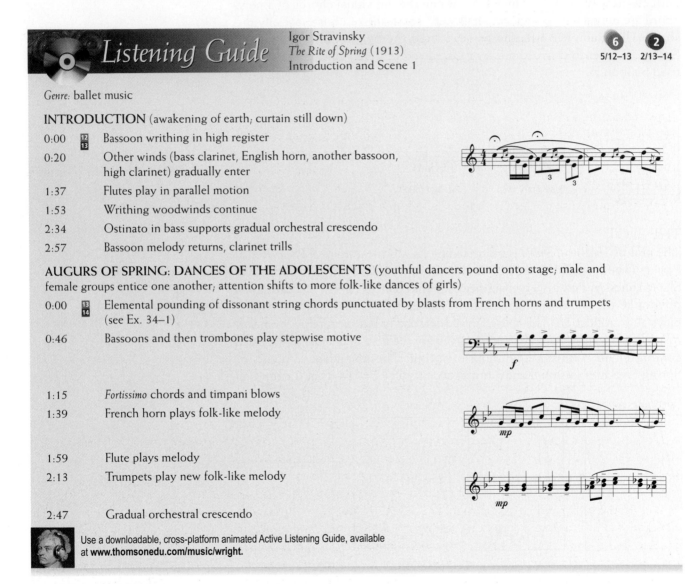

Listening Guide

Igor Stravinsky
The Rite of Spring (1913)
Introduction and Scene 1

6 5/12–13   **2** 2/13–14

Genre: ballet music

INTRODUCTION (awakening of earth; curtain still down)

0:00	12 13	Bassoon writhing in high register
0:20		Other winds (bass clarinet, English horn, another bassoon, high clarinet) gradually enter
1:37		Flutes play in parallel motion
1:53		Writhing woodwinds continue
2:34		Ostinato in bass supports gradual orchestral crescendo
2:57		Bassoon melody returns, clarinet trills

AUGURS OF SPRING: DANCES OF THE ADOLESCENTS (youthful dancers pound onto stage; male and female groups entice one another; attention shifts to more folk-like dances of girls)

0:00	13 14	Elemental pounding of dissonant string chords punctuated by blasts from French horns and trumpets (see Ex. 34–1)
0:46		Bassoons and then trombones play stepwise motive
1:15		*Fortissimo* chords and timpani blows
1:39		French horn plays folk-like melody
1:59		Flute plays melody
2:13		Trumpets play new folk-like melody
2:47		Gradual orchestral crescendo

Use a downloadable, cross-platform animated Active Listening Guide, available at **www.thomsonedu.com/music/wright**.

Listening Exercise 42

6 5/12–13   **2** 2/13–14

Stravinsky
The Rite of Spring

ThomsonNOW
To take this Listening Exercise online and receive feedback or email answers to your instructor, go to *ThomsonNOW* for this chapter.

As you listen to the Introduction of *The Rite of Spring*, you may be shocked by its dissonant, seemingly "disorganized" sound. You will find it difficult to identify a tonic pitch or a familiar scale that governs the music. To "stabilize" the music in the absence of a core tonality, Stravinsky employs several ostinatos*. These ostinatos not only help hold the music together but also impart a feeling of kinetic energy—energy continually being recycled and renewed, like spring itself. The following exercise asks you to focus on the ostinatos in the Introduction and Scene 1. Hearing these ostinatos will not always be easy. Listen carefully to the inner parts. Are ostinatos present? Answer "yes" or "no" below.

1. (0:35–0:56) _____   6. (0:24–0:36) _____
2. (2:08–2:20) _____   7. (1:14–1:22) _____
3. (2:34–2:55) _____   8. (1:23–1:36) _____
4. (2:57–3:10) _____   9. (1:59–2:29) _____
5. (3:28–3:34) _____

10. Judging from your responses, are there more moments in *The Rite of Spring* that make use of an ostinato than those that do not? _____

Following the *succès de scandale* that attended the premiere of *The Rite of Spring*, Stravinsky extracted the music from the ballet itself and presented it as an independent orchestral suite. The music alone was now recognized as an important, if controversial, statement of the musical avant-garde. Later, in 1940, the score of *The Rite of Spring* furnished the music for an important segment of Walt Disney's early full-length animated film, *Fantasia*. For a brief moment, in Disney's *Fantasia*, musical modernism had become mainstream.

music for Walt Disney's Fantasia

ARNOLD SCHOENBERG AND THE SECOND VIENNESE SCHOOL

Ironically, the most radical shoot of musical modernism took root in Vienna, a city with a long history of conservatism. In the early twentieth century, a trio of native Viennese musicians—Arnold Schoenberg (1874–1951), Alban Berg (1885–1935), and Anton Webern (1883–1945)—ventured to take high-art music in a completely new direction. The close association of these three innovative composers has come to be called the **Second Viennese School** (the first, of course, consisted of Mozart, Haydn, and Beethoven).

Arnold Schoenberg, the leader of this group, almost single-handedly thrust musical modernism upon a reluctant Viennese public (Fig. 34–6). Schoenberg was from a Jewish family of modest means and was largely self-taught as a musician. As a young man, he worked as a bank clerk during the day but studied literature, philosophy, and music at night, becoming a competent performer on the violin and cello. He came to know the music of Brahms, Wagner, and Mahler, mostly by playing their scores and attending concerts. Having "left the world of bank notes for musical notes" at the age of twenty-one, he earned a humble living by conducting a men's chorus, orchestrating operettas—the Viennese counterpart of our Broadway musicals—and giving lessons in music theory and composition. Eventually, his own compositions began to be heard in Vienna, though they were usually not well received.

Schoenberg's earliest works are written in the late Romantic style, with rich harmonies, chromatic melodies, expansive forms, and programmatic content. But by 1908, his music had begun to evolve in unexpected directions. Strongly influenced by Wagner's chromatic melodies and harmonies, Schoenberg started to compose works with no tonal center. If Wagner could write winding chromatic passages that temporarily obscured the tonality, why not go one step farther and create fully chromatic pieces in which there is no tonality? This Schoenberg did, and in so doing created what is called **atonal music**—music without tonality, without a key center.

FIGURE 34–6
Arnold Schoenberg, *Self Portrait* (1910).

Expressionism and Atonality

Arnold Schoenberg and his students Alban Berg and Anton Webern were not alone in creating a radically new style of art. As we have seen, there appeared at this same time a powerful movement in the visual arts called Expressionism. **Expressionism** was initially a German–Austrian development that arose in Berlin, Munich, and Vienna. Its aim was not to depict objects as they are seen but to express the strong emotion that the object generated in the artist; not to paint a portrait of an individual but to create an expression of the subject's innermost feelings, anxieties, and fears. In Edvard Munch's early Expressionist painting *The Scream* (1893), the subject cries out to an unsympathetic and uncomprehending world. Schoenberg's statement in this regard can be taken as a credo for the entire Expressionist movement: "Art is the cry of despair of those who experience in themselves the fate of all Mankind" (1910). Gradually, realistic representations gave way to highly personal

National Gallery, Oslo/Erich Lessing/Art Resource, NY/Artists Rights Society (ARS), New York

The Scream, by Edvard Munch.

and increasingly abstract expression. Artists such as Wassily Kandinsky (1866–1944) and Oskar Kokoschka (1886–1980) used harsh colors, macabre images, and distorted figures to show intense psychological states, sometimes with shocking results (see Figs. 33–2 and 34–7). Schoenberg, a personal friend of both Kokoschka and Kandinsky, was himself a painter and exhibited his works with the Expressionists in 1912 (Figs. 34–6 and 34–8). In fact, the music and art of this movement can be described in rather similar terms. The clashing of strong colors, the disjointed shapes, and the jagged lines of the painters have their counterparts in the harsh dissonances, asymmetrical rhythms, and angular, chromatic melodies of Schoenberg and his followers. It is surely not an accident that Schoenberg moved from tonality to atonality in music (1908–1912) at precisely the time Kandinsky and others turned away from realistic representation to abstract expression.

Schoenberg's contemporaries found his atonal music difficult. Not only was there no tonal center, but the melodies were highly disjunct and the harmony exceedingly dissonant (see page 368). Some performers refused to play his music, and when others did, audience reaction was occasionally violent. At one concert on March 31, 1913, the police had to be called in to restore order. Despite this hostility, Schoenberg remained true to his own vision, offering this directive to all creative artists: "One must be convinced of the infallibility of one's own fantasy; one must believe in one's own creative spirit."

the audience riots

Pierrot Lunaire (Moonstruck Pierrot, 1912)

Moonstruck Pierrot, Schoenberg's best-known composition, is an exemplary work of Expressionist art. It is a setting for chamber ensemble and female voice of twenty-one poems by Albert Giraud. Here we meet Pierrot, a white-faced clown from the world of traditional Italian pantomime and puppet shows. Yet in this Expressionist poetry, the clown has fallen under the sway of the moon and changed into an alienated modern artist. Pierrot projects his inner anxiety by means of **Sprechstimme** (speech-voice), a vocal technique that requires the vocalist to declaim the text more than to sing it. The voice is to execute the rhythmic values exactly; but once it hits a pitch, it is to quit

Sprechstimme: *a new vocal technique*

FIGURES 34–7 AND 34–8
(above left) This 1909 Viennese theater poster by Oskar Kokoschka shows the Expressionist affinity for the dramatic and grotesque. The effect is created by the use of strong, almost crude lines and bold, contrasting colors. (above right) As a young man, Schoenberg was undecided whether his future in the arts lay in music or painting. Like many Expressionist paintings before World War I, his *Red Gaze* (1910) gives a sense of the subject's inner terror.

the tone immediately, sliding away in either a downward or an upward direction. This creates exaggerated declamation of the sort one might hear from a lunatic, which is appropriate for Pierrot, given the lunar spell cast upon him.

Poem 6 of *Moonstruck Pierrot* depicts the protagonist's tormented, hallucinatory vision of the suffering Madonna at the cross. Its poetic form is that of a *rondeau*, an ancient musical and poetic form marked by the use of a refrain (set in boldface type on page 380). Traditionally, composers had used the appearance of a textual refrain to repeat the melody as well, thereby creating musical unity (see page 88). However, Schoenberg, the iconoclast, repeats the text but not the music. Thus his music unfolds in an ever-varying continuum, like a stream of consciousness. Perhaps not coincidentally, precisely during the years that Schoenberg was creating this music of intense introspection, Sigmund Freud originated the theory of psychoanalysis, also in Vienna.

The absence of obvious repetition in Schoenberg's music—nothing is allowed to become familiar—places unprecedented demands on the listener. Your first reaction to the dissonant continuum of sound in *Moonstruck Pierrot* may be decidedly negative. Yet with repeated hearings the force of the jarring elements of the atonal style begins to lessen, and a bizarre, eerie sort of beauty emerges, especially if you are sensitive to the meaning of the text.

musical repetition avoided

Arnold Schoenberg
Moonstruck Pierrot (1912)
Number 6, *Madonna*

6   2
5/14   2/15

Genre: art song

(*Sprechstimme* — "speech-voice")

Steig,   O Mut-ter al-ler Schmer-zen, auf den Al-tar mei-ner Ver-se!

Steig, O Mutter aller Schmerzen
Auf den Altar meiner Verse!
Blut aus deinen magern Brüsten
Hat des Schwertes Wut vergossen.
Deine ewig frischen Wunden
Gleichen Augen, rot und offen,
Steig, O Mutter aller Schmerzen
Auf den Altar meiner Verse!
(1:13) In den abgezehrten Händen
Hältst du deines Sohnes Leiche
Ihn zu zeigen aller Menschheit,
Doch der Blick der Menschen meidet
Dich, O Mutter aller Schmerzen.

Arise, O Mother of all sorrows
On the altar of my verse!
Blood from your thin breast
Has spilled the rage of the sword.
Your eternally fresh wounds
Like eyes, red and open,
Arise, O Mother of all sorrows
On the altar of my verse!
In your thin and wasted hands
You hold the body of your Son
To show him to all mankind,
Yet the look of men avoids
You, O Mother of all sorrows.

 Use a downloadable, cross-platform animated Active Listening Guide, available at **www.thomsonedu.com/music/wright.**

Schoenberg's Twelve-Tone Music

When Arnold Schoenberg and his followers did away with tonal chord progressions and repeating melodies, they found themselves facing a serious artistic problem: how to write large-scale compositions in the new atonal style. For centuries, musical structures, like fugue and sonata–allegro form, had been generated by means of a clear tonal plan and the repetition of broad musical themes—repetition created form. But Schoenberg's chromatic, atonal, nonrepeating melodies made traditional musical forms all but impossible. What other formal plan might be used? If all twelve notes of the chromatic scale are equally important, as is true in atonal music, why choose any one note or another at a given moment?

Schoenberg needed a formal plan

By 1923, Schoenberg had solved the problem of "formal anarchy"—the absence of form caused by total chromatic freedom. He discovered a new way of creating music that he called "composing with twelve tones." **Twelve-tone composition** is a method of writing that employs each of the twelve notes of the chromatic scale set in a fixed, predetermined order. The composer begins by arranging the twelve notes of the chromatic scale in a sequence of his or her choosing, forming a "tone row." Throughout the composition, these twelve notes must come in the same order. Music in which elements such as pitch, timbre, or dynamics come in a fixed series is called **serial music.** In twelve-tone music, the twelve-note series may unfold not only as a melody but also as a melody with accompaniment, or simply as a progression of chords, since two or more notes of the row may sound simultaneously. Moreover, in addition to appearing in its basic form, the row might go backward (retrograde*), or upside down (inversion*), or both backward and upside down at the same

setting out twelve tones in advance

time (retrograde inversion). While such arrangements might seem wholly artificial and very unmusical, we should remember that composers such as J. S. Bach in the Baroque era and Josquin Desprez in the Renaissance subjected their melodies to similar permutations. The purpose of Schoenberg's twelve-tone method was to create musical unity by basing each piece on a single, orderly arrangement of twelve tones, thereby guaranteeing the perfect equality of all pitches so that none would seem like a tonal center.

musical permutations

Trio from *Suite for Piano* (1924)

Schoenberg's first steps along this radical twelve-tone path were tentative, and the pieces that resulted were very short. Among Schoenberg's first serial compositions was his *Suite for Piano*, a collection of seven brief dance movements, including the Minuet and Trio to be discussed here. The tone row for the *Suite*, along with its three permutations, is as follows:

Row	*Retrograde*
E F G D♭ G♭ E♭ A♭ D B C A B♭	B♭ A C B D A♭ E♭ G♭ D♭ G F E
1 2 3 4 5 6 7 8 9 10 11 12	12 11 10 9 8 7 6 5 4 3 2 1
Inversion	*Retrograde-inversion*
E E♭ D♭ G D F C F♯ A G♯ B B♭	B♭ B G♯ A F♯ C F D G D♭ E♭ E
1 2 3 4 5 6 7 8 9 10 11 12	12 11 10 9 8 7 6 5 4 3 2 1

Schoenberg allows the row or any of its permutations to begin on any pitch, so long as the original sequence of intervals is maintained. Notice in the Trio, for example, that the row itself begins on E but is also allowed to start on B♭ (see Listening Guide). In the second part, measures 6–9, the exact serial progression of the row breaks down slightly. The composer explained this as a "justifiable deviation," owing to the need for tonal variety at this point. Notice as well that the rhythms in which the notes appear may likewise be changed for the sake of variety. As you listen to the Trio, see if you can follow the unfolding of the row and all its permutations. Listen many times—the piece is only fifty-one seconds long! Its aesthetic effect is similar to that of a constructivist painting of an artist like Theo van Doesburg (see Fig. 34–9). If you like the painting, you might well enjoy Schoenberg's twelve-tone piano piece as well.

FIGURE 34–9
The same rational processes at work in Schoenberg's twelve-tone music can be seen in Theo van Doesburg's *Composition IV* (1917). Notice the retrograde motion: the pattern proceeding downward from the top left is the same as that upward from the bottom right.

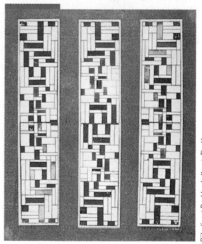

Rijksdienst Beeldende Kunst, The Hague

Listening Guide

Arnold Schoenberg
Trio from *Suite for Piano* (1924)

6
5/15

Genre: twelve-tone music
15

Inversion of row starting on B♭

1 2 3 4 5 6 7 8 9 10 11 12

Row starting on E

Inversion of row starting on F♭

sf

sf

sf

sf

(continued)

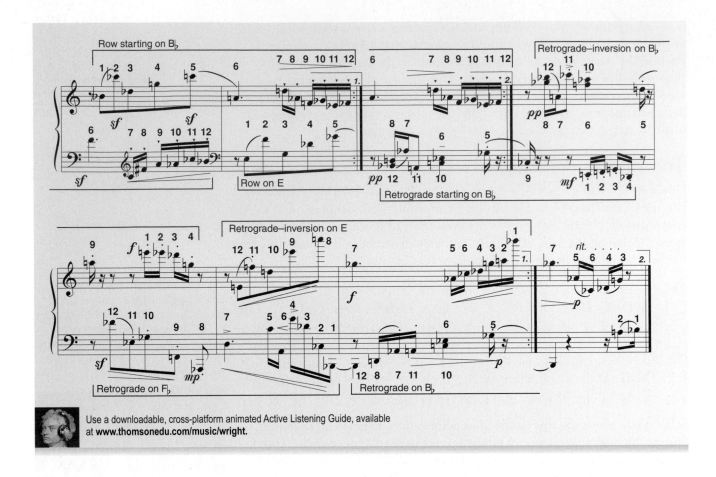

Use a downloadable, cross-platform animated Active Listening Guide, available at www.thomsonedu.com/music/wright.

Schoenberg and posterity

As the years progressed, Schoenberg used his twelve-tone method to construct longer compositions for larger forces. By 1932, he had completed most of a full-length opera, *Moses and Aaron,* and in 1947, he finished a long cantata*, *A Survivor from Warsaw,* that tells of Nazi atrocities in Poland. Both works are in the twelve-tone style throughout. But the listening public never fully embraced twelve-tone music; the style is as inaccessible as Schoenberg's earlier atonal music. For most listeners, it sounds irrational and arbitrary, completely "out of control." Indeed, the twelve-tone system has been called one of the two great failed experiments of the twentieth century, the other being Communism. Schoenberg was philosophical about the public's general dislike of his music: "If it is art, it is not for all, and if it is for all, it is not art."

ThomsonNOW

ThomsonNOW for *Listening to Music, 5th Edition,* and *Listening to Western Music* will assist you in understanding the content of this chapter with lesson plans generated for your specific needs. In addition, you may complete this chapter's Listening Exercise in ThomsonNOW's interactive environment, as well as download Active Listening Guides and other materials that will help you succeed in this course.

Key Words

impresario (**371**)
Ballets russes (**371**)
polymeter (**373**)
polyrhythm (**374**)
polychord (**375**)

Second Viennese
    School (**377**)
atonal music (**377**)
Expressionism (**378**)
Sprechstimme (**378**)

twelve-tone
    composition (**380**)
serial music (**380**)

Russian and Eastern European Modernism

Chapter 35

We naturally tend to assume that Western civilization is shaped primarily by those events that take place in the West itself. In the early twentieth century, however, several events of monumental importance to Western history occurred in Russia and Eastern Europe (Fig. 35–1). In 1917, the West was shaken by the **Russian Revolution,** the overthrow of the Russian tsar by the socialist Bolshevik Party. This turn of events paved the way for the establishment of a Communist-ruled Soviet Union in 1922, a development that led ultimately to the Cold War, which dominated Western foreign policy concerns for decades. We likewise tend to credit the military powers of the West with the defeat of Adolf Hitler and his Nazi regime in the Second World War. But while Western soldiers unquestionably played a vital role, the bulk of the fighting took place on the Eastern Front. Apart from combat in the Pacific, fully 80 percent of soldiers killed in World War II died on the Russian Front—about 11 million Russians and 5 million Germans. Civilian casualties in the East likewise outnumbered those in the West. The number of civilian dead in Russia—victims of war, famine, and government purges—is estimated between 30 and 40 million. These horrors affected all segments of society, in-

events in Russia and Eastern Europe shape the West

FIGURE 35–1
Western Russia and Central and Eastern Europe, early twentieth century.

cluding artists, intellectuals, and musicians. Indeed, it is no exaggeration to say that the three composers discussed in this chapter had their lives ruined by the cataclysmic events that rocked Russia and Eastern Europe in these decades. We begin with Russia.

Stalin prescribes death for avant-garde artists

Progressive artists who worked in the Soviet Union during the dictatorship of Joseph Stalin (r1924–1953) did so under conditions that are incomprehensible today. During the 1920s and 1930s, the ruling Communist Party forcefully confiscated the wealth of the well-to-do and redistributed it collectively among the proletariat. Anything that smacked of "elitism"—anything that could not be immediately understood and enjoyed by the masses—was suspect. Heading the list of likely "subversives" were the names of almost all modern artists, including composers, and especially those who wrote in the atonal* or twelve-tone* style. The Soviet regime encouraged patriotic compositions, in which large choruses sang hymns of praise to the fatherland and to the working class—pieces to promote Communist propaganda. Soviet authorities referred to modern music as **formalism** and branded it "antidemocratic." To be identified as a "formalist" was tantamount to a death sentence. The challenge for a composer working under Stalin was to remain true to a personal artistic vision, yet remain alive.

SERGEY PROKOFIEV (1891–1953)

a life of contradictions

The career of Sergey Prokofiev is full of contradictions and ironies, caused in part by the place he occupied in Russian history. The son of a well-to-do farm administrator, he fled the Russian Revolution in 1917, but later returned to celebrate in music the most murderous of the revolutionaries, Joseph Stalin. Prokofiev was once known as the dissonant, atonal "bad boy" of the St. Petersburg Conservatory, where he received his musical education, but later wrote such pleasantly benign works as *Peter and the Wolf* (1936). He thought of himself above all as a serious composer—the author of seven symphonies, six operas and six ballets, five piano concertos, and nine piano sonatas—but today is remembered mainly for his lighter works: the *Classical Symphony, Peter and the Wolf,* and the film scores *Lieutenant Kijé* and *Alexander Nevsky.*

Classical Symphony (1917)

a return to classical principles

During the summer of 1917, in the midst of the Russian Revolution, Prokofiev composed his *Classical Symphony.* It is written in a style called **Neo-classicism,** one that sought to revive the balanced melodies, lighter textures, and clear forms of earlier music—specifically, of the Baroque and Classical periods. Neo-classicism rejected not only the large orchestra and the emotionalism of the Romantic style but also the extreme sort of dissonance and atonality being advanced by modernists such as Arnold Schoenberg and the Second Viennese School (see page 377). Igor Stravinsky turned to Neo-classicism about this same time, in part because large orchestras were becoming scarce in Europe during World War I. Prokofiev may have turned to Neo-classicism as a way of bringing order to his mind during a chaotic period of Russian history. The next year he fled Russia for the United States.

There is a sense of historical irony in Prokofiev's *Classical Symphony.* It is the irony created by a clash of musical systems and values: those of the eighteenth century against those of the modern world. Prokofiev creates a model of Neo-classicism by invoking the orchestra and the musical forms of Joseph Haydn. He hypothesized: "It seemed to me that had Haydn lived in our day, he would have retained his own style while accepting something new at the same time." The "new" elements of Prokofiev's symphony include a more disjunct, angular melody than Haydn would have written; a harmony that "slides" suddenly to unexpected chords; and frequent, biting dissonances far beyond those employed by Classical composers. What is more, Prokofiev distorts our traditional sense of timing and balance; in this very short symphony, every musical idea seems to end before it has begun. Prokofiev uses Classical forms and procedures, yet simultaneously mocks Classical ideals by means of modern dissonance, imbalance, and unexpected brevity. By juxtaposing the Classical and the modern in a single work, the composer demands that we address the question "What makes musical style?" Thus, as we listen to the *Classical Symphony*, we enjoy the music for its own sake, but we also think about the interaction of contrasting musical styles. Prokofiev's work is simultaneously art and a critique of art.

Classical and modern styles juxtaposed

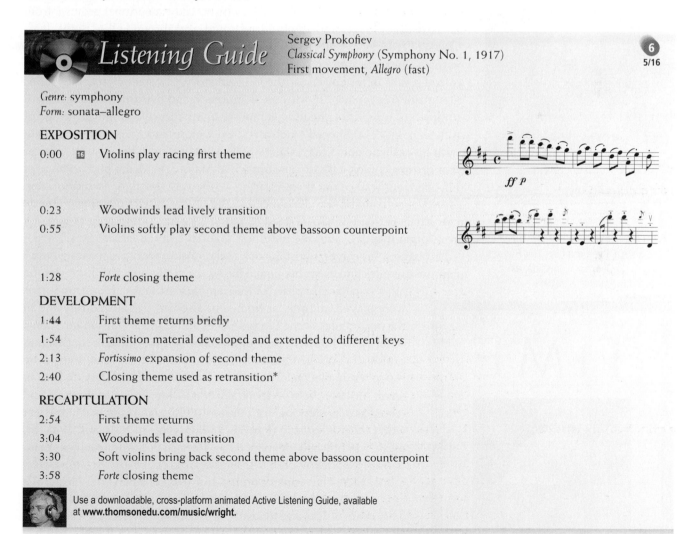

Listening Guide

Sergey Prokofiev
Classical Symphony (Symphony No. 1, 1917)
First movement, *Allegro* (fast)

6
5/16

Genre: symphony
Form: sonata–allegro

EXPOSITION

0:00	16	Violins play racing first theme
0:23		Woodwinds lead lively transition
0:55		Violins softly play second theme above bassoon counterpoint
1:28		*Forte* closing theme

DEVELOPMENT

1:44	First theme returns briefly
1:54	Transition material developed and extended to different keys
2:13	*Fortissimo* expansion of second theme
2:40	Closing theme used as retransition*

RECAPITULATION

2:54	First theme returns
3:04	Woodwinds lead transition
3:30	Soft violins bring back second theme above bassoon counterpoint
3:58	*Forte* closing theme

Use a downloadable, cross-platform animated Active Listening Guide, available at **www.thomsonedu.com/music/wright**.

The end of Prokofiev's life was not a happy one. He voluntarily returned to his Russian homeland in 1934, only to have his works strictly controlled according to Stalin's tastes. (Hitler and Stalin, enemies on the battlefield, had at least one thing in common: they both loathed modern music.) Performances of Prokofiev's music were officially banned in 1948, and to avoid arrest as a musical subversive, the composer renounced musical formalism. That same year, his wife, Lina, was arrested by the secret police for "espionage" and sentenced to an exile of twenty years. In ill health, Prokofiev's output dwindled to nothing. He died within a few minutes of his nemesis, Joseph Stalin, on the night of March 5, 1953. Yet news of Prokofiev's death was withheld for days so as not to deflect attention from the deceased dictator. No flowers could be bought for the great composer's coffin; the funeral of Stalin had, without exaggeration, claimed them all.

FIGURE 35–2
Dmitri Shostakovich.

© Lebrecht/The Image Works

FIGURE 35-3
Shostakovich, the "poster boy" for Russian resistance to German aggression, as presented to Americans in 1941.

© Time Life Pictures/Getty Images

DMITRI SHOSTAKOVICH (1906–1975)

Prokofiev was not the only composer to suffer during Stalin's reign of terror. Dmitri Shostakovich (Fig. 35–2), a few years Prokofiev's junior, experienced even greater trauma.

Born to a musical family, Shostakovich showed exceptional promise from an early age. He had perfect pitch and could play through all of Bach's *Well-Tempered Clavier* by age eleven. In 1919, he entered the St. Petersburg Conservatory, where he studied harmony, orchestration, and composition. After mixed results in his courses at the Conservatory, Shostakovich achieved his first major success in 1925 with the completion and performance of his Symphony No. 1, which earned the composer international acclaim at the age of nineteen. In 1934, Shostakovich attracted widespread attention once again with his realistic opera *Lady Macbeth of the Mtsensk District*. But in 1936, his career prospects took a disastrous turn when Stalin attended a performance of his opera but walked out three-quarters of the way through. Two days later, Shostakovich's music was denounced in the official Soviet newspaper *Pravda* in an article entitled "Chaos Instead of Music." As the composer later said, "I'll never forget that day [and] the bitterness that has colored my life gray."

Throughout his career, Shostakovich's relationship with the Soviet government was complex and ever-changing. During the 1930s and 1940s, he was the most popular composer of Russian high art music. His symphonies were played not only at home but also throughout Europe and in the major cities of the United States and Canada. This international stature gave him a measure of protection; it was difficult for Stalin to exile such a public figure to a work camp, or to execute him, as he did other intellectuals. Indeed, in some years, Shostakovich was "in favor." In 1941, he won the Stalin Medal for service to the state and served as a "poster boy" for the spirit of Russian resistance in the war with Hitler's Germany (Fig. 35–3). But twice, in 1936 and 1948, his music was officially denounced as "formalistic." After each condemnation, Shostakovich hid his most progressive scores (those with atonal or twelve-tone content) and "toned down" the modernist component in the little music that he did allow to be performed. This game of "cat and mouse"—with Shostakovich as the mouse—continued until the composer died from a heart attack in 1975.

Symphony No. 5 (1937)

In his Symphony No. 5, written the year following his first denunciation at the hands of the Soviet authorities, Shostakovich felt compelled to keep his modernist tendencies largely hidden from view. The work was a huge success when it premiered in November 1937, and one critic called it "a Soviet artist's creative answer to just criticism." Shostakovich had been "rehabilitated," at least for the moment. In spirit, Symphony No. 5 resembles the symphonies of Gustav Mahler (see page 333), with their brilliant orchestrations and expressive, emotional character. Yet Shostakovich was fully a citizen of the twentieth century, intent on speaking with a fully modern voice. Here, while the progressive voice is, of necessity, somewhat muted, it can still be heard in the heavy percussion, moderate (but not extreme) dissonance, ostinatos, and "sliding harmonies" of the sort found in Prokofiev's *Classical Symphony* (see page 384). Shostakovich would go on to compose ten more symphonies. While many of these are often performed today, the fifth remains his most popular. The exultant finale seems to signal the ultimate triumph of the human spirit. Yet in light of the circumstances under which it was written, critics still ask: Was the "rejoicing" expressed here truly felt, or was it feigned—forced from the composer? Shostakovich himself suggested the answer when he said, "The majority of my symphonies are tombstones."

"rehabilitated" music

a Romantic and modern symphonic style

Listening Guide

Dmitri Shostakovich
Symphony No. 5 (1937)
Fourth movement, *Allegro non troppo* (fast, but not too fast)

6

5/17–18

Genre: symphony
Form: abbreviated sonata–allegro

EXPOSITION

0:00	17	Percussive sounds as low brasses play first theme

0:40		First theme unfolds continually in brass, strings, and winds
2:29		Trumpet introduces second theme above swirling mass of strings
2:57		Violins sweep along with second theme in heroic fashion

3:32		Low brasses play transition
3:46		French horn plays lyrical solo (variant of second theme)

DEVELOPMENT

4:18		Strings and then winds quietly develop second theme and then fragments of first
5:32		Hints of first theme begin to appear in low strings and then low brasses

ABBREVIATED RECAPITULATION

7:25	18	0:00	First theme returns quietly and somewhat altered with snare drum accompanying
8:25		1:00	First theme grows in intensity

CODA

9:39		2:14	Brasses play first theme slowly; intervals altered to change mode from minor to major
10:12		2:47	Harmony is static, holding on tonic pitch; timpani pounds dominant and tonic pitches

Use a downloadable, cross-platform animated Active Listening Guide, available at **www.thomsonedu.com/music/wright.**

Listening Exercise 43

Shostakovich
Symphony No. 5

6
5/17–18

ThomsonNOW™
To take this Listening Exercise online and
receive feedback or email answers to your
instructor, go to *ThomsonNOW* for this chapter.

In this exercise, you are asked to differentiate modernist musical elements from
those of the earlier Romantic period. Below are listed four (a–d) kinds of sounds
typically found in Romantic symphonies and then four (e–h) types more often
heard in modern ones. Focusing on specific passages of the movement, choose one
of three possibilities listed for you. You should use each letter (a–h) only once.

Elements of Romanticism
a. long, lovely solo by French horn
b. heroic melody carried by violins
c. long, purposeful build-up to
   big climax
d. lengthy cadence signaling that end
   is near

Elements of Modernism
e. heavy percussive sounds,
   particularly from timpani
f. ostinato present
g. moderate dissonance heard
h. harmony sliding from one
   key to another

🔲 1. (0:00–0:17) Which do you hear, a, e, or f? _____
2. (0:25–0:40) Which do you hear, a, e, or h? _____
3. (2:57–3:12) Which do you hear, b, e, or f? _____
4. (3:23–3:30) Which do you hear, b, g, or h? _____
5. (3:46–4:17) Which do you hear, a, d, or e? _____
6. (5:33–5:44 and again at 5:45–6:03) Which do you hear, c, d ,or f? _____
🔲 7. (1:57–2:12) Which do you hear, c, f, or e? _____
8. (2:47–end) Which do you hear, b, d, or h? _____
9. Excepting the addition of a few percussion instruments, the orchestra here
   is essentially that of the nineteenth century, but from which part of the
   nineteenth century?
   a. early nineteenth century   b. late nineteenth century
10. Judging from your responses to questions 1–8, which is true regarding the
    elements of style that Shostakovich has incorporated in this movement?
    a. He has composed it in a predominantly Romantic style.
    b. He has composed it in a predominantly modern style.
    c. He has incorporated elements from both periods in approximately
       equal measure.

BÉLA BARTÓK (1881–1945)

The music of the Hungarian composer Béla Bartók (Fig. 35–4) is decidedly
modern, yet distinctly different in sound from that of Stravinsky or Schoenberg. While it can be atonal, like the music of Schoenberg, it is often highly
tuneful, making use of sweeping melodies. And while it is frequently percussive and highly rhythmic, like the motor-driven sounds of Stravinsky, Bartók's
rhythmic force derives mainly from folk music. Bartók's creative imagination
was fired by folk materials of his native Hungary (see Fig. 35–1). He saw the
return to the simple, direct style of folk music as a way to counter the tendency in Romantic music toward ostentation and sentimentality.

greatly influenced by folk music

The life of Béla Bartók was strongly affected by the turbulent events that
occurred in Eastern Europe during the first half of the twentieth century. He

was born in 1881 in Hungary, but in a part of that nation that was later given over to Romania at the end of World War I. Throughout his life, he was an ardent Hungarian nationalist, and he chose to develop his obvious musical talents at the Academy of Music in Budapest rather than at the German-dominated Vienna Conservatory, to which he had also been admitted. As a student at the academy in Budapest, he studied composition and piano, quickly acquiring a reputation as a concert pianist of the highest quality. By the 1920s, he had achieved an international reputation both as a pianist and as a composer of modernist music. His tours even carried him to the West Coast of the United States, where one newspaper alerted the public to his coming with the following headline: "Hungarian Modernist Advances upon Los Angeles." As both a Hungarian modernist and nationalist, Bartók was an outspoken critic of the supporters of Nazi Germany who gained control of the Hungarian government in the late 1930s. He called the fascists "bandits and assassins," cut off ties with the German firm that published his music, and banned the performances of his works in Germany and Italy, thereby losing considerable performance and broadcast fees. Ultimately, in 1940, he fled to the United States.

Béla Bartók is rare among composers in that he was as much interested in musical research, specifically in the study of Eastern European folk music, as in musical composition. He traveled from village to village in Hungary, Romania, Bulgaria, Turkey, and even North Africa using the newly invented recording machine of Thomas Edison (Fig. 35–5). In this way, his ear became saturated with the driving rhythms and odd-numbered meters of peasant dances, as well as the unusual scales on which the folk melodies of Eastern Europe were constructed.

The musical heritage of Eastern Europe is heard throughout Bartók's music, from his first string quartet (1908) to his great final works for orchestra: *Music for Strings, Percussion and Celesta* (1936), *Divertimento for Strings* (1939), and *Concerto for Orchestra* (1943). This last-named piece was commissioned by the conductor of the Boston Symphony Orchestra for the then-substantial fee of $1,000. It remains Bartók's best-known and most alluring composition.

© Bettmann/CORBIS

FIGURE 35–4
Béla Bartók.

FIGURE 35–5
Béla Bartók recording folk songs among Czech-speaking peasants in 1908. The performers sang into the megaphone of a wax-cylinder recording machine invented by Thomas Edison.

Concerto for Orchestra (1943)

Normally, concertos are written for a single solo instrument—piano or violin, for example—pitted against an orchestra. In Bartók's *Concerto for Orchestra*, however, the composer encourages many instruments to step forward from within the orchestra to serve as soloists from time to time. The spotlight switches from one instrument to another or to a new combination of instruments, each displaying its distinctive tonal color against the backdrop of the full orchestra. There are five movements: The first is "written in a more or less regular sonata form," as the composer says, and makes use of the folk-like pentatonic* scale; the second is a colorful parade of pairs of instruments; the third

© The Art Archive/Corbis

is an atmospheric nocturne*, an example of what is called Bartók's "night music," in which the woodwinds slither around chromatically above a misty tremolo in the strings; the fourth is an unusual intermezzo; and the fifth is a vigorous peasant dance in sonata–allegro form. Let us focus our attention on the fourth movement, *Intermezzo interrotto (Broken Intermezzo)*.

An **intermezzo** (Italian for "between piece") is a light musical interlude intended to separate and thus break the mood of two more serious surrounding movements. But here, as the title *Broken Intermezzo* indicates, the light intermezzo is itself rudely interrupted by contrasting music. At the outset of the movement, a charming theme in the oboe establishes a sophisticated mood. As is usual for Bartók, this melody shows the influence of the Hungarian folksong both in its pentatonic construction (the five notes that make up the scale of the melody are B, C♯, E, F♯, and A♯) and in the way the meter switches back and forth between an even $\frac{2}{4}$ and an odd $\frac{5}{8}$.

Hungarian melodies

EXAMPLE 35–1

After the tune is passed among several wind instruments, an even more ingratiating melody emerges in the strings. It, too, is Hungarian in style. In fact, it is Bartók's idealized reworking of the song *You Are Lovely, You Are Beautiful, Hungary.*

EXAMPLE 35–2

a borrowing from Shostakovich

But the nostalgic vision of the homeland is suddenly interrupted by a new, cruder theme in the clarinet, and it also tells a tale. Bartók had just heard Dmitri Shostakovich's Symphony No. 7, composed in 1942 as a programmatic work designed to stiffen Russian resistance to the German army, which had invaded the previous year. Shostakovich was a Russian hero at that moment (see Fig. 35–3), and Bartók borrowed the theme that Shostakovich had written to signify the invading Germans, believing its simple quarter-note descent to be appropriately heavy and trite.

EXAMPLE 35–3

Thus Bartók's intermezzo can be heard as an autobiographical work in which, as the composer related to a friend, "the artist declares his love for his native land in a serenade which is suddenly interrupted in a crude and violent manner; he is seized by rough, booted men who even break his instrument." Bartók tells us what he thinks of these "rough, booted men" (the Nazis) by

Bartók, an ardent anti-Nazi

surrounding them with rude, jeering noises in the trumpets and woodwinds. Ultimately, he brings back the idyllic vision of the homeland by returning to the two opening themes. As to the soloists in this movement of Bartók's *Concerto for Orchestra*, there are many: oboe, clarinet, flute, English horn, and the entire section of violas.

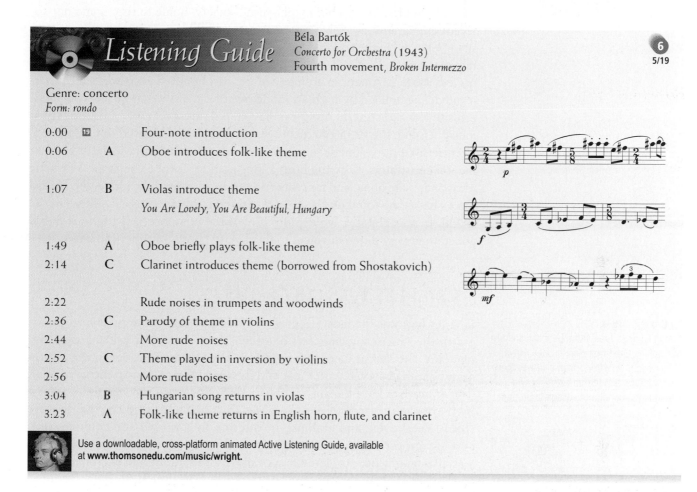

Listening Guide

Béla Bartók
Concerto for Orchestra (1943)
Fourth movement, *Broken Intermezzo*

6
5/19

Genre: concerto
Form: rondo

0:00	**19**	Four-note introduction
0:06	A	Oboe introduces folk-like theme
1:07	B	Violas introduce theme
		You Are Lovely, You Are Beautiful, Hungary
1:49	A	Oboe briefly plays folk-like theme
2:14	C	Clarinet introduces theme (borrowed from Shostakovich)
2:22		Rude noises in trumpets and woodwinds
2:36	C	Parody of theme in violins
2:44		More rude noises
2:52	C	Theme played in inversion by violins
2:56		More rude noises
3:04	B	Hungarian song returns in violas
3:23	A	Folk-like theme returns in English horn, flute, and clarinet

Use a downloadable, cross-platform animated Active Listening Guide, available at **www.thomsonedu.com/music/wright.**

As was true for Prokofiev and Shostakovich, Bartók's last years were not golden. He arrived in New York in 1940 as a refugee from Nazi-dominated Europe and tried to patch together a living by performing and composing. But, aside from his *Concerto for Orchestra*, he had little success and ultimately died of leukemia in New York's West Side Hospital in 1945—a sad ending in an era that brought disillusionment, turmoil, and death to millions.

Key Words

Russian Revolution
    (**383**)
formalism (**384**)
Neo-classicism (**384**)
intermezzo (**390**)

Three American Voices

The United States is a highly pluralistic society, home to recent and not-so-recent immigrants, as well as Native Americans. This cultural and ethnic diversity is reflected in the country's many popular musical traditions including blues, ragtime, jazz, rock 'n' roll, traditional Appalachian music, bluegrass, and country and western. American art music of the past hundred years was equally variegated, exemplified by high-art modernist music of the European type, modernism with a distinctly American flavor, and, most recently, postmodernist music. Unlike the suppressed European composers discussed in Chapter 35, twentieth-century American composers were free to create without governmental constraints. Offering both a "free market" for the exchange of artistic ideas and a safe homeland for ethnic groups from around the globe, the United States has come to enjoy the most diverse and vibrant musical culture in the world. In this chapter, we explore how three composers of high-art music added their very different voices to the diverse chorus of American music.

CHARLES IVES (1874–1954)

FIGURE 36–1
Young Charles Ives in the baseball uniform of Hopkins Grammar School, New Haven, Connecticut. A better baseball player than student, Ives needed an extra year between high school and college to prepare for Yale.

Music Library, Yale University

Charles Ives was the most original and most radical, and arguably the greatest, of the American composers of art music. He was born in Danbury, Connecticut, the son of George Ives (1845–1894), a bandleader in the Union army who had served with General Ulysses S. Grant during the Civil War. The senior Ives gave his son a highly unorthodox musical education—at least by European standards. True, there was the obligatory study of the three B's (Bach, Beethoven, and Brahms), instruction in harmony and counterpoint, and lessons on the violin, piano, organ, cornet, and drums. But young Ives was also taught how to "stretch his ears," as he said. In one exercise, for example, he was made to sing "Swanee River" in E♭ while his father accompanied him on the piano in the key of C—a useful lesson in polytonality*!

Since his forebears had gone to Yale, it was decided that Charles should enroll there, too (Fig. 36–1). At Yale, he took courses in music with Horatio Parker (1863–1919), a composer who had studied in Germany. But Ives's youthful, independent ideas about how music should sound clashed with Parker's traditional European training in harmony and counterpoint. The student learned to leave his more radical musical experimentations—which included, for example, a fugue with a subject entering in four different keys—outside Parker's classroom. Ives became heavily involved in extracurricular activities, including musicals for the Delta Kappa Epsilon fraternity, and maintained a D+ average (a "gentleman's" mark before the days of grade inflation).

When he graduated with the class of 1898, Ives decided not to pursue music as a profession, realizing that the sort of music he heard in his head was not the kind the public would pay to hear. Instead, he headed for New York City and Wall Street, and in 1907, he and a friend formed the company of Ives and Myrick, an agency that sold insurance as a subsidiary of Mutual of New York (MONY). Ives and Myrick became the largest insurance agency in the United States, and in 1929, the year in which Ives retired, the company had sales of $49 million.

But Charles Ives led two lives: high-powered insurance executive by day, prolific composer by night. During the twenty years between his departure from Yale (1898) and the American entry into World War I (1917), Ives wrote the bulk of his 43 works for orchestra (including 4 symphonies), 41 choral pieces, approximately 75 works for piano solo or various chamber ensembles, and more than 150 songs. Almost without exception they went unheard. Ives made little effort to get his music performed—composition was for him a very private matter. By the 1930s, however, word of his unusual creations had spread among a few influential performers and critics. In 1947, he was awarded the Pulitzer Prize in music for his Third Symphony, one he had written forty years earlier! In his typically gruff, eccentric way, Ives told the members of the Pulitzer committee, "Prizes are for boys. I'm grown up."

a double life: businessman by day, composer by night

Ives's Music

Charles Ives was an idiosyncratic, quirky man, and his music is unlike that of any other composer. Ives was a modernist of the most extreme sort. Between 1898 and 1917, he independently devised the same radical compositional techniques—including atonality, polymeter, polyrhythm, and tone clusters—that had begun to appear in the works of Schoenberg, Stravinsky, and the other European modernists. Moreover, Ives was the first composer to use polytonality* extensively, and he even experimented with **quarter-tone music**—music in which the smallest interval is not the chromatic half step (as is the case on the modern piano) but *half* of a half step. Ives's music places great demands on performer and listener alike. It is full of ear-splitting dissonances and dense, complex textures. At the same time, however, it contains many simple, popular musical elements, incorporating patriotic songs, marches, hymns, dance tunes, fiddle tunes, rags, and football cheers—this was Ives's musical America. Ives often combines these familiar musical idioms with melodies of his own, piling one tune on top of another to form a new composite. What results is a jarring kind of **collage art**—art made up of disparate materials taken from very different places. In a manner akin to that of an avant-garde artist who reinterprets fragments of reality in surprising ways (Fig. 36–2), Ives takes the familiar and "defamiliarizes" it, thereby making the old sound very modern.

on his own, Ives invents musical modernism

FIGURE 36–2
In *The Cathedrals of Wall Street* (1939), avant-garde artist Florine Stettheimer reinterprets fragments of reality in surprising ways—just as Charles Ives did in his music. Wall Street was where Ives made his fortune.

Putnam's Camp, Redding, Connecticut from *Three Places in New England* (c1908–1914)

Although he made a fortune in the financial world of Wall Street, Charles Ives was born and died a New Englander. Shortly after his marriage in 1908, he began to compose what he always referred to as his "New England Symphony," though today we call this three-movement programmatic orchestral work *Three Places in New England*. The first movement does homage to an all-black Civil War regiment honored in a monument then (and now) on Boston Common, while the third movement depicts a walk on a misty morning in the Berkshire Mountains in Stockbridge, Massachusetts. The middle movement, *Putnam's Camp*, evokes childhood memories of a Fourth-of-July picnic on the town green in Redding, Connecticut, near Ives's ancestral home. Ives wrote his own narrative program for the movement, and in it *the music of a dream* he suggests that this is music as "seen through" the eyes of a child—perhaps the recollections of Ives himself. At first, the boy recalls the games, bands, and singing on Independence Day, but he soon falls asleep and dreams about the American colonial soldiers in the army of General Israel Putnam, who wintered at Redding during 1778–1779. Reawakening, he again hears the colorful, cacophonous sounds of a small town Fourth of July.

A dream might be termed a "collage of the mind," in which familiar persons and things appear juxtaposed with one another in haphazard sequence. *Putnam's Camp* sounds like a musical dream—tune fragments from many historical periods seem to appear at random. Some of the marches, including "Yankee Doodle" and "The British Grenadiers," date, appropriately, from Revolutionary times, but "The Star Spangled Banner" and Stephen Foster's "Massa's in de Cold Ground" were composed much later. In this piece, Ives shows music to be a particularly effective art in which to reassemble random bits of sonic information (here representing the American musical past), in much the same manner that a dream reassembles random bits of personal experience.

Ives's "musical dream" is a bracing, sometimes shocking vision brought about by musical distortion. For example, the composer typically takes a familiar tune and alters the pitches chromatically or changes the rhythm, usually by syncopation. Notice in Example 36–1 how he modifies the tune "The British Grenadiers," thereby making the familiar unfamiliar.

EXAMPLE 36–1

musical distortion

But most jarring is Ives's use of **polytonality**, the simultaneous sounding of two or more keys. Example 36–2 shows how Ives combines the distorted version of "The British Grenadiers" with his own march tune, presenting the first in the key of E♭ major, and the second in the key of C major. Such tonal clashes add a further element of aural disjunction, making the tunes seem out of phase with each other.

EXAMPLE 36–2

tunes in two different keys

Most polytonality is simultaneous (vertical), but Ives also employs polytonality in linear fashion, taking a standard tune and presenting each successive phrase in a different key, as he does with "Yankee Doodle."

EXAMPLE 36–3

key of B♭   key of C   key of B

The following Listening Guide has been prepared with the aid of Ives scholar James Sinclair, whose edition of *Putnam's Camp,* based upon Ives's manuscripts, was used in the present recording. The Guide attempts to identify the welter of tune fragments Ives drew from his memory of musical America, but even with it and a synopsis of Ives's own narrative program (in italics), *Putnam's Camp* remains a challenging piece. Despite the difficulties, Ives wanted this movement to be fun. As he said to encourage the conductor and instrumentalists prior to a performance in 1931, "The concert will go alright. Just kick into the music—never mind the exact notes or the right notes, they're always a nuisance."

a challenging piece for both performers and listeners

Listening Guide

Charles Ives
Putnam's Camp, Redding, Connecticut
Second movement of *Three Places in New England*
(1908?–1914)

6
5/20–21

Genre: program symphony
Form: ternary (**ABA'**)

A *A boy attends a Fourth-of-July picnic on the village green at Redding, Connecticut.*

0:00 **20** Introduction followed by brisk march tune composed by Ives himself; tune becomes syncopated

0:49   Trumpets and horns play "out-of-phase" fanfare

0:52   Ives's march, to which is added, in flutes and French horn, refrain of Stephen Foster's "Massa's in de Cold Ground"

1:07   "Yankee Doodle"

1:12   Child's song by Ives himself

The boy wanders into a woods in hopes of seeing some old soldiers, but falls asleep.

1:47   Music becomes quiet, and distinctive tunes disappear

B *Dream sequence: Goddess Liberty appears and urges colonial troops to fight on.*

2:25   Shimmering tone clusters*

(continued)

Colonial troops begin to desert.

3:10   Music regains rhythmic profile to simulate stirring of mutinous troops

3:31   Trumpets signal deserters' departure;
              they march away to tune of "The
              British Grenadiers"

General Putnam appears with his own troops; deserters turn around and march with him back to camp.

3:58   General Putnam's troops march to
              "Hail, Columbia," played loudly in
              brass and strings

A' *The boy awakens from the noisy dream and returns to the holiday picnic.*

4:20   0:00   Return of softer child's song in violins, then another, louder march

4:42   0:22   Three tunes at once: violins play Ives's own march, trombones state his own countertheme, and
                      upper winds present second phrase of "The British Grenadiers"

4:59   0:39   Trumpets play "The British Grenadiers"

5:11   0:51   "Out-of-phase" trumpets reintroduce Ives's own march and altered version of "The British Grenadiers"

5:35   1:15   Musical fireworks go off in explosion of sound

5:55   1:35   Piece ends with beginning of "The Star Spangled Banner"

Use a downloadable, cross-platform animated Active Listening Guide, available
at **www.thomsonedu.com/music/wright**.

AARON COPLAND (1900–1990)

FIGURE 36-3
Aaron Copland.

AP/Wide World Photos

Composers working in Europe in the nineteenth century endeavored to establish "national" styles of art music for their respective countries (see Chapter 29). Similarly, in the early twentieth century, the challenge for composers in the United States was to provide this emerging nation with its own distinctive brand of high-art music—to make their learned compositions sound truly American rather than European. Charles Ives did this within his own unique musical world, one full of American marches, patriotic songs, and hymn tunes. Aaron Copland (Fig. 36–3) did much the same, drawing also on cowboy songs and early jazz. But Copland, in contrast to his older contemporary Ives, set his bits of Americana not within a collage of dissonant polytonality, but instead in a conservative backdrop of generally consonant harmony.

Copland was born in Brooklyn of Jewish immigrant parents. After a rudimentary musical education in New York City, he set sail for Paris to broaden his artistic horizons. In this he was not alone, for the City of Light at this time attracted young writers, painters, and musicians from across the world, including Igor Stravinsky (1882–1974), Pablo Picasso (1881–1973),

James Joyce (1882–1941), Gertrude Stein (1874–1946), Ernest Hemingway (1898–1961), and F. Scott Fitzgerald (1896–1940). After three years of study, Copland returned to the United States, determined to compose in a distinctly American style. Like other young expatriate artists during the 1920s, Copland had to leave his homeland to learn what made it unique: "In greater or lesser degree," he remarked, "all of us discovered America in Europe."

he discovered America while in Paris

At first, Copland sought to forge an American style by incorporating into his music elements of jazz, recognized the world over as a uniquely American creation. Then, beginning in the late 1930s, Copland turned his attention to a series of projects with rural and western American subjects. The ballet scores *Billy the Kid* (1938) and *Rodeo* (1942) are set in the West and make use of classic cowboy songs like *Goodbye, Old Paint* and *The Old Chisholm Trail*. Another ballet, *Appalachian Spring* (1944), re-creates the ambience of the Pennsylvania farm country, and his only opera, *The Tender Land* (1954), is set in the cornbelt of the Midwest. It is telling that filmmaker Spike Lee used Copland's music to fashion the soundtrack for his basketball movie *He Got Game* (1998). In the minds of some, the "Copland sound" is as American as basketball!

authentic American elements

Copland's Music

In his most distinctly American works, Copland's musical voice is clear and conservative. He uses folk and popular elements to soften the dissonant harmonies and disjunct melodies of European modernism. Copland's melodies tend to be more stepwise and diatonic* than those of other twentieth-century composers, perhaps because Western folk and popular tunes are fundamentally conjunct and nonchromatic. His harmonies are almost always tonal and often slow-moving in a way that can evoke the vastness and grandeur of the American landscape. The triad, too, is still important to Copland, perhaps for its stability and simplicity, but he frequently uses it in a modern way, as we shall see, by having two triads sound simultaneously, creating mildly dissonant polychords. But perhaps the most important component in the distinctive "Copland sound" is his clear, luminous orchestration. Copland does not mix colors to produce rich Romantic blends, but keeps the four families of instruments (strings, woodwinds, brasses, and percussion) more or less separate from one another. Moreover, his instrumentation typically features a solid bass, a very thin middle, and a top of one or two high, clear tones. It is this separation and careful spacing of the instruments that creates the fresh, wide-open sound so pleasing in Copland's music.

a clear, wide-open sound

The clarity and simplicity of Aaron Copland's music is not accidental. During the Great Depression of the 1930s, he became convinced that the gulf between modern music and the ordinary citizen had become too great—that dissonance and atonality had little to say to most music lovers. "It made no sense to ignore them [ordinary listeners] and to continue writing as if they did not exist. I felt that it was worth the effort to see if I couldn't say what I had to say in the simplest possible terms." Thus he not only wrote appealing new tonal works like *Fanfare for the Common Man* (1942) but also incorporated traditional tunes such as *The Gift to Be Simple*, which he uses in *Appalachian Spring*.

modern music for the ordinary citizen

Appalachian Spring (1944)

Appalachian Spring is a one-act ballet that tells the story of "a pioneer celebration of spring in a newly built farmhouse in Pennsylvania in the early 1800s."

A new bride and her farmer-husband express through dance the anxieties and joys of life in pioneer America. The work was composed in 1944 for the great American choreographer Martha Graham (1893–1991), and it won Copland a Pulitzer Prize the following year (Fig. 36–4). It is divided into eight connected sections that differ in tempo and mood. Copland provided a brief description of each of these orchestral scenes.

SECTION 1

"Introduction of the characters one by one, in a suffused light." The quiet beauty of the land at daybreak is revealed, as the orchestra slowly presents, one by one, the notes of the tonic and dominant triads.

EXAMPLE 36–4

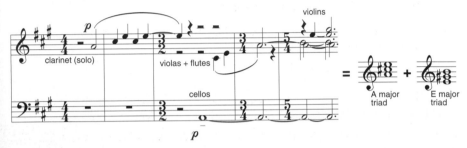

FIGURE 36–4
A scene from Martha Graham's ballet *Appalachian Spring*, with music by Aaron Copland. Here Katherine Crockett dances the role of the Bride (New York, 1999).

Julie Lemberger/CORBIS

While this overlapping presentation of two triads constitutes a polychord*, the effect is only mildly dissonant because of the slow, quiet way in which the notes of the two chords are introduced. The serene simplicity of the introduction sets the tone for the entire work.

SECTION 2

"A sentiment both elated and religious gives the keynote of this scene." The early calm is suddenly broken by a lively dance with a salient rhythm played aggressively in the strings. The dance has all the modern rhythmic vigor of Stravinsky's music, but none of the extreme polymeter*. As the dance proceeds, a more restrained hymn-like melody emerges in the trumpet.

SECTIONS 3–6

Section 3 is a dance for the two principals, a "pas de deux" in ballet parlance, which is accompanied by lyrical writing for strings and winds. Sections 4 and 5 are musical depictions of the livelier aspects of country life, with Section 4 including a toe-tappin' hoedown, while Section 6 recalls the quiet calm of the opening of the ballet.

SECTION 7

Copland's best-known music

"Calm and flowing. Scenes of daily activity for the Bride and her Farmer-husband." For this section, Copland chose to make use of a traditional tune of the Shakers, an extreme religious sect that prospered in the Appalachian region in the early nineteenth century and whose members expressed their spiritual intensity in frenzied singing, dancing, and shaking. Today this tune is famous, having been featured, among other places, in a commercial for General Motors. But the melody has become well known only because of Copland's *Appalachian Spring*. The composer plucked it from an obscure book of folksongs in 1944 because he thought the simple, diatonic* tune (Ex. 36–5) fit well with the American character of the ballet, and because the text of the Shaker song is harmonious with what occurs on stage: "scenes of daily activity."

EXAMPLE 36–5

a Shaker tune

'Tis the gift to be simple,
'Tis the gift to be free,
'Tis the gift to come down where we ought to be,
And when we find ourselves in the place just right,
'Twill be in the valley of love and delight.

In the five variations that follow, *The Gift to Be Simple* is not so much varied as it is clothed in different instrumental attire.

SECTION 8

"The Bride takes her place among her neighbors." Serenity returns to the scene as the strings play a slow, mostly stepwise descent, as Copland says, "like a prayer." The hymn-like melody from Section 2 is heard again in the flute, followed by the quiet "landscape music" from the beginning of the ballet. Darkness has again descended on the valley, leaving the young pioneer couple "strong in their new house" and secure in their community.

an end like the beginning

Listening Guide

Aaron Copland
Appalachian Spring (1944)
Sections 1, 2, and 7

6 6/1–3   **2** 2/16–18

Genre: ballet music

SECTION 1

0:00	**1 16**	Quiet unfolding of triads by clarinet and other instruments
0:45		Soft violin melody descends
1:11		More triads in woodwinds and trumpet
1:36		Oboe and then bassoon solos
2:19		Clarinet plays concluding triad

SECTION 2

0:00	**2 17**	Percussive rhythm (♫ ♩ ♫ ♩) in strings and rising woodwinds
0:19		Rhythm gels into sprightly dance

0:44	Trumpet plays hymn-like melody above dance

1:13	Rhythmic motive scattered but then played more forcefully
2:09	Hymn heard in strings, with flute counterpoint above
2:36	Rhythmic motive skips away in woodwinds

(continued)

SECTION 7

0:00   Clarinet presents Shaker tune

0:36   Variation 1: oboe and bassoon play tune

1:06   Variation 2: violas and trombones play tune at half its previous speed

1:51   Variation 3: trumpets and trombones play tune

2:16   Variation 4: woodwinds play tune more slowly

2:31   Variation 5: final majestic statement of tune by full orchestra

Use a downloadable, cross-platform animated Active Listening Guide, available at www.thomsonedu.com/music/wright.

Listening Exercise 44

Copland
Appalachian Spring

The following exercise asks you to consider the ways Aaron Copland "softens" the more radical aspects of twentieth-century modernist music.

Section I: Introduction

1. (0:00–0:43) Although the opening involves the overlap of two conflicting triads, why does this passage not sound harshly dissonant?
   a. because the notes unfold in succession, rather than sound at once
   b. because the dissonant notes are not all in the same register
   c. because the music is quiet
   d. all of the above

2. (0:45–1:09) Why does this passage sound more like Romantic than modern music?
   a. A primarily stepwise melody is played warmly (with vibrato) by the violins.
   b. A nostalgic-sounding English horn suggests a woodland scene.
   c. An alpine horn call suggests distant mountains.

3. (1:11–2:31) Which family of instruments provides the bulk of the *soloists* for this lovely section?
   a. string
   b. woodwind
   c. brass
   d. percussion

4. (2:19–2:31) In this passage, we hear one of the distinctive aspects of the "Copland sound": the composer spaces the instruments to allow "air" into the middle of the texture. Which is true?
   a. The double basses play a pedal point*, the strings hold softly in the middle, and the clarinet unfolds a triad above.

b. The double basses play an ostinato*, the clarinets hold softly in the middle, and the violin unfolds a triad above.

Section 2: Joys and Anxieties of Pioneer Life

5. The dance theme begins in the strings (at 0:19), and then the hymn-like tune enters in the trumpet (0:44). When the two are together (0:44–1:13), which sounds more aggressively modern?
   a. the trumpet tune moving in long notes
   b. the strings playing the dance in shorter notes

6. (1:22–2:08) Now the lively dance theme dominates. This passage sounds a bit like the music of Igor Stravinsky, a composer whom Copland greatly admired. Which of the following *cannot* be heard in this passage?
   a. strong, irregular accents
   b. a rhythmic ostinato in the flutes and harp
   c. a sweeping melody in the cellos
   d. violent, percussive strokes in the timpani and xylophone

Section 7: Variations on a Shaker tune *The Gift to Be Simple*

7. This section is in theme and variations form. Is this form unique to the twentieth century? Is it a particularly "modern" form?
   a. yes
   b. no

8. This section is likely the best-known passage in all of Copland's music. Which is true?
   a. It sounds like Romantic music, projecting a pleasing, consonant sound, and a regular meter.
   b. It sounds like modern music, projecting percussive sounds, dissonance, and syncopation.

9. We have said that Copland admired the Russian composer Igor Stravinsky. Which of the following is *not* true?
   a. They both wrote ballet music.
   b. They both spent time in Paris.
   c. They both came to the United States as immigrants.
   d. They both liked bright, clean, and carefully spaced colors in their orchestrations.
   e. They both incorporated folk melodies into their music.

10. Comparing Copland's *Appalachian Spring* to Stravinsky's *The Rite of Spring* (❻5/13; ❷2/14), which of the two scores do you judge to be the more radically modern?
   a. Stravinsky's
   b. Copland's

ELLEN TAAFFE ZWILICH (1939–)

By the end of the Second World War, composers such as Ives and Copland had established a uniquely American brand of modernist art music. Consequently, later generations of American composers could work more freely within the tradition of European classical music, without feeling compelled to incorporate distinctively American musical traits. One American composer who might be called, paradoxically, a "traditional modernist" (a modernist working within the European classical tradition) is Ellen Taaffe Zwilich (Fig. 36–5).

FIGURE 36–5
Ellen Taaffe Zwilich

The daughter of an airline pilot, Zwilich was born in Miami and educated at Florida State University. She then moved to New York City where she played violin in the American Symphony Orchestra, studied composition at the Juilliard School, and worked for a time as an usher at Carnegie Hall. Zwilich's big "break" came in 1983, when she became the first woman to win the Pulitzer Prize in music. During 1995–1998, she was the first person of either sex to occupy the newly created Composer's Chair at Carnegie Hall—usher had become director. Today Zwilich enjoys a status to which all modern composers aspire: She is free to devote herself exclusively to writing music, sustained by her royalties and commissions. Recently, the New York Philharmonic and the Chicago Symphony Orchestra each paid five-figure sums for a single new composition.

The tradition of the Baroque concerto grosso* lies at the heart of Zwilich's five-movement *Concerto Grosso 1985*. Commissioned by the Washington Friends of Handel, this work honors the composer George Frideric Handel (see Chapter 14), a leading exponent of the concerto grosso. Zwilich borrows a melody directly from Handel (the opening theme of his Violin Sonata in D major). She also embraces several elements of Baroque musical style: a regular rhythmic pulse, a repeating bass pedal point*, a walking bass*, and a harpsichord*. Yet Zwilich adds twisting chromaticism to Handel's melody (see Listening Guide) and sets it to a biting, dissonant harmony. Most important, she demands an insistent, pounding style of playing that would have shocked Handel. Zwilich's concerto, therefore, uses modern idioms to establish a dialogue with the past. We might call this "Neo-baroque" music—music that is part modern, part Baroque in style. But compositions that heavily reference music from a specific era—be it the Middle Ages, Baroque period, or Classical epoch—are generally referred to as Neo-classical*. This is classical music with a distinctly modern twist.

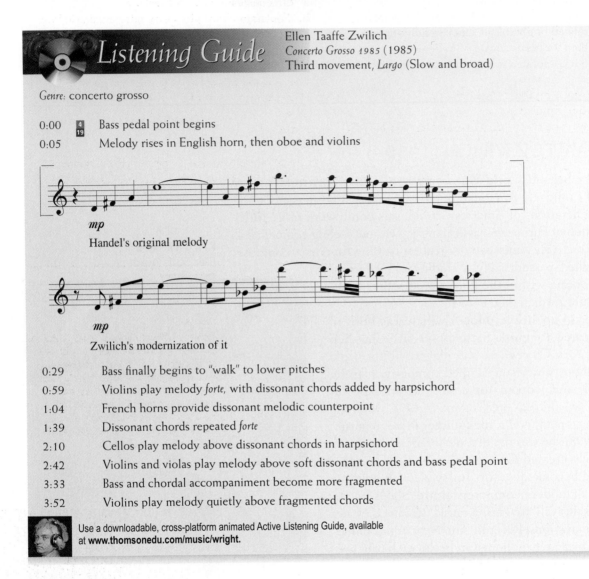

Listening Guide

Ellen Taaffe Zwilich
Concerto Grosso 1985 (1985)
Third movement, *Largo* (Slow and broad)

6 **2**
6/4 2/19

Genre: concerto grosso

0:00	**4 19**	Bass pedal point begins
0:05		Melody rises in English horn, then oboe and violins

mp

Handel's original melody

mp

Zwilich's modernization of it

0:29	Bass finally begins to "walk" to lower pitches
0:59	Violins play melody *forte*, with dissonant chords added by harpsichord
1:04	French horns provide dissonant melodic counterpoint
1:39	Dissonant chords repeated *forte*
2:10	Cellos play melody above dissonant chords in harpsichord
2:42	Violins and violas play melody above soft dissonant chords and bass pedal point
3:33	Bass and chordal accompaniment become more fragmented
3:52	Violins play melody quietly above fragmented chords

Use a downloadable, cross-platform animated Active Listening Guide, available at **www.thomsonedu.com/music/wright**.

Listening Exercise 45

Zwilich
Concerto Grosso 1985

6 **2**
6/4 2/19

ThomsonNOW™
To take this Listening Exercise online and receive feedback or email answers to your instructor, go to *ThomsonNOW* for this chapter.

This movement is scored for strings, two French horns, oboe, English horn, and harpsichord. The following questions pertain to the dialogue Zwilich establishes with the music of Baroque composer George Frideric Handel.

1. The orchestra that Zwilich requires here is *least* comparable in size to which previous orchestra?
   a. the Baroque orchestra
   b. the Classical orchestra
   c. the Romantic orchestra

2. The opening melody is played by an English horn. Is the English horn part of the typical Baroque or Classical orchestra (see pages 130 and 209)?
   a. yes   b. no

3. (0:00) The music begins with a pedal point in the bass. We first met the pedal point in which period in music history (see page 145)?
   a. Baroque
   b. Classical
   c. Romantic

4. (0:59) The harpsichord enters. In which orchestra is the harpsichord traditionally found?
   a. Baroque
   b. Classical
   c. Romantic
   d. modern

5. (0:59–1:38) Which of the following elements from this passage are *not* a typical element in Baroque music?
   a. the harpsichord chords
   b. the very regular rhythm pulsations
   c. the dissonant, disjunct melody

6. (2:10–2:40) Why does this passage sound less modern and more "romantic"?
   a. The rising cellos play with warmth and sentiment.
   b. The harpsichord plays with much vibrato.
   c. The pedal point sounds with much *rubato*.

7. (2:42) The return of the melody here is comparable to a return of what in a Baroque concerto grosso?
   a. the *rondeau*   b. the raga   c. the ritornello

8. (3:52–end) Which of the following is true in this final passage?
   a. The harpsichord plays continuous chords together with a strong bass line, thereby creating the modern equivalent of a *basso continuo*.
   b. The harpsichord plays very different music from the strong bass line, thereby creating the modern equivalent of a cadenza.

9. Knowing that Neo-baroque music is simply one type of music within the larger, general category of Neo-classical music, is Zwilich's *Concerto* a Neo-classical work?
   a. yes
   b. no

10. Which modern composer, discussed in Chapter 35, composed a famous example of Neo-classical music?
   a. Shostakovich
   b. Prokofiev
   c. Bartók

Key Words

quarter-tone music **(393)**   collage art **(393)**   polytonality **(394)**

Postmodernism

Chapter 37

Postmodernism is a philosophy of art that came to the fore after World War II. For postmodernists, art is for all, not just an elite few, and all art is of equal potential—a painting of a Campbell's Soup can (Fig. 37–1), for example, is just as meaningful as a Picasso. Consequently, there is no "high" or "low" art, only art (and maybe not even that). In addition, postmodernism holds that we live in a pluralistic world in which each culture is as important as the next. Indeed, cultural distinctions are seen to be gradually disappearing because of globalization, a process of homogenization made inevitable by instant mass-media communication. Finally, postmodernism is refreshingly egalitarian when it comes to sex and gender, affirming a belief that the creations of, say, gay living black women are just as important as those of straight dead white men.

FIGURE 37–1

The Campbell's Soup Can (1965), painted by Andy Warhol (1930–1987), suggests no distinction be made between "high" art and "low" art.

Postmodernist principles apply to music as well. If all art holds equal potential, then it is no longer necessary to separate classical from popular music—the two styles can even coexist within one and the same composition, as they do, for example, in the tangos of Astor Piazolla (1921–1992) or the film music of Tan Dun (1957–). No longer, according to postmodernism, need there be such distinctions between "highbrow" and "low-brow" music; all music—classical, country, hip-hop, folk, rock, and all the rest—is to be prized in equal measure. John Williams's film music is as important as Igor Stravinsky's ballet scores; Madonna is as worthy of our attention as Mozart.

Finally, postmodernism brings with it a new agenda as to how to create music. Classical formal models, such as sonata–allegro and theme and variations, are no longer operative. Each musical work must fashion its unique form according to the demands and creative urges of the moment. Music no longer need be "goal oriented"; a particular piece does not have to work progressively to a defined point of arrival or climax. In today's musical culture, amplified instruments and electronic music are commonplace in symphony hall and rock arena alike. Traditional acoustic instruments must share the spotlight with newer electric and electronic ones. While Yo-Yo Ma's Stradivarius cello is a cultural treasure, so, too, is Eric Clapton's electric guitar. Postmodernism embraces an egalitarian, pluralistic musical world in which technology plays an important role.

EDGARD VARÈSE (1883–1965) AND ELECTRONIC MUSIC

FIGURE 37–2

Composer Edgard Varèse surrounded by a light sculpture.

The origins of musical postmodernism can be traced to the 1930s and the experimental compositions of Edgard Varèse. Varèse was born in France but immigrated to the United States in 1915 in search of a less traditional artistic environment (Fig. 37–2). After an accidental fire caused the loss of some of the scores he had brought from Paris, he destroyed the rest intentionally, thereby obliterating all traces of his European musical past. Already an extreme modernist, Varèse showed himself eager to step beyond the boundaries of the Western musical tradition and embrace the postmodernist age. But Varèse was a pioneer, in some ways ahead of his time, and musical postmodernism was not to reach full force until the 1960s. Thus, as with many artistic and cultural eras, modernism and postmodernism overlapped for decades. Indeed, in many ways, the two styles still coexist today.

Significantly, Varèse titled his first work written in the United States *Amériques* (1921), suggesting not only a new geography but also a new world of musical sound. Besides the usual strings, brasses, and woodwinds, the orchestra for *Amériques* also required a battery of new percussion instruments, including sirens and sleigh bells, most of which had never been heard in a symphony orchestra. In earlier centuries, composers had typically called on the percussion to provide accentuation. The thuds, bangs, and crashes of these instruments helped especially to delineate the climaxes of the musical structure. Like road signs, they pointed the way but did not constitute the essence of the musical journey. By the 1930s, however, Varèse had radically altered the traditional role of percussion instruments. In *Ionization* (1931), the orchestra consists of nothing but percussion instruments, including two sirens, two tam-tams, a gong, cymbals, anvils, three different sizes of bass drum, bongos, various Cuban rattles and gourds, slap-sticks, Chinese blocks, sleigh bells, and chimes. Here, percussive sounds do not *reinforce* the music; they *are* the music.

an all percussion orchestra

To grasp the significance of an all-percussion orchestra, remember that most percussion instruments generate sounds of indefinite pitch, rather than one continuous frequency or musical tone. Without discrete tones, two essential elements of traditional music—melody and harmony—have been removed. All that remains is rhythm, color, and texture, which Varèse deployed masterfully. Yet having created new percussive soundscapes in *Ionization*, Varèse wanted more. As he said in a lecture in 1936, "When new instruments allow me to write music as I conceive it, [then my shifting sound-masses] will be clearly perceived." Two decades later, the "new instruments" Varèse had envisioned—electronic instruments—became available.

music without a definite pitch

Poème électronique (1958)

Most traditional music around the world is played on acoustic instruments (ones made of natural materials). But shortly after World War II, new technology led to the development of **electronic music** produced by a **synthesizer,** a machine that can create, transform, and combine (synthesize) sounds by means of electronic circuitry. Varèse's *Poème électronique* is an early landmark of electronic music. Here the composer combined new electronic sounds generated by a synthesizer with bits of *musique concrète** (see boxed essay), including taped sounds of a siren, a train, an organ, church bells, and a human voice, all altered or distorted in some imaginative way. Varèse created this "poem for the electronic age" to provide music for a multimedia exhibit inside the pavilion of the Philips Radio Corporation at the 1958 World's Fair in Brussels (Fig. 37–3). Varèse's eight-minute creation was recorded on tape and then played on 425 speakers, again and again, to the 15,000 or 16,000 people who walked through the structure daily. While the music played, a video montage was projected on the inside walls of the building.

FIGURE 37–3
Le Corbusier and Iannis Xenakis, Philips Pavilion, Brussels World's Fair, 1958. The visionary pavilion housed a sound and light show with music provided by Edgard Varèse's *Poème électronique.*

As you listen to *Poème électronique,* you may have one (or more) of the many reactions experienced by those visitors to the Philips Pavilion in 1958: anger, fear, revulsion, curiosity, or awe at the sheer variety and novelty of sound. Startling tones come in rapid succession and then disappear quickly; large, dense masses of sound are suddenly succeeded by thin, airy ones. Three mysterious tones rise chromatically. Squawks, honks, swoops, and animal noises come one after another. What is the artist's message? An ardent postmodernist such as Varèse would say that art need not have "meaning." Is *Poème électronique* really music or merely ingeniously contrived noise? Again, the postmodernist would respond that organized *noise* is just as valid an artistic statement as organized *tones* (music).

Electronic Music: From Varèse to Radiohead

The effect of technology on classical, and especially on popular, music has been nothing short of revolutionary. The earliest experiments with electronic sound—preceding even the first synthesizer—produced something termed *musique concrète*. **Musique concrète** is so called because the composer works, not with sounds written for voice or musical instruments, but with those found naturally in the environment. Another term for *musique concrète*, then, is "found sound." A car horn, a person speaking in a room, or a dog's barking may be captured by a tape recorder and doctored in some way—reassembled and repeated (spliced, mixed, and looped) to form an unexpected montage of sound. Edgard Varèse, working both in New York and Paris, was one of the first practitioners of *musique concrète*, his *Poème electronique* (1958) being a landmark in the history of this sort of synthetic music.

Pop artists, too, quickly began to exploit these musical-technical developments. The Beatles' John Lennon used "tape looping" to create a novel background ambience for his song "Revolution #9" (1968). As Lennon recounted: "We were cutting up [tapes of] classical music and making different size loops, and then I got an engineer tape on which an engineer was saying, "Number nine, number nine, number nine." All those different bits of sound and noises were all compiled. . . . I fed them all in and mixed them live." Lennon also added *musique concrète* (found sound) to a few Beatles songs. "Strawberry Fields," for example, has a piano crash followed by a dog's whistle played at 15,000 vibrations per second. Not to be outdone, the rock band Pink Floyd incorporated the sounds of a clanging cash register into their song, appropriately titled, "Money" (1973). And film-makers, too, jumped on the electronic bandwagon. George Lucas used banging chains to create the sound of the Imperial Walkers for his *Star Wars* epics. To be specific, he recorded, and then modified and layered, the noise of a bicycle chain falling on a concrete floor—a literal example of the principle of *musique concrète*.

What began as esoteric experiments by a few avant-garde scientists and composers soon transformed the world of popular entertainment. The technological development that made this possible was miniaturization. During the 1960s, the large-console tape machine was

W. G. "Snuffy" Walden is an eminently successful TV composer, having created the theme for The West Wing, *as well as scores for* The Drew Carey Show, My So-Called Life, The Street, The Wonder Years, *and many others.*

Listening Guide

Edgard Varèse
Poème électronique (1958)
(beginning)

6
6/5

Genre: electronic music

0:00	5	Large bell, squibbles and zaps, sirens
0:41		Drip-like noise, squawks
0:55		Three-note chromatic ascent sounded three times
1:10		Low sustained noise with rattle, siren, more squawks
1:32		Three-note chromatic ascent, squawks and chirps
2:02		Percussion instruments, siren
2:33		Large bell returns, sustained tones
2:57		More drips, large low crescendo, rattles and zaps

Use a downloadable, cross-platform animated Active Listening Guide, available at **www.thomsonedu.com/music/wright.**

reduced to the portable tape recorder, and then, during the 1980s, microprocessors became small enough to power keyboard-synthesizers. In more recent years, the increasing power, versatility, and availability of the personal computer has facilitated revolutionary changes in the way music is composed, produced, and recorded. Today, almost any aspiring composer or rock band can own the hardware required to produce and manipulate their own sounds. Today's computer-driven synthesizer can generate sounds that are almost indistinguishable from those of a ninety-piece orchestra. Consequently, **computer music** has revolutionized the world of commercial music. The computer-equipped recording studio now generates much of the music we hear on radio and television. The opening music for the series *Law and Order,* for example, begins with tones that sound like those of a clarinet. In fact, these are synthesized (artificially fabricated) sounds created by a computer-driven synthesizer.

Technology has facilitated new processes for the production of pop music. In the 1980s, rap and hip-hop artists began using a technique called **sampling** whereby the rapper or producer extracts a small portion of prerecorded music and then mechanically repeats it over and over as a musical backdrop to the text that he or she raps. And in **scratching,** another technique popular in rap and hip-hop, a creative DJ with one or more turntables manipulates the needles, scratching on the vinyl of the record while other prerecorded sounds loop continually in the background. Perhaps no contemporary rock group has blended songwriting with the manipulation of electronic audio more extensively than Radiohead. For their albums and concert tours, they use not

only analog and digital synthesizers but also "special effects" pedals and distortion filters to reform the audio of their voices and instruments. All these electronic devices and computer processes help give the music of Radiohead its sometimes disembodied, otherworldly quality.

Musician Thom Yorke surrounded by some of the electronic equipment that gives his band Radiohead its distinctive "electronic" sound.

© Frank Micelotti/Getty mages

JOHN CAGE (1912–1992) AND CHANCE MUSIC

If, as postmodernists say, music need not progress in an organized fashion toward a goal, why not just leave it to chance? This is essentially what American composer John Cage decided to do. Cage was born in Los Angeles, the son of an inventor. He was graduated valedictorian of Los Angeles High School and spent two years at nearby Pomona College before going to Europe to learn more about art, architecture, and music. Arriving in New York City in 1942, he worked variously as a wall washer at the YWCA, teacher of music and mycology (the science of mushrooms) at the New School for Social Research, and music director of a modern dance company.

From his earliest days as a musician, Cage had a special affection for percussion instruments and the unusual sounds they could create. His *First Construction (in Metal)* (1939) has six percussionists play piano, metal thunder-sheets,

an affection for percussion instruments

The New York Public Library

FIGURE 37–4
John Cage's "prepared piano." By putting spoons, forks, screws, paper clips, and other sundry objects into the strings of the piano, the composer changes the instrument from one producing melodic tones to one generating percussive impacts.

oxen bells, cowbells, sleigh bells, water gongs, and brake drums, among other things. By 1941, he had collected three hundred percussion objects of this kind—anything that might make an unusual noise when struck or shaken. Cage's tinkering with percussive sounds led him to invent the **prepared piano:** a grand piano outfitted with screws, bolts, washers, erasers, and bits of felt and plastic all inserted between the strings (Fig. 37–4). This transformed the piano into a one-man percussion band that could produce a great variety of sounds and noises—twangs, zaps, rattles, thuds, and the like—no two of which were exactly the same in pitch or color. In creating the prepared piano, Cage was merely continuing along the experimental trail blazed by his spiritual mentor, Edgard Varèse: "Years ago, after I decided to devote my life to music, I noticed that people distinguished between noises and sounds. I decided to follow Varèse and fight for noises, to be on the side of the underdog."

Cage's glorification of everyday noise began in earnest during the 1950s. Rather than engage in a titanic struggle to shape the elements of music, as had Beethoven, he decided to sit back, relax, and simply allow noises to occur around him. In creating this sort of intentionally purposeless, undirected music, Cage invented what has come to be called chance music, the ultimate postmodernist experimentation. In **chance music,** musical events are not carefully predetermined by the composer, but come instead in an unpredictable sequence as the result of nonmusical decisions such as following astrological charts, tossing coins, throwing dice, or shuffling randomly the pages of music to be played. In *Music Walk* (1958), for example, one or more pianists connect lines and dots in any fashion to create a musical "score" from which to play. Such "scores" suggest only vaguely what the musician is to do.

musical "happenings"

The musical "happening" that results is the sort of spontaneous group experience that was to flower during the 1960s. More radical still is Cage's work 0'0" (1962), which allows the performer total artistic freedom. When performed by Cage himself in 1962, he sliced and prepared vegetables at a table on a stage, put them through a food processor, and then drank the juice, all the while amplifying and broadcasting the sound of these activities throughout the hall. Cage's declaration that the ordinary noise made by food processing can be "art" is virtually identical in intent to Andy Warhol's glorification of the Campbell's Soup can (see Fig. 37–1): both typify the kind of postmodernist creation that took hold in New York City during the 1960s.

forcing provocative questions

Naturally, music critics called Cage a joker and a charlatan. Most would agree that his "compositions" in and of themselves are not of great musical value in traditional terms. Nevertheless, by raising profound questions regarding the relationships between human activity, sound, and music, his compositions eloquently articulate his own musical philosophy. By focusing on the chance appearance of ordinary noise, Cage aggressively asks us to ponder the fundamental principles that underlie most Western music. Why must sounds of similar range and color come one after the other? Why must music have form and unity? Why must it have "meaning"? Why must it express anything? Why must it develop and climax? Why must it be goal-oriented, as is so much of human activity in the West?

4′33″ (1952)

The "composition" of Cage that causes us to focus on these questions most intently is his *4′33″*. Here one or more performers carrying any sort of instrument come on stage, seat themselves, open the "score," and play nothing. For each of the three carefully timed movements, there is no notated music, only the indication *tacet* ("it is silent") (Fig. 37–5). But as the audience soon realizes, "absolute" silence is virtually impossible to attain. With no organized sound to be heard during the four minutes and thirty-three seconds that follow, the listener gradually becomes aware of the background noise in the hall—a creaking floor, a passing car, a dropped paper clip, an electrical hum. Cage asks us to embrace these random everyday noises—to tune our ears in innocent sonic wonder. Are these sounds not of artistic value too? What is music? What is noise? What is art?

Needless to say, we have not filled your CDs with four minutes and thirty-three seconds of background noise. You can create your own, and John Cage would have liked that. Sit in a "quiet" room for 4 minutes and 33 seconds and notice what you hear. Perhaps this experiment will make you more aware of how important conscious organization is to the art we call music. If nothing else, Cage makes us realize that music, above all, is a form of communication from one person to the next and that random background noise can do nothing to express or communicate ideas and feelings.

FIGURE 37–5
John Cage's most important book on music is called *Silence* (1966).

Christopher Felver/CORBS

Listening Guide

John Cage
4′33″ (1952)

Genre: chance music

0:00–0:30	First movement—silence (?)
0:31–2:53	Second movement—silence (?)
2:54–4:33	Third movement—silence (?)

JOHN ADAMS (1947–) AND MINIMALISM

Western classical music—the music of Bach, Beethoven, and Brahms—is typically constructed of large, carefully placed units. A movement of a symphony, for example, has themes, which come in a hierarchy of importance, and sections (development and coda, for example), which must be heard in a particular order. A compelling sequence of events leads to a desired end and conveys a message from composer to listener. But what would happen if composers reduced the music to just one or two simple motives and repeated these again and again? What would happen if they focused on what things *are*, rather than

music as it is, rather than what it might become

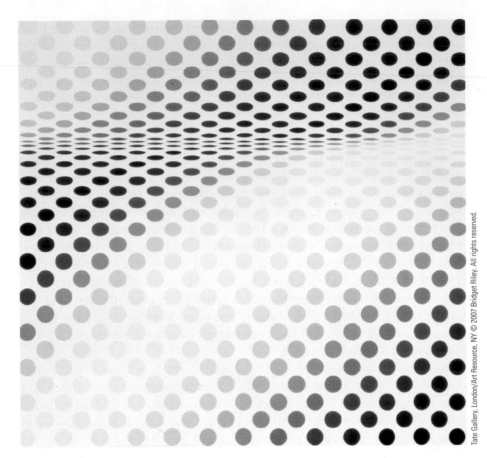

FIGURE 37–6
Briget Riley's Minimalist *Hesitate* (1964) repeats a basic design again and again, much as does the score of Adams's *Short Ride in a Fast Machine*. Indeed, the score itself could be taken to be an example of Minimalist visual art (see Ex. 37–1).

FIGURE 37–7
John Adams. In 2003, Lincoln Center, New York, held an eight-week "Absolutely Adams" festival to go along with its annual "Mostly Mozart" program.

on what these things might *become?* Such is the approach taken by a group of American postmodernist composers called the Minimalists.

Minimalism is a style of postmodern music, originating in the early 1960s, that takes a very small musical unit and repeats it over and over to form a composition. A three-note melodic cell, a single arpeggio, or two alternating chords is the sort of "minimal" element a composer might introduce, reiterate again and again, modify or expand, and then begin to repeat once more. The basic material is usually simple, tonal, and consonant. By repeating these minimal figures incessantly at a steady pulse, the composer creates a hypnotic effect— "trance music" is the name sometimes given this music. The trance-like quality of Minimalist music has influenced rock musicians (Velvet Underground, Talking Heads, and Radiohead) and led to a new genre of pop music called "techno," or "rave" music. Minimalism, in both art (Fig. 37–6) and music, has been mainly an American movement. Its most successful musical practitioners are Steve Reich (1936–), Philip Glass (1937–), and John Adams (1947–) (Fig. 37–7).

John Adams (no relation to the presidents) was born in Worcester, Massachusetts, in 1947 and educated at Harvard. As a student, he was encouraged to compose in the twelve-tone style of Arnold Schoenberg (see page 380). But if Adams counted twelve-tone rows by day, he listened to The Beatles in his dorm room at night. Moving to San Francisco after graduation, Adams developed his own eclectic musical style that blended the learned with the popular, and added increasing amounts of Minimalism, which was then gaining popularity in California. Some of Adams's early scores of the 1980s are strict Minimalist works, but later ones become more all-embracing; from time to time, an operatic melody or a funk bass line, for example, will creep into his constantly repeating, minimal sonorities. In 2003, Adams received the Pulitzer Prize in music for his *On the Transmigration of Souls*, which commemorated those killed in the World Trade Center attacks. Ironically, although Adams is a Minimalist composer, he has been able to extend his ever-repeating blocks of sound into lengthy operas, the best known of which are *Nixon in China* (1987) and *Doctor Atomic* (2005).

Short Ride in a Fast Machine (1986)

To experience the essence of Minimalism, we turn to an early work by Adams, one commissioned in 1986 by the Pittsburgh Symphony. *Short Ride in a Fast Machine* is scored for full orchestra and two electronic keyboard synthesizers*. Example 37–1 shows how the music is composed of short (mostly four-note) motives that continually repeat. There are five sections to this work (we'll call them laps). In each lap, the machine seems to accelerate, not because the tempo gets faster but because more and more repeating motives are added. The effect created is that of a powerful, twentieth-century engine firing on all cylinders. As Adams has said about his Minimalist work, "You know how it is when someone asks you to ride in a terrific sports car, and then you wish you hadn't?"

endlessly repeating ostinatos

EXAMPLE 37–1

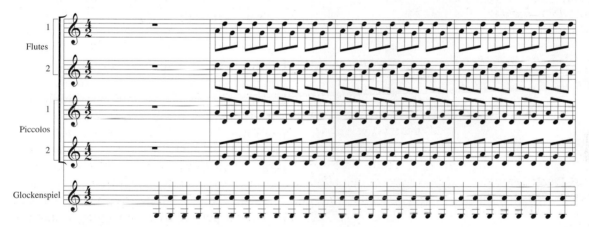

 John Adams
Listening Guide
Short Ride in a Fast Machine (1986)
Delirando (with exhilaration)

6
6/6

0:00	6	Lap 1: woodblock, woodwinds, and keyboard synthesizers begin; brasses, snare drum, and glockenspiel* gradually added
1:06		Lap 2: bass drum "backfires"; motives rise in pitch and become more dissonant
1:47		Lap 3: starts quietly with sinister repeating motive in bass; syncopation and dissonance increase
2:40		Lap 4: two-note falling motive in bass
2:55		Lap 5: trumpets play fanfare-like motives (this is "victory lap")
4:03		Musical vehicle begins another lap but suddenly breaks down

 Use a downloadable, cross-platform animated Active Listening Guide, available at **www.thomsonedu.com/music/wright**.

TAN DUN (1957–) AND GLOBALIZATION

The signs of **globalization**—the development of an increasingly integrated global economy—are everywhere. Computers, cell phones, and MP3 players—all Western inventions—have brought Western, and particularly American, culture to the Far East. The youth of China, for example, can watch most of the newest American films and TV programs, and listen to latest American music, as instantaneously as can students in the United States. Traditional Western musical culture has also infiltrated the Far East. Music students in conservatories in Japan, China, and Korea now study at least some Western classical music. They learn, for example, how to play the piano, a uniquely Western instrument, performing Bach's fugues and Beethoven's sonatas. Today, nearly as many CDs of Western classical music are sold in Japan as in the United States. But commerce—and cultural influence—inevitably flows in two directions. The shorts, socks, and shoes we wear likely came from China, and the automobile in which we ride probably was made (or designed) in Japan. So, too, traditional Chinese music has also made inroads in the West, most emphatically with the Grammy Award–winning film score to *Crouching Tiger, Hidden Dragon* (2000) with music by Tan Dun (Fig. 37–8). As economic barriers are removed, the flow of ideas accelerates, and cultural distinctions begin to blur.

a blurring of cultural differences

FIGURE 37–8
A poster promoting the film *Crouching Tiger, Hidden Dragon*.

No one better personifies "musical globalization" than Tan Dun (Fig. 37–9). Tan was born in Hunan, China, in 1957 and raised in a rural environment full of music, magic, and ritual. During the Cultural Revolution of Mao Zedong, he was sent to a commune to plant rice, but was later summoned to play fiddle and arrange music for a provincial troupe of the Beijing Opera. He first heard Beethoven's Symphony No. 5 when he was nineteen and began to dream of becoming a composer. In 1978, owing to his exceptional knowledge of Chinese folk music, Tan was admitted to the Central Conservatory in Beijing, China's most prestigious music school, where he remained for eight years. In 1986, he received a fellowship to study at Columbia University in New York, and at this time came under the sway of the most progressive styles of modernism. Indeed, some of Tan's compositions of the 1980s have the sort of atonal, dissonant sound that would make Arnold Schoenberg smile.

By the 1990s, however, the sounds of Tan's homeland had crept back into his scores: the pentatonic scale, microtonal pitch slides, scratchy string bowings, vibrant percussion sounds, and the nasal timbres of the Beijing Opera style. Tan's own opera *Marco Polo* (1996) earned him the Grawemeyer Award, classical composition's most prestigious prize. Two years later, he wrote the music for the American thriller *Fallen*, starring Denzel Washington. To create his Oscar- and Grammy Award–winning score for *Crouching Tiger, Hidden Dragon*, Tan worked with Yo-Yo Ma (also of Chinese descent). Ma played the cello solos, which were recorded in New York; these were later patched into the full soundtrack, which was recorded in Shanghai by a Western-style orchestra supplemented by traditional Chinese instruments—a truly global enterprise! Most recently, Tan Dun has worked with Yo-Yo Ma on a series of concerts and recordings called *The Silk Road Project*—a continuing program designed to highlight and integrate the music and instruments of China with those of the Western tradition.

Marco Polo (1996)

Tan Dun's opera *Marco Polo* is an excellent vehicle through which to experience his music and explore the process of musical globalization. It was financed and co-produced by opera companies in Amsterdam, Munich, and Hong Kong, where the first three "premieres" occurred simultaneously. Moreover, the subject of Marco Polo, an Italian explorer who traveled the Silk Road to China in the thirteenth century, offered Tan the opportunity to present the music of several different cultures: Western, Middle Eastern, Indian, Tibetan, Mongolian, and Chinese. In the scene "Waiting to Depart," Marco Polo stands before the sea, looking eastward. The figures of Water and Shadows beckon him to begin the journey of time and space. Marco exists in the present (Western Europe) but envisions the future (the Far East). This we know not from reading the sparse libretto, but from listening to the orchestra. What composer Tan has said about this opera in general applies particularly well to this scene: "I think sounds and different musical cultures guide my own development, leading me through a deeper journey. . . . From Medieval [Western] chants, from Western Opera to Beijing Opera, from orchestra to sitar, pipa and Tibetan ritual horns—the fusion of musical sounds from all corners of the globe is the definition of *Marco Polo* to me."

FIGURE 37–9
Tan Dun.

© Ted Thai/Time Life Pictures/Getty Images

a fusion of the world's music

Listening Guide   Tan Dun
"Waiting to Depart" from *Marco Polo* (1996)

6
6/7

Genre: opera
Situation: Marco Polo stands at the edge of Piazza San Marco in Venice, about to embark on his physical and spiritual journey to the East.

0:00	**7**	Low string drone, like Tibetan chant, and then high string sounds sliding between pitches
0:29		"Reedy" flute plays melody around outline of pentatonic scale (E, F♯, G♯, B, C♯, E)
1:09		(Western) cello continues with melody based on same pentatonic scale
1:42		Romantic-sounding (Western) French horn plays same pentatonic scale
2:02		Voice of Water says, "Listen," accompanied by Chinese pipa*

(continued)

2:14	Voice of Marco says, "Maintain"
2:22	Voices of Water and two Shadows say, "Now journey; listen; now maintain; the journey onward"
3:07	Voice of Marco says, "Preserve; question; read; see"
3:23	Others repeat "Journey," in style of early Western parallel organum*
3:45	Drum and gong enter, then full chorus *fortissimo* with dissonant tone clusters*: "Go; hurry; into; join"
4:34	Low string drone returns, suggesting mystery and vast distances of East

At press time it was not possible to secure a license to reproduce this audio. It is available on Sony Classical CD S2K 62912. The publisher invites instructors to contact Thomson Schirmer for a free copy of this music.

 Use a downloadable, cross-platform animated Active Listening Guide, available at **www.thomsonedu.com/music/wright.**

Key Words

electronic music (**405**)   sampling (**407**)   Minimalism (**410**)
synthesizer (**405**)   scratching (**407**)   globalization (**412**)
musique concrète (**406**)   prepared piano (**408**)
computer music (**407**)   chance music (**408**)

 ## Checklist of Musical Style

Modern: 1900–1985

Representative composers
Stravinsky
Schoenberg
Berg
Webern
Bartók
Prokofiev
Shostakovich
Copland
Zwilich
Gershwin
Bernstein
Sondheim

Principal genres
symphony
solo concerto
string quartet
opera
ballet music
Broadway musical
film music

Melody	Wide-ranging disjunct lines, often chromatic and dissonant; angularity accentuated by use of octave displacement
Harmony	Highly dissonant; dissonance no longer must move to consonance but may move to another dissonance; sometimes two conflicting, but equal, tonal centers sound simultaneously (polytonality); sometimes there is no audible tonal center (atonality)
Rhythm	Vigorous, energetic rhythms; conflicting simultaneous meters (polymeter) and rhythms (polyrhythm) make for temporal complexity
Color	Color becomes agent of form and beauty in and by itself; composers seek new sounds from traditional, acoustical instruments, from electronic instruments and computers, and from noises in environment
Texture	As varied and individual as men and women composing music
Form	A range of extremes: sonata–allegro, rondo, theme and variations benefit from Neo-classical revival; twelve-tone procedure allows for almost mathematical formal control; forms and processes of classical music, jazz, and pop music begin to influence one another in exciting new ways

Postmodern: 1945–present

Nearly impossible to generalize as to musical style; major stylistic trends not yet discernible

Barriers between high art and low art removed; all art judged to be of more or less equal value

Experimentation with electronic music and computer-generated sound

Previously accepted fundamentals of music, such as discrete pitches and division of octave into twelve equal pitches, often abandoned

Narrative music (goal-oriented music) rejected

Chance music permits random "happenings" and noises from the environment to shape a work

Introduction of visual and performance media into written musical score

Instruments from outside tradition of Western classical music (electric guitar, sitar, kazoo) prescribed in score

Experimentation with new notational styles within musical scores (sketches, diagrams, prose instructions)

Representative composers
Varèse
Cage
Glass
Reich
Partch
Adams
Tavener
Pärt
Tan

Principal genres
no common genres; each work of art creates genre unique to itself

PART VII

American Popular Music

Every nation has its popular music, the music all the people know and love, not merely an educated few. Today, CDs of popular music outsell those of classical music by more than ten to one. For the most part, popular music is simple and direct, requiring little or no formal training in music. It is intended to be enjoyed for the moment, without particular concern for lasting artistic value.

The United States has perhaps the most heterogeneous population in the world, and American popular music reflects this richness and diversity. Folk ballads, fiddle tunes, Native American songs, cowboy songs, blues, ragtime,

| 1880 | 1890 | 1900 | 1910 | 1920 | 1930 | 1940 |

AMERICAN POPULAR MUSIC

1880s–1890s Songs of Stephen Foster enjoy popularity

1880s–1890s Blues originates in South

1890–1910 Tin Pan Alley becomes center for creation of popular songs

● 1890s Scott Joplin's ragtime music becomes rage

1900–1920 Classic New Orleans–style jazz originates

CORBIS/Bettmann

1914–1918 World War I

● 1920s "Roaring Twenties" or "Jazz Age"

● 1924 George Gershwin composes "Rhapsody in Blue"

● 1924 Bessie Smith makes her first blues recording in New York

● 1925 Louis Armstrong makes his first jazz recording in Chicago

● 1925 F. Scott Fitzgerald publishes *The Great Gatsby*

● 1929 Stock market crash; beginning of Great Depression

● 1930 Big bands and swing bands emerge

1939–1945 World War II

gospel hymns, military band music, parlor songs, Broadway show tunes, jazz, swing, rhythm and blues, rock, hip-hop, and rap—these are but some among the many musical genres that form the American vernacular tradition. With the advent of jazz in the early twentieth century, American popular music gained prominence throughout the world. Even such classical composers such as Debussy, Ravel, and Stravinsky were captivated, incorporating the infectious rhythms of jazz into their "learned" scores. Today, American—and American-influenced—popular music continues to dominate the airwaves and digital downloads around the globe. Although there are now French rappers and Korean remakers of Michael Jackson–style pop, the original designers of these styles, and much more, were, in the words of Bruce Springsteen "Born in the USA."

© Reuters/Corbis

| 1950 | 1960 | 1970 | 1980 | 1990 | 2000 | 2010 |

AMERICAN POPULAR MUSIC

1945–1955 Charlie Parker and
Dizzy Gillespie generate bebop

● 1950s Rhythm and blues, precursor
of rock 'n' roll, emerges in South

1950s–1960s Elvis is king

● 1957 Leonard Bernstein composes *West Side Story*

● 1964 The Beatles appear on *Ed Sullivan Show*,
launching "British Invasion"

● 1982 Michael Jackson releases *Thriller*,
best-selling album of all time

● 1985 Rap music begins to enter
mainstream charts

1991–1994 Grunge music
peaks in popularity

Photofest

● 2001 Apple releases
first iPod

● 2006
U2 marks thirtieth year
since their formation

CORBIS

Blues and Early Jazz

The origins of blues and jazz are to be found in folk music. Typically, **folk music** springs from rural communities and is passed along by oral transmission. Because folksongs such as "Barbara Allen" and "Tom Dooley" are not usually written down in musical notation, the music and text continually evolve from one generation to the next. Moreover, true folk music is the product not of an identifiable individual but rather of a people's heritage, whether they be Anglo-Irish settlers or West African slaves. Today's popular music, on the other hand, is often created in some form of written musical notation and usually springs not from the community but from the mind of a single known artist or artistic team. Mass communication and easy transportation have blurred many cultural distinctions between ethnic groups in the United States, just as globalization has homogenized cultures worldwide. Despite the diminishing importance of folk music in our daily lives, it is important to recognize that much of today's popular music—blues, jazz, country music, rock, and others—grew out of earlier, unwritten folk traditions.

BLUES

Why, where, and how the blues originated is a story that will probably never be fully told. We cannot even hazard a guess as to who gave this style of singing the name "blues," though the expression "the blue devils" had been used to describe a melancholy mood since Shakespeare's time. All that can be said with certainty is that the **blues** is a form of black folksong that originated in the South sometime during the 1880s and 1890s. Like all true folk music, the blues was passed along by oral tradition, one performer learning directly from another without benefit of written music. Comparisons with other forms of folk music suggest that the blues had two immediate ancestors. First and most important was the work song and field holler (or cry) of the black laborers, which bequeathed to the blues a wailing vocal style, a particular scale (see later), and a body of subjects or topics for singing the blues. The second was the Anglo-American folk ballad, which imparted the regular, predictable pattern of chord changes that characterizes the blues. Blues was first printed as sheet music in 1912 (*The Memphis Blues* and *The Dallas Blues*), and the first blues recordings, all made by black artists, were cut in 1920.

A singer sings the blues to relieve a melancholy soul, to give vent to feelings of pain and anger. Poverty, loneliness, oppression, family troubles, infidelity, and separation are typical subjects of the blues. The lyrics are arranged in a succession of stanzas (usually three to six to a song), and each stanza is made up of three lines. The second line normally repeats the first, and the third rounds off the idea and concludes with a rhyme. At the end of each line, an instrument inserts a short response, called an **instrumental break,** as a way of replying to the cry of the voice. Thus the blues perpetuates the age-old African performing style of "call and response," the form of which is shown in the following stanza from the *Preaching Blues:*

a form of African-American folksong

a succession of stanzas

an African performing style of "call and response"

418

Call	Response
The blues is a lowdown, achin' heart disease,	(instrumental break)
The blues is a lowdown, achin' heart disease,	(instrumental break)
It's like consumption, killin' you by degrees.	(instrumental break)

a stanza of three lines

By the 1920s, the guitar had become the accompanying instrument favored by blues singers. Not only could it supply a solid harmonic support, but it also provided an expressive "second voice" to answer the previous call of the singer. "Bending" the guitar strings at the frets produced a moaning, mournful sound in keeping with the general feeling of the blues.

guitar accompaniment

The object of the blues is not so much to tell a story, as in the white folk ballad, as to express emotion. The voice sometimes moans and sometimes shouts, it is often hoarse and raspy, and it always twists and bends the pitch. Instead of hitting a tone directly, the singer usually approaches it by slide from above or below. In addition, a particular scale, called the **blues scale,** is used in place of a major or minor scale. The blues scale has seven notes, but the third, fifth, and seventh are sometimes flat, sometimes natural, and sometimes in between. The three "in-between" tones are called **blue notes.** The blues scale is an integral part of virtually all African-American folk music, including the work song and spiritual as well as the blues.

EXAMPLE 38–1

blues scale

Good blues singers indulge in much spontaneous expression, adding and removing text and improvising around the basic melody as the spirit moves them. Such liberties are possible because these mournful songs are usually built above the bedrock of the twelve-bar blues* harmonic pattern that repeats, over and over, one statement for each stanza of text (see page 43). Singing the blues most often involves singing in a slow $\frac{4}{4}$ above this simple I–IV–I–V–I chord progression in the following manner:

Vocal lines:	Line 1		break		Line 2		break		Line 3		break	
Chord:	I ———————————				IV————		I ———		V————		I	
Measure:	1	2	3	4	5	6	7	8	9	10	11	12

twelve-bar blues harmony

Sometimes additional chords are inserted between the basic ones for greater harmonic interest. Yet the simplicity of the pattern is its greatest strength. Thousands of tunes have been constructed over this basic harmonic progression, by solo singers, by solo pianists, by New Orleans–style jazz combos, and by rock 'n' roll bands.

Bessie Smith (1894–1937)

Although there have been and are many great blues singers—Blind Lemon Jefferson, Leadbelly, Muddy Waters, and B. B. King, to name just a few—perhaps the greatest of them all was Bessie Smith (Fig. 38–1), called the "Empress of

the Blues." A native of Chattanooga, Tennessee, Smith was "discovered" singing in a bar in Selma, Alabama, and brought to New York to record for Columbia Records. The blues recordings she made between 1924 and 1927 catapulted her to the top of the world of popular music. In her first full year as a recording artist, her disks sold more than 2 million copies, and she became the highest-paid black artist, male or female, of the day. In fact, all of the great blues singers who achieved recording success during the 1920s were women, perhaps because so many of the texts of the blues have to do with male–female relations and are written from the woman's perspective. Tragically, Smith's career was cut short by a fatal automobile accident in 1937.

"Lost Your Head Blues," recorded in 1926, reveals the huge, sweeping voice of Bessie Smith. She was capable of great power, even harshness, one moment, and then in the next breath could deliver a phrase of tender beauty. She could hit a note right on the head if she wanted to, or bend, dip, and glide into the pitch, as she does, for example, on the words "days," "long," and "nights" in the last stanza of "Lost Your Head Blues." In this recording, Bessie Smith is backed by Fletcher Henderson (piano) and Joe Smith (trumpet). The piece begins with a four-bar introduction, after which the voice enters and the twelve-bar blues harmony starts up, one full statement of the pattern for each of the five stanzas of text. Smith continually varies her melody above the repeating bass by means of vocal inflections and off-key shadings. Her expressive vocal line, the soulful, improvised responses played by the trumpet, and the repeating twelve-bar harmony carried by the piano are the essence of the blues.

FIGURE 38–1
Bessie Smith, the "Empress of the Blues," was a physically powerful woman with an exceptionally flexible, expressive voice.

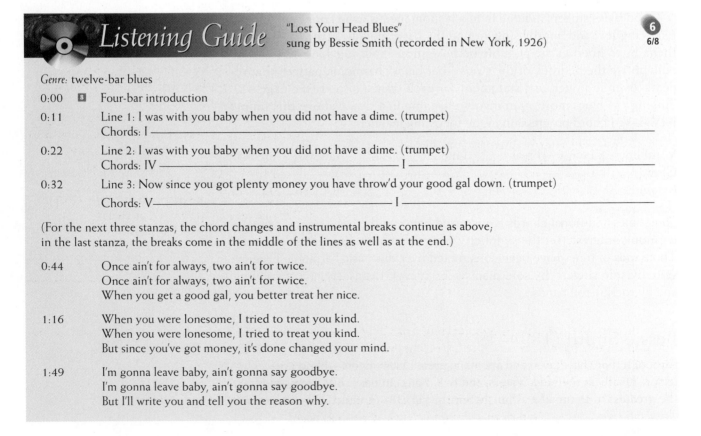

Listening Guide

"Lost Your Head Blues"
sung by Bessie Smith (recorded in New York, 1926)

6
6/8

Genre: twelve-bar blues

0:00   8   Four-bar introduction

0:11   Line 1: I was with you baby when you did not have a dime. (trumpet)
             Chords: I ——

0:22   Line 2: I was with you baby when you did not have a dime. (trumpet)
             Chords: IV ————————————————————— I ——————————————————

0:32   Line 3: Now since you got plenty money you have throw'd your good gal down. (trumpet)
             Chords: V————————————————— I ——————————————————————

(For the next three stanzas, the chord changes and instrumental breaks continue as above;
in the last stanza, the breaks come in the middle of the lines as well as at the end.)

0:44   Once ain't for always, two ain't for twice.
             Once ain't for always, two ain't for twice.
             When you get a good gal, you better treat her nice.

1:16   When you were lonesome, I tried to treat you kind.
             When you were lonesome, I tried to treat you kind.
             But since you've got money, it's done changed your mind.

1:49   I'm gonna leave baby, ain't gonna say goodbye.
             I'm gonna leave baby, ain't gonna say goodbye.
             But I'll write you and tell you the reason why.

2:20	Days† are lonesome, nights are long†.
	Days are lonesome, nights† are so long.
	I'm a good† ol' gal, but I've just been treated wrong.

†Notice vocal "slides" here.

 Use a downloadable, cross-platform animated Active Listening Guide, available at **www.thomsonedu.com/music/wright.**

Listening Exercise 46

Smith
"Lost Your Head Blues"

 ThomsonNOW™
To take this Listening Exercise online and receive feedback or email answers to your instructor, go to *ThomsonNOW* for this chapter.

"Lost Your Head Blues" tells the tale of a "good ol' gal" who has "just been treated wrong." In a format typical of the blues, Bessie Smith belts out five stanzas of text, each with three lines. The questions pertain to issues particular to the genre of the blues. As you listen, pay special attention to the extraordinary power, subtlety, and flexibility of Smith's voice.

1. (0:00–0:10) Which two instruments play during the four-bar introduction?
   a. piano and trumpet
   b. piano and drums
   c. drums and trumpet
2. Within each of the five stanzas of lyrics, the twelve-bar blues harmony is heard how many times?
   a. once   b. twice   c. three times
3. Excluding the partial statement in the four-bar introduction, the full twelve-bar blues pattern is played how many times?
   a. once   b. three times   c. five times
4. Which instrument always sets the harmony (the twelve-bar blues pattern) to support the soloist?
   a. trumpet   b. drums   c. piano
5. Who always presents the "call" (as at 0:11–0:17, 0:22–0:28, and 0:32–0:40)?
   a. trumpet
   b. piano
   c. drums
   d. voice

6. Who always answers with the "response" (as at 0:18–0:21, 0:29–0:31, and 0:40–0:43)?
   a. trumpet
   b. piano
   c. drums
   d. voice
7. How many performers are there in this recording?
   a. two   b. three   c. four
8. Which two performers continually slide into and around (bend) their pitches in the tradition of African as well as European folk singing?
   a. voice and piano
   b. trumpet and piano
   c. voice and trumpet
9. Why does this recording last only three minutes?
   a. because in the 1920s a single side of a 78 record could hold only about three minutes of music
   b. because that is all the time needed to perform the twelve-bar blues pattern once
10. Review three other examples of accompanied singing discussed in this book and identify which is similar to "Lost Your Head Blues"—which is also a sad song built upon a harmonic ostinato*.
    a. Monteverdi, "Powerful Spirit" (page 120)
    b. Purcell, "When I am laid in earth" (page 126)
    c. Mahler, *I Am Lost to the World* (page 334)

The impact of the blues on popular music has been enormous. Many recent pop singers have embraced the blues (the names of some are given on page 43). So, too, have jazz greats ranging from Louis Armstrong ("Gut Bucket Blues") at the beginning of the twentieth century, to Wynton Marsalis ("The Majesty of the Blues") at the end. Equally important, it was from the blues and its offspring, rhythm and blues, that rock 'n' roll was born.

impact of the blues

EARLY JAZZ

Jazz has been called America's classical music. Like America itself, jazz is an amalgam, a mixture of many different influences. Foremost among these, of course, are the traditional musical practices of Africa, as manifested in the spirituals and blues of African-Americans in the South. But jazz also contains European elements: marches and hymns, in addition to fiddle tunes and dances from the British Isles as preserved in the folk music of white Appalachia. The complex rhythms, percussive sounds, and bending vocal style of African-American music merged with the four-square phrasing and strong, regular harmonies of the Anglo-American tradition to produce a dynamic new sound.

Jazz originated about 1910 almost simultaneously in many southern and midwestern cities: New Orleans, St. Louis, Kansas City, and Chicago, to name a few. Because its style was different from city to city and because various other styles of jazz would later evolve—swing*, bebop*, cool*, and jazz-fusion* among others—jazz must be defined in rather general terms. **Jazz** is lively, energetic music with pulsating rhythms and scintillating syncopations, usually played by either a small instrumental ensemble (a combo) or a larger group (a big band). Jazz tends to be polyphonic, since several instruments play independent lines. And it also includes a strong element of improvisation that gives individual performers the freedom to follow their own flights of musical fancy. Tension and excitement are created as virtuosic soloists play off against a regularly changing harmony and a steady beat provided by the rhythm section (usually drums, piano, and a string bass). Playing jazz is like playing a competitive team sport: It requires teamwork, imagination, skill, and endurance, and the outcome is never certain!

Ragtime: A Precursor of Jazz

Ragtime music was an immediate precursor of jazz and shares with it many of the same rhythmic features. To black musicians, "to rag" meant to play or sing music in a heavily syncopated, jazzy style—with "ragged time." Ragtime music originated in brothels, saloons, and dancehalls during the 1890s—the Gay Nineties—and the jaunty, upbeat sound of ragtime captured the spirit of that age. Most rags were written by black pianists who played in houses of ill repute because it was difficult in those years for black musicians to find employment elsewhere. First published in 1897, piano rags took America by storm, with more than two thousand titles appearing in print by the end of World War I. Sold as sheet music of a thin page or two, piano rags moved quickly from the saloon into middle-class homes, where musically literate amateurs played them on the parlor piano.

The undisputed "King of Ragtime" was Scott Joplin (1868–1917) (Fig. 38–2). The son of a slave, Joplin managed to acquire for himself a solid grounding in classical music while he earned a living playing in honky-tonk bars in and around St. Louis. In 1899, he published "Maple Leaf Rag," which sold an astonishing one million copies. Though he went on to write other immensely popular rags, such as "The Entertainer" and "Peacherine Rag," Joplin gradually shed the image of barroom pianist and moved to New York to compose rag-oriented opera.

The "Maple Leaf Rag," which was immensely popular at the turn of the twentieth century, is typical of the style of Joplin and his fellow ragtime composers. Its form is similar to that of an American military march of those same

roots

jazz style

FIGURE 38–2
One of the few surviving images of ragtime composer Scott Joplin.

CORBIS/Bettmann

years, consisting of a succession of phrases (strains), each sixteen bars in length. The harmony, however, is distinctly European, moving in purposeful chord progressions with slight chromatic inflections—Joplin knew his Schubert and Chopin! Yet what makes ragtime so infectious is its bouncy, syncopated rhythm. Syncopation, of course, is the momentary displacement of an accent from on the beat to off the beat (see page 19). In piano ragtime, the left hand keeps a regular "um-pah, um-pah" beat, usually in $\frac{2}{4}$ meter, while the right hand lays on syncopations against it. In the following example from the "Maple Leaf Rag," syncopation (S) occurs when long notes (either an eighth note or two sixteenth notes tied together) sound off (between) the steady eighth-note beats of the bass.

heavy syncopation in the melody

EXAMPLE 38–2

As you follow the Listening Guide, you may be interested to know that the "Maple Leaf Rag" is performed here by composer Scott Joplin himself. This recording was originally made in 1916 not on a vinyl record, but rather on a mechanical piano roll, and only later transferred to vinyl and ultimately to digital format. You will likely be surprised by the slow tempo, but as Joplin warned at the beginning of one of his publications, "Never play ragtime fast."

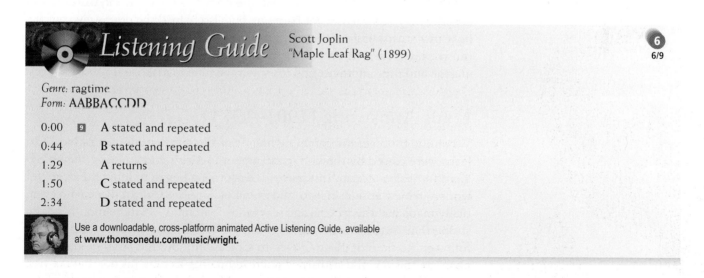

Listening Guide

Scott Joplin
"Maple Leaf Rag" (1899)

6
6/9

Genre: ragtime
Form: **AABBACCDD**

0:00	9	A stated and repeated
0:44		B stated and repeated
1:29		A returns
1:50		C stated and repeated
2:34		D stated and repeated

Use a downloadable, cross-platform animated Active Listening Guide, available at **www.thomsonedu.com/music/wright**.

New Orleans Jazz

Although jazz sprang up almost simultaneously in towns up and down the Mississippi River, its focal point and probable place of origin was New Orleans. Not only was New Orleans the home of many of the early jazz greats—King Oliver (1885–1938), Jelly Roll Morton (1890–1941), and Louis Armstrong (1901–1971)—but it enjoyed an exceptionally lively and varied

New Orleans, a musical and cultural melting pot

musical life that encouraged the development of new musical styles. Culturally, New Orleans looked more toward France and the Caribbean than it did to the Anglo-American North. The city air was filled not only with opera tunes, marches, and ballroom dances from imperial France but also African-American blues and ragtime, and Cuban dance rhythms. The end of the Spanish-American War (1898) brought a flood of used military band instruments into second-hand shops in New Orleans at prices that were affordable even to impoverished blacks. Musicians, black and white alike, found ready employment in ballrooms of the well-to-do, in the bars and brothels of Storyville (a thirty-eight-square-block red-light district in the center of the city), and at parades, picnics, weddings, and funerals associated with the many New Orleans societies and fraternal orders. Music was everywhere. Today, jazz musicians such as Wynton Marsalis, a New Orleans native, are leading the revival of the city and its music following Hurricane Katrina (see Chapter 39).

the style of New Orleans jazz

What marks the sound of **New Orleans jazz**? Syncopation combined with a free treatment of melody. A given march, rag, blues, or popular tune is played with off-beat accents and a spontaneous sliding into and around the pitches of the tune. The rag had strains of sixteen bars, many popular songs of the period had four four-bar phrases, and the traditional blues, as we have seen, consisted of a steady stream of twelve-bar units. Within the square, formal confines of these four-, eight-, twelve-, and sixteen-bar patterns, the New Orleans jazz combo found a security that allowed the solo instruments the greatest sort of freedom of expression. The melody was usually played in some jazzed-up way by a cornet or trumpet; a clarinet supported this lead instrument and further embellished the tune; a trombone added counterpoint against the melody in a lower range; down below, a tuba set the harmonies if the group was marching, but if it did not, that job was handed over to a string bass, piano, banjo, and/or guitar. These same instruments (tuba, string bass, piano, banjo, and guitar), along with the drums, formed the **rhythm section** because they not only set the harmony but also helped the drums give out the beat in a steady fashion. Finally, New Orleans–style bands, then and now, rarely play from written music. They count, or feel, when the chords must change and they improvise and refashion the tune to make it fit those changes.

Louis Armstrong (1901–1971)

When the brothels and gambling houses of the red-light district of New Orleans were closed by the U.S. government in 1917, many places of employment for jazz musicians disappeared. Performers began to look elsewhere for work—in New York, Chicago, and even Los Angeles. One of those who eventually made his way to Chicago was Louis "Satchmo" ("Satchelmouth") Armstrong (Fig. 38–3). Armstrong was born in New Orleans in 1901, and in 1923 followed his mentor, King Oliver, to Chicago to join the latter's Creole Jazz Band. By this time, Armstrong was already recognized by his peers as the best jazz trumpeter alive. He soon formed his own band in Chicago, the Hot Five, to make what was to become a series of landmark recordings. When the vogue of classic New Orleans–style jazz gave way to the sound of the swing band around 1930, Armstrong moved to New York, where he "fronted"—played as featured soloist—a number of large bands. He was an early practitioner of "scat singing"—singing nonsense syllables in jazz style—and eventually became known as much for the gravelly sound of his voice, in songs such as "Hello Dolly" and "Mack the Knife," as for his trumpet playing. His last years

a rags to riches life

were spent in almost continual travel, sent around the world by the U.S. State Department as "Ambassador Satchmo." He died at his home in Queens, New York, in 1971.

Although cut in Chicago, Armstrong's early disks are classics of New Orleans–style jazz. The tune "Willie the Weeper" was recorded by Armstrong's expanded band, the Hot Seven, in 1927. As to who "composed" the piece, we'll never know. Like much folk music, and African-American music in particular, "Willie the Weeper" was worked out by the entire group, following two basic chord progressions, the first in a major key, the second in a minor one. Certainly, none of "Willie the Weeper" was ever written down in musical notation. As Armstrong's drummer, Baby Dodds, said, "We weren't a bunch of fellows to write down anything." Instead, they relied on "head arrangements," a combination of aural memory (remembering the tune and the harmony) and spontaneous improvisation, in which each member of the group took his turn as soloist with the tune. Here the tune in major is sixteen bars long, while the contrasting one in minor lasts eight bars. In a jazz piece of this sort, each presentation of the tune is called a **chorus,** whether played by a soloist or the entire ensemble. The underlying chord progressions and the outline of the melody provide a framework for the spontaneous improvisations of the players during each chorus. Call it what you will—precision abandon, bonded independence, controlled chaos—the joyful exuberance of these extraordinary musicians cannot be denied.

FIGURE 38–3
Louis "Satchmo" Armstrong.

 Listening Guide "Willie the Weeper," played by Louis Armstrong and his Hot Seven (recorded in Chicago, 1927)

 Intro 8

Genre: New Orleans jazz

0:00	8	Four-bar introduction
0:05		Chorus 1 (16 bars): full ensemble; trumpet (Armstrong) and trombone play the tune
0:25		Chorus 2: Armstrong varies tune
0:46		Minor chorus 1 (8 bars): trombone and tuba play tune
0:57		Minor chorus 2: trombone and tuba repeat tune
1:07		Chorus 3: trombone solo
1:28		Chorus 4: extraordinary clarinet solo
1:49		Minor chorus 3: trumpet solo
1:59		Minor chorus 4: piano solo
2:09		Chorus 5: guitar solo
2:29		Chorus 6: Armstrong carries tune
2:49		Chorus 7: trumpet, trombone, and clarinet improvise around tune with wild abandon

Use a downloadable, cross-platform animated Active Listening Guide, available at **www.thomsonedu.com/music/wright**.

Big Bands and Swing

The recordings of Louis Armstrong and the Hot Seven sold as fast as they could be pressed. Jazz became the rage of the 1920s, just as ragtime had been the craze at the turn of the century. It was, in the words of novelist F. Scott Fitzgerald, the "Jazz Age." So popular had jazz become that it was now

© Bettmann/Corbis

Yale Music Library, Benny Goodman Archives

FIGURES 38–4 AND 38-5
(above left) Duke Ellington (seated at the piano) and his big band in 1943. Unlike other band leaders of this time, Ellington was as much a composer and arranger as he was a performer. (above right) Benny Goodman, the "King of Swing," during a radio broadcast in the early 1940s.

big bands play swing music

performed in ballrooms, large dancehalls, and movie theaters, in addition to the smaller bars and supper clubs where New Orleans–style jazz had its home. And just as the small supper club gradually gave way to the ballroom, so, too, did the small jazz combo cede pride of place to the big band—to be heard above the stomping and swaying of many hundreds of pairs of feet, an ensemble larger than the traditional New Orleans combo of five or seven players was needed. Thus was born the big-band era, the glory days of the bands of Duke Ellington (1889–1974), Benny Goodman (1909–1986), Count Basie (1904–1984), and Glenn Miller (1904–1944).

Though not "big" by the standard of today's marching band, the **big band** of the 1930s and 1940s was at least double the size of the New Orleans–style jazz combo. In 1943, for example, Duke Ellington's orchestra consisted of four trumpets, three trombones, five reed players (men who played both clarinet and saxophone), plus a rhythm section of piano, string bass, guitar, and drums—a total of sixteen players (Fig. 38–4). Most big-band compositions were worked out ahead of time and set down in written arrangements called "charts." The fact that jazz musicians now for the first time had to play from written notation suggests a desire for a more disciplined, polished, orchestral sound. The addition of a quintet of saxophones gave the ensemble a more mellow, blended quality. The new sound has little of the sharp bite and wild syncopation of the earlier New Orleans–style jazz. Rather, the music is mellow, bouncy, and flowing. In a word, it "swings." **Swing,** then, can be said to be a popular style of jazz played by a big band in the 1930s and 1940s (Fig. 38–5). The recent revival of "swing dancing" shows that an elegant dance style that is distinctly jazzy can enjoy enduring popularity.

ThomsonNOW
ThomsonNOW for *Listening to Music, 5th Edition,* and *Listening to Western Music* will assist you in understanding the content of this chapter with lesson plans generated for your specific needs. In addition, you may complete this chapter's Listening Exercise in ThomsonNOW's interactive environment, as well as download Active Listening Guides and other materials that will help you succeed in this course.

Key Words

folk music (**418**)
blues (**418**)
instrumental break (**418**)
blues scale (**419**)

blue note (**419**)
jazz (**422**)
ragtime (**422**)
New Orleans jazz (**424**)

rhythm section (**424**)
chorus (**425**)
big band (**426**)
swing (**426**)

CULTURAL CONTEXT

African Influence in American Popular Music

The blues, as we have seen, was greatly influenced by the experiences of African-Americans in the rural South and reflect African musical practices. In fact, almost all forms of twentieth-century American popular music—blues, ragtime, jazz, rhythm and blues, rock 'n' roll, funk, rap, and hip-hop—show, in one way or another, ties to African music. Most of the slaves arriving in the United States came from the western part of Sub-Saharan Africa—from the western part of the continent below the Sahara Desert. Today, the countries of Sub-Saharan West Africa have names such as Senegal, Guinea, Ghana, Benin, and Ivory Coast, though in fact the boundaries of most of these nations are more or less artificial lines drawn by nineteenth-century European rulers. Real unity and loyalty in Africa rests within the structure of the countless tribes, each of which possesses its own history, language, and music. It is the music of the West African tribes that was transported to the Americas and, over the course of time, came to influence and, in some cases, largely shape the traditions of American popular music. But what are the characteristics of African music that are most evident in American popular music?

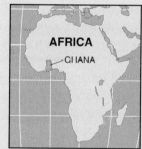

Music as Social Activity

Music permeates every aspect of African life. Africans sing or play while chopping wood, pounding grain, paddling a canoe, harvesting crops, weeding a field, burying a chief, or stamping letters at the post office. Singing keeps the workers together and makes their tasks go faster. When people perform classical music in the West, some play, others listen. Westerners have performers and an audience. In Africa, the audience and the performers are one and the same. Similarly, there is usually no class of professional musician; everyone participates. When transferred to the Americas, these traditions produced the field hollers of the cotton or tobacco pickers and the line songs of the

railroad gangs, all characterized by a call of the leader and the response of the group. The name of the "composer" is not known, for usually it is all the people.

The Importance of Rhythm

Complex harmonies distinguish Western classical music. Subtle melodic gradations characterize traditional Indian and Chinese music. The distinguishing quality of African music, however, is rhythm. Yet rhythm in African music is not like that in Western art music. Western performers invariably start together at a beginning point, an opening downbeat*, and are guided by the regular recurrence of downbeats and upbeats. All musicians lock onto and play with or against this single, common, regulating pulse. In African music, by contrast, the individual parts are far more likely to start independently and to stay that

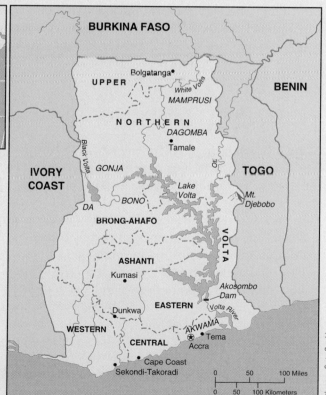

(left) The continent of Africa, and (right) the country of Ghana situated in the western portion of Sub-Saharan Africa.

way. There is usually no common downbeat around which the players gravitate. Each part has its own downbeat, pulse, and rhythm, and often its own meter. What results is polymeter*, a complex of several layers of musical rhythms and meters. We have met polymeter before—specifically, in the music of the European avant-garde (see page 373). The difference between the Western European and the African use of polymeter, again, is the absence in African music of a shared downbeat, as can be seen in this musical example of two African drumming patterns sounding together, each with its own downbeat, rhythm, and meter:

There are always at least two rhythms sounding in African music, which accounts for its complexity. We Westerners perceive it as complex, indeed are often baffled by it, because we can't find a unifying beat to which to tap our feet. The African-influenced Latin pop music and the Afro-Cuban jazz of today seem exciting and energetic because there are so many rhythms and meters sounding at once.

The Importance of Drums

Many musical instruments are indigenous to Africa—flutes, whistles, harps, bells, even trumpets—but it is the drum we immediately associate with African culture. Drums are at the heart of almost all group music-making and all dances. African drums come in a staggering variety of shapes and sizes. There are hand drums, stick drums, water drums, slit drums (a hollowed-out log with a long slit on top), and talking drums. **Talking drums** are those upon which tension can be placed on the drum head by tightening the skin around it. In this way the pitch of the drum can be changed causing it to "speak." African drum makers sometimes place charms within the drum—pebbles from the yard of the village gossip so as to make the drum talk freely, or a bit of skin of a lion to make it roar. When slaves arrived on the shores of America they were often forbidden from using these talking

drums because the masters were afraid that this secret musical language would be used to foment rebellion. Following the Civil War, African drums reappeared. Later, during the 1940s, the insertion of strong drum beats and back beats* helped transform the blues into rhythm and blues and, ultimately, into rock 'n' roll.

Bending the Pitch

Western classical music is one of the few musical cultures that places melody upon a rigid grid of pitches—the unvarying notes of the major and minor scales. Western melodies move directly from one specific frequency to the next with no sliding in between. In large measure this is because Western music, over the course of the centuries, has become heavily dependent upon written notation and fixed-pitch instruments such as the piano and organ. Other non-Western musical cultures—those that rely on the oral rather than the written communication of music—are marked by melodies of subtler nuances of pitch. African music is among these orally communicated musics that allow for greater melodic flexibility or "bending of pitch." The most exciting part of the music is often what happens between the pitches, not on them. African slaves brought their traditional modes of singing with them to antebellum America. *Slave Songs of the United States* (1867) appeared shortly after the Civil War, and in the preface the white editor remarked that black musicians "seem not infrequently to strike sounds that cannot be precisely represented by the gamut [scale]"—a suggestion that the bending blue notes of the blues scale (page 419) were already audible.

Call and Response

The structure of African music is governed in large measure by a principle of performance called "call and response" (see also page 418). In **call and response** singing, a lead singer announces an opening phrase, and the chorus utters a short, simple reply. The soloist returns, extending and varying the call, to which the chorus responds again in simple, stable fashion. The soloist may enter and depart according to his or her whim. The chorus, however, responds at regular and predictable intervals. Instrumentalists can also engage in call and response. A master drummer, for example, can imitate a conversation with a chorus of subordinates. Sometimes the performing forces are mixed: A vocal soloist might engender a response from a chorus of drums. Today call and response remains an important structural feature of African-American spirituals, blues, gospel, and soul. When James Brown, the "Godfather of Soul," sings, "Get up" and we then hear a collective "Get on up," we have a classic example of African call and response.

A Praise-Song from Ghana

As a way of hearing what African music sounds like today—and what it might have sounded like before coming to America—let us examine a traditional drum-accompanied song from Ghana. **Ghana** is a country in West Africa (see map, page 427) somewhat smaller than the size of Texas with a population of 21 million people. In its northeast corner lies a region called Dagomba, which supports a people called the Dagombas who speak a language called Dagbani, one of the forty-four official languages of Ghana. The primary musical instruments of the Dagombas are the drums—specifically, the dondon and the gongon. The **dondon** (see figures) is a talking drum* shaped like an hourglass, with heads at opposite ends.

Leather thongs connect the two heads. Pulling on the thongs increases the tension on the heads and thereby raises the pitch. The **gongon** is a large, barrel-like drum that produces a deep tone. It can also create the rattle-like sound of a snare drum* because a snare string is stretched across the upper part of the face of the drum. Both the dondon and the gongon are struck with a stick in a wrist-flicking motion (see figures). Five or six dondons and one or two gongons typically constitute the "orchestra" for dance music and praise-songs in this region of Ghana.

Kasuan Kura is a praise-song of the Dagombas, a song that tells the history of an important member of the tribe. Its structure is call and response. The vocal soloist relates the history of the honored figure while the chorus repeats the name of this esteemed ancestor "Kasuan Kura" throughout. The piece begins with dondon drummers manipulating their instruments to make them speak. Immediately thereafter (at 0:02), the gongons enter, recognizable by their snare rattle and deeper sound. The gongons play throughout the song, while the higher-pitched dondons come and go. Whenever dondons and gongons are heard together, complex polyrhythm and polymeter result. When gongons merely support the choral response, a rather simple rhythm in a clear duple meter emerges. Thus two musical conversations develop:

A group of dondon and gongon drummers from Dagomba, Ghana.

John Miller Chernoff, Pittsburgh

John Miller Chernoff

The dondon is a talking drum, so called because the player can pull on the leather thongs connecting the two heads to raise the pitch, as we do in our speech.

one between the solo singer and chorus, and a second between the complex dondon-gongon mixture and the simpler rhythmic texture of the gongons alone. In the course of this short piece, the soloist's calls become more elaborate and exuberant, just as the drumming on the dondons grows more excited.

talking drum
(428)

call and
response
(428)

Ghana (429)
dondon (429)
gongon (429)

 Listening Guide

The People of Dagomba, Ghana
Kasuan Kura
(recorded in Ghana by John Miller Chernoff)

 6
6/21

0:00	21	Dondons begin
0:02		Gongons enter
0:12		Solo vocal call accompanied by dondons and gongons
0:16		Choral response accompanied by gongons alone
0:21		Solo call accompanied by dondons and gongons
0:25		Choral response accompanied by gongons alone
0:29		Call and response continues, accompanied as before
1:25		Dondon and gongon patterns become more complex
1:32		Call and response continues to the end

Use a downloadable, cross-platform animated Active Listening Guide, available at **www.thomsonedu.com/music/wright**.

Postwar Jazz

For the United States of America, the first half of the twentieth century was an "age of anxiety" marked by two world wars and the Great Depression. By contrast, the second half of the century was an "age of prosperity" in which the income of most Americans greatly increased. But while many popular musicians became wealthy, jazz artists generally did not. After World War II, much of the attention enjoyed by jazz shifted to other forms of popular music, especially rock 'n' roll and rock. Part of the decline in jazz's popularity was brought about by the artists themselves. They chose to make the jazz melody more abstract and less tuneful, the beat less clear (thus less conducive to dancing), and the music more an artistic statement than a popular success. Jazz, it seemed, was moving away from popular music into the realm of "high" art. This development can be most clearly seen in a new style of jazz that emerged after World War II—bebop.

BEBOP

During World War II, big-band swing jazz was heard at home on the radio, on jukeboxes, at college proms, in hotel ballrooms, in theaters, and even on hastily erected stages on the battlefields of France. With the end of the war, however, swing suddenly fell out of favor with both listeners and practitioners. Many of the best young postwar performers felt that playing from written big-band charts limited their creative freedom. They wanted to return to a style in which improvisation was more important than composition, and in which the performer, not the composer or arranger, was king. Choosing their playing partners carefully, they "jammed" in small, select groups in nightclubs in midtown Manhattan and in Harlem, and in so doing created a new virtuosic style of jazz called bebop.

return of the jazz combo

Bebop, or "bop," is angular, hard-driving jazz played by a small combo without written music. It derives its name from the fact that the fast, snappy melody sounds like the words "bebop, bebop" said quickly. A typical bebop ensemble consists of a quintet of trumpet, saxophone, piano, double bass, and drums—many fewer players than in a big band. The best soloists, among them saxophonist Charlie Parker (1920–1955) and trumpeter Dizzy Gillespie (1917–1993), had astonishing technique and played at breakneck speed. Their passion was improvisation, and the solos they created were more complex than those heard in either swing or New Orleans jazz. They played fast, incorporating "double-time" sixteenth-note runs. They also ornamented the melody with so much embellishment that the original tune soon became unrecognizable. Finally, bebop introduced much more complex accompaniments. In place of the basic triad (see page 40), accompanists now used seventh-, ninth-, and eleventh-chords, making the harmony obscure and dissonant. Only the most gifted performers could keep up with the fast tempo and make these difficult chord changes. Bebop was for an elite few.

a frenetic style of playing

"far out" improvisations above obscure harmonies

FIGURE 39–1
Charlie "Bird" Parker.

Charlie "Bird" Parker (1920–1955)

Perhaps the most gifted of the bebop artists was Charlie "Yardbird" or "Bird" Parker (Fig. 39–1), the subject of Clint Eastwood's film *Bird* (1988). Parker was a tragic figure, a drug-addicted, alcoholic, antisocial man whose skills as an improviser and performer, nonetheless, were greater than any other jazz musician, save Louis Armstrong. Indeed, the lives of Armstrong and Parker make an interesting comparison. Both were born into the extreme poverty of the ghetto, Armstrong in New Orleans and Parker in Kansas City, and both rose to the top of their profession through extraordinary talent and hard work. But Armstrong, an extrovert, viewed himself as a public entertainer as much as an artist. Parker, on the other hand, didn't care whether people liked his music, and he managed to alienate everyone around him including, finally, his longtime friend and playing partner Dizzy Gillespie. He died of the effects of his many excesses, alone and broke, at the age of thirty-four. Parker's personal life may have been a mess, but his inventive style of playing changed irrevocably the history of jazz.

In 1950, Parker and Gillespie recorded a bebop version of a sentimental love song called "My Melancholy Baby" (1911). Like many popular tunes from the early part of this century, "My Melancholy Baby" is sixteen bars long and divided into four four-measure phrases (here **ABAC**). After a four-bar introduction by pianist Thelonious Monk, Parker plays the tune more or less "straight," with only moderately complex elaborations. But when Dizzy Gillespie enters for the second chorus, the ornamentation becomes more complex by means of racing thirty-second notes and continues to do so through the third and final chorus, which Monk and Parker divide. Try to follow the original tune of "My Melancholy Baby" as each soloist embroiders it. As you listen, notice that there is no group ensemble playing at the end and no strong beat. Instead, in bebop, we find frenetic solos for a single instrument set against a quiet, relaxed rhythm section. What results is a music more for listening than for dancing. Bebop is the "chamber music" of jazz, a style designed to appeal to only a small number of aficionados in an intimate nightclub setting.

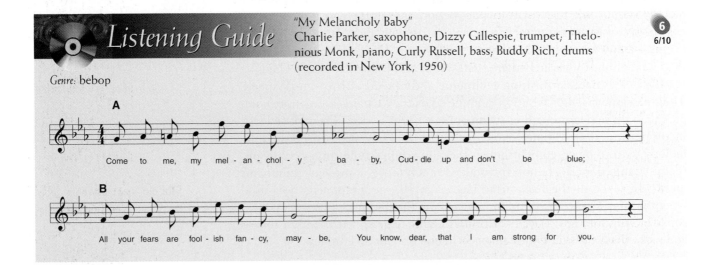

Listening Guide

"My Melancholy Baby"
Charlie Parker, saxophone; Dizzy Gillespie, trumpet; Thelonious Monk, piano; Curly Russell, bass; Buddy Rich, drums
(recorded in New York, 1950)

6
6/10

Genre: bebop

A
Come to me, my mel-an-chol-y ba-by, Cud-dle up and don't be blue;

B
All your fears are fool-ish fan-cy, may-be, You know, dear, that I am strong for you.

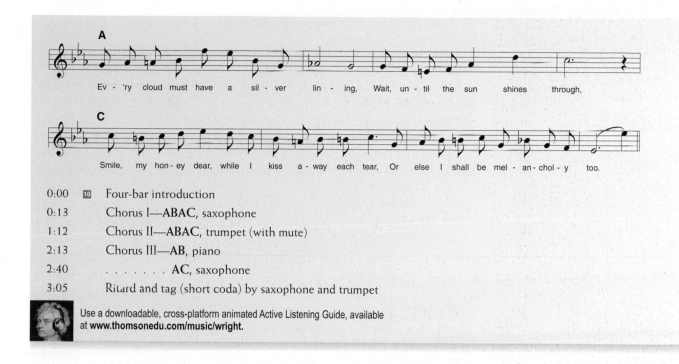

A

Ev - 'ry cloud must have a sil - ver lin - ing, Wait, un - til the sun shines through,

C

Smile, my hon - ey dear, while I kiss a - way each tear, Or else I shall be mel - an - chol - y too.

0:00	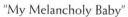 **10**	Four-bar introduction
0:13		Chorus I—**ABAC**, saxophone
1:12		Chorus II—**ABAC**, trumpet (with mute)
2:13		Chorus III—**AB**, piano
2:40		. . . . **AC**, saxophone
3:05		Ritard and tag (short coda) by saxophone and trumpet

 Use a downloadable, cross-platform animated Active Listening Guide, available at **www.thomsonedu.com/music/wright**.

Listening Exercise 47

"My Melancholy Baby"

6
6/10

ThomsonNOW™
To take this Listening Exercise online and receive feedback or email answers to your instructor, go to *ThomsonNOW* for this chapter.

Bebop is a progressive, complex style of jazz with difficult chord changes and dizzying flights of instrumental virtuosity. What makes "My Melancholy Baby" easy to follow is the form: a short introduction, three sixteen-bar choruses, and a short coda. The form is made clear to the listener because there is a change to a new solo instrument at the beginning of each chorus. From one chorus to the next, however, the playing becomes progressively more complex and the tune more heavily disguised by ornamentation. The first five questions help illuminate the musical form, while the second five concentrate on aspects of the bass line.

1. (0:00–0:12) Which instrument solos during the introduction?
   a. saxophone   b. piano   c. trumpet
2. (0:13–1:11) What does the piano do during Charlie Parker's solo in chorus 1?
   a. plays its own frenetic melody against Parker's solo
   b. plays chords quietly in the background
3. (1:12–2:12) During Dizzy Gillespie's trumpet solo of chorus 2, what does saxophonist Parker do?
   a. plays his own frenetic melody against Gillespie's solo
   b. nothing
4. (2:13–3:04) During chorus 3, is Gillespie's trumpet heard?
   a. yes   b. no
5. Which of the forms often employed in classical music is embodied in this piece?
   a. theme and variations
   b. rondo
   c. sonata–allegro
6. Which instrument is playing the bass line in this quintet?
   a. the double bass of the symphony orchestra
   b. the electric bass of the rock band

7. Does the player use a bow or play pizzicato?
   a. bow   b. pizzicato
8. Which figure more accurately reflects the rhythm of the bass?

a.

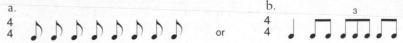

$\frac{4}{4}$ ♩♩ ♩♩ ♩♩ ♩♩   or   b. $\frac{4}{4}$ ♩ ♫ ♫³ ♩

9. Which statement correctly describes the bass line?
   a. It moves mainly in stepwise motion in regular, even notes.
   b. It moves by leaps in highly varied rhythms.
10. This sort of bass line, then, can be said to resemble which musical procedure of the Baroque era?
   a. the ostinato* bass
   b. the walking bass*
   c. the bass pedal point*

COOL JAZZ

By 1950, jazz was no longer young; indeed, it had been around nearly fifty years. Moreover, by mid-century, one could no longer speak of "jazz" and refer to one specific style. The general term "jazz" might refer to one of three sub-genres: New Orleans jazz, swing, or bebop. Bebop was at the forefront, but it was not loved by all—with its fast tempos and biting attacks, bop was almost too hot to handle. An immediate reaction appeared in the form of "cool jazz," which sought to soften bebop's hard-driving sound with a more relaxed feel and less-frenzied solos. Experimentation was also in the air. Making the scene were "modal jazz" (which used new modal harmonies), "electric jazz" (which used electric instruments as well as acoustic ones), and "free jazz" (marked by unpredictable improvisations). The principal practitioner of free jazz was saxophonist John Coltrane (1926–1967). Cool jazz, on the other hand, was molded mainly by the playing of Miles Davis.

an antidote to bebop

Miles Davis (1926–1991)

Miles Davis was born in St. Louis, the son of a well-to-do dentist. He took up the trumpet at age thirteen and two years later was already playing professionally. In 1944, he moved to New York to be near his idols, Charlie Parker and Dizzy Gillespie (on both, see page 432). Naturally, Davis at first emulated their intense, angular style of bebop. But Davis's own, more mellow voice became audible in a series of recordings he made in New York in 1949–1950, later gathered into an album called *Birth of the Cool*. In brief, **cool jazz** rejects the aggressive style of bebop. Instead, it emphasizes lyricism, lower instrumental registers, moderate tempos, and quieter dynamic levels. Davis was not the only exponent of cool jazz—Gerry Mulligan (1927–2002) and Dave Brubeck (1920–) were among the many others—but he was by far the most influential.

To hear the essence of the "cool" in jazz, we turn to the track "Boplicity" from Davis's album *Birth of the Cool*. Instead of a small jazz combo, which typically might consist of five players, Davis assembled for *Birth of the Cool* a group closer in size to a

FIGURE 39–2
Birth of the Cool. Miles Davis at a recording session.

© Hulton-Deutsch Collection/Corbis

big band. Tuba and French horn—unusual instruments for jazz—add sonic weight to the texture, giving the group a sound less like a handful of frenetic beboppers and more like a smooth "big-band" orchestra. Moreover, the solos are distinctly less "hot"—less rapid, less intense. Instead of the high-pitched alto saxophone of Charlie Parker, we hear the lower, smoother baritone saxophone of Gerry Mulligan. Similarly, instead of the flighty buzzing of Dizzy Gillespie's trumpet, we hear Miles Davis's lower, mellower tones. Davis could, of course, play in as high a register as anyone, but he preferred the "cooler" aesthetic of the instrument's lower registers. In "Boplicity," Davis also inserts more space (rests) between his phrases, thereby giving the music a more relaxed, airy feel. Finally, drummer Kenny Clarke's steady $\frac{4}{4}$ beat on the "high-hat" cymbal makes this music good not only for listening but also for dancing.

a slower tempo, a lower range, more space

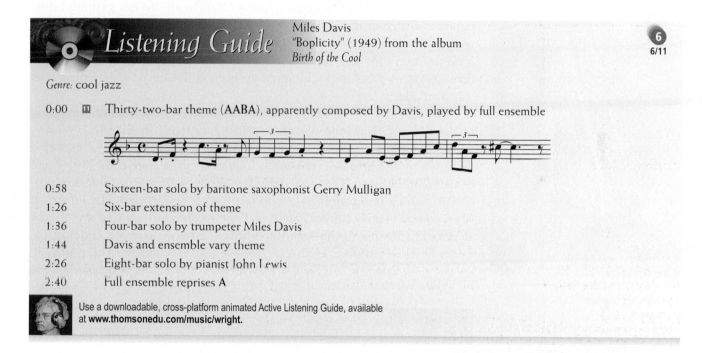

Listening Guide

Miles Davis
"Boplicity" (1949) from the album
Birth of the Cool

6
6/11

Genre: cool jazz

0:00	🎵	Thirty-two-bar theme (**AABA**), apparently composed by Davis, played by full ensemble

0:58	Sixteen-bar solo by baritone saxophonist Gerry Mulligan
1:26	Six-bar extension of theme
1:36	Four-bar solo by trumpeter Miles Davis
1:44	Davis and ensemble vary theme
2:26	Eight-bar solo by pianist John Lewis
2:40	Full ensemble reprises **A**

Use a downloadable, cross-platform animated Active Listening Guide, available at **www.thomsonedu.com/music/wright**.

During the 1970s, jazz began to assimilate some traits of rock. The cause of this stylistic change was simple: money. Jazz recordings—whether swing, bebop, or cool—were not selling. What was selling was rock. So jazz musicians, driven by economic reality, began to adopt the rhythms of the rock drummer and the simple, repetitive harmonies outlined by the bass guitar. **Jazz-fusion** is the name given this mixture of jazz and rock. Young trumpeters, such as Lew Soloff (1943–) and Chuck Mangione (1941–), stopped playing cool like Miles Davis and went off to form jazz-rock bands, such as Blood, Sweat, and Tears; Chicago; and the Chuck Mangione Ensemble. Davis, too, saw the financial handwriting on the wall and began to release jazz-fusion albums. His *Bitches Brew* sold 400,000 copies in its first year, more than any other Davis album. These musicians all made great music—and got rich—not by playing pure jazz but by blending the driving rhythms and repetitive harmonies of rock with the big-band brass sounds and the virtuosity of the jazz improviser. With his smooth style, popular saxophonist Kenny G extended the tradition of jazz-fusion into the 1990s. The moral of the story, as it pertains to the history of jazz and its listening public, is that any popular music without a catchy tune or a finger-snapping beat won't be popular for long.

rock influences jazz

FIGURE 39-3
Wynton Marsalis.

WYNTON MARSALIS (1961–): SPOKESMAN FOR JAZZ TODAY

Our discussion of jazz began in New Orleans, and it ends there as well. Today, our best-known jazz musician is Wynton Marsalis, a native of New Orleans, the birthplace of traditional jazz. He is the son of pianist Ellis Marsalis and the younger brother of saxophonist Branford Marsalis. Being part of a musical family, Marsalis received his first trumpet at the young age of six. To build a virtuosic technique and to "know what makes music great," he studied the classical repertoire, enrolling at the Juilliard School in New York City in 1979. In 1984, Marsalis became the only person to win a Grammy simultaneously as a classical performer (for a recording of the Haydn trumpet concerto) and a jazz performer (for his album *Think of One*). In all, he has garnered nine Grammys, including one for his jazz oratorio *Blood on the Fields*, which also won a Pulitzer Prize in 1997. In 2006, Marsalis was commissioned to compose an opera for the Metropolitan Opera in New York, thereby again demonstrating that, after a hundred years, jazz has become America's own "classical" music.

Most recently, Marsalis has been the driving force to rebuild hurricane-ravaged New Orleans through music. He argues that without music—just as without gumbo—there is no New Orleans. To press his point, he appeared prominently in Spike Lee's documentary film *When the Levees Broke* (2006) and initiated and hosted "Celebrate Jazz Trio: Rebuilding the Soul of America" (2006), which raised millions of dollars for his native city. The efforts of Marsalis and others to resuscitate New Orleans demonstrate that if you want to get the attention of the American public (and raise money), you host the Super Bowl or put on a large-scale popular music telethon, featuring soul, gospel, funk, country, and rock—and a bit of New Orleans jazz, too.

ThomsonNOW™

ThomsonNOW for Listening to Music, 5th Edition, and *Listening to Western Music* will assist you in understanding the content of this chapter with lesson plans generated for your specific needs. In addition, you may complete this chapter's Listening Exercise in ThomsonNOW's interactive environment, as well as download Active Listening Guides and other materials that will help you succeed in this course.

Key Words

bebop (**431**)	cool jazz (**434**)	jazz-fusion (**435**)

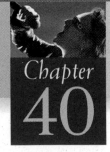

Chapter
40

Tin Pan Alley and the Broadway Musical

The previous two chapters explored genres of American popular music in which oral transmission played a predominant role. Blues, with its origins in folk traditions, was conveyed from one generation to the next with almost no use of notated music. A significant proportion of jazz, too, was and is unwritten—the practice of improvisation, so central to jazz's essence, by definition excludes the use of notation. But some popular music, in contrast, required musical notation. The parlor song, which captured the fancy of mainstream America in the early twentieth century, was published and sold as notated, printed music. This was music you could buy and hold in your hands.

Imagine music before the phonograph, radio, and MP3 player. How would you hear the latest popular songs and choose the ones you liked? Songs could be sampled at a local music store, where a **song plugger** peddled (plugged) them by singing and playing at the piano. Scored for voice and piano, each song was available for purchase as sheet music, usually a single large sheet folded to produce four pages (front, back, front, back). Having purchased the song, one could then sing and play it at home on the parlor piano. In this way, middle-class Americans at the turn of the twentieth century were able to enjoy the latest popular music in their homes, before the advent of the recording industry.

how to buy the latest songs

TIN PAN ALLEY

During these years, the largest cluster of music stores in the United States was in New York City, in an area near Broadway and West 28th Street. So numerous and noisy were the song pluggers in this locale that they sounded like a crowd banging on tin cans, and thus this area came to be nicknamed **Tin Pan Alley** (Fig. 40–1). Here was born the fledgling "music industry" in America. Many of the larger stores in Tin Pan Alley had both "in-house" composers to write new songs on the spot and publishers to print them as sheet music. Copyright laws had recently been strengthened, and some songs became huge financial successes. Charles Harris's "After the Ball Is Over" (1892) earned its publisher $25,000; Harry Von Tilzer's "Only a Bird in a Gilded Cage" (1900) sold 2 million copies in its first year; and George Gershwin's "Swanee" (1919) paid the then-unknown composer $10,000 in royalties in its first year—this when the average annual family income was little more than $1000. The most successful turn-of-the-century songsmith was Irving Berlin, who composed some 3000 songs including "Alexander's Ragtime Band," "God Bless America," "White Christmas" (which sold 40 million records when recorded by Bing Crosby in 1942), and "There's No Business Like Show Business."

Indeed, the Tin Pan Alley song was linked geographically and commercially to the "show business" district of New York, the center of which was just a few blocks up Broadway at 42nd Street. Many Tin Pan Alley songs were made popular by performances of **vaudeville,** an early form of American musical theater involving songs and dances, comedy skits, and the occasional juggler and acrobat. In an effort

FIGURE 40–1
Music stores in Tin Pan Alley in the early twentieth century. George Gershwin got his first job at Jerome H. Remick & Company (center top).

to increase the popularity of their material, some publishers actually paid vaudeville performers to work specific songs into a show—an early form of musical "payola." As the vaudeville show evolved into the Broadway musical, the composers of Tin Pan Alley increasingly came to be associated with the Broadway theaters. Tin Pan Alley itself declined in importance in the 1920s, as radio broadcasts and the phonograph record became commonplace.

George Gershwin (1898–1937)

George Gershwin's career moved from Tin Pan Alley to Broadway and eventually to the classical concert halls of "uptown" New York. Gershwin (Fig. 40–2) was born to Jewish immigrant parents, Rose and Morris Gershovitz, in New York on September 26, 1898. His mother did what many upwardly mobile middle-class matrons then did in America: she bought her family an upright piano on an installment plan. But of all the family members, only young George could play the instrument, picking out every sort of rag, march, and show tune by ear. Soon he was taking formal lessons in classical music, studying Mozart, Chopin, and Debussy. By the age of fifteen, music had become Gershwin's life, so he quit high school and took a job as a song plugger in Tin Pan Alley earning fifteen dollars a week. In 1919, Gershwin stopped plugging the music of others and began to promote his own. With his hit song "Swanee," he became both rich and famous at the age of twenty-one.

from song plugger to famous composer

But mother Gershovitz had not wasted her money on classical piano lessons, for during the 1920s, son George increasingly turned his attention to traditionally classical genres. In three large-scale orchestral compositions (*Rhapsody in Blue*, 1924; Piano Concerto in F, 1925; and *An American in Paris*, 1928), he created something called **symphonic jazz,** a fusion of jazz styles with the idioms and forms of classical music. Later, in 1936, he extended this fusion of jazz and classical to the genre of opera with *Porgy and Bess*, best known for its signature song "Summertime."

In all, George Gershwin composed some 350 songs, many of which were intended for Broadway musicals and films. Among the best known of these is "The Man I Love," an example of what Tin Pan Alley composers would call a **ballad,** a love song in a slow tempo. (Subsequent popular-music genres, from jazz, to rock, to heavy metal, have retained this definition of "ballad.") While the music of "The Man I Love" is exceptionally poignant, its structure is common for a Tin Pan Alley song. After a brief piano introduction and a single verse comes a chorus*, which, as in jazz, provides the main tune. The chorus here is typical, consisting of thirty-two bars in **AABA** form. Gershwin originally wrote "The Man I Love" to be part of his Broadway musical *Lady Be Good* (1924) but withdrew it and later inserted the song in his *Strike Up the Band* (1927)—like many ballads of the period, the amorous sentiments expressed here would be at home in almost any early Broadway musical.

FIGURE 40–2
George Gershwin.

Lebrecht/ColouriserAL/The Image Works

 **Listening Guide**   George Gershwin
"The Man I Love" (1924)

6
6/12

Genre: Tin Pan Alley song
Form: piano introduction, verse, chorus (**AABA**)

0:00   [12]   Piano introduction

0:16   Introductory verse

When the mellow moon begins to beam,
Ev'ry night I dream a little dream,
And of course Prince Charming is the theme—the he for me.
Although I realize as well as you,
It is seldom that a dream comes true,
To me it's clear that he'll appear.

Some- day he'll come a-long,   The man I love;   And he'll be big and strong,   The man I love;

1:15   Chorus, part **A**: accompaniment
slides down chromatically
(see arrows)

Someday he'll come along, the man I love;
And he'll be big and strong, the man I love.
And when he comes my way, I'll do my best to make him stay.

1:46   Part **A** repeats with ornamented
accompaniment

He'll look at me and smile, I'll understand;
And in a little while, he'll take my hand.
And though it seems absurd, I know we both won't say a word.

2:16   Chorus, part **B**: voice
momentarily rises

Maybe I shall meet him Sunday, maybe Monday, maybe not;
Still I'm sure to meet him one day, maybe Tuesday will be my good news day.

2:47   Part **A** repeats with ornamented
accompaniment

He'll build a little home, just meant for two,
From which I'll never roam, who would—would you?
And so all else above, I'm waiting for the man I love.

 Use a downloadable, cross-platform animated Active Listening Guide, available
at **www.thomsonedu.com/music/wright**.

By the 1950s, the parlor song had given way to the rock 'n' roll tune, but
even some of the earliest of these, such as "Rock Around the Clock" and "Jail-
house Rock," sprung from the creative minds of composers based in midtown
New York. As the song composers and publishers of old Tin Pan Alley gradually faded away, their jobs as creators and producers in the music business fell
to midtown record companies such as Atlantic, Decca, and Columbia. These
were the forerunners of today's international "Big Four" record labels: Warner
Music Group, Sony, EMI, and Universal Music.

THE BROADWAY MUSICAL

The Broadway **musical** (also known as the musical comedy) was a form of
American popular musical theater that emerged shortly after 1900. A musical
is based on a "book" (the libretto) and contains "lyrics" (the rhyming verse

needed for the sung portions of the musical). Most of the dialogue in a musical is spoken, but the emotional high points are sung, just as in German *Singspiel** and many light, comic operas. The earliest Broadway musicals were written by native-born Americans, most notably George M. Cohan (*Little Johnny Jones*, 1906, which included "Give My Regards to Broadway") and Jerome Kern (*Showboat*, 1927). The oft-revived *Showboat*, with its signature song "Ol' Man River," is especially noteworthy in that it includes strains of uniquely American music—specifically, blues, jazz, and the Negro spiritual. The treatment of the African-American experience in Kern's *Showboat* and Gershwin's opera *Porgy and Bess* paved the way for other ethnic subjects in American musical theater, like *Fiddler on the Roof* (Yiddish stories) and *West Side Story* (Puerto Rican immigrants).

early musicals on Broadway

The collaboration between composer Richard Rodgers (1902–1979) and lyricist Oscar Hammerstein (1895–1960) marked the beginning of a golden era for American musical theater. In a span of less than two decades, this gifted team produced a succession of blockbuster musicals, beginning with *Oklahoma!* (1943); continuing with *Carousel* (1945), *South Pacific* (1949), and *The King and I* (1951); and concluding with *The Sound of Music* (1959). Their success was unparalleled: *Oklahoma!* ran originally for 2248 performances, and *The King and I* for 4625. Moreover, these were the first musicals in which record sales, movie rights, and touring companies brought in more money than the box office receipts of the original Broadway production. Rodgers and Hammerstein struck gold by blending tasteful (if sentimental) lyrics with uplifting (if square-cut) melodies. The "Broadway songbooks" performed at home today are filled with such standards as "Oh, What a Beautiful Mornin'" (*Oklahoma!*), "You'll Never Walk Alone" (*Carousel*), "Some Enchanted Evening" (*South Pacific*), "Getting to Know You" and "Shall We Dance?" (*The King and I*), and "Climb Ev'ry Mountain" (*The Sound of Music*)—all Rodgers and Hammerstein creations.

musicals by Rodgers and Hammerstein

During the past twenty years, the Broadway scene has been dominated by the megahits of Englishman Andrew Lloyd Webber (*Evita, Cats, Starlight Express,* and *Phantom of the Opera*), which rely as much on dazzling scenic effects and heavily amplified sound as on inspired musical invention. On January 9, 2006, *Phantom of the Opera* had its 7486th performance, surpassing *Cats* as the longest-running show in Broadway history. These British imports, along with the French *Les Misérables* (1987), have put American musical theater into a state of eclipse. At the moment, Broadway offers more revivals of earlier American musicals (*South Pacific, Chicago, Sweeney Todd,* and *A Chorus Line*) and musical-theater versions of movies (*Beauty and the Beast, The Lion King, Spamalot,* and *Mary Poppins*) than new productions.

musicals by Andrew Lloyd Webber

revivals and musical movies

Leonard Bernstein (1918–1990)

One of the most original shows ever mounted on Broadway was Leonard Bernstein's *West Side Story*, a musical as brash and energetic as Bernstein himself. Bernstein was educated at Harvard and at the Curtis Institute in Philadelphia, where he studied conducting. He went on to become one of the great conductor-interpreters of this century. But Bernstein (see Fig. 2–3) was a protean figure of frenetic energy and diverse talents. As a writer of "serious" music, he created symphonies and ballet scores; as a composer in more popular styles, he produced a film score (*On the Waterfront* starring Marlon Brando) and four musicals (*Wonderful Town, On the Town, Candide,* and *West Side Story* with lyrics by Stephen Sondheim); as a virtuoso pianist, he appeared often as a soloist with his own orchestra; as an educator, he introduced a generation of youthful Americans to the joys of classical music through his "Young People's Concerts" broadcast nationally on CBS-TV; and as an advocate for the arts, he exercised influence on presidents, especially John F. Kennedy. America has never enjoyed a more dynamic musical leader than the lion-like Bernstein.

West Side Story (1957)

In *West Side Story,* Bernstein gives the age-old story of Romeo and Juliet a new setting. The feuding Capulets and Montagues are replaced by New York street gangs, one "American" (the "Jets") and one Puerto Rican (the "Sharks"). The scenario crystalized for Bernstein one day during a ride through New York's Spanish Harlem:

> All around, Puerto Rican kids were playing—with a huge causeway as a background in a classic [design of] key, pillars, and Roman arches. The contrast between the setting and the kids was striking, fascinating. Right then and there we had our theme for West Side story—a contemporary setting echoing a classic myth.

The star-crossed lovers are now Tony, former leader of the Jets, and Maria (Fig. 40–3), the sister of the leader of the Sharks and newly arrived from Puerto Rico. They meet at a dance, held not in a Renaissance palazzo but in a high school gym. Juliet's balcony is transformed into Maria's fire escape, and it is here that she and Tony sing the show-stopping duet "Tonight." Ultimately, Tony, trying to make peace, causes the death of the leader of the Sharks and is himself killed, leaving Maria to grieve over his body.

West Side Story is a study in musical opposites. Fast-paced dances for the gangs are set off against quiet duets for the lovers. The gangs' music is dissonant, syncopated, and percussive, much in the style of the musical avant-garde of the early twentieth century (see pages 367–369). The lovers' music, on the other hand, is consonant and melodic, steady in its phrasing and beat. This contrast between the dissonant, syncopated modern style and the melodious Romantic style can be heard in two of the *Symphonic Dances* from *West Side Story.* Both "Mambo," a dance sequence for the gangs, and "Somewhere," a dream song envisioning a distant place of love and friendship, underscore the mood of the onstage action. *West Side Story* is not a musical comedy but a musical tragedy in which competing forces race headlong toward destruction. By distilling the essences of these competing forces into music, Bernstein captures the vitality and the tenderness of this timeless tale.

FIGURE 40–3
Natalie Wood in the role of Maria in Leonard Bernstein's *West Side Story.*

© Mirisch-7 Arts/United Artists/The Kobal Collection

Listening Guide

Leonard Bernstein
Symphonic Dances from *West Side Story* (1957)
"Mambo" and "Somewhere"

6
6/13–14

Characters: the Jets and the Sharks, Tony and Maria
Situation: Friction between the Jets and the Sharks is felt at a high school dance, where gang members strut to the music of "Mambo"; Tony and Maria meet and express their hopes for love.

"MAMBO"

0:00	13	Introduction
0:10		Fast-moving, syncopated theme
0:37		Percussive blasts from percussion and brasses
1:05		Trumpet solo
2:02		Return of theme leads to climax and then fadeout

(continued)

"SOMEWHERE"

0:00	🔢	Cellos tenderly play melody of song "Somewhere"
0:29		French horn plays "Somewhere" melody against counterpoint in oboe
0:55		Strings sweep forward with theme
1:25		Middle strings play "Somewhere" melody against counterpoint in higher violins
1:50		Full orchestra carries melody to climax and then fadeout

Use a downloadable, cross-platform animated Active Listening Guide, available at **www.thomsonedu.com/music/wright**.

In its early years, the Broadway musical was concerned with love, focusing on the problems of the proverbial man-in-the-street and his "gal." *West Side Story*, and more recently *Rent* (see page 315), among others, retains the American setting (indeed, such works are often set in New York itself), but extends the subject matter to racial and social issues. The subjects of today's musicals, however, are less parochial and more exotic, showcasing wicked wizards, ingenious cats, regal lions, and jungle heroes. Appealing to audiences around the world, rather than only to those in New York, the modern musical has become yet another manifestation of musical globalization.

ThomsonNOW

ThomsonNOW for *Listening to Music, 5th Edition*, and *Listening to Western Music* will assist you in understanding the content of this chapter with lesson plans generated for your specific needs. In addition, you may download Active Listening Guides and other materials that will help you succeed in this course.

Key Words

song plugger (**437**)	vaudeville (**437**)	ballad (**438**)
Tin Pan Alley (**437**)	symphonic jazz (**438**)	musical (**439**)

Chapter 41

Rock
MUSIC OF REBELLION

The origins of rock music can be traced to rhythm and blues, a genre that emerged in the southern United States around 1950 (Fig. 41–1). Like earlier blues music (see page 418), **rhythm and blues** followed the twelve-bar blues* chord progression (see boxed essay, page 43), was set to $\frac{4}{4}$ meter, and featured expressive solo singing. But whereas blues was often introspective and mournful, rhythm and blues offered a lively, upbeat aesthetic. The slow tempos typical of earlier blues gave way to much faster, more propulsive rhythms. Drums provided the music a strong, steady beat; electric guitars and basses created a more aggressive sonic texture; saxophones added an expressive "wailing" sound, and often the lyrics were as much shouted as sung. Together, these elements produced a raw, driving, highly danceable musical experience. At first, rhythm and blues was created and played exclusively by black musicians for black audiences. But as many of these musicians and listeners moved to the urban centers of the North in the 1950s, a new white audience, now exposed to the style via radio broadcasts, began to hear and dance to this energized black music. Rhythm and blues became the music of rebellious young Americans, a function that only increased when it evolved into rock 'n' roll.

ROCK 'N' ROLL

The term **rock 'n' roll** was not new to the 1950s. The expression had appeared in popular songs as early as the 1920s, and its roots were older yet. "Rocking" and "rolling," originally nautical terms describing the motion of boats, had been used in African-American circles to describe not only bodily spasms experienced during religious ecstasy but also dance movements, with obvious sexual connotations. In the early 1950s, the expression was given new life by pioneering white radio disc jockey **Alan Freed** (1921–1965), who preferred the name "rock 'n' roll" to the strongly African-American-associated "rhythm and blues." Freed disseminated early rock 'n' roll through radio broadcasts—first in Cleveland, and later in New York—as well as through concerts and dances that fostered racial integration. The demand for rock 'n' roll was unprecedented, and as other stations incorporated the music into their formats, its songs became anthems of defiance for the radio-listening baby boomers. Furthermore, Freed's transmissions were rebroadcast in Europe, extending the genre's popularity to Great Britain and beyond.

The first great exponent of rock 'n' roll was **Elvis Presley** (1935–1977) (Fig. 41–2). Presley began his musical career performing "hillbilly music" (a term used by record executives to designate white southern folk music), singing gospel music in his Pentecostal church and listening to blues and jazz in the black section of Memphis, Tennessee. Elvis combined authentic genres of both black and white American musical traditions. Proof of this can be found on his first record, from July 1954, which features on one side "That's All Right," written by the black Mississippi bluesman Arthur "Big Boy" Crudup, and on the other "Blue Moon of Kentucky," by white bluegrass singer Bill Monroe. All told, Elvis scored an astonishing 149 hits on *Billboard*'s "Hot 100" pop chart. He reached iconic status around the globe not only because of the unmistakable sound of his rich, baritone voice but also through his gyrating style of dancing, seen in numerous television broadcasts and in over thirty feature

FIGURE 41–1

Little Richard (Richard Penniman, 1932–), one of rock 'n' roll's early stars. Along with Chuck Berry and Bo Diddley, he transformed early rhythm and blues into rock 'n' roll.

FIGURE 41–2

"The King is dead, long live the King." The hysteria surrounding Elvis has diminished only slightly since his death in 1977. His retrospective album *Elvis 30 #1 Hits*, released in 2002 on the twenty-fifth anniversary of his death, sold a million copies in the first month. Elvis's estate has generated more income than that of any deceased celebrity.

films. John Lennon's oft-quoted statement, "Before Elvis, there was nothing," is an intentional overstatement, but his words certainly ring true with regard to the explosive impact of Elvis and rock 'n' roll around the world.

The mature style of rock 'n' roll was an amalgam of black rhythm and blues and a broad array of urban and rural influences, some African-American, some white. The girl groups and a cappella* doo-wop ensembles of the 1950s, for example, drew on African-American gospel singing traditions. During that same decade, on the other hand, performers like The Everly Brothers contributed a country music sound, particularly evident in their close vocal harmonies. Although we might naturally assume that rock 'n' roll artists wrote their own songs, the tunes were often composed by professional songsmiths working in the music industry, mainly in New York City. Moreover, some popular entertainers who emerged during this era offered mere dilutions of authentic African-American sounds. Pat Boone, for example, a "sanitized" white contemporary of Elvis, became famous by recording bland but broadly appealing versions of songs first composed and recorded by black musicians like Antoine "Fats" Domino and "Little Richard" Penniman.

rock 'n' roll draws from both black and white popular music

After the arrival of **The Beatles** in the United States from England in February 1964, the full potential of "teen" music was realized (Fig. 41–3). The music and personalities of John Lennon (1940–1980), Paul McCartney (1942–), George Harrison (1943–2001), and Ringo Starr (1940–) had an unparalleled effect on the music and culture of the world. Having started out playing and recording "covers" (songs authored and recorded by others), The Beatles soon developed an unprecedented ability to create original sounds and to compose in new styles. Along with their producer George Martin, these four musicians paved the way for experimentation both in songwriting and in studio recording. In 1967, they created the psychedelic "Strawberry Fields Forever," a song that incorporated astoundingly innovative instrumentation and aspects of

FIGURE 41–3
Although they were together for only a few short years (1960–1970), no pop group has ever equaled The Beatles' musical originality and stylistic variety. Each No. 1 tune was fresh and wildly different from the last.

musique concrète*, and they released a short promotional film for the work that today is considered to be the first modern music video. In the same year, when they assembled the album *Sgt. Pepper's Lonely Hearts Club Band*, The Beatles brought to fruition the thematically unified "concept album," along with lyrics that were to be regarded as serious poetry and album art that provided a sophisticated visual accompaniment to the work's intricate studio recording techniques.

By the time The Beatles disbanded in 1970, they had profoundly changed the world of popular music. Henceforth, artists would be expected to compose their own songs and to release full-length albums rather than singles. Furthermore, The Beatles greatly expanded the boundaries of popular music; their recorded output included such highly disparate styles as rhythm and blues, gospel, country blues, Broadway show tunes, novelty tunes, psychedelic rock, and even In-

Photofest

dian raga*. The various, more sophisticated styles that emerged from rock 'n' roll after The Beatles came to be called simply **rock.**

ROCK

By the late 1960s, the so-called British Invasion initiated by The Beatles had infused popular music with a harder edge. Many groups emulated the styles of such popular black guitarists as Chuck Berry and Bo Diddley. But others, particularly those from the United Kingdom—most prominently, The Rolling Stones, Cream, and Led Zeppelin—were also inspired by older African-American blues singers, particularly the rough, amplified sounds of Muddy Waters, Howlin' Wolf, and Willie Dixon. The British Invasion of the 1960s also revitalized popular music by bringing the sound of the electric guitar, sometimes featured in long improvisations or "solos," to the forefront of rock.

the British Invasion

Perhaps the greatest figure of the early rock era was the African-American guitarist, singer, and songwriter **Jimi Hendrix** (1942–1970), who, like his contemporaries The Beatles, changed forever the range of possibilities for the rock artist. An icon of late-60s fashion, he remains unparalleled in the popular imagination for his unique performance antics, including setting fire to his guitar. Hendrix was arguably the most original, influential guitarist in rock history. He utilized a harmonic vocabulary that ranged from simple blues to complex chords and unusual intervals. His songwriting style extended from the crudely straightforward "Fire" to the eloquent poetry of "Little Wing" (both recorded in 1967). Hendrix's most enduring legacy, however, was his genius in expanding the range of the amplified guitar. Instead of using it solely as a melodic and harmonic instrument, he redefined it as able to produce an assortment of noises, effects, and electronic sounds, such as those employed in his performance of "The Star-Spangled Banner" at the Woodstock Music and Art Festival in 1968. This now-legendary performance has been construed as the guitarist's commentary on a racially divided country whose generations were torn apart by the Vietnam War.

an innovative guitarist

Punk rock crashed onto the scene in the mid-1970s, its self-destructive and nihilistic approach offering a welcome alternative to the mechanistic music and synthetic clothing of the disco craze on the one hand and highly produced, overly orchestrated arena rock on the other. The New York City club music of The Ramones helped shape British groups like The Sex Pistols and The Clash, and all three bands produced seminal albums in the 1970s. The crudely amplified sounds, driving rhythms, and three-chord harmonies of punk music helped to return rock to its working-class roots. Self-proclaimed "nonmusician" Brian Eno began during the early 1970s to conceive of music as a sonic landscape, and his collaborative efforts to incorporate electronica into compositions infused rock with a new timbral sensibility. These innovations in turn inspired the New Wave groups of the late 1970s and early 1980s, like Talking Heads, Devo, and The Police (see page 206).

the elemental sound of punk

By the mid-1980s, the freshest rock sounds were emanating from Metallica and similar heavy metal bands that performed energetic, dissonant songs in somber, minor modes. Ten years later, Kurt Cobain and Nirvana were producing the dark, introspective songs of **grunge.** Both groups revitalized the noises and poetics of rock, re-creating its raw essence for a new, brooding generation of adolescents.

RAP

Rap music, the African-American style that had emerged from New York's South Bronx in the late 1970s, with its attendant hip-hop culture of MCs, DJs, break dancers, and graffiti artists, slowly made its way into the consciousness of America. Initially drawing on funk, disco, and the black preaching tradition, rap became a major cultural force by the 1980s. The group **Run DMC**—Joseph "Run" Simmons (1964–), Darryl "D.M.C." McDaniels (1964–), and Jason "Jam Master Jay" Mizell (1965–2002) (Fig. 41–4)—broke genre barriers with the 1985 album *King of Rock*, which featured a rock guitar accompaniment to the rapping of MCs and scratching* of DJs. The following year, their collaboration with members of the white rock band Aerosmith on the song "Walk This Way" brought Run DMC's sound into heavy rotation on the airwaves, especially via the music video shown on MTV. By the turn of the century, popular white groups like Rage Against the Machine, KoЯn, and Linkin Park were incorporating scratching in their rap-metal textures. In 2004, DJ Danger Mouse (Brian Burton) produced a controversial underground (downloadable) phenomenon called *The Grey Album*, in which he craftily mixed (mashed up) tracks from rapper Jay-Z's *The Black Album* (2003) with those from The Beatles' *White Album* (1968). Like jazz, rhythm and blues, and other earlier styles, the innovation of marginalized African-Americans once again was adopted by mainstream America to produce a novel and authentic music whose broad appeal crossed racial and social boundaries. In a parallel with Elvis Presley, who rose to superstardom largely on the wings of black rhythm and blues, the critically acclaimed white rapper Eminem (1972–) (see boxed essay, page 20), having sold over 50 million albums worldwide, has become the fastest-selling rap artist of all time.

FIGURE 41–4
Run DMC.

© Hulton Archive/Getty Images

EPILOGUE

It is impossible to consider here all of the various types of rock and pop that have arisen over the last fifty years and to laud all its heroes. We cannot neglect, however, at least to mention groundbreaking performers like James Brown, Michael Jackson, and Madonna; song stylists like Aretha Franklin and Mariah Carey; songwriters like Bob Dylan, Joni Mitchell, Paul Simon, and Stevie Wonder; multicultural icons like Mexican-American guitarist Carlos Santana and Jamaican reggae artist Bob Marley; and costumed performers like the flamboyant George Clinton with P-Funk and the unmistakably gimmicky KISS. There is the quintessential "jam" band (that is, improvisation-based) the Grateful Dead, as well as the influential Velvet Underground, Motörhead, and Sonic Youth, three bands all but worshipped by musicians and critics. We need also to single out the important rap groups N.W.A. and

Public Enemy, as well as the tragic personalities Tupac Shakur and the Notorious B.I.G. On the frontiers of rock lie many artistic innovators, from Pink Floyd and Frank Zappa to The Smiths, Radiohead, and Tool. Producers and arrangers like Phil Spector, Brian Wilson, and Rick Rubin are important for the sonic textures they pioneered. This stylistic assortment—folk-rock, Motown, soul, funk, glam, hardcore, reggae, grunge, techno, gangsta rap, dancehall, and a diversity of approaches lumped together as "alternative"—is part of what has become a worldwide phenomenon of popular music.

About popular music, Sting has said, "At its best, it's subversive." Truly, youth music, as part of a general adolescent and postadolescent rebellion, will forever be slippery in style, morphing quickly and thus defying easy labeling. Merely compiling a list, a handful of songs and a few influential artists, as we have done here, leaves out hundreds of significant people and concepts important to the development of popular music in America. The extraordinary vitality and diversity of American popular music, however, requires that it be so.

Key Words

rhythm and blues (442)	Elvis Presley (443)	punk rock (445)
rock 'n' roll (443)	The Beatles (444)	grunge (445)
Alan Freed (443)	rock (445)	rap (446)
	Jimi Hendrix (445)	Run DMC (446)

Glossary

absolute music: instrumental music free of a text or any preexisting program

a cappella: a term applied to unaccompanied vocal music; originated in the expression *a cappella Sistina*, "in the Sistine Chapel" of the pope, where instruments were forbidden to accompany the singers

accelerando: a tempo mark indicating "getting faster"

accent: emphasis or stress placed on a musical tone or a chord

accidental: a sharp, flat, or natural sign that alters the pitch of a note a half step

accompagnato: see *recitativo accompagnato*

acoustic instruments: instruments that produce sounds naturally when strings are bowed or plucked, a tube has air passed through it, or percussion instruments are struck

acoustic music: music produced by acoustic instruments (see above)

adagio: a tempo mark indicating "slow"

Alberti bass: a pattern of accompaniment whereby, instead of having the pitches of a chord sound all together, the notes are played in succession to provide a continual stream of sound

aleatoric music: see *chance music*

allegretto: a tempo mark indicating "moderately fast"

allegro: a tempo mark indicating "fast"

allemande: a stately dance in $\frac{4}{4}$ meter with gracefully interweaving lines

alto (contralto): the lower of the two female voice parts, the soprano being higher

andante: a tempo mark indicating "moderately moving"

andantino: a tempo mark indicating "moderately moving" yet slightly faster than *andante*

antecedent phrase: the opening, incomplete-sounding phrase of a melody; often followed by a consequent phrase that brings the melody to closure

anthem: a composition for chorus on a sacred subject; similar in design and function to a motet

aria: an elaborate lyrical song for solo voice

arpeggio: the notes of a triad or seventh chord played in direct succession and in a direct line up or down

arioso: a style of singing and a type of song midway between an aria and a recitative

art song: a genre of song for voice and piano accompaniment with high artistic aspirations

atonal music: music without tonality; music without a key center; most often associated with the twentieth-century avant-garde style of Arnold Schoenberg

augmentation: the notes of a melody held for longer than (usually double) their normal duration

backbeat: a drumbeat or cymbal crash occurring regularly after a strong beat, as on beats 2 and 4 in a measure with four beats

ballad: a traditional song, or folksong, sung by a soloist that tells a tale and is organized by stanzas; Tin Pan Alley ballad is a love song in a slow tempo

ballet: an art form that uses dance and music, along with costumes and scenery, to tell a story and display emotions through expressive gestures and movement

Ballets russes: a Russian ballet company of the early twentieth century led by Sergei Diaghilev

bandoneon: a square-cut woodwind instrument much like an accordion, except that it is played by pushing buttons rather than keys

banjo: a five-string plucked folk instrument of African-American origin

bar: see *measure*

baritone: a male voice part of a middle range, between the higher tenor and the lower bass

bas instruments: a class of soft musical instruments, including the flute, recorder, fiddle, harp, and lute, popular during the late Middle Ages

bass: the lowest male voice range

bass clef: a sign placed on a staff to indicate the notes below middle C

bass drum: a large, low-sounding drum struck with a soft-headed stick

bass viol: see *viola da gamba*

basso continuo: a small ensemble of at least two instrumentalists who provide a foundation for the melody or melodies above; heard almost exclusively in Baroque music

basso ostinato: a motive or phrase in the bass that is repeated again and again

bassoon: a low, double-reed instrument of the woodwind family

Bayreuth Festival House: an opera house in the town of Bayreuth, Germany, constructed exclusively for the music dramas of Richard Wagner

beat: an even pulse in music that divides the passing of time into equal segments

bebop: a complex, hard-driving style of jazz that emerged shortly after World War II; played without musical notation by a small ensemble

bel canto: (Italian for "beautiful singing") a style of singing and a type of Italian opera developed in the nineteenth century that features the beautiful tone and brilliant technique of the human voice

big band: a mid- to large-size dance band that emerged in the 1930s to play the style of jazz called swing

binary form: a musical form consisting of two units (**A** and **B**) constructed to balance and complement each other

blue note: the third, fifth, or seventh note of the blues scale that can be altered to be sharper or flatter; helps produce the wail of the blues

blues: an expressive, soulful style of singing that emerged from the African-American spiritual and work song at the end of the nineteenth century; its texts are strophic, its harmonies simple and repetitive

blues scale: a seven-note scale in which the third, fifth, and seventh pitches are sometimes flat, sometimes natural, and sometimes in between

bolero: a popular, suggestive Spanish dance for a soloist or couple often performed to the accompaniment of castanets

bongo drum: a pair of small Afro-Cuban single-headed drums created in Cuba c1900; often heard in Latin American dance bands

Brandenburg Concertos: set of six concerti grossi composed by J. S. Bach between

1711 and 1720, and subsequently dedicated to Margrave Christian Ludwig of Brandenburg

brass family: a group of musical instruments traditionally made of brass and played with a mouthpiece; includes the trumpet, trombone, French horn, and tuba

bridge: see *transition*

bugle: a simple brass instrument that evolved from the valveless military trumpet

cabaletta: the concluding fast aria of any two- or three-section operatic scene; a useful mechanism to get the principals off the stage

cadence: the concluding part of a musical phrase

cadenza: a showy passage for the soloist appearing near the end of the movement in a concerto; usually incorporates rapid runs, arpeggios, and snippets of previously heard themes into a fantasy-like improvisation

call and response: a method of performance in which a soloist sings and a group or another soloist answers; particularly favored in African music and genres of African-American music such as the blues

canon (round): a contrapuntal form in which the individual voices enter and each in turn duplicates exactly the melody that the first voice played or sang

cantata: a term originally meaning "something sung"; in its mature state, it consists of several movements, including one or more arias, ariosos, and recitatives; cantatas can be on secular subjects and intended for private performance (see *chamber cantata*) or on religious subjects such as those of J. S. Bach for the German Lutheran church

caprice: a light, whimsical character piece of the nineteenth century

castanets: percussion instruments (rattles) of indefinite pitch associated with Spanish music

castrato: a male adult singer who had been castrated as a boy to keep his voice from changing so that it would remain in the soprano or alto register

celesta: a small percussive keyboard instrument using hammers to strike metal bars, thereby producing a bright, bell-like sound

cello (violoncello): an instrument of the violin family but more than twice the violin's size; it is played between the legs and produces a rich, lyrical tone

chamber cantata: a cantata performed before a select audience in a private residence; intimate vocal chamber music, principally of the Baroque era

chamber music: music, usually instrumental music, performed in a small concert hall or private residence with just one performer on each part

chamber sonata: see *sonata da camera*

chance music (aleatory music): music that involves an element of chance (rolling dice, choosing cards, etc.) or whimsy on the part of the performers; especially popular with avant-garde composers

chanson: a French term used broadly to indicate a lyrical song from the Middle Ages into the twentieth century

character piece: a brief instrumental work seeking to capture a single mood; a genre much favored by composers of the Romantic era

chorale: the German word for the hymn of the Lutheran Church; hence a simple religious melody to be sung by the congregation

chord: two or more simultaneously sounding pitches

chord progression: a succession of chords moving forward in a purposeful fashion

chorus: a group of singers, usually including sopranos, altos, tenors, and basses, with at least two and often many more singers on each vocal part; in Tin Pan Alley songs and Broadway tunes, the main melody of the song; jazz musicians often improvised around it

chromatic harmony: harmony utilizing chords built on the five chromatic notes of the scale in addition to the seven diatonic ones; produces rich harmonies

chromaticism: the frequent presence in melodies and chords of intervals only a half step apart; in a scale, the use of notes not part of the diatonic major or minor pattern

church cantata: see *cantata*

church sonata: see *sonata da chiesa*

clarinet: a single-reed instrument of the woodwind family with a large range and a wide variety of timbres within it

classical music: the traditional music of any culture, usually involving a specialized technical vocabulary and requiring long years of training; it is "high art" or "learned" music that is enjoyed generation after generation

clavier: a general term for all keyboard instruments including the harpsichord, organ, and piano

clef sign: a sign used to indicate the register, or range of pitches, in which an instrument is to play or a singer is to sing

coda: (Italian for "tail") a final and concluding section of a musical composition

col legno: (Italian for "with the wood") an instruction to string players to strike the strings of the instrument not with the horsehair of the bow, but with the wood of it

collegium musicum: a society of amateur musicians (usually associated with a university) dedicated to the performance of music, nowadays music of the Middle Ages, Renaissance, and Baroque era

color (timbre): the character or quality of a musical tone as determined by its harmonics and its attack and decay

comic opera: a genre of opera that originated in the eighteenth century, portraying everyday characters and situations, and using spoken dialogue and simple songs

computer music: the most recent development in electronic music; it couples the computer with the electronic synthesizer to imitate the sounds of acoustic instruments and to produce new sounds

concert overture: an independent, one-movement work, usually of programmatic content, originally intended for the concert hall and not designed to precede an opera or play

concertino: the group of instruments that function as soloists in a concerto grosso

concerto: an instrumental genre in which one or more soloists play with and against a larger orchestra

concerto grosso: a multi-movement concerto of the Baroque era that pits the sound of a small group of soloists (the concertino) against that of the full orchestra (the tutti)

conga drum: a large Afro-Cuban single-headed barrel drum played in Latin American dance bands

conjunct motion: melodic motion that proceeds primarily by steps and without leaps

consequent phrase: the second phrase of a two-part melodic unit that brings a melody to a point of repose and closure

consonance: pitches sounding agreeable and stable

continuo: see *basso continuo*

contrabassoon: a larger, lower-sounding version of the bassoon

cool jazz: a style of jazz that emerged in the 1950s that is softer, more relaxed, and less frenzied than bebop

cornet: a brass instrument that looks like a short trumpet; it has a more mellow tone than the trumpet and is most often used in military bands

cornetto: a woodwind instrument, developed during the late Middle Ages and early Renaissance, that sounds like a hybrid of a clarinet and trumpet

counterpoint: the harmonious opposition of two or more independent musical lines

courante: a lively dance in $\frac{6}{4}$ with an up-beat and frequent changes of metrical accent

crescendo: a gradual increase in the volume of sound

cross stringing: a practice popularized by the Steinway Company whereby the lowest strings of the piano ride up and across those of the middle register, thereby giving the piano a richer, more homogenized sound

cymbals: a percussion instrument of two metal discs; they are made to crash together to create emphasis and articulation in music

da capo aria: an aria in two sections, with an obligatory return to and repeat of the first; hence an aria in ternary (**ABA**) form

dance suite: a collection of instrumental dances, each with its own distinctive rhythm and character

development: the center-most portion of sonata–allegro form, in which the thematic material of the exposition is developed and extended, transformed, or reduced to its essence; often the most confrontational and unstable section of the movement

diatonic: pertaining to the seven notes that make up either the major or the minor scale

Dies irae: a Gregorian chant composed in the thirteenth century and used as the central portion of the Requiem Mass of the Catholic Church

diminished chord: a triad or seventh chord made up entirely of minor thirds and producing a tense, unstable sound

diminuendo: a gradual decrease in the volume of sound

diminution: a reduction, usually by half, of all the rhythmic durations in a melody

disjunct motion: melodic motion that moves primarily by leaps rather than by steps

dissonance: a discordant mingling of sounds

diva: (Italian for "goddess") a celebrated female opera singer; a prima donna

dominant chord: the chord built on the fifth degree of the scale

dondon: a two-headed pressure drum indigenous to West Africa

dotted note: a note to which an additional duration of 50 percent has been added

double bass: the largest and lowest-pitched instrument in the string family

double counterpoint: counterpoint with two themes that can reverse position, with the top theme moving to the bottom, and the bottom to the top (also called *invertible counterpoint*)

double exposition form: a form, originating in the concerto of the Classical period, in which first the orchestra and then the soloist present the primary thematic material

double stops: a technique applied to string instruments in which two strings are pressed down and played simultaneously instead of just one

downbeat: the first beat of each measure; indicated by a downward motion of the conductor's hand and usually stressed

dramatic overture: a one-movement work, usually in sonata–allegro form, that encapsulates in music the essential dramatic events of the opera or play that follows

drone: a continuous sound on one or more fixed pitches

dynamics: the various levels of volume, loud and soft, at which sounds are produced in a musical composition

electronic instruments: machines that produce musical sounds by electronic means, the most widespread instrument being the keyboard synthesizer

electronic music: sounds produced and manipulated by magnetic tape machines, synthesizers, and/or computers

eleventh chord: a chord comprising five intervals of a third and spanning eleven different letter names of pitches

encore: (French for "again") the repeat of a piece demanded by an appreciative audience; an extra piece added at the end of a concert

English horn: an alto oboe, pitched at the interval a fifth below the oboe, much favored by composers of the Romantic era

episode: a passage of free, nonimitative counterpoint found in a fugue

erhu: an ancient two-string Chinese fiddle

"Eroica" Symphony: Beethoven's Symphony No. 3 (1803), originally dedicated to Napoleon but published as the "Heroic Symphony"

etude: a short one-movement composition designed to improve one aspect of a performer's technique

exposition: in a fugue, the opening section, in which each voice in turn has the opportunity to present the subject; in sonata–allegro form, the principal section, in which all thematic material is presented

falsetto voice: a high, soprano-like voice produced by adult male singers when they sing in head voice and not in full chest voice

fantasy: a free, improvisatory-like composition in which the composer follows his or her whims rather than an established musical form

fermata: in musical notation, a mark indicating that the performer(s) should hold a note or chord for an extended duration

fiddle: a popular term for the violin

figured bass: in musical notation, a numerical shorthand that tells the player which unwritten notes to fill in above the written bass note

finale: the last movement of a multimovement composition, one that usually works to a climax and conclusion

flamenco: a genre of Spanish song and dance, with guitar accompaniment, that originated in southern-most Spain and exhibits non-Western, possibly Arab-influenced, scales

flat: in musical notation, a symbol that lowers a pitch by a half step

flute: a high-sounding member of the woodwind family; initially made of wood, but more recently, beginning in the nineteenth century, of silver or even platinum

folk-rock: a mixture of the steady beat of rock with the forms, topics, and styles of singing of the traditional Anglo-American folk ballad

folk music: the traditional music of a distinctive ethnic group or culture passed along orally from one generation to the next, usually emerges from the community and is not attributable to an identifiable individual

folksong: a song originating from an ethnic group and passed from generation to generation by oral tradition rather than written notation

form: the purposeful organization of the artist's materials; in music, the general shape of a composition as perceived by the listener

forte (*f*): in musical notation, a dynamic mark indicating "loud"

fortepiano (pianoforte): the original name of the piano

fortissimo (*ff*): in musical notation, a dynamic mark indicating "very loud"

free counterpoint: counterpoint in which the voices do not all make use of some preexisting subject in imitation

free jazz: a style of jazz perfected during the 1960s in which a soloist indulges in flights of creative fancy without concern for the rhythm, melody, or harmony of the other performers

French horn: a brass instrument that plays in the middle range of the brass family; developed from the medieval hunting horn

French overture: an overture style developed by Jean-Baptiste Lully with two sections, the first slow in duple meter with dotted note values, the second fast in triple meter and with light imitation; the first section can be repeated after the second

fugato: a short fugue set in some other musical form, such as sonata–allegro or theme and variations

fugue: a composition for three, four, or five parts played or sung by voices or instruments; begins with a presentation of a subject in imitation in each part and continues with modulating passages of free counterpoint and further appearances of the subject

full cadence: a cadence that sounds complete, in part because it usually ends on the tonic note

furiant: an exuberant folk dance of Czech origin in which duple and triple meter alternate

gamelan: the traditional orchestra of Indonesia consisting of as many as twenty-five instruments, mostly gongs, chimes, drums, and metallophones

genre of music: type of music; specifically, the quality of musical style, form, performing medium, and place of performance that characterize any one type of music

Gesamtkunstwerk: (German for "total art work") an art form that involves music, poetry, drama, and scenic design; often used in reference to Richard Wagner's music dramas

Gewandhaus Orchestra: the symphony orchestra that originated in the Clothiers' House in Leipzig, Germany, in the eighteenth century

gigue: a fast dance in $\frac{6}{8}$ or $\frac{12}{8}$ with a constant eighth-note pulse that produces a gallop-like effect

glissando: a device of sliding up or down the scale very rapidly

glockenspiel: a percussion instrument made of tuned metal bars that are struck by mallets

gong: a circular, metal percussion instrument of Asian origin

gongon: a large, barrel-like drum indigenous to West Africa

grave: a tempo mark indicating "very slow and grave"

great staff: a large musical staff that combines both the treble and the bass clefs

Gregorian chant (plainsong): a large body of unaccompanied monophonic vocal music, set to Latin texts, composed for the Western Church over the course of fifteen centuries, from the time of the earliest fathers to the Council of Trent (1545–1563)

grito: in mariachi music, an excited, exuberant cry inserted spontaneously by the performers

ground bass: the English term for *basso ostinato*

grunge: a type of alternative rock, inspired by punk rock and youthful rebellion generally, that originated in the northwestern United States and peaked in popularity around 1990

guiro: a scraped percussion instrument originating in South America and the Caribbean

guittarón: literally "large guitar"; a large, six-string acoustic guitar of Spanish origin that provides the bass and essential chords in a mariachi band

Habanera: an Afro-Cuban dance-song that came to prominence in the nineteenth century, marked by a repeating bass and a repeating, syncopated rhythm

half cadence: a cadence at which the music does not come to a fully satisfying stop but stands as if suspended on a dominant chord

half step: the smallest musical interval in the Western major or minor scale; the distance between any two adjacent keys on the piano

harmonics: the secondary tones above a fundamental pitch that, taken in sum, help form the totality of that sound

harmony: the sounds that provide the support and enrichment—the accompaniment—for melody

harp: an ancient, plucked-string instrument with a triangular shape

harpsichord: a keyboard instrument, especially popular during the Baroque era, that produces sound by depressing a key that drives a lever upward and forces a pick to pluck a string

hauts instruments: a class of loud musical instruments, including the trumpet, sackbut, shawm, and drum, popular during the late Middle Ages

hemiola: a rhythmic process in which two bars in triple meter become three bars in duple meter

"heroic" period: a period in Beethoven's compositional career (1803–1813) during which he wrote longer works incorporating broad gestures, grand climaxes, and triadic, triumphant themes

Hindustani-style music: the traditional, or classical, music of northern India

homophony: a texture in which all the voices, or lines, move to new pitches at roughly the same time; often referred to in contradistinction to polyphony

horn: a term generally used by musicians to refer to any brass instrument, but most often the French horn

hornpipe: an energetic dance, derived from the country jig, in either $\frac{3}{2}$ or $\frac{2}{4}$ time

idée fixe: literally, a "fixed idea"; more specifically, an obsessive musical theme as first used in Hector Berlioz's *Symphonie fantastique*

imitation: the process by which one or more musical voices, or parts, enter and duplicate exactly for a period of time the music presented by the previous voice

imitative counterpoint: a type of counterpoint in which the voices or lines frequently use imitation

incidental music: music to be inserted between the acts or during important scenes of a play to add an extra dimension to the drama

instrumental break: in the blues or in jazz, a short instrumental passage that interrupts and responds to the singing of a voice

intermezzo: (Italian for "between piece") a light musical interlude intended to separate and thus break the mood of two more serious, surrounding movements or operatic acts or scenes

interval: the distance between any two pitches on a musical scale

inversion: the process of inverting the musical intervals in a theme or melody; a melody that ascends by step, then descends by step, and so on

invertible counterpoint: see *double counterpoint*

jazz: a lively, energetic music with pulsating rhythms and scintillating syncopations, usually played by a small instrumental ensemble

jazz-fusion: a mixture of jazz and rock cultivated by American bands in the 1970s

jazz riff: a short motive, usually played by an entire instrumental section (woodwinds or brasses), that appears frequently, but intermittently, in a jazz composition

Karnatak-style music: the traditional, or classical, music of southern India

key: a tonal center built on a tonic note and making use of a scale; also, on a keyboard instrument, one of a series of levers that can be depressed to generate sound

key signature: in musical notation, a preplaced set of sharps or flats used to indicate the scale and key

klezmer music: a traditional folk music of the Jews of Eastern Europe that has recently adopted and adapted elements of Western popular music—specifically, rock, funk, and jazz

Köchel (K) number: an identifying number assigned to each of the works of Mozart, in roughly chronological order, by Ludwig von Köchel (1800–1877)

Kyrie: the first portion of the Ordinary of the Mass, and hence usually the opening movement in a polyphonic setting of the Mass

La Scala: the principal opera house of the city of Milan, Italy, which opened in 1778

largo: a tempo mark indicating "slow and broad"

leading tone: the pitch a half step below the tonic, which pulls up and into it, especially at cadences

leap: melodic movement not by an interval of just a step, but usually by a jump of at least a fourth

legato: in musical notation, an articulation mark indicating that the notes are to be smoothly connected; the opposite of staccato

leitmotif: a brief, distinctive unit of music designed to represent a character, object, or idea; a term applied to the motives in the music dramas of Richard Wagner

lento: a tempo mark indicating "very slow"

libretto: the text of an opera

Liebestod: (German for "love death") the famous aria sung by the expiring Isolde at the end of Richard Wagner's opera *Tristan und Isolde*

Lied: (German for "song") the genre of art song, for voice and piano accompaniment, that originated in Germany c1800

London Symphonies: the twelve symphonies composed by Joseph Haydn for performance in London between 1791 and 1795; Haydn's last twelve symphonies (Nos. 93–104)

lute: a six-string instrument appearing in the West in the late Middle Ages

madrigal: a popular genre of secular vocal music that originated in Italy during the Renaissance, in which usually four or five voices sing love poems

madrigalism: a device, originating in the madrigal, by which key words in a text spark a particularly expressive musical setting

major scale: a seven-note scale that ascends in the following order of whole and half steps: 1-1-½-1-1-1-½

mariachi: a type of music popular today in Mexico and the southwestern United States that draws on traditional styles of Spanish and native Mexican music

Marseillaise, La: a tune written as a revolutionary marching song in 1792 by Claude-Joseph Rouget de Lisle and sung by a battalion from Marseilles as it entered Paris that year; it subsequently became the French national anthem

Mass: the central religious service of the Roman Catholic Church, one that incorporates singing for spiritual reflection or as accompaniment to sacred acts

mazurka: a fast dance of Polish origins in triple meter with an accent on the second beat

measure (bar): a group of beats, or musical pulses; usually, the number of beats is fixed and constant so that the measure serves as a continual unit of measurement in music

melisma: in singing, one vowel luxuriously spread out over many notes

melodic sequence: the repetition of a musical motive at successively higher or lower degrees of the scale

melody: a series of notes arranged in order to form a distinctive, recognizable musical unit; most often placed in the treble

metallophone: a general term for a percussion instrument, similar to a xylophone, comprised of a succession of metal bars that are struck by two hammers; an instrument important in the Balinese gamelan

meter: the gathering of beats into regular groups

meter signature: see *time signature*

metronome: a mechanical device used by performers to keep a steady tempo

mezzo-soprano: a female vocal range between alto and soprano

middle C: the middle-most C on the modern piano

minaret: a slender tower attached to a Moslem mosque from which a muezzin (cantor) chants the Islamic call to prayer five times each day

Minimalism: a style of modern music that takes a very small amount of musical material and repeats it over and over to form a composition

Minnesinger: a type of secular poet-musician that flourished in Germany during the twelfth through fourteenth centuries

minor scale: a seven-note scale that ascends in the following order of whole and half steps: 1-½-1-1-½-1-1

minuet: a moderate dance in $\frac{3}{4}$, though actually danced in patterns of six steps, with no upbeat but with highly symmetrical phrasing

mode: a pattern of pitches forming a scale; the two primary modes in Western music are major and minor

moderato: a tempo marking indicating "moderately moving"

modified strophic form: strophic form in which the music is modified briefly to accommodate a particularly expressive word or phrase in the text

modulation: the process in music whereby the tonal center changes from one key to another—from G major to C major, for example

monody: a general term connoting solo singing accompanied by a *basso continuo* in the early Baroque period

monophony: a musical texture involving only a single line of music with no accompaniment

mosque: a temple in which Muslims come to pray

motet: a composition for choir or larger chorus setting a religious, devotional, or solemn text; often sung a cappella

motive: a short, distinctive melodic figure that stands by itself

mouthpiece: a detachable portion of a brass instrument into which the player blows

movement: a large, independent section of a major instrumental work, such as a sonata, dance suite, symphony, quartet, or concerto

muezzin: the principal singer who calls the faithful to prayer daily in the Islamic musical tradition

music: the rational organization of sounds and silences as they pass through time

music drama: a term used for the mature operas of Richard Wagner

musical (musical comedy): a popular genre of musical theater designed to appeal to a general audience by means of spoken dialogue, songs, and energetic dances

musical nationalism: see *nationalism*

musique concrète: music in which the composer works directly with sounds recorded on magnetic tape, not with musical notation and performers

mute: any device that muffles the sound of a musical instrument; on the trumpet, for example, it is a cup that is placed inside the bell of the instrument

nationalism: a movement in music in the nineteenth century in which composers sought to emphasize indigenous qualities in their music by incorporating folksongs, native scales, dance rhythms, and local instrumental sounds

natural: in musical notation, a symbol that cancels a preexisting sharp or flat

Neo-classicism: a movement in twentieth-century music that sought to return to the musical forms and aesthetics of the Baroque and Classical periods

New Age music: a style of non-confrontational, often repetitive music performed on electronic instruments that arose during the 1990s

New Orleans jazz: a style of jazz that originated in that city shortly after 1900 involving a syncopated, improvisatory style of playing built on the tunes and harmonies of blues, parlor songs, rags, and marches

ninth chord: a chord spanning nine letters of the scale and constructed by superimposing four intervals of a third

nocturne: a slow, introspective type of music, usually for piano, with rich harmonies and poignant dissonances intending to convey the mysteries of the night

nonimitative counterpoint: counterpoint with independent lines that do not imitate each other

oboe: an instrument of the woodwind family; the highest-pitched of the double-reed instruments

octave: the interval comprising the first and eighth tones of the major and minor diatonic scale; the sounds are quite similar because the frequency of vibration of the higher pitch is exactly twice that of the lower

octave displacement: a process used in constructing a melody whereby a simple, nearby interval is made more distant, and the melodic line more disjunct, by placing the next note up or down an octave

opera: a dramatic work in which the actors sing some or all of their parts; it usually makes use of elaborate stage sets and costumes

opera buffa: (Italian for "comic opera") a genre of opera featuring light, often domestic subjects, with tuneful melodies, comic situations, and happy endings

opera seria: a genre of opera that dominated the stage during the Baroque era, making use of serious historical or mythological subjects, *da capo* arias, and lengthy overtures

operetta: a light opera with spoken dialogue and numerous dances involving comedy and romance in equal measure

ophicleide: a low brass instrument originating in military bands about the time of the French Revolution; the precursor of the tuba

opus: (Latin for "work") the term adopted by composers to enumerate and identify their compositions

oral tradition: the process used in the transmission of folksongs and other traditional music in which the material is passed from one generation to the next by singing, or playing, and hearing, without musical notation

oratorio: a large-scale genre of sacred music involving an overture, arias, recitatives, and choruses, but sung, whether in a theater or a church, without costumes or scenery

orchestra: see *symphony orchestra*

orchestral Lied: see *orchestral song*

orchestral score: a composite of the musical lines of all of the instruments of the orchestra and from which a conductor conducts

orchestral song: a genre of music emerging in the nineteenth century in which the voice is accompanied not merely by a piano but by a full orchestra

orchestral dance suite: a dance suite written for orchestra

orchestration: the art of assigning to the various instruments of the orchestra, or of a chamber ensemble, the diverse melodies, accompaniments, and counterpoints of a musical composition

Ordinary of the Mass: the five sung portions of the Mass for which the texts are unvariable

organ: an ancient musical instrument constructed mainly of pipes and keys; the player depresses a key, which allows air to rush into or over a pipe, thereby producing sound

organum: the name given to the early polyphony of the Western Church from the ninth through the thirteenth centuries

oscillator: a device that, when activated by an electronic current, pulses back and forth to produce an electronic signal that can be converted by a loudspeaker into sound

ostinato: (Italian for "obstinate") a musical figure, motive, melody, harmony, or rhythm that is repeated again and again

overtone: see *harmonics*

overture: an introductory movement, usually for orchestra, that precedes an opera, oratorio, or dance suite

parallel motion: a musical process in which all of the lines or parts move in the same direction, and at the same intervals, for a period of time; the opposite of counterpoint

part: an independent line or voice in a musical composition; also, a section of a composition

pedal point: a note, usually in the bass, sustained or continually repeated for a period of time while the harmonies change around it

pentatonic scale: a five-note scale found often in folk music and non-Western music

phrase: a self-contained portion of a melody, theme, or tune

pianissimo (*pp*): in musical notation, a dynamic mark indicating "very soft"

piano (*p*): in musical notation, a dynamic mark indicating "soft"

piano: a large keyboard instrument that creates sound at various dynamic levels when hammers are struck against strings

piano transcription: the transformation and reduction of an orchestral score, and a piece of orchestral music, onto the great staff for playing at the piano

pianoforte: the original name for the piano

piccolo: a small flute; the smallest and highest-pitched woodwind instrument

pickup: a note or two coming before the first downbeat of a piece, intending to give a little extra push into that downbeat

pipa: an ancient, four-string Chinese lute

pitch: the relative position, high or low, of a musical sound

pizzicato: the process whereby a performer plucks the strings of an instrument rather than bowing them

plainsong: see *Gregorian chant*

point of imitation: a distinctive motive that is sung or played in turn by each voice or instrumental line

polonaise: a dance of Polish origin in triple meter without an upbeat but usually with an accent on the second of the three beats

polychord: the stacking of one triad or seventh chord on another so they sound simultaneously

polymeter: two or more meters sounding simultaneously

polyphony: a musical texture involving two or more simultaneously sounding lines; the lines are often independent and create counterpoint

polyrhythm: two or more rhythms sounding simultaneously

polytonality: the simultaneous sounding of two keys or tonalities

popular music: a broad category of music designed to please a large section of the general public; sometimes used in contradistinction to more "serious" or more "learned" classical music

prelude: an introductory, improvisatory-like movement that gives the performer a chance to warm up and sets the stage for a more substantive subsequent movement

prepared piano: a piano outfitted with screws, bolts, washers, erasers, and bits of felt and plastic to transform the instrument from a melodic one to a percussive one

prestissimo: in musical notation, a tempo mark indicating "as fast as possible"

presto: in musical notation, a tempo mark indicating "very fast"

prima donna: (Italian for "first lady") the leading female singer in an opera

program music: a piece of instrumental music, usually for symphony orchestra, that seeks to re-create in sound the events and emotions portrayed in some extramusical source: a story, a play, a historical event, an encounter with nature, or even a painting

program symphony: a symphony with the usual three, four, or five movements in which the individual movements together tell a tale or depict a succession of specific events or scenes

Proper of the Mass: the sections of the Mass that are sung to texts that vary with each feast day

punk rock: a rebellious style of rock developed in the United States and Great Britain during the 1970s and exemplified by bands such as the Ramones, the Sex Pistols, and the Clash

qin: an ancient seven-string Chinese dulcimer played with two bamboo sticks

quadrivium: a curriculum of four scientific disciplines (arithmetic, geometry, astronomy, and music) taught in medieval schools and universities

quadruple meter: music with four beats per measure

quarter tone: the division of the whole tone, or whole step, into quarter tones, a division even smaller than the half tone, or half step, on the piano

raga: an Indian scale and melodic pattern with a distinctive expressive mood

ragtime: an early type of jazz emerging in the 1890s and characterized by a steady bass and a syncopated, jazzy treble

rap: a style of popular music closely associated with "hip-hop" that became popular in the United States in the 1980s, mostly among urban African-Americans; it usually involves rapping along with audio processing (sampling and scratching)

realistic opera: a general term for those operas of the nineteenth and early twentieth centuries that deal with everyday, gritty subjects; includes Italian *verismo* opera

rebec: a medieval fiddle

recapitulation: in sonata–allegro form, the return to the first theme and the tonic key following the development

recital: a concert of chamber music, usually for a solo performer

recitative: musically heightened speech, often used in an opera, oratorio, or cantata to report dramatic action and advance the plot

recitativo accompagnato: a recitative accompanied by the orchestra instead of merely the harpsichord; the opposite of *secco* recitative

recorder: an end-blown wooden flute with seven finger holes played straight out instead of to one side

relative major: the major key in a pair of major and minor keys; relative keys have the same key signature, for example, E♭ major and C minor (both with three flats)

relative minor: the minor key in a pair of major and minor keys; see *relative major*

rest: a silence in music of a specific duration

retransition: the end of the development section, where the tonality often becomes stabilized on the dominant in preparation for the return of the tonic (and first theme) at the beginning of the recapitulation

retrograde: a musical process in which a melody is played or sung, not from beginning to end, but starting with the last note and working backward to the first

rhythm: the organization of time in music, dividing up long spans of time into smaller, more easily comprehended units

rhythm and blues: a style of early rock 'n' roll c1950 characterized by a pounding $\frac{4}{4}$ beat and a raw, growling style of singing, all set within a twelve-bar blues harmony

rhythm section: the section within a jazz band, usually consisting of drums, double bass, piano, banjo, and/or guitar, that establishes the harmony and rhythm

Ring cycle: a cycle of four interconnected music dramas by Richard Wagner that collectively tell the tale of the Germanic legend *Der Ring des Nibelungen*

Risorgimento: the name given to the political movement that promoted the liberation and unification of Italy in the mid-nineteenth century

ritard: a gradual slowing down of the tempo

ritardando: in musical notation, a tempo mark indicating a slowing down of the tempo

ritornello: (Italian for "return" or "refrain") a short musical passage in a Baroque concerto grosso invariably played by the tutti

rock: a type of popular music that emerged from rock 'n' roll in the mid-1960s marked by amplified singing, electric instruments, and a strong rhythmic drive conducive to dancing

rock 'n' roll: a type of popular music that emerged from rhythm and blues in the 1950s characterized by amplified singing, acoustic and electric instruments, and a very strong rhythmic drive conducive to dancing

romance: a slow, lyrical piece, or movement within a larger work, for instruments, or instrument and voice, much favored by composers of the Romantic period

rondeau: see *rondo*

rondo: an ancient musical form (surviving into the twentieth century) in which a refrain alternates with contrasting material

rubato: (Italian for "robbed") in musical notation, a tempo mark indicating that the performer may take, or steal, great liberties with the tempo

Russian Five: a group of young composers (Borodin, Cui, Balakirev, Rimsky-Korsakov, and Musorgsky) centered in St. Petersburg, whose aim was to write purely Russian music free of European influence

sackbut: a brass instrument of the late Middle Ages and Renaissance; the precursor of the trombone

sampling: reusing (and often repeating) portions of a previous sound recording in a new song

Sanctus: the fourth section of the Ordinary of the Mass

sarabande: a slow, elegant dance in $\frac{3}{4}$ with a strong accent on the second beat

scale: an arrangement of pitches that ascends and descends in a fixed and unvarying pattern

scena: a scenic plan in Italian opera involving a succession of separate elements such as a slow aria, a recitative, and a fast concluding aria

scherzo: (Italian for "joke") a rapid, jovial work in triple meter often used in place of the minuet as the third movement in a string quartet or symphony

Schubertiad: a social gathering for music and poetry that featured the songs and piano music of Franz Schubert

score: a volume of musical notation involving more than one staff

scratching: sound processing that involves the rhythmical manipulation of a vinyl record

secco recitative: see *simple recitative*

Second Viennese School: a group of progressive modernist composers centered around Arnold Schoenberg in Vienna in the early twentieth century

Sequence: a Gregorian chant, sung during the Proper of the Mass, in which a chorus and a soloist alternate; see also *melodic sequence*

serenade: an instrumental work for a small ensemble originally intended as a light entertainment in the evening

serial music: music in which some important component—pitch, dynamics, rhythm—comes in a continually repeating series; see also *twelve-tone composition*

seventh chord: a chord spanning seven letter names and constructed by superimposing three thirds

sforzando: a sudden, loud attack on one note or chord

sharp: a musical symbol that raises a pitch by a half step

shawm: a double-reed woodwind instrument of the late Middle Ages and Renaissance; the precursor of the oboe

simple recitative: recitative accompanied only by a *basso continuo* or a harpsichord, and not the full orchestra

sinfonia: (Italian for "symphony") a one-movement (later three- or four-movement) orchestral work that originated in Italy in the seventeenth century

Singspiel: (German for "singing play") a musical comedy originating in Germany with spoken dialogue, tuneful songs, and topical humor

sitar: a large, lute-like instrument with as many as twenty strings, prominently used in the traditional music of northern India

snare drum: a small drum consisting of a metal cylinder covered with a skin or sheet of plastic that, when played with sticks, produces the "rat-ta-tat" sound familiar from marching bands

soft pedal: the left pedal of the piano, which, when depressed, shifts the keyboard in such a way that the hammers strike fewer strings, making the instrument sound softer

solo: a musical composition, or portion of a composition, sung or played by a single performer

solo concerto: a concerto in which an orchestra and a single performer in turn present and develop the musical material in the spirit of harmonious competition

solo sonata: a work, usually in three or four movements, for keyboard or other solo instrument; when a solo melodic instrument played a sonata in the Baroque era, it was supported by the *basso continuo*

sonata: originally, "something sounded" on an instrument as opposed to something sung (a "cantata"); later, a multi-movement work for solo instrument, or instrument with keyboard accompaniment

sonata–allegro form: a dramatic musical form that originated in the Classical period involving an exposition, development, and recapitulation, with optional introduction and coda

sonata da camera (chamber sonata): a suite for keyboard or small instrumental ensemble made up of individual dance movements

sonata da chiesa (church sonata): a suite for keyboard or small instrumental ensemble made up of movements indicated only by tempo marks such as *grave, vivace,* and *adagio*; originally intended to be performed in church

song cycle: a collection of several songs united by a common textual theme or literary idea

song plugger: a pianist-vocalist who plugged (peddled) songs in a music store by performing them, thereby allowing the customer to decide which to purchase

soprano: the highest female vocal part

Sprechstimme: (German for "speech-voice") a vocal technique in which a singer declaims, rather than sings, a text at only approximate pitch levels

staccato: a manner of playing in which each note is held only for the shortest possible time

staff: a horizontal grid onto which are put the symbols of musical notation: notes, rests, accidentals, dynamic marks, etc.

stanza: a poetic unit of two or more lines with a consistent meter and rhyme scheme

step: the interval between adjacent pitches in the diatonic or chromatic scale; either a whole step or a half step

stomp: a piece of early jazz in which a distinctive rhythm, with syncopation, is established in the opening bars, as in the opening phrases of the "Charleston"

stop: a knob (or key) on a pipe organ that, when pulled (or pushed), allows a particular group of pipes to sound, thereby creating a distinctive tone color

string bass: see *double bass*

string instruments: instruments that produce sound when strings are bowed or plucked; the harp, the guitar, and members of the violin family are all string instruments

string quartet: a standard instrumental ensemble for chamber music consisting of a single first and second violin, a viola, and a cello; also, the genre of music, usually in three or four movements, composed for this ensemble

strophe: see *stanza*

strophic form: a musical form often used in setting a strophic, or stanzaic, text, such as a hymn or carol; the music is repeated anew for each successive strophe

style: the general surface sound produced by the interaction of the elements of music: melody, rhythm, harmony, color, texture, and form

subdominant chord: the chord built on the fourth, or subdominant, degree of the major or minor scale

subject: the term for the principal theme in a fugue

suite: an ordered set of instrumental pieces, usually all in one key, intended to be played in a single sitting (see also *dance suite*)

sustaining pedal: the right-most pedal on the piano; when it is depressed, all dampers are removed from the strings, allowing them to vibrate freely

swing: a mellow, bouncy, flowing style of jazz that originated in the 1930s

syllabic singing: a style of singing in which each syllable of text has one,

and only one, note; the opposite of melismatic singing

symphonic jazz: music (mostly of the 1920s and 1930s) that incorporates idioms of jazz into the genres and forms traditionally performed by the classical symphony orchestra

symphonic poem (tone poem): a one-movement work for orchestra of the Romantic era that gives musical expression to the emotions and events associated with a story, play, political occurrence, personal experience, or encounter with nature

symphony: a genre of instrumental music for orchestra consisting of several movements; also, the orchestral ensemble that plays this genre

symphony orchestra: the large instrumental ensemble that plays symphonies, overtures, concertos, and the like

syncopation: a rhythmic device in which the natural accent falling on a strong beat is displaced to a weak beat or between the beats

synthesizer: a machine that has the capacity to produce, transform, and combine (or synthesize) electronic sounds

tabla: a double drum used in the traditional music of northern India

talking drum: a drum having a head or heads covered with skin that can be made more or less tight so as to raise or lower the pitch and thereby approximate human speech

tambourine: a small drum, the head of which is hung with jangles; it can be struck or shaken to produce a tremolo effect

tam-tam: an unpitched gong used in Western orchestras

tango: a genre of popular urban song and dance originating in Cuba and Argentina in the nineteenth century; marked by a duple meter with syncopation after the first beat and a slow, sensuous feel

tempo: the speed at which the beats occur in music

tenor: the highest male vocal range

ternary form: a three-part musical form in which the third section is a repeat of the first; hence **ABA**

terraced dynamics: a term used to describe the sharp, abrupt dynamic contrasts found in the music of the Baroque era

texture: the density and disposition of the musical lines that make up a musical composition; monophonic, homo-

phonic, and polyphonic are the primary musical textures

theme and variations: a musical form in which a theme continually returns but is varied by changing the notes of the melody, the harmony, the rhythm, or some other feature of the music

The Well-Tempered Clavier: two sets of twenty-four preludes and fugues compiled by J. S. Bach in 1720 and 1742

through-composed: a term used to describe music that exhibits no obvious repetitions or overt musical form from beginning to end

timbre: see *color*

timpani (kettle drums): a percussion instrument consisting usually of two, but sometimes four, large drums that can produce a specific pitch when struck with mallets

time signature (meter signature): two numbers, one on top of the other, usually placed at the beginning of the music to tell the performer what note value is carrying the beat and how the beats are to be grouped

Tin Pan Alley: a section of New York City near Broadway and West 28th Street where music stores abounded during the early years of the twentieth century; the noise was so cacophonous that it sounded like a crowd banging on tin pans

toccata: a one-movement composition, free in form, originally for solo keyboard but later for instrumental ensemble as well

tonality: the organization of music around a central tone (the tonic) and the scale built on that tone

tone: a sound with a definite, consistent pitch

tone cluster: a dissonant sounding of several pitches, each only a half step away from the other, in a densely packed chord

tone poem: see *symphonic poem*

tonic: the central pitch around which the melody and harmony gravitate

transition (bridge): in sonata–allegro form, the unstable section in which the tonality changes from tonic to dominant (or relative major) in preparation for the appearance of the second theme

treble: the uppermost musical line, voice, or part; the part in which the melody is most often found

treble clef: the sign placed on a staff to indicate the notes above middle C

tremolo: a musical tremor produced on a string instrument by repeating the same pitch with quick up-and-down strokes of the bow

triad: a chord consisting of three pitches and two intervals of a third

trill: a rapid alternation of two neighboring pitches

trio: an ensemble, vocal or instrumental, with three performers; also, a brief, self-contained composition contrasting with a previous piece, such as a minuet or a mazurka; originally, the trio was performed by only three instruments

trio sonata: an ensemble of the Baroque period consisting actually of four performers, two playing upper parts and two on the *basso continuo* instruments

triplet: a group of three notes inserted into the space of two

trivium: a literary curriculum of three disciplines (grammar, logic, and rhetoric) taught in medieval schools and universities

trombone: a brass instrument of medium to low range that is supplied with a slide, allowing a variety of pitches to sound

troubadour: a type of secular poet-musician that flourished in southern France during the twelfth and thirteenth centuries

trouvère: a type of secular poet-musician that flourished in northern France during the thirteenth and early fourteenth centuries

trumpet: a brass instrument of the soprano range

tuba: a brass instrument of the bass range

tune: a simple melody that is easy to sing

tutti: (Italian for "all") the full orchestra or full performing force

twelve-bar blues: a standard formal plan for the blues involving a repeating twelve-measure harmonic support in which the chords can progress I-IV-I-V-I

twelve-tone composition: a method of composing music, devised by Arnold Schoenberg, that has each of the twelve notes of the chromatic scale sound in a fixed, regularly recurring order

unison: two or more voices or instrumental parts singing or playing the same pitch

upbeat: the beat that occurs with the upward motion of the conductor's hand and immediately before the downbeat

vaudeville: an early form of American musical theater involving songs and dances, comedy skits, etc.; a precursor of the musical comedy of Broadway

verismo opera: "realism" opera; the Italian term for a type of late-nineteenth-century opera in which the subject matter concerns the unpleasant realities of everyday life

vibrato: a slight and continual wobbling of the pitch produced on a string instrument or by the human voice

viola: a string instrument; the alto member of the violin family

viola da gamba (bass viol): the lowest member of the viol family; a large six- or seven-string instrument played with a bow and heard primarily in the music of the late Renaissance and Baroque eras

violin: a string instrument; the soprano member of the violin family

virtuosity: extraordinary technical facility possessed by an instrumental performer or singer

virtuoso: an instrumentalist or singer with a highly developed technical facility

vivace: in musical notation, a tempo mark indicating "fast and lively"

vocal ensemble: in opera, a group of four or more solo singers, usually the principals

voice: the vocal instrument of the human body; also, a musical line or part

volume: the degree of softness or loudness of a sound

walking bass: a bass line that moves at a moderate pace, mostly in equal note values, and often stepwise up or down the scale

waltz: a popular, triple-meter dance of the late eighteenth and nineteenth centuries

whole step: the predominant interval in the Western major and minor scale; the interval made up of two half steps

whole-tone scale: a six-note scale each pitch of which is a whole tone away from the next

woodwind family: a group of instruments initially constructed of wood; most make their sound with the aid of a single or double reed; includes the flute, piccolo, clarinet, oboe, English horn, and bassoon

word painting: the process of depicting the text in music, be it subtly, overtly, or even jokingly, by means of expressive musical devices

xylophone: a percussion instrument consisting of tuned wooden bars, with resonators below, that are struck with mallets

Index

Introductory CD Performers List

1. Beethoven, Symphony No. 5, I (exposition), Royal Concertgebouw Orchestra/Bernard Haitink, conductor. Ⓟ 1987 Universal International Music B. V. (1:21)

2. Tchaikovsky, Piano Concerto No. 1, I (opening), London Symphony Orchestra/ Vladimir Ashkenazy, piano/ Lorin Maazel, conductor. Courtesy of Decca Music Group Limited (3:20)

3. R. Strauss, *Thus Spoke Zarathustra* (opening sunrise), Chicago Symphony Orchestra/ Samuel Magad, violin/ Sir Georg Solti, conductor. Ⓟ 1976 Decca Music Group Limited (1:41)

4. Listening Exercise 2, Hearing Meters, Ⓟ 1992 West Publishing Company, Courtesy of Wadsworth/Thomson Learning (4:21)

5. Listening Exercise 3, Hearing Melodies, Ⓟ 1992 West Publishing Company, Courtesy of Wadsworth/Thomson Learning (3:40)

6. Listening Exercise 4, Hearing Major and Minor, Ⓟ West Publishing Company, Courtesy of Wadsworth/Thomson Learning (3:32)

7. Listening Exercise 5, Hearing Melodic Structure, Beethoven, *Ode to Joy* from Symphony No. 9, IV, Karl Böehm, Ⓟ 1981 Deutsche Grammophon GmbH, Hamburg (3:18)

8. Listening Exercise 6, Hearing Phrases and Counting Measures, "Willie the Weeper" (Rymal/Melrose/Bloom), Louis Armstrong & His Hot Seven. Originally Released 1927 Sony BMG MUSIC ENTERTAINMENT. Under License From The SONY BMG Custom Marketing Group, SONY BMG MUSIC ENTERTAINMENT (3:14)

9. Listening Exercise 7, Hearing the Bass Line and Harmony, Pachelbel, Canon in D major, The Stuttgart Chamber Orchestra/ Karl Münchinger, conductor. Ⓟ 1978 Decca Music Group Limited (4:30)

10. Listening Exercise 8, Hearing Chord Changes in the Harmony, "The Listening to Music Blues," Ⓟ 1992 West Publishing Company, Courtesy of Wadsworth/Thomson Learning (1:17)

11. Instruments of the Orchestra, Strings, Ⓟ 2004 Wadsworth/ Thomson Learning, Courtesy of Wadsworth/Thomson Learning (4:02)

12. Instruments of the Orchestra, Woodwinds, Ⓟ 2004 Wadsworth/Thomson Learning, Courtesy of Wadsworth/ Thomson Learning (2:26)

13. Instruments of the Orchestra, Brasses, Ⓟ 2004 Wadsworth/Thomson Learning, Courtesy of Wadsworth/ Thomson Learning (2:22)

14. Instruments of the Orchestra, Percussion, Ⓟ 2004 Wadsworth/Thomson Learning, Courtesy of Wadsworth/ Thomson Learning (:44)

15. Listening Exercise 9, Hearing the Instruments of the Orchestra, Identifying a Single Instrument, Ⓟ 2004 Wadsworth/ Thomson Learning, Courtesy of Wadsworth/Thomson Learning (3:14)

16. Listening Exercise 10, Hearing the Instruments of the Orchestra, Identifying Two Instruments, Ⓟ 2004 Wadsworth/ Thomson Learning, Courtesy of Wadsworth/Thomson Learning (3:18)

17. Listening Exercise 11, Hearing the Instruments of the Orchestra, Identifying Three Instruments, Ⓟ 2004 Wadsworth/ Thomson Learning, Courtesy of Wadsworth/Thomson Learning (2:19)

18. Handel, "Hallelujah" chorus from *Messiah*, The Chicago Symphony Orchestra and Chorus/Sir Georg Solti, conductor/ Margaret Hills, director. Ⓟ 1985 Decca Music Group Limited (3:41)

19. Listening Exercise 12, Hearing Musical Textures, Ⓟ 2006 Craig Wright, Wadsworth/Thomson Learning (3:56)

20. Brahms, *Lullaby*, Anne-Sofie von Otter, Mezzo-Soprano/ Bengt Forsberg, Piano. Ⓟ 1990 Deutsche Grammophon GmbH, Hamburg (1:51)

21. Mozart, Variations on *Twinkle, Twinkle, Little Star*, András Schiff, piano. Ⓟ 1988 Decca Music Group Limited (3:33)

22. Haydn, Symphony No. 94, II, Royal Concertgebouw Orchestra/Colin Davis, conductor. Ⓟ 1982 Universal International Music B.V. (6:14)

23. Tchaikovsky, "Dance of the Reed Pipes," from *The Nutcracker*, Academy of St. Martin In The Fields/Neville Marriner, conductor. Ⓟ 1982 Universal International Music B.V. (2:26)

24. Mouret, *Rondeau* from *Suite de symphonies*, Hannes Läubin, trumpet/Wolfgang Läubin, trumpet/Bernhard Läubin, trumpet/ Norbert Schmitt, timpani/Simon Preston, organ. Ⓟ 1986 Deutsche Grammophon GmbH, Hamburg (1:52)

25. Listening Exercise 13, Identifying Musical Forms, Purcell, *Abdelazer*, The Academy of Ancient Music/Christopher Hogwood, conductor. Ⓟ 1976 Decca Music Group Limited (4:20)